A BRIEF SURVEY OF
MEDIÆVAL EUROPE

HARPER'S HISTORICAL SERIES

Under the Editorship of
GUY STANTON FORD

A BRIEF SURVEY OF
MEDIÆVAL EUROPE

By

CARL STEPHENSON

Professor of History
Cornell University

HARPER & BROTHERS PUBLISHERS

NEW YORK AND LONDON

A BRIEF SURVEY OF MEDIÆVAL EUROPE

Copyright, 1941, by Harper & Brothers

Printed in the United States of America

All rights in this book are reserved.
No part of the book may be reproduced in any
manner whatsoever without written permission
except in the case of brief quotations embodied
in critical articles and reviews. For information
address Harper & Brothers

FIRST EDITION

D-Q

TO

THE SCHOLARLY TRADITION
OF UNIVERSITIES

*Dubitando enim ad inquisitionem venimus; inquirendo
veritatem percipimus*—ABELARD

(see p. 225)

CONTENTS

MAPS

FIGURES

GENEALOGICAL TABLES

(following p. 373)

PLATES

(Between pp. 236 *and* 237)

----

xiii

EDITOR'S FOREWORD

Every work on history, whether it be monographic or many volumed or a text, is in a sense a laboratory report. Physically the laboratory is that infinitely small part of the universe we call the earth. The character of its surface and the changes in cold and heat as it dips and turns and whirls around the sun are conditioning factors in the many experiments to one purpose that are carried on on its surface. The experimenter, the subject, the recorder, and the interpreter are one and the same—man himself.

These experiments and the reports about them go back through many recorded centuries. With the aid of archæology and anthropology they are being pushed still further back into centuries where the records are piecemeal and unconsciously made. Where, as in the centuries here covered, the documents are sometimes scant and seemingly pointless except to him who made them, their steady accumulation, growing availability, and intensive study reveal new meanings and fill in a picture of ages once called dark because men were not fully enlightened about them. A greater light kindled by patient scholars now falls upon them even though the shadows still obscure many points. As a whole the great institutions and movements and the common man and his leaders in the period from the fourth to the sixteenth century are now outlined for us. We know them for what they were and see them as part of the seamless web of the history of mankind from the caveman to ourselves and our fellows in the classroom, in the field, in the marts and factories, and in the public forum.

Still too often even the students of history in universities, whose form and purposes were largely determined in the Middle Ages, turn to what is called contemporary history in an effort to understand their own times. There is really no such thing as contemporary history, as there is no rootless tree and no man without ancestors. A clear and scholarly history like this shows how the institutions and peoples of our own day bear in them the formative influences of the chromosomes and genes of the ages here described, as these ages themselves are in their turn the heirs and transmitting hosts of the *élan vital* of Rome and Greece and Egypt and Israel.

I am sure it is the hope of the author, as it is mine, that these reasons for studying mediæval history and this conception of it—aided by this volume and a good teacher—will survive in every student despite examinations, be they subjective or objective, and final marks even if they are less than an A.

GUY STANTON FORD

PREFACE

This little book is primarily a condensation of my *Mediæval History*, published six years ago. For better or for worse, many colleges have now established an introductory course that, dealing with history in the large, has no use for a text of nearly eight hundred pages. For better or for worse, I have accordingly written a survey of the same period in less than four hundred pages. Because it is half as long as the previous book, it is not supposed to be twice as easy. To condense is always harder than to elaborate—for the teacher and the student, as well as for the writer—and the subject is by no means simple. The more we find out concerning human life in the past, the more complex our problem seems to become. Practically all the facile generalizations that were dear to historians of the nineteenth century have now been proved unsound. I have no substitutes to propose. And I, for one, fail to see that history is made easier by calling it the history of civilization. Anybody who can really explain the growth or decay of a civilization must be ranked among the immortals of historiography.

Our original universities made no distinction between knowing and knowing how to teach. However naïve the schoolmen may now be considered, I am sure that I should never have ventured to write a mediæval history if I had not been giving courses on the subject, and that during six more years of teaching I ought not to have stopped learning. Evidence to this effect may, I trust, be found in some of the following sections—particularly those dealing with intellectual, social, and economic developments. It is only too certain that in all respects my knowledge is still in need of improvement. But the best we can do is to set down what we happen to think at a given time, or our hosts of eager students would have no history books. My opinions, like those collected by Abelard, should be read *inquisitionis causa*.

With few exceptions, the maps, figures, and plates are as they were in the *Mediæval History*, merely rearranged to suit the new organization of the subject matter. The genealogical tables and chronological charts have been retained in full, although they include more detail than is actually needed here. The list of suggested readings and the index are revisions of those published earlier. Obviously, therefore, I remain deeply indebted to the associates mentioned in the previous volume—two of whom, George L. Hamilton and Nathaniel Schmidt, we shall no longer see in their accustomed places.

A number of friends have more especially helped me in the preparation of this volume. The suggestions of President Guy Stanton Ford have, as always, been most welcome. Mr. Henry H. King of the Cornell University Library has again saved me from all sorts of errors. My colleagues in the Department of Fine Arts and in the College of Architecture have contributed to a better selection of plates. Professor Harry Caplan, whose devotion to the classics does not prevent his appreciation of things mediæval, has been good enough to criticize my entire manuscript.

CARL STEPHENSON

Cornell University
   March, 1941

A BRIEF SURVEY OF
MEDIÆVAL EUROPE

INTRODUCTION

PRELIMINARY DEFINITIONS

The student who takes up a history of the mediæval period, or of the Middle Ages, may properly wish to know what is meant by those conventional terms. In the present instance no more is implied than particular attention to the history of Europe from Roman times to the opening of the sixteenth century. How the age called mediæval differed from that called ancient should be clear from what is said in the first few chapters; whether a sharp distinction can be drawn between the age preceding 1500 and the one following is a question which can hardly be answered until that date has been reached. Meanwhile there is no need for worry about any marked peculiarity of mediæval men in general. They will be found to have varied quite as much as the men of more recent centuries. Fortunately, we do not have to begin with an abtruse definition of the mediæval.

The term "mediæval"

It should, however, be realized that, while attempting to describe the past, we must use a modern vocabulary. And although most of our current words can be expected to have a reasonably precise connotation, a number of those in constant use by historians, as well as by journalists, are all too often misunderstood. Three—"state," "nation," and "race"— are especially apt to be confused in popular writing. Before we apply them to the Roman world, accordingly, we should be careful to explain what we mean by them.

"State" and "nation"

Today, as in ancient times, a state has a territorial basis. It not only can be named; it also can be drawn on a map. All residents of such a territory, without regard to personal likes and dislikes, are subject to the supreme authority of the government there established. For example, when a citizen of Mexico crosses an imaginary line to the north, he ceases to be bound by Mexican law and becomes bound by that of our country. Yet, normally, he will still be considered a Mexican. Although he leaves his state behind, he bears with him his nationality—a matter that is not so easy to define. Speech is sometimes a guide to nationality, sometimes not. Frenchmen and Germans, we know, are likely to speak respectively French and German. But a man who speaks French may be a Canadian; a man who speaks German may be a Swiss. A person whose native tongue is Spanish can belong to any one of a dozen nations. Descent, furthermore, is not the determining factor in nationality, or there would be—to mention a single instance—no American nation. Here, as in Europe, nationalism is ultimately resolved into little more than the feelings of a people. Men who declare themselves a nation are one; a nation is said to be self-determined. Recently there has been a tendency for every nation to demand a government of its own, to insist on being also a state. This sort of nationalism, however, is a late development; it does not appear in the early centuries of European history. The Romans, though quite familiar with the territorial state, had no concept of the national state. To them a nation (*natio*) was merely a people whose common origin was indicated by a common custom which had nothing to do with political status or aspiration. Therefore, when nations are referred to in the chapters immediately following, the term should be understood thus vaguely—as having no significance other than what it had for the Romans.

Alleged races of Europe

The word "race" has a very different meaning. A man may change his state by moving away from it, or his nation by transferring his affections; but he cannot change his race, for that is born with him. Properly understood, a race is a people marked off from others by hereditary characteristics—for instance, the black skin of the Negro. Although, up to a certain point, color is a useful guide in identifying race, it utterly fails when we come to consider the white inhabitants of Europe. The question of primary interest to us is whether these peoples can be classified in distinct races according to some other scheme.

It is still the confirmed habit of many authors to speak of a Latin, Celtic, Slavic, Germanic, or even an Anglo-Saxon race. Yet such differentiation is based on language; and language, however significant in the history of civilization, is not inherited. We cannot be safe in assuming that two groups were related by blood descent because they spoke kindred tongues; there are too many known instances of a population that changed its language as the result of conquest or intermarriage. So, of more recent years, it has become fashionable to divide Europeans into other races—such as Mediterranean, Alpine, and Nordic. Men of the first type are short and slender, with dark complexions, black eyes, and skulls that measure more from back to front than from side to side. Those of the second have medium complexions, brown eyes, round heads, and thickset frames. The Nordics are tall, fair, blue-eyed, and, like the first group, long-headed. As a matter of fact, a traveler crossing the continent of Europe from south to north can readily perceive these three types predominating in the regions for which they are named. But are they, as a popular school of writers would have us believe, the three fundamental races of Europe through whose antagonisms and interminglings the entire history of the western world can best be explained?

The more closely the theory is examined, the weaker it appears. In the first place, it rests almost solely on modern observation of physical characteristics and takes for granted the primitive invasion of the continent by three races bearing those characteristics. Aside from a few scattered bones and certain vague remarks by ancient authors, we have no evidence concerning the appearance of early European peoples. Secondly, the theory assumes that stature, complexion, skull-formation, and the like are purely hereditary. But this is denied by many scientists, who point out that climate, diet, and other environmental factors may produce radical alterations of human physique within a relatively short period. Thirdly, the selection of three races, as set forth above, is quite arbitrary from the mathematical point of view. People classified according to one pair of opposites—e.g., tall and short—fall into two groups. If a second test is then applied—such as complexion—four groups are defined. And as each added distinction doubles the number, five tests result in thirty-two groups. Of all these, which are the original races and which are mixtures?

Race and culture

Although there obviously are superior breeds of men, as there are of domestic animals, we cannot in the former case be sure how the better strains were produced. Presumably they are all the result of intermixture. As far as the known history of Europe is concerned, the biologically pure race is a figment of the imagination—and so is the alleged relation between a particular set of physical characteristics and various intellectual, spiritual, or moral traits. Even if we admit that certain features of coloring and bone-formation are the true marks of an original race, we are still left to wonder precisely what they may have to do with political genius, commercial shrewdness, artistic skill, or any of the other qualities that make a people great. The historian's pre-eminent task, at any rate, is to deal with cultures; for the relative superiority of a people can be judged only from what it has accomplished.

CHAPTER I

THE ROMAN WORLD

----

1. THE RISE OF THE ROMAN EMPIRE

Our study of European history begins with the Roman The Republic power at its height. This starting-point is convenient for several reasons. Although it excludes direct consideration of the more ancient period, it enables us to review the developments of that period in their culminating stage—when for the first time the entire Mediterranean world was organized as a political unit. And for the ensuing age such a review is of prime importance. To understand the salient features of European history for the next thousand years and more, the student must have a knowledge of the Roman Empire and its civilization.

The germ from which the Roman Empire sprang was a settlement of Latin-speaking people on the Tiber in Italy. To the contemporary Greeks these early Romans could have appeared hardly more than a crude farmer-folk. Yet, from the time we first hear of them, they displayed a surpassing genius for military and political organization. By the end of the third century B.C. the Romans had secured undisputed control of the Italian peninsula; within another hundred years they had conquered Spain, northern Africa, and southern Gaul. Being drawn into the troubled waters of the east, the Romans then crushed the monarchies of Syria and Macedon, made Egypt a protectorate, and so rounded out their dominion of the Mediterranean shores. Most of the territories that were to comprise the Roman Empire were thus in some fashion brought together, but their integration was a long and troublesome process.

Rome, now commanding a host of allied and subject peoples, remained essentially what it had been before—a

5

city-state on the Tiber, formally styled the Republic (*res publica*, or commonwealth). Its citizens were the privileged body of Italians who alone enjoyed equal rights under the Roman law, and upon whom in theory the government ultimately depended. Actually, the effective power was restricted to the senatorial aristocracy, the few families who, by controlling the elections, named the magistrates and dictated their policies. The supreme direction of the republic—civil, military, and religious—was called the *imperium* (whence eventually our word "empire"), but as yet it was held by a group of officials styled consuls and prætors. Some of them ruled at home; others administered outlying regions (*provinciæ*, provinces) designated by the senate. For a long time the ancient constitution had worked efficiently, as the amazing success of the republic bore witness; then, in the closing century of the pre-Christian era, the system broke down. Devised for a small city-state, it proved inadequate for the Mediterranean world.

The principate of Augustus
Nearly a hundred years of political disorder, marked by a bitter conflict between the old senatorial aristocracy and its popular opponents, ended with a new settlement carried out by Augustus. At least officially, he avoided the precedent set by his uncle, Julius Cæsar. The latter, after conquering Gaul, had championed the popular cause against the senate and so gained the life dictatorship, which was virtually monarchy without a royal crown. Augustus preferred compromise in the form of a dyarchy—joint rule by the senate and himself, the first man (*princeps*, eventually "prince") of the state. Although referred to by modern historians as the empire, the régime of Augustus is more properly called the principate, for as yet the title *imperator* was little more than the designation of a victorious general.

Theoretically, therefore, the administration of Augustus made no sudden change with the past; the republic remained unaltered, except that it now had a principal magistrate and commander-in-chief elected for life. The senate was kept, not merely as an order of supreme social honor, but as a governing council for the city of Rome and for those of the provinces that required no large body of troops. The highest officials, both civil and military, were normally landed aristocrats. For a while they were still chosen by the ancient assemblies, which also voted formal laws; later these functions in one way or another came to be exercised by the senate and the *princeps*. Although Roman citizenship thus lost much of its political significance, in other respects it continued to be a valuable privilege, the more highly prized because Augustus opposed any lavish extension of the right into the provinces. And since membership in the Roman legions had always been restricted to citizens, this policy placed an inevitable check on territorial expansion. Failing to secure the line of the Elbe, Augustus made the Rhine and the Danube his northern defense. To the east the Parthians were held along the upper Euphrates and the edge of the Arabian desert. In Africa the Sahara provided a natural frontier to the south. These were to remain the principal boundaries of the Roman Empire until its collapse in the fifth century.

Another primary concern of Augustus was the municipal system, on which the whole imperial structure rested. Roman dominion had never been a matter of sheer military occupation. First in Italy and then outside it, the Romans had extended their sovereignty by means of perpetual leagues. Each city-state, while recognizing the superior authority of Rome in some particulars, remained autonomous in all else. Except as specified by solemn treaty, every community was free to govern itself and to develop its own native institutions. Following what had already become an established Roman policy, Augustus now sought, as rapidly as was practical, to organize new city-states throughout all the more backward territories. In the east the Romans generally constructed their municipalities after Greek models, merely continuing the process of Hellenization begun by Alexander the Great. In the west, where Roman dominion had been imposed on more barbarous countries, the urban plan together with the civilization that accompanied it was thoroughly Latin. By the opening of the Christian era the shores of Gaul, Spain, and Africa were dotted with flourishing colonies of Italian settlers and with native communities that rivaled them in prosperity and culture. To advance this work of Romanization to the frontiers on the north and south continued to be a primary object of the principate.

Succession to the principate

The rule of Augustus has been emphasized in the foregoing pages because it was one of the great political successes in history. Two hundred years after his death the principate remained very much as he had designed it. But with the passage of time the power of the senate had more and more been overshadowed by that of the *princeps*. To the unforgiving remnant of the old aristocracy this was tyranny and usurpation. As the honor passed from Augustus to unpopular members of his house, the ancient feud blazed up again and various Cæsars wreaked their vengeance in bloody deeds which famous historians have delighted to recount. Their scandalous narratives are now being corrected by the study of more sober records that reveal a smoothly running government controlled by experts, and millions of provincials thankful to it for the boon of an undisturbed life. To the Mediterranean world at large the prince who assured the blessings of the great Roman peace was indeed the master of the state. The opposition of a few senatorial families led merely to their extermination and to the advancement of more loyal men to fill the gaps in the ranks. By the second century after Christ the transformation was complete. Public opinion had recognized the prince as the actual ruler of the whole Roman territory; the title *imperator*, like the names Cæsar and Augustus, had come to mean "emperor."

Even the problem of the succession now appeared to have been solved. In 68, on the death of Nero without heirs, the senate had shown itself incompetent to meet such an emergency, merely ratifying whatever nomination was made by the nearest military force and thereby encouraging the various armies to advance on Rome in support of their rival candidates. In 96, however, the senate took advantage of a similar opportunity to install a worthy man named Nerva. He designated the illustrious Trajan as his heir and successor; and according to the same plan Trajan was followed by Hadrian, Antoninus Pius, and Marcus Aurelius. These were the five "good emperors," under whom the Roman world enjoyed unbroken calm for nearly a hundred years (96-180).

Judged by our best historical standards, the empire of the second century was in a healthful condition. Its military system, especially to modern eyes, seems a marvel of efficiency; for, without the mechanical aids of today, it kept an enormous expanse of territory in a peace that has since remained proverbial. Thanks to the virtually continuous efforts of the emperors, the frontiers had been greatly strengthened since the time of Augustus. Tremendous lines of fortification were thrown across wild regions where neither desert nor river afforded adequate protection—as in the newly acquired provinces of Britain and Dacia, and in Germany, to connect the Rhine and the Danube (see Map II). Along the frontiers were distributed small fortresses (*castella*) held by permanent garrisons, and at wider intervals the great legionary camps (*castra*), which often attracted a considerable urban population. In the earlier period most of this construction had been of earth and timber, but in the course of time masonry was substituted—of such massive strength that much of it has lasted even to our own day. And the magnificent paved highways, which linked the military outposts with the cities of the interior, were also destined far to outlast the state that built them.

Further evidence of Roman vigor in the second century is provided by the remains of countless cities in what had recently been semi-barbarous country. Throughout the west in particular the progressive extension of the city system marked an increasing population and an advancing frontier of civilization. According to the normal pattern, the *civitas* was not precisely a city in our sense of the word, but a city-state that included a considerable territory about an urban

The empire in the second century

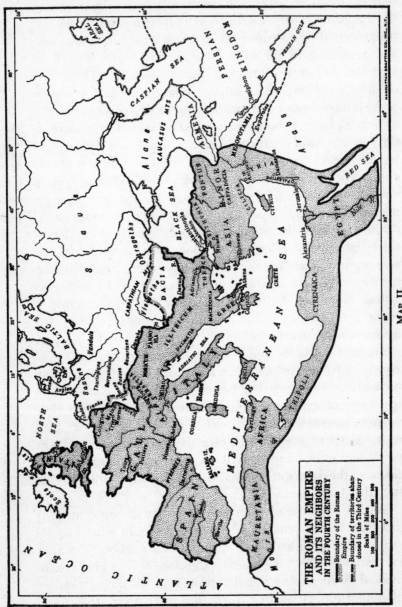

THE ROMAN EMPIRE
AND ITS NEIGHBORS
IN THE FOURTH CENTURY

▨▨ Boundary of the Roman
  Empire
━━━ Boundary of territories aban-
  doned in the Third Century

Scale of Miles
0 100 200 300 400 500

MAP II.

center (*urbs*). Its governing body was a miniature senate, usually termed *curia*, which elected the necessary magistrates from its own number. Every citizen of the local community, on acquiring a certain amount of property, was officially enrolled in the list of *curiales*, persons eligible for membership in the *curia* and so for other political honors. During the second century, as is attested by many inscriptions, such rank was highly prized and competition for city offices remained keen, although to hold one might entail the expenditure of a small fortune. The social importance of this municipal aristocracy—the curial class of the west together with its eastern counterpart—can hardly be exaggerated. Constantly increased by the rise of successful men from below, it constituted a sort of imperial bourgeoisie, from which the more exalted orders of the state were in turn recruited.

It is characteristic of the age that four of the "good emperors" were by origin Spaniards, and under their rule, very naturally, provincials more and more came to enjoy equality with Italians. By the time of Marcus Aurelius full Roman rights had been granted to better-class communities on all sides. Even the senatorial order had become imperial in scope. The personal household of the prince had developed into an elaborate civil service, in which the places earlier held by freedmen were eagerly sought by members of the noblest families. The true Rome was no longer a dominant city, but a world empire.

2. GRÆCO-ROMAN CULTURE

A fact of great significance for the later development of Europe was the cultural difference between the eastern and western halves of the Roman Empire. In the latter the extension of Roman dominion generally implied the Latinization of the inhabitants. Throughout Illyricum, the upper Danubian provinces, Gaul, Spain, northern Africa, Britain, and all Italy, except the Greek colonies of the south, Latin became the ordinary speech of the educated classes. And together with the language, they tended to acquire an outlook

The Latin west and the Greek east

on life, a mental discipline, a mould of character, that can only be described as Roman. It should, however, be remembered that the Greeks of southern Italy had originally taught the Romans the elements of civilization and that, as long as the Roman Empire persisted, it remained under direct Greek influence. Further description of Latin culture may therefore be postponed until the nature of that influence is better understood.

To the deathless glory of ancient Greece no feeble tribute need be attempted in these pages. By the time of the principate the classic age of Hellenism was long past; the old homeland was depopulated; Athens had yielded pre-eminence in art and letters to the new-grown cities of Syria and Egypt. Those countries, ever since the triumphant campaigns of Alexander, had been progressively Hellenized. While much of the peasant population might retain its native speech and custom, the urban aristocracy became Greek. To be accepted by educated persons, whatever their descent, books had to be written in Greek; ideas had to conform to Greek habits of thought; works of art had to follow the Greek canons of taste. And these æsthetic and intellectual standards were left unchanged by the Romans, who had little to teach the easterners except in matters legal and military.

Sculpture   Numberless critics have commented on the exquisite beauty—a beauty of grace and simplicity—achieved by the earlier Greeks, whether they wrought in words or in marble. Thus the sculptors of ancient Athens excelled in depicting humanity at its noblest. Avoiding the imperfections of the individual, they sought to represent ideal persons, and did so with a magic touch that the subsequent world has never quite recovered. But though the artists of the Hellenistic age—the period following Alexander—abandoned the antique standards of beauty, they maintained great skill with less exalted themes, such as the pathetic and the comic; and they brought portrait sculpture to a new height of perfection. The continued excellence of this art may be judged from the statues of the early Roman emperors, which were presumably by Greek hands. For in such work—as in the engraving of gems, the designing of coins, the carving of reliefs, or any of the finer crafts—the supremacy of the Greeks was recognized throughout the Mediterranean world. To a certain degree the same truth holds in the sphere of architecture; yet in it the Romans made original contributions of lasting importance.

The classic architecture of ancient Greece is best exempli- **Archi-** fied by the Doric temple, and pre-eminently by the Parthe- **tecture** non of Athens. There the primary unit of construction is a horizontal slab, or architrave, supported by columns. In the Doric temple the architrave bears a decorative frieze with a projecting cornice above it, and these three parts are together called an entablature (see Figure 1). Greek buildings of the Hellenistic period remained structurally the same, though more elaborate capitals came to be used on the columns. The Ionian order is characterized by volutes at the corners of the capital; the Corinthian, by a larger capital decorated with acanthus leaves. But the

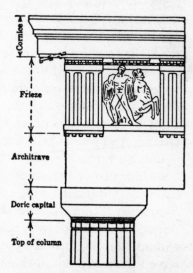

FIGURE 1.—GREEK ENTABLATURE.

Corinthian style was not invented till late and was popular mainly in the west. For the Romans, evidently, the loveliness of the Parthenon had no appeal. Their temples, though constructed on the Greek plan, were chiefly noteworthy for magnificence of size and ornamentation. All too often the Roman taste preferred the florid and the pretentious, was willing to combine incongruous elements for the sake of a grandiose effect. These failings are especially prominent in the great monuments erected by the later emperors.

It is not such buildings that entitle the Romans to distinguished rank in the history of architecture. Rather it is their more utilitarian works—forts, aqueducts, amphitheaters, basilicas, and the like—in which for the first time the principles of arch-construction were well developed. Upon these principles a number of great architectural styles were to be evolved by later generations. Yet to the Romans of the early empire, apparently, a mere arch was not a thing of beauty. When putting up a bridge, they thought of it as no more than a useful piece of masonry, and so left the arches plain—and to our eyes charming (see Plate II). But when they employed the same structural method in a more formal edifice, they sought to embellish the exterior by framing the arches with quite unnecessary columns and entablatures superficially attached to the walls. In the famous Colosseum, for example, the three tiers of arches are thus set off by the Doric, Ionian, and Corinthian orders one over the other—a bit of ostentation never found in the works of ancient Greece. And similar criticism may be applied to the Roman triumphal arches.

Greek literature and science   In imaginative literature, as in the other Greek arts, there had been a distinct falling off even before the advent of the conquering Romans. The famous books of antiquity continued to be studied with passionate zeal, but too commonly without the production of anything that might in turn deserve such study. So, in the field of poetic composition, it is chiefly the preservation of the old classics for which we have to thank the Greeks of tne Hellenistic age. Prose writing, on the other hand, remained noteworthy, and with the establishment of the principate gained actual brilliance. The period from Nero to Marcus Aurelius (58-180) witnessed the careers of Dio Chrysostom, rhetorician and moralist; Plutarch, author of the enormously popular *Parallel Lives*; Arrian, scholarly biographer of Alexander the Great; and Lucian, a clever and original satirist. And although the schools of philosophy produced no such towering genius as Plato, they were still thronged with students who not infrequently made important contributions to intellectual research.

For the majority of educated men philosophy retained its traditional interest—as a system of thought purporting to explain the universe and man's place in it. Yet in the later age an increasing number of scholars turned their attention to that phase of the ancient study which we know as science. The change was largely due to the influence of Aristotle who, in preference to metaphysical speculation, had emphasized the observation of natural phenomena and the formulation of general principles from the data thus learned. Science, as Aristotle very well knew, is valid only to the extent that it is verified, and cannot advance without fresh research. Some of his disciples, regarding the master's words with undue reverence, sanctified his mistakes and failed to continue what he had only begun. So physics made too little progress and the biological sciences languished. Splendid work, nevertheless, was done in mathematics and medicine.

These were subjects in which the Greeks had long excelled. **Mathematics: Ptolemy** The early philosophers had all been interested in problems of arithmetic and geometry, and had demonstrated the fundamental importance of such problems in music and astronomy. How mathematical study continued to attract the best minds of the Hellenistic schools is shown by the writings of Euclid, Eratosthenes, Hipparchus, Apollonius, and Archimedes in the third and second centuries B.C. Adding the first principles of trigonometry to an exhaustive analysis of geometry, they applied this knowledge to a description of the physical universe and its constituent parts. The earth they agreed was round and, like the sun and the planets, was contained in the sphere of the fixed stars. As to the center of this revolving universe, however, there was dispute: Eratosthenes made it the sun, Hipparchus the earth. The latter theory, by much ingenious figuring, was brought into fair agreement with the observed facts and so came to be accepted by Ptolemy, the last great mathematician of the ancient world. His principal book—written about A.D. 150—not only combined the best work of his predecessors on geography and astronomy but contributed much that was original, including a masterly exposition of trigonometry. There was good reason why the *Almagest*, as it came to be known by the Arabs, should remain a standard text for over a thousand years.[1]

Medicine: Galen

Comparable service to medicine was rendered by Galen, a native of Pergamon contemporary with Ptolemy. Galen, too, wrote towards the close of a long and honorable tradition, for Greek medicine had been illustrious since the time of Hippocrates, the late fifth century B.C. From that day to this the Hippocratic writings—partly by the master, partly by followers—have enjoyed high renown for their sanity and fine ideals. The older physicians, however, had been handicapped by lack of technical information; and this failing was in some part corrected by the medical schools of the Hellenistic age, which extended the list of useful drugs and, through dissection, greatly advanced the science of anatomy. Thus, when Galen wrote his monumental treatises, he could incorporate a relatively large amount of new material. The modern student, to be sure, finds them dull reading, and considers absurd a physiology based on theories of soul, spirits, and bodily humors.[2] Yet Galen had an encyclopædic knowledge of medical practice and, for his age, an excellent understanding of the pertinent sciences. Even the mystic reverence for a divine plan that pervades his writing recommended it the more strongly to the learned world of the next fifteen centuries.

Latin literature

In richness of content as in artistic perfection Greek literature is unquestionably superior to the Latin. Indeed, the Romans generally admitted that in the finest of composition the Greeks remained their masters. Nevertheless, by the time of the principate, Latin had been developed into one of the world's great literary languages. Such poets as Catullus, Horace, Vergil, and Ovid, while borrowing their meters from

---

[1] See below, p. 92.
[2] See below, p. 94.

Greece, produced immortal verse. And Latin prose attained classic excellence in the work of Cæsar, Cicero, Sallust, Livy, and Seneca. During the period between Nero and Marcus Aurelius poetry somewhat declined, being represented by two specialized forms: the light epigrams of Martial and the heavy satires of Juvenal. But the earlier standard of prose writing was well maintained in the elegantly turned letters of Pliny the Younger, Quintilian's famous book on rhetoric, the popular *Lives of the Cæsars* by Suetonius, and the distinguished works of Tacitus.

As a whole, this literature clearly displays the Latin genius for the practical. The Romans were always more successful in discussion of law, politics, and morals than in the loftier flights of imaginative thought. Compared with the Greeks, they produced little great poetry. The best of their historians cannot be ranked with Thucydides. They contributed nothing to mathematics or natural science. The only philosophy to be adopted by many Latin writers was the later Stoicism, which, divorced from metaphysical argument, provided the educated Roman with a sort of ethical religion. The keynote in the Stoic doctrine is will power—self-control through reason, the divine element implanted in man by the Creator. All men, having in this respect the same original endowment, are equally the sons of God and so brothers to one another. The parts assigned them in the world's drama may vary, but human character remains constant. If a man is true to his real self, he is true to nature; he will then understand the divine order that governs the universe and will ask no other reward.

Stoicism in the west

Stoic ideas gained widespread popularity through the writings of Cicero and Seneca, and, as will be seen, came to pervade the works of the jurists. But the two best expositions of western Stoicism are the *Discourses* of Epictetus, a slave at the court of Nero, and the *Meditations* of the emperor Marcus Aurelius—both of which, very significantly, were written in Greek. All things, says Epictetus, are of two sorts: those which are in our power and those which are not. Outside our power are worldly fame and fortune—wealth, office, family, even our bodies. He who concentrates his devotion on such matters is truly the slave, for he is always at the behest of others. Our reason, on the contrary, is our own. The free man is one who has steeled himself to cherish only that which he can himself control, for he is beyond all hurt. "I must die. But must I die groaning? I must be imprisoned. But must I whine as well? I must suffer exile. Can any one hinder me from going with a smile, with a good courage, and at peace?"

Epictetus was a slave and a cripple, but he is quoted by the emperor Marcus Aurelius, who tells himself: "You are a little soul burdened with a corpse." A spider, he meditates, is vastly proud of itself when it has caught a fly; one type of man when he has netted a small fish; another—referring to one of his own campaigns—when he has routed the Sarmatians. Marcus reminds himself that all things happen in accord with universal nature; that before long he, like Hadrian and Augustus, will be nothing. And he concludes: "Let it be your hourly care to do stoutly what your hand finds to do, as becomes a man and a Roman." Such was the creed of the men who ruled imperial Rome while it was at its height. But could that creed survive in an age of mounting ignorance and despair?

3. THE DECLINE OF THE ROMAN EMPIRE

The Severi (193-235) Even before the end of the second century the waning prosperity of the empire was indicated by reports of financial distress in certain municipalities and by the increasing difficulty of checking the barbarians on the northern frontier. To contemporaries these seemed minor troubles, but they were symptomatic of the desperate conditions to follow. The unworthy son and designated heir of Marcus Aurelius was murdered in 193, and the succession to the purple again became an ugly problem. In the armed conflict that ensued the victor proved to be an African general, Septimius Severus, who founded a short-lived dynasty ending in 235. One of the Severi, Caracalla, is famous for a decree extending Roman citizenship to virtually all free inhabitants of the empire—the formal culmination of a process begun long before. A much more significant change effected during the same period was the transformation of the principate into a military despotism. Terrorizing the senate into subservience, the Severi lavished money and privilege upon the army. High civil offices tended to be filled with soldiers, and their point of view determined the chief policies of state. Such an administration, it must be admitted, was not unjustified; the absolute necessity of strengthening the imperial defenses was soon to be fully appreciated. But the legions needed no encouragement in the belief that they were the masters of Rome. With no law governing the succession, every popular commander was a potential emperor awaiting a good opportunity for advancement. It is no wonder that assassination so often provided one.

When such a fate claimed the last of the Severi in 235, the result was a prolonged civil war in which none of the contestants seemed able to win a decisive victory. While one emperor held the city of Rome, others dominated the provinces. And as the legions followed their champions to distant battlefields, the frontiers were left open to hordes of wandering barbarians. For the first time the Roman populace became familiar with tribal names that future centuries were to make increasingly formidable. Alamans and Franks seized coveted lands along the Rhine and carried their pillaging raids far into Gaul. Goths broke into the Danubian provinces, slew an emperor who tried to stop them, and, taking to the sea, looted the ancient cities of the Ægean. Meanwhile Roman dominion in Asia all but collapsed before the attack of a reconstituted Persian kingdom. Thus, by the second half of the third century, the Roman Empire had actually disintegrated. In the absence of any central authority, the provinces were organized into shifting groups under local chieftains—a condition resembling that which became chronic a century and a half later.

Civil war (235-70)

For the moment, however, the disorder was merely the prelude to a new era of stabilization. The work was begun by Aurelian, who rose from the ranks to be hailed as the Restorer of the Empire. In five short years (270-75) he disposed of all rival princes and re-established the old frontiers except that he abandoned to the barbarians all land to the north and east of the Rhine and the Danube (see Map II). Aurelian's murder by a petty conspirator was a calamity that threatened once more to plunge the world into chaos; fortunately, another soldier-emperor soon took up the unfinished task and brought it to a successful conclusion. This was Diocletian, a Dalmatian of humble birth, who attained the purple in 284 and ruled without serious opposition until 305, when he abdicated. His enactments, formally recognizing the principle of absolute monarchy, so strengthened the empire that it remained intact for another hundred years. The problem of the succession, it is true, continued to cause trouble in spite of Diocletian's attempted solution; for the legions persisted in their ancient habit of installing emperors by force. Yet there were no prolonged civil wars. During most of the fourth century the government was in the hands of such able soldiers as Constantine (306-37), Valentinian (364-75), and Theodosius (379-95), who well maintained the traditions of Aurelian and Diocletian.

Their system of government must be recognized as an honest effort to cope with realities. Believing that the preservation of political unity demanded military despotism, they subordinated everything and everybody to the one consideration. The emperor was now the sovereign lord, officially endowed with royal titles and insignia. His person and all that belonged to him were sacred. His will, expressed in formal edicts, was the public law of the empire. He was the fountain of justice, the source of all authority. He commanded the armies and named their officers: immediately below himself, the masters of horse and foot; for the legions on the frontiers or in the field, generals (*duces*, eventually "dukes"); and under them, of course, a host of subordinates.

Sharply distinguished from the military hierarchy was that of the civil service, also created by imperial appointment. The provinces, now much smaller than they had been, were grouped in thirteen dioceses, each under a vicar; the dioceses in four prefectures, each under a prefect. And special agents (*agentes in rebus*) were sent out on regular missions to inspect the activities of local officials and report to the master of offices who, together with the other heads of departments, sat in the emperor's advisory council (*consistorium*).

Through this bureaucratic system the efficiency of the government was sufficiently improved to prevent a relapse into anarchy; yet the Roman peace was still precarious, and constant attention had to be given to the problem of imperial defense. The emperors of the fourth century, rightly mistrusting the strength of the old frontiers, organized field armies with an increasing proportion of heavy-armed cavalry to support the stationary legions on the borders, and greatly extended the work of local fortification. Aurelian had earlier taken the ominous step of encircling Rome with walls; now every important city was turned into a garrisoned fortress. And as the task of personally controlling the entire machine, civil and military, proved too great for one man, Diocletian's example was generally followed in having a co-emperor to share the responsibility. Under such conditions the natural policy was to take the Latin and Greek halves of the empire as the two administrative units. In the west Rome by tradition remained the imperial city; but in the east a new and stronger capital was built by Constantine on the site of the ancient Byzantium, a small peninsula that juts into the Bosphorus. Thus arose the great city of Constantinople, dominating the narrow passage between the Mediterranean and the Black Sea, and itself defying attack from either side—a position of enormous military and commercial importance to every government that has since held it.

Meanwhile another consequence of Diocletian's absolutism had become more and more prominent: as service of the state was identified with service of the emperor, nearness to his

Administrative division of the empire

The imperial court

sacred person came to be the test of all social distinction. On working up the ladder of civil or military preferment, a man acquired increasing honor, together with resonant titles of proportionate dignity. And when he approached the top, he found himself in the imperial court, participating in a ceremonial routine of oriental magnificence. There his associates were the great officers of the household, the heads of the governmental departments, the masters of horse and foot, the "most noble" members of the emperor's family, the patricians (*patricii*) whom the emperor addressed as his "kinsmen," and the lesser gentlemen who were merely his "companions" (*comites*, eventually "counts"). The senatorial order still existed as a decoration, though the actual senate was no more than a municipal council for the city of Rome. Long past were the days of the early principate, when Cæsar himself was proud to be a Roman citizen, the subject of no one.

Growth of a caste system

The lower ranks of men experienced an even more significant change of fortune, to appreciate which we must review the economic distress of the empire in the third century. As noted above, certain military and financial difficulties had appeared under Marcus Aurelius; while the Roman peace was yet unbroken, the government had begun to suffer from a shortage of troops and from dwindling revenues. Then to the ravages of civil war were added those of pestilence. The population sharply declined and the loss could not be made up. Lands ceased to be cultivated; urban properties stood vacant; taxes remained unpaid. To meet their obligations, various emperors debased the coinage and so drove good money out of circulation. The poverty of the masses deepened and became chronic. The state, though rescued from destruction, was bankrupt; wide regions were depopulated; many cities were faced with starvation. In a frantic effort to check the encroaching ruin, Diocletian resorted to desperate measures, which were continued and amplified by his successors. The result was what amounted to an official system of castes.

The government was able to restore the coinage, but not **The army**
the wealth of the people. Cash remained so scarce that the
state had to collect most of its taxes in kind. As a consequence, its employees were in turn compelled to accept
produce for at least part of what was owed them. Even land
was used for paying wages—as, for example, those of 'the
troops. And this policy completed the dominance of the army
by rude peasants drawn from the border districts, men who
would accept land in return for service. By the time of
Constantine the mobile legion of ancient Rome had thus
been transformed into a sort of professional militia, domi-
ciled along one section of the frontier and largely recruited
from barbarian tribesmen.

Whenever possible, too, the government employed the **Trade and**
time-honored system of requisitioning animals, conveyances, **industry**
materials, and services. Placed at the discretion of rapacious
subordinates, such exactions became a never-ending plague
for the rural population. But the merchant and the artisan
were by no means exempt from similar oppression. For a
long time the trades regarded as essential to the state had
been organized under highly privileged associations termed
collegia. Among them, for instance, were the millers, bakers,
and others who helped to supply the capital with food; the
carpenters and masons who constructed public buildings;
the craftsmen who furnished arms for the legions; and the
men who transported necessities by sea or land. As times
grew worse and public credit became insecure, business men
naturally hesitated to undertake contracts that meant certain
loss. So edicts were issued to compel the performance of
the customary duties, and finally to prohibit the member
of a *collegium* from quitting his position, or his heirs from
refusing the same responsibility. Every trade and every profession, by the extension of this iniquitous system, tended
to become a hereditary servitude, and all prospect of commercial revival through private initiative was destroyed.

Equally important developments took place in connection **Agriculture**
with agriculture. Under the republic a good many estates

had been worked by slave labor, but the establishment of general peace had ended the supply of cheap slaves and made such a method of agricultural exploitation unprofitable. Then, if the proprietor lacked cash for the employment of hired labor, he had to settle his lands with peasants who, in return for plots assigned to each, would contribute a share of the crops and perform necessary labor. A settler of this sort, holding by perpetual lease, was called a *colonus*. Legally he was a freeman; and so he remained, although in the fourth century his freedom ceased to be very desirable. According to Diocletian's fiscal reorganization, each assessment district was made liable for a number of land-tax units, which thenceforth tended to become a fixed charge on that particular territory. And since the amount of the tax depended not only on the character of the land but also on the number of cultivators, the latter had to be turned into a stable asset. The law forbade the *colonus* to leave; he and his children after him were attached to the estate, to be bought and sold along with it.

The ruin of the cities
An even worse fate befell the aristocracy of the provincial cities. In the second century, as noted above, the rank of *curialis* was still highly prized; two hundred years later it had become a sort of official slavery. The unfortunate dignitary, being held responsible for the taxes assessed on the *civitas*, had to make up a constantly mounting deficit. He and his heirs remained shackled with their wretched honor. If in despair he ran away, he might, like a fugitive *colonus*, be captured and brought back. The only fortunate man in this miserable company was the great landlord who, through imperial favor, attained the senatorial order and so escaped the baneful liability for ordinary municipal office. Retiring to his country estate and the protection of his retainers, he could defy the tyranny of governmental officials and spend his days in the society of friends like himself.

The decay of culture
The culmination of these unhappy developments was the ruin, in all but exceptional regions, of urban life and culture. Through the multiplication of cities the frontier of

civilization had for hundreds of years steadily advanced; through the influence of the cities the east had tended to become Greek and the west to become Latin. As the reverse process set in during the third century, it naturally brought a relapse towards more primitive conditions—in the east oriental, in the west barbarian. The decrees of the later emperors thus betray a much graver deterioration than the passing of the semi-republican principate; they show that vitality had somehow gone out of the state. And if we compare the culture of the third and fourth centuries with that of the preceding age, the same fact is brought home to us even more convincingly.

The decay of the arts during the period between Marcus Aurelius and Diocletian is no less than shocking. The fine series of imperial statues comes to a melancholy close; even the heads on the coins cease to be real portraits. The later triumphal arches prove the failure of all skill in the carving of relief; so that Constantine, finally, was reduced to filching decorations for his arch from the monuments of his predecessors. Meanwhile, except in the field of jurisprudence,[3] there had been an abrupt decline of Latin literature. No historian arose to take the place of Tacitus, no poet to take that of Juvenal. Towards the end of the second century we encounter the names of Aulus Gellius, a collector of anecdotes, and Apuleius, a collector of stories; after them ensues a blank. And in the meantime Greek thought had been overwhelmed by the wave of oriental mysticism that will be considered in the following section.

What was the cause of this degradation, which was to culminate in the so-called Fall of Rome? All sorts of answers have been given to the question. Learned writers have attributed the decay of the empire to such diverse influences as sin, slavery, barbarian attack, official tyranny, racial deterioration, epidemics, exhaustion of the soil, lack of applied science, and Christianity. To repeat the arguments that have been marshaled against these and similar contentions is im-

Alleged causes of Roman decline

[3] See below, pp. 70-71.

possible in a brief review of the subject. Suffice it to say that in general they have been proved untrue or inadequate. One point, however, the discussion has made increasingly plain: the strength of the empire depended on the strength of its component city-states, the ancient centers of political and cultural life throughout the Mediterranean world. And the prosperity of the cities, it is generally admitted, was dependent on commerce, which assuredly declined from the third century onward. But when we ask why commerce declined and why it failed to revive, we obtain no positive answer. Even if modern economists were more certain in the explanation of crises and depressions, we should still find the ancient records too scanty to warrant definitive conclusion.

The essential poverty of the west

We are thus left with the conviction that the Roman Empire suffered from an economic malady which, up to the present, experts have failed to diagnose. Perhaps this economic malady was itself a result and not a cause. At any rate, it is worth remarking that the imperial structure seems to have depended on wealth drawn principally from the eastern provinces. The Latin world, judged by modern standards, was thinly populated. Most of the western cities, being centers of military and civil administration rather than of economic production, were relatively small. Like the great city of Rome, they in many cases were mere agglomerations of consumers, dependent on food directly or indirectly supplied by the state. The Romans, except in such matters as money-lending and tax-farming, developed slight talent for commerce. Even after they had become the rulers of the Mediterranean, shipbuilding, sea trade, and the more important manufactures remained in the hands of Greeks. Large-scale production in the west was therefore restricted to raw materials, the market for which was largely a creation of the government. Left to itself, the western half of the Roman Empire was doomed to impoverishment and political chaos, while the eastern half was able not only to survive but even to regain a certain degree of prosperity.

How, as the empire disintegrated, these conditions determined the fate of European civilization will be seen in the following chapters.

4. THE NEW RELIGIONS

From the very outset Greek thought had been remarkable for its rejection of traditional authority and its insistence upon fresh research. Not infrequently, as we now realize, Greek scholars had tended to reason on the basis of insufficient data, had allowed fancy to outstrip observation. The validity of their method, nevertheless, was amply demonstrated by the most brilliant advance in science that the world had yet seen. And although their schools of philosophy differed in the solutions offered to various problems, all believed in man's capacity to learn about himself and the universe through the normal human faculties. This attitude was in sharp contrast to the prevalent mysticism of the orient. In all ages the typical mystic has despaired of man's unaided capacities. Truth, he believes, can be reached only by contemplation, by shutting oneself off from the world and communing with the infinite through the medium of the soul. Regarded from this point of view, the acceptance of Neo-Platonism by the scholarly world of the third century was equivalent to a declaration of intellectual bankruptcy.

Neo-Platonism is a modern term used to distinguish the system of Plotinus (d. 270) and his followers from the original teachings of Plato. Divorcing Plato's "idealism" from its context, Plotinus combined it with various non-Greek elements to form the alleged quintessence of philosophy and religion. But the conclusion of all his labor was to deny what the Athenian philosophers had held most dear; for he came to preach the ultimate futility of thought and the consequent need of inner revelation through ecstatic vision. Neo-Platonism thus tended to justify the acceptance of any religion that appealed to the emotions. Although a select few might remain loyal to the metaphysics of Plotinus, most men would find an easier way to reach the same goal. By this time, in-

The failure of Greek philosophy

deed, many an oriental mystery had come to attract the learned as well as the illiterate.

The
oriental
mysteries

In an earlier age, presumably, the Romans had found spiritual exaltation in the worship of their ancient deities; yet, long before the establishment of the principate, the official cult had ceased to be more than legal formalism. Educated men regarded the traditional stories of gods and goddesses—whether Greek or Latin—as sheer myth, and rejected all religious doctrines that could not be embraced under such a creed as Stoicism. On the other hand, the uneducated, to whom philosophy could offer slight consolation, naturally turned to the new faiths imported from the east. They offered what the legalistic ceremonial of the official temples could not provide: the emotional appeal of a highly sensuous ritual, the certainty of truth mystically revealed, and the assurance to the purified initiate of life in a blessed hereafter. They demanded only what every man could give—faith. And to all alike they promised a reward more precious than wealth could buy. It is no wonder that, with the progressive ruin of state and society, they numbered their converts by the million.

Eventually one of these oriental faiths was to gain supremacy throughout the Roman world, but for several centuries it had to strive against many rivals for popular favor. Earlier mysteries—such as those associated with Bacchus, god of wine, and Demeter, goddess of the harvest—celebrated the principle of fertility and, by depicting the return of vegetation to the earth, symbolized the initiate's entrance into a new spiritual existence. These elements, together with many others, were combined in the worship of the Phrygian Cybele, whom the west knew as Magna Mater. According to the sacred legend, she restored the slain Attis to life through the power of her love; and about this theme of death and resurrection was developed a cult that became widely influential under the principate. Meanwhile a similar myth concerning the resuscitation of Osiris by Isis, an Egyptian goddess, had become the germ of another religion, remarkable for its hierarchy of priests, its elaborate liturgy, and its positive doctrine of immortality. A third popular mystery was that of Mithras, which originated from Persian sun-worship. According to the latter system, known as Zoroastrianism, man's nature, like the universe, is the scene of perpetual strife between the two gods of light and darkness, the forces of good and evil. The individual, to escape the realm of darkness after death, must hold to the light, must follow a strict code of morality. As an aid in the struggle for righteousness, the cult of Mithras offered constant spiritual fortification. To gain admission to it, the candidate had to be purified through an elaborate ceremony. Thereafter he was said to be reborn.

By the third century these mystic religions had borrowed much from one another. To all of them, for example, a sacrificial meal, in which the participant symbolically partook of the divine substance, had become a common feature. All, likewise, tended to absorb the ancient astrology of the Babylonians, such as the lore connected with the signs of the zodiac and the division of time into periods of seven days, each named for a heavenly body or its presiding deity. Some of these cults had originally been marked by license rather than restraint; but, with the passage of time, all came to emphasize ethical teaching. Barbarous ritual was softened and crude mythology was explained in terms of Hellenistic philosophy. All gods could thus be regarded as manifestations of one supreme power, and all dogmas as reflecting the same essential truths. The greatest appeal of the new religions, however, lay in the fact that each offered a divine intermediary through whom the individual could obtain salvation. The Christian faith was but one of many; how it came to receive universal acceptance is a story of truly epic character. *Common elements*

According to the familiar account of the Gospels, Jesus was born—while Augustus still ruled at Rome—in the Judæan town of Bethlehem. Having been recognized by John the Baptist as the prophesied Christ, the Messiah of the *The Christian religion*

Hebrews, He devoted His life to preaching the kingdom which God was about to restore to His people. But this kingdom, said Jesus, was not the earthly monarchy that the Jews had dreamed of re-establishing; it was a spiritual kingdom, to enter which a man must be born again in the spirit. Precise observance of the traditional law was of no avail; the outward act was less than the inward thought. In heaven the faith of a little child was of greater worth than all the learned holiness in the world. Finally, because of His bitter attack upon sacred tradition and vested interest, Jesus was sent to death on the cross—a punishment commonly assigned to thieves and other criminals. The martyrdom served only to advertise an obscure cause. The small band of the faithful proclaimed that Christ had risen from the dead and that, through His abiding spirit, they were able to perform all wondrous works. Their fervor rapidly made converts, one of whom was the apostle Paul. In his own vivid words he tells us how he had never known the man Jesus; how he preached the gospel of the risen Christ, seen in blinding glory on the road to Damascus. And as the result of his preaching, the Christianity that spread across the Roman Empire was Pauline Christianity. Thanks to his Greek education, Paul was able so to present an essentially Jewish religion that it could be understood throughout the Mediterranean world.

Compared with its rivals, Christianity obviously had many points of superiority. In the first place, the story of Jesus is compellingly beautiful—vastly superior, as a mere story, to the theme of any other oriental mystery. And it is itself the expression of a religious idea. Telling of a savior who died to redeem all men, it requires no symbolic interpretation. Furthermore, the ethical teachings of Jesus lay at the heart of His gospel; they were not a supplement borrowed from Greek philosophy, intelligible only to the learned. Christianity, as the event proved, appealed to all. It did not, like the cult of Mithras, exclude women; nor did it, like the cults of Cybele and Isis, exalt a feminine principle at the expense of others. Lastly, the Christian religion took over from Judaism an uncompromising monotheism. It was a religion that declared every other to be false, a religion at once exclusive and aggressive. Therein lay an avowed hostility to the Roman imperial system that was to invite persecution; yet therein lay also the strength that was to bring triumph.

The concept of a church distinct from the state was originally foreign to Roman, as it had been to Greek, thought. Under the constitution of the republic and of the principate, one set of magistrates held all political functions—civil, military, and religious. Any man legally elected was considered competent to ascertain the will of the gods by formal divination or to preside over the public ceremonial of worship; no especially sanctified priesthood was necessary. And as long as the Roman citizen outwardly submitted to the official deities, he was free to believe anything he pleased. Citizens of other communities were permitted to maintain any faith that did not conflict with the general peace of the empire; yet, as a sign of their proper reverence for the dominant state, they were commonly required to recognize by solemn act the cult of its living embodiment, Augustus—a formality as ordinary to that age as an oath of allegiance is to ours.

Roman religious policy

Such requirements, in a polytheistic world, could be expected to offend nobody. The believer would willingly admit one more god to the Pantheon; the skeptic would regard an additional ceremony as a matter of no importance; even the devotee of an oriental mystery, while preferring one manifestation of divine truth, would normally concede that there might be many others. In this polytheistic world the Jew was an exception. To him all faiths except his own were sheer idolatry, an abomination in the sight of the Lord; he would never conform to the official system of Rome. But since the Jewish religion, with its strict observance of a peculiar law, could never be popular enough to be dangerous, the Romans wisely accepted it as a national institution and exempted its followers from emperor-worship. Even after the destruction

Polytheism and Judaism

of the Jewish state (A.D. 70) and the consequent dispersion of the Jews throughout the provinces, their religious beliefs and practices were still tolerated.

Early Christian persecutions

To the Christians no such liberty was extended. Although the Roman government seems for a time to have considered Christianity a mere sect of Judaism, by the close of the first century the distinction between the two had become eminently clear. Most of the Jews would have nothing to do with the new faith, which, on the other hand, had spread rapidly through the Gentile population. The Christians held that they had been freed from the Hebrew law and, to emphasize the fact, celebrated the first day of the week in place of the Jewish sabbath. Yet in their monotheism they remained as intolerant of other creeds as the Jews. In Roman eyes, consequently, the Christians were no better than seditious conspirators. Their associations were declared illegal; to be a Christian was to commit a crime. Thus it came about that the Christians were persecuted, not merely by notorious tyrants, but also by the very best of the emperors. Trajan, Hadrian, Antoninus Pius, and Marcus Aurelius, in so far as they tried to enforce the law, were necessarily hostile to those proscribed by it.

One of our earliest and best sources on the Christian persecutions is the letter written to Trajan by Pliny the Younger, then governor of Bithynia. He reports that he has discharged all suspects who have made offerings of wine and incense to the statue of the emperor. Those who refused he has handed over to execution.

Nevertheless, they affirmed that this was the sum total of their guilt. On a certain day they would meet before dawn and sing in alternate verses a song to Christ as a god. They would bind themselves by oath, not for the sake of criminal acts, but as an engagement not to commit fraud, theft, or adultery, not to break faith and not to refuse the surrender of a pledge when it was demanded. It was their habit then to disperse, although they reassembled later in order to partake of food.

Trajan replies that Pliny has acted very properly. The governor should not himself undertake to ferret out these people, nor should he listen to anonymous accusations. But when Christians are regularly denounced and found guilty, they should be punished according to law.

History has often proved that, merely as a matter of state policy, a little persecution is worse than none. The fact that the Roman government was so moderate prevented its staying the progress of the outlawed cult. And the joyous courage with which the condemned welcomed martyrdom proclaimed the quality of their faith and converted many a spectator. Then, with the paralysis of the state in the third century, the Christians gained a prolonged respite. Even when the emperors once more found time to devote to the religious problem, their edicts were chiefly directed against the making of Christian converts—a tacit confession that the duty of punishing the offenders was becoming arduous. Diocletian's reform of the administration inevitably brought fresh troubles on the Christian communities; but the persecution was short-lived, for the ancient policy of Rome was reversed by the illustrious Constantine.

The end of the persecution

According to the famous story, Constantine was leading an army against one of his earlier rivals when he beheld in the sky a blazing cross with the motto IN HOC VINCE (In This Conquer). And all we know of the man indicates that he believed himself the recipient of a mystic revelation through which he won a decisive victory and gained possession of Rome. Abandoning sun-worship, he not only professed Christianity for himself but also brought up his children in the faith. Christian symbols were placed on his military standards, his coins, and his monuments. Now, for the first time, official decrees gave the Christians toleration throughout the empire and permitted them to form legal corporations. It should be remembered, however, that Constantine did not make Christianity the state religion, for the older cults still retained their ancient prerogatives. The latter were indeed attacked by Constantine's sons, but their acts were repealed by Julian, who devoted his brief reign (361-63) to an attempted revival of paganism. Valentinian then restored the system of Constantine and, finally, Theodosius undertook the suppression of all faiths except that of the officially recognized church—a revolution of momentous import for the future of Europe.

CHAPTER II

THE BARBARIAN INVASIONS AND THE CHRISTIAN CHURCH

1. THE BARBARIANS BEFORE THE INVASIONS

The more important peoples inhabiting lands beyond the Roman frontiers in the third century were, in Africa, the Moors or Berbers; in western Asia, the Arabs and the Persians; on the central Asiatic plateau and the Caspian steppe, the Ural-Altaic nomads; and to the northwest of them, in Europe, the Slavs, the Germans, and the Celts (see Map II). Of these language groups, the first three can be taken up more conveniently in the next chapter. The others must now receive a few words of introduction; for, beginning in the fifth and sixth centuries, they vitally affected the destinies of the European provinces. *Frontier peoples*

From the Ural-Altaic group, named after a vague homeland extending from the Ural to the Altai Mountains, have emerged such famous peoples as the Scythians, Sarmatians, Huns, Bulgars, Avars, Magyars, Mongols, Tartars, and Turks. Originally they were all nomadic—i.e., wandering; for nomads owe their sustenance to flocks and herds and must constantly move from one pasture to another. Thus having no settled habitation, they restrict their household belongings to tents and the few utensils that can easily be carried on horseback. Among them wealth consists of animals, to guard which is the principal task of the men; other labor is turned over to the women. And they have, of course, no need of any political organization beyond the customary discipline of the tribe, enforced by its chief. *The Ural-Altaic nomads*

To the ordinary occupations of pastoral life the Asiatic nomads added those of professional marauders. Magnificent horsemen, inured from infancy to all extremes of hardship, they covered amazing distances in wastes that others found impassable. Throughout all exposed regions the scourge of their raids was unceasing. Normally these raids were merely for loot; but occasionally, as the result of economic pressure in the homeland, a migrating horde would bring ruin to far-distant lands. Such episodes are familiar in the history of China, India, Persia, Syria, and even Egypt. Nor did Europe escape, for the Caspian steppe gave the nomads an easy highway to the heart of the continent. In the fourth century it was the Huns who, driving westward along this route, terrorized the peoples then dwelling across the Roman frontier. The Huns, we are told by the chroniclers of the empire, resembled beasts rather than men—with their squat bodies, bowlegs, and ugly faces marked by prominent ears, flat noses, slanting eyes, swarthy skins, and bristling hair. And behind their repulsive exterior, enhanced by the filthiness of their habits, lay a stark ferocity that daunted their more civilized antagonists.

The Slavs

Prominent among the victims of these nomads were the Slavs, first mentioned as a fair-haired people living to the north of the Pontic steppe in what is now central Russia. We know remarkably little about the Slavs in ancient times, but in the early Middle Ages their rôle was generally that of the hunted and oppressed. Probably their geographic position—between Asiatic raiders from the south and Germanic raiders from the north—had much to do with their misfortunes. Thousands were driven by alien conquerors to till distant lands. Other thousands were carried into captivity and sold throughout the markets of the west; so that the name that by derivation meant "glorious" eventually became our word "slave."[1] Yet through it all, developing a marvelous power of endurance, they lived and multiplied. As more warlike nations killed one another off or pushed westward to despoil the Roman provinces, the Slavs took over the vacated lands. Without a single battle to win the

[1] See below, p. 115.

attention of chroniclers, they made the plains of eastern Europe almost solidly Slavic.

In a much earlier age the Celts—or, as the Romans called them, the Gauls—had inhabited the forests of northern Europe as far east as the Elbe. Thence, in a great migration that for a time threatened to wipe out the little republic of Rome, they swept over the Alps into Italy and across the Rhine into the country which was thereafter known as Gaul. A first wave of invaders, the Gaels, occupied the islands off the northwest coast; then the better part of the principal island, which thereby got a permanent name, was conquered by a second wave, the Britons. The languages of these two peoples have persisted as Gaelic and Welsh; but with the Latinization of Gaul the Celtic dialects of that region disappeared, except for an occasional place name. And meanwhile the Gauls, whom all the ancient writers describe as of the Nordic type, had lost their original traits through mingling with the native Mediterranean stock.

The Celts

The peoples whom the Romans knew as *Germani* are first heard of in the lands bordering on the Baltic. Moving south behind the Celts, they took over the country between the Elbe and the Rhine, where they were held in check by the military defenses of the Roman Empire. For the early Germans we have two principal sources: the *Commentaries* of Cæsar (55 B.C.) and the *Germania* of Tacitus (c. A.D. 100). And of the two the latter is the more valuable, although the author wrote with an eye to reproving his luxury-loving compatriots. Thus, when Tacitus paints an idyllic picture of German marriage customs and family life, we may suspect a little exaggeration for the sake of a moral lesson. The actual Germans whom we encounter in the pages of history—even the most primitive of them—were by no means so pure. Yet, on the whole, Tacitus gives us a reliable account, in many respects confirmed by later records.

The Germans

With regard to the appearance of the Germans he repeats the general verdict: "fierce blue eyes and reddish hair; great bodies, especially powerful for attack, but not equally patient of hard work; little able to withstand heat and thirst, though by climate and soil they have been inured to cold and hunger." Cæsar describes them as living mainly by pasturage, together with fishing and hunting; Tacitus emphasizes rather their agriculture. None of the German tribes, he says, lived in cities; even within their villages each man's house was surrounded by a considerable open space. As much land was occupied by the villagers as they needed for the raising of grain, and the fields were distributed among them according to their rank. Because they had land to spare, they changed the arable yearly and so avoided exhausting the soil. The German freeman, however, was a warrior rather than an agricultural laborer. During intervals of peace he spent his time in loafing, gambling, and beer-drinking, while all necessary work was left to women and dependents. The German slaves, adds Tacitus, were not household servants like those of the Romans, but peasants (*coloni*) holding plots of land from which they paid a share of the produce.

Only the menfolk had any part in public life. The German youth, on attaining man's estate, received a formal gift of arms; thereafter he bore his shield and spear on all public occasions. Political organization was slight. The formal assemblies were military gatherings in which the chief men submitted proposals; if the warriors approved, they clashed their weapons. Although some of the German tribes had kings, they were little more than leaders in war. The kindred group remained powerful, defending its members and collecting compensation for injuries done them. And the tribesmen were free to form voluntary associations for the sake of warlike adventure and booty. A well-known chief might thus attract a considerable band of followers. The relationship was highly honorable to both parties: the followers obtained equipment and food, while in return they provided the chief with a distinguished retinue and made possible his greater exploits. Together they fought and enjoyed the profits of victory; or, in case of bitter fortune, together died. Of this institution, known as the *comitatus*, much will be heard in later chapters.

Tacitus gives an extensive catalogue of German tribes, but few of them are ever heard of outside his pages. By the time of Marcus Aurelius the Marcomanni and the Quadi had become dangerous on the upper Danube, and their power was broken only with the utmost difficulty. Then, in the third century, a new series of Germanic peoples came to threaten the whole imperial frontier in Europe. The Goths, striking south from the Baltic, crushed the Sarmatians and overran the Danubian provinces. There, as remarked above, they were finally checked by Aurelian, though he was forced to leave them in possession of Dacia. To the north, meanwhile, had emerged three powerful confederations: the Alamans ("all men"), to whom Aurelian abandoned the triangle between the two great rivers; the Franks (i.e., "the free") on the lower Rhine; and to the east of them the piratical Saxons (or "axemen"), feared on both sides of the British Channel. This was the situation when, in the fourth century, the terrific onslaught of the Huns brought increasing pressure on the already weakened defenses of the empire.

The Roman government had long been suffering from a shortage of troops. Diocletian's military system called for a total force of possibly half a million men; if enough Romans could not be found, the emperors had to hire barbarians. So, in one way or another, streams of Moors in Africa, of Arabs in Syria, and of Germans in Europe entered the imperial service. The auxiliary divisions had from the earliest time been non-Roman; by the fourth century even the citizens in the legions were such as Augustus would never have recognized. Besides, through extension of another ancient precedent, whole tribes had been admitted to the empire as allies (*fœderati*), to whom lands had been assigned in return for an engagement to patrol the frontier. Thus Valentinian's successor in the west, Gratian, formally established large bodies of Franks in what is now Flanders. And about the

Germanic peoples of the third century

Germans in the Roman service

same time Valens, emperor in the east, made a similar bargain with various chieftains of the Visigoths, or West Goths, who had appealed to him for protection against the Huns.

All this was ordinary enough; it was merely an unfortunate accident that the latter arrangement had tragic consequences. While the Goths were crossing the Danube, they became involved in a violent quarrel with certain high-handed officials. Both sides called in 'reinforcements, and the result was the battle of Adrianople (378), in which Valens was slain. But for the moment there was no further trouble. The new emperor, Theodosius, quickly restored peace by carrying out the original agreement, and during the rest of his reign the Goths faithfully guarded the frontier, as thousands of other *fœderati* were already doing. The affair hardly marks the beginning of an epoch either for the Romans or for the barbarians.

2. THE INVASIONS OF THE FIFTH CENTURY

Roman and barbarian

To explain the history of the fifth century it is necessary first of all to make clear the distinction between Roman and barbarian. Today in America we all know of prominent men who are commonly referred to as Swedes, Italians, Poles, or the like; but who, nevertheless, are American citizens and worthy members of the community. Legally their descent is of no importance. Culturally it may or may not be, according to the degree of their Americanization. The situation was very much the same in the Roman Empire. A man was often called a Frank or a Goth because he came of a Frankish or a Gothic family, although he was quite as Roman as the law could make him, and although the better Romans of his day themselves had dubious ancestries. The really significant question was the extent to which a particular citizen had absorbed Latin culture. As a matter of fact, the empire of the fourth century was filled with semi-barbarous Romans. The only difference between the armed forces on the two sides of the frontier was that the one was paid by the emperor and, presumably, was better equipped and better disciplined. And since the military service was the surest road to political preferment, the higher offices of the state were frequently held by men of recent barbarian extraction. No one doubted their ability, or their desire to be good Romans. Acquiring wealth and power, they inter-married with the noblest families of the empire; for German blood, in particular, was no social disgrace. On the contrary, the admiration of Roman ladies for Nordic beauty had stimulated a brisk trade in blond wigs made of imported barbarian tresses.

Thus we find a Vandal soldier named Stilicho rising to high favor under Theodosius and his incompetent son Honorius, who succeeded as western emperor in 395. Stilicho—*patricius*, master of troops, and eventually father-in-law of the new emperor—became actual ruler of the west. Yet he remained unsatisfied, longing also to control the east, which had been placed under the sovereignty of Arcadius, the second incompetent son of Theodosius. In that design he failed, for the main consequence of his intrigue was to encourage another adventurer like himself. This was Alaric, king of the Visigoths, i.e., the elected chief of the Gothic *fœderati* whom Theodosius had stationed along the Danube. Having extorted some sort of military commission from Arcadius, Alaric led his Goths towards Italy, where Stilicho was already faced by a number of other rebels. By calling all available troops from the northern frontiers, however, Stilicho succeeded in holding off his enemies until, in 408, the jealous Honorius had him executed on a charge of treason. The result was chaos, for the emperor merely shut himself up in the impregnable fortress of Ravenna and let happen what would. So, although Alaric invaded Italy, his negotiations with Honorius came to nothing. In revenge he then starved Rome into submission and gave the proud city to his troops for three days' pillage (410). Shortly afterwards he died in the midst of plans for transporting his army to Africa.

The succeeding events may be passed over in still briefer

Honorius, Stilicho, and Alaric

review. Under the weakling sons of Honorius and Arcadius
the two halves of the empire drifted farther and farther
apart. The east, as will be seen in a later chapter, continued
much as before and even recovered strength; but the west
sank to irretrievable ruin, Before the death of Honorius the
imperial administration, and with it the imperial defense,
had utterly collapsed. Across the frontiers, now stripped of
regular troops, poured hosts of barbarians, to do what they
pleased with the unfortunate provinces. Britain, early abandoned to its fate, was overrun by Picts from beyond the
northern wall, Scots from Ireland, and Saxons from the
continent. Northern Gaul was occupied by Franks, Alamans,
and Burgundians, while the Vandals and their allies took
Aquitaine and Spain. The Visigoths, in the meantime, had
entered a sort of Roman alliance through the marriage of
their new king, Alaric's brother, to a sister of Honorius.
Acting under an official commission, they now invaded southern Gaul and inflicted so terrific a defeat on the Vandals
that the latter abandoned Spain and crossed the strait to
Africa (429). There Gaiseric, recently elected king of the
Vandals, quickly secured the whole territory west of Tripoli,
organized it as an independent state, and made it the base
for piratical expeditions to the north and east.

Meanwhile the Huns had extended their ruthless dominion from the Caspian to the Rhine, and had respected
the Roman territory only because the eastern emperor, Theodosius II, had regularly paid them blackmail. Now, under
a new and vigorous leader named Attila, they decided on
wider operations, and it was fortunate for the government
at Constantinople that they struck at Gaul rather than
Greece. Although the western emperor, Valentinian III,
could be expected to do nothing, his able master of troops,
Aëtius, took the field against the invaders. And, thanks to
the aid of the warlike Visigoths, he won the famous battle
of the Catalaunian Fields, in the region now called Champagne (451). That battle, however, merely diverted Attila
towards Italy; the decisive event was his sudden death two

years later. Thereupon his horde broke up and the Huns ceased to be a menace.

In spite of this respite, conditions in the west became steadily worse. Valentinian III had Aëtius put to death and was himself assassinated in revenge (455). Gaiseric, seizing the favorable moment, brought his Vandals up the Tiber and systematically looted the capital for the second time. The government of Italy then fell to a series of military bosses, commanders of the German mercenaries; and they set up and pulled down emperors at pleasure until, in 476, one Odoacer decided it was a useless formality. Deposing the last of the puppets, he sent the insignia of the vacant office to the eastern emperor, Zeno, who in return allowed him the traditional title of *patricius*. In theory the empire was again united under one Augustus; actually, with the removal of the shadow-emperor, Italy had been turned into a barbarian state like those already established by Vandals, Visigoths, Burgundians, Franks, and Saxons in the other western provinces. The reality, of course, was by no means hidden from Zeno, but for the moment he accepted the fiction. Eventually he tried, in a way, to reassert his authority.

The end of the western emperors (476)

Among the Germanic peoples freed by the death of Attila were the Ostrogoths, or East Goths, who were then admitted to the empire as *fœderati* in the station earlier held by the Visigoths. They were under several kings, one of whom had a son named Theodoric. The boy, being sent as a hostage to Constantinople, there acquired a warm admiration for Roman ways and absorbed at least a modicum of Greek and Latin culture. And there, after his elevation as king, he continued to enjoy imperial favor, acquiring the rank of Roman citizen, *patricius,* and master of troops. He was even designated as one of the two consuls for the year 484. But as Theodoric united all the Ostrogoths under his command and displayed ambitions like those of his predecessor Alaric, Zeno determined to get rid of him by commissioning him against Odoacer. In 489, consequently, Theodoric led his Ostrogoths to Italy, which he conquered and, after the treach-

The rise of Theodoric the Ostrogoth

erous murder of Odoacer, ruled without challenge until his death in 526. The further significance of his reign, together with contemporary developments throughout the west generally, will be explained in a later section.

3. THE CHURCH IN THE FOURTH AND FIFTH CENTURIES

Christian tradition and the Bible

Christianity, as remarked above, was one of several mystic faiths that, originating in the east, swept through the Roman Empire. In the first century it remained very obscure; in the second century it gained sufficient prominence to awaken an increasing hostility on the part of the government; in the third century it grew so strong that persecution of its followers came to be recognized as useless; and, finally, in the fourth century it became the official religion of the state. Meanwhile—in the course of bitter conflict with the Jews, with the empire, and with pagan sects—the church had developed a powerful organization. Whatever the controversies that were to arise over this development a thousand years later, there were none in the fourth century. So, without raising the question of absolute truth, which must remain a matter of faith, we may restrict our attention to the theory and practice of the church as it then was.

The ultimate authority, to which appeal was made for the settlement of all disputes, was the sacred tradition of the faithful. Part of that tradition was contained in the Scriptures, but the acceptance of such writings as divinely inspired was itself traditional. In ecclesiastical history a collection of authoritative books is called a canon. The Christian Bible includes two such canons, known as the Old and New Testaments. The Old Testament of the Christians was not the original Hebrew canon, but a Greek version called the Septuagint, which had been drawn up for the use of Hellenized Jews in Alexandria, and which included various books that had never been written in Hebrew. The New Testament was a subsequent compilation that took form as the result of Christian usage. As late as the time of Constantine, although the Epistles of Paul, the four Gospels, and the Acts of the Apostles were universally recognized, opinions were still divided with regard to the Apocalypse, the epistles attributed to other disciples, and certain additional writings. The final determination of the canon, therefore, came only with the formal organization of the church in the period immediately following.

In the meantime, however, all Christian communities had come to hold certain fundamental doctrines: especially that Christ, the Son of God, had founded His church on earth to provide men with a new means of salvation—the holy sacraments. A sacrament, to use the phrase that was to become official, is the "outward sign of an inward grace." The outward sign is the ceremonial; the inward grace is the grace of God spiritually transforming the recipient. According to this view, every sacrament is a mystery, a miracle that produces results otherwise unobtainable. The sacrament of baptism, for instance, is held to wash away the sin inherited by the child from his first parents, Adam and Eve. On becoming old enough to know right from wrong, he is admitted to the Christian congregation by another sacrament, confirmation. Henceforth he is bound to confess his sins and, on proving his repentance, he receives absolution, together with a temporal penalty—prayer, fasting, or the performance of other holy works—assessed in proportion to the evil that he has committed. This is the sacrament of penance, performed like baptism for one individual. On the other hand, the celebration of the eucharist, popularly known as the mass, is rather a community service, in which the congregation meets to commemorate the last supper of the Lord and through the sacramental bread and wine enters into mystic communion with Him.

The sacramental system

To administer sacraments like these the ordinary person was held to be obviously incompetent; the supernatural powers of the church had been entrusted to a sacerdotal class, admission to which was itself a sacrament—that of ordination. The justification of this idea was the theory of the apostolic succession. The apostles, it was affirmed, had re-

Theory of the apostolic succession

ceived divine authority from Christ, who had laid His hands upon them and so commissioned them to continue the work He had begun. They in turn, by the same ceremony, had commissioned others; and upon their successors, the ordained clergy, devolved the power of administering the sacraments and governing the church. But the apostolic authority, according to this doctrine, was given in its entirety only to the bishop (*episcopus*). The priest (*presbyter*) was his subordinate, empowered to administer all the sacraments except confirmation and ordination. And below the priesthood a number of lesser grades came to be recognized, of which the highest was that of deacon.

Territorial organization

It was only after the legalization of Christianity that ecclesiastical government came to be based on a territorial plan borrowed from the Roman Empire. The unit was the *civitas*, the bishop's diocese or see (from *sedes*, seat), in which stood his cathedral church (from *cathedra*, the episcopal chair). The diocese was subdivided into parishes, both urban and rural, each of which was entrusted to a priest named by the bishop. Earlier, on the death of a bishop, the man to be consecrated in his place had been chosen through a somewhat informal election, in which popular acclaim was frequently a decisive factor. Later, as the episcopal office gained prominence in society and politics, it became a prize to be secured through influential patrons, or even to be fought over by rival factions. So the actual choice of a bishop was gradually taken over by the clergy of the diocese, and little was left to the populace beyond a sort of confirmatory applause.

A much more troublesome problem concerned the relative dignity of bishops. For both civil and ecclesiastical administration a number of *civitates* were combined to form a province. One city in each province served as the metropolis, and the bishop of such a city, styled metropolitan or archbishop, normally enjoyed the right of consecrating all bishops within his jurisdiction. Thus far there was general agreement, but the higher grades were a subject of dispute. Applying the imperial system of organization in its entirety would demand prelates corresponding to the vicars and prefects. And would not the supreme rank then have to be shared by the bishops of Rome and Constantinople? Although such a rigorous hierarchy of ecclesiastical offices was never actually established, it might well have been if the empire had not disintegrated. As long as the emperors ruled the Roman world, the church tended to be governed according to their ideas. And they unquestionably regarded it as a department of state, administered by public officials under the sovereignty of Augustus. The peculiar authority of the clergy extended only to matters of faith and religious discipline; their acts, like those of other subjects, depended for legality upon imperial decree.

In this connection the policy of the fourth-century emperors with regard to heresy is very illuminating. The concept of heresy had already become clearly defined in the earlier period—as a doctrine advanced in the name of Christianity but denounced by the church as contrary to the orthodox faith. Thus the attempt of the so-called Gnostics to combine Christianity with Neo-Platonic mysticism had been rejected by the general agreement of the Christian leaders. In the time of Constantine, however, more serious controversies arose within the organized church itself. In 314 a council of western bishops called by the emperor at Arles condemned the Donatists—a fanatical group which, rebelling against the bishop of Carthage, asserted that the validity of a sacrament depended on the personal character of the minister. Then, a few years later, a priest of Alexandria named Arius began a dispute that was to have much graver consequences. With what seemed to him unescapable logic he argued that Christ, being the Son of God, must have been younger than the Father; must, indeed, have been a creature rather than a divinity in the absolute sense. Otherwise, said Arius, Christians would have to admit that they were worshiping two gods. Eloquent champions, notably Athanasius, at once arose to defend the traditional faith. They insisted that, although the doctrine of the Incarnation

The empire and heresy

necessitated belief in the humanity of Jesus, Christians must also believe that He was truly God as well, or their customary worship of Him would be no better than idolatry.

The Council of Nicæa (325)

In 325, accordingly, Constantine summoned the bishops from all Christendom to decide the question of Arianism in a great meeting at Nicæa, the first general council in the history of the church. Before the assembled prelates, perhaps three hundred in all, the emperor appeared in person to urge the cause of unity. The result was a nearly unanimous declaration condemning the views of Arius and prescribing the formula of Christian belief that, with later amendments, is known as the Nicene Creed. Nevertheless, in one form or another, Arianism persisted in the eastern provinces, and was thence carried to the Germans by missionaries—among them the famous Ulfilas (d. 383), first bishop of the Goths and translator of the Bible into their language. As will be seen, the conversion of these barbarians to unorthodox Christianity was to cause them much trouble when they came to rule parts of the empire. For in the meantime Theodosius had secured final outlawry of Arianism in the Council of Constantinople (381) and had established severe penalties to crush heresy throughout the Roman territory.

Theory of the Petrine supremacy

From these facts it is evident that, according to the imperial theory, the normal government of the church rested with a hierarchy of bishops corresponding to the hierarchy of civil officials, and that any major cause of dispute should be submitted by the emperor to a general council of bishops and settled by his promulgation of their decision. But from an early time this theory had been opposed by another, to which the tragic events of the fifth century inevitably gave fresh prominence. Christian tradition, said the upholders of the latter theory, was essentially that handed down by the apostles and preserved in the churches which they had founded: especially Antioch, Alexandria, and Rome. By the test of apostolic foundation, of course, Constantinople had no claim to superior rank. Rome, on the other hand, was the city where, by ancient tradition, the apostles Peter and

Paul had both been martyred, and where Peter had been the first bishop. Furthermore, according to the Gospel of Matthew (xvi, 18-19), Peter was the rock on which Christ had built His church, the keeper of the keys to the kingdom of heaven, the holder of the power to bind and loose. As Peter had been the head of the apostles, so his successor, the bishop of Rome or pope,[2] was the head of all bishops, the supreme authority of the Christian Church.

To state this theory was one matter, to enforce it quite another. Of the popes during the first two Christian centuries little more is known than the list of their names. It is only after the time of Constantine that the sources begin to reveal certain popes as distinct individuals who play an active part in the affairs of the universal church. Thus Damasus I (366-84) appears as the author of a digest setting forth the beliefs and practices of the Roman see, including a definite assertion of the papal supremacy. He also proclaimed what was thereafter to be the official canon of the New Testament and, as will be explained below, commissioned the illustrious Jerome to revise the Latin translation of the Bible. From his successor, Siricius (384-99), come the oldest extant papal decretals—formal letters on questions of law and doctrine submitted to Rome for decision. And with Leo the Great (440-61), an inspiring leader in an age of political ruin, control by the papacy was accepted by most local churches of the west.

The early papacy

In the east, on the other hand, the papal sovereignty was bitterly opposed. There the emperor remained powerful, summoning councils to decide religious disputes and warmly supporting the claim of Constantinople to equality with Rome in ecclesiastical privilege. This, assuredly, was one important cause of dissension between east and west. Another was the fundamental incompatibility of Greek and Latin theologians. The latter, for example, readily accepted

Religious divergence between east and west

---

[2] This title is merely a form of the Latin *papa* (father). It could be used in addressing any priest, but in the west, as a mark of special honor, it came to be reserved for the Roman bishop.

Leo's practical judgment on the combination in Christ of both human and divine natures. But the former continued violent controversy on the same subject despite the papal decision, the action of a general council, and an attempted compromise by the emperor. The result was a chronic disunion among the churches of the eastern provinces and an intermittent schism between Rome and Constantinople that was to determine the course of many famous events.

Problems of the official church

Whatever may have been the theory, it is obvious that in practice the church of the fifth century was very different from what it had been in the days of Roman persecution. Christianity then was not a faith for the ease-loving and indifferent; there was no worldly advantage in holding ecclesiastical office. But the conversion of Constantine made Christianity fashionable. The clergy attained social and political prominence. The local churches, through gifts and bequests, acquired extensive property. Finally, the decrees of Theodosius compelled all Roman subjects, except the tolerated Jews, to become ostensibly Christian. In reality, many of them remained pagan, especially throughout the country districts—as the word itself implies (*paganus,* a rustic). And even more of them, although they assumed the Christian name, remained pagan at heart; for the earlier situation had been reversed. To be a Christian was now a matter of law, rather than of religious fervor. Being a practical institution, the church had to take the people as they came and mould its requirements to suit the great majority; but in so doing it could hardly satisfy those who demanded a more rigorous Christianity. For them—"the religious," as they were significantly called—the church came to provide an ascetic life primarily devoted to worship and meditation.

Monasticism

The establishment of this peculiarly religious discipline came through monasticism—literally "living alone," for the original monk was a hermit. Retiring into solitude, he found a cave or built a cell where he could attain holiness through constant prayer and the mortification of the flesh. Such a life is relatively easy in a warm dry climate; so it is not strange that the first noteworthy development of Christian monasticism was in Egypt. There, early in the fourth century, the famous St. Anthony became head of a hermit community, for which he finally drew up a set of rules—a system greatly elaborated by St. Pachomius a few years later. These Egyptian monks, though they might be assembled for meals and worship, still occupied separate dwellings. What we know as a monastery—a house where the monks all live together, participating in the same routine existence—was instituted toward the close of the same century by St. Basil, a Greek of Asia Minor. And in those countries that follow the traditions of the Greek Church, the Basilian Rule has remained standard down to the present. For a long while, however, the influence of St. Anthony continued strong throughout both east and west. In Syria great renown for piety was won by extremists like St. Simeon Stylites (d. 459), who lived for thirty years on top of a pillar, gradually increasing its height to sixty feet. In Italy and Gaul, though the weather tended to discourage pillar saints, Christian hermits soon appeared on all sides; and, by the opening of the fifth century, there were many communities of the Pachomian type —even some for female ascetics, or nuns. From such beginnings western monasticism was to have a remarkable development in the next two hundred years; but for the moment we must interrupt the story in order to consider the relation of the church to learning.

The fact of primary significance in this connection is that, with the decay of the Roman Empire, education in the west came under control of the church, which naturally changed the older system to accord with Christian ideals. In the time of the principate it had still been customary for Romans of good birth to learn Greek as a matter of course, and even to attend schools in Greece for advanced work. By the fifth century this was no longer true. Most western scholars were thenceforth ignorant of Greek and to them, accordingly, the finest thought of the ancient world became inaccessible. Meanwhile, too, the other Roman studies had lost all contact

The church and education

with the realities of life. Traditionally the mark of a cultured gentleman was training in grammar and rhetoric—what we should recognize as literature and public speaking. But the goal of his ambition was now merely to compose and pronounce declamations on conventional subjects in a conventional way. He was not interested in practical questions; he never said anything simply and directly. His themes had to be drawn from classical sources; his argument had to proceed by the weaving together of literary allusions; his style had to be elevated, intricate, and ornate. The curse of Latin letters in the schools of the later empire was this craze for artificial rhetoric. Christians might well condemn it, not merely for its paganism, but also for its uselessness.

The church, to be sure, recognized grammar as of fundamental importance. A knowledge of Latin was essential to all ecclesiastical writing, and to learn good Latin one had to go to the pagan classics. But the means ought to be subordinated to the end—the practical needs of the Christian religion. So, while the church might frown on the traditional rhetoric of the schools, it welcomed such popular works as Priscian's *Institutes of Grammar* and the textbooks and translations of Boëthius. The latter, while living at the court of Theodoric the Ostrogoth, could still maintain the tradition of pagan letters in his famous *Consolation of Philosophy*; but he had no successors. The intellectual leadership of his world had already passed to the great ecclesiastical writers known as the church fathers. Until the later fourth century the outstanding exponents of Christian thought were mainly Greeks. Then, on the eve of the barbarian invasions, the list of eminent Latin fathers began with St. Ambrose, St. Jerome, and St. Augustine, whose lives richly illustrate the general facts set forth above.

St.
Ambrose
(d. 397)

In an earlier age Ambrose would doubtless have risen to command armies and rule provinces, for he was the son of a high Roman official and himself possessed the talent and training for a distinguished civil career. As it was, however, he left the service of the state to become bishop of Milan.

then the residence of the emperor Theodosius. Excellently educated in Greek as well as Latin, Ambrose made a conscientious study of theology and wrote a number of books on practical religion. Yet he was more distinguished as a preacher. Through his sermons, we are told, hundreds of men and women were inspired to renounce the world and adopt the life of ascetics. And as spiritual director of Theodosius he had much to do with shaping the imperial policies. On one famous occasion, when the emperor's commands had resulted in a massacre at Thessalonica, Ambrose refused to admit him to divine service until he had publicly shown contrition for his sin. This he did, appearing before the congregation in the garb of a penitent; and the lesson was driven home for all to understand, that even Augustus was only human and was therefore subject to the discipline of the church.

In Jerome we find one of the few persons ever raised to sainthood[3] for purely scholarly labors. Although brought up as a Christian in Dalmatia, he seems at first not to have taken the faith very seriously. He was, he tells us, enamored of pagan letters rather than of religion. Subsequently, as the result of an illness and what he believed to be a miraculous vision, he abandoned his sinful passion for rhetorical study and vowed exclusive devotion to the church. After spending a number of years as a hermit in Syria, he took holy orders and in 382 became secretary to Pope Damasus. And it was on the papal urging that Jerome undertook a new Latin version of the Scriptures—a task for which he was eminently fitted, having a thorough knowledge of Greek and at least a smattering of Hebrew. Jerome first began the translation of the New Testament, and soon finished it. The Old Testament caused him much more trouble; for he realized the importance of using Hebrew manuscripts as well as the Greek Septuagint, and he was not proficient enough in the former

St. Jerome (d. 420)

---

[3] By the ceremony of canonization, the church came to recognize as saints those exceptionally holy persons who were deemed worthy of special honor. Prayer might be addressed to a saint for his aid in securing divine grace.

language to proceed without the assistance of Jewish experts. Consequently, it was not until he had returned to Syria, after the death of Damasus, that Jerome was able to complete his undertaking. Meanwhile he had produced an amazing quantity of other writings: essays on Chrisian archæology, controversial tracts, and numerous letters, many of them in praise of the monastic life. But his greatest accomplishment was the Latin text of the Bible which, with the addition of certain translations from the Septuagint, became the official Vulgate of the western church.

St.
Augustine
(d. 430)

Almost exactly contemporary with Jerome was the great African bishop Augustine, whose life is so familiar to us from his own *Confessions*. Like Jerome he was early enrolled in the church, but drifted away from it to develop a passion for rhetoric; so that he eventually became a teacher of the subject in Carthage. Thus, among the sins bewailed in the *Confessions*, he emphasizes his delight in Latin poetry, his love of the theater, and his "damnable and vainglorious pride" in profane wisdom. Craving intellectual certainty, he joined the sect of Manichæans, who held a modified form of Zoroastrianism.[4] But he eventually rejected their teachings in favor of Neo-Platonism, which he, being ignorant of Greek, did not distinguish from the philosophy of Plato. Then, having obtained appointment as a teacher of rhetoric at Milan, he came under the influence of Bishop Ambrose. From him Augustine learned that the Old Testament should be interpreted symbolically, and that the New Testament had much in common with Platonism. Hitherto he had been repelled by the form of the Christian Scriptures; now he reread them with growing interest, especially the Epistles of Paul, in whom he found a kindred spirit. And while he was thus engaged, he first heard the story of St. Anthony and Christian monasticism. The result was an emotional crisis, in the midst of which the voice of a child at play seemed to Augustine a divine urging to "take up and read." Taking up Paul's Epistles, he read the text (*Romans,* xiii, 13-14) bid-

[4] See above. p. 29.

ding him "put on the Lord Jesus Christ and make not provision for the flesh." Thus ended all his questionings. He abandoned his profession, together with a contemplated marriage, returned to Africa, and adopted the life of a monk in his old home. Thenceforth, even after he had been elected bishop of Hippo, his principal energies were devoted to the defense and exposition of the Christian faith. He died in 430 during the siege of his cathedral city by the Vandals.

The details of Augustine's life are of profound significance in the history of Europe; for the intellectual dominance of the church throughout the succeeding age is summed up in his creed of scholarship—rationalism subordinated to mystic faith. He left his mark on virtually every great problem that has remained to vex the theologian: especially the origin of evil, predestination, divine grace, human will, and the nature of salvation. On these subjects he wrote a number of learned works, but for the average reader his views are best presented in the little volume entitled *De Civitate Dei*, "Concerning the City of God." To refute the allegation that the sack of Rome in 410 was due to the Romans' desertion of their ancient gods, Augustine appeals not merely to history but to all revealed truth. The fortunes of persons and the fate of empires, he says, are but episodes in the scheme of divine providence. The City of Man is imperfect and temporary; the City of God is perfect and everlasting. In magnificent perspective Augustine then depicts the design of the Creator: God and the angels, Satan and the demons, the creation of the world, the fall of Adam and its consequences for mankind, human history under the Old Dispensation, the coming of Christ and the nature of His redemption, the church and the sacraments, the end of the City of Man, and the perpetual triumph of the City of God.

Despite the turgid rhetoric so dear to the African rhetorician, this is one of the world's great books. Centuries were to elapse before Christian scholarship could hope to equal its epic grandeur.

The City of God

4. THE WEST IN THE SIXTH CENTURY

As the result of events described above, a series of Germanic peoples had established themselves on Roman soil by the second half of the fifth century. Sometimes they held legal commissions, sometimes not. In any case it was they who now ruled the occupied territories, which, without regard to a theoretical persistence of the empire, we place on the map as barbarian kingdoms (see Map III). Of these states the most thoroughly Roman was that of Theodoric in Italy. Under him the ancient system of government remained intact. The Ostrogoths, settled on lands assigned to them, held to their old customary law, which was unwritten; but for Roman citizens Theodoric issued an official code embodying the principles of their own civil law. The best Latin scholars of the day were his secretary, Cassiodorus, and his counselor, Boëthius. Scrupulously loyal to the emperor as his rightful sovereign, Theodoric in every way tried to act as a good Roman. And he assuredly provided the best administration that Italy had had since the death of Theodosius.

Three other barbarian kingdoms were relatively civilized: those of the Visigoths in Spain and southern Gaul, of the Vandals in Africa, and of the Burgundians in the country named after them, Burgundy. In these regions, as in Italy, the kings appropriated part of the land for their followers, preserved what they could of the imperial government, and issued codes of Roman law for the native inhabitants. But of these three peoples only the Visigoths remained formidable. The Vandal kingdom weakened rapidly after the death of Gaiseric in 477, while the Burgundians came under a sort of Ostrogothic protectorate. All the barbarian establishments in the southwestern provinces, it should be noted, rested on the same basis. The invaders were at most a few tens of thousands ruling native millions by virtue of military strength. Once that was broken, the conquerors vanished—absorbed into the conquered population, to whom they had already tended to be assimilated. Biologically, the intermixture had

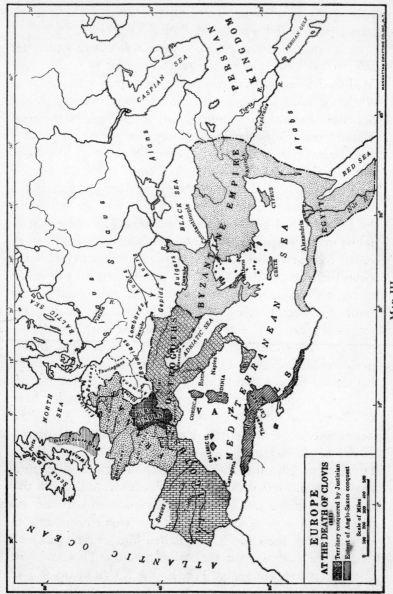

EUROPE
AT THE DEATH OF CLOVIS
(511)

Territory conquered by Justinian
Extent of Anglo-Saxon conquest

Scale of Miles
0   100   200   300   400   500

MAP III.

little if any significance; culturally, it served only to accelerate a process of barbarization begun long before.

Britain and Gaul

In the northwestern provinces conditions were altogether different. Britain, one of the last territories to be incorporated in the empire, had never been thoroughly Romanized. While the south and east of the island were overrun by the Germanic barbarians whom we call Anglo-Saxons, the west relapsed into Celtic barbarism like that prevailing in Ireland. Between these two forces Latin culture tended to disappear altogether. Meanwhile the left bank of the Rhine had been so densely settled by Franks and Alamans that it has since remained a German-speaking country. To the south the invaders had generally been converted to Arian Christianity before leaving their old homes. The northern peoples, on the contrary, were still heathen; and the fact that, being somewhat isolated, they kept their primitive traits had much to do with their political destinies. If, for example, the Franks had been less fiercely warlike, they could hardly have become a great European power during the sixth century.

The Frankish kingdom

In 481 a certain Chlodovech or Clovis, of the family known as Merovingian, became king of a Frankish band that had settled in and about the city of Tournai. A thoroughly cruel and unscrupulous barbarian, he quickly showed himself to be also a remarkably able commander. An initial victory over a local chieftain named Syagrius gave him possession of the territory between the Seine and the Loire. Then, turning against the Alamans, he defeated them near Strasbourg and seized the upper Rhinelands. And about this time, through the influence of his Burgundian wife, he was converted to orthodox Christianity—a momentous step in his career, for the church now hailed him as the champion of the true faith against the Arian heretics. To Clovis the rôle was entirely congenial. Forcing the Burgundians to join forces with him, he marched against the Visigoths and crushed them in a decisive battle near Poitiers (507). At this point the Ostrogothic king, Theodoric, intervened to keep the Franks away from the Mediterranean, preserving Septimania for the Visigoths and taking Provence for himself. Clovis, however, annexed the rest of Aquitaine and, before his death in 511, rounded out his dominions to the north by murdering or deposing all the other Frankish kings.

The new-grown power of the Franks did not end with Clovis. Although his four sons often fought each other, they co-operated well enough to carry out a number of successful offensives. Especially after the death of Theodoric in 526, they took advantage of troubled conditions in Italy to occupy Burgundy and Provence. In central Germany they had already subjugated the Thuringians. Now, in the Danube valley, they extended their rule over the Bavarians and the rest of the Alamans. The combination of all these territories makes a brave showing on the map; actually they were held together by no more than force of arms, and under the later Merovingians they rapidly fell apart. Frankish ascendancy brought no real unification. Aquitaine and Provence kept a good part of their Roman culture; the other regions were more or less dominated by Germanic custom. Yet the Frankish monarchy had at least been strong enough to discourage attack on the part of the suddenly revived empire.

This revival, as will be more fully explained in the next chapter, resulted from the ambitious policy of Justinian (527-65). Dreaming of a restored Roman dominion in the west, he carried through a number of glorious but short-lived conquests. A disputed succession to the throne gave him a pretext for intervention first in Africa, then in Italy, and finally in Spain. The decadent Vandal kingdom fell before a single expedition in 533. The Ostrogoths, on the contrary, put up a valiant resistance that was crushed only after a desperate war covering nearly twenty years (535-53). In Spain the imperial adventure gained merely the Balearic Islands and a patch of the opposite coast. At the death of Justinian, accordingly, the Visigoths still held most of the peninsula, together with Septimania. The rest of Gaul, including Provence, remained in the hands of the Franks, to whom, rather than the emperor, the barbarians of the upper

Conquests of Justinian

Danube were subject. The regained territory in Africa did not extend all the way to the straits and was constantly threatened by the Moors. Italy and the adjacent islands had been recovered, but at a frightful cost. Rome, left virtually intact by the plundering Visigoths and Vandals, was now a mass of wreckage, as were many of the other great cities. And with the destruction of urban culture, ancient institutions could not long survive. This was the end of classic Italy.

The Lombards in Italy

To complete the distress of that unhappy country, the Lombards now appeared on the scene. A Germanic people reputed to be utterly savage, they had for some time been settled on the middle Danube as the military allies of the emperor. Then the death of Justinian had brought an unfavorable shift of policy at Constantinople, and the approach of the Avars[5] forced them to move westward in 568. Breaking through the northern defenses of Italy, they conquered the Po valley—or Lombardy, as it came to be called—and most of the interior to the south of the Apennines. But the empire, thanks to its control of the sea, maintained posession of the greater cities and the adjacent coasts—including Ravenna, headquarters of. the principal governor or exarch, and a number of military districts, each under command of a duke (see Map IV). Isolated by the Lombard conquests and neglected by the failing government at Constantinople, these lands were thrown more and more on their own resources. Nor were the Lombard territories better united. Although the invaders elected a series of kings, they had little real authority in the north and none at all over the principalities of Spoleto and Benevento.

Pope Gregory the Great (590-604)

Under such conditions the people of Italy, and of the west in general, naturally turned for leadership to the pope, not merely as the successor of St. Peter, but as the upholder of the glorious Roman tradition. Recently Justinian's conquest of Italy, together with his attempted dictation in religion, had precipitated a violent dispute with the pope. Now that the imperial cause was again declining, the papacy was con-

[5] See below, pp. 72-73.

ITALY
AFTER THE
LOMBARD INVASION

Lombard territories
Byzantine territories

Scale of Miles
0   25   50   100

Drave R.

FRIULI

Trent

Milan   Verona
Pavia   Aquileia   Trieste
Brescia Padua
Mantua   Istria
Turin   Vicenza R.
         Bologna   Pola
                    Ravenna

EXARCHATE
OF RAVENNA   Rimini

Genoa

LOMBARDY

LIGURIA

Florence
Pisa   Ancona
         PENTAPOLIS
TUSCANY
    Siena   D. OF
         Perugia Spoleto
              SPOLETO

CORSICA

D. OF ROME   BENEVENTO

Rome

Foggia

Capua   Bari
Aversa Benevento   Brindisi
Naples D. OF NAPLES
    Salerno   APULIA
              Tarentum
                    Otranto

SARDINIA

TYRRHENIAN

SEA

CALABRIA

Trapani   Palermo   Messina
                    Reggio

SICILY

MEDITERRANEAN   Girgenti   Catania
                    Syracuse

Carthage
TUNIS   SEA

MALTA

CROATIA

DALMATIA

Save R.

Spalato

ADRIATIC

SEA

MANHATTAN DRAFTING CO. INC., N.Y.

MAP IV.

fronted with a splendid opportunity—and found a great man
to grasp and develop it in Gregory I. Of his early life little
is known except that he was born of a noble family about
540, received a good Latin education, and by 573 had risen
to high office in the city of Rome. Then, suddenly, he abandoned his worldly career and turned his ancestral mansion
into a monastery, where he himself became one of the
brothers. Within a few years, however, he had left his seclusion to receive holy orders and eventually to act as special
agent of the pope in Constantinople. There he remained for
about seven years, vainly urging the distracted emperor to
consider the needs of Italy. Returning to Rome, Gregory
once more sought the peace of his monastery; and once more,
in 590, he was drawn back into the world, this time to occupy
the papal throne.

**His
writings**

Gregory, as will be seen, proved himself a great statesman
and administrator, but he was loved and revered by succeeding generations primarily on account of his books. Written
in a plain, straightforward style, they—unlike the works of
Augustine—could be well understood by any one who knew
Latin. They were, in fact, designed to be popular rather than
scholarly: simple expositions of theology, allegorical inter-
pretations of Scripture, practical sermons, and moral discourses adorned with a wealth of pious anecdotes. In the
Dialogues, for example, Gregory relates a series of marvelous
stories about holy men and women to show how, through
the power of God, they were able to escape the wiles of
Satan, to perform all sorts of miracles, and, dying, to be assured of paradise. The most widely read of all Gregory's
books, however, was the one entitled *Pastoral Care*, a manual
on the character and duties of the bishop. He, says Gregory,
is the pastor of the flock, who must teach by example as well
as by words. Although he should be an educated man, he
must above all else have a sympathetic understanding of
human nature, so that he may distinguish one kind of people
from another and vary his instruction accordingly. So Gregory enumerates thirty-six pairs of opposites and devotes a

chapter to the admonitions that should be given in each case—homely advice from one who was himself a wise and faithful shepherd.

On assuming control of the Roman see, Gregory's attention was at once demanded by the Lombard war, which had now continued for over twenty years. As a practical statesman with long experience in the east, Gregory realized that the empire could never regain its lost territory and that, for the sake of the Italians, peace should be arranged on the basis of existing conditions. This policy he vigorously upheld in the face of all imperial opposition, and eventually he had the satisfaction of seeing it put into effect. By the end of the sixth century the emperor had formally recognized the Lombard conquests and had thus accepted a balance of power that was by no means unfavorable to the papal interest. By that time, too, like many other bishops of the west, the pope was tending to acquire political authority. Through pressure of necessity and of public opinion, Gregory seems to have become *de facto* ruler of his city, superintending its defense and acting as its spokesman in diplomatic negotiations. With or without imperial authorization, the groundwork was thus being laid for the temporal power of the papacy—a development of great significance for the age to come.

Another of Gregory's permanent concerns was the so-called patrimony of St. Peter, the mass of private estates owned by the Roman see. His careful administration of such property, scattered throughout Italy and the adjoining regions, is prominently reflected in his correspondence. Indeed, his attention to detail is no less than amazing when it is remembered that such matters were a very small part of his official duties, which were now coming to be world-wide. In his dealings with the prelates of the east Gregory could do little more than reiterate a claim to sole headship for the see of St. Peter. Throughout the west, on the other hand, his supremacy was not merely asserted but actually enforced. In Italy the papal authority was generally recognized both within and without the Lombard territories. In Africa, like-

His statesmanship

wise, Gregory's supervision of all major ecclesiastical affairs was constant and efficient. In Spain he won a splendid victory through the conversion of the Visigothic king to the orthodox faith. Nor was there any serious opposition to the theory of papal government in Gaul. The problem there was to maintain even a semblance of Christian unity and discipline; for conditions in the semi-heathen Merovingian kingdom grew steadily worse as the grandsons of Clovis became involved in a series of murderous feuds. Yet an ultimate reform was made possible through Gregory's support of a new monastic system, the beginnings of which we must now briefly consider.

Irish monasticism and Gregory's mission

It has earlier been noted how, by the fifth century, primitive monasticism of the Egyptian type had spread as far west as Gaul. There it attracted a man of British origin who, on taking holy orders, was renamed Patricius or, more familiarly, Patrick. Having in his youth been captured by pirates from Ireland, he now returned to that savage country with the hope of Christianizing it, and before his death in 461 he had actually succeeded in converting the greater chieftains together with their followers. The result, since the Irish were so completely isolated from the rest of the Christian world, was a peculiar system of ecclesiastical government, in which the clan was the unit and the priests were also monks. The majority of the people, it is to be feared, remained as wild as before; yet many of the new converts adopted Christianity with such zeal that within a hundred years the Irish monasteries had acquired great renown for their religious austerity, their pious learning, and their missionary activity. From the sixth to the eighth century, in fact, the scholars of Ireland led all western Europe, acquiring a remarkable knowledge of Greek as well as Latin literature, and producing illuminated manuscripts that still rank as artistic masterpieces. Meanwhile Irish missionaries, headed by St. Columba (d. 597), had revived Christianity among the Celtic tribes of Britain and introduced it to at least some of the Anglo-Saxon peoples.

This was the situation when Pope Gregory determined on

a British mission of his own and selected for it a group of monks from the monastery that he had founded at Rome. Their landing in Kent (597) marks the beginning of a new epoch in the history of northwestern Europe; for thenceforth the Christianization of those regions proceeded under the papal authority, to which even the Irish eventually submitted. It is therefore important, before the consequences of Gregory's mission are further studied, to make clear the character of his missionaries. Coming from his own monastery, they were of course believers in the discipline under which he had lived and to which, as pope, he gave his official blessing—that of St. Benedict.

The few known facts in the life of Benedict are provided by Gregory's *Dialogues*: that he was born in Nursia of a noble Roman family; that, disgusted with fashionable life in the capital, he left the world and became a hermit; that the fame of his sanctity soon attracted many disciples; and that for the best of them he finally established the renowned monastery of Monte Cassino. There he died towards the middle of the sixth century, after composing the rule that was to serve as a basis for all Latin monasticism. It was, in fact, intended as such from the beginning; for its provisions clearly apply to monasteries in general, and contemplate, not the creation of a new institution, but the reform of an old one. The keynote is practicality. Benedict says that he is offering merely "a little rule for beginners"—a discipline adapted to the needs of ordinary men who wish to enter "a school for the service of God." For one who has proved his saintliness through long preliminary training the solitary life may be desirable; for others it is dangerous. So Benedict writes only for cenobites, "the best kind of monks," who live in religious communities. And in regulating such a life he naturally passes over accepted principles to emphasize his innovations.

St. Benedict and his rule

Much, for example, is taken for granted by the Benedictine vows: stability, conversion of life, and obedience. The brother gives up his old life and adopts that of the monk;

he resigns his own will and becomes subject in all ways to the abbot, the elected head of the community; and he swears to remain permanently in that community, for without special authorization he may not set foot beyond its walls. The monastic life implies the obligations of chastity and poverty. The first Benedict does not refer to; the second he dwells on at length. A monk shall own literally nothing; whatever he uses is the property of the community, distributed and administered by the abbot. The latter, accordingly, is not simply a moral leader; he is, under the rule, the absolute governor of the monastery. His office is of such vital importance that Benedict devotes page after page to his duties and necessary qualifications. There lay one of the fundamental distinctions between the old system and the new. And it was supplemented by another, the stability of the Benedictine. Under what was henceforth to be the official Roman usage, monks were the regular clergy, living by a rule (*regula*) and remaining wholly apart from the secular clergy, who served the church in the world (*sæcula*).

The monastic routine

Every Benedictine house was thus an autonomous unit— a cloistered community devoted solely to the religious discipline prescribed by the rule. The principal obligation of the Benedictines, as of all monks, was divine worship, but in their case it was a routine of eight daily "offices," in which all the brothers took part. Although hours were set for repose, meditation, and prayer, the Benedictine had no private quarters. He ate in the common refectory and slept in the common dormitory. And a fixed proportion of his time was taken up with manual labor, for all necessary tasks in and about the monastic buildings—such as gardening, repairing, cleaning, cooking, waiting on table, and the like— were assigned to groups of brothers by the abbot. He, presumably, could also provide for scholarly pursuits, which are hardly mentioned in the rule and were certainly not considered essential; for it was expected that many of the monks would be illiterate. In matters of diet, also, much was left to the abbot's discretion. According to the local climate, the season of the year, and the needs of the individual, he could vary the usual ration of food and drink. In every case, however, the brother was assured of adequate sustenance, as he was of sensible clothing, a comfortable bed, and uninterrupted sleep. The extreme asceticism of the Irish and Egyptian hermits had no place in the Benedictine monastery.

On the whole, nothing better illustrates the practical character of the Latin genius than the brilliant success of this monastic system, the work of two eminent Romans in the service of the church.

CHAPTER III

THE BYZANTINE EMPIRE AND THE RISE OF ISLAM

----

1. JUSTINIAN AND HERACLIUS

The empire in the east

While the western half of the Roman Empire disintegrated in the course of the fifth century, the eastern half persisted without noteworthy change. Indeed, conditions somewhat improved in the east after the death of Theodosius II in 450. Such emperors as then came to be proclaimed by the troops and installed by the senate at Constantinople, though far from brilliant, were fairly competent. The menace of the Huns passed, the Ostrogoths were diverted westward, and for the moment the Persians ceased to be dangerous. Economically, the east had always been the productive part of the empire, and in Constantinople the government possessed a commercial center of growing prosperity. With no further obligations towards the western provinces, it had at least a good chance of keeping what it still held. But all that could be reasonably hoped for was a successful defense. When new attacks upon the Danube and the Euphrates were already threatening, it was folly to contemplate a great western offensive—the policy that was now to be adopted by an ambitious emperor.

Justinian (527-65)

Justinian was the nephew and designated successor of Justin, an Illyrian peasant who had risen to be commander of the palace guards and finally emperor in 518. First informally under his uncle and then as official sovereign, Justinian ruled the empire for nearly half a century. And during most of that time he enjoyed the collaboration of the empress Theodora—said in her younger days to have been an actress of more than dubious reputation. However this may be, she was a devoted wife to Justinian and in many ways contributed to the brilliance of his reign. He, it should be emphasized, was a Latin of Illyria, educated in the Roman law and devoted to the Roman tradition. To him it seemed natural to dream of restoring the empire in the west and, on finding conditions favorable to the project, actually to attempt it. How—thanks to the victories of his great generals, Belisarius and Narses—he regained the provinces of Italy and Africa has been seen in the foregoing chapter. At the time these conquests seemed indeed glorious. But the glory was dearly bought—through the withdrawal of the best troops from the Danube, the payment of disguised blackmail to the Persians, and the exhaustion of the imperial resources.

To the grievances of extortionate taxes and military requisitions the emperor's religious policy added a host of others. A fervent Christian, deeply interested in theology, Justinian strove for complete uniformity—the inclusion of all Roman subjects in one church dominated by himself. Accordingly he confirmed and stiffened the edicts of his predecessors against heretics and pagans. The schools of Athens, with their proud history running back to the days of Plato, were closed; at Constantinople and elsewhere all persons suspected of "Hellenism" were excluded from the teaching profession. Furthermore, the emperor tried to enforce a theological compromise on various subjects disputed in earlier councils of the church. The result was to drive even more of the eastern clergy into opposition, as well as to assure open conflict with the papacy at Rome. In the troubled years that ensued, these animosities were to prove a chronic weakness of the imperial government.

His religious policy

Yet, whatever judgment may be passed on Justinian's military and ecclesiastical policies, there can be no doubt of his greatness as a legislator; for his *Corpus Iuris Civilis* has been in continuous use since it was first promulgated. That famous work was drawn up by a commission of distinguished lawyers under the presidency of Tribonian. To them the emperor gave two principal tasks. The first was to produce the *Code*, a collection and revision of the formal decrees that, since the reign of Diocletian, had become the sole form of

His Code

legislation. A number of lesser compilations had already been made—notably one named for the otherwise insignificant Theodosius II. This Theodosian Code, though now superseded in Justinian's own dominions, remained in use throughout much of the west and continued to inspire collections issued by many barbarian kings.

The jurists and the *Digest* The second and harder task of Justinian's commission was to codify the writings of the jurists—an enormous library of jurisprudence that had accumulated during the past five hundred years. In the ancient Roman court the judge was merely an ordinary citizen agreed on by the parties to a suit. Being unacquainted with legal technicalities, the judge commonly sought advice from a jurist, a man whose profession was the systematic study of the law. At first the jurists had no official standing; later, under the principate, the government came to designate certain ones whose opinions, of necessity asked in many cases, should be authoritative. The institution was remarkably successful, for it permitted the law, without interruption of its practical working, to be gradually developed according to theoretical ideals. In particular, it was the influence of the jurists that tended to amalgamate the law of citizens (*ius civile*) with the law of non-citizens (*ius gentium*) even before the edict of Caracalla[1] made the distinction wholly obsolete.

The principles that guided the jurists throughout this work of amalgamation may be briefly stated as follows. One was that the *ius gentium*, being drawn from the usages of many communities, could be treated as a system of equity to supplement the old *ius civile*, which was the custom of a single privileged group. Another was that this *ius gentium* could in turn be supplemented by appeal to abstract right. For, under the influence of the popular Stoic philosophy, the jurists believed in a natural law (*ius naturale*), the knowledge of which was implicit in human reason. The Creator, by endowing all men with rational faculties, had given them a common responsibility to observe the dictates of nature,

[1] See above, p. 19.

the fundamental principles that underlay the enactments of particular states. Justified in this way, constant amendment and reinterpretation adapted the *ius civile* to the needs of a great empire. By the time of Diocletian the process was complete; the whole Mediterranean world lived under one uniform Roman law.

Also by that time the ancient procedure of the Roman courts had yielded to a more despotic system of adjudication, under which all judges were imperial officials empowered to decide cases on their own authority. Yet classic jurisprudence retained its importance, for the judgments of the courts still had to follow established rules. To facilitate the work of his magistrates, Justinian thus ordered an official condensation of all the jurists' writings, and the result was his immortal *Digest*. Citing over fifteen hundred books by some thirty-eight authors, the *Digest* is arranged analytically according to a plan worked out in the *Institutes*, a textbook of first principles separately published by the commissioners. What is known as the *Corpus Iuris Civilis* is therefore made up of three distinct parts: the *Code* (with a supplement of later decrees called *Novels*), the *Institutes*, and the *Digest*. And of these three it is the latter two that have always been vitally significant. Even revised statutes are quickly outmoded; but while Roman law remains a living system, an exposition of its structure can never become obsolete.

Another permanent contribution of Justinian to the world's culture was his magnificent church of St. Sophia (see Plate II), first converted into a mosque, and later into a museum by the Turkish government. Although this church is the greatest monument of the style known as Byzantine, there are many others, especially the churches raised by Justinian and Theodora at Ravenna. Very remarkably, Byzantine architecture owed almost nothing to the Greeks, being essentially a development of the Roman arched construction. Thus the eastern builders discarded the Greek entablature (see Figure 1), which was altogether unnecessary in the Roman system, and made their arches spring directly

Byzantine architecture

from the supporting columns (see Plate IV, Sant' Apollinare in Classe). In connection with the dome, also, they effected a great improvement by designing a graceful means of placing the round superstructure over a square opening. This device, which first appeared in the church of St. Sophia, is called a dome on pendentives and can best be understood by examining the diagram (Figure 2). To suit the changed environment, the capitals of the columns were carved in new ways; otherwise sculpture was little used in the Byzantine church, the exterior of which was left entirely plain. But the smooth interior surfaces were made to blaze with color. Variegated marbles, often stripped from pagan temples, were used in rich profusion, together with brilliant mosaic in designs borrowed from the orient.

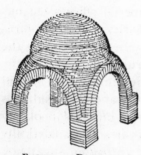

FIGURE 2.—DOME ON PENDENTIVES.

Conquests of the Avars and Persians

Compared with his achievements in architecture and jurisprudence, Justinian's conquests were ephemeral. The emperors who came after him were faced with an impossible task. While vainly trying to hold extended positions in the west, they lost a great part of their ancient heritage in the east. Africa for a time was successfully defended because no formidable enemy appeared on that flank; but most of Italy was taken by the Lombards, and the Visigoths soon reduced the province in Spain to a few cities on the coast. In Asia, meanwhile, the imperial frontier was threatened by a new Persian offensive, and to the north the Danubian provinces were overwhelmed by another incursion of nomads. These were the Avars, whose drive into Europe largely repeated that of the Huns in the previous century. Though Attila's great horde had long since broken up, many of the tribes that had taken part in his raids still inhabited the steppe—among them the Bulgars along the lower Danube. These peoples, together with a host of new recruits from Asia, were now united under the Avar khan, who by the end of the sixth century ruled a vast tributary domain between the Black Sea and the Baltic.

For the empire the situation was already desperate when, in 602, Justinian's third successor, Maurice, was slain by mutinous troops, who then forced the senate to enthrone their ruffianly leader, Phocas. The immediate result was that the government lost all control over the provinces. While the Persians broke into Syria, the Avars, with their allies and Slavic dependents, seized the interior of the Balkan peninsula and largely resettled it. In Illyria, the homeland of Justinian and many other great Romans, Latin culture was permanently destroyed. In Macedonia and Thrace the Greeks were driven back on the coasts. For a while it seemed likely that the Avars would take Constantinople itself. And the advance of the Persians had in the meantime continued unchecked. Completing the reduction of Syria by the capture of Damascus, Antioch, and Jerusalem, they proceeded to invade Asia Minor and Egypt.

It was at this point that Heraclius reversed the situation through one of the most astonishing campaigns in history. The son of the provincial governor in Africa, he headed an expedition against Phocas in 610 and, after deposing the usurper, was rewarded with the throne. A dozen years were then spent in building up the imperial resources. Finally, with a small army, he crossed to Asia and by a flanking march established a base in Armenia. Operating from there, he blocked all the attempts of the Persians to combine their scattered forces, and then resumed the offensive. His good fortune still held, for he was able to celebrate Christmas, 627, at Nineveh, where he had just defeated Chosroës II, the Persian king. No further action was necessary. Chosroës was overthrown by a palace revolution and his successor at once signed peace, restoring the frontier as it had been under Maurice. The citizens of Constantinople, who had meanwhile withstood a siege by the Avars, thus had good cause for rejoicing when Heraclius returned in 629. Happily, they

Heraclius
(610-41)

could not know that the emperor's heroic work in Asia was soon to be undone by an outpouring of tribesmen from the Arabian desert.

2. ARABIA, THE ARABS, AND MOHAMMED

Semitic peoples

Arabia, like the central Asiatic plateau, has served as a vast reservoir of nomadic peoples. It is a roughly quadrangular peninsula, which to the north abuts ón the rich and famous countries of Mesopotamia and Syria (see Map V). Time and again these lands have been swept by great migrations from the south. Such, it is generally held, was the common origin of the peoples known as Semitic: Assyrians, Chaldæans, Hebrews, Phœnicians, Aramæans, and others. But their invasions took place in very ancient times. Until the seventh century neither Greeks nor Romans encountered anything more serious than petty raiding from the direction of the Arabian desert, the interior of which remained unknown to them.

The Bedouin Arabs

That region today is much as it has been throughout recorded history. It is still the home of the Bedouin Arabs, whose mode of life is quite like that of the primitive Hebrews pictured in the Old Testament. The Bedouins, being purely nomadic, move with their flocks in unending routine—north in summer and south in winter, as dictated by the scanty vegetation of the desert. Their ordinary beast of burden is the camel, but their horses, bred for speed and endurance, have been famous for many centuries. Among the Bedouins the patriarchal system is universal. Family groups, each under the absolute rule of a chief man, are united to form a tribe headed by a sheik. The tribes have no use for centralized government and resist all interference with their time-honored habits, which include cattle-stealing from each other, the raiding of caravans, and the looting of any country that may be exposed to attack. The dignity, courtesy, and hospitality of these desert Arabs are proverbial, and according to their own peculiar standards—which do not exclude professional robbery and bloody feuds—they

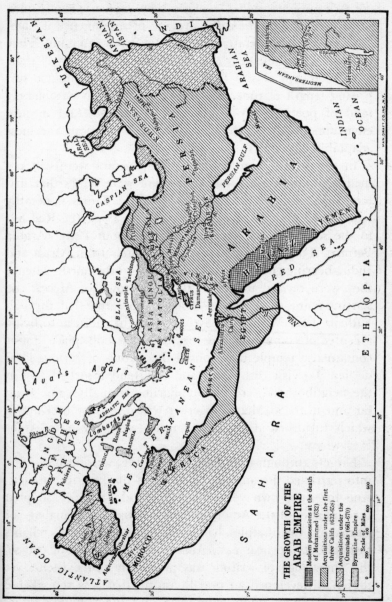

MAP V.

THE GROWTH OF THE
ARAB EMPIRE

▨ Moslem possessions at the death
of Mohammed (632)

▩ Acquisitions under the first
three Califs (632-658)

▨ Acquisitions under the
Ommiads (661-670)

▨ Byzantine Empire

Scale of Miles
0   200   400   600   800

are strictly honorable. Generally they have a splendid physique, and among them the average of intelligence is high. Though quite illiterate, they are far from ignorant. They can recite from memory the genealogies, not merely of their great men, but also of their great horses throughout a surprising length of time. They have always been passionately fond of poetry, story-telling, and discussion. And in new environments they have proved themselves among the most adaptable of peoples.

Trade and town life
In the seventh century most of the Arabs were still nomadic, but in certain localities there were tribes that had long since adopted a settled mode of life. This was notably true in the Hejaz, the region extending along the Red Sea to the south of the Roman province about Petra (Arabia Petræa). To Jidda, especially, came vessels from Africa and India, bearing goods for trans-shipment to the north. Thence they were carried inland to the little town of Mecca, the starting-point of the great caravan route that led through Yathrib (later Medina) to Syria. Mecca, in addition to being a center of commerce, was regarded as a holy place; for it contained a temple that housed the statues of various local deities. To visit this shrine and to attend a sort of fair in the neighborhood, crowds of pilgrims annually came from far and near. So Mecca, together with the tribe of Kuraish which furnished its ruling families, was known to Arabs everywhere.

Largely through the influence of trade, writing had come into restricted use among the Arabs of the frontier districts. And for their own vernacular they had naturally adopted the alphabet of the Aramæans; for Aramaic, the language of Christ and the disciples, had long been spoken by merchants throughout the near east. Among the Bedouins, of course, the knowledge of writing was practically non-existent; yet they had developed an oral literature that was remarkable for the richness of its vocabulary and the vividness of its imagery. Inevitably, too, there had been some infiltration of foreign religions: Zoroastrianism on the northeast, Judaism and Christianity on the northwest. The peoples of the interior, however, remained untouched by these influences. They still honored various local gods and goddesses, like those of Mecca, and they cherished numerous superstitions about sacred wells, enchanted rocks, evil spirits of the desert, and the like. Such were the conditions now to be revolutionized by the preaching of a new prophet.

Mohammed was born at Mecca about the year 570. His family though belonging to the tribe of Kuraish, was not wealthy, and as a boy of nine or ten he was left an orphan. Thus coming under the care of an uncle, Mohammed spent his youth in comparative poverty—a period of which we know nothing except that he became thoroughly familiar with contemporary methods of trade. Of formal education he could have had little; that he ever learned to write has been denied. In his travels with caravans, however, Mohammed unquestionably picked up a great deal of miscellaneous information. As a trader, he would have the opportunity of meeting men from different lands; as an intelligent Arab, he would store in his memory much of what they told him. And as there were many Arabic-speaking Jews and Christians, such a smattering of their doctrines as he later displayed would not be hard to obtain. We may be positive that he never read their Scriptures.

By the age of about twenty-four Mohammed had so far perfected his professional training that he was employed as commercial agent by a wealthy widow of Mecca named Khadija. And after he had successfully led a caravan to Syria on her behalf, he became the lady's husband—her third. Being now a man of substance and leisure, he could devote himself to the problems of faith and conduct that must first have attracted his attention long before. The traditional polytheism of the Arabs, he felt, was wrong; there was only one true God (Allah), the creator of all things, in whose sight man must live righteously in order to win salvation on the awful day of judgment that momentarily impended. When the last trump sounded, the good would be raised to

Mohammed and his teachings

the everlasting joys of paradise, while the bad would be cast into the flames of hell. Mohammed insisted that his God was the God of the Jews and of the Christians—the God testified to by the prophets, including Moses, Abraham, Noah, and Jesus. And even as the prophets of old had received direct commissions from the Almighty, might not he, Mohammed, be made the intermediary of a new dispensation from on high?

It was not until he was over forty and had spent much time in prayer and fasting that Mohammed became convinced of his prophetic mission. The angel Gabriel, as he told his wife and a few intimate friends, brought him divine messages according to which he was to restore religious purity. But when he began to preach his revelations, he had little success. The majority of the Kuraish bitterly opposed the upstart prophet, who denounced their traditional worship, and with it many of their business interests. They ridiculed Mohammed as a crazy poet. His teachings, they said, were absurd. How could God restore them to life after they had turned to dust and dry bones? Why should they believe a simple fellow from among themselves, who ate like them and walked like them in the market? If he had a divine commission, let him show them an angel or work for them some evident miracle. To which Mohammed replied with eloquent stories about the persecution of the ancient prophets and with lurid descriptions of the hell that yawned for unbelievers.

The Hegira (622)   Finally Mohammed decided to leave Mecca for a more sympathetic environment. At Yathrib there was a considerable colony of Judaized Arabs, some of whom professed a willingness to recognize him as their promised Messiah. Furthermore, the long-standing feuds of rival tribes in that neighborhood had proved inconvenient for all parties. The upshot was that the men of Yathrib made a solemn treaty with Mohammed, swearing to accept whatever peace he might dictate and to protect him and his followers as members of their own families. So, in 622, the prophet and his little band left Mecca, breaking all connection with their own groups of kinsmen—the famous Hegira, from which Mohammedans reckon their time. Yathrib was now renamed Medina (City of the Prophet), and from there Mohammed continued the promulgation of his divine messages, now turned from short exhortations in a highly poetic vein to detailed edicts on social and political problems.

At Medina, too, Mohammed proclaimed the formal principles of his religion—officially called Islam, submission to God. One who has made this submission is a Moslem. His confession of faith is extremely simple: "There is no God but Allah, and Mohammed is His prophet." After ceremonial ablution with water or with sand, he should pray at certain fixed hours of the day, and these prayers are accompanied with a mild discipline of bodily postures resembling athletic exercises. Service in a mosque is merely common prayer under the guidance of a leader, for there has never been a true Mohammedan priesthood. At first the faithful had prayed with their faces turned towards Jerusalem; later, when Mohammed found that most Jews rejected his teachings, he substituted Mecca. To that holy place the Moslem should make a pilgrimage at least once during his life. He should, furthermore, give alms for charitable and pious ends, and he should fast from sunrise to sunset during the sacred month of Ramadan.

Islam and the Moslems

These were and are the major requirements of Islam, to which Mohammed from time to time added a large number of moral precepts—rather modifications of existing custom than radical innovations. To a limited degree polygamy and slavery were both retained. The prophet himself, after the death of Khadija, took many wives, often making such alliances for the sake of political advantage. Yet in various ways he sought to ameliorate the condition both of slaves and of women. Sexual promiscuity, which earlier had been common, was severely punished. The primitive system of the blood feud, by which the family avenged wrongs done to its members, was limited by enforcing the acceptance of compensation when that was rightfully offered. The Arabs were already acquainted with taboos in connection with food and drink, and Mohammed wisely refrained from adding any very rigorous prohibitions. Moslems should abstain from the flesh of all animals slaughtered in the name of any god except Allah, as well as from pork and from wine. But the latter restrictions, it should be noted, could work no great hardship on the Bedouins. As the mark of a national cult, the new discipline was eminently sensible in its moderation.

The Koran

With respect to all these matters our primary source of information is the Koran (Recital), a collection of Mohammed's sayings, which in its present form dates from just after the prophet's death. And as the compilers—except for an opening prayer—merely placed the 114 chapters in decreasing order of their length, the Koran is devoid of logical coherence. To read and appreciate it as a whole is extremely difficult; each fragment must be taken as it was originally uttered—as a separate message delivered on a particular occasion. Thus understood, the Koran is magnificent. To the student of law and institutions the later chapters promulgated at Medina are the most instructive; but as literature, revealing the very heart of Islam, the earlier ones are superior. Most of them, being short, are to be found towards the end of the book. In form they resemble modernistic verse, being made up of irregular lines without definite meter or rhyme pattern, but with rhythmic cadences and combinations of syllables based on resemblances of sound. Although Mohammed considered the term an insult, he really was a poet, and a great one.

Mohammed's triumph

As a religion, Islam was founded during the prophet's ministry at Mecca. His later life was devoted to the establishment of an organization to enforce its dominion; and since there was no pre-existing Arabian state, his system was of necessity semi-political. At Medina Mohammed was confronted by all sorts of problems. He had to prescribe details of worship and everyday morality for his followers.

He became involved in conflicts with the Jews and other local inhabitants who, refusing to recognize his prophetic mission, opposed his authority on all occasions. He had to consider means of spreading the faith among the Bedouin tribes. But all such matters depended on the outcome of the Meccan war that had inevitably followed the Hegira. This war was marked by three major events: the battle of Badr (624), in which the Moslems defeated a force outnumbering them three to one; their successful defense of Medina against an enemy offensive in 627; and, three years later, their triumphant entry into Mecca. Mohammed made wise use of his victory. Justified by a special revelation which declared that the local temple had originally been founded by Abraham, Mohammed simply purified it by casting out the idols. Thus, consciously or unconsciously, he made the revolution easy for the Kuraish to accept. As a matter of fact, they soon found that, by guarding Islam's holiest shrine, they stood to gain infinitely more than they had ever thought to lose. And with that testimony to the might of Allah, all resistance crumbled.

To the mass of his converts the sudden death of Mohammed in 632 was a frightful calamity. But his work was done. Within ten years after leaving Mecca as a fugitive he had returned as a conqueror. His fame had spread throughout the length and breadth of Arabia; and while as yet the Bedouin tribes had by no means all submitted to his dominion, the war that he had proclaimed against the enemies of Islam was to bring an amazing series of triumphs.

His death (632)

3. THE CALIPHATE AND THE ARAB EMPIRE

The first problem raised by the unexpected death of Mohammed was how to perpetuate the organization he had founded. On this point, strangely enough, the prophet had announced no revelation; yet it was one that could hardly have escaped consideration by his relatives and associates. In spite of his many weddings, Mohammed was survived by only one child, Fatima, the daughter of Khadija. She was married to Ali, the prophet's cousin, and by him had two

Abu Bakr and Omar (632-44)

sons. If the headship of the Moslems should be declared hereditary like that of an ordinary family, the office would fall to Ali; but he was more remarkable for piety than for ability. In preference to him, Mohammed's confidence had been given to Abû Bakr, one of the earliest converts to Islam. So it was Abu Bakr whom an informal assembly of the faithful hailed as caliph (successor of the prophet). And whatever hostility was still nourished by Ali's legitimist faction soon collapsed before the wonderful success of the newly established government.

Only two years remained to the aged Abu Bakr, but his work was carried to a glorious conclusion by his talented friend and counselor, Omar. Their primary concern was the prosecution of the holy war preached by Mohammed. This, it should be emphasized, was properly directed against idolaters alone; for the Koran (ch. ix) commanded that they be slain unless they accepted the true faith, while the People of the Book—i.e., Jews and Christians—were to be subjected and made to pay tribute. To win the adherence of the desert Arabs, the Moslems shrewdly combined force with persuasion. On the one hand they launched energetic campaigns against the tribes of central and southern Arabia; on the other they organized a number of highly profitable raids into Syria and Mesopotamia. The result was a triumphant advance that proved irresistible. The Bedouins, having so much to gain and so little to lose, everywhere flocked to the standard of Islam.

Omar, on succeeding to the caliphate, could see the whole of Arabia virtually won, and magnificent opportunities awaiting concerted Moslem efforts to the north. There the Arab raids had already progressed beyond the stage of pillaging expeditions and everything favored the development of more ambitious projects. In Persia a prolonged civil war had followed the great defeat of five years earlier and the monarchy was badly discredited. In the Roman Empire conditions were hardly better. To the crushing burdens imposed by Justinian had now been added the cost of the Persian war. Political discontent, occasioned by religious controversy as well as by economic distress, was widespread in both Syria and Egypt. Outside the Greek aristocracy of the greater cities, the government had few loyal supporters. Against these enfeebled states Omar could now direct a host of devoted adherents—warlike tribesmen from the desert, eager for spoil and adventure, inspired by the fanatic enthusiasm of a new faith. And to lead his armies in battle he could rely on excellent commanders of proved ability. One of them, Khalid, must be ranked among the great generals of all time.

It was in 634, while leading a raid in Syria, that Khalid was first confronted by a Roman army. Instead of retreating to the desert, he called up other bands of raiders and defeated it. Two years later, after taking Damascus, he was met by a greater force, and again he displayed military genius. Falling back on the Yarmuk (see the insert in Map V), he trapped the imperial army between two converging defiles and annihilated it. The battle was decisive, for it ended eight centuries of Roman rule in Syria. Within four years the last fortress of Palestine had surrendered and the Arabs were beginning an attack on Egypt. And since the local authorities made hardly a show of resistance, that province too was soon occupied—the last tragic news to reach the dying Heraclius. Meanwhile the Moslem raids in Mesopotamia had led to another surprising triumph. Five years after a small invading force had beaten off the best troops of the Persian king (637), his monarchy was broken and he was a fugitive. The banners of Islam had advanced beyond the Nile on the west, and far beyond the Tigris-Euphrates on the east.

Conquest of Syria, Egypt, and Persia

Rather detailed treatment has been given to the beginnings of this great Arab Empire because it so deeply affected the fortunes, not only of the Roman Empire, but of the entire Mediterranean world. Its later development may be reduced to a brief outline, with emphasis upon features of lasting importance. One of these was the transformation of

The Ommiad caliphate at Damascus (661-750)

the caliphate. Originally, as we have seen, it was a personal
leadership of the faithful held by a sort of elected president
with headquarters at Medina. Such an office and such a
capital were obviously unsuited to the needs of the empire
that had appeared by the middle of the seventh century.
Largely on that account the Moslem ranks had become more
and more divided by a series of bitter rivalries: between the
Meccan aristocracy and the other Arab families; between
the original tribesmen and the mass of new recruits brought
in by conversion to Islam; and—an older dispute—between
the supporters of Ali and the supporters of the existing
caliphate.

These issues all came to be involved in an insurrection
against Omar's successor, Othman—a man distinguished only
by the fact that he belonged to the powerful Ommiad family
of Mecca. The result of the insurrection was the murder of
Othman and the proclamation of Ali as caliph.. But Othman's
cause was maintained by his kinsman Muawiya, the governor of Syria; and it was he who finally triumphed, securing
general recognition as caliph after the death of Ali in 661.
Muawiya's victory had important consequences. In the first
place, the caliphate was now placed on a dynastic basis, for
it remained in the possession of the Ommiad house during
the next ninety years. Secondly, the political center of Islam
was shifted from Arabia to Syria, as the new line of caliphs
made Damascus their capital. And this was much more than
a change of residence. The caliphate was henceforth a sort
of territorial monarchy, with an elaborate system of administration largely borrowed from the Roman Empire.

**The Arabs
on the sea
and in
Africa**

The advance of Moslem conquest, interrupted by the civil
war, was resumed as soon as the state had been reorganized
under Muawiya. In the far east the Arabs quickly overran
the ancient kingdom of Persia and, thanks to zealous recruits from the native population, were soon pushing their
raids into the lands of the Turks, Chinese, Afghans, Thibet-
ans, and Hindus. To the westward, meanwhile, even greater
progress had been made. As governor of Syria, Muawiya had

already built a navy and established the Moslem power on the sea by destroying a Roman fleet in 655. As caliph he energetically continued the same policy, and under his successors it brought decisive results. While the armies of the Arabs drove into Asia Minor, their ships attacked Constantinople itself and so cut the communications between the imperial capital and the province of Africa. A preliminary campaign in that direction, launched by the governor of Egypt, had failed on account of opposition from the Moors. But towards the end of the seventh century the conciliatory policy adopted by the Ommiad government was rewarded with complete success. Carthage fell in 697 and the whole southern coast of the Mediterranean came into the hands of the Moslems.

Furthermore, as the Moorish tribes of the adjoining desert now became enthusiastic converts to the Mohammedan faith, they supplied the Arab conquerors with eager volunteers for new expeditions. Thus it came about that in 711 the Moslem governor of Africa authorized one of his lieutenants, a certain Tarik, to lead a force of Moors into Spain, where the Visigothic kingdom persisted mainly through default of vigorous enemies. Skirting the rock that still bears his name (Gibraltar, *Jebel Tarik*), he landed at Algeciras and proceeded towards Cadiz. The king of the Visigoths tried to drive back the invaders, but instead suffered a crushing defeat. And as reinforcements came up from Africa, the Visigothic state soon went the way of Persia. Within seven years the Moslems had reached Septimania beyond the Pyrenees, and within a further seven years they were raiding the plains of central Gaul. What had begun as a mere plundering expedition had thus turned into another momentous triumph for Islam.

If now we examine the tremendous empire established by the Arabs within a hundred years after the death of Mohammed, certain conclusions are at once impressed upon us. In the first place, it is hard to believe that so great a political revolution could have been accomplished by mere

Conquest of Spain

The nature of the Arab Empire

religious zeal. Religion could have provided only the final impetus to other forces that had been gaining strength for many centuries—especially economic pressure. We may be sure that, on the side of the conquered, the mass of the people either welcomed, or at least did not oppose, the invaders; and that, on the side of the conquerors, their homeland had become greatly overpopulated—perhaps, as has been alleged, through the increasing desiccation of the interior. Secondly, the notion that Mohammedanism was a religion of the sword, forced upon defenseless masses by a bloodthirsty horde of fanatics, is the exact contrary of the truth. The caliphs, following the instruction of the Koran, deprecated unnecessary slaughter of non-Moslems, or even their compulsory conversion, because they were to be the financial support of the government. It was only later, when the great wars were over, that true believers had to pay any kind of tax.

The empire of the Arabs, therefore, was essentially a political structure. On taking over the administration of the conquered lands, they carefully preserved anything that might be turned to their own advantage. The provincial organization of Romans or Persians they left intact, merely substituting Arabs for natives in the topmost offices. Subordinates, as long as they proved loyal to their new masters, remained unmolested, even though they clung to their old religions. Accordingly, the only persons to suffer complete ruin were the members of the ancient aristocracy. To lesser men—such as peasants, laborers, small traders, and civil servants—the Moslem conquest was a blessing rather than a calamity. Their burdens under the new régime could be no heavier than those already borne, and by the easy process of accepting Islam they could themselves enter the favored class in the state. Hundreds of thousands quickly grasped the advantages offered by the new faith, and throughout the centuries down to the present their descendants have largely remained Mohammedan. The further significance of these facts in the history of culture will be seen in the next section.

But before that subject is taken up, a few words are required on the character of the later caliphate.

The first decisive checks to the expanding power of Islam were administered in the second quarter of the eighth century. As will be explained below, they were the work of a new leader among the Franks and a remarkable emperor at Constantinople. But a contributing factor was the weakening of the caliphate. The legitimist party, surviving all defeats, had continued its bitter opposition to the Ommiads and so attracted to its standard an increasing host of malcontents. Prominent among the latter were those who, for one reason or another, wanted the caliph to be a religious head rather than a Cæsar; also the inhabitants of Persia, who on principle objected to any government out of Syria. Such persons held that, since the line of Ali had been killed off in the earlier fighting, the mantle of the prophet had fallen to the Abbasid house—so-called because it was descended from Abbas, an uncle of Mohammed. Finally, after many insurrections had been put down, a revolutionary movement in 750 gained such headway that it carried all before it. The Ommiads—except for one survivor who fled to Spain—disappeared in a general massacre, and the caliphate was thenceforth held by the Abbasids.

The Abbasid revolution (750)

The immediate result of this revolution was the establishment of the capital in Mesopotamia, eventually in the newly built city of Bagdad on the Tigris. There such caliphs as al-Mansur (754-75), al-Rashid (786-809), and al-Mamun (813-33) lived in great splendor—like the gorgeous despots of ancient Persia rather than the Arab chieftains who had earlier commanded the faithful. In spite of the magnificence, however, the caliphate had lost its strength. The shifting of the government to the east was the signal for the western lands to declare their independence, saving only the nominal recognition of the caliph's religious headship. Long before the close of the ninth century his actual rule was restricted to one small portion of the Moslem dominions, and even within it he more and more came under the dictation of his Turkish

The later caliphate

bodyguard. There were yet to be many caliphs, but the Arab Empire was a thing of the past.

4. THE CULTURE OF THE MOSLEM WORLD

Linguistic and commercial unity

Although the Moslem world had politically disintegrated, it continued to possess a distinctive civilization. From the Oxus and the Himalayas to the Sahara and the Pyrenees, society and culture were very much the same. Despite the endless quarrels of Mohammedan theologians, all recognized the sanctity of the Koran and obeyed the command that it should not be used in translation—a fact that assured the supremacy of Arabic among the educated classes. By the eighth century, of course, relatively few who spoke that language were of pure Arab descent; they were not even all Moslems. Thousands of Hindus, Parsees, Jews, and Christians learned the dominant tongue and so, by combining the contributions of a dozen scattered countries, gave Islam under the Abbasids a culture of amazing richness and variety. Yet, even if we admit that Arabic civilization was the work of a very heterogeneous population, the Arabs deserve the chief credit. It was that talented and adaptable people who built the empire and established the traditions which governed its destiny.

The linguistic unity of the Arab dominions was naturally a great stimulus to commerce. The Moslem conquests by no means ruined the cities of Syria, Egypt, and Africa. Their economic connections with Greece and Italy were, it is true, largely destroyed; but, to make up for the severance, they were now brought into much closer contact with Persia and the orient. The caravan trade of central Asia naturally fell into the hands of the Arabs, who had long been expert in that business. They brought the precious goods of China and the Indies direct to the ports of Syria. On the north they had access to the Black Sea, and through the nomads of the steppe dealt largely in furs and slaves from eastern Europe. From Egypt they penetrated into Ethiopia, and from the Sahara into the gold-bearing countries about the Niger. By sea their

ships linked the coasts of India, Persia, Arabia, and eastern
Africa as far south as Madagascar. Much of this traffic converged on Egypt, where Alexandria and Cairo enjoyed un-
paralleled prosperity through the trans-shipment of merchandise bound to the west. The Mediterranean, except for
the Adriatic and the Ægean, became virtually the sole possession of the Moslems; from the mountains of Asia Minor
to those of Spain the shores of the mainland, together with
the adjacent islands, were all theirs.

The art of the Arabs was typical of their civilization. Ele-   The arts
ments from the four corners of the earth were combined to
produce a strikingly original result. In architecture, as is
shown by the eighth-century mosque at Damascus (see Plate
II), they adapted the Byzantine style of construction to their
own needs and tastes by adding such features as minarets—
slender towers from which the muezzin calls the faithful to
prayer—and horseshoe arches. Through the latter, in fact,
the buildings of the Arabs can almost always be identified,
although in the later mosques—as at Cairo, Bagdad, and Cordova—the arches are sometimes pointed or cusped (see Figure
3). As far as decoration was concerned, the Moslem artists

Round   Pointed   Horseshoe   Cusped   Flamboyant

FIGURE 3.—ARCHES.

were somewhat handicapped by the fact that they were forbidden to represent either men or animals. But they came
to excel in all lawful ornamentation. Following models already perfected in the orient, they drew charming patterns
from flowers and leaves, either naturalistic or conventional;
and from geometrical figures they developed the intricate
and graceful designs that are still known as arabesques.
These decorative schemes were applied not only in architecture but also throughout the minor arts that flourished

everywhere under Moslem patronage. No lengthy description of such productions can be given here; it need only be remarked that the Arab craftsmen were especially famous for tooled leather, carved ivory, brocaded silk, pile carpets, enameled pottery, luster ware, and the work called damascening after the city of Damascus—the inlaying of gold and silver upon steel and brass.

Literature
Poets had flourished in Arabia long before Mohammed's time, and, although he was not very favorable to the profession, it continued to enjoy great honor. As the Arabs spread over the world and increasingly adopted city life, the older poetic forms naturally became obsolete and popular demand shifted from conventional tales of tribal warfare to matters of personal experience—in other words, towards lyric themes. Yet the old passion for story-telling lived on; tales from every land were reworked and put into writing. This was the origin of the collection known as the *Thousand and One Nights*, which in some measure reflects the early Abbasid age. As would be expected, the Arabs also maintained a high standard in historiography. Merely to list the names and works of important Moslem historians between the seventh and tenth centuries would fill a page of print—a catalogue that must be left to more specialized books on the subject.

Science and philosophy
For the rudiments of science and philosophy, on the other hand, the Arab conquerors were indebted to the lands which they invaded. There, especially in the cities of Syria and Egypt, they found great schools with traditions of study running back to the golden age of Athens. But all the standard texts were in Greek; they had to be translated before the cause of higher education among the Moslems could be far advanced. And as soon as conditions favored the undertaking, the needed intermediaries were readily found. Since the time of Justinian various groups of Christians, driven from the empire as heretics, had extended their missionary efforts far into central Asia, and through their agency many Greek works had already been put into Persian and Aramaic. Besides such persons, numerous Hellenized Jews had by now

made a thorough study of Arabic. Accordingly, as the Abbasid caliphs gave the project their generous support, the work of translation was rapidly carried out. By the end of the ninth century the great body of Greek scientific learning—Aristotle, Hippocrates, Galen, Euclid, Archimedes, Ptolemy, and many additional authors—had been made available to the student of Islam.

The mass of writings to which the Arabs thus fell heir was already a strange mixture, combining classic philosophy and science with mystic elements from Neo-Platonism. To this mixture the Arabs contributed the sacred tradition of the Koran, together with considerable lore from Persia, India, and even China. The result was an original advance in thought that can best be appreciated by examining the works of a few outstanding scholars. For example, a Christian Arab named Hunain ibn Ishaq (d. 877) acted as the chief advisor of the caliph al-Mamun in educational matters. He and his pupils ransacked the old Greek cities for manuscripts and formed at Bagdad one of the greatest libraries in the world. But Hunain, as a practising physician, was particularly interested in medicine. He superintended the translation of Galen and many of the Hippocratic books, made numerous commentaries on these classics, compiled a huge medical encyclopædia, and wrote a number of special studies based on his own experience, including the earliest known treatise on the eye.

Of Hunain's contemporaries two may be singled out for particular attention, al-Kindi and al-Khwarizmi. The former has the distinction of being called the first Arab philosopher. He was, at any rate, the first Arab to make an extensive study of Aristotle and so to become interested in the reconciliation of Greek thought with orthodox Moslem theology—a project that was to occupy his successors for many centuries. Al-Kindi was a sort of universal scholar, writing not merely on logic and metaphysics but also on meteorology, optics, specific gravity, and music. The reputation he came to enjoy may be judged from the fact that, rightly or wrongly, no less than

Ninth-century scholarship

265 books are attributed to him. No such imposing list of works bears the name of al-Khwarizmi. Yet he was to have a momentous influence on European thought; for he produced the first known exposition of our everyday arithmetic and the treatise through which the science of algebra came to have that designation, as well as various books on trigonometry, astronomy, and geography. The connection between al-Khwarizmi and modern mathematics must be left for later treatment; that between him and ancient mathematics may receive a few words of explanation.

Arabic mathematics

Since the caliphate of al-Mansur the Arabs had been acquainted with the great work of Ptolemy, which they called *al-Majisti*—later made into *Almagest*. From it they obtained not only the theoretical science of trigonometry but also the basis for all their geographical and astronomical studies. Geometry, too, they learned from Euclid and other Greek writers, together with a few algebraic processes. The nine symbols that we know as Arabic, on the contrary, came from India. In themselves they are not especially significant; for any series of marks, arbitrarily agreed upon, will do as well. It is the zero that allows those symbols to be arranged in columns and so, under a decimal system, to represent tens, hundreds, thousands, and the like. To explain the origin of modern arithmetic, we must therefore explain the origin of the zero.

The Greeks and Romans, using letters for numerals and having no zero, had been forced, like other ancient peoples, to make their larger computations on some sort of abacus—an instrument with counters set in grooves or strung on wires. With an abacus addition and subtraction are easy, multiplication is not difficult, and division is at least possible. But the Greek or Roman, after working his problem, had to write his answer in numerals that by no means corresponded to the columns of his abacus. The Hindu, with his nine symbols, was not much better off; for how would he represent a vacant column on the abacus? Precisely who first thought of inventing a symbol to stand for such a vacant column we do not know. But it was al-Khwarizmi who first described that simple device in a book that has come down to us; and, having such a book, the harassed mathematician could throw his abacus away. It was likewise al-Khwarizmi who seems, by combining Greek and Hindu elements, to have perfected what we know as algebra. The name, at any rate, is derived from the title placed on one of his books.

Thus established, Arabic scholarship in the following centuries made excellent progress, only a brief summary of which can be given here. Philosophy remained essentially Aristotelian, in orthodox circles largely subordinated to religious mysticism. But later Moslem society produced a good many free-thinkers, of whom the greatest was Ibn Rushd of Cordova, better known as Averroës (d. 1198). Medicine continued to flourish and reached a new height of excellence in the work of the illustrious Ibn Sina, or Avicenna (d. 1037). Much profitable study was also given to the mathematical subjects, especially astronomy, for the benefit of which the caliph al-Mamun had erected a fine observatory at Bagdad. There and in other centers the Arab astronomers perfected such instruments as the astrolabe for determining the movements of heavenly bodies, and enormously enlarged the tables of observations made by the Greeks. Among other significant contributions may be mentioned the system of measuring music invented by al-Farabi (Alpharabius) and the splendid research of al-Haitham (Alhazen) in the field of optics. *Later developments*

A remarkable feature of Arabic science in general was its practical aspect, for the greatest scholars kept a lively interest in common things. A chemist, for instance, might discuss paint, dye-stuffs, and glass-making, as well as the theoretical composition of the universe. Many handbooks of useful knowledge were thus composed on various phases of manufacture, commerce, and agriculture—including encyclopædias of animals, plants, trees, stones, metals, and the like. Through the experience of foreign trade the Arabs came to lead the world in navigation and geographical science. It was they who seem to have made the earliest use of the magnetic com- *General features of Arabic science* pass. To the Latins they introduced paper-making and block-printing, originally learned from the Chinese. Their knowledge of fireworks, drawn from the same source, was probably the foundation for the later invention of gunpowder. That the west learned from them the use of the bow for stringed instruments is certain; that it also learned from them much about music and lyrical composition is probable. As will be seen in a subsequent chapter, the importance of Arabic influence upon higher education in mediæval Europe is incalculable.

To our eyes, of course, the Arab scholars perpetuated and developed many absurd ideas. For example, their alchemists spent much time in the vain search for a medium by which to transmute metals. Despite all their original work in medicine, they held to the physiology of Galen with its physical, animal, and natural spirits resident in the brain, the heart, and the liver, and its four bodily humors—blood, phlegm, yellow bile, and black bile—that gave rise to the sanguine, phlegmatic, choleric, and melancholic temperaments. Their astronomy was based on the Ptolemaic system, according to which the earth was the center of the universe and was surrounded by the spheres of the seven planets—the moon, Mercury, Mars, the sun, Venus, Jupiter, and Saturn—and finally by that of the fixed stars. And with all this they naturally accepted the ancient lore of the Chaldæans and Persians as to the influence exerted by the heavenly bodies on the destinies of men.

The fact nevertheless remains that, for all its shortcomings, Arabic science was the best that the learned world had yet produced. Without the Ptolemaic astronomy, the Galenic physiology, and the Aristotelian physics as elaborated by Arab scholars, the splendid discoveries of Galileo, Harvey, and Newton would have been impossible. The casting of a horoscope then seemed no more mysterious than the prediction of an eclipse. If the sun could affect the growth of crops and the moon could control the movement of the tides, why could not Mars govern the course of a war, or Venus that of a love affair? And before we condemn alchemy as sheer foolishness, we should remember that to the Arabs the true elements were the earth, air, fire, and water of Aristotle; and that even the elements of the modern chemist are now being transmuted.

5. THE BYZANTINE EMPIRE

By the close of the seventh century the Roman Empire of the east had been reduced to a mere fragment. The Arabs had taken the provinces of Syria, Egypt, and Africa, and had gained control of the southern Mediterranean. The Roman position in Spain had been lost to the Visigoths, and most of Italy to the Lombards. Avars and Slavs had wiped out Latin civilization in the Balkans. What was left to the emperor was actually a Greek kingdom deprived of all but a modicum of Roman character. Accordingly, it has come to be known in historical writing as the Byzantine Empire—an apt designation, for the well-spring of its life was the city originally called Byzantium.

Signifi- cance of the name

At the opening of the eighth century it was as yet questionable whether even this fragment of the empire could survive the Moslem attack. That it did survive was largely due to the ability of a general named Leo. Having waged a number of victorious campaigns in Anatolia, he was raised to the imperial throne in 717—just in time to organize the defense of the capital against a last great assault by the caliph's fleet. Again, after months of bitter fighting, the Bosphorus was successfully held, and the opportune weakening of the Ommiad state ended the danger of a renewed offensive. Leo consequently was left in possession, not only of the remaining territory in Europe, but also of Asia Minor as far as a line extending from the Taurus Mountains to the Armenian Highlands (see Map V). And the respite now gained in the Moslem war was turned to good advantage by a thorough reform of the administration, both civil and military.

Leo III (717-40)

Leo's religious policy was not so fortunate. During his early life in southern Asia Minor he had become well acquainted with Mohammedanism, as well as with various Christian sects that condemned many beliefs and practices of the orthodox—especially what they termed the pagan ceremonial of the established church. While sympathizing neither with heretic nor with Moslem, the emperor seems to have been convinced that both were right in at least one respect: the customary use of images and pictures in Christian worship was hardly better than idolatry. In 725, accordingly, he officially denounced it and launched a violent campaign of iconoclasm (image-breaking). Though zealously supported by many of the educated, the decree was intensely unpopular with the mass of the people. Riots broke out both in Greece and in Italy. For opposing the imperial will the aged patriarch of Constantinople was ousted from office, but in Rome no such action was possible. From the beginning the pope gave vigorous support to the traditional cause and eventually pronounced excommunication[2] against all who accepted the iconoclastic program. East and west thus came once more into religious conflict, which intermittently continued until the use of images was formally restored by imperial edict in 843.

Political decadence

Meanwhile, with the passing of the Moslem danger, the Byzantine government had fallen into a chronic state of incompetence. The history of the capital becomes a wearisome recital of palace revolution and intrigue, more and more dominated by refined but·vicious women. Such was the regent Irene, who had her own son blinded and deposed that she might reign as empress (797-802). After Irene had finally been deposed by one insurrection, a series of others, together with foreign invasions, kept the empire in constant turmoil. And for a long time no improvement was visible in the character of the sovereigns, which reached its low ebb with Michael III (842-67), popularly known as "the Drunkard." Being passionately fond of chariot-racing, he singled

[2] In the broadest sense of the term, excommunication meant separation from the Christian community, exclusion from the sacraments. Throughout the mediæval period it was the principal weapon used by bishops to enforce their decrees. When two bishops denied each other's authority by mutual excommunication, the result was a schism.

out from among his low-born companions a Macedonian horse-trainer named Basil and loaded him with honors. From the office of chief equerry Basil eventually rose to be co-emperor; and when Michael gave signs of transferring his affections, Basil secured undisputed title to the throne by having him murdered. Thus, strangely enough, was founded the remarkable Macedonian dynasty, under which the Byzantine Empire enjoyed a last interval of glory.

For all its inauspicious beginning, the reign of Basil I was not unsuccessful. He carried out a much-needed reform of the administration and once more established religious peace by restoring images to the churches. His son and grandson were men of scholarly tastes who, maintaining Basil's efficient government, encouraged a noteworthy revival of Greek learning. Then, in the tenth century, three soldier-emperors—Nicephorus Phocas, John Tzimisces, and Basil II—took Cilicia, Cyprus, and Antioch from the Moslems and, subjugating the Bulgarians, regained the Danube frontier. The change of dynasty, however, had brought no change of morals at the Byzantine court; in this respect the record becomes even more fantastic. The empress Theophano, we are told, acquired that rank by helping her husband to murder his father; she then poisoned this first husband in order to win a second one, who through her connivance was assassinated by his nephew; but the latter, ungratefully, sent her to a convent and married her daughter. Whatever may be made of all this scandal—and it is significant that every one then took such stories for granted—Theophano's second husband was Nicephorus Phocas and his nephew was John Tzimisces, who were both distinguished rulers. It was through a liberal policy of recognizing emperors-by-marriage that the Macedonian house maintained its power for nearly two hundred years.

The Macedonian dynasty

If now we turn from the subject of Byzantine politics to that of Byzantine culture, we find a more edifying tale. After the sixth century, to be sure, the empire can hardly be said to have progressed in any phase of civilization, but it tena-

Byzantine culture

ciously clung to what it then had. By that time, despite the Roman origin of the imperial institutions, Latin had become so unfamiliar throughout the east that Justinian's law books had to be translated into Greek. And this language was by no means what it had been. In its spoken form Greek had come to reflect the cosmopolitanism of the capital, being intermixed with Latin, oriental, and barbarian elements. Even the vernacular of the educated was no longer classic in vocabulary, syntax, or pronunciation. Nevertheless, it remained so close to the ancient language that the latter could be kept inviolate for all formal writing. Under such circumstances literary education could hardly be other than static. The boy of good family continued to study grammar and rhetoric as they had been studied for centuries. He learned Homer and other poets by heart, and he gained an intimate knowledge of Herodotus, Thucydides, and the great orators —a pagan tradition that the eastern church was never able to break down.

This system had the obvious merit of preserving and honoring some of the greatest works that have ever been written. Its fault was that, by ignoring the spirit of the classics and maintaining an absolute devotion to old forms, originality was discouraged. The multitude of authors remained content with imitations, commentaries, and anthologies. Verses written in the traditional meters based on quantity lacked the vigor of the new Christian poetry that followed the popular pronunciation, with stressed syllables and rhyme. Prose works that attempted to be literary were generally inferior to those dealing with more practical matters, such as technical essays on civil and military administration. A relatively high standard was kept in biography and in historical memoirs. The ancient skill in philosophical discussion to some extent survived among the theologians. But scientific research all but disappeared; of the later Greek scholars there is not one who deserves mention as a worthy successor of Galen and Ptolemy. In that respect the Byzantine civilization was vastly inferior to the Moslem.

How much the Latin world was to learn from both civilizations will be seen in the following chapters. As far as the Byzantine Empire was concerned, its influence upon western Europe was especially significant in four ways: in commercial and maritime activity through the agency of the Venetians, in military tactics and engineering through that of the crusaders, in architecture and the decorative arts through that of Italian artists, and finally in the study of the Greek classics through that of the later humanists. These influences, though important, were hardly decisive in shaping Latin culture, which remained fundamentally different from the Greek—an antagonism that is particularly evident in ecclesiastical history. The recurrent disputes between the churches of Rome and Constantinople were to culminate in a schism that has remained unhealed since the eleventh century. The sphere where Byzantine contributions proved most significant was rather the Balkan peninsula, together with the lands beyond the Danube.

About 861 two brothers, Cyril and Methodius, went from Constantinople to preach Christianity among the Slavs. And to facilitate the translation of the Scriptures into the language of their converts, Cyril invented a modified Greek alphabet—one that has since been known as Cyrillic. Although the jealousy of western prelates finally drove the two missionaries out of Moravia, their work had permanent results in the Balkan country. There, with the collapse of the Avar power,[3] both the Serbs and the Bulgars had organized independent states; and before the close of the ninth century both had accepted Christianity. In the latter case this involved also a change of language; for the Bulgar khan, Boris I, made official the Slavic vernacular that since then has been used by his people. In the next century Christianity, together with the authority of the Greek Church, was extended from Bulgaria to Russia, the origin of which will be considered in the following chapter. Even today the consequence of this cultural advance is quite apparent. The Byzantine sphere of influence is still distinguished by the prevalence of the Cyrillic alphabet or one derived from it.

[3] See below. p. 104.

CHAPTER IV

THE CAROLINGIAN EMPIRE

1. THE FORMATION OF THE CAROLINGIAN EMPIRE

The rise of the Carolingians

By the middle of the seventh century the imposing kingdom of the early Merovingians had completely disintegrated. The old Frankish territory was divided between Austrasia and Neustria, rival states that had long been engaged in a savage war (see Map VI). To the south Burgundy was organized as a separate kingdom, while Aquitaine was virtually independent under a local duke. To the east, with the decline of the Frankish power, the Alamans, Bavarians, and Thuringians had naturally tended to throw off all allegiance to it. Nor was any improvement in the situation likely to be expected of the kings, for they had degenerated into mere puppets controlled by their more important ministers. All real authority in Austrasia had thus come to be exercised by the chief of the royal household (*maior domus*), inaccurately known to historians as the mayor of the palace, and the office had become hereditary in the family that was to win renown under the name Carolingian (see Table I).

Charles Martel (714-41)

The first of the line to gain a noteworthy success was Pepin II who, after defeating the Neustrians in 687, was able to recombine the two fragments of the old Merovingian dominion. This unification became permanent through the remarkable achievements of his son Charles. The latter, by a series of vigorous campaigns into Burgundy, Aquitaine, and the Germanic lands to the east, enforced his authority on all sides and so re-established the Frankish kingdom as it had been under the sons of Clovis. But while he was thus engaged, a more formidable enemy appeared to the south— the Moorish conquerors of Spain, who from their base in Septimania now extended their raids into southern Gaul.

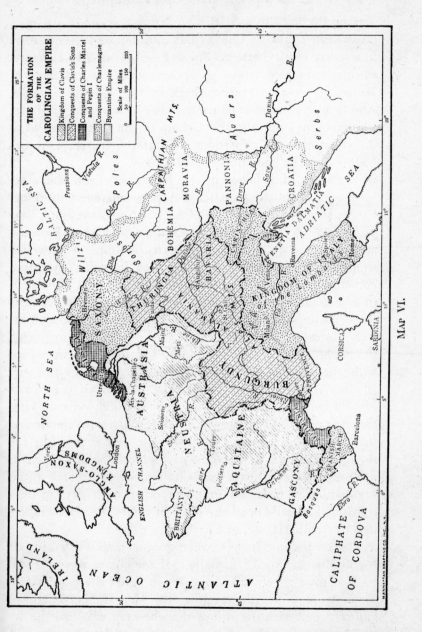

MAP VI.

THE FORMATION
OF THE
CAROLINGIAN EMPIRE

Kingdom of Clovis
Conquests of Clovis's Sons
Conquests of Charles Martel
and Pepin I
Conquests of Charlemagne
Byzantine Empire

Scale of Miles
0   50   100   150   200

ATLANTIC OCEAN

NORTH SEA

BALTIC SEA

IRELAND

ANGLO-SAXON KINGDOMS

York

London

ENGLISH CHANNEL

BRITTANY

NEUSTRIA

AUSTRASIA

Soissons
Seine R.
Tours
Poitiers
Loire R.
AQUITAINE
Garonne R.
GASCONY
Basques
SPANISH MARCH
Barcelona
Ebro R.
CALIPHATE
OF CORDOVA

Utrecht
Aix-la-Chapelle
Mainz
Metz
SAXONY
Bremen
Weser R.
Elbe R.
THURINGIA
Soissons
BURGUNDY
PROVENCE
Rhone R.

WILZI
Oder R.
Poles
Vistula R.
Prussians
DANES

BOHEMIA
MORAVIA
CARPATHIAN MTS.
BAVARIA
Augsburg
Danube R.
Salzburg
CARINTHIA
PANNONIA
Avars
Drave R.
Save R.
CROATIA
DALMATIA
Serbs

THE ALPS
KINGDOM OF ITALY
of the Lombards
Milan
Venice
VENETIA
Ravenna
Spoleto
Rome

ADRIATIC SEA

CORSICA

SARDINIA

MANHATTAN DRAFTING CO. INC. N.Y.

Taking the field in 732 with an army composed in part of heavy-armed cavalry, Charles met and defeated the invaders in a great battle between Poitiers and Tours. His victory, since it coincided with the weakening of the caliphate at Damascus, gave a decisive check to the Moslem advance. And from it Charles obtained not only his surname of Martel (the Hammer) but also the acclaim of the western world as the champion of Christendom. Naturally, therefore, it was he to whom the pope now turned for aid.

The disturbing factor in the Italian situation was a rejuvenated Lombard monarchy. A new and energetic king, having subdued the duchies of Spoleto and Benevento, now proceeded, on the north, to attack the exarchate of Ravenna and, on the south, to threaten the city of Rome. No effective support could at any time be expected from the Byzantine emperor, and at this particular moment he was embroiled in a violent controversy with the western church over the iconoclastic program.[1] To the pope it must have seemed utterly absurd that he, the actual ruler of the Roman duchy, should be the subject of a distant and incompetent prince with whom he had forbidden all good Christians to have any dealings. The Frankish mayor, on the other hand, had proved himself a heroic and loyal son of the church—a true king lacking only the regal crown. The logic of events demanded that the two outstanding powers of the west should ally for their great mutual advantage. Charles Martel, as it happened, was unwilling to embark on an Italian adventure and, as the Lombard state relapsed into temporary inactivity, matters continued to drift until the office of mayor had been inherited by Pepin III, son of Charles.

Pepin, king of the Franks (751-68)

The crisis came in 751, when another ambitious king of the Lombards, Aistulf, actually took the city of Ravenna. Almost at once an embassy from Pepin asked the pope a momentous question with regard to the Merovingian kingship, and returned with the answer that the man who had the actual power better deserved the crown than the one who had

[1] See above, p. 96.

not. Accordingly, a great assembly of the Franks elected and solemnly proclaimed Pepin as their king. The last of the Merovingian puppets was sent to a monastery, and the house of Clovis ended in oblivion. Three years later, when Aistulf demanded the recognition of his sovereignty over the duchy of Rome, Pope Stephen II crossed the Alps into Gaul and, adopting the ritual of the ancient Hebrews, anointed Pepin with consecrated oil—as king of the Franks and *patricius* of the Romans. The latter title, vague as it was, definitely implied to contemporaries that the Frankish king was in some measure to be lawful sovereign in the imperial city. And the sequel proved that the recognition was no mere gesture. Pepin invaded Italy, defeated Aistulf, took the exarchate away from him, and bestowed it on the pope.

By this famous donation Pepin brought into existence the Papal States of history—an irregular territory extending across the peninsula from Rome in the west to Ravenna in the east. Otherwise he made no change in the Italian situation, but devoted the remainder of his life to affairs nearer home. Following up a campaign that he had earlier launched, he finally took the whole of Septimania from the Moors and so brought his frontier to the line of the Pyrenees. And by actively supporting the efforts of Christian missionaries—a work of which more will be heard in a later section—he extended his dominion over the Frisians beyond the lower Rhine. In 768 Pepin died, leaving his enlarged kingdom to be shared by two sons; but, with the early death of one, the entire inheritance fell to the other, whom the world knows as Charles the Great or Charlemagne.

As soon as he had secured undisputed possession of the throne, the new king proved his military genius by the energy and effectiveness with which he advanced the great projects of his father and grandfather. The first of these projects was the subjection of the Lombards, whose king, Desiderius, the pope accused of seeking to undo Pepin's settlement. In one campaign Charlemagne ended that danger. Occupying northern Italy, he deposed Desiderius, and himself assumed

Conquests of Charlemagne

the crown of the Lombards (774). Then, without attempting the reduction of the southern Italian provinces, he turned his attention to the conquest and Christianization of the Saxons, the fierce Germanic people who inhabited the country north of Thuringia and east of the Rhine. The task was a difficult one, completed only after a general uprising had been cruelly suppressed. Thereafter, in spite of sporadic insurrection, Saxony constituted an integral part of the Frankish kingdom.

To supplement his conquest of northern Germany, Charlemagne next led an army down the Danube and ousted the Bavarian duke, who had been conducting himself very much as an independent prince. And from the position thus gained Charlemagne proceeded to deal with the Avars. Two hundred years earlier they had built up a considerable empire that extended far into the Balkans. Now, however, their power was so far decayed that the victorious Franks were able to take even the great Rings, the central camps where the Avars had piled the accumulated booty of a thousand raids. Towards the close of the eighth century, therefore, Charlemagne could draw his eastern boundary from the Baltic to the head of the Adriatic. All along the frontier lay a series of territories with a special military organization. These marches, or marks, included, to the south of the Danube, Croatia and Pannonia; to the north of it Moravia and Bohemia, mainly inhabited by the Czechs; and, to the east of the Saale and Elbe, the lands of various other Slavic peoples. Against the Danes, similarly, a march was created in the region that was later to become known as Holstein (see Map VI).

At the beginning of his reign Charlemagne seems to have been convinced that he might easily conquer Spain. On the fall of the Ommiad caliphate at Damascus Abd-ar-Rahman, last survivor of the ill-fated dynasty, made good his escape to Cordova. There, from 756 on, he ruled as emir, successfully defying the authority of the Abbasid caliph, who therefore urged the Frankish king to dethrone the usurper. But an expedition of Charlemagne in 778 utterly failed, and on the return journey his army was ambushed by the Christian Basques in the pass of Roncevaux—an incident that was to inspire a glorious epic of the feudal age. To Charlemagne it probably served merely as a warning not to pursue fantastic projects beyond the Pyrenees. Thenceforth he adopted a defensive policy towards the Moors and sought to acquire only enough territory for the organization of a frontier district. The result, after the capture of Barcelona, was the establishment of the Spanish March, which remained an outpost of northern influence for many centuries to come.

Meanwhile a matter of surpassing interest had diverted men's thoughts from such paltry events as the taking of a Spanish fortress. This was nothing less than the revival of the imperial office in the west, to explain which entails a brief review of the preliminaries. To his father's titles, king of the Franks and *patricius* of the Romans, Charlemagne had added a third by acquiring the crown of the Lombards. But the Lombard kingdom included neither Rome nor Ravenna; when Charlemagne acted as sovereign in those regions, it was presumably by virtue of his Roman patriciate. Whatever the theory may have been, he exercised a very real authority over the Papal States; so, when serious trouble broke out in Rome, he was called upon to settle it. In 800 Pope Leo III was driven from the city by a violent insurrection. Taking refuge with Charlemagne, he appealed for reinstatement, while the opposing faction, to justify its revolt, filed a series of grave charges against the fugitive. Charlemagne accordingly proceeded to Rome and there held a great council of clergy and laity, which eventually decided that the pope should clear himself by swearing his innocence on the Gospels. This he did on December 23 and was forthwith recognized as the lawful holder of the papal insignia.

Two days later Leo presided over the Christmas festival in St. Peter's church. After saying mass, and while Charlemagne was praying at the altar, the pope placed a diadem on his head and the assembled throng shouted: "To Charles Augustus, crowned of God, great and pacific emperor of the

The imperial coronation (800)

Romans, life and victory!" Are we to believe, as we are told by the official annalists, that the ceremony took Charlemagne entirely by surprise and that he was actually displeased at the high honor so unexpectedly thrust upon him? The statement is incredible. The stage was too carefully set for the affair to have been other than premeditated. The tradition of an indestructible Roman Empire still charmed the minds of men, including that of Charlemagne himself. The west had had no resident emperor since 476; now, as the reward of the Frankish might, one was again installed. The assumption of the imperial title was the logical climax of Charlemagne's whole career. He must have willed it.

Byzantine recognition   In strict theory, of course, Leo had no more right to bestow the crown than Charlemagne to assume it; but a pope had earlier given a Frankish king the title of *patricius* and it was now superseded by the title of emperor. The revolution had been so gradually brought about that the final step was natural enough. Although the Byzantine court might register a protest, it would hardly trouble any one in the Latin world, for at that moment the holder of the purple in the east was the notorious Irene.[2] Besides, the acquiescence of Constantinople might ultimately be purchased. To that end Charlemagne devoted earnest efforts, and just before his death he was assured that, in return for the cession of Dalmatia and Venetia, his newly acquired rank would be recognized by the Byzantine emperor. Yet, after the formalities had been concluded, Charlemagne was still essentially the warrior Frank—speaking his native German, wearing the barbarian costume, and delighting in the traditional sports of his people. And when we more closely examine his state, we find it as slightly Roman as his personal character.

2. CAROLINGIAN SOCIETY AND INSTITUTIONS

The royal authority   As far as government was concerned, the Carolingian Empire was merely an enlarged Frankish kingdom, for Charlemagne ruled Lombardy in much the same fashion as his

[2] See above, p. 96.

other dominions. Like his Merovingian predecessors, he had three principal functions: to command the army, to administer justice, and to protect the church. He was not supposed to be absolute. He neither claimed nor exercised arbitrary control over the ancient laws of his people. His nearest approach to imperial legislation in the Roman sense was the establishment of judicial reforms and other extraordinary measures with the counsel and consent of his great men. In such cases, however, we generally hear of Charlemagne's decisions, not from formal edicts, but from capitularies, sets of instructions to the royal officials. Occasionally a capitulary would be restricted to a single subject—the administration of the royal estates, the improvement of education, the organization of the Saxon territory, or the like. More often it would embody a haphazard group of enactments dealing indiscriminately with church and state, and with both the public and the private affairs of the emperor.

Immediately under Charlemagne was the royal household, an institution derived, through adaptation by the Merovingians, from the court of Diocletian. Charlemagne's household included the chamberlain, who acted as governor of the palace and of the royal treasure; the seneschal, who managed the king's food and in some degree supervised the estates that produced it; the butler, who had charge of the royal cellar and vineyards; and the marshal or constable, who through control of the stable had obtained high command in the army. Another important officer of the household was the chaplain, the superior of the priests who administered the sacraments to the king and his family, and of the clerks who wrote his letters and drew up his legal documents. It was not till considerably later that the writing office (*scriptorium*) acquired a separate head called the chancellor.

Officers of the household

As in Merovingian times, the all-important agents of the central government throughout the provinces were the counts, appointed by the king to act during his pleasure. Each normally combined judicial, military, financial, and

Counts and missi

other executive functions within a small district, frequently an old Roman *civitas*. But along the frontiers wider regions were assigned to counts of the border, styled marquises (German *markgraf*, margrave) or dukes, each of whom was apt to have authority over a number of ordinary counts. All such officials, in the absence of a trained civil service, were merely Frankish noblemen, who in addition to grants of land customarily received a share of the revenues they collected. To keep an effective check upon the counts was therefore the king's great difficulty. Charlemagne met it principally through personal activity, for he was continually moving about at the head of his troops. With the same end in view, he also revived a practice which had formed part of the Roman system, but which had lapsed under the Merovingians. According to a famous capitulary of 802, distinguished laymen and ecclesiastics were to be sent out (*missi*) as inspectors. They were to superintend the entire government of both church and state, listening to all complaints, investigating the facts through sworn witnesses, and reporting back to the emperor. They were, indeed, to see that everybody, in or out of office, did what he ought to do—a noble ideal which, it is to be feared, even the best of *missi* could not wholly live up to.

Law and justice

With regard to justice generalization is impossible, except to say that it was a matter of local custom. Barbarian princes of the previous age had often issued codes to govern the settlement of disputes among the various groups of their subjects, but by the eighth century the old national distinctions had long since broken down. Whether a man lived under the Roman law or under some variety of barbarian law had become largely accidental. Each little region had its own usages administered by its own court. There, under the presidency of the count, judgments were rendered by the assembled suitors, or a select number of them (Latin *scabini*, French *échevins*), who knew what rules and penalties ought to be enforced. The character of this customary law varied according to the dominant tradition of the countryside: in the south it was fundamentally Roman; in the north it was almost purely Germanic.

Among the Franks, as among the Anglo-Saxons and other barbarian peoples, the idea of crime had scarcely emerged. Although the administration of justice brought the king numerous fines and fees, such acts as homicide, assault, and theft remained primarily offenses against the individual and his kindred. If the kinsmen were not bought off, they might seek revenge by proclaiming a blood feud. The killing of a man thus necessitated the payment to the relatives of his *wergeld*, a sum determined by his social rank. Wounding called for compensation in proportion to the value of the part affected, and other wrongs, notably insults, had to be atoned for in the same way. So the law books of the Germanic kings are mainly tariffs of the amounts charged for every sort of injury. But they also give us much information about judicial procedure. Trials were extremely formalistic. The plaintiff (A), having summoned the defendant (B) and got him to court, accused him by means of a solemn oath. The court then decided how B should clear himself. In the case of compurgation, B first swore his innocence and then produced a stated number of oath-helpers, each of whom had to swear by a letter-perfect formula that B's oath was pure. In the case of ordeal, B might have to plunge his arm into boiling water or carry a heated bar of iron for a certain distance. He was acquitted only if, after being bound up for three days, the arm or the hand was pronounced clean— i.e., apparently, not infected.

In connection with military obligations, too, the earlier distinction between Roman and non-Roman had disappeared under the Merovingians. In time of war the king treated all able-bodied men as Franks, liable for service when called. But by the time of Charlemagne far-reaching modifications of the primitive system were being rapidly introduced. Each person, in proportion to his means, was required to possess certain weapons and defensive armor. And since the obligation of serving at one's own cost for a period of three months

Military service

was burdensome, the emperor restricted it to men owning particular amounts of land—amounts that varied according to the distance from the scene of war. For this purpose, therefore, estates came to be assessed in a rude unit known as the manse or hide—the land presumed requisite for the support of a single family. Great landlords were made responsible for one soldier from every so many hides. Small men were grouped together so that their joint contributions would support one of them on the campaign.

For the procuring of mounted troops similar arrangements were even more essential. The emperor might, of course, require certain properties to furnish horses instead of men; but to obtain a force of expert cavalry something better was demanded than casual levies made through the counts. This truth had long been appreciated. Charles Martel and Pepin, needing a stronger army and lacking funds for hiring cavalry, solved the difficulty, we are told, at the expense of the church. To their most reliable followers they gave ecclesiastical lands as life estates, or benefices, and in return specified service with horses and arms. Presumably such military benefices had already been created out of property belonging to the king; at any rate it became increasingly common, in the second half of the eighth century, for all great men thus to provide contingents of trained horsemen. Charlemagne deliberately encouraged the practice, providing that in time of war armed retainers might follow the standard of the lord whom they served. This development of feudal tenure, as will be more thoroughly explained below, had momentous significance for the future of Europe.

Taxation   In financial organization likewise, the monarchy remained fundamentally as it had been in the earlier age. The two great political concerns of the royal administration, justice and military defense, were largely taken care of through gratuitous service on the part of the individual subject. In the same way the maintenance of public works, the housing and provisioning of royal agents, and the transportation of men and materials were secured by direct requisition. An endless plague of such exactions had, in fact, continued to afflict the countryside since the days of the Roman Empire. Nor was there any interruption in the levy of indirect taxes, now called *thelonea,* tolls. On the other hand, the ancient system of taxes on land and persons had so far decayed that only indistinct vestiges of them henceforth appear in the records. Charlemagne invented no new imposts to take their places. Tribute might be collected from subjected peoples, but the nearest approach to a general tax throughout the empire was the practice of taking contributions, styled gifts (*dona*), from the great men when they attended the formal assemblies. That they in turn recouped themselves by requiring similar offerings from their followers is extremely probable. Finance, like military service, was tending to become a matter of seignorial arrangement—that is to say, a matter brought under the control of the lordly class in society.

The bulk of Charlemagne's income, plainly, was got from his own estates, for he was the greatest landowner in the kingdom. This side of the emperor's activity is known to us in intimate detail from his famous capitulary concerning his villas, which contains minute instructions as to how they should be managed. Each villa was placed under a steward called *maior* or *villicus,* responsible to a superior official who acted as superintendent for a considerable number of such properties. The steward saw to the cultivation of the estate and had the produce carried to central barns, where the superintendent kept it for the disposal of the emperor. Each steward, according to the capitulary, was to make out an annual statement, describing the sources of income under his care and listing everything that was produced: grain, hay, fruits, nuts, vegetables, wine, beer, vinegar, oil, flax, hemp, honey, wool, hides, horns, tallow, meat, lumber, firewood, domestic animals and fowls, eggs, dairy products, game, fish, and all manufactures. He was to keep account of all the tenants and their respective obligations; to see that there were skilled artisans for the production of all necessary articles; to make an inventory of all buildings, tools, and furnishings;

The royal estates

and to attend to a dozen other matters as well. And from extant reports made by the emperor's agents we may see that his regulations in this connection were actually enforced.

Charlemagne, regarding himself as the anointed of God and the successor of Theodosius, constantly asserted a general power of supervision over the church. He very plainly held that Rome was under his supreme jurisdiction, and that the pope should exercise no more than the autonomy befitting so distinguished a prelate. The pope, on his side, seemed to acquiesce in the imperial leadership, having good reason for personal gratitude and apprehending no threat of an immediate dictatorship. So Charlemagne's capitularies regularly included measures affecting both clergy and laity. Even when problems of a purely ecclesiastical nature arose, it was through his initiative and under his presidency that action was taken by the bishops in council. They, in fact, were quite submissive to his desires, for episcopal elections were under his control. And by nominating candidates to be chosen by the monastic chapters he virtually appointed abbots also. Both groups of prelates, it should be noted, had come to hold extensive temporal power by grant of the emperor or his predecessors. Even under the Merovingians great ecclesiastics had often received charters of immunity, by virtue of which each beneficiary was assured that within a specified territory he should be immune from the authority of the count and should there exercise the regalian rights himself. Originally, perhaps, he was obliged to make an equivalent return to the king; but eventually the effect of an immunity was to give the immunist the profits of justice, tolls, military service, and other dues that normally would have accrued to the state. By the ninth century all important prelates had thus become actual princes, sharing the king's sovereign rights and equaling the counts in official dignity.

Turning now to the subject of economic conditions in the Carolingian Empire, we encounter a number of highly controversial problems. The view here maintained is that western Europe suffered a progressive decline from the third century onward. This decline was not primarily the result of the barbarian invasions, but was undoubtedly stimulated by them. In both Gaul and Italy conditions were much worse in the sixth and seventh centuries than they had been in the fifth. Meanwhile the widening separation between east and west had removed from the latter the major part of its shipping industry and sea trade. And by the eighth century the encroaching power of the Arabs had definitely broken most of the ancient routes across the Mediterranean. With Africa, Spain, and Septimania in the hands of the Moslems, and with Italy torn by chronic warfare, the lands to the northwest of the Alps were further isolated. Charlemagne's state was entirely a construction of the mainland; for he left Dalmatia, Venetia, and southern Italy to Byzantine control and had little success against the Moors of Spain. However brilliant the Carolingian Empire may have superficially appeared, it brought no economic improvement of any significance.

Commercial decay was thus unchecked, with the consequence that society became more and more thoroughly agrarian. By the ninth century the overwhelming mass of the population lived through agriculture and so fell into two main classes: the few, who constituted the aristocracy of landlords, and the many, who constituted the servile or semi-free peasantry. Such a society had no conspicuous place for a town-dwelling class of traders. Small industry, of course, continued, for people had to have manufactured articles; but production was localized on the great estate. As described in Charlemagne's capitularies, artisans were attached to the villa and subordinated to its agrarian routine. Ordinary trade shrank to petty dealings in a neighborhood market, which, being held on a single day in the week, attracted no resident population of professional merchants. It is significant also that the only money coined under the Carolingians was silver pennies; and since the minting privilege was widely distributed, each little region came to have its own currency—a situation that bespeaks small transactions on the part of people who were chronically poor. From the east, it is true,

The decay of commerce

bands of wandering merchants, generally called Syrians, still penetrated into the remote provinces of the west. All the evidence, however, tends to show that they were relatively few in number and that on their infrequent visits they brought articles of luxury that could be afforded only by the very wealthy. Commerce of this kind is of practically no importance in building up the economic resources of any country.

The Carolingian cities

As has been remarked, Moslem Africa and Spain remained in close touch with Egypt and Syria, and so developed a brilliant culture that was wholly foreign to the lands across the Pyrenees. Some of the Italian ports, too, never lost contact with the great metropolis of Constantinople; and while the Franks fought for control of the interior, the city of Venice, under Byzantine protection, arose on the lagoons of the upper Adriatic. The Carolingian Empire witnessed no such development. Although Gaul was dotted with places which were called *civitates* and which still bore their Latin names, that fact by no means proves the persistence of a truly urban civilization. Many of the cities in the western Roman Empire had never been more than centers of administration and defense, and in the succeeding period that character became the rule. From archæological investigation it is clear that even a great metropolis like Cologne or London had lost all but a few of its inhabitants long before the time of Charlemagne. Counts and bishops, to be sure, often used Roman cities for their capitals, but the persons whom they attracted were principally soldiers, clerks, and serving-men, supported like their masters by the labor of peasants on adjoining estates. Economically, these cities were not centers of production. Socially, they had no peculiarity to mark them off from the countryside. Politically, they lacked every vestige of true municipal organization.

Growth of the manorial system

As far as rural life was concerned, there can be no doubt that the Roman villa persisted under the barbarian conquerors. The model for the Carolingian manor was the great estate of the later empire. There we encounter the division of the arable between the proprietor and the tenants, so that each of the latter had his own plot in return for rents and labor owed to the former. The cultivators included slaves (*servi*) as well as the theoretical freemen called *coloni*. But all of them had come to be settled in much the same way, and through imperial legislation the *coloni* were as firmly attached to the estate as if they had been slaves. By the fifth century the mass of the agricultural population in the west had already become an economically dependent peasantry. And as the greater landlords rapidly acquired grants of immunity, the dependence of the peasantry tended to become also political. These agrarian arrangements were in general left unchanged by the barbarians, who merely took over a share of the existing estates and allowed them to be cultivated as before. Even the distinction between the invaders and the native Romans soon vanished. By the time of Charlemagne there was a single agrarian aristocracy, throughout Gaul usually speaking a Latin dialect, but in dress, habits, and disposition remaining predominantly barbarian. Beneath the ruling class a variety of Roman dependents, poorer German settlers, captives in war, and other subjected persons had been fused into the villein class of the Middle Ages. Many, perhaps most, of the peasants were legally free; yet they were economically unfree, being reduced to the position of *coloni*. The *servus*, too, had become what we know as a serf; and to designate the rightless bondman a new word was introduced—*esclave* or slave, derived from the tribal name of the unfortunates then being sold in the markets of the west.[3]

Along with the development of manorialism—the economic subjection of the masses to the greater landlords— the records of the Frankish kingdom reveal a striking growth of dependent tenure on the part of landlords themselves. During the troubled centuries that followed the collapse of the western empire, the lot of the small proprietor became increasingly hard. Often, to secure protection or other advantage, he would give his land to a church and receive it

Benefices and precariæ

[3] See above, p. 36.

back as a benefice, a life estate to be held in return for a nominal payment. Sometimes an ecclesiastic or a layman would, on his own initiative, grant such an estate in order to have valuable service performed by the recipient. And very much the same result would ensue when a man requested land to live on and obtained it by virtue of a similar agreement. In the latter case the holding was technically called a *precaria*, because it was received in answer to formal prayer (*preces*); but it was also a benefice, because it was alleged to be a boon (*beneficium*) conferred by the donor.

The names are a matter of secondary interest. The really important point is that, whatever the preliminaries, a certain property while owned by one man was actually possessed by another. Under Roman law a "precarious" tenure had been one enjoyed during the pleasure of a grantor. As developed under Frankish law, however, the *precaria* or benefice became a form of legal possession—whether for a term of years, for one life, for several lives, or for an indefinite period. Here we find an important element in the growth of the institutions called feudal. But what was eventually to become known as a fief (*feudum*) was only a special kind of benefice— one held by a vassal in return for military service. To understand feudal development, therefore, we must turn our attention to the earlier history of vassalage.

Vassalage and the Carolingian policy　　According to many famous scholars, the mediæval relationship of the vassal to his lord (French *seigneur*, Latin *senior*) was derived from that of the Roman client (*cliens*) to his patron (*patronus* or *senior*). The weakness of the argument is that, for all the persistence of a few vague Latin words, the two institutions were utterly unlike. The vassalage of the feudal age was essentially honorable and military.[4] The clientage of Rome, on the contrary, was merely a form of economic dependence; on helping to swell some wealthy man's escort, the poor man received donations of money, food, and clothing. It would thus appear more reasonable to find the origin of vassalage in the Germanic *comitatus* de-

[4] See below, pp. 139-40.

scribed by Tacitus.[5] In so far as the aristocracy of the eighth
and following centuries was primarily warlike, it must have
been descended from the warrior class of the conquering
barbarians. Through appeal to an ancient tradition of that
class, the Carolingians attempted to strengthen their dubious
authority in an overgrown kingdom. Important offices in
church and state were now increasingly given to royal vassals;
soon it became the rule that only they should hold such
offices. Thanks to endowment with rich benefices, royal
vassals supplied the king with an enlarged force of expert
cavalry. And as the royal vassal came to have important political functions, so he came to enjoy high political privilege.
In particular, his military benefice brought him official immunity—the delegation of certain governmental powers
within a restricted territory.

By adapting and developing old institutions, the Carolingians thus carried out what may properly be termed the
feudalization of their state; although, of course, they could
not foresee the ultimate consequences of their policy. That
the policy was not in itself vicious will be apparent from the
later discussion. The Carolingian Empire could not be saved
by any set of royal enactments—good, bad, or indifferent.

3. THE CHURCH AND EDUCATION UNDER THE CAROLINGIANS

It is very significant that, when Charlemagne sought to
revive learning in his empire, his inspiration came not from
Mediterranean lands but from the British Isles. Their earlier
history, accordingly, must at this point be briefly reviewed.
By the end of the sixth century most of Roman Britain had
been occupied by the Anglo-Saxons, who remained divided
into a series of petty kingdoms: Northumbria, East Anglia,
Mercia, Kent, and the East, Middle, South, and West Saxons
(Essex, Middlesex, Sussex, and Wessex—see Map VII). In
the north the Picts were struggling to defend the highlands
against a horde of Scots from Ireland. Some of the Britons,
whom the Anglo-Saxons called Welsh, still held the moun-

Anglo-Saxon peoples

[5] See above, pp. 38-39.

tainous regions of western Britain. Others, fleeing from the invaders, had crossed the Channel to the Armorican peninsula, thenceforth known as Brittany, where they established the Celtic speech and customs that have persisted down to the present.

MAP VII.

Success of the Roman mission

This region, as well as most of Britain, naturally came to be visited by zealous Irish monks,[6] who found new opportunities for missionary effort in the lands to the east. The famous St. Columban (543-615) was thus attracted first to the wilder parts of Gaul, where he established a number of religious communities; then to the country of the Alamans, where a great monastery came to bear the name of his dis-

[6] See above, p. 64.

ciple, St. Gall. But while the influence of Irish monasticism was being carried to the very frontiers of Christendom, Pope Gregory the Great had proclaimed his support of the Benedictine system and had sent Augustine with other Benedictine monks as missionaries to Britain. Having converted the king of Kent, they extended their activities into the neighboring kingdoms, and so encountered the rivalry of the Irish. In 664 the dispute between the two groups was laid before a council at Whitby by the Northumbrian king, whom for the moment the Anglo-Saxon states generally recognized as overlord. The decision, rendered in favor of the pope, made it necessary for ecclesiastical organization to conform with Roman usage; soon a number of territorial bishoprics had been created and combined in the two provinces of Canterbury and York.

For the continent, too, this decision had momentous consequences. As Irish influence yielded to Roman even in the British Isles, it became impossible for Columban's foundations to maintain their original independence. By the end of the seventh century the Benedictine system had definitely gained supremacy in the Latin world, and Anglo-Saxon monks, devoting themselves to the papal service, had superseded the Irish as leaders of missionary enterprise among the Germans of central Europe. About 690 Willibrord, a Northumbrian educated in Ireland, undertook the task of converting the Frisians who inhabited the estuary of the Rhine. He was so successful that some five years later he was consecrated bishop of Utrecht under the name of Clemens. Then, shortly before his death, he was joined by one Winfrid, a West Saxon monk. But Winfrid's stay in Frisia was brief. Having—under the name of Boniface—secured direct authorization from the pope, he transferred his activities to the Austrasian border, where he soon reported thousands of converts among the Thuringians and other Germanic peoples.

Hitherto all effort towards Christianizing these districts had been sporadic. Irish monks and other volunteers had

St. Boniface (680-754)

founded monasteries and local churches without the slightest supervision on the part of any central authority, for the chaotic conditions that prevailed throughout the Merovingian dominions had prevented decisive action by the monarchy. Now, with the effective backing of the Carolingian house as well as of the papacy, Boniface was able to create a unified ecclesiastical system for this entire East Frankish territory. Older monasteries were reformed and new ones established on all sides—chief among them the illustrious Fulda. Bavaria and Thuringia, together with the adjacent country, were divided into bishoprics under the jurisdiction of an archbishop at Mainz, eventually Boniface himself. Yet, as an old man of seventy-four, Boniface still longed for a fresh world to conquer. Resigning his see, he resumed his missionary career among the Frisians and was there slain by heathen pirates in 754. As Augustine had begun a new epoch for Britain, so Boniface, a product of the earlier mission, began a new epoch for Germany. A century and a half of religious history serves as a commentary on the statesmanship of Pope Gregory the Great.

The Dark Age in the west What, in the meantime, had been the fate of arts and letters in the old Roman provinces of the west? The period following the calamitous fifth century has, with considerable justice, been termed the Dark Age. The darkness was that of ignorance, which extended far beyond the range of academic instruction. Whether we examine archæological or literary remains, the conclusion is the same: there had been an appalling degradation of culture. It was not merely the study of the classics but the ability to read and write that was threatened with extinction. The spoken Latin, even of the upper classes, had drifted so far from literary Latin that a knowledge of the former was a hindrance rather than a help in formal composition. No one as yet dreamed of writing in the crude vernacular, though such polished languages as French, Provençal, Italian, and Spanish were eventually to develop from it. And, to judge from the works of the comparatively learned, the quality of education had rapidly deteriorated. The depth was reached in later Merovingian Gaul, where the king's official documents prove that his clerks were ignorant of the simplest grammatical rules, and where the best handwriting had become a grotesque scrawl.

The attitude of the church fathers towards scholarly pursuits has already been well illustrated in the views of Ambrose, Jerome, Augustine, and Gregory. All four were fundamentally mystic in that they insisted on the primary need of faith and to it subordinated the rational faculties. Their intellectual labors, though often profound, were consecrated to pious ends: to refute pagans and heretics, to expound the truths of revelation, and in all practical ways to advance the cause of Christianity. A passionate delight in literature or learning for its own sake they were inclined to regard as sinful. Thus Gregory admonished the proudly erudite to forsake their "foolish wisdom" for the "wise foolishness of God." The opinions held by the great monastic leaders were apparently much the same, but the varieties of religious discipline that they advocated permitted considerable divergence in practice. The Irish monks, commonly acting as priests among the people, had especial need of education; and since Greek was no stranger to them than Latin, they developed extraordinary zeal in the study of both languages. Many of them, in fact, came to have a deep regard for the classics, which they copied and recopied with loving care. Yet their conscious purpose was solely the promotion of the true faith.

Benedictine monasticism seems to have given somewhat less encouragement to scholarship during these early centuries. Although the subject is hardly referred to in the rule, Benedict obviously took for granted a certain amount of study and clerical work. The monastery had to have missals for the routine of divine service and books to be read aloud at mealtime or privately read by those brothers who were literate. To provide for such needs, younger monks received appropriate instruction, which, occasionally, boys from the outside might be permitted to share. Nevertheless, the Bene-

Monastic education

dictine monastery was not primarily an educational institution; the religious life that it enjoined was essentially worship alternating with manual labor. Furthermore, through the Benedictine insistence on the separation of the regular from the secular clergy, the monastery lost whatever functions it had earlier had in the training of priests. It became an isolated community subject to the benevolent despotism of its abbot. If he chanced to have scholarly leanings, his house might become famous for its learning; but such a development was exceptional. In this early time the average monastic school was a small group of brothers studying penmanship and Latin composition; the average monastic library was a press containing perhaps a score of books, mainly religious in nature.

Degrada-
tion of
the secu-
lar clergy

The secular clergy was thus left responsible for the work of the church in the world. To carry on this work effectively, priests had to have some education. If it could not be obtained in monasteries, the bishops would have to provide it. Although the cathedral school eventually became a prominent feature of ecclesiastical organization, such institutions remained very obscure in the pre-Carolingian period. And we may be sure that, at least in Gaul, the priesthood of that time was generally debased. Too frequently even the bishops were worldly and ignorant, spending their lives in family feud, political intrigue, warfare, hunting, and other favorite pursuits of the semi-barbarous noblemen. Those exceptional priests who were competent to act as intellectual leaders found their energies so absorbed by the Christianization of new countries, or the attempted reform of old ones, that much scholarly endeavor was beyond them. It is not remarkable that, under these circumstances, the seventh and eighth centuries were a singularly unproductive age in literature and learning. Authors worth mentioning in the history of European thought were exceedingly few, and such as there were had a mental outlook that to us seems childlike. If they were the great teachers, what shall we think of their pupils?

In Gaul Gregory of Tours (538-94), the honest and informative historian of Christianity among the Franks, had no worthy successor. Italy produced no writer to be compared with Gregory the Great. Justinian's conquest of Roman Africa, however beneficial in other respects, brought no revival of Latin scholarship. In Spain, on the other hand, the church preserved a relatively superior culture, the chief exponent of·which was Isidore, bishop of Seville from about 600 to 636. He was a prolific author, writing on theology, history, literature, and various sciences. Finally, towards the close of his life, he composed a summary of his teachings and gave it the title of *Etymologies*. The book had an enormous success, for it served as a manual of universal knowledge throughout the next five centuries. From it, therefore, we may gain a more complete picture of what constituted wisdom in the Dark Age than from any other one volume.

The key to the compilation is provided by its title. Isidore believed that the essence of a thing was indicated by its name: through the derivation and significance of the latter, one could understand the former. So his book is little more than a series of definitions based, often enough, on purely fanciful etymology. For example, he says that "night (*nox*) is so called . . . because it injures (*noceat*) the eyes"; "man (*homo*) is so called because he was made of earth (*ex humo*), as is told in Genesis"; "the liver (*iecur*) has its name because in it is resident the fire (*ignis*) that flies up into the brain and is thence spread to the eyes and the other senses and members." In this way Isidore introduces a series of topical essays, which together review all the traditional subjects of instruction. His information, to be sure, was sometimes a little better than is displayed in these passages, because he sometimes copied from more reliable sources. In no case can we attribute much critical insight to Isidore himself, for he merely compiled a scrapbook from earlier writings. Often he adopted statements that were flatly contradictory, and occasionally he seems to have quite misunderstood what he repeated. The contrast between the book's pretensions and its actual substance is ridiculous; yet the author, we should remember, was doing what he could to enlighten a desperately ignorant world.

Bede

For a better standard of intellectual achievement we must turn from the continent to the British Isles, where by the eighth century the learning of the Irish monks, as well as their missionary zeal, was being taken over by Anglo-Saxons. The greatest scholar of the age was Bede, a Northumbrian who spent the greater part of his life in the monastery of Jarrow, dying there in 735. It was presumably through the tradition of the Irish schools that Bede had so remarkable a knowledge of Greek and Latin letters, but with it he combined a devotion to the papal ideals that was characteristic of the Anglo-Saxon monks. His erudition was wholly subordinated to the practical ends of Christian education. Even an unconscious delight in literature as an æsthetic study is never revealed in his many writings, which were in the main commentaries on Scripture, useful compilations, and textbooks. His essay on chronology deserves special mention because it was largely responsible for our system of dating in years of the Christian era. His *Ecclesiastical History of the English* is the best historical composition of the age.

The Carolingian reform of education

One of Bede's contemporaries, it should be noted, was the illustrious Boniface, who had spent many years in teaching before he undertook his great missionary enterprise. And while he was on the continent, his work was by no means restricted to converting the heathen. Clearly it was he and his associates, rather than Charlemagne, who inaugurated the reform of the Frankish clergy. But it was characteristic of the new king that he should assume the initiative in advancing a cause which he considered essential to the welfare of church and state. Under his father, Pepin, a number of teachers had already been attached to the royal court for the instruction of young nobles. From this nucleus Charlemagne now developed his famous palace school, bringing over the Northumbrian Alcuin to superintend it. As the director of the cathedral school at York, which had been founded by a pupil of Bede, Alcuin represented a noble tradition, and in every way he was eminently fitted to carry out Charlemagne's plan. To Aix-la-Chapelle, the king's favorite residence, he attracted teachers from all sides: English, Irish, Italians, and Spaniards, as well as Franks from Gaul and Germany. Within this early generation there were few noteworthy authors; yet they, by imparting to their students an enthusiasm for learning, inspired the production of many influential books in the next century. On men from this group Charlemagne conferred great abbeys and bishoprics, entrusting to them the task of organizing local schools, collecting libraries, reproducing ancient texts, standardizing the services of the church, and improving the quality of ecclesiastical music. Such projects, backed by the amazing energy of the king himself, rapidly stimulated the cultural advance that is often known as the Carolingian Renaissance. The description is somewhat exaggerated. What was actually done was to make more general a system of education that already existed in isolated communities, particularly those of the British Isles.

Although in minor respects some of the Carolingian scholars may have surpassed Bede, on the average they were distinctly inferior. Alcuin's own books were not at all remarkable, consisting chiefly of dialogues on the liberal arts and of commentaries on the Scriptures. In both respects his work was continued with great success by his pupil, Hrabanus Maurus, who rose to be abbot of Fulda (d. 856). The more popular writings of Hrabanus included a universal encyclopædia, which was only a revision of Isidore's *Etymologies*; a long essay on the education of the clergy, which was largely a compilation of extracts from the church fathers; and many volumes of Biblical interpretation, which of course used the allegorical approach. These products, on the whole, were characteristic of Carolingian scholarship, which but rarely wandered into the more dangerous fields of original speculation. A profound thinker was out of place in the ninth century; it was the very mediocrity of Hrabanus that assured his renown.

Among the other writers at the Frankish court two of the

Carolingian scholars

better known were historians: one who ended and one who began his career during the reign of Charlemagne. Paul the Deacon, a monk of Monte Cassino, spent only a few years in the north; then, returning to Italy, he devoted the rest of his life to composing a *History of the Lombards*. The book has enjoyed great popularity because it is filled with a variety of engaging legends; but, for that same reason, it is not a very trustworthy source, and the author unfortunately did not live to describe the age of which he had direct knowledge. In every way a finer scholar was Einhard, a young Frank who came from Fulda to complete his education in the palace school. There he gained the friendship of Prince Louis and, after the latter had inherited the throne, continued to enjoy high favor at the imperial court. Einhard thus was able to pursue a literary career without becoming either priest or monk, and while a mere layman to write the most remarkable biography of the early Middle Ages. Being steeped in the Latin classics, he consciously set out, as a second Suetonius, to describe the deeds of another Cæsar, the late emperor Charlemagne. This is a fact of great significance in appraising Einhard's work; for, as he constantly borrowed language from his model, his statements cannot always be taken literally. The *Life of Charlemagne*, nevertheless, is a brilliant piece of literature and parts of it have great historical worth. In particular, the graphic picture of the aged emperor is unforgettable and should be read by every one interested in the Carolingian age.

Einhard, it is clear, prized literary study as something beyond an element of practical education. He felt that, within limits, admiration of the classics was not incompatible with Christian character, and prominent clergymen occasionally shared his attitude. For instance, Lupus, abbot of Ferrières, devoted much more time to pagan letters than to theology. At the same time many other students are known to have attempted imitations of classic authors. To modern eyes the most noteworthy of them was John the Scot, an Irishman who came to Gaul about the middle of the ninth century and who seems never to have secured ecclesiastical preferment. His knowledge of Greek was so excellent that he even tried his hand at verses in that language. But his truly significant accomplishment was a book called *On the Division of Nature*— a reconcilation of Neo-Platonism and Christianity, which few if any of his contemporaries could have understood. John the Scot was the only man of the period whose mentality approached that of the great church fathers, and he had no intellectual heirs. As a matter of fact, the age was one in which original investigation could hardly flourish, and an uncritical devotion to the ideals of ancient authors could lead only to affectation. The really significant issue was the advancement of such practical education as had been advocated by Gregory the Great.

In theory the instruction given by the Carolingian schools, whether attached to monastery or cathedral, was based on the traditional scheme of the seven liberal arts. They were divided into two groups: the *trivium*, consisting of grammar, rhetoric, and dialectic; and the *quadrivium*, consisting of arithmetic, geometry, astronomy, and music. What of all this did the student actually get? In the first place, he would learn to read and write Latin—in itself no mean accomplishment, for Einhard tells us that even the great emperor never learned the art. Having gained a knowledge of elementary Latin, the youth could proceed with the popular textbooks of Priscian, Boëthius, Isidore, Bede, Alcuin, and Hrabanus. Besides, if he were to perfect his style, the leading masters agreed that he should have at least selections from the pagan classics. And the more zealous learner would not stop with a mere understanding of grammatical construction; according to the ancient tradition, the first of the liberal arts included most of what we should call the study of literature. This, however, was a secondary consideration, pursuit of which depended on the talents and sympathies of the instructor.

In rhetoric and dialectic ordinary education was restricted to the reading of standard treatises by Alcuin and his prede-

The seven liberal arts

cessors. Classical rhetoric had lost all meaning except as it might be adapted to the needs of the Christian preacher. To be effective, however, he now had to speak in the vernacular, and he would probably find the homilies of Gregory the Great more useful than theoretical discussions of the ancient art. Dialectic, too, had slight practical importance in the Carolingian age; and even if curiosity impelled a student to exhaust all his authorities, he could not progress very far. After working back to Boethius, he could read in translation Porphyry's *Isagoge* and the elementary logic of Aristotle. Of Plato nothing beyond a portion of one dialogue was available in Latin. All the rest of Greek philosophy and science, aside from scattering quotations, remained unknown in the west.

The learning imparted under the head of the *quadrivium* had therefore become negligible. Neither the Romans nor the Greeks before them had been able to do much with arithmetic, because they had continued to use letters as numerals and without specific values based on position—a system under which addition and subtraction remain formidable operations, while multiplication and division are almost impossible. Now that even Euclid's geometry was lacking in the western libraries, the Carolingian scholar could not be expected to be very proficient in advanced mathematics. On the theoretic side he had only such essays as those of Boëthius, Isidore, and Bede; on the practical side he was interested in nothing more abstruse than determining the date of Easter. Music had been included in the *quadrivium* through the Greek discovery of the mathematical ratios underlying the musical scale; but the notion of music as a liberal art was now little more than a vague tradition, and the actual technique of playing instruments or of singing was hardly a subject of academic instruction.

The development of handwriting

Accordingly, aside from fundamental training in grammar, the education offered by the Carolingian school was very superficial, consisting of little more than definitions and catchphrases. Compared with the contemporary learning of the Moslem world, that of the Latin west was puerile. Yet, if it had not been for the enthusiasm of Charlemagne and his helpers, our irreparable losses of ancient literature would have been immensely greater, for many a classic has come down to us through a single manuscript written in some Frankish monastery. To the obscure scholars of the eighth and ninth centuries our modern culture is also indebted for the system of letters in which this book is printed—a remarkable development of which only the first stage may be considered here. For all formal writing the Romans had originally employed the square letters known to us as capitals, but in the later centuries a more rounded hand gained popularity because it was easier to use. Meanwhile, as the breakdown of oriental commerce took papyrus out of the western market and compelled the use of parchment, the factor of economy became increasingly potent. To get more words on a page, the scribe had to use smaller letters and squeeze them closer together. Some, to preserve their distinctive shapes, were extended above the line, some below. The ultimate result was the form of writing called minuscule—little letters, with capitals inserted for emphasis—as distinguished from majuscule, which consisted only of large letters.

The precise way in which this evolution came about is a highly technical and somewhat controversial subject. Here it need only be remarked that by the eighth century there were several well-defined minuscule hands: the Irish, from which was derived the Anglo-Saxon; the so-called Visigothic, which had been devised in Spain; and the Beneventan, which was employed in southern Italy. Through the migrations of scholars and the interchange of manuscripts, all these hands became known in Gaul, where the Carolingian revival of learning produced a growing demand for handsomely and legibly written books. Through this demand was eventually developed the Carolingian minuscule, characterized by the rounded form of its letters and its general distinctness and simplicity (see Figure 4). Written in this beautiful hand and illuminated in color—the method of decoration perfected by the Irish monks—a manuscript became a treasure of art

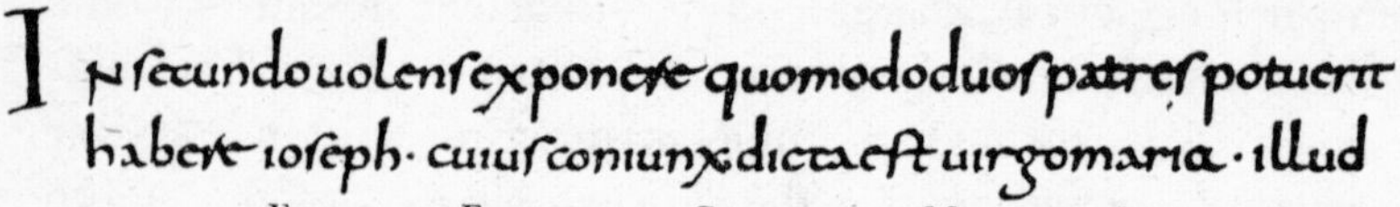

I p̄ secundo uolens exponere quomodo duos patres potuerit habere ioseph. cuius coniunx dicta est uirgo maria . illud

FIGURE 4.—EXAMPLE OF CAROLINGIAN MINUSCULE.*

as well as of erudition. It was no wonder that, indirectly, the books of the ninth century later became the models followed by the printers of Italy, from which our most popular type has been inherited.

Narrow scope of the Carolingian revival

Outside the narrow field of Latin education there was no Carolingian Renaissance. Vernacular literature as yet did not exist, except in the form of heroic tales chanted by wandering minstrels. Einhard tells us that Charlemagne had these "ancient barbarian poems" put into writing; none of them, unhappily, has survived, and we may only guess that they were somewhat like the sagas preserved from a later age. As far as the fine arts were concerned, we have only one Carolingian monument of any importance. Einhard says that Charlemagne constructed at Aix-la-Chapelle "an extremely beautiful basilica," adorned with gold, silver, and bronze. And since the materials could not be procured elsewhere, he had them brought from Rome and Ravenna. The emperor's church is still preserved as a chapel within the cathedral of Aix-la-Chapelle. It is, as Einhard implies, built in the Byzantine style; but it is not imposing, being only a domed octagon some forty-seven feet across. Was not this pathetic little imitation of Roman grandeur somewhat typical of Charlemagne's whole imperial structure?

4. THE RUIN OF THE CAROLINGIAN SYSTEM

Weakness of the Carolingian Empire

We have already seen that Charlemagne's state, though officially styled Roman Empire, was essentially the enlarged Frankish kingdom. So modern writers have aptly called it

* The Latin reads as follows: In secundo uolens exponere quomodo duos patres potuerit habere ioseph. cuius coniunx dicta est uirgo maria. illud . . .

the Carolingian Empire—an empire which, despite a vague Roman tradition blessed by the church, owed its real strength to the personal might of a semi-barbarian ruler. For the empire of Charlemagne had no truly imperial system of administration and lacked the economic resources on which one could be based. There was as little solidarity among the dominions of the emperor as there had been among those of his Merovingian predecessors, and the common bond of religion was devoid of political significance. How long would such a hasty agglomeration of disparate lands and peoples hold together when it passed to a prince who, being no military genius, could not enforce his authority by a continuous series of campaigns? Or could even a Charlemagne successfully defend so broad a territory if it were assailed on all fronts by formidable antagonists?

As a matter of fact, Louis, who fell heir to the entire empire in 814, was far from being another Charlemagne. Excellently educated and sincerely devoted to the ideals of the church, the new emperor deserved his nickname of "the Pious." In personal morality he was, moreover, a distinct improvement over his father. But he was neither a general nor a statesman, and before long the political situation had got completely out of hand. To aggravate the trouble caused by local insurrection and foreign invasion, a bitter conflict arose among the emperor's own sons, and it was still raging when he died in 840. By that time the rivals had been reduced to three. Lothair, the eldest, was king of Italy and emperor. Against him, to check his assertion of supreme authority, were arrayed Louis the German, king of the East Franks, and Charles the Bald, king of the West Franks—an alliance that produced the famous Strasbourg Oaths. A contemporary tells us how Louis first swore unfailing loyalty to Charles, using the *lingua romana* (i.e., Romance, French) so that his brother's retainers could understand him; and how Charles followed, using the *lingua teudesca* (i.e., *Deutsch*, German). Besides, he reports the forms that were then em-

Charlemagne's successors

ployed, and from them we gain valuable information concerning the two languages in the ninth century.

More important from the political point of view was the final settlement forced upon Lothair in 843. This was the Peace of Verdun, which extended the kingdom of Charles to an irregular line running along the Scheldt and the upper Moselle to the valley of the Rhone, and which brought the

MAP VIII.

kingdom of Louis to the Rhine, excluding Frisia on the north. Lothair was thus left with the kingdom of Italy, plus Provence, Burgundy, Alsace, the western Rhinelands and the Low Countries (see Map VIII). The fact that such a straggling territory, devoid of all cohesion, was thought a fit portion for the eldest son proves the absence of foresight in the treaty. And whatever solidarity was possessed by the other sections was purely accidental, for nationalism played no part in the politics of the ninth century. Nevertheless, the Peace of Verdun was to have permanent results. It marked the first stage in the dissolution of the Carolingian Empire.

While Lothair's middle strip was soon broken into half a dozen fragments, the kingdoms to the west and east maintained at least a superficial integrity, becoming known respectively as France and Germany. But before their later fortunes can be sketched, something must be seen of the peoples who were then threatening their frontiers.

Although Scandinavian freebooters had occasionally appeared in earlier times, it was not until the ninth century that their raids became a source of terror throughout the Christian northwest. The fundamental cause of the outpouring was undoubtedly overpopulation. Besides, the advancing authority of various local kings tended to drive adventurous spirits abroad, and the defenseless condition of the neighboring countries, quickly advertised by the success of preliminary expeditions, encouraged a growing stream of marauders. For the character and activities of these northerners we are dependent on the accounts of Christian chroniclers, supplemented by archæological evidence and the Icelandic sagas.[7] But the latter, being written at a much later time, give traditional stories in poetic form and must be used with great caution. What we actually know about the primitive Scandinavians in their old homeland is slight; the main facts can be very briefly stated.

In the first place, it should be remembered that Denmark, Norway, and Sweden are political units which hardly existed in Carolingian times. Although it may be convenient to speak of Danes, Norwegians, and Swedes as invading southern lands in the ninth century, those names should be understood as merely indicating the vague regions from which three groups of invaders came. Commonly they called themselves Vikings, meaning creekmen or men of the *fjords*. Being still heathen, they showed no mercy to Christian churches or clergymen. It was, indeed, the wealth of the monasteries and cathedrals that chiefly attracted them; for their primary object was loot. But they also took delight in sheer devastation. Often they put entire settlements to the torch and slaughtered the in-

The
Vikings

[7] See below, p. 239.

habitants with a cold fury that spread universal horror. In such respects they closely resembled the original Anglo-Saxons who had terrorized the shores of Roman Britain.

As far as institutions were concerned, the Vikings could contribute little that was new to the semi-barbarous society of the west; their customs were very much the same as had earlier been common to all the Germans. The *comitatus* described by Tacitus reappears in the wandering band of warriors led by the Scandinavian *jarl*. In the material arts of civilization, as in matters of education and morals, the Vikings were learners rather than teachers. Only in one respect they were manifestly superior to the peoples they despoiled: they were beyond doubt the greatest sailors of western Europe. In open boats, propelled by oars or small sails, they not only skirted the coasts of Europe from the Baltic to the Mediterranean but constantly made long voyages into the stormy Atlantic, where days had to be spent beyond the sight of land.

Viking raids and conquests

As the Scandinavian peoples spread across the seas, geographic position naturally dictated the directions they normally took. The Swedes, facing east, were attracted to the southern shore of the Baltic and thence through the interior by the river routes that led to the Black Sea. Along these routes slaves and furs had long been carried by Avars and other Asiatics to be sold to the Moslem traders of the Caucasus or the Christian traders of Constantinople. Now that the Avar power had been broken, the northerners encountered no serious opposition; lured by opportunities for brigandage, they eventually established themselves on the Dnieper and extended their raids to the ports of the Black Sea. So, by the end of the ninth century, they had gained the attention of Byzantine writers, who called them Russians (*Rhos*) or Varangians. From these beginnings, as will be seen in a following chapter, a great empire was to be developed in eastern Europe.

To the west, meanwhile, the Norwegians and Danes had been led to attack the British Isles and the Atlantic shores of the continent. Long before the close of the eighth century Viking raiders had begun to make annual visits to Ireland and Britain, and within the next hundred years both islands had been ravaged from end to end. Everywhere the great religious houses, ancient centers of Irish and Anglo-Saxon learning, were looted and burned. The kingdoms of Northumbria, East Anglia, and Mercia were practically wiped out. The cathedral cities of southern Britain were repeatedly taken; even London was sacked. On the continent it was the same story. Beginning with inroads in Frisia, the Northmen, as they were generally known to the Franks, gradually pushed their fleets along the coasts to Aquitaine and Spain. In 859 a great expedition actually rounded Gibraltar and plundered the Mediterranean shore as far east as Italy. Nor did the inland districts escape. Sailing up the larger rivers, the Vikings often captured a walled city or built a fortified camp; thence, by means of horses taken from the unfortunate inhabitants, they rode across country, spreading desolation far and wide. From such practices it was only a step to effect permanent conquests. Sometimes, as in eastern Ireland, the native population was subjected and forced to supply the conquerors with food; sometimes, as in what the Anglo-Saxons called the Danelaw and in what the Franks called Normandy, colonists were brought from the homeland to occupy the devastated regions. The political significance of these settlements will be considered below.

One important cause of the Viking successes on the continent was assuredly the lack of Carolingian defense by sea, and this same lack permitted a continuous scourge of Moslem raids along the Mediterranean shores. All danger of Moorish incursions across the Pyrenees, it is true, had been ended by the campaigns of Pepin and Charlemagne; but the independent emirs of Tunis soon launched an active maritime offensive and continued it throughout the ninth century. While Sicily was being systematically conquered, other Moslem forces ravaged Sardinia and Corsica, terrorized the coasts of Provence and Italy, and even preyed on the commerce

Moslem raids and conquests

of the Adriatic. About the time that the sons of Louis the Pious were swearing the Peace of Verdun, the Moslems took Messina and made it a base for further operations on the mainland. In 846 the great church of St. Peter outside the walls of Rome was looted and burned; and not long afterwards the monastery of Monte Cassino suffered the same fate. As late as the tenth century it was still problematical whether the Italian peninsula would remain a Christian possession.

The Hungarian invasion

To increase the misery of the Carolingian lands, another horde of Asiatic nomads now appeared on the eastern frontier. Because of their affinity to the ancient Huns these invaders came to be generally known as Hungarians, but they have always called themselves Magyars. Like their predecessors, they were apparently forced to migrate by some sort of disturbance in the homeland and they came by the same route, over the grasslands of the Pontic steppe. Crossing the Dniester in the closing years of the ninth century, they advanced into the plain between the Carpathians and the Danube. There the remnants of the Avars quickly became amalgamated with the newcomers, so that ever since then the territory has been known as Hungary. According to all contemporary descriptions, the invaders were of the primitive nomad type—savage horsemen, repulsive in appearance, rapacious and pitiless. While the Frankish lands of the west were still suffering from the inroads of the Vikings, those of the east were devastated by the Hungarians. Unchecked by the feeble defenses of the empire, they drove through Bavaria, Venetia, and Lombardy. In the following years they turned north, desolating Thuringia, Saxony, and the Rhine valley. Some of their bands even penetrated as far west as Burgundy.

Degradation of the empire

From the mere recital of these tragic events it should be evident that the glory of the Carolingian Empire did not long survive its founder. Conditions were bad under Louis the Pious; under his sons they became infinitely worse. Although the royal brothers indulged in fine talk about imperial unity and Christian co-operation, their acts continuously belied their words. While their subjects were being slaughtered by heathen marauders and Moslem pirates, they presented a most unedifying example of selfishness, cruelty, and bad faith. It was only during intervals between dynastic quarrels that their attention was given to the defense of the country, and then their efforts were singularly ineffective. Their reigns merely prepared for the general disintegration that followed. Lothair's middle kingdom was the first to disappear, for he divided it among his three sons (see Table I). None of them is worth mentioning except Lothair II, after whom his nondescript territory was called *Lotharii Regnum*, Lotharingia or Lorraine. By the last quarter of the ninth century all three of these sons were dead and their lands were being fought over by their relatives and by local usurpers. By that time, too, the Vikings were beginning to turn from mere plundering to systematic conquest. As the disorder increased, the empire was momentarily reunited under Charles the Fat, a son of Louis the German; but in the face of a new invasion he quickly proved his incompetence and so was dethroned in 887.

The deposition of Charles the Fat marked the end of Charlemagne's empire. Despite the titles held by later kings, it was thenceforth as dead as the empire of Constantine. Nor did the old dynasty long survive. In the eastern kingdom the throne was given to Arnulf, an illegitimate member of the house, because he had the reputation of being an energetic fighter, and he intervened in Italy long enough to be crowned emperor. He was succeeded, however, by a mere child, with whose death in 911 the line came to an end. In the western kingdom the events of 887 led the magnates to proclaim the valiant Odo, count of Paris; and his descendants, after a hundred years of rivalry with the later Carolingians, finally gained undisputed possession of the throne as the Capetian dynasty. While France and Germany thus became independent states under elected kings, the old middle kingdom utterly vanished. The northern end, Lorraine, for a while was obtained by the French king; then it was taken from him by the German. To the south lay the two petty kingdoms of Burgundy and Provence, and beyond the Alps the theoretical kingdom of the Lombards or Italy—the scene of a murderous

warfare that defies narration. The imperial title, disgraced
by the local princes who last held it, eventually went begging.

Since, according to the Carolingian ideal, church and state
were but two phases of one administration, it was inevitable
that both should be affected by the calamities of the ninth
century. Down to the time of Charles the Bald learning and
literature continued to flourish at the Frankish courts. Then,
as all central authority collapsed and the principal seats of
education were destroyed by barbarian or Moslem invaders,
the little that remained of Latin culture was threatened with
extinction. At the same time the papacy, after a short period
of brilliant leadership sank so low as to forfeit any claim
to the respect of Christendom. Nicholas I (858-67), the ablest
man to hold the see of St. Peter in many generations, asserted
his rights in three important respects: by compelling Lothair
II of Lorraine to take back a wife whom he had unlawfully
repudiated, by enforcing direct papal jurisdiction over the
Gallic bishops in the face of opposition from the powerful
archbishop of Reims, and by excommunicating the Byzantine emperor for arbitrarily deposing the patriarch of Constantinople. But Nicholas died prematurely, and his successors had the misfortune of becoming immersed in local politics and so of losing their spiritual headship of Europe. By
the tenth century the popes had actually been reduced to
the rank of ignoble puppets controlled by vicious Roman
nobles and their equally vicious women.

The age thus seemed to be one of complete ruin. Yet,
obscurely, forces of regeneration were at work. From the
welter of armed conflict, massacre, and desolation that marked
the close of the eighth century new political units were to
emerge—characterized by regard, not for tradition, but for
sheer necessity. These political units were small, the fragments into which the empire and its component kingdoms
had broken. As a rule, they lacked the appearance of sovereignty, being styled duchies, marquisates, or the like; but
they had the great merit of military efficiency. And among
them the strongest were what we recognize as feudal states—
a term that demands fuller discussion in a separate chapter.

CHAPTER V

FEUDAL SOCIETY AND THE REVIVAL OF URBAN LIFE

----

1. FEUDALISM AND THE FEUDAL ARISTOCRACY

To introduce the present discussion it should be remarked that only one peculiar combination of customs can properly be described as feudal—the one developed in the older parts of the Frankish kingdom and thence spread far and wide throughout mediæval Europe. Whether the customs of other peoples in other ages may be called feudal by analogy is a somewhat dubious matter which may here be passed over. We are concerned merely with the original feudalism. That term, of course, implies some kind of system built upon fiefs (*feuda*); but the latter, as already noted in the foregoing chapter, presupposed the personal relationship known as vassalage. There could always be vassals who, like the "companions" depicted by Tacitus, had not been endowed with fiefs; there could never be a fief without a vassal to hold it. The truth of this statement will become apparent as we more closely examine particular feudal institutions.

Vassalage and homage

Of prime importance was the Frankish ceremony of homage, which can certainly be traced back to early Carolingian times and was probably older. Through Christian influence it had come to be associated with an oath of fealty, sworn on the Gospels or on holy relics. Such an oath, however, was often prescribed for all subjects of a ruler and did not in itself create the bond of vassalage. To become a vassal a man had to perform homage. Coming before A, the prospective lord, B knelt, placed his two hands between those of A, and acknowledged himself A's man (French *homme*). A then raised B to his feet and kissed him, thereby accepting his homage and recognizing him as vassal. Thenceforth the pair were supposed to be bound by a permanent tie of mutual loyalty and support—a relationship portrayed by the feudal epics as to the highest degree sacred and honorable.[1] In real life, unfortunately, the relationship was not so ideal. Lords and vassals often quarreled over their respective rights, exchanged defiances, and engaged in bitter warfare. As will be seen from the study of actual cases, the effectiveness of vassalage depended on a number of variable factors, notably the character and political ambitions of the persons concerned.

Vassals and fiefs

In this connection it must always be remembered that vassalage and lordship are relative terms. Since all vassals might themselves be the lords of other men, neither term designated an exclusive group. To be a vassal was by no means disgraceful. On the contrary, vassalage was the equivalent of gentility; for by ancient tradition the vassal was a member of the warrior class. Besides, by the eleventh century, it had become exceptional for vassals to live in their lord's household; instead they had normally received lands on which to set up their own domestic establishments and in return for which they had agreed to give special services. As a fief-holder, the vassal possessed, not merely a certain acreage, but organized estates that included peasant cultivators free and unfree. And over the local population he exercised political as well as economic control, assessing a variety of public dues and charges, raising fortifications, and administering justice. In other words, the vassal belonged to the agrarian aristocracy, the governing class in the feudal state.

In many cases the privilege thus enjoyed by a feudal lord could be justified by a grant of immunity or other delegation of authority by the king. Frequently, however, the lord's title rested on nothing more than sheer usurpation; for the later Carolingian age was one in which men followed ——

> The good old rule, . . . the simple plan,
> That they should take who have the power
> And they should keep who can.

[1] See below, pp. 240-41.

By the end of the tenth century, as will be explained more fully in the next chapter, the French king had lost all effective control over his realm as a whole. His principal officials—usually styled dukes, marquises, or counts—had come to hold what amounted to hereditary sub-kingdoms. And often enough their authority was contested by a number of their own vassals, both ecclesiastic and lay. To make hard and fast generalizations about such arrangements is impossible; they were the result, not of systematic planning, but of circumstance. Each territory had its own custom, which must be individually studied to be understood.

Yet, despite all local variation, the common political character of fiefs gave rise to certain common principles. One was primogeniture. Land could be easily divided. An office could not be, and the fief was a sort of office even when it was not styled a dukedom, a marquisate, or the like. The furnishing of troops was itself a state service, the value of which depended on a personal responsibility. So feudal law, unlike Roman and Germanic law, came to require that a fief should pass in its entirety to the eldest son. This principle involves what is commonly known as the inheritance of fiefs, also an established custom by the end of the tenth century. What was actually inherited, however, was the right to obtain the fief on certain conditions. Vassalage was not hereditary. The son had no legal title to his father's fief until he had performed homage for it, and he was not permitted to do that until he had reached man's estate. A girl, since she was no warrior, could be neither a vassal nor a fief-holder. It was only in default of male heirs, and after she had been married to a proper vassal, that a daughter could legally inherit a fief. Meanwhile it remained in the lord's hands and technically ceased to be a fief at all. *Inheritance of fiefs*

Wherever fief-holding had not degenerated into a mere fiction, it was held to imply a contract between the two parties. Along with his fief the vassal received from his lord a guarantee of protection and justice; in return he owed the lord various forms of service and assistance. Very commonly *Feudal tenures* the fief bore a specific obligation for mounted soldiers, or knights[2]—in which case the vassal was said to hold by knight service. Occasionally he was bound to furnish arms or other objects of value, or to perform some duty at court; such tenures are usually classified as serjeanty. By a sort of legal fiction, a church might obtain a fief to be held by free alms —to owe no service except prayer for the donor's soul or the souls of his ancestors. But this tenure was not always enjoyed by ecclesiastics. Most bishops and abbots held at least part of their lands by knight service and—through a special compromise that exempted them from personal service—supplied their quotas by granting fiefs to vassals. In any case, the obligation resting on the fief was not supposed to be indefinite. Service, as a rule, could be demanded no more than once a year and, when troops were provided, only for a fixed term—in northern France forty days.

Suit to court Whatever the nature of his tenure, the vassal regularly owed suit to the lord's court: that is to say, he had to attend the lord whenever summoned. At irregular intervals great assemblies would be held for ceremonial purposes, and on these occasions the lord would submit to his men for their approval projects of general interest to his territory. Such times would also be appropriate for celebrating a son's knighthood or a daughter's marriage. Often, however, the court would be held for the sake of administering justice, in which connection the vassal, if not appearing as defendant or plaintiff, would be called as a judge. For the feudal court, though presided over by the lord, was legally the body of suitors themselves, who rendered decisions according to recognized custom. The vassal, therefore, claimed the right to judgment by his peers, his social equals. Even when he came to trial, he kept his gentleman's weapons, appealing for a decision by judicial combat. The two parties, after God had been solemnly invoked to defend the right, fought it out and the victor was held to be justified in his contention.

The vassal, furthermore, owed hospitality to his lord. This

2 See below, pp. 144-45.

was a very expensive obligation when the latter came with **Hospitality and aid** a large retinue and made a protracted stay; so the exaction of entertainment was frequently limited by written charter or commuted into a money payment. Besides, if the lord incurred some extraordinary expense, the vassal was usually liable for a contribution called aid. The occasions varied from region to region; in northern France an aid was commonly due when the lord knighted a son, celebrated the wedding of a daughter, or was captured and held to ransom. In case the lord was a clergyman, the installation of a successor or the necessity of a trip to Rome provided a good excuse for seeking pecuniary assistance. The general rule always held good, however, that the vassal was not subject to arbitrary taxation; if subsidies were wanted for purposes other than those recognized by custom, or if service was needed in addition to what was definitely owed, the lord had to ask his men for a voluntary grant.

More profitable than the aids were those perquisites of the **Feudal incidents** lord that we know as the feudal incidents. Relief was a sum, often defined as the first year's income from the fief, that was paid by an heir on securing possession of a fief. Wardship was exercised by a lord over an heir who was under age, and it included the right to the income from the fief during such minority. Marriage, in the technical sense, was the lord's power of approving the husband chosen by the heiress to a fief—a privilege that commonly led to the selection of the highest bidder in a sort of private auction. Escheat was the return of a fief to the lord's possession when a vassal died without heirs. Forfeiture was the penalty for felony— the confiscation of the fief should a vassal refuse to perform his owed service. But the penalty was easier to declare than to enforce. A rebellious vassal could always justify his action by alleging default on the part of the lord, and the issue would be left for determination by force of arms. Finally, it should be noted that, since none of the ordinary incidents could be expected from ecclesiastical fiefs, the lord by way of compensation generally took over the lands of a dead prelate and treated them as his own until a successor was installed.

The services and incidental revenues just enumerated were received by any feudal lord from lands granted as fiefs to vassals. What remained in his own possession was called his demesne (less technically, domain), and from it he received the manorial income that will be described in the following section. Each vassal could in turn give fiefs to vassals of his own and so provide for part of the service required by the lord. But, to support himself and his family, he would have to keep at least some of his lands in demesne. The profit in fief-holding, we may say, arose only from the surplus of demesne income over and above the cost of the owed service. From these facts it should be apparent that a particular village could be included within any number of fiefs, being held of one another by any number of vassals. Eventually, however, it would be directly managed as demesne of some landlord. Below the feudal hierarchy and supporting it by their labor were always the peasants.

The gulf between the two classes was hard to cross. A man of low birth, though not actually unfree, could rarely become a fief-holder. Through the service of a prince—by acting as administrative agents of some sort—even serfs occasionally gained wealth and power; yet in the eyes of the gentry they never lost their base blood, and it was long before the origin of their families could be forgotten. And to keep the peasant youth from the military class, there was not merely the handicap of social prejudice but also the professional training required by the code of chivalry. This term (derived from the French *chevalier*, horseman) refers to the set of customs that were generally held to regulate knighthood. During the early feudal age the boy of noble birth, unless destined for a clerical career, was not expected to have an education in letters. Since his profession was to be that of a warrior, his training was essentially military. While still a child, he began his lessons in riding and in the use of weapons. His graduation from this rude school was the attainment of knightly rank, but first he had to pass through two preliminary grades. Commonly he would serve in some feudal court as page (French *valet*), learning how to conduct himself in polite society and continuing his martial exercises. Later, in his early teens, the youth would rise to be a knight's assistant or squire (French *écuyer*, shield-bearer). Eventually he would be allowed to ride to battle with his elders and, after proving his fitness, would be knighted—usually by the lord at whose court he had been brought up, though the honor could be conferred by any knight. In the final ceremony of *adoubement*, when the candidate was formally invested with the arms and armor of a mature man, we may clearly see the perpetuation of an ancient custom described by Tacitus.[3]

Primitive chivalry was therefore non-Christian, and originally it had no feminine implications. It was simply the standard of conduct adopted by members of the warrior class to govern their relations with one another. The knight should be brave to the point of foolhardiness. He should fight according to certain accepted rules, scorning tricks and strategy as savoring of cowardice. He should be loyal to his friends. He should keep his plighted word. He should treat a conquered foe with gallantry. Yet, although the gentleman was chivalrous towards social equals and their womenfolk, he felt no such obligation towards the baseborn. In this respect, as in all, his attitude was intensely aristocratic. The fact that in contemporary records *miles* (Latin for soldier) always means the mounted fighter summarizes a whole chapter in the history of warfare. And the virtual equivalence of knight, noble, and vassal well illustrates the social constitution of the early feudal age.

For the study of chivalrous ideals our best sources are the French epics, which also give us precious information concerning feudal warfare. But the most vivid picture of the eleventh-century knight is to be found in the famous Bayeux Tapestry, an embroidery made as a decoration for the nave

The Bayeux Tapestry

[3] See above, p. 38.

of the cathedral in that city and still preserved in the local museum (see Plate I). It is a strip of linen twenty inches wide and over 230 feet long, with scenes worked in colored worsted to describe the Norman Conquest of England. Although the story thus told is interesting as a partisan tradition, the great historical value of the tapestry lies in its realistic presentation of contemporary life. Probably completed before 1100, this unique work allows us to be positive with regard to many odd details of military activity, of domestic habits, and above all of costume.

Civil and military costume

Laymen of every class commonly wore tunic and hose: a loose-fitting jacket belted at the waist and a sort of tights pulled on over the legs. For warmth or ceremony a man might also throw over his shoulders a mantle, fastened on the right side to leave the sword-arm free. Women were dressed in robes of almost classic simplicity extending from the chin to the ground. For outdoor wear both sexes had cloaks fitted with hoods for use in bad weather. Defensive armor in the early period was not elaborate. The knight's lower legs remained unprotected except for strips of cloth or leather wound like modern puttees from the knees to the shoe-tops. Over the upper body he wore a hauberk, a shirt of link mail slashed at the bottom. His head was covered with a helmet, a conical steel cap with a narrow extension in front to serve as a nose-guard, and with mail attached to the rear to hang down over the nape of the neck. On the left arm he bore a kite-shaped shield some four feet long, generally decorated with a fanciful design, though regular coats of arms hardly came into use before the twelfth century. For offense the knight's weapons were principally a cross-hilted sword, slung on a belt at the left side, and a lance about eight feet long that was held couched in the right hand.

Feudal warfare

These facts help us to understand the character of feudal warfare. The obligation for knight service was heavy: one knight would include not merely the warrior himself but also a supply of expensive arms and armor, a change of horses, perhaps a squire and his mount, a number of grooms and other servants, and finally enough food to maintain all these men and animals for the specified period. Through feudal tenure the ruler of a mediæval state obtained a whole army with a minimum outlay of cash, but even among the knights who led the attack discipline was slight. Each gentleman considered himself the ally rather than the subordinate of the commander. Fighting for the lord did not at all prevent a vassal's fighting for himself; except through acquisition of booty and captives, he stood to make nothing from the campaign. Pitched battles were infrequent; when one occured, it resolved itself into a series of individual affrays—of charges and countercharges with lances atilt, followed by hand-to-hand combat with sword and axe. There would be a magnificent display of knightly prowess—and little generalship. Although one side might gain much in honor and plunder and prisoners, the opposing force would largely escape, to fight again on some more fortunate day.

Feudal warfare, as a matter of fact, was normally restricted to skirmishing between roving bands and to devastating the enemy's territory. During most of the time the efforts of the combatants would be concentrated in and about castles. In the ninth century the castle, or *burg*, had been primarily a center of refuge from the invading Northmen; now, at least in France, it had become a specialized form of stronghold adapted to the needs of a feudal chieftain and his garrison of professional warriors. This form, after its two essential parts, is called the motte-and-bailey castle (see Figure 5). The bailey was a courtyard surrounded by a moat, an earthen embankment, and a palisade of tree trunks—or a series of such fortifications. Friends gained admittance by means of a gate and a drawbridge that could be let down for their special benefit. Enclosing houses, stables, and other necessary buildings, the bailey constituted the outer defense of the castle. The motte was its more inaccessible portion—a hill or artificial mound protected by a separate line of entrenchments. Here stood the donjon, a wooden tower with its own

The feudal castle

drawbridge giving access to what we should call its second story. Such a crude fortress, in an age that had forgotten Roman siegecraft, could offer stout resistance to attack, but —as illustrated on the Bayeux Tapestry—it was especially vulnerable to fire. In the twelfth century, therefore, castles generally came to be reconstructed in massive stonework.

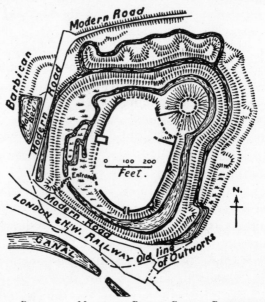

FIGURE 5.—PLAN OF A MOTTE-AND-BAILEY CASTLE: BERKHAMPSTEAD.*

Feudal amusements

The feudal noble, carrying his warlike prejudice into the realm of sport, was passionately fond of tournaments. The contests familiarized by romantic fiction were essentially pageants, involving a maximum of display and a minimum of bloodshed. In the primitive age, however, the tournament was a real fight, differing from a battle in the field only in that the former was deliberately arranged in advance.. One was as deadly as the other, and in both the victor claimed as spoil the horses and accouterments of the vanquished. Next to fighting, the noble loved hunting—riding down

* Taken from E. S. Armitage, *Early Norman Castles of the British Isles,* Fig. 9 (John Murray: London, 1912).

stags and other large game with dogs. So every prince maintained wide preserves in which he and his retainers enjoyed a monopoly of the chase. A more gentle pastime, in which the ladies frequently joined, was hawking—the taking of herons, pigeons, waterfowl, rabbits, and other small game by means of trained falcons. When condemned to remain indoors, the feudal baron, like his barbarian ancestors, spent most of his time in gambling, drinking, and feasting. Dice had been taken over from the Romans, and from them too had probably been learned a form of backgammon known as tables. Chess was introduced in western Europe after the crusade of 1095.

Throughout the grape-raising provinces of the Roman Empire wine remained the standard drink, but in the more purely Germanic regions of the northwest its place, except in wealthy homes, was taken by beer. The quantities consumed by the average person were such as to stagger the imagination of the modern tippler; and temperance was equally unknown in eating. The nobleman's favorite meat was game—often a deer or a boar roasted whole—accompanied by smaller dishes of fowl, pasties, vegetables, and fruit. On fast days, when the meats disappeared, the platters were filled with fish and eggs. Bread and cheese were of course staples. Sweets, on the contrary, were rare because the sole available sweetening was honey, and spices were found only on the tables of the great. As far as cooking was concerned, we are led to believe that quantity, rather than quality, was the main consideration. And what we know as table manners were hardly known; the appetite of the hunter and the fighter raged unchecked by an etiquette of delicacy.

Food and drink

Princes commonly had castles as their chief residences; yet all classes of nobles spent much time in manor houses on favorite estates. In any case, the center of domestic life was the great hall, which according to modern standards was picturesque rather than comfortable. Heat was supplied by open fires, the smoke from which found its way out past the grimy rafters overhead. As windows were generally unglazed,

The baronial hall

the weather had to be kept out by means of shutters. The walls were hung with arms, banners, and trophies of the chase. The floor often was merely hard-trodden earth covered with straw or rushes, where the ever-present dogs made themselves at home. Light was furnished by candles. Here the lord sat in state to receive homage or to confer with his vassals in formal court. Here was spread the festive board, with the company seated on benches in order of rank. Here of an evening took place whatever literary entertainment the age afforded—tales of heroic deeds chanted by wandering minstrels. And here finally, after the lord and his family had retired to their chambers, would be laid the pallets of retainers and guests who could not be accommodated elsewhere.

The position of women

The feudal gentleman did not have to be a very competent administrator. Customary arrangements made the superintendence of landed property largely a matter of routine. The care of the house and servants was chiefly left to feminine management. Occasionally we hear of some extraordinary lady who, on the death of her husband, continued his work by playing a dominant rôle in politics and warfare. Normally, however, the feudal age accepted the maxim that woman's place is the home. Although we have every reason to believe that love was important in society even before it became a fashionable theme in literature, marriage within the aristocracy was regularly dictated by dynastic and financial interest. The first obligation of the wife was to bring the inheritance of a fief, or at any rate a handsome marriage portion; the second was to bear at least one son. And if she were unfortunate enough to fail in the latter duty, a complaisant bishop was usually at hand to declare the wedding invalid. In this respect, as in others, early feudal Europe was a very masculine world.

2. THE MANORIAL SYSTEM AND THE PEASANTRY

The manor

The political significance of feudalism will be considered in the following chapter. Here we are concerned with its economic significance, or—to be more precise—with the economic conditions which it presupposed. For feudalism proper was not a stage in economic evolution; rather it was a peculiar form of political organization developed by the Carolingian kings. Since the basis of the state was then agrarian society, fiefs normally consisted of the rural properties that we call manors. Yet it is important to remember that, at the opening of the eleventh century, the manorial system was practically universal throughout western Europe, while feudalism was not. A manor remained exactly the same, whether or not it was held by a vassal in return for feudal service.

The manor (Latin *manerium*, a dwelling house) may be defined as an agricultural settlement controlled and exploited by a lord, and thus sharply distinguished from a free village where the inhabitants work primarily for their own benefit. Fundamentally, therefore, the manor was an estate like the villa of the later Roman Empire. But the authority of the mediæval lord, thanks to the lavish dispersal of royal privilege, had generally come to be political as well as economic. Through long usage, rights that we should classify as public and private were inextricably confused, and it made no difference to the men of that age whether particular institutions were five hundred or only two hundred years old. The manorial system flourished on all sides because under it, and under it alone, the mass of the people found the possibility of livelihood. The lord owed his dominant position not so much to his own rapacious greed as to the defenseless condition of the countryside and the vital needs of the inhabitants. The manorial organization was a simple administrative machine that ran on and on with a minimum of supervision; yet that minimum was essential and only a lord could provide it.

The chief purpose of this manorial organization was of course agriculture, concerning which absolute generalization can hardly be made. Customs varied according to the climate, the soil, and the aptitudes of the people. Statements applied to a fertile plain will not hold true for a mountainous re-

Agriculture

gion or a country of marsh and dune. No one method of
tillage could be successful in vineyards, orchards, and corn-
fields. What may be described as standard agricultural practice, however, was the one that prevailed throughout those
regions of Europe where feudal institutions were earliest
and most fully developed. There the staple crop was wheat
or rye, for the raising of which plowing is essential. And in
that operation certain common factors everywhere tended to
produce uniform results. The soil, on account of shallow
working, was very heavy; the plow, being only a light blade
fastened on a wooden frame, was light. Draft animals, because of poor breeding and undernourishment, were small
and weak. Merely to prepare a field for planting commonly
required a team of eight oxen—which, together with a plow,
the average peasant did not possess.

The open-
field system

The solution, obviously, was co-operative agriculture. Economic necessity, apart from the need of protection, forced
the country population to dwell in villages and pool their
resources. Within such a settlement each household contributed towards a common fund with either labor, materials, tools, or animals; and it logically followed that each
should have an equal portion of the harvest. If, however,
the member of the community had his land all in one place,
the returns would vary according to the fertility of the allotment. So the usual plan was to equalize the holdings by
forming them of strips scattered in all sections of the arable.
And since the strips were not individually fenced, the whole
arrangement is known as the open-field system. It will be
noted that the basis was co-operation, not communism.
While all plowing, harrowing, sowing, reaping, and the like
were done by the villagers working together, in the end
each received only what was raised on his own acres. Even
the so-called rights of common were units of property attached to the individual holdings. The peasant was entitled
to pasture a certain number of beasts on whatever fields
were not at the moment bearing crops and on whatever waste
land the manor included. He might also have a share of

meadow, which was carefully set aside as the only source of hay. And in the nearby woods he could gather a limited quantity of fallen timber and could turn loose his pigs to gather feed as best they might.

The open-field system should not be confused with the three-field system, which had an entirely different origin. Experience had long proved that land continuously devoted to the raising of wheat, rye, barley, or oats would quickly become exhausted. We know that the cause is the depletion of nitrogen, which must be replaced before another good harvest of grain can be secured. This is done today by applying a fertilizer or by planting a nitrogen-producing crop, such as peas, beans, clover, or alfalfa. In the feudal age nobody understood the scientific rotation of crops. Vegetables were grown only in separate plots and hay was obtained only from natural meadows. There were no manufactured nitrates to buy. Manure was scarce because domestic animals were few. So the only available method of preventing exhaustion was that of occasionally permitting the land to lie fallow. In the case of the two-field system the arable was divided into two portions, which would alternately be turned into pasture. The three-field system was more economical except in comparatively barren regions. Under it one-third of the land rested every year; of the remainder one-half was planted with a spring crop and the other half with an autumn crop. The fallow was only scantily refertilized through the plowing under of weeds and through incidental manuring by animals put out to graze; yet the process was sufficient to maintain the agricultural routine for an indefinite period.

The three-field system

Together with his arable and rights of common, each peasant also had his own house—the meanest sort of hut, commonly made of wattle plastered with mud and covered with a roof of straw thatch. Adjoining it was a small plot of land on which he could have a vegetable garden and keep a few geese or chickens. His clothes and belongings were of the poorest. His furniture would be little more than a rude table and a bench or two, his beds only bags of straw laid

The peasant's home

on the floor. His principal food was black bread, supplemented by dairy produce, eggs, and coarse vegetables. Occasionally he might enjoy a fowl; normally he could not afford meat. Game and fish he was forbidden to take. Sheep, cows, and oxen were too precious for slaughtering, except when the approach of winter and the lack of fodder made it imperative—and then the cost of salt led to insufficient curing. He had, however, a plentiful supply of home-brewed beer or, in favorable regions, of very ordinary wine.

The manor house and the inland   A traveler through the countryside in the feudal age would have no difficulty in perceiving the subjection of the agricultural village to seignorial control, for the settlement would be dominated by the manor house. In this age it was normally built of wood. Sometimes, especially when used by the lord as a dwelling, it was defended by a moat and a drawbridge. Often, however, the manor house served merely as administrative headquarters under the charge of a resident steward. Surrounding it, in any case, was the lord's close, containing gardens, fruit trees, beehives, barns, stables, and other outbuildings. Here was stored the produce from the estate, together with the usual wagons and agricultural implements. The lord generally had his own meadow; but his arable, as a rule, consisted of acre strips scattered among those of his tenants. And like them he would pasture his beasts on the common. All labor required to maintain the lord's particular property—known as the manorial demesne or inland—was left to be done by the peasants. They cultivated the lord's arable along with their own, harvested the crops, threshed out the grain, and disposed of it according to instructions. To see that all rightful obligations were performed, so that the estate would show the normal profit, was the responsibility of the steward, assisted by subordinates chosen from among the peasants. The steward also held the manorial court for the settlement of disputes, the trial of persons accused of petty offenses, and the general enforcement of the lord's authority. In all such matters law was held to be, not the will of the lord or of his steward, but the custom of the manor as stated by the best men of the locality.

The lord and his peasants

The fact that the entire feudal class was supported, directly or indirectly, by the peasants should not be taken to imply that in general the latter were cruelly treated. During wartime, of course, the people of the countryside were the first to suffer from the enemy's attack, and there were always barons who acted like brigands towards the defenseless tenants of others. But a lord would naturally be considerate of his own men, for without them his lands would be worthless. The peasant's life, however bad it may seem in comparison with modern conditions, was reasonably secure. Under the lord's protection he was assured at least of subsistence; even serfdom was infinitely better than the constant fear of death by violence or starvation. And many, perhaps most, peasants were not of servile status. Except in England after the Norman Conquest, serfdom and villeinage were by no means synonymous. The serf was by origin the Roman *servus*, the bodily property of a master. The villein (*villanus*), on the contrary, was simply the ordinary villager who, no matter what his obligations were, legally remained like the Roman *colonus* a freeman. Actually all lived under much the same régime. The serf could not be sold apart from the estate to which he belonged, and either law or economic necessity made the free peasant also a mere appurtenance to the soil he cultivated.

Peasant obligations

The obligations of a peasant community cannot, therefore, be rigorously classified according to the status of the persons liable. About all that can be affirmed is that the baser tenants were generally responsible for unrestricted service, whereas the freer tenants were not. But the only sure test of such arrangements was local custom, which was hardly the same in any two places. The variety of rents, for example, was endless. Although each peasant owed the lord definite payments, the time when they were due might be any season of the year, and the specified amounts might be anything produced on the manor. Virtually every peasant was also obliged to perform labor service, or *corvée*, for it was only through such labor that the lord's inland was taken care of. Here again, however, there was wide variation. Lowest in the scale were the men said to be *corveable a merci*, bound to do whatever was commanded at any time. The average villein owed rather a number of days each week, together with extra days for sowing and harvest, and a fortunate few might be free of all *corvées* except such work on special occasions. While ordinary *corvées* had to do with agriculture, others were more political in character. So the burden of repairing roads, bridges, and castles naturally fell on the peasants. It was they who cut the timber, dug the moats, hauled the supplies, and made themselves generally useful on military campaigns.

Cotters and artisans   How the peasant spent his time is accordingly no mystery; for it must be remembered that, when he was not toiling for the lord, he had his own household to support. In this enterprise he had the assistance of his wife, sons, and daughters, all of whom customarily labored in the fields. And since the service owed the lord consisted of certain units due from the peasant's land as a whole, it could be performed by any able-bodied man. We frequently hear of poor villeins who had no arable in the village, but only huts and gardens. These cotters, as they were often called, could always be obtained when extra help was needed, for it was only by doing odd jobs that they could pick up a living. Exceptional in another way were the skilled craftsmen who might be placed at specialized tasks instead of ordinary labor. One villein, for example, would maintain a smithy for the repair of iron tools and another would have charge of the local mill. And along with the smiths and the millers—whose name is yet legion—there might also be peasants who in some degree served as masons, carpenters, leather-workers, and the like. Such an artisan still lived primarily by cultivating his own lands, following his trade as a sort of *corvée* and paying his rent in articles of manufacture. Even the parish priest held a share of the arable, while devoting most of his time to the saving of souls.

Whether legally free or unfree, the peasant and his family constituted a valuable asset within the estate. If a son entered the church, he was lost to the manor; so it was everywhere the rule that such a step could not be taken until the lord's permission had been obtained, and that might not be gratuitous. For the same reason a daughter could not be wedded outside the manor without the payment to the lord of a sum known in French as *formariage*, in English as merchet. On the peasant's death his land passed as a matter of course to his children, but the lord generally claimed the chattels or the best beast as a token payment styled heriot or *mainmorte*. Occasionally we also find villeins contributing a yearly head tax (*chevage*) in recognition of their personal subordination. And the whole rural community was usually liable for tallage or *taille*—a more or less informal contribution that was taken sometimes annually, sometimes only when there was special need. In this way, if in no other, the villein could be prevented from accumulating undue wealth. Special payments

Within the manor the lord also enjoyed certain customary monopolies. Game and fish could be taken only by his permission, and poaching was severely punished. The villein was allowed to gather fallen branches in the woods either for fuel or for minor building purposes, but the lord's license was required for the cutting of green timber. Sometimes the lord had his own mint, and he normally held control of local trade. This was exercised by issuing regulations known as bans, the proceeds from which were called *banalités*. He thus established official weights and measures and enforced their use in the market, levying customary tolls on articles displayed for sale. Commonly he had the only lawful winepress, mill, and bake-oven. And for the service that the peasant was forced to accept he had to contribute a percentage of his wine, flour, or bread. In this same category may be included the lord's income from the manorial court —the fees collected from parties to suits and the fines as- The lord's monopolies sessed for violations of law. Justice in the feudal age was highly regarded as a source of profit, and all too often, especially when enforced over other people's tenants, was the pretext for sheer extortion.

Manorial and feudal income

The items enumerated in this section, when combined, will be seen to constitute the manorial income that the baron received from his demesne. His feudal income was what he obtained from infeudated estates; but that, as may easily be seen, was ultimately derived from some vassal's manorial income. Eventually every obligation of a superior, whether layman or ecclesiastic, was passed down the scale to the peasant at the bottom. To appreciate this truth is to understand the economic structure of feudal society, and accordingly to perceive how the development of new economic resources, by changing the fundamentals of human existence, would tend to revolutionize both church and state. A great revival of trade and industry could hardly fail to have momentous results for the future of Europe.

3. THE REVIVAL OF COMMERCE AND THE GROWTH OF TOWNS

Evidences of economic recovery

Of the many centuries that had elapsed since the disruption of the Roman Empire, the eleventh was the first to witness positive signs of economic recovery in western Europe. There was then, for one thing, a noteworthy increase of population. Armies of younger sons made possible the great feudal expeditions into Britain, Spain, Sicily, and Palestine that will be described in the next chapter. At the same time we hear of a greatly enhanced commercial activity, of new trading settlements along highways and water routes, of projects to expand the cultivated area by draining swamps and clearing forests, and of the rural colonization that accompanied such projects. In the later Roman period a vicious cycle of impoverishment and depopulation had brought ruin to whole provinces of the empire. Now the reverse process brought renewed prosperity. The cause was assuredly no increase in human fecundity. It was not that the men of the eleventh century had more offspring, but that more of their offspring were permitted to survive and have offspring of their own. More jobs made it possible for more people to live, and the needs of these people led in turn to the appearance of still more jobs.

As usual when economic phenomena are concerned, it is hard to say precisely what was cause and what was result. We may, however, be reasonably certain of a few relationships: that the increase of agricultural production was necessitated by the growth of new trading centers, where the population was dependent on imported food; and that, of course, these centers arose to meet the demands of reviving commerce. We may also find significance in the fact that the tenth century was a period of political stabilization—marked by the emergence of new and efficient states, the absorption of the Vikings and Hungarians into the European system, and the organization of French society on a feudal basis. But the problem of how and why the Dark Age was succeeded by the marvelous Age of the Crusades is too complex to be taken up in an introductory chapter. The interaction of economic, political, and cultural developments must be left for later discussion, our present attention given to preliminary questions regarding trade routes, mercantile colonization, and the rise of the class known as bourgeois.

In the first place, it should be remembered that we are dealing primarily with the Latin world—the countries dominated by the Roman Church, which were mainly Italy, France, the British Isles, Germany, Scandinavia, and the lands of the North Slavs. To the east lay the Greek world, consisting of the Byzantine Empire together with the Slavic states under its cultural influence: principally Serbia, Bulgaria, and Russia. To the south was the great Moslem world, which at its height included Spain, most of the Mediterranean islands, Roman Africa, Egypt, Syria, and other vast territories in Asia. The Moslems were thus able, when they chose, to prevent all direct contact between Christian Europe and the far east, to force all trade between those regions to pass through their hands. And their control of Spain and

The Latin world and its neighbors

Morocco broke the Latin world into two reaches of seacoast joined only by overland communications: a southern area on the Mediterranean and a northern area extending from the Bay of Biscay to the Baltic.

Trade routes: The Mediterranean

The center of the southern area was of course Italy, from which in the days of Roman prosperity lines of traffic had crossed the sea in all directions. But for many centuries regular trade had ceased to flow along most of the ancient routes —interrupted, as it was, by the piracy of barbarian peoples, by the political separation of east and west, and finally by the Moslem conquests. In this respect Charlemagne's pseudo-empire, being essentially a creation of the mainland, had brought no improvement; and its collapse in the ninth century, together with the continued decline of the Byzantine power, had encouraged a fresh series of Moslem offensives. Under such conditions Italian shipping had all but disappeared. The one notable exception was provided by Venice, the new commercial city that arose on Byzantine soil at the head of the Adriatic. Then, in the first half of the eleventh century, a holy war against the Moslem on the sea was launched by the Genoese and Pisans, who were thereby able to gain rich trading advantages in Corsica, Sardinia, Sicily, and Africa. And with the crusade the Italian merchants found themselves in position to reopen direct communications with Syria, carrying eastward the armies of pilgrims with their horses and necessary supplies, and bringing westward cargoes of oriental products.

Roads and rivers

This revival of the old sea routes linking Europe, Asia, and Africa inevitably brought new life to the land and river routes that ran north from Italy. The great Roman highways, which had originally been built to join the capital with the provinces, included two coast roads: one from Genoa to Marseilles and Spain, the other from Aquileia to Trieste and Dalmatia. Between them extended fanwise two sets of roads across the Alps: those crossing by the western passes to the valley of the Rhone and those crossing by the eastern passes to the upper valley of the Rhine and Danube.

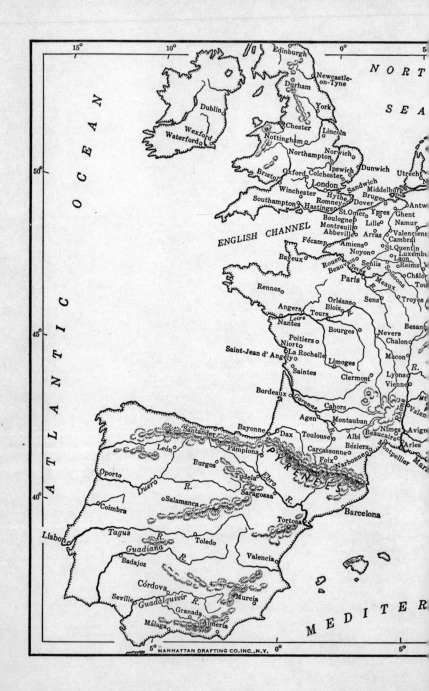

TOWNS OF
WESTERN EUROPE
IN THE
THIRTEENTH CENTURY

Scale of Miles

0   50   100   150   200

Thence other paved highways paralleled the military frontiers and led through Gaul to the ports of the Atlantic and the North Sea. But, whenever possible, the mediæval merchant preferred to travel by water, restricting his overland carrying to short journeys between rivers. So the Garonne, Loire, Seine, Somme, Scheldt, Meuse, and Rhine provided important routes to the west and northwest; the Ems, Weser, Saale, and Elbe to the north (see Map IX).

In ancient times the waters of the Atlantic had been slightly used for commerce. The only northern sea route that the Romans had found indispensable was the one crossing the Channel to Britain. But by the eleventh century enormous changes had been made in the political map of Europe. Beyond the Rhine what had been a wilderness inhabited by savage tribes had now been brought within the pale of Christendom, as had much of the Slavic borderland, northern Britain, Ireland, and parts of Scandinavia. In the ninth century the Vikings had appeared on the continent as pillagers and destroyers; during the next two hundred years they had been absorbed into older states or had founded new and vigorous states of their own, while their fleets had been diverted from piracy to peaceful trade. Thus the waterways of the Viking freebooters now served as commercial links connecting the lands bordering on the Baltic and the North Sea. And through the mediation of the Russians, who controlled the so-called Varangian route from the Dnieper to the Gulf of Finland, the northern region was brought into economic contact with the Black Sea and the Caspian, and so with the Arab and Byzantine Empires.

In the history of the world the commercial prominence of Italy was no new phenomenon. The unprecedented development was rather that which now took place in the northwest. A glance at the map will show how Flanders served as the focal point for the great routes of the eleventh century. Goods brought by land and water through central France, down the Rhine, westward from the Baltic, or eastward from the British Isles, all easily converged on the

The northern seas

The commercial importance of Flanders

little marquisate founded in the ninth century by Baldwin Iron-Arm.[4] In Roman times that district had been largely uninhabited, being held merely as a military frontier. Now, on the contrary, it rapidly became a great center of population and wealth, a source of enormous power for its fortunate rulers, and on that account the object of wars and political intrigues that have continued down to our own day. Of secondary economic importance in the northwest region were Picardy, Normandy, the middle Rhine valley, the Île de France, and England. Central France remained backward, but the French Mediterranean coast, advantageously situated between Spain and Italy, tended to share the prosperity of the latter two countries.

Towns and trade

The connection between these developments and the revival of urban life in western Europe is obvious. On all sides towns and trade grew up together. No important trade route could exist apart from towns, and every great town arose on a trade route. This connection serves to explain many important facts. The outstanding features of urban life, which were to have profound influence on the culture of Latin Christendom, were very new in the Age of the Crusades. By the close of the twelfth century scores of communities in western Europe were enjoying extensive liberties, sometimes including rights of self-government. Two hundred years earlier such privileged communities had not existed. What amounted to a social revolution had been produced by economic advance during the intervening period. Some writers, it is true, have traced the municipal institutions of the Middle Ages back to Roman tradition or to the primitive customs of the Germans; but careful analysis of the problem indicates that they have been misled by treacherous words.

The transformation of old cities and _burgen_

We have already seen that the "cities" of the Carolingian Empire could have been little more than military and administrative centers. And the fortifications erected by kings and princes in the ninth and tenth centuries were hardly

[4] See below, p. 178.

towns in our sense of the word.[5] Whether situated in France, Germany, or England, and whether called *château, burg*, or *borough*, such a fortress had few if any urban features. Even when a walled area included an official market, the latter was by itself insufficient to support a mercantile population of any considerable size. Some trade, of course, persisted all through the Dark Age, but the professional merchant and the free artisan remained very exceptional. By the twelfth century the situation had been radically changed. Thenceforth, through the influence of revived commerce, cities tended to become truly urban centers. At the same time "borough" (*burg, bourg*) acquired the meaning of a privileged town, the citizen of which was known as a burgess, burgher, or bourgeois. That these words all came to denote a townsman, rather than the defender of a fort, resulted from the transformation of the place where he lived. Although most of the pertinent evidence is contained in charters and other documentary sources, much valuable information in this connection has of recent years been obtained through the study of local topography. By examining the traces of early fortifications and other archæological remains, we may often find out when and how a particular town developed.

The Roman city of Cologne, for example, was a walled rectangle of approximately 239 acres, in one corner of which only a small remnant of the ancient population continued to live throughout the period that followed the barbarian invasions. By the opening of the eleventh century, however, a new settlement of merchants had appeared on the bank of the Rhine outside the wall. Within another hundred years three additional suburbs had been fortified, and finally, in 1180, a new wall was erected to enclose an area of about three times that of the original city. Scores of other communities can be proved to have grown in much the same way. Along routes that had earlier been used by the Romans it was natural that the new settlements should be formed

Types of urban growth

[5] See below, pp. 177, 181.

in or about the old cities or camps of the Romans. In more recently organized states, where no such positions existed, the settlers were attracted to other centers, usually the castles of the local prince. Particularly fine examples of such development can be seen in the great towns of Flanders: Ghent, Bruges, Arras, Ypres, Saint-Omer, and others. What is still called the Vieux-Bourg (Old Burg) at Ghent was the primitive fortress of the count—a triangle of about twenty-five acres at the intersection of two rivers. But the town of Ghent grew from the New Burg or Port—a trading quarter that by the eleventh century had appeared across the river to the south. When surrounded by a wall in 1191, it had already come to include over two hundred acres, and this was only the beginning of a rapid expansion that, with occasional interruption, has continued down to the present.

Throughout France and Italy most mediæval towns will be found, like Cologne, to have developed on the sites of old Roman cities, and a similar origin can of course be attributed to a number of English towns: London, York, Lincoln, Canterbury, Exeter, Winchester, and others. Beyond the Rhine, however, most of the German towns developed, like Ghent, in conjunction with an earlier *burg*, as is often testified by their names (Magdeburg, Merseburg, Quedlinburg, etc.). And the early history of many English boroughs—e.g., Bristol, Nottingham, Oxford, and Norwich —also resembled that of the Flemish towns. Occasionally a fortified cathedral or abbey served as the nucleus of an extensive urban settlement—as at Durham, Bury St. Edmunds, Vézelai, and St. Gall. But without the advantage of a good commercial location, neither church nor castle nor Roman fortress could ever become more than it had been in the previous age. Towns grew up in mediæval Europe as naturally as they have grown up in modern America, through the operation of natural forces that no one could entirely foresee or control. Although kings and princes frequently tried to create towns by deliberate planning, it was only rarely that their experiments produced urban communities of the first rank. The majority of the new foundations (*villes neuves*) remained comparatively small.

At the bottom of the list was a host of settlements that were hardly more than agricultural communities—groups of peasants attracted to a particular region for the sake of bringing it under cultivation. Yet the least of these colonists, or *hôtes*, was distinctly superior to the ordinary villein, being free of all manorial obligations except fixed rents and a few stated services. Lorris, a little town situated in the vineyard country of the upper Loire, was evidently planned as a center for the local wine trade. Its liberties, guaranteed by a charter of the French king Louis VI,[6] were enormously popular, for they were later extended to upward of a hundred other semi-rural places. Among the greater commercial towns established through princely enterprise may be mentioned Freiburg-im-Breisgau, founded in 1120 by Conrad, duke of Zähringen, on the main road connecting the Rhine and the Danube; Newcastle-upon-Tyne, founded before 1135 by Henry I of England below the castle after which it was named; and Montauban, founded in 1144 by Alphonse, count of Toulouse, on the Tarn, a tributary of the Garonne. Other famous examples, especially in eastern Germany, will be cited in subsequent chapters.

Newly founded towns

By whatever process the result was attained, the typical town of the later Middle Ages appears to have been essentially a mercantile settlement—a colony of persons engaged in commerce and allied activities. Only a restricted number of the inhabitants would be merchants in our sense of the word. The mass of the townsmen would be rather artisans and laborers. Many, in fact, would still be employed in agriculture, for the increase of the population inevitably stimulated the production of food and raw materials in the immediate neighborhood. And since transportation by land depended largely on domestic animals, wide pastures remained a vital necessity. In spite of its rural features, however, the town was economically very distinct from the sim-

The town as a mercantile settlement

[6] See below, p. 202.

ple village. The town had a continuous market, where an
increasing number of persons made a living through buying
and selling at a profit. There a man could earn enough for
himself and his family through his craft alone, and so be
come entirely independent of any manorial organization. In
the smaller towns, which served chiefly as distribution cen
ters for agricultural produce, a limited number of manu
facturers could exist merely by supplying the local residents
with articles of daily use—such as clothing, leather goods
tools, and food. Occasionally some community, becoming
famous for the excellence of its work, would export manu
factures to far distant lands and accordingly develop industry
on a much larger scale.

**Sea trade
and ships**

Pre-eminent among such communities came to be the cities
of Italy and Flanders, but originally their prosperity de
pended rather on their location with regard to the great
trade routes by sea and land. Business always flourished
where cargoes had to be unloaded for trans-shipment, and in
this respect seaports or places towards the mouths of rivers
tended to have the advantage. For example, we find among
the outstanding mediæval towns Venice, Pisa, Genoa, Mar
seilles, Bordeaux, Rouen, Ghent, Liège, Cologne, Bremen
Hamburg, London, York, and Bristol. And it should be
noted that important towns like Arras, Bruges, and Lübeck
which the modern maps show apart from navigable water
were situated on streams readily ascended by mediæval ships
Much trading continued to be carried on in long fast boats
propelled by oar. Such were the galleys of the Mediterranean
as well as the Viking ships of the north, and they were al
of very shallow draft. For bulky cargoes slow round-buil
sailing ships were preferable, but even these remained com
paratively small in northern waters. The largest were those
constructed by the Genoese and Venetians for use on the
crusades—with two or even three decks, and with raised "cas
tles" at bow and stern to accommodate noble passengers
By the thirteenth century such vessels were sometimes a

hundred feet in length, with a beam of nearly half that amount.

During the earlier period we have very scanty information concerning the life and habits of merchants on land. The roads, we know, were so bad that wagons were of little use and goods had to be carried on pack animals. Many regions, furthermore, were infested by robbers, and every feudal boundary was made the excuse for collection of tolls. Under these conditions merchants came to travel in bands, accompanied by escorts of armed men. And since journeys of this sort entailed careful planning and a considerable outlay of money, they naturally led to the organization of merchant unions called gilds or hanses. Such associations are first definitely heard of in the twelfth century, when princes came to guarantee their liberties in formal charters. By that time, however, many gilds were already old, holding valuable privileges in widely separated countries. At London, for instance, the Flemings, the men of Cologne, and the men of Rouen were enjoying special rights long before the Norman Conquest.

Another prominent feature of reviving commerce in twelfth-century Europe was the fair. The rural market, normally held once a week for the exchange of local products, played no part in the distribution of articles imported from abroad. The men who engaged in that business needed larger gatherings attended by merchants from all the neighboring towns. Religious festivals might provide occasions that could be turned to profitable advantage by merchants; but as a rule the fair owed its formal establishment to a territorial prince, who guaranteed special protection to all persons coming to a certain place at a certain time every year. Annual fairs, each lasting for several days, were eventually organized in series; so that the great traders arranged their trips in order to attend as many as possible. Thus they disposed of merchandise in large quantities, while small dealers obtained stocks for resale or for use in manufacture and the lord of

Gilds

Fairs

the fair got a handsome revenue from stallage, the fees charged for displaying goods in stalls.

Articles of trade
With regard to the articles distributed, nothing more than a brief indication can be attempted here. A large proportion of the finer manufactures still came from the Moslem countries of Spain, Africa, and Asia—especially silks, rugs, and other luxurious fabrics; damascened arms and armor; and artistic products in the precious metals, ivory, earthenware, and other materials. The demand for oriental spices, drugs, dyes, perfumes, and gems was constant, and was greatly stimulated by the crusades. Many of our common words, by their derivation from the Arabic or Persian, show that they originally denoted imports from the east: e.g., sugar, syrup, cotton, gauze, satin, damask (from Damascus), muslin (from Mosul), scarlet, azure, lilac, spinach, artichoke, orange, lemon, apricot, camphor, and saffron. By the twelfth century, however, the Moslem cities were coming to be rivaled by those of Italy. Venice, in particular, soon became famous for glass-making, metal-working, and other skilled crafts. By that time, too, the woolen cloth of Flanders was finding a ready market throughout Europe. Other regions of the north and west exported principally food and raw materials. There was a flourishing trade in salt, which was obtained either from mines or from marshes on the seacoast. Iron was in great demand. Stone and wood were scarce in some countries. French merchants carried wine to England and returned with wool and hides. The Germans from the Baltic brought oriental goods that had been transported across Russia, as well as furs, lumber, naval stores, and amber.

It was in connection with this sort of trade that the towns developed in the twelfth century. Even the greatest of them were still commercial rather than industrial—and they would not seem very great to us. In those days a city of twenty-five thousand was relatively huge. Yet even the ordinary town, of from five to ten thousand, was an island of privilege sharply contrasted with the surrounding country.

4. URBAN INSTITUTIONS IN THE TWELFTH CENTURY

Throughout most of mediæval Europe the elementary bourgeois liberties were very much the same; without regard to the peculiarities of individual charters, the minimum demands of townsmen in the twelfth century can be readily summarized. First of all the bourgeois enjoyed free status. No matter what his origin, the man who lived in a town unchallenged for a year and a day secured complete liberty. The town air, it was said, made him free. To be more exact, it was his residence on privileged soil that broke any ties of personal or manorial subjection to an outside lord. In legal theory the town was a sort of territorial immunity, created by a holder of political authority. It is, therefore, a mistake to explain the mediæval town as a servile community that gradually or suddenly became emancipated. And the principle thus enforced was merely the expression of a social fact: the mercantile pursuits of the inhabitants were incompatible with villeinage. Men would not come to a place as merchants or laborers unless they could have unhampered control of their bodies and of whatever they might acquire.

Bourgeois liberties: Free status

The personal freedom of the bourgeois tended to carry with it exemption from all the typically servile or manorial obligations. Rents usually were very small, being set at a nominal figure to attract settlers. Other services were defined in advance and were owed, as a rule, by the entire community, rather than by individuals. A member of the community thus held his land on extremely advantageous terms. He could freely sell or lease any part of it, and keep the proceeds. He could even dispose of it by will; for bourgeois land, unlike the acres of the villein or the fief of the noble, was not bound by inflexible rules of inheritance. This free tenure, peculiar to the bourgeois class, is known by various names in various countries, but is familiar in English law as burgage. That it, rather than any other mediæval tenure, anticipated what we know as ownership of real property is obvious.

Burgage tenure

Justice

Another almost universal feature of early municipal charters was the promise to the men of the town that they should not be tried outside it. The reason was that the bourgeois community enjoyed a peculiar law, and to secure its benefits the member had to be exempted from courts where justice was administered according to feudal or manorial custom. Townsmen naturally objected to procedure devised for knights or peasants; they demanded forms of action by which debts could be collected, contracts could be enforced, and property rights in land and chattels could be safeguarded. These advantages were obtained in the town court because there the judgment-finders were bourgeois. Although the presiding magistrates might be appointed by the ruler, the court itself was made up of prominent citizens who were familiar with the established custom of the locality. Each of the older communities had its own law, and a pre-existing system of this sort was usually proclaimed as the standard whenever a new town was founded. Thus Freiburg-im-Breisgau followed the law of Cologne, and a dozen other places later received that of Freiburg.

Mercantile privileges

The chief mercantile privilege of the bourgeois was his right to sell freely in the town market. Any one from the outside, even the citizen of a nearby town, was a foreigner against whom the municipal tolls served as a protective tariff. Frequently it was provided that certain articles could there be manufactured or sold only by members of the local community, that they had the first right to buy certain kinds of imports, or that all merchants coming within a certain region had to display their goods in the town. All these and many other regulations would have to be administered by men familiar with the details of business—in other words by such a group as decided the law. Often the leading townsmen were combined in a gild having charge of all buying and selling; in that case the men who controlled the court were likely also to be the governors of the gild. In any case the community had to have some sort of mercantile organi zation, and by easy transition this might develop into formal self-government.

What the townsman chiefly wanted, however, was not political authority but legal and economic freedom—the opportunity to make a living where and as he pleased, without being subject to the arbitrary control of a manorial lord. On his side, the prince who founded the town was swayed by equally practical motives. He had learned from experience that trading communities could not be managed like agrarian estates. He was willing to renounce all the rights objected to by bourgeois populations. He was willing even to rent lands at a nominal figure, abandoning to the men who took them the chance of profit on future sales. Yet his action was by no means altruistic. He hoped to make a fortune out of the revenue that would later accrue to him if the settlement flourished. The greater and more prosperous the town, the more he could expect by way of tolls, profits of justice, and other incidentals. Wealthy communities were always glad to pay well for new privileges or for the confirmation of old ones. And by politic negotiation handsome subsidies might be secured from townsmen who appreciated the worth of a benevolent patron.

The interests of the lord

Sharply distinguished from the great majority of towns, which enjoyed merely the elementary bourgeois liberties, were the few that had at least some measure of autonomy—the group generally known as communes. Such great towns first developed it Italy, and there, strangely enough, the city to assume leadership had been unknown to antiquity. While the older urban centers of the west were threatened with extinction, Venice took form and prospered. Until the time of Justinian the low-lying region of Venetia had been thinly populated. Thenceforth, however, its marshes came to afford refuge to thousands of immigrants fleeing from the disorders of the inland regions. To gain a living in such an environment, the newcomers naturally turned to the established industry of salt-making and to coastwise trade. Then, as the Lombards took Ravenna, the settlements along the Venetian

The communes: Venice

shore found their unbroken connection with Constantinople of enormous advantage in commerce. And their pre-eminence on the Adriatic was definitely assured when Charlemagne abandoned the duchy to the Byzantine emperor. Within the next hundred years an increasing population gathered at the Rialto, the lagoon that experience proved to be the most favorably situated—and the illustrious city of Venice, as poets have sung, was born of the sea.

Being built on islands and a shore cut by numerous streams, Venice from the outset used waterways for streets. On the west the city was isolated from the mainland by a great expanse of swamp that made it virtually immune from military attack; to seaward lines of sandbars constituted a naval barrier of even greater strength. Although in theory part of the Byzantine Empire, by the opening of the eleventh century the city was actually a republic, holding dominion over a considerable portion of the coast. The duke of Venetia had now become the doge of Venice—no longer an appointed official, but an elected magistrate who ruled by the advice and consent of the local aristocracy. In every respect Venice henceforth acted as a sovereign state; it coined money, signed treaties, and waged war. Venetian fleets assumed an active offensive against the Dalmatian pirates, the Moslems of Sicily, and various rival communities on the Adriatic. When, later in the eleventh century, the Venetians joined the Byzantine emperor against the Normans,[7] it was as allies rather than subjects and in return for the splendid privilege of free trade throughout the imperial lands, including the city of Constantinople itself.

Genoa and Pisa

Following the lead of Venice, though without the advantage of a Byzantine connection, Genoa and Pisa rose to great prosperity in the course of the eleventh century. While the sea belonged to the Moslems, these cities had remained obscure. Then, as the Moslem power weakened, they launched a Christian offensive in the western Mediterranean. By 1095 they had come to dominate the coast from Sicily to Barce-

[7] See below, pp. 182-83.

lona, together with the islands of Corsica and Sardinia, and they had extorted special privileges from the emirs of northern Africa. How their fleets made possible the success of the First Crusade will be seen in the following chapter. Their reward was the allotment of trading quarters in the towns of the Syrian coast and a series of valuable concessions from the rulers of the newly organized Latin states. Meanwhile Genoa and Pisa had tended, like Venice, to became autonomous republics. Before the end of the eleventh century both cities appear as communes, governed by groups of elected magistrates styled consuls.

During that same time, or within the next few years, extensive rights of self-government were secured by a host of other towns in northern Italy—such as Siena, Florence, Lucca, Milan, Pavia, Brescia, and Bologna. Each of these municipalities had, of course, its own history, influenced by peculiarities of local custom and the varying attitude of persons in authority. In general, however, the commune arose as a sworn association of citizens—both noble and plebeian —for the maintenance and extension of their liberties. Though occasionally it might be formed with the consent and support of the existing government, it was more frequently a revolutionary organization that achieved its ends by means of insurrection. When, as was generally the case in Lombardy, the city had been legally subordinated to the bishop, the outbreak was primarily directed against his power. But the commune might also be employed as an effective weapon against a lay prince. Whatever the preliminaries, the ultimate result was the establishment of a *de facto* republic based on a league of citizens sworn to advance their common interests by persuasion, boycott, or force of arms. In the absence of an efficient monarchy, northern Italy thus tended to become a mosaic of city-states; for each commune sought to assure its lines of communication by annexing a considerable district outside the walled area.

It should also be noted that, consciously or not, these city-states held to the classic tradition of an urban nobility. The

The Lombard and Tuscan communes

aristocratic families of Venetia identified themselves with the rising city of Venice. They lived in it, ruled it, and, through investment in ships and commercial enterprise, prospered with it. Similar customs prevailed among the Lombard and Tuscan communes, which always attracted a good proportion of the local gentry. There business and politics were generally controlled by a few great families who engaged in bitter feuds with one another and raised the fortress-like palaces that still dominate many an Italian street. In Spain and southern France, likewise, it was not unusual for the nobility to prefer urban residences or even to take part in municipal affairs. But in northern France and the adjacent regions the nobility was essentially an agrarian class. Living in the country, the feudal baron despised the town-dweller as an inferior, and his chivalrous prejudice may yet be detected in the implications of our word "bourgeois."

Northern communes: Flanders and Picardy

Italy was long to be characterized by the complete sovereignty of its city-states; elsewhere the extent of urban self-government depended on the sympathies and powers of local princes. By 1100, as already remarked, flourishing towns had grown up about various *burgen* in Flanders, especially at Ghent, Bruges, Arras, Ypres, and Saint-Omer. And since the counts generally favored the ambitions of the bourgeoisie, each of these towns obtained the right to elect its own *échevins*—magistrates who, under the superior authority of the count, had charge of the municipal administration. Each, furthermore, seems to have had a gild merchant, which included all local traders and so held monopolistic control of local business. Unlike the communes of Flanders, those of Picardy usually rose to power through violence. The latter region was sprinkled with old Roman cities that earlier had been little more than fortified centers of government under the resident bishops. By the opening of the twelfth century, however, most of these cities had attracted a considerable population of merchants and artisans, who commonly occupied separate quarters beyond the walls. And as the bishops, or other lords, refused to make any sort of concessions, their bourgeois rose in revolt and formed sworn associations much like those of Lombardy. Beginning at Cambrai, the revolutionary movement spread to Saint-Quentin, Laon, Beauvais, and other places. Sometimes the rising failed and sometimes it succeeded. But eventually—and often through the intervention of the French king—most of the Picard cities became self-governing under boards of elected magistrates styled *jurés*.

In Normandy we have clear evidence that the merchants of Rouen were organized as a powerful gild even before the duke's conquest of England. From Henry I the city apparently received at least some political rights, but it is only at a later time that we definitely learn of a communal administration headed by a group of elected *jurés*. In his island kingdom Henry also gave a remarkable charter to London —the first known grant of formal self-government to an English town. In this respect, as in all others, the rest of the boroughs lagged far behind the metropolis. Until the closing years of the twelfth century most of them enjoyed only the elementary bourgeois liberties of free status, burgage tenure, the right to organize a gild merchant, and the like. Special mention, however, should be made of the Cinque Ports. As the name implies, there were originally five (Hastings, Sandwich, Dover, Romney, and Hythe); later the number was increased. According to a custom dating from the reign of Edward the Confessor (d. 1066), each of them was bound to furnish the king a certain number of ships for fifteen days' service annually and in return enjoyed freedom from toll throughout England, together with other privileges. Under the Normans the Cinque Ports gained even more extensive liberties and eventually became self-governing. From this unique confederation, directed by the constable of Dover Castle, the king secured a regular navy for many centuries.

In twelfth-century Germany the most advanced town both economically and politically was Cologne, where, by way of exception, municipal development seems to have continued

Normandy and England

Germany

without serious opposition from the local bishop. Before
1100 the city had a flourishing gild merchant, and within
the next fifty years a communal organization under elected
magistrates took form. The other cities of the Rhine valley—
such as Mainz, Trier, Worms, Strasbourg, Frankfort, Constance, and Basel—became self-governing only in the following century. The same statement will apply to the leading
towns of the Danube, headed by Ratisbon, and of eastern
Germany, where the foremost urban center was Magdeburg.
As yet the only great town of Holland was Utrecht, and on
the Meuse Liège was hardly rivaled by Namur and Verdun.

**Central
and
southern
France**

The central regions of Lorraine, the Burgundies, Champagne, and Auvergne remained comparatively backward.
The towns on the upper Seine and Loire—even Paris and
Orleans—were of second rank as late as 1200. Brittany had
no towns of any considerable size. Along the Bay of Biscay,
however, La Rochelle, Bordeaux, and Bayonne were becoming important for sea trade, especially in wine. Throughout
Toulouse and Provence, meanwhile, the revival of commerce in the western Mediterranean naturally brought new
life to such Roman cities as Marseilles, Arles, Nîmes, Bé-
ziers, Montpellier, Narbonne, and Carcassonne. By the middle of the twelfth century at least a dozen of these towns
had peaceably obtained extensive liberties from their respective lords and, following the example of the Italian
communes, had installed magistrates called consuls. In Spain
most of the great cities were still held by the Moslems in
the twelfth century. Of those in Christian hands the only one
to attain prominence in European commerce was Barcelona.

The preceding pages have, of course, merely introduced
a very large and complex subject. Europe in the thirteenth
century was vastly different from what it had been in the
tenth—how different may be realized when we have had
occasion to examine the political and cultural changes of
the intervening age. And when that point is reached, something more may be said regarding urban development in
the later period and the revolutionary effect of such development upon the life of both peasantry and aristocracy.

CHAPTER VI

POLITICAL AND ECCLESIASTICAL RECONSTRUCTION

....

1. FEUDAL FRANCE AND FRENCH INFLUENCE

By the opening of the tenth century not only Charlemagne's empire but also the three kingdoms of his grandsons had practically disappeared, being resolved into such fragments as could be politically managed. In Germany the change was to some extent legalized when, on the death of the last Carolingian in 911, the magnates raised one of their own number to the vacant throne. If Conrad of Franconia, the new king, had ever thought of governing the entire kingdom, he soon abandoned the idea and recognized as his actual equals the three great dukes of Saxony, Suabia (earlier Alamania), and Bavaria (see Map X). He could, indeed, do nothing else; for the kingdom was paralyzed by the Hungarian raids and in most cases the duke had risen to power through a revolutionary movement inspired by local patriotism. Nor was the situation greatly modified under Henry the Fowler (919-36), whose activities as king merely continued what he had begun as duke of Saxony. It was to defend the valleys of the Elbe and Weser that he constructed his famous *burgen*—fortified camps to serve as centers of military and civil administration. And it was on the Unstrut, a tributary of the Elbe, that he won his great victory over the Hungarians in 933. Even the conquest of Lorraine, which had earlier been seized by the French king, was accomplished with little or no co-operation from the other dukes, whom Henry left to enjoy virtually sovereign powers in their own territories. How Otto, Henry's illustrious son, was led to reverse this policy, and how the reversal affected the destinies of his country, will be seen in the following section.

In France, meanwhile, the disintegration had been car-

**France:
Origin
of the
Capetian
dynasty**

ried even further. Charles the Bald, with a view to checking
the ravages of the Vikings, had established three great
marches in the northern part of his kingdom: Burgundy—
which should not be confused with the kingdom of Burgundy, or Arles—under one of the local counts; Flanders
under an adventurer called Baldwin Iron-Arm; and Neustria, the region between the Seine and Loire valleys, under
a similar adventurer, Robert the Strong. And Robert's son,
Odo, count of Paris, was chosen king by the western magnates when Charles the Fat was deposed in 887.[1] Odo's title,
however, was bitterly contested by the descendants of Charles
the Bald; and it was only after a hundred years of rivalry,
and the extinction of the direct Carolingian line, that the
Parisian house secured undisputed claim to the throne. Hugh
Capet, great-grandson of Robert the Strong (see Table II),
was elected in 987 and thenceforth the ruling dynasty came
to be named for him, Capetian.

**Feudal
states of
the north**

By that time northern France had been divided into the
feudal states that were to dominate its history for over two
centuries. The duchy of Burgundy was held by a branch of
the royal family; but these Capetian dukes, obtaining neither
riches nor power from their backward country, remained
comparatively obscure. Flanders, on the contrary, grew into
a strong principality, as the descendants of Baldwin Iron-
Arm acquired additional fiefs on both sides of the French
frontier, and as the revival of commerce brought increasing
wealth and population to the new Flemish towns. Brittany
had no such good fortune. Though generally styled one of
the French duchies, it was a wild region which had scarcely
formed part of the Frankish kingdom and which continued
to be the scene of barbarous warfare over the ducal title.
Adjoining Brittany on the Channel lay the territory conquered and largely resettled by the Vikings in the previous
century—since 911 formally recognized as a fief held of the
French crown by the duke of the Northmen or Normans.
Since then Normandy had become an integral part of feudal

[1] See above, p. 137.

EUROPE
AT THE TIME OF
THE FIRST CRUSADE

Kingdom of France
Capetian Domain
Kingdom of Germany
Kingdom of Arles
Kingdom of Italy

The Holy Roman Empire included these three kingdoms

Scale of Miles

0   100   200   300   400   500

France. The inhabitants, converted to Christianity, had quickly adapted themselves to their environment and made its customs and language their own. It was essentially as Frenchmen that the Normans were to lead a series of great expeditions in the eleventh century.

What was known after 987 as the royal domain was by origin the march of Neustria, but of the splendid principality held by Hugh Capet's ancestors little was left when he finally obtained the crown (see Map X). To the west the Norman duchy shut him off from the sea by including the lower Seine valley, together with the city of Rouen. And to north and south he was now hemmed in by the lands of powerful vassals who had taken advantage of the previous rivalry to make themselves all but independent. Thus the count of Troyes, by accumulating a mass of little fiefs, had built up the great county of Champagne, while on the western side of the king's territory two ambitious viscounts had created the rival counties of Blois and Anjou. The latter, in particular, was a solidly organized state, and its rulers gained a reputation for political shrewdness as well as for warlike ferocity. Hugh Capet, therefore, had only the Ile de France—a narrow strip extending north to Laon and south to Orleans, with its center at Paris. The kingdom of Charles the Bald was no more than a tradition, for below the Loire the king had even less authority than he had above it.

The south of France, indeed, was a country entirely foreign to the north—one having its own language, Provençal, and enjoying its own customs, which in many respects were Roman rather than Germanic. The great barons of the north regularly attended the royal court, performed their homage, and provided whatever slight service they owed in addition. But the princes of the south recognized the Capetian solely by dating their acts according to the year of his reign. Foremost among these southern states was the duchy of Aquitaine, which from the tenth century on was held by the counts of Poitiers. Earlier a Carolingian subkingdom, it reached from the Loire to the Garonne and

The Capetian domain

Feudal states of the south

from the Bay of Biscay to the Rhone, and because of its very size was not always thoroughly controlled by the duke. Between the Garonne and the Pyrenees the Gascons were governed by their own duke until, in the later eleventh century, Gascony was absorbed into Aquitaine. Finally, on the Mediterranean, lay the two important principalities held by the counts of Toulouse and Barcelona, respectively the old Septimania and the old Spanish March.

Political significance of feudalism

Many historians have repeated the assertion that feudalism was virtually the equivalent of political disintegration, being incompatible with an efficient central government. The statement is misleading. It is true that the feudal age coincided with the decay of the Carolingian Empire and of the greater kingdoms that took its place; but the cause of the decay was not feudalism. The feudal relationships worked very effectively in many small states of the tenth and eleventh centuries—the only political units which then had any real existence in the Latin west. The rulers of those states found the system of feudal tenures the best means of governing their territories, for in that way alone they could provide for their administrative, judicial, and military needs. That the French king could not enforce his rights was due to his own weakness, not to a paralyzing effect of feudalism. The great lack of the first four Capetians—Hugh Capet, his son, grandson, and great-grandson—was a well-integrated principality, and this lack was first supplied by Louis VI, whose reign will be discussed below. The model states of the eleventh century were rather Flanders, Normandy, and, after the Norman Conquest, England.

The kingdom of England

The Anglo-Saxon territories, as remarked above, were still devoid of all political unity at the time of the Viking attack. Consequently the Danes, as all the invaders were known in Britain, easily conquered most of the little kingdoms north of the Thames. But Wessex, thanks to the valiant defense of King Alfred (871-901), was preserved intact and ultimately enlarged by the annexation of all lands below the Thames and of about one-half of Mercia. Under Alfred's successors this greater Wessex was rapidly extended by the occupation of the Danelaw (see Map VIII), to become what has thenceforth been known as the kingdom of England. To the west the peninsula of Wales lay outside English control, as did northern Britain, where various tribes of Picts and Scots had united to form the state called Scotland. England, with an effective administration centered in royal boroughs,[2] remained peaceful until the close of the tenth century. Then the weak rule of Æthelred brought a renewal of foreign invasion and, in 1016, the conquest of his whole kingdom by Canute (Knut) of Denmark.

This conquest was not like those of the Scandinavian pirates in the ninth century. The Danes, Swedes, and Norwegians had now been generally Christianized, and were already organized into the three kingdoms that have since remained traditional. Of these Denmark was the furthest advanced; its king, Canute, was an able and enlightened man whose dominions eventually included Norway, part of Sweden, and the Viking settlements on the southern shore of the Baltic. If England had continued to be a Scandinavian dependency, its history would have been vastly different. But Canute's incipient empire fell apart after his death, and in 1042 the English crown was given to Edward the Confessor, son of Æthelred by his queen, Emma of Normandy. Edward, therefore, was half Norman in blood, and since the troubled days of his infancy he had lived in Normandy. Returning to his native land, he brought with him a considerable group of Norman companions, and for a time they dominated English politics. Later it was Godwin, a Saxon nobleman, who gained the ascendancy; his daughter Edith was married to Edward and, when the latter died in 1066, her brother Harold was proclaimed king. Thereupon the Norman cause was revived by Duke William who, declaring that Harold had sworn to support his claim to the English throne, at once prepared an expedition to cross the Channel.

The final episode in this complicated story was the battle

The Danish Conquest (1016)

---

[2] Cf. the *burgen* of Flanders and Saxony, above, pp. 164, 177.

of Hastings (14 October 1066), where William's knights broke the shield-wall of the English infantry and where Harold himself was numbered among the slain. Assuming the royal crown, William crushed all local resistance and proceeded to organize his conquered kingdom as he thought best. Since inheriting the duchy of Normandy as a mere boy in 1035, he had made it one of the best-governed principalities in Europe. To England he now extended the feudal system with which he was familiar, proclaiming the rule that every bit of English soil was by ultimate title his—either held in his own hands or held of him as part of some fief. Although the change introduced a new French aristocracy, which was long to dominate all phases of English life, it hardly affected the mass of the people, which was already a dependent peasantry. And with the ancient manorial arrangements the Conqueror preserved much of the local government—the shires and the hundreds, their courts, their customary law, and their fiscal organization. But all this was now subordinated to a central government that was essentially feudal. The king's own court was henceforth a feudal court; his army was a feudal army, supplied through feudal tenures; the sheriffs, the old royal officials in charge of the shires, became Norman viscounts, ruling the countryside from recently constructed feudal castles.

While the Norman duke was thus engaged in an enterprise that was to affect the entire future of England, some of his humbler subjects were drawn into equally significant adventures in other lands. The Hauteville family, in particular, had an amazing career. There were twelve brothers, sons of an obscure Norman gentleman named Tancred (see Table VI). Most of them, compelled to seek fortune away from home, were attracted to southern Italy, where the unceasing wars of Greeks, Lombards, and Moslems offered good opportunities for mercenary service. From such employment the Hauteville brothers gradually turned to the more profitable business of fighting for themselves. Organizing a volunteer army, they seized castles in the interior, developed brigand-

age on a large scale, and finally undertook the actual conquest
of the surrounding country. It was at this stage in the game
that the command passed to a younger Hauteville called
Robert Guiscard (the Sly), who by sheer native force and cleverness completed the reduction of the southern peninsula.
In 1059, for reasons to be explained below, he was accepted
by the pope as a vassal and formally recognized as duke of
Apulia and Calabria. Next his brother Roger was placed
in charge of a holy war against the Moslems of Sicily, with
the result that by the end of the century the whole island had
been taken—and the foundations thus laid for a second great
Norman kingdom.

Another theater of constant warfare was the Spanish peninsula, where the Ommiad caliphate of Cordova, after reaching
its height of splendor in the early tenth century, was now
broken into a number of independent emirates. This situation naturally provided the opportunity for a Christian offensive, which might have gained headway somewhat earlier
if the Christians, too, had not suffered from disunion. At the
eastern end of the Pyrenees the old march of Charlemagne
had become the autonomous county of Barcelona. To the
west the Basque mountaineers, fighting with equal zeal
against all invaders, had successfully defended themselves
against both Frank and Moslem and thus made possible the
emergence of two little kingdoms, Aragon and Navarre. In
the mountains of Asturias, meanwhile, other Christians had
similarly maintained their independence, and so formed the
nucleus of a Galician state that grew into the kingdom of
León, extending south to the Douro River. And a frontier
region on the east, named for the castles built to defend it,
became the kingdom of Castile. In the eleventh century León
and Castile, which for a while were united under one king,
both extended rapidly (see Map X). Navarre, after reaching
the Ebro, found the way blocked by Aragon, which in turn
was barred by the emirate of Saragossa. Finally a great Christian victory at Barbastro in 1065 opened the way for the annexation of the lower Ebro valley in the next century.

*The
Spanish
kingdoms
and the
French
in Spain*

These conquests could hardly have been made by the little Spanish kingdoms had they been dependent solely on their own resources. From the beginning of their offensive, however, they had drawn an endless supply of recruits from the French principalities to the north. In the eleventh century the illustrious monastery of Cluny,[3] and later the papacy, gave active support to the holy cause of fighting the Moslem, issuing widespread appeals for enlistment and holding forth the promise of great spiritual benefits to any who should die on so sacred an undertaking. As would be expected, a host of volunteers came from the nearby lands of Gascony, Toulouse, and Aquitaine; but men of the northern baronies also crossed the Pyrenees in large numbers. And many of these adventurers won fine Spanish fiefs at the expense of the infidel. Eventually the royal house of Portugal was to trace its descent from a Burgundian knight who secured a border county along with the hand of a León princess.

To the men of eleventh-century France the crusade of 1095 came merely as the most glorious in a series of French enterprises.

2. THE REVIVAL OF THE EMPIRE AND OF THE PAPACY

Otto the Great (936-73)

Up to a certain point the kingdoms of France and Germany developed along parallel lines. In each all real power tended to fall into the hands of local princes; in each the Carolingian dynasty was supplanted by kings elected from among those princes; and in each a princely house finally obtained a semi-hereditary claim to the throne. If the descendants of Henry the Fowler had continued his policy, they would have remained, like the early Capetians, actual rulers of a principality with the kingship held as a sort of honorary title. But Henry's son, who came to be known as Otto the Great, was not satisfied with such a rôle. Leaving Saxony to be administered by subordinates, he turned to the enforcement of his authority throughout Germany as a whole. The inevitable result was a far-reaching insurrection. The dukes of Lor-

[3] See below, pp. 188-89.

raine, Franconia, Suabia, and Bavaria, though willing to accept Otto's election and even to act as household officials at his coronation, would brook no interference with their local affairs. And in this attitude they were supported by many of the higher clergy. Fortunately for the king, the risings did not all occur at once; he was able to crush them in detail and, reasserting the Carolingian tradition, to appoint new dukes, generally members of his own family.

The plan was a complete failure, for even a royal son or son-in-law found it easier to champion local sentiment than to oppose it, and a fresh insurrectionary movement awaited only a favorable opportunity. It was provided by the king's ambitious projects abroad. Before 952 Otto had gained three noteworthy successes outside Germany. He had defeated the Czechs of Bohemia, now organized as a Christian state, and compelled their king to accept his overlordship. He had forced similar recognition from the youthful king of Arles and so extended his sovereignty westward to the Rhone. Finally, to complete his title to the old middle kingdom of Lothair, he had crossed the Alps, married the widow of one Italian king, and exacted the submission of another. From this adventure he was recalled by a German rebellion, combined with a renewed Hungarian offensive. Despite the apparent odds, Otto was able to reassert his mastery. Having crushed the rebels, he won a crowning triumph over the Hungarians on the Lech in 955—a decisive victory, for it ended the last great Magyar invasion of Germany.

By 961 all was again quiet; with the frontiers secure and the duchies temporarily in loyal hands, Otto was free to resume his Italian enterprise. On the invitation of Pope John XII, one of the notorious profligates who disgraced the Roman see at this unhappy time, Otto crossed the Alps with a formidable army, occupied Lombardy, and assumed the Italian crown. In the next year he was crowned emperor by the pope—and what historians know as the Holy Roman Empire had come into existence. Then, as the pope came to repent his hasty action, Otto took Rome by storm, had John

The Holy Roman Empire

deposed, and procured the election of his own secretary. Momentarily he even thought to conquer the rest of the peninsula, but abandoned the project in favor of a treaty with the Byzantine emperor. Thereby he secured the hand of a Greek princess for his eldest son, together with the promise of the southern Italian duchies as her marriage portion. The remaining years of his life the king devoted primarily to ecclesiastical reform and, thanks to his control of the papacy, he eventually obtained the erection of a new archbishopric at Magdeburg, with jurisdiction over the Slavic marches to the east. Dying in 973, he left a magnificent heritage to his son, Otto II, who had already been crowned emperor as well as king.

The successors of Otto the Great

To understand the policy of Otto the Great is to understand that of his successors for over two hundred years. Thenceforth, generation after generation, the kings of Germany were to try to rival Charlemagne, but few of them were to equal the success of Otto. Glorious as it was, his example proved the bane of German politics. Under its talented ruling house Saxony might have been made the nucleus of a powerful state with infinite possibilities of expansion to the east— or perhaps to the north, for as yet there were no Scandinavian kingdoms of any strength. Otto, however, chose to abandon Saxony and to attempt the government of Germany through personal control of the dukes, while he pursued imperial ambitions in Burgundy and Italy. For the sake of a pseudo-Roman grandeur, too many of the men who followed Otto on the throne forgot to be German. Striving for an empire, they failed to secure even a duchy.

With these remarks to serve as an introduction, the next century of German history can be passed over in briefest outline. Otto II ruled for only ten years (973-83). He put down several revolts, fought the Bohemians, and died in the midst of a futile campaign to enforce his claim to the southern duchies of Italy. His son Otto III (983-1002) lived only to be twenty-two. Brought up under the tutelage of his Greek mother, he spent all his time in Italy, where, surrounded by officials with Byzantine titles, he indulged in imperial play-acting while his kingdoms relapsed into anarchy. His one noteworthy act was the installation of Gerbert, his illustrious teacher, as Pope Silvester II.[4] Since Otto III died without direct heirs, the magnates proclaimed Henry II, a grandson of Otto I's brother (see Table IV). Although his reign was not spectacular, he somewhat restored the credit of the monarchy by devoting most of his time to the defense of Germany, which was now threatened by a new Slavic attack under the command of the Polish king. The latter, finally, was forced to submit and like the Bohemian king to recognize German overlordship.

With the death of Henry II in 1024 the house of Saxony, by descent on the male side, came to an end; but the German electors, remaining loyal to the dynastic principle, chose a Franconian noble named Conrad, the great-grandson of Otto I's daughter. So the new line of kings, known as the Salian or Franconian house, was merely the old under another name. There was no innovation either in theory or in practice. Conrad put down several revolts, spent a year in Italy, secured the imperial crown, fought the Slavs, and reasserted German overlordship in Poland and Bohemia. The outstanding event of his reign was the acquisition of a third royal crown, when, *added* the last king of Arles died without heirs in 1032. Seven years *to Kingdom* later Conrad's dominions passed to his son Henry III who, happily, enjoyed a rather uneventful reign (1039-56). Aside from a minor war in Lorraine, his empire remained generally peaceful, and externally it had no dangerous enemies. German influence, already dominant in Poland and Bohemia, was now extended over Hungary, which had recently emerged as a Christian kingdom. Altogether, Henry III held a magnificent pre-eminence in Europe; the speciousness of his imperial glory was not to be proved until it was inherited by his less fortunate son.

Meanwhile a development of the greatest significance had begun to affect the relations of all Christian princes to the

The Franconian kings (1024-1125)

[4] See below, pp. 220-22.

**The feu-
dalization
of the
church**

church. Since the evil days of the later ninth century there had been no general reform of ecclesiastical institutions. Occasionally a wise ruler, like Alfred in England or Otto I in Germany, had been able to bring about a noteworthy improvement; but throughout the greater part of Europe conditions grew worse during the tenth century. In many religious houses, especially those under lay abbots, the ancient discipline was entirely forgotten. Bishops, when they were not actually vicious, were commonly submerged in secular affairs; and in these respects even the popes set a bad example. Besides, ecclesiastical properties and offices had in general been turned into fiefs, to be secured by the methods that were everywhere in vogue among laymen. On all sides bishoprics, abbacies, parishes, and other preferments were solicited from patrons by means of suitable presents. And the successful candidate naturally recouped himself from his subordinates. Bishops charged priests for ordination; the priests took fees from the people for the administration of the sacraments. The rule of celibacy for clergymen in the Roman Church above the grade of sub-deacon was everywhere relaxed. Priests and even bishops were frequently married, and so came to endow their children with estates that were supposed to maintain religious service. The church, like the Carolingian Empire, was threatened with dispersion among a host of feudal dynasties.

**The abbey
of Cluny**

The reform movement, when it finally gained headway, was thus directed against the subjection of the church to lay control, especially as the result of clerical marriage and simony,[5] the buying of ecclesiastical office. Under the existing circumstances it was natural that the leadership of the movement should be assumed by the monastery of Cluny, founded, with papal confirmation, by the duke of Aquitaine in 910. According to the terms of its establishment, that famous abbey was to be strictly governed under the rule of St. Benedict; the monks were to choose whom they pleased as abbot with-

[5] The sin of Simon Magus (*Acts*, viii, 18), who offered money for the gift of the Holy Spirit.

out the intervention of any person; and the abbot thus elected was to be independent of all ecclesiastical authorities except the pope. The original Benedictine system had all too often resulted in domination by some local magnate and in the decadence of religious life. Now, as the new community acquired wide renown for purity and zeal, many ancient monasteries became affiliated with it under priors named by the abbot of Cluny. The resulting group of houses, known as the Congregation of Cluny, eventually numbered over three hundred and exerted great influence throughout western Europe —principally by means of preaching and political agitation, for the Cluniac monks paid little or no attention to scholarship.

Worthy as it was, however, the cause of reform could have slight success without the backing of temporal authority, and most princes were reluctant to abandon established custom. The first noteworthy convert to the new religious movement was the emperor Henry III. On his accession in 1039 he immediately undertook to remove all taint of simony from his court and to enforce the rule that no son of a clergyman could hold any honor under the crown. But Henry III never dreamed of relinquishing his control of ecclesiastical affairs. Like Charlemagne, he regarded the church as a department of the royal government, and by his official acts he soon demonstrated that in this respect no distinction would be made between Germany and Italy. Crossing the Alps in 1046, Henry was confronted by the unusual spectacle of three rivals claiming to be pope at the same time. This scandal he summarily ended by having all three deposed in assemblies of the clergy. Then he procured the election of a German successor, and on the death of the latter he virtually appointed three other popes. Of them the second was Leo IX, whose pontificate marked the resumption by the papacy of spiritual leadership in Europe.

In the first place, Leo personally launched a vigorous campaign to root out simony and clerical marriage, holding councils for that purpose in Italy, France, and Germany. And

Henry III and ecclesiastical reform

Leo IX and the Greek schism

while he was thus engaged in traveling about the country, he actively sought to restore the papal influence over the great prelates and temporal princes of the west. Meanwhile the Norman conquests in southern Italy had given rise to fresh unpleasantness with the Byzantine government. At first Leo thought to advance his interests at Constantinople by joining forces with the emperor. But the Normans had no difficulty in defeating both the imperial and the papal armies. Then, while the pope's attitude was still in doubt, the head-strong Michael Cerularius, patriarch of Constantinople, precipitated a religious crisis. Reviving an ancient quarrel, he denounced all the peculiar usages of the Latins—such as saying that the Holy Spirit proceeded from the Father and the Son (*Filioque*), shaving the faces of priests, and eating eggs in Lent—and closed all churches in his capital where they were in force. Leo accordingly had no choice. Shortly before his death in 1054 he signed peace with the Normans and excommunicated[6] the patriarch. The latter. taking advantage of the vacancy at Rome, induced the weak emperor to reverse his policy and agree to the acts of a synod that formally condemned all followers of the Roman discipline. The schism between east and west, thus renewed in 1054, has remained unhealed down to the present and has had many evil consequences. The blame, no doubt, will always be differently assessed by persons of different faiths, but in any case little of it can justly fall on Leo IX.

Gregory VII and Henry IV

The pontificate of Leo is also important for the rise of a remarkable Italian with a German name, Hildebrand, who became archdeacon under Nicholas II (1058-61). As the pope's chief assistant, Hildebrand is generally credited with two significant measures which were then enacted. One was the formal alliance with the Normans in southern Italy, recognizing Guiscard's conquests as a papal fief, blessing his brother's expedition against the Moslems of Sicily, and assuring the pope of their armed support in case of a German attack upon Rome. The other was the famous electoral de-

[6] See above, p. 96 n.

cree of the same year, 1059, which vested the control of papal
elections in the cardinal clergy of Rome.[7] The new plan was
merely the adaptation of a custom that was already widespread—having a bishop elected by the cathedral chapter, the
clergy attached to the service of the bishop's church. But at
Rome the change was especially momentous in that the initiative in papal elections was given to the cardinal bishops,
while the emperor was left with no function beyond that of
confirming an accomplished act.

The election of Nicholas II in 1058 had gone uncontested
by the imperial court because Henry III had died two years
earlier, leaving an infant son to succeed as Henry IV. During
the minority Germany was administered by a regent—first
the queen mother and then the archbishop of Cologne, who
kidnaped the young king to secure control of the government.
Again in 1061 a Roman candidate was proclaimed as Pope
Alexander II, and under him Hildebrand continued to guide
the papal policy, deciding among other important matters to
bless the Norman duke's conquest of England as a means of
ousting a rebellious archbishop of Canterbury. Finally, in
1073, Hildebrand himself was raised to the papal throne with
the tumultuous acclaim of the Roman populace, and his accession as Gregory VII was promptly recognized by Henry
IV. The king, in fact, could do nothing else; for at that
moment he was fully occupied with a great revolt in Saxony.
By 1075, however, the rebels had been forced to submit, and
Henry at once changed his attitude towards the papal administration.

Gregory, meanwhile, had boldly suspended a number of
German prelates for opposing his decrees against clerical marriage and simony. Then, early in 1075, he struck at what he
considered another root of evil by prohibiting lay investiture: kings and princes might still be allowed to exercise
some influence in elections, but ecclesiastical office could be
actually conferred only by an ecclesiastic. To the announce-

[7] The cardinal bishops, priests, and deacons are by definition those who
are closest to the hinge (cardo) or axis of Christendom, i.e., Rome.

ment of this decree Henry made no reply and in other ways showed his antagonism to the papal program. Gregory, therefore, sent him a warning letter, threatening excommunication unless he at once proved his good faith. Henry, dazzled by his recent victory in Saxony, now threw aside all caution and announced to the world that he intended to re-establish his imperial control over the papacy. Summoning his bishops to a council at Worms in January, 1076, he easily inspired them to condemn Gregory as a usurper and declare him unfit to hold office. The pope, on receipt of an insulting letter to this effect, at once pronounced Henry excommunicate and, as a rebel against divine authority, deprived of his regal estate; his subjects, released from their oaths of fealty, were urged to elect another king in his place.

Canossa (1076)

Gregory's judgment was not merely a heroic gesture; he had clearly appraised the situation in Germany. Before the next winter the princes, welcoming the papal authorization of revolt, had declared their king deposed unless he could secure absolution within twelve months. But Henry, in spite of his occasional rashness, was intelligent and brave. He realized that, to avoid complete ruin, he had to come to terms with the pope. So, crossing the Alps in December, he made his way to Canossa, the Tuscan castle in which Gregory was then being entertained. There Henry appeared as a penitent, barefoot and clad in coarse wool. And there, after three days of humiliation, he was finally received by the pope and absolved of his sin—a famous episode that has rightly been regarded as a great moral victory for the church. Gregory, like Ambrose in the fourth century, had proved that, in so far as a king was a man, he was subject to ecclesiastical discipline; that the relations of church and state could be resolved into a question of right and wrong, over which the successor of St. Peter had supreme jurisdiction.

The triumph of Gregory's ideals

Otherwise the victory lay with Henry, who had now gained time to rebuild his fortunes. Although the rebels went ahead with their plans and set up a rival king, Henry was once more in complete control by 1080. Again he broke with Gregory and, leading an army into Italy, took Rome and installed an anti-pope who crowned him emperor (1084). In the next year Gregory died at Salerno, where he had taken refuge after his Norman allies had captured Rome and, with their usual recklessness, sacked it. At the end he is reported to have exclaimed: "I have loved righteousness and hated iniquity; therefore I die in exile!" Nevertheless, the cause for which he lived and died had suffered no lasting defeat. Henry's attempt to dominate Italy had served only to weaken his hold on Germany, where insurrection followed insurrection and his own son eventually turned against him. Long before his death in the midst of this wretched struggle, the papacy had regained complete independence. And the ideals of Gregory VII, maintained by his successors, carried the Roman see to a new height of renown in the glorious Age of the Crusades.

3. THE FIRST CRUSADE

Towards the close of the eleventh century a number of factors combined to produce the great movement known as the crusade. Three of these factors have already been examined: the growth in France of a feudal aristocracy that tended to swarm into the surrounding regions; a commercial revival that brought to old cities a new population eager for mercantile expansion; and the emergence of a reformed papacy that ardently laid claim to the moral leadership of Europe. Two factors in the east remain to be examined: the final weakening of the Byzantine Empire and the rise of a formidable Turkish power in Asia.

Factors producing the crusade

On many occasions the Byzantine state had shown remarkable ability to recover from apparent ruin—as under Heraclius and Leo III. Once more, under the Macedonian dynasty, a period of utter weakness was followed by one of surprising vigor. Despite the iniquitous means by which the members of the house secured the throne, they maintained a high standard of scholarship and artistic production, greatly advanced the cause of Christianity among the heathen Slavs,

The Byzantine Empire and the Slavs

and restored the glory of Roman arms on land and sea. Greek influence, already dominant among the Serbs and Bulgarians, was now extended to the Russians—the Vikings and their allies who by the middle of the tenth century had built up a considerable state with its capital at Kiev on the Dnieper. Down to about that time the princes of Kiev bore Scandinavian names, from then on Slavic. For example, it was Igor who led an attack on Constantinople between 941 and 945. His wife and successor was Olga, but their son was called Svyatoslav and his son was the famous Vladimir, whose dominions extended from the frontiers of Poland to the Black Sea. About 988 Vladimir accepted peace with the emperor Basil II, agreeing in return for commercial and other privileges to respect the imperial frontier and to accept Christianity for himself and his people. This promise he faithfully kept, and thereby the Russians were brought within the pale of civilized nations—a cultural triumph for the Byzantines that was to prove far greater than their military conquests.

Conquests of the Seljuk Turks

Politically, the empire was once again to suffer a bad relapse. The remaining members of the Macedonian house, principally two women, reigned until 1056; then the usual palace intrigues raised to the throne a series of very ordinary, if not incompetent, rulers. It was during this period that Venice became entirely independent, that the other Italian provinces were lost to the Normans, and that the patriarch of Constantinople forced an open breach with the papacy. Meanwhile the Byzantine possessions in Asia were coming to be threatened by a fresh Moslem offensive. In this the driving force was not the caliphate, which had long been helpless, but the Seljuk Turks, one of the many nomadic tribes that, adopting Mohammedanism, had entered the military service of Moslem princes in Khorasan. By 1038 Togrul Beg, grandson of Seljuk, had established himself as autonomous sultan of Nishapur, and in another seventeen years he had taken Bagdad, rescued the caliph from a local chieftain, and substituted his own control. Inheriting his father's office in 1063, Alp Arslan (Brave Lion) completed the subjection of Persia and Armenia. And when Romanus IV brought up the imperial army to defend the frontier, Alp Arslan annihilated it at Manzikert (1071).

The result of this one battle was not only the loss by the Byzantine Empire of all Asia Minor, except a few places on the coast, but also the destruction of its military power. Anatolia, which for hundreds of years had supplied the government with the best of its generals and civil servants, was now resettled by wild tribesmen from central Asia, and down to the present it has remained solidly Turkish. Alp Arslan, however, did not long survive his great victory. Dying in the next year, he was succeeded by Malik Shah (1072-92), under whom the Seljuk power reached its height. While Asia Minor was organized as the sultanate of Roum (i.e., Rome), a new Turkish offensive was launched against Syria, the conquest of which was completed by 1080. So it came about that the successors of Romanus at Constantinople, unable to recover what they had lost or perhaps to defend what they still possessed, appealed to the pope for the aid of western Christendom.

The appeal was well calculated to awaken interest at Rome. Already the papacy had formally blessed the Christian war in Spain, the Norman conquest of Sicily, and the various enterprises undertaken by the Genoese and Pisans against the emirs of Africa. Some of these expeditions had also been encouraged by a guarantee of extensive indulgence—the assurance to any one who participated that his previous obligations for penance would be largely remitted. Besides, under Hildebrand's energetic guidance, the papacy had definitely formulated a policy of active intervention in European politics to enforce the Petrine supremacy and to advance the cause of ecclesiastical leadership throughout the world. The predecessors of Gregory VII had, for instance, backed William the Conqueror against a schismatic king of England and Robert Guiscard against schismatic Greeks in Italy. Gregory himself was willing to take a much more ambitious step; in 1080 he decided to support a Norman expedition against the Byzantine Empire. So in the following year Guiscard, with the

The Byzantine appeal and the papal policy

able assistance of his son Bohemund, launched a drive which he hoped would carry him to Constantinople. After taking Corfu and Durazzo, however, Guiscard was compelled to recall his troops against Henry IV of Germany, and the continuance of his eastern campaign was brought to a sudden end by his death in 1085, two months after that of Gregory VII.

Urban II and the Council of Clermont (1095)   Within ten years conditions again favored an ambitious papal program. The aging Henry IV had abandoned all pretensions across the Alps, and a young and energetic man had been raised to the Roman see as Urban II. A noble of Champagne who had left the world for the monastery of Cluny, Urban had been selected by Gregory VII to be his trusted assistant. As pope, Urban proceeded to devote his splendid talents to enforcing the ideals of his departed master. While the Byzantine emperor, now Alexius Comnenus, thought merely to obtain a force of western mercenaries to fight a war for the recovery of his territory, Urban conceived of a magnificent Latin enterprise, organized and controlled not by any secular prince but by the papacy—a great Christian offensive that should absorb and surpass the lesser offensives already begun. So he crossed the Alps into France and in November, 1095, presided over a council at Clermont, to which the clergy and nobility streamed from all directions. And there Urban, a Frenchman speaking in the vernacular to a French audience, delivered his epoch-making appeal.

The Turks, he reminded his hearers, had but recently, after almost destroying the Byzantine Empire, seized the holy places in Palestine. What a noble work it would be to rescue the Lord's sepulcher from their foul hands! And who should assume this most sacred obligation if not the Franks—a people long distinguished for purity of faith, and a people famed beyond all others for prowess in arms? Here, crowded in by sea and mountain, they inhabited a country that hardly produced enough food to support them; there, on the contrary, lay the Promised Land of Israel, "flowing with milk and honey." Let them cease from their murderous wars and dissensions. Let them rather join in one blessed enterprise, to wrest from the infidel the lands defiled by his presence, knowing that God would grant them not merely a rich earthly reward but also imperishable glory in the kingdom of heaven. So Urban concluded, and the entire assemblage, we are told, shouted as with one voice, "*Dieu le veut*—God wills it!"

The cry thus raised was soon echoed throughout Europe, for the agitation was at once taken up by a host of official and unofficial preachers. On all sides hundreds of men vowed adhesion to the sacred cause and each of them, as prescribed by the pope, marked his new status by sewing on his garments a cross made of cloth. Thus the volunteer became known as a *croisé*, and his expedition as a *croisade*, or crusade. Every crusader, together with his family and all his possessions, was brought under the protection of the pope and, by a plenary indulgence, was assured of immediate entrance into paradise if he died in the course of the war. But it was one thing to enlist pilgrims for a crusade and quite another to bring an effective army into Syria. While crowds of ill-advised enthusiasts at once set out for the Holy Land, only to be slaughtered or turned back, the real crusaders gathered in bands under the princes of their respective countries and did not start until the autumn of 1096. And since as yet no one dreamed of going direct by sea, the plan was to make a general rendezvous at Constantinople, where the emperor promised to supply additional provisions and troops.

Enlistment of crusaders

The leaders of the host were all French, being actual barons of France or the relatives and associates of such persons. This, as Urban had clearly realized, was quite inevitable if his project was to succeed. All the famous military exploits of the previous years had been carried out by French armies, and little co-operation could be expected from Henry IV and his German followers. Thus, among the more eminent princes who took the cross were Hugh, count of Vermandois, brother of the worthless Philip I of France;[8] Robert, duke of Normandy, son of William the Conqueror; and

Leaders of the crusade

[8] See below, p. 202.

Robert's brother-in-law, Stephen, count of Blois. None of these three, however, was equal in ability to Robert, count of Flanders, the son of a renowned adventurer who had already made the pilgrimage to Jerusalem. And the neighboring house of Boulogne contributed no less than three important chiefs: Eustace, Godfrey, and Baldwin, of whom the second had been named by Henry IV to the undesirable duchy of Lower Lorraine.[9] An imposing contingent from the south of France was headed by Raymond, count of Toulouse, who enjoyed a great reputation on account of his piety, wealth, and experience in the Spanish wars. Nevertheless, the best general in the Christian host was unquestionably Bohemund, son of Robert Guiscard. Having seen action in Italy, Sicily, and Greece, he was familiar with the peoples of those countries and, to some extent, with their languages. Guiscard's duchies had been inherited by Bohemund's brother; so he had no great expectations at home and was naturally attracted by the crusade as a fresh opportunity for eastern conquest. With him went another Hauteville soldier of fortune, his nephew Tancred.

Eastward advance (1096)   By the end of 1096 the various crusading units, advancing down the Danube or across Macedonia, had finally made their way to Constantinople. There Alexius demanded that all the leaders should become his vassals for whatever lands they might capture; and eventually, in spite of much resistance, all agreed to some sort of oath. Accordingly, in the spring of 1097, the great host crossed the strait and laid siege to Nicæa. Mediæval chroniclers, who have been followed by various modern writers, exuberantly reckoned the crusaders by hundreds of thousands. Such numbers, if our estimate is restricted to knights, must be divided by ten. Although to our eyes an army of twenty to thirty thousand is not impressive, it was tremendous for the eleventh century. And against it the Turkish princes could bring no equivalent force, for all Moslem unity in Asia had again vanished after the death of Malik Shah. The Christians, therefore, had a good pros-

[9] See below, p. 209.

pect of success if only they could hold together; but it soon appeared that they were by no means united in their counsels. The mutual distrust of the Greeks and Latins was nearly equaled by that of the southern and northern French, and it was only for brief moments that the bitter rivalries of so many feudal chieftains could be submerged by religious enthusiasm.

In June, 1097, Nicæa fell and was immediately given to the emperor. Then, while the latter diverted his forces to conquer the Ægean coast, the crusaders struck bravely across the interior of Anatolia. Despite the unaccustomed heat and a grave shortage of food, they maintained their advance, routing the Turks at Dorylæum in July and by September crossing the Taurus Mountains into Cilicia. Here, on the very border of the Promised Land, the host began to disintegrate. While Tancred, nephew of Bohemund, entered Tarsus, Baldwin of Boulogne struck towards the upper Euphrates, where he eventually secured Edessa. The rest of the crusaders, vainly awaiting the support of Alexius, spent the winter before the walls of Antioch. It was not until an Italian fleet arrived in the spring of 1098 with supplies and siege engines that the city could be closely invested. On June 3, thanks to the generalship and diplomacy of Bohemund, it surrendered—five days before a large relief army was brought up by the emir of Mosul. But Bohemund again distinguished himself by leading a counter-attack that drove off the besieging Turks (June 28).

Capture of Antioch (1098)

This battle was decisive in many ways. In the first place, it produced an open breach between the Latins and the Greeks. Bohemund, defying the emperor who had abandoned the crusaders in their hour of need, obtained definite title to the principality of Antioch. Because of the Roman-Greek schism, the pope found no occasion for intervening on behalf of the discredited Alexius. And since the ships of Genoa and Pisa had now established direct contact with Syria, Constantinople no longer dominated communications with the west. The crusade thus became an independent Latin ven-

Capture of Jerusalem (1099)

ture, the course of which was left to be determined by the
generals in the field. The victory, furthermore, opened the
road to Jerusalem, on which the crusaders, after much wran-

MAP XI.

gling between the Norman and southern French factions,
ultimately advanced in 1099. The Italian fleet once more
brought needed supplies and reinforcements. In July 15, less
than six weeks after the enraptured crusaders had first sighted
the Holy City, its walls were stormed. Strangely enough, the
man who had launched the great enterprise survived but did

not live to celebrate its triumphant conclusion. Urban II died at Rome on July 29, just before the glad news arrived.

The immediate result of the crusade in the east was the organization of four Latin states in Syria: the county of Edessa, originally held by Baldwin of Boulogne; the principality of Antioch, which passed from Bohemund to Tancred; the county of Tripolis, finally created as a sop for Raymond of Toulouse; and the kingdom of Jerusalem, which carried with it a theoretical superiority over the other three (see Map XI). The first man to rule at Jerusalem was Godfrey of Lorraine, though merely with the title, Lord of the Holy Sepulcher. It was his brother Baldwin who, on moving from Edessa, assumed the royal crown on Christmas, 1100. Shortly afterwards, to provide recruits for the holy war and to facilitate Christian enterprises in Palestine, the Knights Templars were organized under the supreme command of a Grand Master and with branches throughout the Latin world. The Knights of St. John, or Hospitallers, who had already appeared as a band of volunteers pledged to care for sick pilgrims, now adopted an organization like that of the Templars. And later a third military order, that of the Teutonic Knights, came into existence. In the west, as already remarked, the crusade served to enrich the Italian cities and, more generally, to accelerate economic and cultural revival throughout western Christendom. But, above all, the success of the crusade was logically reflected in the exaltation of the power that had conceived the undertaking. It was more than coincidence that the mediæval papacy attained its height during the Age of the Crusades.

Results

4. CHURCH AND STATE IN THE TWELFTH CENTURY

Since the twelfth century is almost exactly the period between the death of Urban II and the election of Innocent III, the following sketch may be taken as an introduction to the famous career of the latter. The greatest triumphs of the church during this period—those won in the fields of art, learning, and practical religion—will receive attention in the

The rise of the Capetians

next chapter. Our present task is merely to pass in brief review over the dynastic rivalries of the twelfth-century kings
and emperors, to estimate the significance of their governmental policies, and to see how all such activities were eventually drawn into the sphere of papal influence.

**Louis VI
(1108-37)**

For England as well as for France an event of prime importance was the rise of the Capetians. At the accession of
Louis VI in 1108 the prospects of the French royal house
seemed far from brilliant. Up to that point the successors of
Hugh Capet (see Table II), as if content with great exploits
on the part of their barons, had themselves accomplished
little. Under Louis's father, Philip I, the prestige of the
crown had, indeed, sunk lower than ever. From the beginning the Capetian had enjoyed no real authority throughout
the kingdom as a whole; he now lost control even of his subordinates in the Île de France—the *prévôts* who collected his
revenues and the *châtelains* who held his castles. In every
direction lawless vassals made the roads unsafe for travel and
terrorized the churches of which the king acted as patron.
Obviously, before the Capetian could hope to be a real king,
he would have to make himself master of his own principality.
To this undertaking Louis VI devoted his life.

Year after year, with the support of neighboring abbots
and bishops, the indefatigable Louis assembled a small force
and led it against some local brigand or rebellious official.
Gradually the royal cause triumphed: the king's castles were
put into the hands of loyal vassals, his courts were effectively
administered, revenue once more flowed into his treasury,
economic production rapidly increased. Like other progressive lords of the day, Louis issued charters of liberty for the
benefit of peasants who would settle on his waste lands, or
of merchants who would develop such trading centers as
Lorris.[10] To Paris and Orleans, as to most towns under his
immediate authority, he made no formal grants of self-government; but on ecclesiastical territory, forcing the churches
to accept the inevitable, he helped to found communes in

[10] See above, p. 165.

Laon, Amiens, Beauvais, Soissons, and several other places. Against the great barons of either north or south Louis's resources were inadequate to win him any noteworthy success. It was therefore a stroke of splendid fortune that William X of Aquitaine decided to give his only child, Eleanor, in marriage to the king's son. Thanks to this match, Louis VII could incorporate in his domain a magnificent duchy beyond the Loire.

In England, meanwhile, William the Conqueror had been succeeded first by William II and then by Henry I, who reunited his father's possessions by taking Normandy from his elder brother Robert. Henry, of whose government something will be said below, reigned with marked success. His main trouble arose over the succession to the crown. Being left with only a daughter, Matilda, he forced his barons to recognize her as their future queen and married her to his bitterest rival, Geoffrey Plantagenet, count of Anjou. But on Henry's death in 1135 strong factions in both England and Normandy refused to accept the Angevin and instead proclaimed Stephen of Blois, a son of the Conqueror's daughter (see Table III). In the resulting war, though Geoffrey and Matilda secured Normandy for their son Henry, they failed to oust Stephen from England. And it was during this conflict that Louis VII came to the throne of France.

The Angevin succession in England

A pious, well-intentioned man, he very nearly ruined the Capetian cause by a series of political blunders. In the first place, he joined Conrad III of Germany in a futile crusade, and all that saved the royal government was the fact that he could turn it over to Suger, a trained minister of his father. Even Suger, however, could not prevent Louis from being shocked by the flirtatious habits of his wife, the granddaughter of a famous troubadour,[11] and in 1152 Louis persuaded the ecclesiastical authorities to annul his marriage. Thereupon Eleanor at once accepted a match with the young Henry of Anjou, who thus added her duchy to the possessions already inherited from his father and mother. The king,

[11] See below, p. 242.

having amiably permitted the union of Normandy, Anjou, and Aquitaine, still remained inactive when Henry took up arms against Stephen, won recognition as heir to the English throne, and occupied it in 1154. The damage had then been done. It was merely an aggravation of the Capetian misfortunes that Henry later asserted his feudal lordship over Wales and Scotland, extended his dominion into Ireland, married a son to the heiress of Brittany, and built up powerful alliances in Germany, Spain, and Sicily.

Government of Henry II (1154-89)

The ruler of what is sometimes called the Angevin Empire is most familiar as Henry II of England; yet it should be remembered that he was primarily a continental prince, who could devote only a minor part of his time to his island kingdom. The fact that, among all the kings of England, none has left a greater impress on the institutions of that country is eloquent testimony to his political genius. On assuming the crown, Henry's initial task was to restore the governmental system of his grandfather, which had completely lapsed during the troubled reign of Stephen. Under Henry I the permanent court surrounding the king had already contained a nucleus of professional ministers—men especially trained in law and administration, whose loyalty was often rewarded by appointment to high office in church or state. In particular he seems to have organized the exchequer,[12] the royal court sitting for financial business round a checkered table that was used as a sort of abacus for reckoning accounts. With the accession of Henry II the exchequer again met regularly, and its annual records, known as pipe rolls, are all thenceforth extant. From these and other documents we obtain detailed information concerning Henry II's income. We find that, more and more frequently, he substituted a money payment known as scutage for the knight service of his barons; that, especially from the boroughs, he developed another very profitable tax called tallage; and that he enormously in-

---

[12] "Exchequer," "checker," and "chess" are three forms of the same word, the Arabic name of the famous game introduced into western Europe after the First Crusade. On the abacus, see below, p. 222.

creased the crown revenues by a reform of his judicial administration.

The English common law

Henry I had often sent out members of his central court as itinerant justices to try royal pleas, cases reserved for the king's personal jurisdiction, and to hold inquests, special investigations by means of juries.[13] The jury was a group of men selected on account of their presumptive knowledge and sworn (*jurati*) to give a true answer (*veredictum*, verdict) to a particular question. William I, for example, had asked juries from the hundreds to provide him with information regarding all the manors of England—material which was finally combined in the huge volume called *Domesday Book*—and the same procedure had frequently been used for other administrative purposes. Henry II greatly extended the employment both of itinerant justices and of juries. From his ordinances we first hear in detail of grand juries, which were drawn from the local communities and instructed to present the names of suspected criminals, as well as of petit juries, which were as yet restricted to the trial of civil cases, mainly disputes over land. Men presented by a grand jury were still tried by ordeal, while judicial combat remained the ordinary form of trial in all baronial courts. But as the superiority of the king's jury procedure became evident, it was adapted to the needs of all freeholders, whether or not they were tenants of the king. So the feudal law, as well as the ancient custom of the Anglo-Saxon courts, tended to be superseded by a growing body of royal law, known as the common law because it was common to the whole realm.

Ecclesiastical relations

Henry received his first decisive check when he tried to determine the relations of church and state; for, like his grandfather, he was opposed by a zealous archbishop of Canterbury. Under Henry I the holder of that see had been the famous scholar Anselm.[14] As the king, following the established Norman tradition, had continued to dictate ecclesiastical elections and to treat bishops and abbots like other royal

---

[13] Cf. procedure under Charlemagne's *missi*, above, p. 108.
[14] See below, p. 223.

vassals, Anselm, taking to heart the principles of Gregory VII, had raised the issue of lay investiture. In 1106, however, the two parties had finally agreed to a compromise: prelates were to be elected by the proper ecclesiastical bodies in the king's presence; those elected should then perform homage before receiving from him their lay fiefs; but investiture with the ring and staff, the symbols of spiritual office, had to be from the hands of a clergyman. Since investiture had thus ceased to be a subject of controversy, it was another matter that caused trouble for Henry II—the trial of criminous clerks. The king held that, although purely ecclesiastical cases, such as wills and marriages, might be finally disposed of in ecclesiastical courts, convicted murderers and thieves should be punished according to the royal law, whether or not they had ever received holy orders.[15] To this sensible proposal Thomas Becket, royal chancellor and archbishop of Canterbury, refused to agree. And since he was unfortunately martyred by would-be friends of the king, the latter was never able to put through his reform; for hundreds of years numberless English criminals went virtually scot-free by pleading benefit of clergy and reading a text of Scripture to prove their privileged status.

Philip Augustus (1180-1223)

The excellence of Henry II's governmental machine was demonstrated by the fact that it ran efficiently under Richard I—a fine soldier who deserved his nickname of Lion-Heart (*Cœur de Lion*), but who left his kingdom to be ruled by ministers while he won renown on the crusade.[16] Meanwhile, in 1180, the Capetian throne had been inherited by Philip II, son of the inglorious Louis VII by a second wife. As a mere youth, Philip displayed the wisdom that was to gain for him the surname of Augustus. Neither chivalrous nor especially pious, he was greatly inferior to Louis VII in traditional goodness; yet there can be no question as to which was the better king. Philip's crafty self-control and hard intelligence, though they brought him few warm friends, enabled

---

[15] Cf. trials for heresy, below, p. 355.
[16] See below, p. 216.

him to redeem his father's mistakes and triumphantly to resume the policy of his grandfather. His first success was to
make good his claim to the marriage portion of his wife, a
daughter of the Flemish count, and so to acquire Artois to-

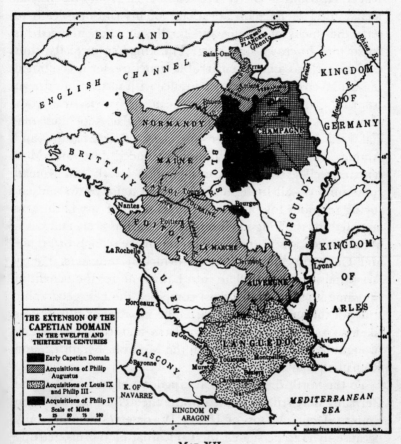

MAP XII.

gether with the upper Somme valley (see Map XII). As far
as breaking the Angevin power was concerned, he could,
while Henry II lived, merely hope for a future opportunity.
And although Philip abandoned his crusade to plot against
Richard, he won little glory until the sudden death of the
latter brought the ignoble John to the English throne. Before

completing this story, however, we must turn our attention to events in central Europe.

The kingdom of Sicily

While Henry I was strongly organizing one Norman kingdom in England, another was created in southern Italy by Roger II, count of Sicily (see Table VI). Attaining his majority in 1112, he took advantage of his cousin's death to seize the duchy of Apulia and finally, in 1130, induced his papal lord to crown him king. The kingdom of Sicily, thus established, was a most remarkable structure, for it combined the feudal custom of northern France with institutions drawn from all parts of the Mediterranean. Its rulers, who commonly spoke a French or Italian vernacular, kept their official records in three other languages: Greek, Latin, and Arabic. The polyglot population included Jews and Moslems as well as Christians of both the Greek and Roman communions—all living under their customary laws and enjoying religious toleration. And loyal men of any faith were accepted for the king's civil service, as for his army and navy. While Greek was virtually unknown in the schools of France and Germany, one of Roger's principal ministers, Henry Aristippus, translated Plato into Latin, and for the benefit of the same king the Arab Idrisi composed the best geographic study of the age (see Figure 14). The mixture of culture was likewise reflected in Roger's palaces and churches, which brought together elements from the Moorish, Byzantine, and Romanesque styles.[17]

The Holy Roman Empire

To the north the theoretical kingdoms of Italy, Arles, and Germany were still combined in the theoretical Holy Roman Empire. Henry V, son of Henry IV, deserves mention only because in 1122 he signed the Concordat of Worms, settling the investiture controversy on much the same terms as had earlier been agreed to in England by Henry I and Anselm. Otherwise his reign was marked by a steady decline of the royal authority and the multiplication of small autonomous principalities held by feudal tenure. The Italian kingdom, in particular, became a mosaic of petty states among which

---

[17] See below, pp. 249-52.

the urban communes gained an increasingly dominant position. In the kingdom of Arles the German was also a foreigner. Even at home his monarchy, despite the semi-hereditary position of the Franconian house, remained a sort of personal leadership, utterly lacking the efficient machinery of government that characterized the Norman kingdoms of England and Sicily. Having ousted the old ducal families and largely broken up the old duchies, the German kings found themselves equally powerless before the host of lesser barons who now held direct of the crown.

Thus, in the twelfth century, there was no longer a duke of Franconia. Lorraine had been divided into the two duchies of Upper and Lower Lorraine; and, as the latter rapidly disintegrated, the name of Lorraine came to be applied only to the former. The duchy of Suabia, though weakened by the rise of various local houses, was still relatively important, because it had been given by Henry IV to a certain Frederick of Hohenstaufen together with the hand of his daughter Agnes (see Table VI). Bavaria, too, had been reduced, first by the creation of a new duchy in Carinthia, and then by the separation of two frontier districts called the North Mark and the East Mark.[18] To what was left of the old duchy Henry IV appointed a South German nobleman by the name of Welf or Guelf, and the office had been inherited by Henry the Black, whose son was married to a daughter of Lothair, duke of Saxony (see Table V). The latter, like the dukes of Suabia and Bavaria, was a newcomer, elevated by Henry IV after he had crushed the old ducal family established by Otto the Great.

These relationships, however uninspiring to the modern reader, assumed great importance for all Germans when Henry V died without direct heirs in 1125. If the principle of hereditary succession were still to be applied, as it had been in 1024, the crown would now pass to Frederick, duke of Suabia and son of Henry IV's daughter. But the electors de-

Guelf vs. Hohenstaufen

---

[18] Later famous as Austria (Osterreich), though now restored to its ancient name of Ostmark.

termined to assert their independence and so proclaimed a man without the slightest hereditary claim—Lothair, duke of Saxony. The determining factor in this election was Lothair's alliance with the Guelfs, who as dukes of Bavaria were bitterly hostile to their Hohenstaufen neighbors in Suabia. And the Guelf victory began a civil conflict that continued intermittently for upward of a hundred years. Under Lothair the Hohenstaufen leaders revolted and were put down. Then, on Lothair's death, the electors deliberately passed over his son-in-law, Henry the Proud, who combined the duchies of Bavaria and Saxony, to choose Conrad of Hohenstaufen. Thereupon the Guelfs took arms, and it was only after a prolonged war that Conrad found the opportunity of joining Louis VII of France on his mismanaged expedition to the Holy Land.

Frederick I (1152-90) On the death of Conrad, the electors gave the crown to his nephew Frederick, for the latter was half Guelf by descent and bore an excellent reputation. The new king, nicknamed Barbarossa by the Italians on account of his reddish beard, ranks among the greatest of mediæval Germans. As a soldier he was rivaled only by Richard Lion-Heart, who in other respects was his inferior. Even those who disliked Frederick as a matter of principle agreed that he was a worthy foe— a thoroughly imperial figure like Otto the Great or Charlemagne. It was, indeed, the tradition of those men that colored his whole career and, while lending a certain grandeur to his reign, ultimately proved its curse. The quest for a pseudo-Roman glory led to Italy, which remained a strange land to the German. And by diverting his attention from his own country, Frederick played into the hand of Henry the Lion, duke of Saxony and Bavaria, who led the anti-monarchical faction and, by marriage to Henry II's daughter, was allied with the powerful house of Anjou.

Defeat in Italy Frederick's first Italian expedition in 1154 brought him the imperial crown as a reward for helping Pope Hadrian IV against various local rebels and the opportunity of proclaiming his regal authority in a great diet at Roncaglia. Four years later, after arranging a settlement with the Guelfs, he held a second diet at Roncaglia, and there issued a series of grandiloquent constitutions, asserting his right to appoint officials, levy taxes, and administer supreme justice throughout his Italian kingdom. And when Milan headed an insurrection of the Lombard communes, he took the city after a protracted siege and destroyed it. Having come into violent controversy with the papacy, he now occupied Rome, drove out Alexander III, Hadrian's able successor, and installed an anti-pope. Yet Frederick's triumph was only the beginning of a long war in the course of which the papal cause steadily advanced. By 1168 Alexander had regained his capital through the support of his Sicilian vassals, had found allies among the Guelfs in Germany, and had organized the great Lombard League, a defensive combination of virtually all the city-states of northern Italy. Milan was rebuilt and a new fortress, named Alessandria in honor of the pope, was constructed to offset the imperial position at Pavia. Frederick, though deserted by the Guelfs, accepted the challenge and again invaded Italy. But in 1176, after vainly besieging Alessandria, his army was overwhelmed at Legnano by the united forces of the league. Alexander's victory was complete, as Frederick promptly acknowledged by granting him formal recognition. Finally, by the Peace of Constance in 1183, the allied cities obtained the guarantee of what amounted to the *status quo* in Italy, having merely to accept the reservation of certain theoretic rights on the part of the emperor.

In Germany, on the other hand, Frederick proved that he was still master, for by 1182 he had confiscated the duchies of Henry the Lion and forced him to crave the royal pardon on bended knee. The fall of the Guelf chieftain brought about a momentous change in the map of Germany. The historic duchies of Saxony and Bavaria were never reconstituted. Although a local margrave came to be styled duke of Saxony, his holdings were confined to the eastern border, and it was only a fragment of the old Bavaria that eventually

Success in Germany

passed with the ducal title to the house of Wittelsbach. Austria, recognized as a separate duchy, became increasingly prominent, as did Brandenburg, another frontier state. And between them the kingdom of Bohemia, though still ruled by a native dynasty, was more and more subjected to German influence. Meanwhile a great work of recolonization was carried out in the region to the east of the Elbe, which had been laid waste by the Poles in the previous century. Here, too, may be perceived the effect of commercial revival, for the Saxon princes—both the Guelfs and their local rivals— brought hundreds of Flemish and Westphalian peasants to drain and cultivate the marshy wastes along the Baltic. At the same time economic considerations led to the founding of many famous towns. For example, Henry the Lion created a flourishing center for the Bavarian salt trade at Munich, and in his other duchy he was largely responsible for the estab- lishment of a mercantile settlement at Lübeck—a project that had a greater success than all the Italian expeditions of all the emperors combined!

Henry VI and the Sicilian succession

For Frederick Barbarossa there are only two other events to chronicle. Profiting by the fact that the great Alexander III had only short-lived and mediocre successors, the em- peror in 1184 had the satisfaction of marrying his son, already crowned as Henry VI, to Constance, daughter of Roger II and potential heiress of the Sicilian kingdom. Lastly, as a fitting close to his picturesque career, he took a splendid army to join Philip of France and Richard of England on the crusade. But he never reached the Holy Land, being drowned, as the result of an unexplained accident, in a little river of Cilicia. Thus, in 1190, Germany came under the sovereignty of Henry VI—a man of a harsh and cruel disposi- tion who nevertheless proved to be an efficient ruler and a shrewd diplomat. Besides, he had amazing luck. Through the complaisance of the aged pope, Celestine III, he not only secured the imperial crown but also, with the opportune death of Roger II's last grandson, made good his claim to the kingdom of Sicily. Following up this success, and the joyful news that his wife had presented him with a son, Henry launched plans for making the imperial office hereditary and for including in a greater crusade the capture of Constantinople and the reunion of the Roman world. His magnificent design was never to be put to actual trial. Stricken by fever in 1197, Henry died at the age of only thirty-two. And through one of the most dramatic reversals in history his reign introduced a new age of splendor, not for the empire, but for the papacy.

5. INNOCENT III AND THE QUESTION OF A PAPAL THEOCRACY

The death of Henry VI was shortly followed by that of the ninety-year-old Celestine, and the cardinals, realizing that the moment was critical, gave the vacant throne to a young and vigorous man with a known talent for practical affairs. They chose well, for Innocent III, as the new pope saw fit to be styled, ranks among the greatest statesmen of Europe—a bishop sincerely devoted to the traditions of his see, and yet a politician and diplomat of superlative skill. In the contest for the German crown, as was to be expected, Innocent favored Otto, son of Henry the Lion, in preference to a younger son of Frederick Barbarossa. Then, as the victorious Otto failed to carry out his promises, Innocent shifted his support to the youthful Frederick of Sicily, son of Henry VI and ward of the papacy. Meanwhile, however, the conflict between the houses of Guelf and Hohenstaufen had inevitably been drawn into that between the Angevins and the Capetians.

Papal intervention in European politics

John, having succeeded his brother Richard as ruler of the Angevin lands, soon provided the French king with the opportunity he had long awaited. As the consequence of John's insolent refusal to attend his lord's court when summoned, Philip declared forfeit all fiefs held by his felonious vassal and, with astonishing good fortune, proceeded to take most of them. Innocent, to force the submission of Philip in the matter of a royal divorce, at first gave encouragement to John. Later, to coerce John into accepting his settlement of a disputed election to the see of Canterbury, the pope blessed Philip's plan for the conquest of England. It was only after much devious maneuvering that Innocent found himself in position to back the alliance of Philip and Frederick against that of John and Otto.

The battle of Bouvines (1214), in which the forces of the Angevin-Guelf coalition were decisively beaten, was therefore a victory for the pope as well as for the French king. Otto quickly lost all but a few scattered supporters, and the young king of Sicily gained general recognition as Frederick II of Germany. John, through sheer negligence, had earlier permitted Philip to occupy Normandy, Anjou, Poitou, and Auvergne, and had only bestirred himself in time to save the rest of Aquitaine (see Map XII). After Bouvines there was no one to challenge the Capetian conquest. Philip became the master of his kingdom, many times more powerful than any one of his remaining vassals. And as he extended to all his dominions the administrative system of the annexed territories, what we recognize as the mediæval French constitution began to take form. For England John's loss of Normandy, though long considered a shame and a disgrace, eventually proved an enormous benefit. The island kingdom, instead of being merely the outlying possession of a continental prince, came to be a state regarded for its own sake. Norman barons who had hitherto held fiefs on both sides of the Channel now had to choose which they would be, English vassals or French vassals. The first step in the direction of an English nationality had perforce been taken.

The papal monarchy

As far as the papacy was concerned, Innocent now seemed on the verge of establishing a Roman theocracy by combining the spiritual with the temporal headship of the Christian world. Long before his time the Roman Church, in so many ways the true heir of the Roman Empire, had come to be recognized as an absolute monarchy. For the Latin world constituted a single ecclesiastical unit, within which the pope was sovereign—held supreme authority in all matters, legislative, executive, or judicial. His actual administration, naturally, was entrusted to a host of subordinates. Chief among them were the cardinals, whom he frequently summoned to meet with him in consistory, a sort of cabinet to which he customarily submitted important questions for discussion. Besides he appointed the ministers who acted as his judges, secretaries, financial experts, and the like, and who together made up his great central *curia*. To enforce his decisions, he dispatched on all sides special emissaries called legates, with powers superior to those of any local prelate. Normally, of course, each diocese was governed by its own bishop under the supervision of the metropolitan, and from time to time the bishops of a whole province, or of a larger region, would meet in council to legislate on matters of general concern. Their acts, however, could always be set aside by papal edict, just as the ruling of any ordinary court of canon law could be reversed at Rome. And, as had now come to be generally acknowledged, even a more comprehensive assembly of the church could only give advice to the chief pontiff. In 1215 Innocent III held a great Lateran Council, to which ecclesiastics streamed from the four corners of Christendom; but its function was merely to hear and to applaud the promulgation of the pope's decrees.

By this time too the traditional theory of the emperors, that the church was merely a department of state, had been discredited along with its official sponsors. However effectively it might be enunciated at Constantinople, it had little cogency when proclaimed by men who were hardly respected as kings of Germany. Ecclesiastical advocates, on the other hand, could cite famous authorities, headed by St. Augustine, to the effect that the state was but the handmaid of the church. For all temporal government, they asserted, was simply the consequence of Adam's sin, which had first brought evil among men and so had necessitated the maintenance of armies, courts, and penal laws. Ultimately, therefore, the decision of all political questions must depend on the power of distinguishing the good from the bad; and that power lay with the church, whose supreme head was the

Theories of church and state

bishop of Rome. Innocent III, implicitly accepting this theory, sought to enforce it by whatever means he could find. As ruler of the Papal States, protector of the Lombard League, and guardian of the Sicilian kingdom, he dominated the Italian peninsula. In Germany he had helped to depose two kings and to install others. John of England, threatened by French invasion and baronial revolt, had agreed to hold England as a papal fief. The kings of Poland, Hungary, Portugal, Aragon, and Denmark had also acknowledged themselves vassals of the pope. An even more splendid prospect of extending papal influence throughout the east had now been opened up by his surprising crusade. Yet, when we review Innocent's policy in that connection, we discover another side to the picture.

Innocent and the crusade

Two factors had largely contributed to the victory of the original crusade: the success of the papacy in uniting the Christians of the west for the sake of a holy war and the failure of the Moslems to make common cause against them. The twelfth century had brought a sad reversal of fortunes. While the zeal of the Christians yielded to political and commercial ambitions, a new Turkish power gained control of both Syria and Egypt. The great hero of the Moslem offensive was Saladin, who, having risen to be sultan at Cairo, secured the emirates of Mosul and Damascus and at last, in 1187, took Jerusalem. Earlier the fall of Edessa had inspired Louis VII and Conrad III to lead the so-called Second Crusade, which never got beyond Anatolia. The Third Crusade of 1189-92, aimed at the recapture of Jerusalem, was hardly more successful. Although Richard of England won great fame by the storming of Acre, the Holy Sepulcher remained in Moslem hands. So Innocent, on assuming the papal office, immediately set out to organize a fourth great expedition; and since the kings of Europe were busily engaged in fighting one another, he seemed to have an excellent chance of directing it. On assembling at Venice in 1202, however, the crusading host found that it lacked funds to pay for its transportation. The majority of the crusaders therefore accepted a Venetian proposal that, to cancel the debt, they should capture the rival city of Zara, although it belonged to the king of Hungary, an orthodox Christian and a vassal of the pope. After carrying out this proposal in the face of Innocent's objection, most of the crusaders proceeded, not to the Holy Land, but to Constantinople. There they first drove

MAP XIII.

out a usurping emperor, then took the empire from his ungrateful successor, and finally divided it up among themselves. Baldwin of Flanders acquired the imperial title, while his principal followers carved out fiefs in Greece and the Venetians extended their dominion over most of the Byzantine islands and the adjacent waters (see Map XIII).

Nothing better illustrates the limitations of the papal theocracy than this Fourth Crusade, which turned out to be no crusade at all. It was not until the Byzantine Empire had been conquered in flat disobedience of papal orders that

The papal
theocracy
in actuality

Innocent saw fit to accept the facts and turn them to advantage. And if we closely examine his political victories in Europe, we find that they too were of dubious worth. For example, his apparent success in dealing with the Holy Roman Empire resulted in the coronation of Frederick II, which proved to be no blessing for Innocent's successors. The papal lordship over isolated states like Portugal was rendered advantageous by local conditions that were subject to change at any moment. The vassalage of the English king was a mere by-product of the Angevin-Capetian war and it came to impose very embarrassing obligations on the pope. When the revolting barons extorted *Magna Carta* from John,[19] Innocent at once quashed the charter, ordered the barons to submit, and forbade the projected invasion of England by Philip Augustus. But the French king, who on the pope's demand had reluctantly taken back a repudiated wife, would not allow him to dictate the royal conduct in any essential matter of state. The English barons, headed by Innocent's own nominee to the see of Canterbury, maintained their stand. They had actually received Prince Louis of France and recognized him as their lord when John saved the papal cause by suddenly dying.

It would thus appear that Innocent's success was due, not to the general acceptance of the theocratic ideal, but to his own superlative skill in diplomacy, aided by a very fortunate turn of events over which he had no real control. The design of a world-wide Christian commonwealth was doomed to failure by two principal facts: that succeeding popes could not all be men of Innocent's peculiar genius and that the rivalries of European politics were as little compatible with Christian idealism then as they are today. Merely to superintend the legal and financial administration of the papal monarchy was a tremendous responsibility. How, in addition, could any pope think of acting as a sort of moral dictator in all national and international affairs, disciplining

[19] See below, pp. 282-83.

temporal rulers for their misdeeds in public as well as in private life? If, in the changing world of the thirteenth century, the papacy chose to devote its chief attention to government and diplomacy, would it not gravely endanger its spiritual leadership?

CHAPTER VII

THE GROWTH OF MEDIÆVAL CULTURE

---

1. THE REVIVAL OF LEARNING

Throughout the dismal period that followed the collapse of Charlemagne's empire very few men were able to devote their time to scholarship, and among those who somehow managed to keep alive the traditions of the Carolingian schools almost none produced anything original. The intellectual history of the Latin world between 850 and 1050 is, indeed, distinguished by only one great name—that of Gerbert, who died as Pope Silvester II in 1003. Little is known of his early life apart from the fact that he was born in Aquitaine and, after studying grammar at the monastery of Aurillac, visited the county of Barcelona, where he became very proficient in mathematics. Later, for the sake of training in dialectic, he attended the cathedral school of Reims and there became a famous master. When teaching the *trivium*, we are told, he introduced his students not merely to the standard textbooks but also to the great poets and prose writers of Rome. And his numerous letters show him to have been an ardent collector of books, building what for that age was a splendid library of the classics. Yet to us, as to his contemporaries, Gerbert's most remarkable work was in the field of the *quadrivium*. He demonstrated the mathematical basis of music by means of vibrating strings, and for instructing his students in astronomy and arithmetic he used a number of inventions which then seemed utterly marvelous.

According to his pupil Richer, Gerbert constructed two spheres. One was solid and on it he marked the poles, the horizon, various other imaginary circles, and both the northern and the southern constellations. The second was an ar-

FIGURE 6.—AN ARMILLARY SPHERE: FRONTISPIECE TO THE *Epitome of Ptolemy's Almagest*, by Johannes Müller (Regiomontanus), Venice, 1496.

millary sphere—i.e., one made of concentric metal bands like bracelets, each representing a planetary orbit, with a ball for the earth in the center and on the outside a belt carrying the signs of the zodiac (see Figure 6). Gerbert's abacus was even more wonderful; for with it, Richer says, he could solve problems involving numbers so large that they could hardly be expressed in words. It had twenty-seven columns, in which he distributed counters made of horn and inscribed with nine symbols—variations, as we know, of the nine Arabic numerals. Since neither the abacus nor the Ptolemaic system had been expounded by the Latin authors commonly used in the schools of the west, it is clear that Gerbert must have obtained most of his mathematical learning in Spain, and the fact that he was familiar with the nine Arabic numerals shows that his information was derived from an Arabic source. Apparently, however, it came through some indirect channel; Gerbert knew neither Greek nor Arabic, and he made no use of the zero, with which educated Moslems had been familiar for over a hundred years.[1]

Gerbert's influence

A Frenchman and a teacher in a great cathedral school of France, Gerbert stood at the forefront of the educational revival that was to culminate in the university of Paris; by examining his scholarly interests we are introduced to those of many succeeding generations. In the field of mathematics Gerbert's influence was profound. He inspired a whole series of writings on the abacus, awakened curiosity with regard to astronomical science, and so helped to bring about the translation of the pertinent Greek and Arabic works. From Gerbert, too, many pupils acquired a lasting enthusiasm for grammar—chief among them Fulbert, under whom the cathedral school of Chartres became the foremost center of classical study in western Christendom. Dialectic, another topic emphasized by Gerbert, likewise flourished in the eleventh century. And as an increasing number of students came

[1] See above, pp. 92-93.

to be fascinated by the logical art, many were attracted to a problem left unsolved by their standard texts.

Porphyry's *Isagoge*, being merely an introductory essay, refers to the subject of universals as one of great importance, but does not go on to explain it. Nor was it thoroughly treated by the works of Aristotle then available in Latin.[2] The scholars of the eleventh century were therefore led to answer for themselves such questions as arose concerning the existence of universals and particulars. For example, can we recognize an individual thing as an apple without first having an idea of apple in general? Is then our knowledge of this universal, apple, derived from our knowledge of particular apples, or vice versa? Can the former exist apart from the latter? If so, where does it exist? And is it a thing (*res*)? Although the traditional dialectic of the schoolmen was Aristotelian, their philosophic attitude, under the influence of St. Augustine, remained Neo-Platonic. So the orthodox generally held that all knowledge is based on divine ideas implanted in the human reason by the Creator; and certain doctors, without very careful definition, came to affirm that universals are *res*—the dialectical position called "realist." On the contrary, a well-known teacher named Roscellinus boldly advanced the "nominalist" thesis, that universals are not *res* but *nomina* (names), which are no more than *voces* (sounds). The more conservative schoolmen, ably led by Anselm, abbot of Bec and later archbishop of Canterbury, at once denounced the view of Roscellinus as heretical, being directly opposed to the revealed truths of religion. And Anselm's opinion was confirmed by a council at Soissons in 1092, which compelled Roscellinus to retract at least some of his statements before he was allowed to continue teaching.

At this point the discussion was taken up by a young Breton named Peter Abelard. In a famous autobiography he tells us how, enamored of dialectic, he abandoned a noble inheritance to become an "emulator of the Peripatetics," wandering from school to school in search of the best in-

Dialectical argument

Abelard (1079-1142)

[2] See above, p. 128.

struction; and how, inevitably, he came to Paris, where William of Champeaux was defending the realist position. Undertaking to refute the master's thesis, Abelard did so with such effectiveness that he was encouraged to set up a school of his own in the outskirts of the city. But the hostility of the ecclesiastical authorities soon compelled him to resume his travels, and it was only after he had repeatedly proved his ability at the expense of other teachers that, about 1115, he secured official appointment in the cathedral school of Paris. There, as we know from many sources, he won a prodigious success, attracting students in unprecedented numbers by the keenness of his intellect and the charm of his exposition. There, too, occurred the love idyll with Héloïse which so quickly turned into tragedy—an immortal story that all should read in the letters of the two unfortunates themselves. Abelard's life thenceforth became a succession of miseries: vain attempts to find peace in monastic seclusion alternating with returns to public teaching that always culminated in worse trouble. Abelard, inordinately proud of his own cleverness and bitterly intolerant of ignorance or stupidity, was never one to avoid altercation. To the very end he was involved in fierce controversy. Appealing to Rome against his condemnation by a provincial council, he was taken ill on the way to plead his cause before the pope and died at Cluny (1142).

His logic   Abelard was unquestionably one of the greatest figures in the intellectual history of Europe. To the study of dialectic —as appears from his recently printed works on that subject—he made a contribution of fundamental importance. The question then at issue could be resolved into this: What does logic deal with? By denying that it deals with things (*res*), Abelard placed himself squarely in the nominalist camp. But, said he, a distinction must be made between *vox* and *sermo*—between the sound of a word and its meaning. The latter is the true universal, for the sound is only a particular. To that extent Roscellinus had been mistaken, and to that extent Abelard was willing to accept a compromise.

Thus the way was cleared for understanding logic as the study of concepts—a conclusion which few would now care to dispute, and which in Abelard's day prepared the schools for the more advanced logic of Aristotle, then about to appear in translation.

Abelard's second great contribution was virtually the definition of systematic theology. During the previous centuries there had, of course, been extensive writing on theological subjects, but no attempt had been made to combine and analyze the results. To almost any theological question that might be raised the student would find a number of different answers. This fact Abelard clearly demonstrated in his famous book *Sic et Non*, which lists 158 queries concerning such matters as faith and reason, the Persons of the Trinity, the angels, Adam and Eve, human nature, sin, and the sacraments. After each query he quotes appropriate extracts—from the Old and New Testaments, Jerome, Ambrose, Augustine, Gregory the Great, Isidore of Seville, Bede, and other authors, as well as from the decrees of councils and the letters of the popes. His object—and there is no reason to question his sincerity—is stated in the prologue: he desires to stimulate inquiry, the key to wisdom. These opinions (*sententiæ*), he says, have been collected because they are to some extent contradictory. The contradiction can be explained in various ways and sometimes can be reconciled. Sometimes, however, it cannot be; then the best authority must be taken. In any case the student must work out the problem for himself, and he must first realize that a doubt exists as to the proper answer. "For by doubting we come to inquiry, and by inquiring we perceive the truth." — His theology

Abelard's chief antagonist was Bernard of Clairvaux, a Burgundian noble who, about the time that Abelard began formal teaching, entered the monastery of Cîteaux. There an English abbot, Stephen Harding, had established a reformed discipline based on literal observance of the Benedictine rule, and there Bernard quickly proved his talent for spiritual leadership. As abbot of a daughter house at Clair- — St. Bernard (d. 1153) vaux, he came to have extraordinary influence throughout Europe—on account of which, very largely, the Cistercian order enrolled 343 abbeys before his death in 1153. Bernard was pre-eminently a monk, and a very conservative one. Like the order to which he belonged, he was devoted to a primitive austerity of Christian conduct. The most eloquent preacher in the west, he fiercely denounced the growing luxury of the age—its wicked delight in magnificent architecture, orchestral music, secular literature, and rationalistic study. To Bernard a man like Abelard, who scorned the mystic faith of his ancestors for the sake of intellectual vanity, was a grave menace to Christian society.

Abelard's influence

Yet Abelard was by no means—as his nineteenth-century admirers liked to believe—a freethinker. He never disputed the authority of the church or the truths that it declared a matter of sacred tradition. He merely insisted that, to supplement revelation, one could rightfully employ the reason with which man had been endowed by the Creator. In support of this opinion he could cite the greatest doctors of Christendom. He could, in fact, argue that any one who denied it was himself open to prosecution as a heretic; for how could a Christian hold that Christianity was contrary to reason? It was only when teachers allowed their academic discussions to question the established beliefs of the church that they encountered serious trouble. Roscellinus, as we have seen, was disciplined for advancing a logical argument that, his opponents declared, was contrary to Christian dogma. Earlier a certain Berengar of Tours had been condemned by a provincial council for denying that the bread and wine in the sacrament of the eucharist were substantially flesh and blood.[3] But he had been mildly treated by Gregory VII, who permitted him, after signing a rather vague retraction, to live in peaceful retirement.

Peter Lombard's Sentences

As far as Abelard was concerned the local judgments against him were never upheld at Rome, and within another

[3] The dogma of transubstantiation was first promulgated by Innocent III in his Lateran Council of 1215.

hundred years the soundness of his position had been attested by the whole development of ecclesiastical education. All the great scholastics had followed in his train. The illustrious Peter Lombard, for instance, was one of Abelard's actual pupils. Before Peter's election as bishop of Paris in 1159, he like his master had made a collection of theological *sententiæ*, but had added careful arguments to reconcile the differences of opinion or, when reconciliation was impossible, to decide where the weight of authority lay. The book was enormously successful, for it became a standard text in the schools and has remained in use down to the present. The theology of Abelard, which thus became a prominent subject in the scholastic curriculum, was characterized by two outstanding features. In the first place, it was deductive, being essentially the development of general principles taken from authoritative sources. Secondly, it was practical, in that it came to be the required preparation for high office in the church.

Both features also characterized the contemporary study of law. For a thousand years the church had been accumulating a mass of legal rules, or canons, in the form of Biblical precepts, papal decretals, acts of councils, decisions of courts, and opinions of learned men. But little had as yet been done with the material beyond the making of incomplete collections. Now, about 1148, an Italian monk named Gratian published his monumental *Concordance of Discordant Canons*. The *Decretum*, as Gratian's book was popularly called, is precisely the same kind of work as Peter Lombard's *Sentences*, being at once a code of laws and an exposition of their principles. It is analytically arranged according to hundreds of separate problems, under each of which the pertinent canons are quoted and a logical solution is proposed for the settlement of disputed points. Immediately accepted as the basic text for the use of all canonists, it in turn elicited a library of weighty commentaries and supplementary collections. And though unofficial in origin, it was eventually

*Gratian's
Decretum*

placed at the beginning of the great papal compilation entitled *Corpus Iuris Canonici*.

The re-
vival of
juris-
prudence

The choice of a name reminiscent of Justinian's *Corpus
Iuris Civilis* was, of course, no accident, for the systematic
study of the canon law was directly influenced by that of the
Roman law. The latter as a customary system had never
gone out of use in Italy and southern Gaul, but the little
instruction that had continued to be necessary in no way
depended on the *Corpus* of Justinian. The all-important *Digest*, in particular, remained virtually unknown in the west
until, towards the close of the eleventh century, its discovery
led to the revival of jurisprudence in the Italian schools.
After an obscure early development this study came to be
especially prominent at Bologna. There, following the
method first rendered famous by Irnerius, generations of
glossators, as they were called, lectured on the *Digest*, ex-
pounding it by dialectical argument, and illustrating difficult points through citation of the *Code*. And there the same
method was applied to ecclesiastical jurisprudence, when
that came into existence. Accordingly, as the ensuing age
became more and more legalistic, a host of young men,
trained in one or both of the two laws, were able to enter
upon profitable careers in church or state.

Transla-
tions from
Greek and
Arabic

For the study of law and theology practically all the
needed sources were available in Latin, but other fields were
not so well provided. In response to scholarly demand, therefore, an extensive work of translation from Greek and
Arabic was begun and rapidly advanced in the course of the
twelfth century. At one time it was usual to attribute this
sudden activity to the influence of the crusades. It is now
evident, however, that the average crusader was as little interested in books as had been the average Venetian merchant. Almost none of the translating was done in Syria, and
comparatively little of it at Constantinople. The more important centers of the work were Spain and Sicily; and although the latter country included a number of men who
had a thorough knowledge of Greek, most of the popular

translations were made from Arabic texts. The translators came from many lands, as is indicated by their names: Adelard of Bath, Robert of Chester, Rudolf of Bruges, Hermann of Carinthia, Gerard of Cremona, John of Seville, and the like. Among them, by 1150, they had translated the geometry of Euclid, together with the trigonometry, algebra, and arithmetic of al-Khwarizmi—from whom the last-mentioned subject came to be called algorism. By that time, too, the more advanced logical essays of Aristotle had appeared in Latin, to take their place as the New Logic in the prescribed dialectic of the schools. And by the end of the century western scholars were also supplied with Latin versions of Ptolemy, Galen, Hippocrates, Archimedes, Apollonius, and other Greek authors, as well as scores of books by al-Kindi, al-Farabi, Ibn Sina (Avicenna), and other Arabs. The *Metaphysics*, *Physics*, and lesser scientific writings of Aristotle were, for the most part, translated early in the thirteenth century, together with a mass of Arabic commentary, especially that of Ibn Rushd (Averroes).

The scholarly interests of the Latin world are clearly revealed in this list of outstanding textbooks. By the close of the twelfth century the schools of France, Italy, and the neighboring countries had adopted a course of instruction that emphasized logic, mathematics, and general science as a preparation for professional training in theology, law, and medicine. The curriculum thus defined kept grammar as an elementary study, through which the youth obtained merely the ability to write and speak correct Latin. And since the Latin that he had to use was a rapidly growing, highly technical language, he was normally unwilling to spend much time on the niceties of classical style. So the study of literature as an end in itself tended more and more to be disregarded. The masterpieces of Greek prose and poetry remained unknown; many Latin authors were almost wholly neglected. In the eleventh century there had been a noteworthy development of literary study in the French schools, notably at Chartres, and in the later period a few distin-

Education at the close of the twelfth century

guished writers were still devoted to the tradition of the
ancient grammarians. For instance, John of Salisbury—a talented Englishman who died as bishop of Chartres in 1180—
continued to bewail the passing of the old liberal education.
Instead of acquiring wisdom through wide and leisurely
reading, he declared, students were being swept away by the
craze for dialectic, a much overrated subject that could never
be the foundation of true culture. But, for all his wit and
erudition, he was defending a lost cause. The ideals of the
rising universities were set by Abelard, rather than by John
of Salisbury.

2. THE BEGINNINGS OF THE UNIVERSITIES

**Original
nature
of the
university**

The rapid expansion of advanced study during the twelfth
century naturally implied a huge increase in the number of
teachers and pupils. Being attracted to certain great centers
of instruction, they tended, like merchants or artisans, to
become self-governing and eventually to gain legal recognition. Such an educational unit is what we know as a university, but the word acquired that meaning by a very
gradual process. At first the Latin *universitas* was merely
one of several vague terms that could be applied to any association of people. All men teaching or studying in a particular place might be so referred to, or the same designation
might be applied to a separate union of masters or of students. In other words, the university was at first a gild, or
perhaps a combination of gilds. No specific dates can be
assigned to the emergence of the oldest universities; they
gradually took form in the course of the twelfth century. A
second group arose through migration—when for some reason a number of masters and students came to establish themselves in a new center. Finally, when the models had been
perfected, it became usual for princes, lay or ecclesiastical,
to found universities by formal charter.

Bologna

For a long time after the year 1100 no one could have
predicted which of many schools would eventually dominate
western education. By 1200, however, the issue was settled:

the mother universities of Europe were to be Bologna and Paris. At Bologna the great attraction was the teaching of civil and canon law by the successors of Irnerius. These masters seem from an early time to have formed gilds, there styled colleges, for the regulation of their common affairs, particularly the qualifications demanded for admission to their own ranks. The students, having already completed a course in arts and being of mature age, were left to shift for themselves. And they, in the absence of all control by cathedral school or royal government, proceeded to organize gilds of their own, which they called universities. Before the end of the twelfth century two such universities had come into existence at Bologna: the cismontane, including the Italian "nations," and the transmontane, including those from beyond the Alps. But the two acted together through groups of deputies, each headed by a rector, and so came to be thought of as one. The completed organization was first used to force concessions from the municipal authorities— to secure, by threat of migration, a schedule of fair rents and prices. Then the students turned on the masters, who of course were dependent on them for fees. It was provided that each master should give a certain number of lectures and cover a certain amount of work in a certain way. He had to agree to supervision by student inspectors, who fined him if he did not begin on time and quit on time, or if he left town without permission. Even on the occasion of his wedding he was allowed only one day off!

Thus at Bologna, while the masters' colleges retained the **Paris** granting of degrees, they were definitely subordinated to the students' university. At Paris, on the other hand, it was the masters' gilds, or faculties, that from the outset controlled the students. Most of the latter, having come for work in arts, were boys in their teens, for whom their teachers would naturally be held responsible. In the time of Abelard such matters of discipline were still regulated by the chancellor, the head of the cathedral school. But by the close of the twelfth century his authority had become merely nominal.

The crowds attracted to the study of dialectic and allied subjects had quickly spread beyond the cloister of Notre-Dame and across the Petit-Pont to the left bank of the Seine, which—from the scholarly language there spoken—became known as the Latin Quarter. Under these changing conditions the academic population came to demand extensive rights of self-government and, as was usual in university towns, had frequent altercations with the civil authorities. One such affair in 1200 led to important consequences. Having intervened in a student riot, the Parisian police were clumsy enough to kill certain high-born Germans. In protest, all the masters suspended teaching and threatened to leave the city unless the king gave immediate redress. Philip Augustus acted promptly to avert so calamitous an event, throwing his *prévôt* into jail and issuing a charter that confirmed the exemption of his *scholares* at Paris from all but ecclesiastical jurisdiction.

Having secured formal recognition of their clerical immunity, the Parisian masters proceeded with equal determination to assert their independence of the episcopal authority. And at least some of their established customs were confirmed in 1215 by a legate of Pope Innocent III, who had himself studied at Paris. According to the statutes thus made, a master of arts had to be at least twenty years of age and to have completed six years of academic work; but in order to teach theology he had to be at least thirty-five, with ten additional years spent in that study. The master was to maintain a decent exterior and wear a dark-colored gown reaching to his heels. A student had to be enrolled under a particular master, who would be responsible for him and have the right to discipline him. Both students and masters were permitted to form associations to defend their rights and to aid one another in charitable enterprises. Through the development of this principle the university of Paris took definite form in the course of the next hundred years. The faculty of arts, subdivided into four nations, gained the supremacy by sheer force of numbers; so that its rector became the acknowledged superior of the deans elected by the other faculties—those of theology, law, and medicine—and accordingly the head of the university. The chancellor, to be sure, still held the right of issuing the final license to teach, but he could do little more than accept candidates recommended by the faculties.

Although the universities of Paris and Bologna used much the same method of teaching, they continued to emphasize different studies. At Bologna jurisprudence always dominated and very little attention was given to arts or theology. For those subjects the student went by preference to Paris, where canon law was of secondary importance and civil law was not taught at all. In the twelfth century we hear vaguely of a university at Salerno which was renowned for instruction in medicine, but in the next century leadership in that field passed to the newer universities of Padua, formed in 1222 as an offshoot of Bologna; Naples, founded outright by the emperor Frederick II in 1224; and Montpellier, gradually developed under the joint patronage of the pope and the local princes. About the same time another distinguished university emerged at Orleans, and it quickly became the foremost center of legal study outside Italy. Oxford University seems to have originated towards the close of the twelfth century through the settlement of certain masters who had earlier been at Paris. Cambridge, the second English university, began through a migration from Oxford in the thirteenth century. The first Spanish university to be permanently successful was established at Salamanca by the king of León about 1220. Germany had no university until the fourteenth century, when such institutions were set up at Prague, Vienna, Erfurt, Heidelberg, and Cologne. By that time universities had likewise arisen in Angers, Toulouse, Pavia, Florence, Lisbon, Cracow, Buda, and a score of other places.

For all these younger institutions the two older ones continued to serve as models—Paris generally throughout the north and west of Europe, Bologna generally throughout

Younger universities

Degrees and graduation

the south. It should not be imagined, however, that the two academic organizations were really very different. The students at Bologna, with few exceptions, had already completed the arts course before coming there to study law. The dominant element in the university of Paris was the faculty of arts, consisting mainly of young men who, having spent six years of preparation, were teaching arts while they continued as students of theology, law, or medicine. In other words, the ruling groups of both universities were masters of arts engaged in work for advanced degrees. Such a degree could be awarded only by the proper gild, whether styled faculty or college; for the degree signified admission to the gild. *Doctor, professor,* and *magister* were synonymous terms; all of them meant "teacher." So LL.D. (*Legum Doctor*), M.D. (*Medicinæ Doctor*), and S.T.P. (*Sanctæ Theologiæ Professor*) were the titles of men competent to teach respectively civil and canon law, medicine, and theology. These degrees we still recognize as professional; but the degree of A.M. was by origin equally professional, marking the person formally admitted to the gild of arts teachers. Even the baccalaureate fitted into the same plan of professional advancement. The grade of bachelor—it was not really a degree at first and was not prized for its own sake—entitled the youth, after four years of competent study, to give preliminary instruction in elementary subjects.

As in the ordinary gild, the man who had passed the required tests was formally invested with the insignia of his profession—in this case the cap and gown peculiar to his chosen field. The final ceremony was his inception or commencement—his beginning of professional activity. No legal hindrance then remained to prevent his entering upon actual instruction; all he needed was a vacant room over a tavern and enough student fees to make his lectures worth the giving. It was only later, when endowed chairs had been set up by rival municipalities or by wealthy patrons, that the new graduate was confronted by the unhappy distinction between a degree and a faculty appointment. But in the meantime other splendid opportunities had arisen. Lucrative positions in church and state were opened to trained theologians, canonists, and jurists. It became possible to earn a good livelihood by practising law or medicine. And for any of these learned professions the fundamental requirement was the doctorate—the certified fitness of a man to teach the subject.

Numerous sources provide us with detailed information concerning student life during this early age of the universities. To judge from contemporary sermons, the typical student was a prodigal roisterer who respected neither God nor man—such a fellow, indeed, as often plays the hero's rôle in the *fabliaux*.[4] And the verdict of the preachers and storytellers is to some extent borne out by the writings of the students themselves, as well as by the records of the courts. Yet, allowing for the laxer standards of the time, we may well believe that conditions then were very much as they are now: the average student was law-abiding and conscientious, although his wilder brethren were always the more conspicuous. Of routine matters—such as disputations in the classroom, dinners to celebrate graduation, and the hazing administered to the unfortunate freshman or *bejaunus* (*bec jaune*, yellow beak)—we have many descriptions. Manuals for student use provide Latin words and phrases for everything that could be thought of, and incidentally illustrate daily life in the university community. Even more remarkable are the letters exchanged by students and parents. Well adorned with rhetorical flourishes and appropriate quotations from Scripture, the models kept by professional letter-writers were inspired by very practical motives. Almost invariably the student asks for money and is chiefly interested in a good excuse for being short of cash. Sometimes the father replies simply and generously. More often he takes occasion to deliver a lecture on the evils of sloth and extravagance.

Among the youths who sought an education there were at all times hundreds of boys from poverty-stricken homes, for

Student life

Residential colleges

[4] See below, pp. 245-46.

the church offered the base-born the surest means of advancement. And it is greatly to the credit of the mediæval university that it recognized scholarship without regard to social distinction; many a peasant's son rose to fame as master and author. Yet, at the beginning, such a student found life desperately hard. His chief trouble was the question of lodgings. Wealthy students and masters maintained separate quarters; the rank and file clubbed together in co-operative houses; the poorest starved in garrets and cellars. The foundation of the mendicant orders[5] brought aid to a good many youths; but those who did not want to be friars remained at a disadvantage. So, about 1258, Robert de Sorbon endowed a hall at Paris for sixteen deserving seculars, candidates for the degree in theology—a noteworthy event in the history of culture, for it marked the beginning of the famous Sorbonne,[6] oldest of residential colleges. Similar establishments at Paris soon came to house the bulk of the university population, both masters and students; and from there the practice spread far and wide, attaining great popularity especially in England.

Meanwhile the development of the educational system that is technically called scholastic had raised problems of serious concern to the organized church. Before they can be understood, however, attention must be shifted to other prominent features of mediæval civilization.

3. VERNACULAR LITERATURE

Ecclesiastical origins

It was once usual to explain the sudden perfection of vernacular literature in the twelfth century as the final stage of a slow evolution out of folk-tales, folk-songs, folk-plays, and the like. But since none of the supposed primitive forms have ever been found, scholars now prefer a less fanciful explanation: that the prototypes of the vernacular masterpieces should rather be sought in the Latin literature of the church. For hundreds of years there had been virtually no educated

[5] See below, pp. 264-66.

[6] After the theological faculty had come to reside in the Sorbonne, the name was generally applied to that faculty.

Duke William Knights Earl Harold

Duke William Embarks for England

SCENES FROM THE BAYEUX TAPESTRY

PLATE I.

St. Sophia (Constantinople)

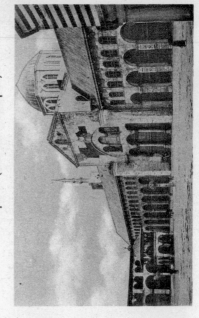

Great Mosque (Damascus)

The Colosseum (Rome)

Pont du Gard (Nîmes)

PLATE II.

Saint-Sernin (Toulouse)

Cathedral of Pisa

Abbey of Laach

Sant' Ambrogio (Milan)

PLATE III.

Sant' Apollinare in Classe (Ravenna), Interior

Sant' Ambrogio (Milan), Interior

PLATE IV.

Abbey of Vézelai, Interior

Saint-Trophime (Arles), Main Portal

PLATE V.

Abbaye-aux-Hommes (Caen)

Durham Cathedral

Notre-Dame (Paris)

Amiens Cathedral

PLATE VI.

Lincoln Cathedral

Salisbury Cathedral

PLATE VII.

Notre-Dame (Paris), Chevet

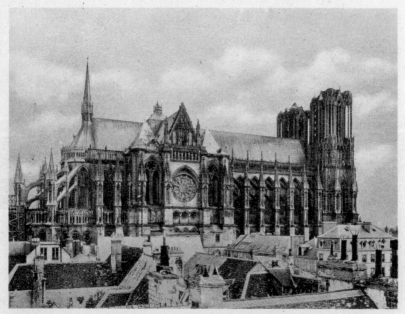

Reims Cathedral, North Side

PLATE VIII.

Amiens Cathedral, Interior

Westminster Abbey, Interior

PLATE IX.

Abbey of Vézelai, Portal

Chartres Cathedral, Main Portal

PLATE X.

Virgin of the Salutation (Reims)

Vintage Capital (Reims)

Mont-Saint-Michel, Cloister

PLATE XI.

Kenilworth Castle (England)

PLATE XII.

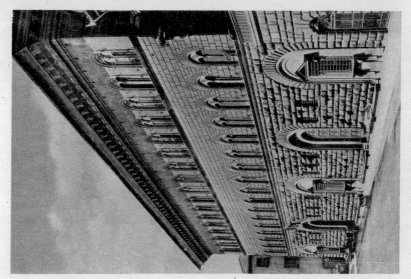

Medici Palace (Florence)

Cloth Hall (Bruges)

PLATE XIII.

Van Eyck, "The Man With the Pink"

Illumination from the Duke of Berry's "Book of Hours"

PLATE XIV.

Giotto, "The Descent From the Cross"

Masaccio, "The Tribute Money"

PLATE XV.

Ghiberti, Bronze Doors of the Baptistery (Florence)

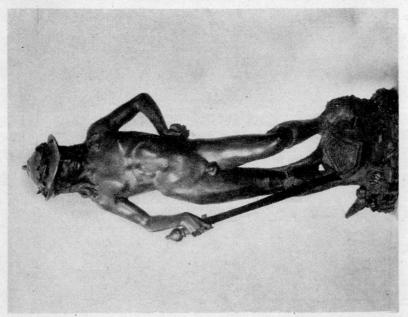

Donatello, "David"

PLATE XVI

persons outside the clergy; and the clergy, it should be remembered, were by no means all priests or monks. Most
clerks were men who had taken minor orders, to become
students in the schools or—as the word came to imply—
secretaries and accountants. When employed, they frequently
served in baronial households; when unemployed, they lived
by their wits. As a class they were remarkable neither for
piety nor for virtue; many of them, in fact, were notorious
rascals. Yet, because they were not responsible holders of
churchly office, they were the more likely to give free play
to whatever talents they might have for original composition.

The language normally employed for all official or formal
writing was Latin, which, though not classical in either vocabulary or syntax, was an admirable medium of expression.
The days when even the better-educated had been unable to
write correctly were long past. In the twelfth century the
Latin of the schoolmen, according to contemporary standards, was entirely grammatical. And how could it remain a
living language unless it met the demands of changing environment? A glance at the appendix of a modern dictionary
will show how rapidly English has admitted new words and
invented new meanings for old ones. In precisely the same
way mediæval Latin was adapted to the needs of government
officials, business men, lawyers, physicians, theologians, scientists, and other experts, as well as to less technical use by
preachers, chroniclers, biographers, story-tellers, and the like.
The great bulk of this literature was intensely practical; yet
all of it was not on that account lacking in beauty. From
the æsthetic point of view, the greatest prose of the age is
to be found in the liturgy of the church—rhythmic Latin
chanted to the accompaniment of gorgeous ceremonial. A
similar majestic quality pervades many of the documents issuing from the chanceries of great ecclesiastics. A papal bull,
for instance, has a sonorous timbre that to the trained ear is
very characteristic.

Mediæval Latin: Prose

In Latin, as in Greek, the best mediæval poetry did not
follow classic models, but used the system with which we are

Poetry

familiar—rhyme and a meter based on accent. Monks, priests, and schoolmen turned out an enormous quantity of such poems on religious themes; and although most of it was distinctly mediocre, occasional pieces have remained justly famous. Especially the great Latin hymns of the twelfth and thirteenth centuries rank among the world's artistic master-pieces. Equally remarkable, yet wholly different, are the lyrics known as Goliardic, the authors of which appear to have been principally students, the wandering clerks who were not displeased at being called sons of Goliath (i.e., Philistines). This poetry, written in the Latin of the schools, is on the whole delightfully fresh and gay. It has the wit and irreverence of youth, together with a sensuous outlook on life that ascetics would consider sheer paganism. The favorite themes, as of most lyrics, are love and the beauties of nature. The execution varies from ordinary ditties with affected invocations of Cupid and Venus to the truly exquisite *Dum Diane vitrea* and *De ramis cadunt folia.*[7] The collection also includes a variety of frivolous jingles, sometimes with a beg-ging motive, as well as a number of splendid drinking songs. And here the opinion may be ventured that the finest of all the Goliardic poems is, appropriately enough, the *Confes-sion of Golias,* in which the author, one styled the Archpoet, completes the recital of his sins by requesting that, with the wine at his lips, he may end his days in the tavern.

Literary use of the vernacular

From these facts it should be evident that the ranks of the mediæval clergy included many writers with a talent for either prose or poetry. We may, indeed, suspect that the same man would often produce songs both sacred and pro-fane. Abelard was a hymn-writer as well as a dialectician, and he tells us himself that his poems in praise of Héloïse were widely sung in France. Heloïse adds that he was skilled not only as a poet but also as a composer of music. Although, unfortunately, his love songs have not come down to us, the

[7] See the admirable translations by Helen Waddell, in her *Mediæval Latin Lyrics,* pp. 265, 275; and for the Confession of the Archpoet, p. 171.

Goliardic verse enables us to guess their general character. Presumably they were in Latin. Yet, if he had wanted to, could he not have used his native Romance? Others were then beginning to do so—with the result that, within another hundred years, vernacular literature had won great and lasting triumphs. This, surely, would have been impossible had not the church, directly or indirectly, supplied the preliminary training.

From the seventh century on, Anglo-Saxon was used not only for the royal laws, or dooms, but also for other kinds of literary production. The *Anglo-Saxon Chronicle*, a monument of early Germanic prose, was begun under King Alfred and continued into the twelfth century. Meanwhile a considerable body of Anglo-Saxon poetry had been composed: warlike songs, of which the finest are those celebrating the battles of Brunanburh and Maldon; hymns and other religious compositions, notably those ascribed to Cædmon; and a number of strangely beautiful lyrics in a minor key, such as *The Seafarer* and *The Wanderer*. But the most famous Anglo-Saxon poem is *Beowulf*—a heroic tale of weird adventure in which, despite the author's Christianity, the central theme is plainly heathen. The material of *Beowulf* thus appears to have been largely drawn from older sagas, traditional stories that had long been current among the Germanic peoples of the Baltic region. ^{Anglo-Saxon}

In German itself only fragments remain of what must once have been a rich literature. The *Nibelungenlied*, familiarized by Wagnerian opera, was written in Austria about the year 1200 and is imbued with the romantic chivalry then fashionable. Beneath the embellishment, however, may readily be detected an ancient legend about a magic treasure guarded by a dragon—the same legend that, remarkably enough, appears as the *Volsungasaga* in the Icelandic collection known as the *Edda*. Evidently the Norse, on finding new homes beyond the sea, there preserved the popular literature of Scandinavia in isolation from continental influ- ^{The Norse sagas}

ence. The Icelandic sagas, when put into writing in the twelfth and thirteenth centuries, thus retained much of their primitive character. Some of them, like the *Volsunga-saga*, are wholly legendary; some, on the other hand, glorify the adventures of actual persons—as, for example, the finding of Vineland the Good by Leif Ericsson. In either case the sagas provide us with much valuable information concerning the earlier age, though the task of separating the original elements from the accretions of later centuries is one that demands the attention of an expert—and the experts often disagree.

The chansons de geste

From such pieces as survive we may at least be sure that the primitive saga was chanted to the accompaniment of a harp. The thoughts and feelings of the individual author are of no especial significance. Interest is concentrated on the tale itself, which is dramatic, idealized, and intensely serious. Poetry of this sort is called epic and is recognized as characteristic of a particular stage in cultural development. But the Icelandic sagas and the Anglo-Saxon *Beowulf*, however fine, remained apart from the main current of western civilization. The more typical epics of mediæval Europe are the *chansons de geste*—as the name literally implies, songs of great deeds. Whatever the influence upon them of ancient Frankish sagas, none of which are extant, the *chansons de geste* appear to be unified compositions of the eleventh and twelfth centuries rather than popular tales that gradually took form. They are written in French and, while borrowing names and episodes from Carolingian times, they faithfully reflect the society and thought of feudal France.

The *Song of Roland* is not only the earliest and best of the *chansons de geste* but one of the finest poems in all literature. The author seems to have been a Norman clerk named Turold, who wrote under the immediate inspiration of the Spanish wars in the later eleventh century. The meter of the poem, like its language, is simple. There is no rhyme, but instead a rude assonance, by which the final syllables throughout a group of lines have the same vowel sound.[8] The story is that of Roland, count of the Breton march, who, according to Einhard, fell in the pass of Roncevaux when the rear-guard of Charlemagne's army was attacked by the Basques. But in the *chanson* the antagonists become Moslems instigated by a Frankish traitor; Roland becomes the champion of Christendom, the paragon of chivalry, who with sublime courage leads the Franks in desperate battle against overwhelming odds. Despite the wise counsel of Oliver, his loved companion-in-arms, Roland refuses to call for aid by sounding his horn until the fight is practically over and the few remaining Franks are doomed. Then, as the Moslems retreat before the advance of the main host, Roland dies in possession of the battlefield—a martyr to the Faith, whose soul is borne to paradise by the blessed arch-angels of God. For all its talk of Christianity, however, the real theme of the epic is vassalage. Roland is all that a noble vassal should be, all that the feudal knight could dream of being—the ideal of the fiercely warlike and naïvely religious aristocracy that spent itself on the First Crusade.

These *chansons de geste*, being chanted like the earlier sagas, obviously presumed at least a little musical knowledge on the part of the minstrel. Precisely what it was we have no way of discovering; but we are well informed with regard to ecclesiastical music. From an early time the church, for the major part of its service, had declared official the system known as plain chant. Under it certain limited scales are used in prescribed ways; the length of the notes is not rigorously defined, being varied to suit the rhythm of the Latin that is being sung; and all voices carry the same part in unison, without instrumental accompaniment. For less formal music, however, many instruments remained in common use: various kinds of harps, lyres, guitars, pipes, and horns, as well as a sort of organ in which water was used to compress the air. Furthermore, particularly through the experience

Mediæval music

---

[8] The meter and, to some extent, the assonance of the original are very happily reproduced in the translation of C. K. Scott-Moncrieff.

of monastic choirs, it became usual in Carolingian times for music to be sung in several parts—for example, with what we should call tenor and bass above and below the central melody. And by the same time, presumably through the influence of Arabic writers, Latin scholars were beginning to explain the division of music into regular measures, with an exact plan of designating the length of individual notes. From ecclesiastical usage, therefore, a writer of popular songs could learn much about musical as well as literary composition.

Lyrics of the troubadours

The relationship of music to vernacular literature becomes especially important in connection with the songs of the troubadours.[9] The earliest known examples—eleven lyrics dealing principally with love—bear the name of William IX, duke of Aquitaine (d. 1127), but they cannot have been actually the first. His verse reveals a finished rather than a primitive art and, although his native land was Poitou, he wrote in the dialect of Limousin, the language that is somewhat erroneously called Provençal. William, obviously, adopted an established literary form, the origin of which we are left to guess. It was not at all classical, and there is no evidence that it had been gradually evolved out of folk poetry. The more probable supposition is that the preliminary experimentation had been carried out by clerks already familiar with poetical expression in Latin. There is also the possibility of an Arabic tradition obscurely received from the Moors who had long ruled the province of Septimania. In the twelfth century, at any rate, an increasing number of southern French gentlemen devoted themselves to the writing of lyrics, which they set to music and sang to the accompaniment of a guitar.[10] And since the manuscripts, using the ecclesiastical system of musical notation, often indicate the tune along with the words of a poem, we may in some measure know how the troubadour's lay sounded to the fair lady who had inspired it.

[9] Provençal *troubadour*; French *trouvère*, a finder or composer.

[10] It is significant that the troubadour played his guitar with a bow and that this musical device was introduced by the Arabs.

The work of the troubadour, being intensely personal, was always known under his name. Thus from the twelfth and thirteenth centuries we have poems by some four hundred troubadours, and we know of many others whose writings have perished. Noble birth, though usual, was by no means essential to the success of a troubadour. For example, Bernard de Ventadour, one of the earliest and finest of Provençal poets, was the son of a domestic servant; Jaufré Rudel, who wrote the exquisite song of a distant love,[11] was a baron of Limousin; Marcabrun, famous for his invention of new literary forms, was a foundling; Bertran de Born, the comrade of Richard Lion-Heart, was a viscount of Périgord. From southern France the new literary fashion quickly spread to all the neighboring countries. Eleanor of Aquitaine, first at the Capetian and then at the Angevin court, continued to patronize a number of distinguished troubadours—with the result that, in the second half of the twelfth century, it became fashionable to write love songs in French. Meanwhile the feudal aristocracy of the north had retained its devotion to the old *chansons de geste*, which had come to form regular cycles dealing with a number of legendary dynasties. In them, as in the *Song of Roland*, the love motive hardly appeared. Now, under the influence of the troubadours, a different sort of long poem came to be especially popular—one dominated by a new code of politeness, *courtoisie*, in which the ancient masculine chivalry gave way to the glorification of women.

This literary form, composed in rhymed couplets to be read rather than chanted, became known as the romance. The subject matter is what will still be recognized as romantic: beautiful damsels, gallant knights, cruel husbands, sinister magicians, benevolent fairies, talking animals, mysterious forests, enchanted palaces, perilous quests, and the like. Love is always prominent and the exotic element is strong. The authors, finding no romantic charm in the old-

The romance: Marie de France

[11] See especially Helen Waddell's translation in her *Wandering Scholars*, p. 205.

fashioned epics, borrowed from antiquity themes concerning Alexander the Great, Æneas, and the siege of Troy. Yet, no matter when the scene was laid, the characters were made to act and talk like lords and ladies of feudal France. The famous cycle of King Arthur, mythical leader of the fifth-century Britons, began in much the same way. Some of the Arthurian material may have come into France by way of Brittany, but most of it seems rather to have been derived from Norman writers in England. Of the latter the most influential was Geoffrey of Monmouth (d. 1154), whose Latin *History of the Britons*, a combination of legend and sheer fancy, became a mine of treasure for poets and story-tellers. Among the first to dip into it was Marie de France, of whom nothing is known except that she was a well-educated Frenchwoman at the court of King Henry II and Queen Eleanor. From her pen we have about a dozen romances or, as she called them, lays. They include stories of a knight who changes himself into a falcon in order to visit his imprisoned lady-love (*Yonec*), of a fairy princess who carries her human lover to Avalon (*Lanval*), of a werewolf (*Le Bisclavet*), and of amorous adventures on the part of various Arthurian barons (e.g., *Gugemar*).

Chrétien de Troyes   Like Marie de France, Chrétien de Troyes in the later twelfth century took old materials and rewrote them to suit the *courtoisie* of the fashionable world. But by his time society was more sophisticated. Ovid's *Art of Love* and similar compositions in the vernacular were enjoying a great vogue. So, when Chrétien retold an ancient tale, he adorned his pages with elaborate pictures of beauty and chivalry in luxurious surroundings and with eminently polite conversations; and he constantly emphasized the psychology of love. Each of his romances is, in fact, a sort of problem play. For instance, his *Lancelot* turns on the conflict between a knight's honor and his love for a lady. In *Erec et Enide* the plot concerns the tests that one lover may properly demand of the other. These and other stories of the same type, after delighting the countless generations that have intervened, may still be read in the verse or prose of all European nations, and may even be heard in the form of grand opera from the stage of a metropolitan theater. There is, nevertheless, a limit to the enjoyment that one can receive from such literature. Sooner or later the world of make-believe, with its people who could never have lived and its events that never could have happened, grows tiresome. And after one has read a certain number of conventional lyrics, the charms of *belle Yolanz, belle Aiglentine,* and *belle Amelot* begin to pall. One longs for a point of view other than that of the fine gentleman with a fatal attraction for both queens and peasant girls.

Such a reaction in the thirteenth century helped to popu larize the *fabliaux*—stories composed in rhymed verse and, to judge from the subject matter, intended for the market place rather than the baronial hall. Being written for the sole purpose of provoking a laugh, they ignore all chivalrous prejudice. Members of the nobility rarely appear and, when they do, are treated as ordinary persons. And since peasants are considered too stupid to be interesting, it is the bourgeois class that receives the chief attention. The typical merchant is rich, but in all matters apart from his business apt to be a fool. The hero is generally the wandering clerk, a clever rascal who makes the most of any opportunity, whether for love, for gain, or for sheer amusement. When one of these fellows arrives, the sensible burgher locks up his valuables—also his wife and daughter; for, according to the *fabliaux*, women are never to be trusted. However beautiful and intelligent, they are devoid of morals. Equally unprincipled are priests and monks, who excel only in hypocrisy and amply deserve the grief that always befalls them. These, of course, are stock characters—such as today win laughs in the films and comic strips. It is not to be supposed that bourgeois audiences of the thirteenth century actually believed that there were no virtuous women or honest clergymen. The spice of the jest lay in depicting the opposite of what would be found in pious or romantic literature.

Modified
forms of
romance

Although some of the *fabliaux* are cribbed from the Latin classics and in others the wit does not rise above the level of plain smut, a good many are both funny and original. Applied to the romance, satirical humor of the same kind produced the well-beloved cycle of Reynard the fox. Drawing from German folklore as well as from the ancient fables of Æsop, the authors—we know merely that they were French clerks—built up a mock epic about King Noble the lion and his unruly vassals, who include Bruin the Bear, Isengrim the wolf, Tybert the cat, Chantecleer the cock, and others in addition to the reprobate hero. Reynard lives by thievery, plays cruel tricks on all his associates, lies his way out of court—and keeps the reader's sympathy throughout. His fame is still attested by the fact that in France any fox is *un renard*. Inevitably, too, the realistic touch came to be applied to the traditional romance, and the result, among lesser pieces, was the utterly charming *Aucassin et Nicolette*. The story is remarkable for both form and substance. The unknown writer not only alternates prose and verse with singular artistry; every now and then he turns an apparently conventional narrative in a very unconventional way—as when Aucassin admits that he would prefer hell to heaven, or when the cripple is miraculously cured by a glimpse of Nicolette's leg. We are even introduced to a human villein, who dries the hero's tears by ·describing his own wretched existence.

Allegories

Meanwhile romantic literature had also come to be affected by a very different influence. This was allegory, the form of mystic interpretation extensively used by the schoolmen. If a Christian meaning could be found in the Hebrew Bible or in the works of pagan antiquity, why could not one be read into the tales of King Arthur and the Round Table? So the ancient materials were again reworked to produce a new cycle of prose romances—the famous series that is built round the quest for the Holy Grail. About the same time Guillaume de Lorris set another literary fashion with his allegorical *Romance of the Rose*.[12] Here the Rose typifies the Lady sought by the Lover, who is aided or impeded by Idleness, Danger, Evil-Tongue, Fear, Shame, Fair-Welcome, Reason, and the like. His device, being quickly adopted by a host of other writers, proved especially popular in dramatic representations—the morality plays that for hundreds of years delighted audiences with more or less realistic impersonations of the virtues and vices.

For the beginnings of the mediæval drama we must, of course, look to an earlier age, when on special occasions the liturgy of the church was enlarged by the insertion of added features. At Easter, for example, the choir might present the story of the Resurrection, or at Christmas that of the Nativity. From merely singing the sacred story, the participants came to act it out, with appropriate costumes and stage effects. Thus arose the religious plays called mysteries, the themes of which were taken not only from the Bible but also from the lives of popular saints—a practice that allowed the introduction of many a homely touch drawn from real life. At first the mystery, being a supplement to the regular service, was presented inside the church and in Latin. Later the performance was often transferred to the porch or to a stage erected beyond it. And since the object of the play was to instruct the people, it might to good advantage be put in the vernacular. A very early example of such composition is the *Mystère d'Adam*, written in the first half of the twelfth century. The parts were of course taken by clergymen, and for their benefit the stage directions are in Latin; but the dialogue is in French verse, amazingly spirited and with a touch of subtle wit that is wholly delightful. Though ecclesiastical drama might become more elaborate, it could hardly be more effective.

In the literary use of the vernacular during the twelfth and thirteenth centuries France led and Europe followed.

Growth of the drama

German literature

---

[12] For the additions by Jean de Meun, see below, p. 355.

The southern French set the fashion in lyric; the northern
French in all other forms of poetic composition, as well as
in prose—with Villehardouin's memoirs of the Fourth Crusade and Joinville's life of St. Louis.[13] Anglo-Saxon had virtually disappeared as a literary language after the Norman
Conquest of England. And although the old Germanic traditions were yet maintained in far-off Iceland, they had been
generally abandoned on the continent. From the twelfth
century on, German writers devoted a good part of their
time to translating and adapting the poetry of France. Much
of their work, being mere imitation, was naturally inferior;
but by the thirteenth century certain German developments
of the Arthurian cycle—especially the *Tristan* of Gottfried
von Strassburg and the *Parzifal* of Wolfram von Eschenbach
—had attained striking originality. And the ranks of the
local troubadours, or *Minnesinger*, had come to include at
least one great lyric poet, Walther von der Vogelweide. Born
of a noble family in the Austrian Tyrol, Walther began his
literary career at Vienna; subsequently, as a professional
poet, he wandered from court to court, finally to be rewarded
with a small fief from the emperor Frederick II. Walther's
later poetry thus tended to be of the bread-and-butter variety, and to suffer from overly intricate meters and rhyme
patterns. His finest lyrics are those of his youth—simple love
songs like the famous *Unter den Linden*.

Spanish and Italian literature

In contemporary Spain and Italy the literary models were
likewise French and Provençal, and most poets, when they
came to use their own vernacular, were satisfied with copies
and adaptations. Yet the great Spanish epic of the Cid, a
semi-legendary character of the earlier wars, began to take
form in the twelfth century—with the *Poema del Cid*, of
which only a fragment remains. We have no Italian epic or
lyric for another hundred years, and nothing especially remarkable before Dante, whose glorious career will be
sketched in a later chapter.

[13] See below, pp. 280-81.

4. ROMANESQUE AND GOTHIC ARTS

The languages evolved from Latin in the Middle Ages we Origins of Roman-esque call Romance, whereas the architecture that was evolved from Roman elements during the same period we call Romanesque. In French both ideas are expressed by the same word, *roman;* and that usage is more logical than ours, for the parallel between the two developments is very striking. In eastern Europe, as already remarked, the sixth and following centuries witnessed the perfection of the architectural style known as Byzantine, which, with modifications, came to be widely used throughout Moslem countries. In parts of Italy, too, Byzantine influence remained strong—especially at Venice, where as late as the eleventh century the church of St. Mark was modeled after that of St. Sophia at Constantinople. Yet, despite a few borrowings of this sort, the separation of the Latin and Greek worlds was no less decisive in art than in other phases of civilization. When, with the economic recovery of western Europe, the local prelates were able to undertake new and monumental structures, they generally preferred what they considered the true Roman tradition and designed their churches on a basilican plan.

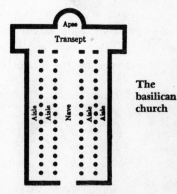

The basilican church

Extensively used by the Romans for public meetings, the basilica was a simple rectangular building divided lengthwise by rows of columns into a nave and aisle (see Figure 7). Illumination was provided by a clerestory—the section over the nave, elevated above the rest and set with windows (see Figure 8). The principal

FIGURE 7.—GROUND PLAN OF A BASILICAN CHURCH.

entrance was normally at one end of the nave; the other end was frequently rounded to form an apse, where, on a raised platform, the Romans placed the chair of the presiding officer. For that, however, the Christians substituted their altar and, when constructing a new basilica, oriented it so that the apsidal end would be towards the east. To north and south, furthermore, they often added a transept, bringing the whole into the shape of a Latin cross. The interior,

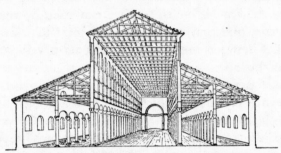

FIGURE 8.—SECTION OF A BASILICAN CHURCH.

plentifully supplied with light, could be gorgeously decorated —with marble columns, inlaid panels, gilding, fresco, and Byzantine mosaic.[14] But all this splendor was only too likely to be ruined by fire. While the walls of the basilica might easily be made of brick or stone, the roof, in order to be held on its fragile supports, had to be of timber—and such roofs often caught fire and burned.

Romanesque construction

The main problem confronting mediæval builders was therefore the covering of the entire building with stone vaults, and out of their experience in this connection were evolved the great structural systems known as Romanesque and Gothic. For vaulting a rectangular area the Romans had employed two devices. The simpler was the barrel vault, a half-cylinder of masonry, the weight of which was equally distributed along the supporting walls. In the other case the area was divided into squares, and over each of these bays, as they are called, two barrel vaults were made to intersect at right angles (see Figure 9). The weight of such a cross

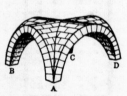

FIGURE 9.—CROSS VAULT.

[14] For example, Sant' Apollinare at Ravenna, Plate IV.

vault was concentrated at the four corners (A, B, C, D), which were joined by four semi-circular arches (AB, BC, CD, DA) and by two groins (AC, BD). In the basilican church the aisles could readily be cross-vaulted; for the thrust of the arches towards the nave could be counteracted by the weight of heavy clerestory walls resting on sturdier columns, while that towards the outside could be met by placing buttresses, thick fins of masonry, against the exterior walls. The more difficult task was to vault the nave. Transverse lines from column to column would divide it into oblong rather than square bays. How could half-cylinders of different diameters be made to intersect on the same plane? And how could the clerestory walls be buttressed over the aisle roofs? So builders rarely attempted to cross-vault a nave. Instead they raised a barrel vault, and its mass tended to doom both clerestory and colonnade. Since the walls on which the vault rested had to be of uniform thickness, they could not be pierced for windows of any useful size; and to support such walls slender columns had to be replaced by enormous piers.

The Romanesque church with a vaulted nave consequently has a low, gloomy interior, characterized by massive stonework, extensive flat surfaces, and strongly marked horizontal lines. These principles necessarily hold good whether the building was put up in Italy, Germany, France, Spain, or England, although minor differences of style could be produced by varying the arrangement of the essential parts or the decoration of the exterior. Scores of examples could be given, but space permits mention of only a few. The cathedral of Pisa, dedicated in 1118, is justly renowned for its leaning bell-tower, its arcaded façade, and its sumptuous interior, adorned with varicolored marbles. Structurally, however, it is somewhat primitive. Only the aisles are cross-vaulted; the nave is covered by a timber roof, which permits the retention of a windowed clerestory and of antique columns to support it (see Plate III). The contemporary buildings of Lombardy, less elegant in form and materials, are

Italian Romanesque

better illustrations of Romanesque construction. Among them the most interesting is the church of Sant' Ambrogio at Milan, the rebuilding of which was begun in the eleventh century. Here the nave is divided into five bays, each corresponding to two in the aisles and so obtaining a square outline. Three of the bays are cross-vaulted, with heavy diagonal ribs set along the groins; one is barrel-vaulted; and one is topped by a low octagonal tower to admit light over the altar. Without such illumination the interior would be very dark, for a continuous gabled roof covers the church and there is no clerestory at all (see Plates III and IV).

German and French Romanesque

Since the greater Romanesque churches of Germany, like the cathedral of Pisa, were originally built with timber roofs over their naves, they have little to offer by way of innovation in vaulting. Their chief originality lies in their general design. Often they were planned with a western as well as an eastern apse and with the main entrance, consequently, on one side. Sometimes they have two transepts. In any case the ends of the church are commonly marked by groups of three towers, as in the famous abbey of Laach (see Plate III). French Romanesque, on the contrary, held to the tradition of a single transept and a single apse, with a place thus reserved for a western façade—one of the glorious features in all the Gothic cathedrals of France. Furthermore, the French architects came as a rule to enlarge the apse by adding a number of concentric chapels, so perfecting what is known as the *chevet*. An early example of the completed design is to be seen in the monumental church of Saint-Sernin at Toulouse.[15] But even here, it should be noted, the covering of the nave with a barrel vault reduced the clerestory windows to a row of mere port-holes.

Indeed, the normal system of Romanesque construction throughout Lombardy, Provence, southern France, and Spain called for cross vaults over the aisles and a barrel vault over the nave. In the churches of Saint-Trophime at Arles and of Notre-Dame at Clermont-Ferrand, for instance, the nave

---

[15] The tower and steeple over the crossing are later additions; see Plate III.

is covered by solid masonry shaped on the outside to form
a gabled roof and on the inside a barrel vault—an enormous
weight borne on thick walls buttressed over the aisles by
quadrant vaults, quarter-cylinders of stone that leave no
room for clerestory windows (see Figure 10). The interior
of such a building is inevitably dark; its beauty is one of
strength and majestic proportion. By way of compensation,
therefore, the exterior was often
handsomely decorated. Thus the
church of Saint-Trophime has an
especially fine cloister and a magnificent portal, on which elaborate
carvings are happily combined
with plain surfaces (see Plate V).
Compared with this sculpture,
which clearly suggests classic inspiration, that of Vézelai, a Burgundian abbey begun in the later
eleventh century, seems barbarous
(see Plate X). Yet, for all its
crudeness, the sculpture of Vézelai has extraordinary vigor—an
original quality that marks the
emergence of a new art rather
than a reminiscence of the past.

FIGURE 10.—SECTION OF
NOTRE-DAME (Clermont).

The abbey of Vézelai is also
remarkable for the cross-vaulting of the nave, through which
the bold designer obtained a relatively high clerestory (see
Plate V). What he did not understand was how to buttress
the transverse arches from the outside; so, if it had not been
for subsequent improvements, the vault would have collapsed. The solution of his problem came with the invention
of the flying buttress. Frequently, in the case of a barrel-
vaulted nave, continuous support had been provided along
the sides by means of quadrant vaults under the aisle
roofs (see Figure 10). When cross-vaulting was similarly employed, such a quadrant vault would logically be reduced to

Gothic
construc-
tion: The
flying
buttress

a series of curved buttresses placed against the points that needed support. But these points, if a high clerestory were erected, would be far above the aisle roofs. No matter— some adventurous builder, ignoring tradition, brought the buttresses out from their concealment and made them "fly" through the air to meet any thrust from the interior arches. And his device made possible the architecture misnamed Gothic.[16]

The rib-and-panel vault

Two other prerequisites for this development were the pointed arch and the ribbed vault. Neither was new in the twelfth century. The Arabs, long before, had used pointed arches for the sake of variety in decoration, and in a number of Romanesque churches barrel vaults had been designed with a pointed section to reduce the outward thrust on the walls (see Figure 10). The great architectural advance came with the adoption of the unconventional form in order to simplify cross-vaulting. As noted above, trouble had been experienced in putting a cross vault over an oblong area. Half-cylinders of different diameters could not be made to intersect without resorting to clumsy expedients. But eventually the fact came to be realized that, if the half-cylinders were pointed, the task could be accomplished easily and elegantly; for the height of a pointed arch can be varied without changing its breadth. Meanwhile, from at least as early a time as the planning of Sant' Ambrogio at Milan, diagonal ribs had sometimes been set along the groins of a cross vault. And experience proved that, under such conditions, lighter stone could be used to cover the intervening

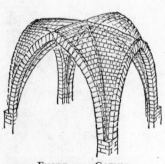

FIGURE 11.—GOTHIC VAULT.

[16] It had, of course, no connection with the Goths. As the result of the fifteenth-century reaction against the mediæval styles, the term Gothic came to be used as a synonym for barbarous; see below, p. 351.

spaces. Thus the weight of the vault would be reduced and a considerable saving made in the cost of materials. The next step was to turn these ribs into pointed arches and make them intersect at the geometrical center of the bay, whatever its shape might be. Finally, without regard to the traditional surfaces, thin slabs of stone could be arched from one rib to the next (see Figure 11).

The Gothic skeleton

The Romanesque building, no matter what its decorative pattern, had continued to be a series of walls holding up a roof. The perfected Gothic building, on the contrary, was a towering framework of slender masonry piers and arches supported from the outside by flying buttresses. As far as stability was concerned, it needed no walls, even after the vaults had been completed and slanting timber roofs had been placed over them to keep off the weather. When architects came to appreciate this truth, they enlarged the windows of aisle, clerestory, and apse, so that glass filled virtually the entire space from one pier to the next. The interior was

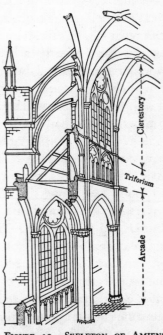

FIGURE 12.—SKELETON OF AMIENS CATHEDRAL.

thus flooded with light; the massive columns, the heavy arches, the extensive wall spaces that had characterized the Romanesque style disappeared. The three horizontal stages of the nave—arcade, triforium, and clerestory—were still indicated by delicate mouldings, but their height was enormously increased and all structural members received soaring outlines that rose from the pavement to the crown of the vault (see Figure 12).

The development sketched above can be traced step by step in the churches of northern France. By the middle of the twelfth century pointed-arch construction had come to be well understood, but the buildings then erected were likely to keep such vestiges of the Romanesque as round-arched windows, massive piers, and cylindrical columns. Even the cathedral of Notre-Dame at Paris retained the old-fashioned columns in the nave, whereas the transept and apse were finished in the more advanced style of the later century. Discrepancies of this sort are, in fact, characteristic of almost all the great French cathedrals; one portion of the church would be antiquated before another was started, and continual changes would be introduced as the work progressed. To appreciate the masterpieces of Gothic, we must therefore compare individual features rather than entire structures. Among all the Gothic façades, that of Notre-Dame at Paris may be hailed as the loveliest, by virtue of its rather primitive simplicity, its graceful proportion, and its complete harmony (see Plate VI). That of Amiens is marred by its superstructure—an addition made long after the body of the church had been erected. That of Chartres combines Romanesque towers with one masonry spire of the twelfth century and another of the sixteenth. That of Reims, though symmetrical, is excessively ornate, reflecting the tendency of the later Gothic to degenerate into meaningless decoration. But the monumental plan of this cathedral deserves all the praise it has received (see Figure 13). The exterior of the nave, with its series of pinnacled buttresses, has great dignity and charm (see Plate VIII). And its double-aisled transept leads to a magnificent apse set with five semi-circular chapels. The cathedral of Paris, too, is famous for its *chevet*—internally, a marvel of Gothic vaulting; externally, an intricate pattern that artists along the Seine never tire of sketching (see Plate VIII).

The beauty of a Gothic masterpiece, it should be noted, arises directly from its structural design, to which all decorative effects are rigorously subordinated. To give windows a fancy outline, to spread exuberant sculpture across a façade, or to cover a roof with spires and pinnacles is not and never has been to produce a Gothic building. Any one who has imagined that the Gothic style implies a lavish display of ornament should study the interiors of such cathedrals as Chartres, Reims, and Amiens. There he will find, aside from the pictures in stained glass, only the simplest of designs. The capitals and an occasional moulding are carved in unostentatious patterns, and a little delicate tracery may be

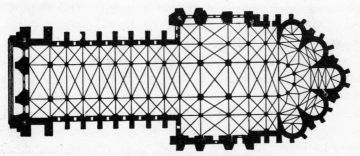

FIGURE 13.—GROUND PLAN OF REIMS CATHEDRAL.

added to set off the openings in the triforium and elsewhere. That is all, except for an almost incredible refinement of structural outlines. In the undecorated stonework of nave, transept, aisle, and apse, rather than in some accidental feature of the exterior, is to be seen the acme of Gothic art (see Plate IX). And in mere point of size these buildings are impressive. The nave of Chartres reaches a total height of 106 feet, that of Reims 125 feet, and that of Amiens 141 feet. Only one Gothic structure is still loftier—the cathedral of Beauvais, which collapsed twice in the course of construction and was never finished.

Perfected in the Ile de France, the Gothic style quickly spread to the adjoining provinces and by the close of the thirteenth century had come to exert an influence throughout the Latin world. The results on the whole were mediocre. In the southern regions pointed-arch construction was

The spread of Gothic to the south and east

at best an imported fashion which never wholly displaced
the older Romanesque and which rarely was well developed.
To the Italians, in particular, Gothic was largely a system
of decoration—one that too often degenerated into a riot of
peaks and spikes and pointed openings. In Germany there
was little Gothic construction before 1300, and what there
was merely followed French models. In some cases, as at
Worms, a rib-and-panel vault was placed over a purely
Romanesque nave; in others a larger portion of the church
was rebuilt in the perfected style. At Strasbourg a pleasing
effect was obtained; but the pretentious cathedral of Cologne, which was not finished until the nineteenth century,
is generally felt to lack refinement. For all its plainness,
German Romanesque is artistically superior to the German
adaptations of Gothic. From this point of view the more significant advance in architecture was made by the English.

Roman-
esque and
Gothic in
England   In Britain a new and glorious age of church-construction
was begun by the Normans, for the Saxons had never been
great builders. The style introduced by the conquerors was
of course the Romanesque of Normandy, best exemplified
by the two abbeys founded at Caen by William I and his
wife Matilda. Both now have various features that were
added at a later time. But, below the superstructure of the
towers, the Abbaye-aux-Hommes still preserves the original
façade—a massive and rather grim design that, greatly elaborated, reappears in the magnificent cathedral of Durham (see
Plate VI). Many other famous churches retain portions of
the old Norman work, which can everywhere be identified
by its tremendous bulk and strength, as well as by its simple
ornamentation in zigzags, diamonds, and other geometrical
patterns. This architecture, before the close of the twelfth
century, was generally superseded by the form of Gothic
that is locally known as Early English. Its chief characteristic
is the pointed arch, frequently introduced for decorative effect only. Of the churches actually based on pointed-arch
construction an especially fine example is Lincoln Cathedral
(see Plate VII). Salisbury Cathedral, for the most part erected

between 1220 and 1258, is perhaps the most symmetrical expression of the Early English ideal. But here, as in many of the English cathedrals, the relatively low vaults are supported by massive walls that render flying buttresses unnecessary—a system of construction that is modified Romanesque rather than Gothic (see Plate VII). Judged by the contemporary French standard, the purest English Gothic is to be found in Westminster Abbey, which is built on a complete framework of ribs and buttresses.[17]

French pre-eminence in mediæval architecture as a whole **Gothic** has often been disputed, for many critics continue to prefer **glass** a Romanesque or semi-Romanesque style to the logically perfected Gothic of the Île de France. In the decorative arts, however, French pre-eminence throughout the Age of the Crusades is unquestioned. For the best sculpture of the twelfth and thirteenth centuries we must turn to the cathedrals of Chartres, Reims, and Amiens. And the stained·glass of these same churches remains the despair of the modern artist. One factor in the success of the mediæval craftsman was that he never treated a window as other than a flat translucent surface. Attempting neither realism nor perspective, he gained his effect by the simplest of means. His figures were outlined by the strips of lead in which the pieces of glass were set, and for this glass only solid colors were used, with details of face or costume indicated by a few pencil touches. The great rose windows, placed to catch the rays of the setting sun, are geometrical designs of plain glass set in stone tracery. The principal windows of nave and aisle, on the other hand, commonly portray stories from the Bible or the lives of the saints. Here are to be found the most graphic examples of symbolic art—scenes from the Old and New Testaments to show the harmony of the Scriptures, animal fables to illustrate the life of Christ by mystic analogy, and the like.

---

[17] The eastern end of the church is original Gothic of the thirteenth century; the western façade is an unfortunate addition designed by Wren and built in the eighteenth century. See Plate IX.

Much the same generalization holds true of the major sculptures on a mediæval cathedral. They were placed there to teach lessons as well as to adorn the building. So, before we judge the work of the artist, we must remember what he was hired to do. It was the ecclesiastical authorities who dictated all the principal designs; and many of the latter had to follow traditions already established in Romanesque and Byzantine usage—for example, the four beasts of the apocalypse which may be seen over the main portals of Chartres and Saint-Trophime (see Plates V and X), or the pictures of the Last Judgment to be found on many of the great churches. The art of such carvings, being conventional and symbolic, could never be made to portray actual people and actual things. The artist had somewhat greater latitude when statues were ordered. Yet even here he generally had to produce sculptures of sacred persons, of characters from Biblical history, and of saints—to express a religious ideal rather than to depict living people.

The skill with which the Gothic statuary of the thirteenth century was made to observe these prerequisites, and at the same time to be intrinsically beautiful, is one of the world's artistic triumphs. It is an absurd legend that all mediæval art is stiff and lifeless. The twelfth-century sculpture that adorns the façade of Chartres is, to be sure, distinctly primitive in certain respects. The statues beside the main portals are elongated like columns and resemble in their complete rigidity the forms of Byzantine mosaic; yet the faces are strongly individual and sometimes very handsome (see Plate X). This, we may say, is the sculpture of the transition. When we turn to the perfected Gothic style of the thirteenth century, we find that sculpture has lost its archaic stiffness and is characterized throughout by charming ease. The principal statues, still imbued with religious idealism, have become lifelike from head to foot. Famous Gothic masterpieces of this kind decorate the façade of Amiens, the porches of Chartres, and virtually the whole cathedral of Reims. Against the walls of that church, for example, stand the marvelous draped figures of Mary and Elizabeth, almost Athenian in their dignity and grace (see Plate XI). And the minor sculptures of Reims, compositions in which the artist was allowed to enjoy much greater freedom, are often very fine—especially the capitals carved with scenes from the French countryside (see Plate XI). This is naturalistic art of a high order. All that was necessary for its further development was to end its subordination to architecture, and such independence was actually brought about in the period that immediately followed.

5. THE PROBLEM OF ECCLESIASTICAL REFORM

To sketch the achievements of the twelfth and thirteenth centuries in arts and letters is to pay constant tribute to the influence of the church, which for the better part of a thousand years had been the dominant institution of the Latin world. It should always be remembered, however, that the church controlled much which it could not create. The armies and fleets that made possible the capture of Jerusalem were not in themselves clerical. The fact that a boy learned to read and write in an ecclesiastical school was no assurance that he would produce ecclesiastical books. A cathedral was designed by architects and built by skilled workmen, not by the bishop who ordered its construction. And the money with which he bought materials and hired labor was amassed principally through contributions by the faithful. In other words, man-power and talent and wealth were devoted to the service of the church because of its inspiring hold on the minds of the people. This it could not afford to risk for the sake of outworn prejudices or ambitions.

The church and the world of the thirteenth century

At the opening of the thirteenth century the church was faced with a number of grave problems. As remarked in the previous chapter, the papacy was pledged to a tradition of political intervention and dictation that, to be even moderately successful, required an Innocent III in the Roman see. Could the magnificent dream of Christian unification, however promising in the days of Urban II, be actually realized a hundred years later? All subsequent experience with the crusades had proved that, from the papal point of view, times had sadly changed. Economically, the western states were already emerging from the feudal age. On all sides ambitious princes were developing stronger governments, with ministers trained for professional service and with revenues drawn from the mounting wealth of the towns. Could the church, as was vitally necessary for its continued strength, maintain the loyalty of the bourgeois class? Ecclesiastical organization had been perfected to meet the demands of an agrarian society; urban populations, rapidly growing outside that organization and living a life utterly foreign to its traditions, had found themselves misunderstood and neglected. Now, within such bourgeois environments, the universities were taking form. How could the church effectively govern the new associations of unruly masters and students? And how could it secure the reconciliation of the new learning—mainly the work of pagans and Moslems—with the sacred principles of Christianity?

Anti-clerical agitation

In the course of the twelfth century anti-clerical movements, almost invariably led by townsmen, steadily gained headway. One current of criticism runs through the *fabliaux* and other bourgeois writings, to culminate in a series of great satirical works that will be examined in a later chapter. But these compositions, like the Goliardic literature, hardly go beyond coarse jesting and irreverent burlesque; they attack the corruption of the church rather than the church itself. The same can be said of the preachers who denounced the clergy as politicians and money-getters, exhorting them to return to the pure simplicity of apostolic times. For example, Arnold of Brescia, an eloquent theologian who had studied at Paris, gained a large following in the Italian cities by advocating the abolition of clerical property. Arrested by Frederick Barbarossa at the request of the pope in 1154, Arnold was hanged by the Roman authorities as a rebel— not, it should be noted, as a heretic.

Peter Waldo (Pierre Valdo), a well-to-do merchant of

Lyons, rose to fame through popular agitation of much the same kind. It was about 1170 that he, inspired by the precepts of the Gospel, devoted all his wealth to charity and organized a group of Poor Men to engage in work among the people. Although the original project was approved by Pope Alexander III, Waldo soon embroiled himself with the local clergy. He and his Poor Men were accused of unauthorized preaching in the course of which, by means of a Provençal translation, they interpreted the Bible to suit themselves. So in 1179 the pope ordered Waldo to submit to episcopal authority—and he replied that he must obey God rather than man. Finally, in 1184, the Waldensians were excommunicated and driven from Lyons. As a proscribed sect, they quickly developed heretical doctrines, reviving the Donatist assertion that the validity of a sacrament depended on the character of the minister[18] and establishing their own forms of worship without an ordained clergy at all. Like the later Protestants, they tended to discard all dogma and practice that were not specifically mentioned in the New Testament. Their missionary zeal was prodigious. Spreading into southern France, Spain, Italy, and the Rhinelands, they merged with various other groups of ecclesiastical rebels, such as the converts recently made by Arnold of Brescia.

The Waldensians

It was not, however, the Waldensians whom the rulers of the church most detested; rather it was a totally different sect, the members of which called themselves Cathari (i.e., the Pure). Apparently originating in the Byzantine Empire through a combination of earlier heresies, Catharism was brought by traders to the growing towns of Italy and southern France, where by the time of Innocent III its supporters were generally known as Albigensians, from the city of Albi in the county of Toulouse. Their success was due in large measure to popular dissatisfaction with the established church. It was the especial boast of the Albigensians that, without a richly endowed clergy, they attained a higher standard of morals than was dreamed of by orthodox Chris-

The Albigensians

[18] See above, p. 47.

tians. Besides, their doctrines had certain practical advantages. Like the ancient Manichæans,[19] they maintained two disciplines: one for the ordinary man and one for the perfected. The latter was pledged to rigid asceticism, including celibacy and a vegetarian diet. The former had only to revere his bet.ers until, at the last moment, he might be fully initiated and so die in purity. Any one who thus ended his life was assured of paradise. The soul of the impure man was doomed to inhabit a lower animal; for, according to the Albigensians, there was neither a hell nor a purgatory. In the absence of a strong central authority, their theology varied somewhat from congregation to congregation; but in general it was based on a sharp dualism of spirit and matter, light and darkness, good and evil.

By the close of the twelfth century the Albigensian heresy had attained such proportions in southern France that the ordinary agencies of the church were powerless to combat it. Most of the local clergy were suspect, and the efforts of papal investigators and missionaries broke down before the indifference or hostility of the princes. Innocent III, as usual, acted circumspectly; but in 1208 the murder of his legate at the court of Raymond VI, count of Toulouse, precipitated a crisis. Declaring Raymond excommunicate and deprived of his county, Innocent offered the lands and goods of his heretical subjects to any Christian warriors who would enlist in the sacred cause. This was the famous Albigensian Crusade, the political results of which will be seen in the next chapter. As far as heresy was concerned, the pope's holy war was unquestionably effective. The Albigensian cause, together with the prosperity and culture of Languedoc, fell in ruin. Innocent's successors were left with merely the task of stamping out the remnants of dissent—one for which they found invaluable assistants within the new mendicant orders.

St. Francis of Assisi Between heresy and sainthood the gulf is normally thought of as wide and deep. Yet Peter Waldo and Francis of Assisi began their public careers in almost identical fashion. The

[19] See above, p. 54.

son of a prosperous cloth merchant, Francis in his earlier years was known as a gilded youth of luxurious tastes and fastidious ways. Disliking his father's business, he became a soldier. He was captured in the course of a local war and while in prison experienced a severe illness. Then, on his return home, a series of incidents revealed a change in his character. Instead of avoiding lepers, he gave them personal care. He renounced all his wealth and dressed himself as a hermit. Being convinced that, while praying, he had received a divine command to "repair My house, which is everywhere falling into ruins," he began, with a few other volunteers, to rebuild various abandoned churches in the neighborhood of Assisi. It was not until he chanced to hear the reading of Christ's commission to the apostles[20] that the true purport of his call became clear to him.

Francis took literally the admonition to "provide neither gold nor silver nor brass in your purses, nor scrip for your journey, neither two coats nor yet staves; for the workman is worthy of his meat." Henceforth he devoted himself to absolute poverty, traveling barefoot and living by charity while he preached the Gospel and ministered to the sick and needy. Soon he was joined by a band of followers, the nucleus of what quickly became a far-reaching organization, for the success of the movement was immediate. Especially in the towns the Franciscans caused a sensation. Here were men who, by example as well as by words, revived the simple faith which Jesus had inspired in His disciples. Francis called himself and his men the Friars Minor, that is to say, the Lesser Brothers. It was indeed as a kindly brother that he treated every one, including the meanest outcasts of society. In all nature he found a keen and reverent delight. And in gratitude he wrote hymns of praise to God, employing, not the language of formal worship, but the Italian vernacular. One of these songs, fortunately, has come down to us. In it he thanks the good Lord for brother sun who lights the day; for sister moon and the stars; for brother wind and sister

20 *Matthew*, x, 7-10.

water and brother fire, so gay and strong; for mother earth, who sustains us by her fruits; and, lastly, for sister death.

Happily for the church, it was at that moment headed by a great statesman. Innocent III, appreciating the opportunity that lay before the papacy, was careful to guide, rather than to antagonize, the reforming energy of the friars. They were at once authorized to maintain their desired poverty, not merely as individuals but as a group, and to preach repentance. And shortly afterwards Innocent sanctioned a similar organization for the followers of one Dominic, a Spaniard who had long been engaged in missionary work among the Albigensians. Before the middle of the century both Franciscans and Dominicans had come, under papal control, to adopt elaborate constitutions and to carry their religious activities to the ends of the Christian world.

Thus, as will be more fully shown in the closing chapter, the papacy acquired a vast army of preachers, scholars, and charitable workers who, among them, solved the greatest problems confronting the church. Thanks mainly to the Franciscans, the spiritual needs of the masses, in and out of towns, could be better satisfied. Thanks mainly to the Dominicans, heretics could be more effectively refuted and the new learning of the schools brought into magnificent agreement with the traditional ideals of Christian education.

CHAPTER VIII

CHURCH AND STATE IN THE LATER MIDDLE AGES

··

1. THE HOLY ROMAN EMPIRE AND EASTERN EUROPE

Frederick II, son of Henry VI, was unquestionably a Hohenstaufen; yet few mediæval kings were less German than he
was. He and his reign are to be explained rather by the fact
that, as the grandson of Roger II, he fell heir to the Sicilian
kingdom, and with it to the tastes and talents of the Hauteville dynasty. Left an orphan at the age of four, Frederick was
brought up in his native land of Sicily under the wardship of
Innocent III. He never saw Germany until 1211, when he
was elected king in opposition to Otto IV. By that time he had
been declared of age, had been married to Constance of
Aragon, and by her had a son, Henry (see Table VI). During
his youth he had played a cautious game, remaining in all
ways submissive to his papal guardian; but this docile exterior
had come to conceal a fully matured character. At eighteen
Frederick II was a statesman who had already determined his
policies, a many-sided genius who was soon to astonish the
world.

To secure Innocent's support in Germany, Frederick had
formally repeated the broken promises of Otto and had sworn
that, as soon as he obtained the imperial crown, he would
confer upon his infant son the sovereignty of Sicily, to be
held under papal wardship. Later, on Innocent's proclamation
of a new and greater crusade, Frederick had taken the cross.
But in 1216 Innocent was succeeded by Honorius III, an
elderly and benevolent cleric who, though a good administrator, lacked all cleverness as a politician. Frederick, taking
advantage of the favorable situation, now postponed his crusade and, through grant of extraordinary privileges, induced
the German magnates to accept Prince Henry as king. By

*Frederick
II and the
papacy*

thus abandoning Germany in order to concentrate attention upon Italy, Frederick reversed the policy to which he had been solemnly pledged. In 1220, nevertheless, the amiable Honorius crowned him emperor, and it soon became apparent that the coronation had confronted the papacy with a very real danger. Frederick II's design was no such dream of Roman imperialism as had dazzled his predecessors. To create an actual kingdom of Italy, he had only to annex a few northern provinces to the magnificent state inherited from Roger II. Within six years, thanks to the pope's enthusiasm for the future crusade, the emperor had pretty effectively asserted his authority throughout the peninsula.

Frederick's crusade (1228-29)

The first challenge to Frederick's ambition came with the installation of a new pope in 1227. Gregory IX was not only an eminent student of canon law but also a fiery champion of the papal tradition. Ecclesiastical penalties, he declared, would at once be imposed if the promised crusade were further postponed. Frederick, as it happened, now had a personal interest in the project, for he had recently taken as his second wife the heiress of the kingdom of Jerusalem. After he had actually embarked, however, he came down with a disease then prevalent among his troops and was forced to return for medical treatment. Thereupon he was promptly excommunicated by the pope and, remaining unrepentant, was still under the ban of the church when he again sailed for Palestine in 1228. On his arrival, Frederick continued his unorthodox behavior. Making skillful use of local jealousies among the descendants of Saladin, he secured by treaty what had been the despair of all Latin hosts for the past forty years. The Christians received possession of Jerusalem, as well as a strip of territory connecting it with Acre, in return, merely, for a guarantee that resident Moslems could freely worship in their two great mosques. Within a year after leaving Italy Frederick victoriously entered the Holy City and there assumed the royal crown—a remarkable crusade, which triumphed in the face of papal excommunication, and without a battle.

The success of Frederick's expedition failed to abate Gregory's hostility. While Christian rule was being restored at Jerusalem, the pope was absolving the emperor's subjects from their oaths of fealty and calling upon the faithful to invade and conquer the imperial dominions. It was not until 1230 that Frederick obtained absolution after agreeing to rather severe terms. The peace, though hailed as a great ecclesiastical victory, was only the prelude to another extension of Frederick's power. With his crusade officially blessed, the emperor now resumed his European projects where they had been dropped three years before. At this time, for example, he published the famous decrees that made his Sicilian kingdom into a sort of enlightened despotism. An insurrection in Germany caused him only momentary embarrassment; a graver threat was the revival of the Lombard League by the communes of northern Italy. But Frederick II was more fortunate than his grandfather Barbarossa had been. In 1237 it was the communal army that went down to crushing defeat at Cortenuova. The inevitable result was a fresh crisis with the papacy. An exchange of violent recriminations was followed by open war, in which Gregory allied with the defeated league, and Frederick began the systematic reduction of the Papal States. The death of the pope brought no more than a lull in hostilities; for his successor, Innocent IV, renewed the conflict after a few years of apparent reconciliation. Finally, in the midst of further conspiracies and revolts, the great emperor suddenly died (1250).

Italian activities

Frederick's hope of creating a real Italian kingdom thus remained unfulfilled; yet his reign should not, on that account, be considered a failure. Quite apart from his imperial ambitions, his achievements as king of Sicily were sufficient to rank him among the world's greatest statesmen. His *Liber Augustalis* was the finest secular code to be issued since the time of Justinian. Being drawn up by "civilians" at the royal court, the work was, of course, inspired by Roman example; but its substance was drawn from the legislation of his Norman predecessors. For every major feature of Frederick's gov-

Legislation and economic administration

ernment precedents had existed under Roger II—for his combination of Latin, Greek, and Arabic institutions; for his monopoly of warfare and of military fortification; for his improved method of detecting and trying criminals; and for his toleration of Jews and Moslems. It should not be imagined, however, that Frederick believed in complete religious liberty. Although any of his subjects could lawfully be converted to Christianity, the Christian, under penalty of death as a heretic, was required to maintain strict orthodoxy.

Frederick's administration was especially noteworthy in the economic sphere. Throughout the Sicilian kingdom he abolished all internal tolls and substituted a tariff (Arabic *tarif*) collected at the state frontier. He established a series of monthly fairs, each held in a different region. He negotiated commercial treaties with the Moslem princes of northern Africa. He proclaimed royal monopolies in salt, iron, tar, hemp, and silk. By experimentation on his own estates and by offering inducements of various kinds, he sought to improve agriculture and the breeding of domestic animals. He made special efforts to introduce the date palm, indigo, sugarcane, cotton, and other Asiatic plants. His minting of *augustales* in 1231 marked the resumption of gold coinage in Latin Europe.[1] He encouraged immigration, colonized waste lands, and founded a number of new towns. He was the first to call representatives of the bourgeoisie to meet with the barons and other important persons in regularly constituted assemblies.[2]

Habits and interests

Like his Norman predecessors, Frederick lived in a semi oriental magnificence that amazed and somewhat shocked his Christian contemporaries. We need not entirely believe all the scandalous stories that were told about him by his enemies —as that he maintained a harem. Yet he very likely did bathe on Sunday! And his reputation for skepticism was undoubtedly based on fact. Frederick was not characterized by a childlike faith; a highly educated man, with a knowledge of Latin

[1] See below, p. 319.
[2] See below, p. 337.

Greek, and Arabic in addition to the Romance vernaculars, he took keen delight in all intellectual problems. For the sake of study, as well as of display, he kept a wonderful menagerie that, among other strange birds and beasts, contained ostriches, parrots, monkeys, leopards, panthers, lions, camels, a giraffe, and a great royal elephant. His own book, *On the Art of Hunting with Birds,* is not simply a manual of falconry; it is introduced by a general sketch of ornithology and includes much that the author had learned through personal observation. Under such patronage the pre-eminence of the Sicilian court in the arts and sciences became even greater than before. European civilization is deeply indebted to this most original of mediæval emperors.

The death of Frederick II introduced an age of political chaos for central Europe. The emperor's eldest son, Henry, was already dead; his second son, who for some years had reigned in Germany as Conrad IV, died in 1254. Thereupon the Sicilians, defying the papal authority, recognized Frederick's illegitimate son Manfred, a handsome youth with much of his father's brilliance and popularity. But in 1266 Manfred was slain in battle with Charles of Anjou, a French prince to whom Pope Clement IV, also a Frenchman, had offered the crown of Sicily. This action, though quite in accord with feudal law, involved the peninsula in a series of ruinous wars and brought lasting discredit to the papacy. By the end of the thirteenth century the kingdom of Italy had ceased to exist and the kingdom of Sicily had been broken up. In the Holy Land, meanwhile, Frederick's restored kingdom had come to a melancholy end with the Moslem capture of Acre in 1291. Thereafter the great crusade was merely a glorious memory. *Italy after Frederick II*

The later thirteenth century also witnessed the final disintegration of Germany. Even while Frederick II lived, his northern kingdom had been virtually abandoned to the local princes. With the disappearance of the Hohenstaufen dynasty, they for a time continued to rule the country without a king at all. And when they finally agreed to hold an election, they *Germany: Rudolf of Habsburg (1273-91)* deliberately chose an obscure Alsatian landgrave named Rudolf of Habsburg. The new king very sensibly accepted conditions as he found them. He never went to Italy and even at home made no effort to revive the monarchical power. Instead he devoted his energy to improving the fortunes of his own family—a project in which he won remarkable success. Rudolf's opportunity arose when Ottokar, king of Bohemia, refused to recognize his accession or to attend his court. After the rebel's fiefs had been declared forfeit, Rudolf took the field against him and slew him in battle. Seizing Austria, Styria, Carinthia, and Carniola, which Ottokar had held of the German crown, Rudolf gave them to members of his own house. Thus was established a Habsburg dominion on the upper Danube that was to persist until 1918 (see Map XIV).

Charles IV (1346-78) The later history of mediæval Germany may be passed over very briefly. The kingdom remained as a sort of theoretical union symbolized by an elected king, but the latter had no real power beyond what he might enjoy as the ruler of a hereditary principality. The royal office was chiefly valuable because it enabled the holder to enrich himself and his family through the acquisition of vacant fiefs. It was in this way, as we have seen, that the Habsburgs first gained prominence. It was in the same way that Henry of Luxemburg, elected in 1308 because of his poverty, advanced the fortunes of his house. For his son he obtained the kingdom of Bohemia, which was inherited by his grandson (see Table VIII). The latter, who also acquired the German crown as Charles IV, deserves special mention because he gave the Czechs of Bohemia an excellent government, based on a wise reform of their ancient institutions, and because he there founded the illustrious university of Prague. In Germany, furthermore, his reign was memorable for the promulgation of the so-called Golden Bull of 1356, which confirmed and regulated the traditional procedure used in royal elections. It recognized seven electors: the archbishops of Mainz, Trier, and Cologne, together with the king of Bohemia, the count palatine of the

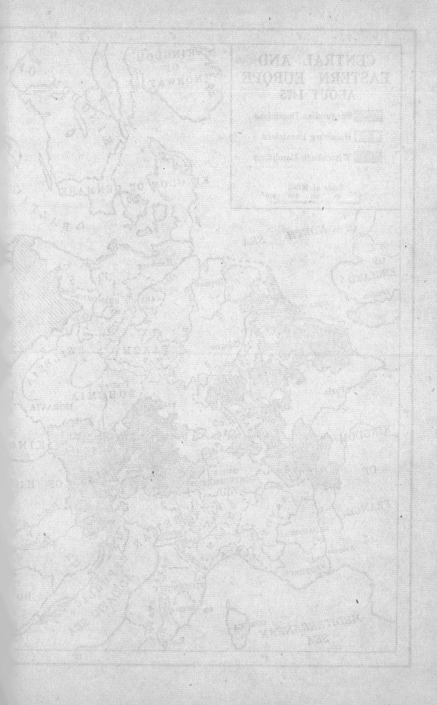

CENTRAL AND EASTERN EUROPE ABOUT 1475

Burgundian Dominions

Habsburg Dominions

Wittelsbach Dominions

Scale of Miles
0   50   100   150   200

KINGDOM OF NORWAY

KINGDOM OF DENMARK

BALTIC

NORTH SEA

KM. OF ENGLAND

London

Hamburg

Bremen

MARK OF BRANDENBURG

Elbe R.

Weser R.

Ems R.

Oder R.

ZEELAND

HOLLAND

Utrecht

GELDER-LAND

FLANDERS

ARTOIS

Calais

Cambrai

PICARDY

BRABANT

HAINAULT

Liège

Cologne

SAXONY

SILESIA

KIN

LUXEM-BURG

Trier

Mainz

ALSACE

Prague

BOHEMIA

MORAVIA

Paris

Seine R.

Rhine R.

LORRAINE

FRANCHE COMTÉ

PALATINATE

BAVARIA

AUSTRIA

Danube R.

KING

KINGDOM OF FRANCE

DUCHY OF BURGUNDY

SWISS CONFEDERATION

TIROL

Salzburg

STYRIA

CARINTHIA

OF HU

Rhone R.

SAVOY

MILAN

VENETIAN REPUBLIC

Venice

MANTUA

CARNIOLA

Drave R.

Save R.

CROATIA

BO

DAUPHINÉ

Avignon

PROVENCE

GENOA

MODENA

PAPAL STATES

FLORENCE

SIENA

Tiber R.

ADRIATIC SEA

MEDITERRANEAN SEA

CORSICA

Rome

Rhine, the duke of Saxony, and the margrave of Brandenburg. The electors were to assemble within a month after a king's death and, if at the end of thirty days they had failed to reach a decision, they were to be put on a diet of bread and water until they did so. By other articles which guaranteed the vested interests of the great princes, Charles assured the persistence of the monarchy. Under his plan, it is worth noting, the papacy lost all opportunity of reviewing the action of the electors, and future kings were encouraged to assume the imperial title without coronation at Rome. The popes of course protested; but since the emperor no longer asserted any control over Italy, they had no valid cause of complaint.

Under Sigismund, son of Charles IV, the Luxemburg house attained its height of glory, for a while combining the three crowns of Bohemia, Germany, and Hungary. But Sigismund's reign, disturbed by the Hussite wars and the Ottoman conquests in the Balkans,[3] was far from happy; and on his death without heirs the Habsburgs acquired the major part of his dominions (see Table VIII). This, of course, was only one of many dynastic relationships to affect the later history of Germany, which had now been broken into scores of little principalities. In the present connection it is impossible even to name the local states. And of the many unions established for the sake of common defense only two can be mentioned. One was the Hansa, the great association of German towns, which will be discussed when we come to the subject of Baltic trade. The other was the Swiss Confederation, founded in 1291 by the mountaineers of Uri, Schwyz, and Unterwalden as a means of assuring their rights of self-government. The Habsburgs, who had held political control over this territory, vainly sought to enforce their authority. The league—greatly strengthened by the inclusion of other cantons, together with the towns of Lucerne, Zürich, and Bern—won a decisive victory at Sempach in 1386 and thenceforth enjoyed complete independence.

Origin of the Swiss Confederation

Turning our attention to eastern Europe, we find that by

[3] See below, pp. 278, 360.

Eastern European peoples

1250 two major changes had been made in the political map. As a consequence of the Fourth Crusade, the Byzantine Empire had all but disappeared, while another great horde of Asiatic nomads—the Mongols or Tartars of Jenghis Khan and his successors—had destroyed the Russian state and subjected its inhabitants.[4] For the Christian lands farther west it was sheer good fortune that the Mongols now diverted their energies towards Mesopotamia, where in 1258 they took Bagdad and slew the last of the Abbasid caliphs. The three kingdoms along the German border thus escaped serious danger: Hungary, which included Croatia and so reached the Adriatic; Bohemia, which had been definitely incorporated in the Holy Roman Empire as a fief of the German crown; and Poland, which like Hungary had thrown off its earlier dependence on Germany. To the north along the Baltic lived a series of peoples who were still for the most part heathen: between the Vistula and the Dwina the Prussians, Lithuanians, and Letts, speaking an Indo-European language that was neither Slavic nor Germanic; farther eastward the Livs, Kurs, Esths, and Finns, speaking a variety of Ural-Altaic dialects.

The Teutonic Knights and the revival of Poland

If the Polish monarchy had remained as strong as it had been two hundred years earlier, the southern Baltic coast might have had an altogether different fate. But by the thirteenth century Poland had badly weakened, and the Germans, already in possession of Mecklenburg and Pomerania, found nothing to prevent their advance into Prussia (see Map XV). The project of Christianizing another heathen land naturally received the support of the papacy, with the result that in 1230 the direction of the Prussian war was given to the Teutonic Knights. This religious order, like the Templars and Hospitallers, had originally been founded as an organiza-

[4] The city republic of Novgorod maintained its independence, and so became affiliated economically with the Hansa (see below, p. 326). The nucleus of modern Russia was the principality of Moscow (Muscovy), whose rulers led a successful revolt against the Tartars towards the close of the fourteenth century and then, in the course of the next two hundred years, subjected all their Russian rivals.

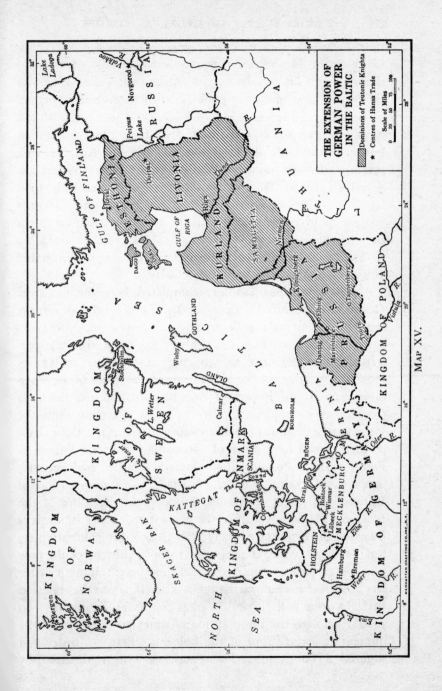

THE EXTENSION OF
GERMAN POWER
IN THE BALTIC

☆ Centres of Hansa Trade

▨ Dominions of Teutonic Knights

Scale of Miles

0   20   50   75   100

MAP XV.

tion of crusaders in Palestine; now, with the victorious advance of the Moslems, its activity was gradually diverted to the north. In 1237 it absorbed a similar order, the Knights of the Sword, that had been established by a missionary bishop in Livonia, and together the two won great success. Within a hundred years the whole Baltic coast from the Pomeranian border to the Gulf of Finland was held by the Knights, who there, under the nominal control of the papacy, exercised sovereign powers. On all sides they carved out fiefs to be held by German barons, settled the devastated areas with German peasants, and, co-operating with the Hansa,[5] built new towns for the benefit of German merchants. Much of their work has never been undone. Prussia, especially, became a thoroughly German country, and so remains today.

Once its conquest had been completed, however, the great German order rapidly decayed. By the second half of the fourteenth century the Teutonic Knights were suffering from the evil consequences of material prosperity. And at this particular time Poland came to enjoy a dramatic revival of strength. A series of able kings restored the unity of the kingdom, gave it an improved constitution, and extended its frontiers to include Galicia on the south. Then, in 1386, the Poles won a great diplomatic victory by marrying the heiress of their crown to Jagiello of Lithuania, thereafter known as Ladislas II of Poland. Since Jagiello's father had recently taken the Ukraine from the Tartars, the incorporation of Lithuania brought the Polish kingdom to the shore of the Black Sea. It was even more important that the Lithuanians followed the example of their ruler in accepting Christianity; for the Poles, without prejudice to holy church, could now join forces with a people who had long been waging a bitter war against the Teutonic Knights. The climax in the renewed struggle came with Jagiello's great victory at Tannenberg in 1410. Although the intervention of other powers limited the immediate acquisitions of the Poles, the Prussian order had suffered a fatal blow. The Peace of Thorn, dictated by

[5] See below, p. 326.

Jagiello's grandson in 1466, awarded West Prussia to Poland in full sovereignty, while the Teutonic Knights were to hold East Prussia merely as a fief of the Polish crown.

In the Balkans, meanwhile, the Byzantine Empire was entering upon the last dismal stage of its long history. Although a Greek emperor regained the throne at Constantinople in 1261, he could not restore the empire even as it had been in the twelfth century. The control of the Ægean, with its islands and the coasts of the Peloponnesus, was kept by Venice; much of Greece remained in the hands of French barons; and the emperor's possession of his other European provinces was disputed by the revived kingdoms of Bulgaria and Serbia (see Map XIII). First one and then the other of these states, under rulers who had assumed the imperial title of tsar, threatened to reduce the whole peninsula and to take the city of Constantinople. But each eventually fell back exhausted. Nor could any more Christian co-operation be expected from the Italians, Hungarians, and Poles than from the Bulgars, Serbs, and Byzantines. It had been proved by sad experience that the Latins were quite as willing to fight one another as to fight schismatic Greeks. Like the project of re-uniting the eastern and western empires, Innocent III's dream of healing the breach between the two churches had long since faded when the Balkan scene was invaded by a new enemy, the Ottoman Turks.

The tremendous drive of the Mongols in the thirteenth century, though checked on the Syrian frontier by the Mamelukes of Egypt,[6] destroyed the caliphate of Bagdad, together with the last remnants of the Seljuk sultanate. One of the immediate results was a westward migration of nomads from the interior, especially into the borderlands of Christendom, where opportunities for loot and conquest were most promising. Among such invaders of Anatolia was a band of Turkish Moslems who, under a chief named Osman (d. 1386),

The Balkan states

The rise of the Ottoman Turks

[6] Originally the slaves who constituted the palace guard of the sultan, the Mamelukes became the rulers of Egypt during the crusade of St. Louis and so remained until the time of Napoleon Bonaparte.

established themselves to the northwest of Dorylæum. This was the beginning of the remarkable dynasty called Osmanli or Ottoman. Orkhan, son of Osman, took Nicæa and, by seizing the adjacent coasts, forced the Byzantine emperor to abandon his last Asiatic province. Then, as befitted his enhanced dignity, Orkhan assumed the title of sultan and made his conquests into a territorial monarchy. To him in particular would seem to be due the splendidly organized Turkish army with its famous corps of Janissaries, entirely recruited from the families of subjected Christians.

Meanwhile, through employment as imperial mercenaries, the Turks had become very familiar with the situation in the Balkans and so had been encouraged to send raiding expeditions across the strait at Gallipoli. Finally Murad, Orkhan's successor, launched a major European offensive. Taking Adrianople in 1361, he adopted it for his capital and thence delivered a series of crushing blows against the disunited forces of the Christians. The subjection of the Bulgarians brought the sultan's power to the Danube and the Black Sea. The overwhelming defeat of the southern Serbs resulted in his conquest of all Macedonia. And when the Slavs of the northern Balkans finally decided to renounce their local jealousies for the sake of a counter-offensive, they suffered the same fate. At Murad's death the little that remained of Serbia was a tributary state of the Turks; the Byzantine Empire had been reduced to hardly more than the city of Constantinople.

The fall of Constantinople (1453)

The invasion of Anatolia by another Asiatic horde under Timur in 1402 gave the hard-pressed Greeks a brief respite; but in the following years the Ottoman advance again proved irresistible. Under Mohammed I and Murad II Turkish dominion was extended throughout most of Asia Minor, and a number of crusades, led by heroic kings of Hungary and Poland, were eventually thrown back. By the middle of the century the Ottomans were rapidly pushing into Bosnia and Wallachia as well as into southern Greece (see Map XVI). Constantinople, long doomed, surrendered to Mohammed II in 1453. Except for the pale ghost in the west, there was no longer a Roman Empire.

MAP XVI.

2. FRANCE, ENGLAND, AND THE DECLINE OF THE PAPACY

The year 1223 saw the passing of Philip Augustus, who had brought the French monarchy to a new height of power. So unquestioned was the Capetian authority that the king had found it unnecessary to crown his son during his own lifetime, and Louis VIII inherited the throne as a matter of course. Aside from this fact, his brief reign is memorable only for his participation in the Albigensian Crusade, originally proclaimed by Innocent III in 1208. As the result of earlier expeditions, the county of Toulouse had been taken from Raymond VI and given to Simon de Montfort, a French adventurer who had proved his military genius by a series of brilliant victories. But Simon's heir had been unable to prevent Raymond VII, son of the old count, from regaining his

Louis VIII and the acquisition of Toulouse

patrimony. So, with the blessing of the church and at its expense, Louis VIII now set out to conquer the disputed territory for himself. Having stormed Avignon, he received the submission of many other cities and was on the point of capturing Toulouse when he suddenly fell ill and died.

Louis IX and his crusade

It was fortunate that the able Blanche of Castile was now proclaimed regent for her infant son Louis IX. She promptly defeated the hostile moves of various ambitious barons and extorted an advantageous treaty from Raymond of Toulouse. That portion of the county which had already been taken was to remain in the king's hands; the rest should pass with the hand of Raymond's daughter to one of the king's brothers. Accordingly, when Louis IX assumed control of the government, Capetian rule had actually been extended to the shore of the Mediterranean (see Map XII). By this time, too, the great Angevin principality had been reduced to a mere fragment of the old Aquitaine, popularly called Guienne. Although Burgundy and Brittany remained virtually independent, neither was at all formidable. Flanders, since Baldwin IX had secured the crown of the Latin Empire,[7] had rapidly come under the dominance of the French court and was now on the verge of a paralyzing civil war. Blois and Champagne, once again separated, were held by peace-loving vassals. As the future was to show, the greater peril to the monarchy lay in the new practice of conferring feudal estates, or appanages, on members of the royal house (see Table II).

Being delivered from the necessity of constant war against jealous princes, Louis IX could devote his energies to whatever projects lay near his heart. It was thus possible for him to be a successful king of France and at the same time to lead a saintly life; for he was canonized by the church in 1297. As between these two phases of his career, it was of course the latter that especially impressed his contemporaries and inspired the justly famous memoirs of Joinville, which were written long after the king's death. Louis, beyond doubt, was deeply and sincerely religious. All the acts of his reign testify

---

[7] See above, p. 217.

to the fact that he was fundamentally a mystic whose first thought was for heaven. While governing his kingdom as a matter of duty, he always found time for prayer, meditation, and ascetic practices. He seems to have married and reared a family principally for reasons of state; at any rate, Joinville says that for five years on end he never heard the king refer to wife or children. Even among his intimates, though always kind and gentle, Louis remained strangely detached— a man to be revered rather than loved. In all matters of belief he was exceedingly conventional, and, in taking the cross against the advice of his mother and of all his ministers, incredibly naïve.

With a pathetic ignorance of the Saracens and their world, he led a fine army across the sea in 1248, only to have it captured, together with his royal person, in a mismanaged campaign on the lower Nile. The net result was a frightful loss of life and the payment of a huge ransom to the Moslem victors. Later, on the persuasion of the pope, Louis agreed to support his brother, Charles of Anjou, for the Sicilian crown—another costly and far from creditable venture. Finally, as an old man, he insisted on undertaking a second crusade, this time against Tunis. And when the inevitable pestilence hit the army while still on shipboard, Louis was among the first of its victims. Joinville, who lived to thank God that he had refused to join this foolish expedition, frankly declared that those who had encouraged the king to go committed mortal sin. If he had stayed in France, he might have lived to do a great deal of good, but since his departure the kingdom had never been the same.

A king whose heart was thus set on visionary crusades would naturally tend to follow a pacific policy in other respects. Louis made no attempt to profit by the misfortunes of the Hohenstaufen dynasty; nor did he take advantage of a feeble administration in England to complete the conquest of the Angevin inheritance. Had he done so, he might have saved his country from the horrors of a long war; instead, he agreed to a treaty by which the English king was to obtain double

Government of Louis IX

his present fief, plus a considerable sum of money, in return for his abandonment of all claim to Normandy, Anjou, and Poitou. In the sphere of domestic government Louis's reign was less noteworthy for the establishment of new institutions than for the development of old ones—and precisely what the king's personal influence was in such matters is somewhat conjectural. For both France and England it was an age of rapid legal and constitutional progress which was carried on by an army of trained civil servants with or without much royal supervision.

In both countries the great central organ of government was the king's feudal court, or *curia regis*. Normally it consisted of a few permanent ministers; but to grant aids, proclaim campaigns, or transact other extraordinary business, it might be expanded by a general summons to all royal vassals. Already filled with professional judges and administrators under Philip Augustus, this *curia* in thirteenth-century France tended to break into separate groups, each with a special function. So, under Louis IX, we find two subdivisions maintaining their own peculiar records: the *chambre des comptes*, which had charge of the king's revenues, and the *parlement*, his court of justice at Paris. In all such matters of central organization the French kings had much to learn from Norman-Angevin example. Thence too came many lessons in local administration. Under Philip Augustus and his successors districts within the royal domain were assigned to officials called bailiffs (*baillis*) in the north and seneschals (*sénéchaux*) in the south, who exercised very much the same powers as the English sheriffs. And to supervise the working of his government, Louis IX regularly sent out *enquêteurs*, royal agents like the itinerant justices of England, empowered to hear complaints and to hold investigations (*enquêtes*).

The English government and Magna Carta

In England Henry II's governmental system had continued to run smoothly in spite of his sons' many distractions. It was, in fact, the efficiency of that system which enabled the unpopular John to act despotically and so to invite a general insurrection of the barons in 1215. Momentarily yielding, the king agreed to the baronial demands by issuing the famous *Magna Carta*, in which he promised to do many things and not to do many others. And although the pope declared the original charter null and void, it was reissued in modified form and repeatedly confirmed under succeeding kings. *Magna Carta* was not, as nineteenth-century scholars generally believed, a great monument of national liberty. Its concession of privileges to the "freemen of England" could not apply to the mass of the people, which was still thoroughly servile. Interpreted in the light of contemporary usage, the Great Charter will be found to contain little beyond provisions dictated by baronial interest. Most of the articles were conservative or perhaps reactionary. The barons wished, first of all, to define the rights of the king as feudal lord and so to prevent a number of unwarranted exactions. Furthermore, they sought to undo much of Henry II's reform by restoring to their own courts some of the cases that had been diverted to royal courts. A few articles deserve to be called progressive because in certain particulars they recognized the king's improvement of justice. But *Magna Carta* itself established virtually nothing that was new. Even by insisting that the king was below the law, it enunciated no revolutionary principle. There were many things that a feudal prince was not supposed to do; the difficulty was to prevent his doing them if he were powerful enough to defy the threat of insurrection. The problem was an old one and to it *Magna Carta* brought no solution. The final article of the original grant merely set up a baronial committee to hear complaints and to authorize war against the king if he failed to give redress; and even that was dropped in the reissues.

Aside from continuous quarrels over the enforcement of *Magna Carta*, leading eventually to a short-lived Barons' War, the reign of Henry III (1216-72) was politically uneventful. England, sharing in the great cultural advance that has been described in the preceding chapter, remained essentially French in civilization. The most distinctively English developments of the age were in the sphere of law and administration

Edward I and the common law

—developments to which no exact dates can be assigned, but which tended to reach a culminating stage under Henry III's statesmanlike son, Edward I. By that time the royal courts, thanks to ingenious extension of the common law by the king's judges, had secured almost a monopoly of important judicial business. Ecclesiastical courts still enjoyed a variety of powers. The boroughs and certain other localities long preserved their own peculiar customs. Baronial courts continued to deal with servile tenures and to claim other prerogatives, though their criminal jurisdiction was strictly interpreted as a delegation from the monarchy. Jury trial, established only in civil disputes by Henry II, had now become regular also in case of indicted criminals. Such a person, after Innocent III's prohibition of ordeal, could no longer be tried in the old way and was compelled to submit the question of his guilt or innocence to a specially selected panel of jurors.

By the time of Edward I there had also been a significant evolution of the English courts; as in France, the *curia regis* had tended to subdivide into a number of distinct organizations. The first to take form was the exchequer, which kept the financial accounts of the kingdom and sat as a court of law for fiscal cases. In the thirteenth century it came to have a separate personnel under a chancellor of the exchequer, the official who is today an important member of the British cabinet. The second offshoot from the central *curia* was the court of common pleas, permanently set apart for the trial of cases between private citizens. Suits to which the king was a party normally followed his person until Edward I constituted another permanent court styled the king's bench. The three great courts of common law, thus fixed at Westminster, remained essentially unchanged until the nineteenth century. Below them were the circuit courts, held in the counties by regularly empowered justices on mission. And exceptional matters of all kinds could yet be taken to the king by means of petition—the procedure that later gave rise to the supplementary legal system called equity.

Even more significant for the history of England and of the world was the development of the assembly that became known as parliament. The word long retained its literal meaning—a talking or discussion, rather than a particular group of men. In thirteenth-century England it was especially applied to deliberations of the king's central *curia*. Established custom, as set forth in *Magna Carta*, required that for all scutages and extraordinary aids the king had to secure the consent of the baronage. And since the lesser barons were only too glad to avoid the expensive journey to court, parliaments came to include only the greater barons, lay and clerical—those who were summoned by individual letters. This group, later known as the house of lords, was therefore the original parliament, which then constituted, as it still constitutes, the supreme court of England. But for business other than judicial, parliaments also came to include deputies of the counties and boroughs. In particular, the mounting cost of the royal government necessitated more and more frequent demand for special subsidies—a regular system of taxation in place of the occasional aids, scutages, tallages, and the like of the previous century. Experience proved that the best results were obtained from a uniform levy on the personal property of all classes and that, to facilitate assessment, all classes should be asked to make a voluntary grant. Under Henry III the sending of representatives from the counties and boroughs for such purposes was only occasional; under Edward I it became normal. The result, by the middle of the fourteenth century, was that an official parliament had to include, in addition to the ancient council of the barons, two burgesses chosen in each borough and two knights chosen in each county court. Eventually these men from the English communities combined as one body and so were called the house of communes or, as we know the term, commons.

The development of parliament

Edward I, of course, could not foresee that his enlarged parliament, by controlling the royal income, would eventually establish what we understand as a constitutional form of government. In his day the more important issues appeared to

The conquest of Wales

be his relations with the French king and with his rivals in Britain. Long before his accession the mountainous peninsula between Bristol Channel and the Irish Sea had come to be divided into two main portions: the southeast under a series of Norman lords marchers and the northwest under a Welsh prince who acknowledged himself the vassal of the English king. In 1272 Llewelyn, prince of Wales, foolishly refused the accustomed homage and thus gave Edward a good excuse for marching against him. Finally, after Llewelyn had submitted and again rebelled, his country was incorporated with England and has so remained down to the present—leaving only a memory to be perpetuated by the title, Prince of Wales, that is borne by the king's eldest son. A more important consequence of the Welsh war was Edward's reform of the army. From experience in the field Edward learned how to supplement a force of knights with light-armed troops, especially infantry equipped with long-bows; and this military lesson, coinciding with the king's policy of weakening the nobility, led him to supersede the old feudal tenures by a system of voluntary enlistment and pay. The superiority of the army thus formed was soon demonstrated in Scotland.

The conquest and loss of Scotland

Although the English kings had long claimed a vague overlordship in the north of Britain, Edward was the first of them to exercise any real authority there. His opportunity arose from a disputed succession to the throne in 1290. Having been invited to arbitrate the affair, he awarded the crown to John Balliol. The new king, in accordance with a previous agreement, duly became Edward's vassal, but rebelled when his lord called on him for service in France. Thereupon Edward took his army north, deposed Balliol, and set up a government of his own. A Scottish insurrection under William Wallace led only to another English victory. Using his long-bows to prepare for a cavalry charge, Edward annihilated the Scottish array at Falkirk in 1298 and once more established his rule throughout Britain. The Scots, however, refused to submit. A new uprising was headed by Robert Bruce, who assumed the crown in 1307, just before Edward was succeeded by his incompetent son. Attempting to punish the Scottish rebels while ignoring the military lessons of his father, Edward II suffered crushing defeat at Bannockburn in 1314—a battle that established the independence of Scotland for the next three centuries.

Meanwhile, in 1285, the French throne had passed to Philip IV, whose handsome face won him the nickname of Philip the Fair. Otherwise little is known of his personality. Either through weakness or through stealth he allowed everything to be done for him by his ministers, principally laymen trained in the new universities and devoted to the traditions of the civil law. Whatever the reason, Philip IV identified himself with an ambitious, mercenary, and unscrupulous government, which carried out measures of serious consequence both to France and to Europe as a whole. One of his chief concerns was of course the relation to the crown of the ancient French principalities. Failing an opportunity to secure a great fief by escheat or forfeiture, the king inevitably sought to undermine the baron's power by extending direct control over his subjects. Languedoc, the old county of Toulouse, had now been wholly incorporated in the royal domain and Philip IV, by marrying the heiress of Champagne, had recently acquired that glorious territory. Since Burgundy and Brittany were of secondary importance, the royal attention would naturally be concentrated on Guienne and Flanders.

Philip IV of France (1285-1314)

Edward I, in lawful possession of Guienne, could be counted on to resist all French encroachment and to push his claim to the lands promised by Louis IX but never received. The count of Flanders was a much weaker antagonist. To all practical intents his state was a union of great self-governing cities, whose prosperity depended on the cloth industry and so upon the importation of wool from England. By threat of embargo the English king could normally force the count into alliance, although the Flemish aristocracy, fearing the urban mob, tended to be strongly pro-French These issues are worth emphasizing because they lay at the root of the so-called Hundred Years' War that began in the

Flanders and Guienne

next century. Edward I and Philip IV engaged in only brief hostilities, the former encouraging the count of Flanders to oppose French aggression, the latter supporting the rebel Scots under Wallace. When the two kings signed peace in 1298, each deserted his allies. Edward, as we have seen, thereupon conquered Scotland, while Philip conquered Flanders. But the mass of the Flemish population, consisting largely of weavers and their apprentices,[8] refused to accept French domination. Having seized control of their cities, the burgher militias met and defeated an invading French army at Courtrai in 1302—the first great victory of infantry over cavalry since the advent of the feudal age in Europe. Although Philip somewhat repaired his fortunes in later campaigns, he was soon persuaded to abandon his design of annexing Flanders and to restore the count; for in the meantime he had become embroiled in a much greater controversy with Pope Boniface VIII.

The papacy and the Sicilian question

It has already been noted that the papacy, in order to break the Hohenstaufen power, had given the Sicilian kingdom to a brother of Louis IX, Charles of Anjou. The latter, dazzled by his success in Italy, failed to perceive any danger to himself in the rise of Aragon across the Mediterranean to the west. A new era had begun for that little kingdom in 1150, when it was acquired through marriage by a count of Barcelona. Henceforth established on the sea, Aragon was pushed southward at the expense of the Moors, finally to include, under James the Conqueror (1213-76), the port of Valencia and the Balearic Islands (see Map XVII). It was his son Peter III who now, being married to a daughter of Manfred, showed an interest in the kingdom of Sicily. In 1282, when the Sicilians rose in revolt and massacred all the French on the island, Peter happened to be nearby with a fleet. Having once landed and accepted the crown from the rebels, he refused to yield, even when the pope proclaimed a crusade against him. Although Charles of Anjou, and after him his descendants, continued to style themselves kings of Sicily, they had no

8 See below, p. 322.

authority in the island of Sicily, which remained loyal to the house of Aragon. This was the origin of the famous Two Sicilies, still marked on the political map of Europe in the middle of the nineteenth century.

The test of a good politician is success. In their effort to be successful, the popes of the thirteenth century had forgot-

MAP XVII.

ten that there are nobler ambitions—and that popes could not always succeed. By identifying themselves with the Angevin cause in Italy, they suffered defeat along with it. The papacy, as a secular power, never recovered from the Sicilian disaster; and the ensuing war of revenge against Aragon served only to proclaim the utter degradation of the crusading ideal. Within the cardinal college the natural result was a violent anti-French reaction, which carried into power the unfortunate Boniface VIII (1294-1303). He was a man of considerable ability, especially in law and business administration. Despite the charges hurled against him by his enemies, he appears to have been rather a misguided enthusiast than a monster of corruption. The principles to which he gave his passionate devotion had been consecrated by centuries of tradition. But times had changed. The papacy had lost much of its moral force and it was now pitted against strongly organized states, not the pseudo-Roman emperors of a bygone age.

Boniface
VIII *vs.*
Philip IV

The first sensational move of Boniface was to forbid all secular princes to levy taxes on the clergy without papal authorization. Though based on good ecclesiastical theory, the decree could not be enforced. In the face of prompt action by Edward I and Philip IV, and of a feud with the Colonna faction in Italy, Boniface reluctantly modified his position. Then, encouraged by the defeat of his local enemies and by the enthusiastic celebration of a papal jubilee in 1300, he repeated his earlier prohibition and followed it with an admonition to Philip IV that the French could not fail to regard as insulting. Philip's reply, though supported by a representative assembly of the nation,[9] coincided with his defeat at Courtrai. So Boniface did not hesitate to continue his offensive with the bull *Unam Sanctam*,[10] declaring in extreme form the theocratic ideal of the papacy: that the bishop of Rome is the supreme authority on earth in both spiritual and temporal matters and, the judge of all others, is himself responsible to God alone. The sequel to this pontifical utterance would have been ludicrous had it not been so tragic. Nogaret, one of Philip's ablest and most unscrupulous ministers, joined with the more vindictive members of the Colonna faction in seizing the pope when he happened to visit Anagni. Although soon released, the aged Boniface never recovered from the shock. Broken in mind and spirit, he died only a month later. So disgraceful an affair was in itself no moral victory for the French king. That he could turn it to advantage is further proof of the discredit into which the papacy had fallen.

[9] See below, p. 295.

[10] The formal decrees of the popes are called bulls and are commonly known by the first few words of the Latin text.

In 1305, after the death of a short-lived successor, the papal office was conferred on the archbishop of Bordeaux, who assumed the name of Clement V. If some had expected him, as the vassal of the English king, to be unfriendly to Philip, they were quickly disillusioned. Clement at once quashed the offending decrees of Boniface and gave full absolution to those who had insulted him at Anagni. Then, delaying his journey to Rome, he co-operated with the French king in the notorious trial of the Templars. The members of that distinguished order, though no longer engaged in crusading, enjoyed the amassed wealth of earlier generations and actively continued in the banking business.[11] This was itself equivalent to treason in the eyes of a government that consistently persecuted all money-lenders. The Templars in France were arrested and accused of horrid crimes. Nogaret, placed in charge of the investigation, secured useful confessions by the application of torture. Finally, in 1314, Clement abolished the order and bestowed most of its property on the Hospitallers, who were still engaged in charitable work. But in France the royal government kept the Templars' cash and refused to surrender their lands until a variety of alleged expenses had been paid.

Clement V and the fall of the Templars

Meanwhile Clement had established himself at Avignon, in a territory that had come to the pope as a result of the Albigensian Crusade. Though not legally in the French kingdom, the city was encircled by Capetian holdings. And as a majority of the cardinals came to be Frenchmen who detested Italy, the temporary sojourn lapsed into a permanent residence. Clement was thus the first of six French popes who maintained their government at Avignon. Life was indeed pleasanter and safer on the Rhone than on the Tiber. But the peace and comfort of Avignon were more than counterbalanced by the fact that, to remain there, the popes had to absent themselves from their proper see. The very essence of their authority was the Roman episcopate; separation from the Petrine city, except in case of dire necessity, could be no

The "Babylonian Captivity" of the papacy

[11] See below, pp. 319-20.

less than a scandal in the eyes of the devout. Personally the Avignon popes were by no means inferior to most of their predecessors. They were, however, more successful as jurists and administrators than as religious leaders. While the inspirational failure of the church was bewailed by a growing multitude of the faithful, the popes seemed chiefly concerned with the maintenance of a luxurious court and the raising of unprecedented sums to support it. How the situation, bad as it was under the Avignon papacy, became infinitely worse with the Great Schism of 1378 will be seen in a later section.

3. THE HUNDRED YEARS' WAR

The fundamental issue

What is popularly known as the Hundred Years' War was an intermittent conflict between the French and the English kings that lasted into the second half of the fifteenth century. Its outbreak is generally placed in 1337, when Edward III took up arms against Philip VI. But by indulging in hostilities with each other these two kings followed a precedent that was already two centuries old; for practically every king of England since the Norman Conquest had at some time fought a king of France. The underlying cause was always the same: the English king held of the French king certain great fiefs over which the latter consistently tried to gain control. In other words, the so-called Hundred Years' War was merely the continuation of an ancient struggle—one in which the French naturally had the military advantage, though they often failed to use it; and one which logically ended when the English had at last abandoned their continental possessions. If these facts are appreciated, much of the romantic detail that popular accounts have rendered famous may be passed over as relatively insignificant. In the following sketch emphasis will be placed rather on those events which have an important bearing on social or constitutional development.

The Valois succession (1328)

First of all, a few words must be given to the matter of the royal succession. By the opening of the fourteenth century primogeniture had been recognized as governing the inheritance of both the English and the French crowns. In England, furthermore, inheritance had already been admitted on the female side of the house (see Table III); in France the question remained open until 1328, when the last son of Philip IV died without a male heir (see Table II). Thereupon Edward III of England, an ambitious man who had succeeded the deposed Edward II in 1327, laid claim to the throne as the son of Philip's daughter. But a council of French magnates decided that, since regal power had already been refused to a woman, no woman could give such power to her son. Philip of Valois thus won the royal title, and Edward accepted the decision, which was thenceforth the established law of France.[12] Even if the decision had gone the other way, the crown would eventually have passed, not to the English claimant, but to Charles of Navarre (see Table II).

It is therefore evident that, when Edward III reasserted his claim ten years later, his action was dictated by the outbreak of war in Flanders. The situation there remained unchanged by the accession of new sovereigns. Philip VI, by extending military rule over the county, induced Edward to reply with an embargo on English wool. The Flemings once more rebelled and under Jacob van Artevelde, a wealthy merchant of Ghent, signed a commercial treaty with Edward. Then, as the latter declared himself king of France and quartered his arms with the French lilies, they gave him political recognition. Securing control of the sea with the help of his Flemish allies, Edward was able to send annual raiding parties across the Channel. But in 1345 Artevelde was murdered and, to remedy the situation in Flanders, Edward landed in Normandy and marched north with an army of about ten thousand. At Crecy in the Somme valley he was overtaken by Philip with a force that outnumbered his two to one. The ensuing battle, nevertheless, was a brilliant victory for Edward, who turned to good advantage the tactical innovations of his grandfather. He dismounted his cavalry and grouped

Crécy (1346)

---

[12] The principle of succession thus defined really had nothing to do with the ancient Frankish custom called the Salic Law; that tag was falsely attached by lawyers to justify an action already taken.

them in three battalions on the crest of a hill. On the flanks of each battalion he stationed archers equipped with the English long-bows. Philip's knights charged bravely time and again, but, faced by a deadly storm of arrows, could not reach the enemy position. And when at last the English men-at-arms swept down the hill, they carried all before them.

Poitiers (1356) and its results

The immediate consequence was Edward's capture of Calais, which, recolonized by English merchants, he turned into a useful base for future operations and a commercial rival to the Flemish towns. Otherwise the war reverted to its previous routine of pillaging expeditions and local skirmishes. By the middle of the century the command of the English forces had passed to the king's eldest son, known as the Black Prince, while Philip VI had been succeeded by John. Like his father, the new king was a gallant gentleman, fond of chivalrous display and courteous entertainment, but utterly devoid of ability either as a statesman or as a general. After long delay, John in 1356 set out with his army to rescue Languedoc from the Black Prince. The English, again badly outnumbered, stood near Poitiers and, repeating the tactics of Crecy, won another victory of the same sort. Some two thousand French knights fell on the field and an equal number were taken prisoner, including the king and his youngest son. This catastrophe brought France to the verge of ruin. While the king passed a pleasant captivity in England, the royal authority collapsed throughout his kingdom. Hostilities were suspended by a series of truces, and the mercenary companies, now generally employed by both sides, proceeded to live off the country. Before long hardly a French province had escaped devastation or the payment of heavy blackmail. Meanwhile, too, all regions had been swept by the plague, which contemporaries called the Black Death.[13]

The nominal ruler of France during this unhappy period was the dauphin[14] Charles, as yet an inexperienced youth.

[13] See below, p. 336.

[14] The count of Vienne had become known as the dauphin, and his county as Dauphiné, because he had a dolphin in his coat of arms. When the territory was acquired by Philip VI, the stipulation was made that it, together

Placed in a hopeless situation, he could do no more than yield to the leaders of the estates general. For over half a century it had been customary for the king to summon great assemblies of the clergy and nobility, together with deputies elected by the towns, in order to secure the grant of taxes, the authorization of military levies, or the approval of other extraordinary measures. Occasionally a single body had been called for the entire kingdom, as was first done by Philip IV in 1302 to gain support against Boniface VIII. But such meetings of estates general had been infrequent; the more usual practice had been to hold two assemblies, one for the north at Paris and one for the south at Toulouse. This was the plan followed in 1356, and the estates had already met when the disaster of Poitiers produced a sudden crisis. With the king and the aristocracy wholly discredited, the popular spokesmen at Paris—especially Etienne Marcel, head of the local gild merchant—were able to combine and carry through all the reforms that earlier estates had urged in vain.

The estates general and the Grande Ordonnance

The *Grande Ordonnance* of 1357, accepted by Charles in desperation, provided that the royal council should be filled with ministers nominated by the estates. The latter should meet regularly, whether called by the king or not; and when not in session, they were to be represented by a standing committee. No tax could be levied, no military force could be raised, no truce could be signed except by authorization of the estates. They were to appoint deputies (*élus*) to collect all subsidies that might be granted, and generals (*généraux*) to receive the money, pay the troops, and submit accounts for audit. This great enactment, if it had continued in force, would have made France, like contemporary England, a constitutional monarchy. But the increasing disorder throughout the country eventually allowed the patient dauphin to revive and even to enhance the royal authority. By 1358 the Parisians, led by Marcel, had set up what amounted to a revolutionary commune; and their example was being followed in

with the appropriate title, should be regularly held by the heir to the French throne.

other towns when the peasants in the adjacent country rose in the famous Jacquerie.[15] The insurrection, quickly suppressed by a combination of feudal forces, served only to discredit popular movements of all kinds. By the end of the year Marcel had fallen a victim to a Parisian reaction and the dauphin had regained his capital.

Government of Charles V (1364-80)

In 1360 peace was signed with the English, and John recovered his freedom on the promise to pay a huge ransom and to cede Guienne in full sovereignty to Edward III. John's spendthrift habits, however, prevented his meeting even the first payment; so, chivalrous to the end, he went back into captivity in England and there died (1364). The dauphin, already old in experience, assumed the royal title and at once proceeded to earn the name by which he was to be known—Charles the Wise. To direct the English war, recommenced since the failure of John's peace, Charles found a talented collaborator in his constable, Bertrand du Guesclin. Together, he and the king reformed the French army by organizing it in permanent companies, pacified the countryside, improved the system of local fortification, and, by developing a sensible strategy of defensive warfare, gradually forced the English back. Meanwhile Charles also reconstituted the royal government. Earlier the estates had granted to John, as a means of paying his ransom, a considerable revenue for an indefinite period—excise taxes on salt, wines, liquors, and other merchandise, together with a direct tax on certain kinds of real property. Subsequently, when the estates objected to new imposts which Charles sought to levy, he agreed to drop them on condition that the old ones should be made permanent. And with the taxes the king took over the machinery of collection set up by the estates. Henceforth the *élus* and *généraux* were royal officials, and estates ceased to be called except for particular regions that had come to enjoy special liberties. The fiscal system that was to characterize the French monarchy until the Revolution of 1789 thus appears as the work of Charles V. In his day, at least, royal

[15] See below, p. 336.

absolutism meant the re-establishment of order throughout a distracted country. Apparently, too, it meant the turning of defeat into victory; for at the king's death in 1380 the English possessions in France had been reduced to three patches of territory about Calais, Bordeaux, and Bayonne.

Charles V's triumph, though mainly the result of his own intelligent effort, was aided by the contemporary weakening of England. Edward III, outliving the military glory of his youth, soon proved himself a bad king—a quite unprincipled man who cared for nothing but his own ease, and so by choice maintained a corrupt administration. During the last years of his reign, as the Black Prince sickened and prematurely died, the efficiency of the English leadership, both military and civil, inevitably declined. Even the death of the old king in 1377 brought no immediate improvement, for he was succeeded by a nine-year-old grandson, Richard II, who very naturally accepted whatever ministers were then in office. Political discontent, reinforced by the economic grievances of the age,[16] reached a climax in 1381, when the government sought to raise money for the French war through an unpopular poll tax. Insurgent artisans from Kent joined insurgent peasants from Essex in a march on London. Admitted by sympathizers inside the walls, the rebels terrorized the city for two days and dispersed only on being assured by the young king that he would redress their grievances.

Richard II, however, quickly disillusioned his many friends. In quashing the charters of emancipation granted to the peasants and in ruthlessly suppressing all further risings, he had the warm support of parliament. But he proceeded to alienate that support by asserting despotic powers and seeking through force of arms and legal chicanery to remove all limitations on his authority. As a consequence, the leaders of parliament in 1399 threw their support to Henry of Lancaster who, heading a baronial revolt, had succeeded in capturing the king. Richard was formally deposed by parliament, and the duke of Lancaster, as a grandson of Edward III, was pro-

England under Edward III and Richard II

---

[16] See below, p. 336.

claimed as King Henry IV. This Revolution of 1399 was momentous in more ways than one. In the first place, it established the Lancastrian dynasty and in so doing passed over an elder branch of the royal house, whose claims were eventually acquired and reasserted by the duke of York (see Table III). Secondly, it consecrated various principles of parliamentary government which, surviving a Yorkist victory and reaction, have since remained fundamental to the English constitution.

Principles of parliamentary government

In the course of the fourteenth century parliament had come to be legally constituted and defined. To be so named, a meeting of the king's great court had to include both lords and commons, regularly summoned according to established precedent. The former already made up, as they still do, the official peerage of England—dukes, marquises, earls, viscounts, and barons by right of inheritance or royal patent, together with a number of spiritual peers. The house of commons, formed earlier in the century by the union of the burgesses and the knights of the shires, was now definitely organized under an elected speaker. Turning the pressure of the war to their own advantage, the two houses had adopted the practice of refusing grants of money or troops except on certain conditions and so had forced Edward III to recognize a number of parliamentary principles. These principles, confirmed by the Revolution of 1399 and notably developed under the Lancastrians, were chiefly the following. No restatement or modification of the law should be made except by statute—a formal act of the king in parliament. Earlier the houses had presented vague petitions; henceforth they normally drew up the desired statute in the form of a bill and asked the king to sign it. No tax, direct or indirect, should be levied by the king unless it had been granted by parliament, and any such grant should originate in the house of commons. Moneys thus obtained by the king should be expended only as appropriated by parliament, which, to enforce its authority, had the right of auditing the royal accounts. Besides, various liberties of members—the freedom to attend parliament without molestation, to introduce petitions, and to engage in debate—were regularly guaranteed, as well as the customary rules of electoral procedure.

Until the death of Henry IV in 1413 the English government was thus mainly concerned with domestic problems, and the war in France continued to languish. From the French point of view this was indeed fortunate, as will be apparent when we consider the calamity that had befallen the proud monarchy of Charles V. His son and heir, Charles VI, proved to be thoroughly incompetent and, to make a bad situation worse, became intermittently insane. As the royal authority thus weakened, a bitter feud developed between two factions at court: one headed by the king's younger brother, Louis, duke of Orleans; the other by the king's uncle, Philip, duke of Burgundy (see Table VII). The latter, having shared his father's captivity in England, had been rewarded with the Burgundian duchy when it escheated to the crown in 1361; and to that he had added not only Franche-Comté, a fief of the Holy Roman Empire, but also Flanders, acquired through fortunate marriage to the heiress of the county. Thanks especially to this latter acquisition, the duke of Burgundy had become a great and powerful prince, whose strategic position on the frontier led him to pursue an aggressive policy in both France and Germany. But Philip's ambition to control the French government was continually thwarted by Louis of Orleans, who preferred to use his high favor at court for his own advantage. So John the Fearless, inheriting the old quarrel along with the Burgundian territories, adopted the simple expedient of having the duke of Orleans assassinated in 1407. The immediate consequence was the outbreak of a murderous civil war that paralyzed France for a generation.

Outbreak of civil war in France

Accordingly, when the young and vigorous Henry V acceded to the English throne, he at once set out to glorify the Lancastrian dynasty by reconquering the lost heritage of the Angevins. In 1415 he landed on the coast of Normandy and, leading about ten thousand men, advanced along the Somme. At the moment Paris, together with the insane king, was in

Henry V and the battle of Agincourt (1415)

the hands of the Orleanist faction, chiefly nobles of southern France under the count of Armagnac, father-in-law of the youthful duke. To the Armagnac government the bitter experience of the previous century was as nothing. With incredible folly a glittering array of knights proceeded to attack Henry V at Agincourt precisely as their ancestors had attacked Edward III at Crécy. The result was the same. The English repulsed and slaughtered a force that outnumbered them three to one. While Henry then completed the reduction of Normandy by taking Rouen, the Burgundians drove their discredited rivals from Paris and took over the royal administration. The fifteen-year-old dauphin Charles fled south with his Armagnac friends; Queen Isabelle, to maintain her position at court, came to terms with the victors. John of Burgundy now had the responsibility of meeting the English and so opened negotiations for peace with the Armagnacs. But in 1419, while arranging final terms with the dauphin, he was stabbed by a feudist who thought only of avenging Louis of Orleans.

The Peace of Troyes (1420)

The Burgundian reply was the Peace of Troyes signed in 1420 between Charles VI and Henry V. Actually, of course, the treaty was the work of Philip, the new duke of Burgundy, aided by the shameless queen. The dauphin was repudiated as being no lawful heir; on the death of Charles VI his throne should go to his "only true son," Henry of England, now married to the princess Catherine. But Henry was not to enjoy his triumph for long; before the end of 1422 both he and the unfortunate Charles VI were dead and the newborn child of Henry and Catherine was proclaimed king of both realms. Momentarily the change of sovereigns hardly affected the political situation. Two royal uncles, the dukes of Gloucester and Bedford, were installed as regents, and in France the latter proved himself an able soldier. Acting in co-operation with the Burgundians, his armies continued to advance, occupying the country north of the Loire and in 1428 laying siege to Orleans. The uncrowned Charles VII, who was recognized only in the southeast, remained sunk in apathy, apparently indifferent to the fate of his kingdom. Yet his cause was by no means hopeless. If only he would shake off the Armagnac tutelage and assert the powers inherent in his kingship, he would gain widespread sympathy. The English hold on Paris and the north could not survive the loss of Burgundian support and, in the face of a national awakening, Duke Philip might well abandon his allies in order to keep his fiefs. Through one of the most amazing episodes in history the king was to learn his proper rôle from an illiterate peasant girl.

For the early life of Jeanne d'Arc we have only one documentary source of any great value—the testimony that she herself gave at her trial in 1431. She had been born, she then declared, in the village of Domrémy on the Lorraine border, the daughter of one Jacques Darc[17] and his wife Isabelle. She was not sure of her age; she thought that she was about nineteen—which would make the date of her birth about 1411. She had no book-learning, knowing "neither A nor B," but her mother had taught her to say her prayers, and also to spin and sew. In this domestic skill she took pride; she was no mere shepherdess, for at home she had never tended animals. It was in her father's garden, at noon on a summer's day, that she had first heard a voice from heaven. She had been frightened, but had finally come to know that it was St. Michael who spoke to her. Surrounded by angels, he had often appeared before her eyes, and had told her again and again that she must "go into France" and raise the siege of Orleans. On later occasions she frequently reported having talked with angels while persons beside her failed to see or hear anything extraordinary. The historian may therefore conclude that her experiences were purely subjective, and beyond that he need not go. There is no good reason for doubting the girl's honesty. Her messages must have been very real to her. Otherwise, how could she have acted as she did?

Jeanne d'Arc and the relief of Orleans (1429)

[17] This was the original spelling of the name; it was later changed to d'Arc when the family was declared noble.

The region about Domrémy, though isolated by the Burgundians, was still being held for Charles VII by a detachment of royal troops. Their captain, persuaded of Jeanne's divine mission, gave her a suit of armor and an escort of

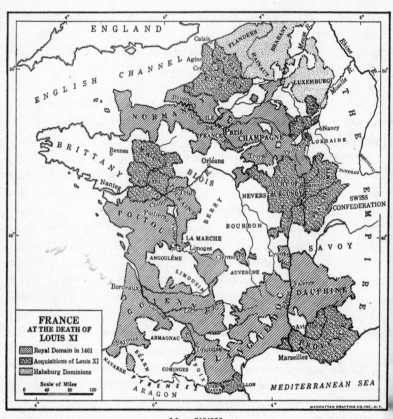

MAP XVIII.

six soldiers. With them Jeanne made the long and perilous journey to the castle of Chinon on the Loire (see Map XVIII). There she found Charles and, after being carefully examined, convinced him that she had been miraculously sent to aid him. So, at the head of the king's army, she set out for Orleans. Since the French fervently believed that they were being led by an angel from heaven and the English feared her as a devil from hell, Jeanne's success in relieving the city can be readily understood. Within a few weeks her victorious advance had cleared the way to Reims where, standing at the king's side, she saw him crowned. If Charles had now displayed any nobility of character, his success would have been even more brilliant. But he listened to the advice of jealous ministers and gave scant support to the heroic maid, who by no means regarded her mission as ended. By a most remarkable proclamation she had announced that, with God's help, she would drive the English "out of the whole kingdom of France." While the king resumed his old life and signed a truce with the Burgundians, Jeanne therefore continued the war. During a vain attack on Paris she was wounded; finally, in 1430, a brave sortie before the walls of Compiègne led to her capture by a Burgundian soldier. Charles, to his everlasting discredit, made no offer of ransom; the English were only too glad to do so.

The tragic sequel was inevitable. By that time the witchcraft delusion had taken firm hold on the minds even of the educated.[18] In English eyes Jeanne was unquestionably a witch; the matter of her condemnation was merely a detail. At Rouen, in the spring of 1431, she was placed on trial before a special court of French clergy headed by the bishop of Beauvais, who had been driven from his diocese by the royal advance. He and his associates, of course, gave her no chance of acquittal. In spite of a courageous and witty defense, the court declared her guilty of heresy. At the reading of the accusation, Jeanne broke down and confessed her guilt; but later, after being sent back to jail, she reasserted her unflinching faith in her mission and denounced her confession as sheer cowardice. The court thus had the pleasure of sentencing her as a relapsed heretic. Given over to the secular government, she was burned in the public square of Rouen.

Her trial and death (1431)

The death of Jeanne d'Arc was hailed with delight by the English and their partisans; yet, by making their pitiful cap-

18 See below, p. 368.

tive a martyr, they did not better their cause. Alive, the
maid had not proved invincible; dead, she became the inspiration of a patriotic cause. Although its progress was slow,
the demand for a national monarchy eventually grew so
strong as to overcome even the inertia of Charles VII. In
1435 he succeeded in buying a separate peace with Philip of
Burgundy, and the ruin of the English cause in northern
France was assured by the death of Bedford before the end
of the same year. A series of truces permitted the king to
re-establish the military and financial administration of his
grandfather. And when hostilities were renewed about the
middle of the century, the triumphant march of the French
could not be checked. Having regained Normandy, they
invaded Guienne. Bordeaux fell in 1453 and the war was
over. Now at last Charles decided that something ought to be
done for Jeanne d'Arc; it should not stand on the record that
so glorious a king had been saved by a witch. Accordingly,
by papal authorization, the case was reopened at Rouen in
1456. The errors in the previous trial were blamed on the
deceased bishop of Beauvais and, after a prolonged eulogy
of the poor burned girl, the judgment was reversed—belated
thanks for the winning of a crown and the reinvigoration of
a kingdom.

4. THE COUNCILS, THE PAPACY, AND THE NEW DESPOTS

The long-continued residence of the popes at Avignon was
finally ended by Gregory XI, who, shortly after the return to
Rome, died there in 1378. Of the sixteen cardinals who now
had to choose a successor eleven were Frenchmen. Had they
been voting at Avignon, their action would undoubtedly have
been different; but in the midst of the wildly excited Roman
populace, and just before a mob broke into the Vatican, they
named an Italian who was crowned as Urban VI. Almost at
once they repented their action. So, encouraged by Charles V
of France, they withdrew to Anagni, where they declared
the previous election void on account of intimidation and
elevated the bishop of Geneva as Clement VII. Thereupon

Urban excommunicated all the old cardinals and replaced them with new ones. Clement, establishing himself at Avignon, replied with anathemas of his own, and the Great Schism had begun. On earlier occasions disputed elections had usually ended after a few years of quarreling, when one of the contestants died or abdicated. Now, however, th opposing forces were so evenly balanced that their conflict threatened to last indefinitely. For each could justify its position by weighty argument, and the peoples of Europe took sides according to their political sympathies. France, together with Scotland, Aragon, Castile, Navarre, and some of the German states, supported Clement. England, Portugal, and Flanders joined the emperor and most of the Italians in recognizing Urban.

As the century drew to a close, and all Europe seemed to be falling into chaos, the university of Paris launched an energetic campaign to heal the schism. The efforts of Christians were to be directed towards securing the abdication of both popes in favor of a single candidate, towards obtaining some other settlement through arbitration between the two, or, as a last resort, towards the calling of a general council with jurisdiction over the whole matter.[19] The first plan broke down when Clement's successor, Benedict XIII, ignored his solemn pledge and refused to abdicate. The second plan led merely to the comedy of 1407-08. Benedict and a new Roman pope, Gregory XII, having agreed to an interview, actually got within sight of each other at Lucca; but while one was on land, the other was on the sea, and neither could be persuaded to forsake his element! Disgusted by this farcical performance, a majority of the cardinals from the two camps made common cause and, in defiance of both popes, summoned a general council to meet at Pisa in the following year. Although it lacked hearty support in various countries, the council proceeded to adopt drastic measures. Benedict and Gregory, after their refusal to appear for trial, were declared guilty of heresy and deposed from office. The

The Council of Pisa (1409)

[19] For discussion of the conciliar theory, see below, pp. 357-58.

combined group of cardinals then undertook to fill the vacant office and finally installed the Neapolitan John XXIII. But the latter failed to oust either Gregory or Benedict, and the net result of the council's activity was the establishment of a third papal government.

The Council of Constance (1414-18)   The very fact that the situation was thus made worse united all western Christendom in support of a new council, which was summoned to Constance by John XXIII in co-operation with the emperor Sigismund. In the autumn of 1414 the great assembly came together and, after long discussion, adopted a method of organization that had been proposed by the Parisian spokesmen. The right of voting, instead of being restricted to prelates, was extended to all doctors of theology or of canon law, and for deliberative purposes the council, like a university faculty, was divided into nations. The first of these measures assured a majority to the reforming party; the second prevented domination by the Italians, for they constituted only one of four (later five) nations. John XXIII had called the council in the expectation that it would support him against the other two popes. On the contrary it treated him as merely one of three rivals; and when he denounced its action, it declared him deposed—a judgment which he accepted after his arrest by the emperor. Gregory XII, to avoid a less dignified fate, wisely decided to resign. There remained only the obstinate Benedict XIII, who shut himself up in a Spanish castle and launched anathemas against a hostile world until he died in 1422. But in the meantime he had been recondemned and thereafter ignored.

While thus taking effective steps to end the schism, the council affirmed its orthodoxy by convicting John Hus of heresy[20] and began protracted debates on the reform of ecclesiastical government. After the lapse of two years, however, little agreement had been secured. The many who joined in denouncing the notorious corruption of the church fell into violent dispute as soon as any specific change was advocated. In the meantime the papal throne had remained vacant,

[20] See below, p. 360.

for the majority of the members insisted on the adoption of reforms as a necessary preliminary to the holding of an election. Finally, towards the end of 1417, general weariness forced a compromise. It was decided that the articles already accepted by the nations should be enacted as a basis for future legislation and that the cardinals, reinforced by deputies from the nations, should forthwith elect a pope. Six decrees were accordingly promulgated, the more important of which concerned the holding of general councils in the future. The first of these councils should be called in five years, the second seven years later, and thenceforth one every ten years, except that in case of schism a council should meet even without being summoned. The sixth decree enumerated eighteen points with regard to which the newly elected pope should establish reforms in consultation with the present council. All eighteen had to do with papal rights and practices: such as his taxes and other revenues, his powers of appointment, appeals to his court, his granting of dispensations and indulgences, the constitution of the cardinal college, and the offenses for which a pope might be tried before a general council.

In the election that followed, the papal throne was given by unanimous vote to an Italian, a member of the Colonna family who took the name of Martin V. A man distinguished for political adroitness rather than for statesmanship, Martin inevitably took advantage of the council's growing fatigue to reassert the papal authority. One or two measures of no far-reaching consequence were proposed by him to the entire assembly and there adopted. Shortly afterwards the separate nations accepted a few meager promises as partly satisfying their demands. Finally, in the spring of 1418, the pope announced the dissolution of the council on the ground that it was no longer needed. In the general rejoicing over the unification of the church, the program of thorough reform that had occasioned so much talk seemed now to be forgotten. Reluctantly observing the decree issued at Constance, Martin summoned a general council at Pavia in 1423, but

Martin V (1417-31)

it was attended only by a few Italian prelates who did nothing beyond providing that the next council should meet at Basel in 1431. That assembly, on the contrary, attracted a large number of clergymen, especially from the lower ranks; for in the meantime a series of crusades against the Hussites in Bohemia had signally failed.[21]

The failure of the councils

Martin V died just after the council met at Basel and his successor, Eugenius IV, proved to be a much less skillful politician. Already embroiled in a series of Italian feuds, he soon involved himself in open conflict with the council as the result of its conciliatory policy towards the Hussites. The pope's rôle in this affair was far from glorious; yet it was he who enjoyed the final victory. The council, having asserted its superiority over the papacy and forced Eugenius to accept its earlier decisions, proceeded to defy his authority still further by adopting a series of reforms. But eight years had passed and the council now consisted of only a few determined radicals. When in 1439 they went so far as to set up an anti-pope, their cause was ruined; for a renewed schism was the last thing Europe desired. Only a dwindling remnant continued in session, ultimately to declare the dissolution of the council in 1449. When in the next year Nicholas V, successor of Eugenius, celebrated the restoration of Christian peace by a great jubilee at Rome, the conciliar movement was dead.

The relapse of the papacy

Unhappily for the church, the prospect of reform died with the councils. The decrees of Basel were ignored except as the greater princes of Europe chose to re-enact them. The papacy, to the great distress of many loyal supporters, not only failed to extirpate the ancient abuses but allowed them to be aggravated. Apparently secure in the enjoyment of absolute monarchy, the popes in the closing decades of the fifteenth century once more became submerged in Italian politics. Distinguished as temporal rulers and as devotees of the new Renaissance culture, they forfeited all respect as leaders of Christendom and even as exponents of common decency.

[21] See below, p. 360.

How this papal relapse was logically followed by the great Protestant Revolution must be left for explanation in some other volume. To complete the present sketch of political conditions after the Hundred Years' War, it remains only to mention a few outstanding developments in France, England, and Spain.

Charles VII, the king who owed his crown to Jeanne d'Arc, lived on until 1461. He had been cordially detested by many persons, including the dauphin Louis, who had finally run away to the Burgundian court. There he was splendidly entertained by Duke Philip, the most resplendent prince of the age. To Burgundy, Franche-Comté, Flanders, and Artois Philip had added by inheritance or purchase virtually all the other Low Countries (see Map XIV). By treaty in 1435 Charles VII had given him possession of the Somme valley and had relieved his French fiefs of all royal taxes and services. In return for his hospitality, Philip doubtless expected a further reward from the future king, but in that he was disappointed. The dauphin was quite willing that some one else should pay his expenses until he came to the throne; when that happy moment arrived, he assumed the position of an absolute monarch who required no advice from a ducal cousin. Although Louis XI suffered from the physical degeneration of the Valois house, having a poor cadaverous body that was hardly strong enough to hold itself up, his intelligence was unsurpassed. Indefatigable and relentless, he knew precisely what he wanted and, to attain his ends, willingly sacrificed whatever stood in his way. The least chivalrous of kings, he went to war only as a last resort and customarily relied on diplomacy, in which he proved himself a master of consummate skill. To those who opposed him he appeared a hateful tyrant; even his loyal subjects complained of his harsh administration and heavy taxes. Yet whoever served him faithfully received just treatment, and his revenues were spent, not to adorn his court, but to preserve and strengthen his kingdom.

Since Philip the Good was now too old to engage in active

Louis XI vs. Charles the Rash

revenge against the faithless king, that task devolved upon his son Charles. Athletic, handsome, and likable, the young prince was not only a brave knight but also an able and intelligent ruler. The fatal flaw in his character was indicated by his nickname, Charles the Rash (*le Téméraire*). Throwing himself into a series of grandiose projects, he scorned all advice and proudly maintained his course in the face of any odds. The striking contrast between him and the king of France gave to the struggle that now commenced between them an epic grandeur—made it a worthy theme for the great chronicler who happened to be present. Philippe de Commines was a Flemish nobleman who rose to be councilor and chamberlain at the Burgundian court. Later prevailed on by Louis XI to enter the royal service, he remained in it until the king's death. Being then removed from political office, Commines devoted his last years to the writing of his memoirs, the finest historical composition in Europe since the decay of ancient culture.[22]

The fall of Burgundy

During the first decade of his reign Louis had to withstand as best he could a combination of discontented princes led by the duke of Burgundy. Time and again, as Commines so graphically tells us, the king accepted defeat and signed a humiliating peace, only by some kind of chicanery to slip out of his commitments. Eventually he escaped reprisal because the duke had evolved the magnificent design of uniting his scattered territories and so of reconstituting the ancient Lotharingia.[23] By 1475 Charles had almost realized his ambition. But the diplomacy of Louis XI frightened the Habsburg emperor into refusing a Burgundian alliance and built up a coalition to defend the local states of Alsace and Lorraine. Foremost among the French allies were the Swiss who, having gained their independence through the paralysis of the royal power in Germany, had no liking for the new and powerful monarchy that was emerging on their western border. In their earlier wars they had found that massed infantry armed

[22] See below, p. 347.
[23] See above, p. 137.

with long pikes could successfully oppose charging cavalry, and through similar tactics they now astonished Europe by breaking the military power of Burgundy. Twice in 1476 Charles sought to punish the troublesome mountaineers, and twice he was defeated. Before the walls of Nancy in the next year he insisted on again attacking a Swiss position. The result was the same, except that on this occasion the duke himself remained on the stricken field.

The delight of Louis XI and the dismay of certain French nobles when they heard the news are vividly described by Commines. The emotions were justified, for henceforth the king was to be undisputed master of his realm. Despite the fact that Charles had left an heiress, Louis proceeded to confiscate his fiefs as escheat to the crown. Without difficulty the royal troops occupied Picardy, Artois, Burgundy, and Franche-Comté, although the last was imperial territory. He likewise sought to take Flanders, but there he overreached himself. The Flemings rallied to the support of Charles's daughter Mary, who was a native of their country, and she, in revenge for the royal perfidy, accepted marriage with Maximilian of Austria (see Table VIII). Thus a Habsburg prince was installed as ruler of the Netherlands and claimant of the whole Burgundian heritage—an event of prime importance for the future of Europe. Meanwhile, however, Louis had obtained another windfall. The extinction of the Angevin house, also descended from a brother of Charles V (see Table VII), gave him the duchy of Anjou and the counties of Maine, Bar, and Provence (see Map XVIII). Aside from Flanders, only one of the great French fiefs was still independent of royal control —the duchy of Brittany, which was to be acquired through marriage by Louis's son, Charles VIII.

As far as internal government was concerned, Louis XI ruled France as the unrestricted heir of Charles V. There was, in fact, no substitute for royal absolutism; a parliamentary government like that of England had no place in a kingdom devoid of institutional unity. Louis XI called only one meeting of the estates general—when, during his early

Government of Louis XI

years, he needed support against a feudal coalition. Later, as resistance to the king's will utterly collapsed, he used only provincial estates and assemblies of notables who could be counted on not to oppose him. By the close of the century Louis had thus come to enjoy the taxes that remained under the arbitrary control of the king until the critical year of 1789. They were (1) the *taille*, a direct tax paid in general by the non-noble classes; (2) the *aides*, indirect taxes on sales of various articles; and (3) the *gabelle*, a tax on salt. The second and third were usually farmed out to syndicates which advanced the king definite sums for the privilege of making the collections. The first was normally apportioned among fiscal districts called *généralités* and *élections* after the *généraux* and *élus* who administered them. There was, however, no uniformity. In some regions, notably Normandy and Languedoc, the royal tax had to be voted and assessed by local assemblies. So the kingdom was said to include two kinds of provinces: the *pays d'états* and the *pays d'élection*. This distinction, together with the hundred others that affected the administration of law for particular persons, classes, and communities, remained to the very end characteristic of the Old Régime in France.

The English civil war and the Tudor accession

In England, meanwhile, events had pursued an opposite course. The Lancastrian dynasty, which had attained so glorious a height with the Peace of Troyes, ended amid the horrors of civil war and massacre. Henry VI grew up to be a virtuous man, utterly devoid of political ability. Under more favorable circumstances the ruinous consequences of the king's incompetence might have been avoided through the employment of wise ministers. But he was surrounded by ambitious courtiers who thought only of their own private interests. Among them the more prominent figures were the king's relatives—a prolific tribe claiming descent, legitimate or illegitimate, from the children of Edward III, and intermarried with practically every baronial house of England. Under the feeble administration of Henry VI their feuds disturbed the entire country. The king, tainted by descent from Charles

VI, became hopelessly insane and, as in France, this misfortune helped to precipitate a murderous conflict. The leader of the anti-Lancastrian party was Richard of York, heir of the boy whose rights had been passed over by parliament in 1399 (see Table III). In 1453, when the birth of a son to Henry VI precluded the possibility of a peaceful succession, York raised the standard of revolt.

Although the war which thus began never involved more than small bands of noblemen and their retainers, it was an extremely sanguinary affair. Before it was over, the English nobility had been very nearly exterminated. From the military point of view the battles were insignificant, and their political results may be briefly summarized. Richard of York was slain in 1460, but his cause triumphed eleven years later when his son gained undisputed title to the throne as Edward IV. Then, after Edward's brother Richard had murdered his two nephews to secure the crown, he was defeated and slain in 1485 by Henry Tudor. The latter was a Lancastrian adventurer whose claim to the throne was at best dubious (see Table III). But his victory in battle, confirmed by his marriage to a daughter of Edward IV, by the ratification of parliament, and by the judicious execution of other relatives, assured the triumph of the new dynasty. Under the Tudors the kingdom of England, despotically administered, was again to be a European power.

The third of the great western monarchies at the close of the fifteenth century was Spain, a much more recent creation. **The new monarchy of Spain** In the preceding pages it has been seen how Aragon became an important state through union with Catalonia and the conquest of the Moorish territory to the south. At the same time the kingdom of Castile, finally combined with León, had pushed its dominion to the Mediterranean at Murcia and to the Atlantic at Cadiz, thus restricting the Mohammedans to the little territory of Granada (see Map XVII). On the west coast Portugal had established itself as an independent kingdom, and to the north Navarre had come to be ruled by a series of French princes. This was the situation at the end of the thirteenth century, and in general it remained unchanged for the better part of two hundred years. Taking advantage of the chronic civil wars in Spain, Louis XI obtained possession of two Catalonian provinces, Roussillon and Cerdagne, and so brought his frontier to the crest of the Pyrenees. But in another affair he was taken by surprise. In 1468 a group of Castilian rebels submitted on condition that Isabella, the sister of their unpopular king, be recognized as heiress of the crown, and in the following year she married Ferdinand, the prince apparent in Aragon. First brought together by personal union in 1479, the two kingdoms were finally made into one, the kingdom of Spain. Its territory, as Ferdinand conquered Granada and the southern half of Navarre, came to include the entire peninsula with the exception of Portugal. Its government, as Ferdinand made himself independent of the local estates, or *cortes*, became an absolute monarchy. Its anti-French policy, as Ferdinand arranged a momentous alliance with the house of Habsburg, was to remain a dominant factor in the European wars of the next two hundred years.

CHAPTER IX

SOCIETY AND CULTURE IN THE LATER MIDDLE AGES

----

1. THE BOURGEOISIE AND THE GROWTH OF CAPITALISM

During the thirteenth century the bourgeois class continued to grow in numbers, in wealth, and in privilege. *Villes neuves* appeared by the hundred, especially in the more backward regions. Since practically all the great towns of Italy, France, Spain, and England had emerged before 1200, the more important of the new foundations were in the northeast of Europe. There, for example, we find Berlin, Dresden, Prague, Rostock, Stralsund, Danzig, Königsberg, Riga, and the other trading communities that were soon combined in the powerful Hansa.[1] As Wales, Scotland, and Ireland had earlier adopted urban models from Norman England, so in the following period the Slavic and Scandinavian countries adopted theirs from Germany. And comparison of municipal charters shows that on all sides bourgeois status remained essentially uniform, implying the elementary liberties sketched in a previous chapter. With regard to the older towns generalization is harder, for by the thirteenth century they had developed widely different institutions. Judged according to their degree of autonomy, they fell into two main groups. In the first were the communes of Italy, which henceforth acted as sovereign republics; the free cities of Germany, which held direct of the weakening empire; and the industrial centers of Flanders, which had come to dominate the whole country. In the second group were the towns subject to the western monarchies or to the German princes, which at most enjoyed such limited rights of self-government as those of the English boroughs.

The towns and their constitutions

[1] See below, pp. 325-26.

315

In the twelfth century the larger town had ordinarily been governed by a single board of elected magistrates; in the thirteenth it was more usual for such a board to be expanded into a number of courts and councils under the general direction of one principal official. The typical Italian commune thus came to be ruled by a *podesta*, frequently a foreigner installed by rival factions as a means of avoiding civil conflict. The chief municipal magistrate in German-speaking regions was commonly styled *bürgermeister*, in French-speaking regions *maire*; and through French influence the latter title became usual also in the greater English boroughs. The precedent was set by London, which took advantage of Richard's absence on the crusade to regain the self-government lost under Henry II.[2] Thenceforth the city was administered by a mayor and a board of aldermen elected by the citizens in local districts called wards—the custom that was eventually imported from England to our own country. It should be noted, however, that many towns continued to prosper without a mayor or an equivalent officer and that, no matter what the precise nature of the constitution, local affairs were normally controlled by the wealthier citizens. Even before it came to be officially recognized, oligarchy was the rule rather than the exception.

The craft gild

Earlier, the more substantial men of a town had often been united in a gild merchant; but that had now been generally superseded by a series of craft gilds, each of which included persons engaged in only one trade. The essence of such a gild's power was its control of a particular industry, the official monopoly that enabled it to exclude outside competition and to prescribe elaborate rules governing production. According to the universal practice, a boy entering upon a trade first had to serve as apprentice for a number of years, during which he received at most his board and lodging. Having learned the craft, he became a journeyman, a man working by the day (*journée*), and so he remained until he was able to start in business for himself. To be

---

[2] Because of its support of Stephen; see above, pp. 175, 203.

ranked as a master, he commonly had to produce a master-piece, a sample of his work that met the standards of the gild. Naturally, too, the master would have to accumulate a certain amount of capital before he could set up an establishment of his own; but his outlay would not be great, and to our eyes his business would remain very small. In any craft that catered solely to the local inhabitants, the number of the latter would determine the number of masters who could make a good living. The gild system, by its intensely conservative regulations, discouraged individual enterprise for the sake of unorthodox gain; so the master could hardly expect to rise above the ordinary standard of bourgeois comfort. Men in one craft usually owned or rented little shops along a single street. There each of them not only produced his wares but also sold them at retail. And there, in the upper stories that projected over the street, he lived with his family.

What we generally recognize as capitalism is not, therefore, to be found in the business of the ordinary craft gild. Nevertheless, capitalism did develop in the Middle Ages, and on a relatively large scale. The origin of the capital itself is no great mystery. Men seem to have acquired it then precisely as they do now—through savings or earnings of one sort or another. Having acquired it, the more venturesome would seek investment by which to increase their wealth. One good opportunity was already provided by urban real estate; for the physical expansion of mediæval towns rapidly converted arable and waste into building lots that could be leased to individual tradesmen at a handsome figure. The establishment of a *ville neuve* was often made possible by shrewd merchants who furnished the necessary capital and recouped themselves by securing title to the best land about the market place. The foundation of many a bourgeois fortune was thus laid in the twelfth and thirteenth centuries. But it is ridiculous to assert, as has been done by a certain school of historians, that the sole origin of capital in the Middle Ages was the unearned increment of land. Although

Capital-istic enterprise

most business was then organized on a small scale, numerous merchants were able to make a profit over and above what they needed to live on. Profits of this kind, as well as accumulated rents, could be advantageously invested in a number of new-grown enterprises.

Italian
influence
in business

In all such matters the men of northwestern Europe looked for instruction to the Italians; and among them the original experts were the Venetians, who had undoubtedly benefited from their early association with the Byzantine Empire. Through the Norman kingdom of Sicily and the Latin states of the crusaders, Italians had also learned much from the Arabs. Whatever the exact origin of the practices, the following had become well known by the thirteenth century. For the building of ships and the financing of voyages beyond the sea, wealthy men often formed companies. Therein every member, by contributing a share of the cost, became entitled to a share of the profit. And the risk was minimized by a system of marine insurance quite like that which is still in common use. Similar arrangements, of course, could be applied to other commercial ventures: the transportation of goods by land, the wholesaling of food and raw materials, manufacturing, and the like. Since Italy had become the foremost distributing center for articles imported from the east, it was natural that before long Italians would try to produce certain of the articles themselves. Frederick II, as we have seen, was keenly interested in projects of this sort; but the greater success was eventually won by the cities to the north, especially Florence. Before the end of the thirteenth century Italian artisans had already developed flourishing industries for the production of glass, silk and linen fabrics, armor, jewelry, and other luxurious wares. The only northern region to witness a comparable development was Flanders, where the larger towns had become world-famous, not only for their usefulness in the trans-shipment of imports, but also for their manufacture and exportation of woolen cloth.

Activities like these presuppose a ready supply of sound

money. During the Carolingian period no coin had been minted in western Europe except the silver penny (*denarius*); so the shilling, the mark, and the pound had been units of weighed money, and the only gold pieces in circulation had been of Arabic or Byzantine origin.[3] And as princes had constantly debased the silver coinage in order to pay their debts more cheaply, it had gradually been turned into bronze. Just before the end of the twelfth century, accordingly, Venice led the way towards a monetary restoration by minting a penny of fine silver worth twelve of the old ones. This was called a big penny (*denarius grossus*), and in the next hundred years such coins—particularly the *gros tournois*[4] of France and the sterling of England—came to have wide circulation throughout the northwest. Shortly afterwards the coining of gold was resumed by the emperor Frederick II and by the great Italian republics—as familiar words still bear witness, for the ducat was named after the *ducatus* of Venice and the florin after Florence.

The subject of money is today associated with that of banking, and the association goes back at least to the thirteenth century. The Italians, naturally enough, set the example in both. The simplest and oldest of banking transactions was money-changing, for time out of mind travelers had been compelled to convert the currency of one region into that of another. Wherever trade was active, numbers of men came to specialize in that business, and from it they were quickly drawn into credit operations of various kinds. Suppose, for example, that A of Lombardy sold spices to B of Flanders, while C of Lombardy bought cloth from D of Flanders. By canceling B's debt against C's, the actual transfer of cash would be reduced to a mimimum. And if agents of the leading importers and exporters met at regular intervals for a mutual balancing of accounts, the result would be what we know as a clearing house. Activities of this sort

[3] Hence the name bezant that was applied to such a coin.

[4] I.e., a penny of Tours; cf. the German *groschen*. The derivation of the English sterling is doubtful; but it was not from easterling, an alleged reference to the Hansa merchants.

became a normal feature of the thirteenth-century fairs—especially those of Champagne, a yearly cycle of six great assemblies for the wholesale distribution of goods, held in Troyes, Provins, and other nearby towns. In all such periodical centers of trade and in all the more important cities the banking firms of Italy, indiscriminately called Lombards, came to maintain regular agents. Through them, as through the international organization of the Knights Templars, financial operations in any country of Europe, or in almost any country of the Mediterranean, might be readily carried out. A crusader, for instance, might buy a letter of credit which he could cash in a Syrian port; a pope could send funds to his legate in Dublin; a king could pay by draft for crown jewels to be bought in Constantinople. And despite the prohibitions of ecclesiastical law, the Lombards did a flourishing business in money-lending.

Money-lending

The church, by citing various texts from the Bible, had forbidden the taking of usury. To read certain authors, one would suppose that such prohibition tended to paralyze all credit operations in the Middle Ages. But it is an instructive fact that, even in the days of Innocent III, the utmost pressure of ecclesiastical authority could not even prevent ordinary buying and selling on Sunday. And in connection with the lending of money the church itself taught Christians how to circumvent the canon law. In the earlier Middle Ages, when a prince needed a loan, he normally applied to a wealthy prelate, who would be quite willing to provide the necessary gold or silver in return for a mortgage on good real estate. During the term of the note the lender enjoyed the income from the land; then, should the principal remain unpaid, he continued his possession indefinitely. By the thirteenth century, however, the lending business had been largely taken over by the great merchants. Officially, they never took usury; instead they collected rents, remuneration for services, or damages for alleged injury. Eventually they coined the word "interest" to designate the sum charged for a loan. The rising cost of government, together with the more luxurious standard of aristocratic life, progressively aided the cause of the bankers. As always happens, economic necessity made short work of an inconvenient prohibition, and the law was modified to fit the facts.

Among the money-lenders of Europe there were many Jews, but their importance in the financial history of Europe has often been exaggerated. Since the Carolingian period, when Jews were prominent in what little trade persisted between Moslem and Christian countries, the situation had radically changed. The big money-lending business of the thirteenth century was not in the hands of Jews, whose operations were generally confined to less progressive regions where banking was not monopolized by Christians. In such localities the Jews, as long as they remained useful to the rulers who protected them, enjoyed a dubious security; but they were herded into particular quarters of the towns, forced to wear a distinctive garb, placed under all sorts of legal restrictions, and periodically stripped of their earnings. Not infrequently a combination of debtors would join in buying from the government a cancellation of their notes; so the unfortunate lender, in order to anticipate the eventual loss of his principal, had to charge an exorbitant rate for his loans. At best the Jews were merely tolerated, and every now and then religious prejudice, fanned by economic jealousy, led to savage persecution. For example, the Jews were driven from England by Edward I, while in France Philip IV proscribed not only them but also the Lombard bankers and the Knights Templars.

Meanwhile the major industries of the Italians and the Flemings had come to depend on an economic organization very different from that of the local craft. Growing in response to a widespread demand, these industries depended on wholesale exportation; and undertakings of such large scope required capitalistic management that, for obvious reasons, could not be supplied by the ordinary master of a gild. All the prominent industrial centers thus came to be dominated by the big business men, who were financiers

Capitalistic industry

rather than manufacturers. In Flanders, for instance, the expansion of the cloth industry was made possible by the great wholesalers, or clothiers as they were later known in England. The clothier bought the raw material, paid weavers to make it into cloth, and sold the finished product throughout the markets of the world. As a class, therefore, the clothiers were capitalistic employers, inevitably affiliated with the bankers and the landed aristocracy of the towns. Under the clothiers the master craftsmen were reduced to little more than hired artisans, doomed to a precarious existence which their gilds were powerless to remedy. When, as the result of political disturbance, they were thrown out of work, their only recourse was insurrection. So, in the industrial centers of both Italy and Flanders, the wars of the fourteenth century were constantly embittered by social antagonism.

Urban population

During the previous three hundred years western Europe had enjoyed an almost uninterrupted advance of prosperity, which can be fairly well measured by the growth of the new urban centers. To our eyes, of course, mediæval towns were not large. Except for Venice and one or two of its Italian rivals, no western city of that age could possibly have had 100,000 inhabitants. The foremost Flemish communes, like Ghent and Bruges, had only half as many and yet were relatively huge. Even London, with about 25,000, was far above the average; for the ordinary town would have a population of from 5,000 to 10,000. However insignificant these figures appear to us, they were very respectable when judged according to Roman standards.[5] By the thirteenth century western Europe had clearly surpassed whatever prosperity it had experienced in ancient times. Later, however, conditions tended to become stabilized. The process of urbanization was halted, and along with it the progress of the bourgeois class. As it became harder for artisans to improve their lot by moving to newly developed regions, their discontent increased. And as the devastations of war and pesti-

[5] See above, p. 26.

lence ruined the European markets, such discontent was fanned into revolutionary activity. This is one of the major factors that must be taken into account when we seek to explain the popular insurrections of the fourteenth century.

2. THE MEDITERRANEAN, THE BALTIC, AND THE NEW ROUTES

In the thirteenth century the sea trade of the Latin west was still divided between two disconnected areas: to the north the Baltic, together with the adjoining reaches of the Atlantic, and to the south the Mediterranean. The greatest commercial power within this latter area was Venice, which had long dominated the Adriatic and now, as the result of the Fourth Crusade, sought to enforce a monopolistic control throughout the Ægean, the Bosporus, and the Black Sea. Politically, Venice was characterized by the unbroken and effective rule of a closed oligarchy. The final step in that direction was taken in 1298, when eligibility for governmental office was restricted to certain great families— those listed, with a continuing record of births and marriages, in the official Golden Book. While the other Italian cities were constantly disturbed by civil wars and revolutions, Venice silently disposed of all malcontents, to remain synonymous with political stability throughout the mediæval period. *Venice and Genoa*

Among the more turbulent rivals of Venice front rank had long been held by Genoa and Pisa, but these two were also involved in a bitter feud with each other. Finally, in 1284, the Genoese succeeded in destroying the Pisan fleet and so became free to join the restored Greek emperor in breaking the Venetian hold on Constantinople. Until the second half of the fourteenth century Venice and Genoa remained fairly well balanced in strength. Then, in the last of their furious wars, Venice captured a besieging fleet by a heroic counter-attack and was able to dictate terms of peace in 1381. Genoa, continually distracted by civil conflict, thereafter abandoned the race for commercial supremacy. The Venetians, on the other hand, vigorously pushed their advantage. To meet a possible threat to their communications across the Alps, they had already adopted a policy of territorial expansion; eventually, by employing mercenaries, they established their control over the Adige valley and the region to the west as far as Brescia and Bergamo (see Map XIV). Meanwhile their dominance in the eastern Mediterranean had come to be challenged by the Ottoman Turks. The Venetian policy, however, had always opposed fighting the Moslems except when commercial advantage lay in that direction. Even the Turkish conquest of the Balkans failed to inspire them with crusading ardor, for by treaty with the sultan they still retained their privileges in the Levant. It was not until the Ottoman advance endangered their positions on the Adriatic and the Ægean that they actually went to war. This was the beginning of a gradual Venetian decline, for which the Turkish victories were merely in part responsible. The decisive factor, as will be seen in the pages immediately following, was rather the diversion of trade to the new Atlantic routes.

Florence and the Lombard communes

Very little need be said here of the other Italian republics, among which a large part of the peninsula came to be divided. The ruin of the Hohenstaufen kingdom and the later collapse of the Angevin power left a host of petty states to fight with one another for the next five hundred years. In the meantime Italy long continued to hear the old names of Guelf and Ghibelline.[6] The latter, an Italian substitute for Hohenstaufen, had come to designate the party of the imperialists; the former to designate their opponents, the papalists. So the Angevins were Guelfs and the Aragonese were Ghibellines. Traditionally, Florence and Milan were Guelf, while Pisa and Pavia were Ghibelline. But the alignment was at most a matter of vague loyalty. Florence, for example, had no desire for a papal government and might be willing to fight either Milan or the Angevin king. Indeed, the traditional epithets soon lost all but a local significance, to be tossed back and forth in feuds of city against city and

[6] Said to be a corruption of Waiblingen, a family estate of the Hohenstaufen.

of faction against faction. At Florence a Ghibelline coalition, aided by Manfred, took the city in 1260. Then, six years later, the power of the Guelfs, under a new and more democratic constitution, was restored by Charles of Anjou. His death brought further changes in the government, accompanied by fierce contests between nobles and gildsmen, between the greater and the lesser gilds, and between rival groups of nobles—in all of which such popes as Boniface VIII played an active and not disinterested part. Such was the environment that influenced Dante Alighieri and, after him, so many other distinguished artists.

By that time, in most of the greater cities, effective political authority had been secured by some kind of despot. Sometimes he was a dictator set up by a form of election, sometimes the descendant of an imperial official, sometimes an adventurer who obtained power by sheer violence. Almost invariably he was thoroughly unscrupulous, resorting when he thought best to legal trickery, force of arms, or assassination. Thus Milan was governed for over a hundred years by the Visconti, who rose from comparative obscurity to be imperial vicars and then dukes, related by marriage to the greatest houses of Germany, France, and England. Under their aggressive rule Milan became the head of a considerable state, extending north to Switzerland and south to Parma. On the east, however, Milan was checked by Venice and in Tuscany by Florence. The latter republic, after continued disorders under one constitution or another, eventually came to be governed by the richest man in town— the banker, Cosimo de' Medici (d. 1464). Although he held no office, being merely what in America is called a political boss, his ascendancy was unquestioned; and it passed like an actual principality first to his son and then to his grandson. It is a famous irony of history that the Medici coat of arms, an arrangement of "medical" pills, lingers on as the sign of the ordinary pawnbroker.

Turning now to the Baltic, we find a significant development of the thirteenth century in the league of German **The Hansa**

towns called the Hansa. The name had no peculiar significance, for it was often applied in northern countries to
any gild or association of merchants. At London, for instance, the men of Cologne had enjoyed special privileges
since long before the Norman Conquest; and when their
hansa was confirmed by Henry II in the twelfth century, it
had already been joined by traders from other cities on
the Rhine. Similarly, with the extension of German commerce throughout the Baltic, Lübeck became the center of
a growing confederation which included the neighboring
towns of Hamburg, Stralsund, and Rostock, as well as the
German colony of Wisby on the Swedish island of Gothland.
By the later thirteenth century this group, or some of its
members, had secured valuable concessions in many quarters
—notably in connection with the fur trade of Russia, the
cloth trade of Flanders, and the fish trade of Norway and
Sweden. As, by mutual agreement, the western and eastern
groups of German towns now pooled their interests and
perfected an organization to administer their common affairs, the combination became *par excellence* the Hansa.

By the early fourteenth century the league had enrolled
all the older German towns on rivers flowing into the Baltic
or the North Sea, together with the new German towns
along the coasts of Prussia, Livonia, and Estonia. It maintained factories—permanent trading establishments, with
warehouses and docks—at Novgorod, Bruges, Bergen, and
London; and in each of these places it enjoyed exclusive
control over the sale of Baltic products (see Map XV). Although the Hansa sought to give its members such protection
as they failed to obtain from the enfeebled monarchy, it
was not a political, much less a national, organization. Held
together solely by mercantile interest, it had no formal constitution, no common seal, no official head, and no capital.
Its only organ of government was a congress which met in
a convenient place whenever the need arose for extraordinary measures. On such occasions Lübeck, by virtue of commercial pre-eminence, was normally deputed to speak for

the confederation and so came to be regarded as its chief. Cologne ranked second and was followed in no fixed order by Hamburg, Bremen, and Wisby. We sometimes hear of a Hanseatic congress representing well over fifty towns, but the lesser communities rarely bothered to send deputies and no list of members was ever published. The only penalty that could be inflicted on a rebellious member was exclusion from the monopolies controlled by the league. Conversely, the maintenance of the Hansa's privileges abroad depended on the power of withholding shipping from a recalcitrant port. It was by an embargo on all trade with the Baltic that Bruges in 1307 and Novgorod in 1392 were forced to submit. And the same weapons normally sufficed to preserve favorable relations with foreign princes. The Hansa encountered formidable opposition in only one direction—from the reinvigorated kingdom of Denmark.

At one time or another the Danish kings had claimed portions of the southern Baltic coast, as well as Scania, the tip of the Scandinavian peninsula. The Baltic provinces they had now abandoned to the Teutonic Knights; Scania, on the other hand, they still coveted, for it was of great political and economic importance. Whoever held it and the adjacent islands controlled not only the entrance to the Baltic but also the profitable herring trade. During the earlier years of the Hansa this strategic position formed part of the Swedish kingdom, and there the merchants were quite willing that it should remain, even after Magnus of Sweden (1319-65) inherited the crown of Norway. Then, about the middle of the fourteenth century, the able Waldemar IV of Denmark defeated Magnus, took Scania, and, seizing the island of Gothland, sacked Wisby. Although Waldemar's act was ostensibly directed against the Swedes, the Hansa took the unprecedented step of going to war as the ally of Magnus, and eventually, after taking Copenhagen, dictated the Peace of Stralsund in 1370. Thereby the Hansa obtained free passage of the Sound and free trade throughout Danish territory. Hanseatic commissioners were to have charge of

The Danish war and the height of the Hansa

the herring market, as well as possession of four royal castles
until the cost of the war had been defrayed by the king. It
was even agreed that no successor was to be placed on the
Danish throne without the consent of the Hansa.

The league, to be sure, soon abandoned its right to interfere in royal elections. Waldemar, dying in 1375, was succeeded by his daughter Margaret, who devoted her long
reign to the project of a united Scandinavia. At Calmar in
1397 the three kingdoms finally agreed to union under
Margaret—a settlement that was to have lasting consequences; for Norway, detached from Sweden, remained under
Danish control for some hundreds of years. Meanwhile, by
rigorously enforcing its commercial privileges, the Hansa
long continued to gain in wealth and power. Its decline in
the fifteenth century was only in part due to the inevitable
hostility of the Baltic states; the fundamental cause was the
gradual diversion of trade to the west and south. The Hanseatic towns, like the Italian republics, had attained their
height of prosperity while the Baltic and the Mediterranean
were two isolated regions. As the two came to be joined by
new maritime routes, commercial ascendancy passed to the
more convenient ports of the Atlantic seaboard.

The economic decay of Flanders

Another phase of this economic shift is to be seen in the
industrial and commercial decay of Flanders. Throughout
the thirteenth century, as earlier, the bulk of English wool
was exported to the Flemish cities, where it was made into
cloth and sold in large quantity—especially to Hanseatic
merchants for distribution in the north and to Italian merchants for distribution in the south. During the fourteenth
century, however, the Venetians developed the practice of
sending convoyed merchant fleets through the Strait of Gibraltar and thence along the coast to England and the
Netherlands. Italian merchants thus found it a simple matter
to buy wool in London for the benefit of manufacturers in
their own cities. Besides, as a political move in the course
of the French war, Edward III established colonies of Flemish weavers in England, and within a hundred years English

cloth came to be well known in the European market. By the time of the Tudors there was no wool to be exported from England; it had all been absorbed by the great English cloth industry that has since led the world. In the meantime,

FIGURE 14.—IDRISI'S MAP OF THE WORLD.
(South is towards the top of the map.)

the ship-owners of England, France, Spain, and Portugal had learned to follow the example of the Venetians and, by undertaking Mediterranean voyages of their own, to win profits that had earlier gone to Flemish middlemen. But to appreciate the ultimate significance of these maritime adventures, we must briefly re-examine the economic position of the Moslem world.

The seven centuries that had elapsed since the establishment of the Arab Empire may be said, from the commercial
point of view, to fall into two clearly marked divisions.
During the first the Moslems enjoyed a virtual monopoly
of trade throughout central and western Asia, northern
Africa, and the adjoining waters. Then, in the eleventh century, the fleets of the Italian cities—co-operating with Christian hosts in Spain, Sicily, and Syria—drove the Moslems
back and gained dominion over the Mediterranean. Thenceforth it was the Italian merchants who controlled the
carrying of oriental products between the ports of the Levant
and those of western Europe. The Arabs, however, still
maintained their supremacy in the caravan trade across the
Asiatic plateau and in the sea trade that linked the coasts
of India, Persia, Arabia, and eastern Africa. So Idrisi, the
Arab geographer of Roger II,[7] could mark these regions on
his map, together with the land of Ghana (Guinea) on the
western shore of Africa. Such, essentially, remained the extent of geographic knowledge down to the opening of the
fifteenth century. Various Christians had crossed Asia—a
journey made famous by the writings of the Venetian Marco
Polo[8]—and its outline was fairly well known. On the other
hand, all of Africa except the extreme north was only a
matter of hearsay to Europeans. Idrisi's map, without offering the possibility of circumnavigation, had shown a west-
ward-flowing river (presumably the Senegal) which had a
common source with the Nile. This tradition backed by
various legends about a Christian country in the interior
(really Ethiopia) might well lead to speculation about establishing direct contact between Europe and the Indies. Yet
what state could be expected to show any interest in such
a project during the early fifteenth century?

As it happened, only Portugal had the westward outlook

[7] See Figure 14 and above, p. 208.
[8] See Marco's famous memoirs of his trip to the court of Kublai Khan, his
experiences there, and his return. The story was dictated by Marco during his
later imprisonment by the Genoese.

and the freedom from other preoccupations to encourage experimentation with African voyages. And Portugal, though recognized by the papacy as a kingdom since 1179, was too small to contemplate an ambitious program of exploration. What ended in revolutionary discovery began very modestly indeed. Prince Henry of Portugal (1394-1460) held two important offices: the headship of the Order of Jesus, which had fallen heir to the local possessions of the Templars, and the governorship of Ceuta, a small Portuguese conquest across the strait from Gibraltar. In the former capacity he hoped that his crusaders, like the Teutonic Knights, might win new lands and peoples for Christianity. In the latter he sought to break into the remunerative slave trade carried on by the Moorish chieftains. These two motives combined to inspire a series of expeditions down the African coast in search of the fabled Ghana and its marvelous river. After the Azores, the Canaries, and Madeira had been occupied, his mariners crept past the inhospitable shores of the Sahara and finally reached the Promised Land to the south. Thence came shiploads of negro captives to be Christianized—and sold at a huge profit. Thence too came precious cargoes of gold dust, ivory, and other tropical products. Even before Prince Henry's death the Portuguese had forgotten the sacred crusade for the sake of commercial enterprise on a grand scale.

The ensuing adventures are a familiar story which the present volume can hardly begin to retell. Once having started, the Portuguese made rapid progress. In 1482 Diego Cam found the mouth of the Congo. A few years later Bartolomeo Diaz rounded the Cape. In 1498 Vasco da Gama actually completed a voyage to the Indies and back again. But this success had already been anticipated by Ferdinand of Aragon, who—without such great hesitation as has been attributed to him—backed the undertaking of one Christopher Columbus. Daring as he was in sailing straight west into the unknown, Columbus launched no startling theory by doing so. The sphericity of the earth had been taught

Portuguese exploration and the New World

in all Latin schools since at least the intellectual revival of the twelfth century and had, of course, been believed by educated Moslems for centuries earlier. The discovery of America, if not the circumnavigation of Africa, resulted from the application of mediæval science. Both, assuredly, were but logical consequences of a commercial expansion that had begun in the Age of the Crusades.

3. THE DECAY OF THE MANORIAL SYSTEM AND OF FEUDALISM

The reaction of the towns upon the country

In the twelfth century, as already noted, it became increasingly common for territorial lords to attract settlers of one sort or another by granting them formal charters of liberty. Under such a grant the peasant, whatever his earlier status, could become free by acquiring a legal residence in some particular place. The town-dwelling class or bourgeoisie, though engaged in commerce and allied activities, must originally have been recruited, to a large degree, from the rural population. Meanwhile, too, a multitude of free villages had been established in much the same way for the purpose of bringing new land under cultivation. The inhabitants of these villages, generally known as *hôtes*, constituted a very superior class within the peasantry. They were exempted from all arbitrary exaction of labor, produce, and money. By meeting obligations known in advance, they were assured of whatever profits they could earn. Like bourgeois, they could at any time sell their holdings, pack up their chattels, and move to a more favorable locality. There was, in fact, no sharp distinction between agrarian colonists and the lower rank of urban colonists; for most towns were small and even the great ones included many persons who lived by raising vegetables or by keeping domestic animals.

The all-important characteristic of these settlers in town or village was that, whatever their precise occupation and however poor they might be, they were not subjected to any manorial organization. To that extent they were economically emancipated. By the close of the thirteenth century considerable areas had thus come to be entirely populated by freemen—notably the reclaimed lands along the North Sea and the recently colonized regions beyond the Elbe. Besides, free communities enjoying a variety of special privileges were thickly scattered all through western Europe. The serf who somehow got away to such a community, and stayed there, would quickly cease to be a serf. But what of the old manors, the thousands of agrarian estates that constituted the hereditary wealth of the feudal aristocracy? To have any cultivators left, did the lords have to emancipate them *en masse*? There is little evidence to support such a conclusion. All fresh demands for labor had been met by natural increase of the population—especially through the migration of younger children to the new centers of employment. Despite the phenomenal growth of the bourgeois class, western Europe remained solidly agrarian except in a few favored regions. And throughout most of the anciently settled land the manorial system had scarcely been changed as late as the fourteenth century.

By that time, of course, an increasing number of serfs had been freed by individual charters of manumission, but this is a matter of relative unimportance. Since manorial organization was not invariably, or even usually, founded on personal servitude, its decay cannot be explained as the result of personal emancipation. The manor, for reasons set forth in an earlier chapter, must be regarded as an agrarian community whose life depended on a traditional routine of labor and a traditional equalization of the returns. Whether the peasant was legally free or unfree, he contributed his share of the labor and received his share of the returns. Accordingly, there could be no true emancipation of the peasantry as a whole until the ancient manorial organization had been generally abandoned—and that would amount to an economic revolution. Such a revolution did take place, though its course was very gradual and its effects were perceptible at different times in different countries. The key to a fuller understanding of its nature may be found in the fact that serfdom disappeared first in those regions where

Economic emancipation

mercantile development was furthest advanced—as, for example, in Flanders and northern Italy.

It has already been remarked that an immediate result of urban growth in the twelfth century was an increased demand for food and raw materials, which in turn led to the rapid expansion of the cultivated area. From the outset this expansion was largely dominated by capitalistic enterprise. Whether undertaken by the original landlord or by speculators who secured title from him, the reclamation of forest, swamp, and waste was inspired by the hope of profit. The ancient manors had been considered mere sources of goods to be consumed. The new agrarian settlements, on the other hand, were established in order to obtain goods to be sold. Even the individual peasants were engaged in a sort of business. They, as well as the lords to whom they paid their rents, depended on the cash markets that were now becoming available on all sides. And wherever facilities were best for the sale of agricultural produce in large quantities, it was inevitable that rural estates of the ancient type would be adapted to the new environment. In other words, the manors of the more progressive regions would be turned, essentially, into colonist villages.

Commutation and the end of serfdom

Under these improved economic conditions a great lord, instead of trying to produce everything he needed on his own estates, concentrated on whatever he found most profitable and bought the rest in the urban market. So, in the course of time, whole districts came to be devoted to particular kinds of production: for example, wheat and rye where the soil was richest, butter and cheese where the pasturage was best, wine where the finest grapes could be grown. And since it was now to the interest of the lord to obtain as much as he could at the lowest possible cost, he might decide that he would be better off without the old manorial arrangements. By substituting money rents for all the miscellaneous services of his peasants and hiring laborers with the proceeds, he not only would be relieved of administrative troubles but would also have his work better done. Commutation, thus carried out, necessarily implied the establishment of a cash economy in place of the time-honored co-operative agriculture. The manor ceased to be an agrarian community and became a group of individual tenants. The personal relationship of peasant to lord came to have no importance. As long as the rents were paid, the lord would not care who held the strips. One tenant could accumulate as many as he pleased; everybody was free to sell out and leave if he chose to do so.

Fundamentally, therefore, the emancipation of the peasantry seems to have been brought about through the influence of commercial growth upon the agrarian organization of the Dark Age. As far as western Europe was concerned, it may be said to have been well under way by the end of the thirteenth century, but not to have reached its culmination for another three hundred years. In both England and France the manorial system was still the rule during the fourteenth century. Then, as those countries recovered from the evils of the early fifteenth century, it rapidly declined and all but disappeared in the sixteenth. Thereafter serfdom was unknown to the English law, and no more than a memory remained in copyhold,[9] a form of hereditary tenure in return for a fixed rent. In most of the French provinces a similar development took place; the Revolution of 1789 found relatively few serfs to free and only vestiges of manorial custom to abrogate. To the eastward emancipation progressed much more slowly. Serfdom was not abolished in Prussia until 1807, in Russia not until fifty years later.

From the view here expressed it follows that in general the improvement of the peasants' condition was hardly the result of their own revolutionary activity. We hear of no such activity during the earlier period, when society was most thoroughly agrarian. Then, in the fourteenth century, there were three great risings, for which peasants were at

Peasant insurrections in the fourteenth century

[9] So-called because the tenure was said to be by copy of court roll—i.e., a manorial record. It has only recently been superseded by a modern form of ownership.

least in part responsible: the insurrection of 1323-28 in West
Flanders, the Jacquerie of 1357 in northern France, and the
Great Revolt of 1381 in England. But discontented artisans
were also prominent in the first and third; and the second
occurred after the example had been set by the Parisians
and other townsmen. Each of the three was undoubtedly
aggravated by local grievances—especially the tyranny of the
Flemish aristocracy, the collapse of the royal authority after
the battle of Poitiers, and the corruption of the government during the minority of Richard II. More fundamental
were a variety of economic ills that now tended to become
chronic. By the opening of the fourteenth century the material progress of the previous three hundred years had begun
to slacken. As old towns ceased to grow and fewer *villes
neuves* were established, the demand for commodities fell
off. It became increasingly difficult for a craftsman to rise
in his profession, or to secure employment at all. Peasants
who had been led to hope for immediate betterment were
sharply disappointed when war, famine, and pestilence made
the times even worse, and were thoroughly enraged when the
governing classes adopted reactionary measures.

Our sources are fuller for the English rising than for
those on the continent. The Great Revolt was the aftermath
of the Black Death, which about the middle of the fourteenth century ravaged England as well as the other European countries. The epidemic is now known to have been
plague, a germ disease carried by fleas that infest many small
animals. Originating in Asia, the Black Death was carried by
rats to all the great ports of Europe and thence spread inland by the panic-stricken inhabitants. Some towns, we are
told, lost a half or three-quarters of their population; many
villages were practically wiped out. Perhaps, in all, a third
of the English perished. In any case rural mortality was so
high that food stocks became depleted, prices rose to unprecedented levels, and agricultural labor was at a premium.
Parliament, under control of the land-owning class, sought
to re-establish normal conditions by the Statute of Laborers,

which imposed heavy penalties on runaway villeins and on men who demanded higher wages than had hitherto prevailed. This policy of the government, together with its notorious inefficiency and its attempts to levy an unpopular tax, precipitated the insurrection. However justified, it was a complete failure. As already remarked, the concessions made to the rebellious serfs were later annulled and emancipation came only in the course of gradual economic improvement. The Great Revolt of 1381 is of particular interest to historians because it so well illustrates the new social antagonisms of a transitional age.

Ultimately, of course, the feudal aristocracy was to be vitally affected by the influx of gold and silver from America; for the decrease in the value of money turned manorial rents into mere token payments. But in the Middle Ages the commutation of villein services, for reasons already seen, worked to the advantage of the landlords. It was rather the undermining of feudal tenure by the growth of a cash economy, supplemented by a revolution in warfare, that weakened their position in society. By the opening of the fourteenth century the rulers of progressive states, such as England and France, had ceased to depend on their ancient feudal and manorial income. Instead they had come to develop a system of regular taxes paid by all classes of subjects. And as an increasing proportion of these taxes came to be taken from the new wealth of the bourgeoisie, it was inevitable that the latter should demand and secure a greater share in the government. The introduction of townsmen into the old feudal councils is a prominent feature of constitutional development in the later thirteenth century. Whatever the precise nature of the representation obtained—in the assemblies of Frederick II, in the *cortes* of the Spanish kings, in the estates general of Philip IV, or in the parliaments of Edward I—the phenomenon was essentially the same. It constituted a legal recognition of bourgeois importance and denoted a proportional decline in the prestige of the feudal aristocracy.

The decline of the feudal aristocracy

With regard to contemporary changes in warfare only a
meager outline can be attempted here. Throughout the
thirteenth century armies continued to be thoroughly feudal.
The knight still fought in the old way, using the weapons
of his ancestors, though his defensive armor became increasingly elaborate as mail was extended over his arms
and legs, and as his head came to be covered by a great
helmet with a visor to be pulled up over the face. The
castle, too, retained its ancient importance, but palisades
and blockhouses had now been replaced by walls and keeps
of solid masonry. The stone keep was at first a square tower
placed against the side of the wall that enclosed the bailey.[10]
Along the top of this wall ran a parapet, behind which a
continuous walk provided advantageous positions for the
defenders. Outside was a deep moat, whenever possible filled
with water. Such a fortress was an enormous improvement
over the eleventh-century castle and yet proved to be vulnerable in many respects. Experience on the crusade taught
men the use of battering-rams, catapults, and other siege
engines, which were found to be particularly effective when
directed against corners. In the thirteenth century, therefore, the old distinctions of motte and bailey and of wall
and keep were abandoned. The castle became an integrated
structure, with round towers and bastions placed at intervals
so as to command every portion of the wall. Even if, by
means of scaling-ladders, the enemy took one section, it
could be entirely isolated from the rest. And the defenders
gained an even greater advantage when fortifications were
built in concentric rings, as at Krak-des-Chevaliers in Syria
(see Plate XII).

In the course of the fourteenth century, however, the
ancient dominance of the feudal array on the battlefield was
definitely broken. Courtrai, Crécy, and Poitiers were noteworthy victories of skillfully used infantry over the best of
cavalry forces. And in the following century the *coup de
grâce* to the traditional system was administered by the

[10] See Plate XII, Kenilworth Castle, the windows are a later addition.

Swiss, when they destroyed the proud armies of Charles the Rash. Although knights—now dressed in entire suits of plate armor—were still fighting at the opening of the sixteenth century, it had come to be recognized that, at least for defense, they had to be reinforced with units of pikemen, archers, and other infantry. Besides, artillery had already proved its effectiveness for certain kinds of warfare. What ever may be decided with regard to the origin of gunpowder,[11] there seems to be no doubt that the gun was a western invention of the fourteenth century and that its earliest form was a sort of cannon that fired balls of stone. For a long time it was a very crude weapon, almost as dangerous to the attackers as to the attacked. But as cannon were gradually improved, they became more useful, especially in besieging fortifications. By the end of the fifteenth century the feudal castle had lost all military significance. With its moats filled, and with windows cut in its massive walls, it was henceforth to be merely a palatial dwelling—as the word *château* now implies.

In the light of the facts detailed above, it may readily be understood why chivalry became decadent in the later Middle Ages. During the early feudal age the essence of vassalage had been the personal loyalty of a man to a single lord; the fief had been a quite subordinate factor. Subsequently, as one man might accumulate a dozen fiefs and for them owe homage to as many lords, how could he remain a Roland at heart? Lawyers, it is true, invented the saving distinction of liege homage, by which the claims of the chief lord were recognized as paramount; but by this time the spirit of ancient feudalism was already passing. Chivalry, under such conditions, became more and more an aristocratic affectation, overlaid with the *courtoisie* of the fashionable romance. At the opening of the twelfth century *adoubement* was still the barbarian custom of giving arms to the noble youth who had proved his manhood on the field of battle. By the end of the thirteenth it had been made into an elaborate cere-

The decadence of chivalry

[11] See below, p. 363.

monial—half mystic sacrament, to conform with the ideals of the church, and half courtly pageant, to delight the eyes of high-born ladies. In the fourteenth century it suffered further degradation. The lower the noble sank in real importance, the more extravagantly he flaunted his pride of birth and his feudal traditions. Although men were probably no less brutal in the primitive period, they lived a life that better comported with their character. They were quite frank in their coarseness, not having learned to affect a refinement which they did not possess. The chivalrous ostentation of Philip VI and Edward III ill concealed their actual worthlessness. The more useful example for the subsequent age was set by such unchivalrous princes as Charles V.

4. ARTS AND LETTERS

The "Italian Renaissance" and vernacular literature

On approaching the subject of artistic expression in the fourteenth and fifteenth centuries, all writers have long been expected to fix their attention upon a so-called Italian Renaissance. The expression, as first used by historians of a hundred years ago, designated a rebirth of ancient culture which, dispelling the darkness of the mediæval period, ushered in the age called modern. This Renaissance, it was alleged, began with the classical studies of the Italian humanists, was continued by the artists who rediscovered the beauty of antique monuments, and culminated in the glorious achievements of the sixteenth and seventeenth centuries. Today, of course, few if any historians would subscribe to the theory as stated above. Yet the phrases popularized by the older school remain in common use and, at least when they appear without proper qualification, may still be very misleading. Within the brief space that remains it is proposed to give, not a series of definitions or redefinitions, but a review of actual developments in the various cultural fields.

The splendid advance of vernacular literature during the Age of the Crusades has already been described in a preceding chapter. At the close of the thirteenth century the pre-eminence of the French in prose writing, as well as in all forms of poetic composition, was uncontested, although a number of remarkable works had appeared in German and Spanish. The fourteenth century, with its accumulated miseries for France, brought a marked decline in the quality, if not in the quantity, of French literary production. Too many poems now came to be written according to established formulas and to lack all freshness or sincerity. Prose likewise suffered from the contemporary decadence of feudal society. Froissart's famous chronicle of the Hundred Years War never rises above the level of elegant gossip—the superficial narrative of a Flemish shop-keeper hopelessly dazzled by the false chivalry of his day. And with the death of Froissart, about 1400, France entered upon a period of utter demoralization that hardly ended before the accession of Louis XI. It is therefore understandable why, in certain phases of intellectual and artistic activity, the leadership of Europe now passed to the Italians.

The illustrious Dante Alighieri owed his literary career **Dante** to the fact that, in the course of a municipal revolution (1265-1321) encouraged by Boniface VIII, he was exiled from Florence in 1302. For nearly a score of years, as the son of a prominent lawyer, he had taken an active part in the troubled politics of the republic and had been intimately associated with a number of talented artists and scholars. He had received a good education, presumably of the scholastic type then prevalent, and he had assuredly come under the influence of the vernacular poets. Some Italians, loyal to an ancient tradition, still wrote in Provençal; others, adopting a fashion set under Frederick II, preferred one of the native dialects. Dante, for reasons that he was subsequently to expound at length, followed the example of the latter group. Writing lyrics, he was naturally led to celebrate a beautiful lady whom he was compelled to adore from a distance, but his treatment of the familiar theme was distinctly original. The story is told in Dante's first book, the *Vita Nuova*—the New Life, to which he had been introduced by Beatrice. Actually, she was the wife of another Florentine gentleman and, according to Dante's own account, she had only spoken to him once, when he chanced to meet her on the street. Yet she had inspired the young poet to compose a series of mystic sonnets, which are included in the *Vita Nuova*; and, after her premature death in 1290, she had come to be his spiritual guide, leading him ever upward towards ultimate truth. Although Dante later took a wife and lived with her happily, it was not she whom he glorified in poetry, but the idealized Beatrice.

During his exile Dante produced a number of interesting works—some in verse and some in prose, some in Latin and some in the vernacular. His final preference, defended in one of his learned essays, was for a courtly Italian, which should combine the best features of all dialects within the peninsula; and in this language, essentially the speech of his native Florence, Dante finally wrote his immortal *Commedia*. The *Divine Comedy*, as it is generally known, is unlike anything else that has ever appeared. Though epic in scope and solemnity, it is by no means an impersonal narrative. In a way it is a tale of adventure, but the adventure is such as no man could really have and the hero is Dante himself, who relates in the first person what he has seen and heard. The author is thus permitted to express his own emotions whenever he pleases, giving to many passages an intensely lyric quality. The subject-matter of the poem is equally remarkable, for it deals with the entire universe— God and the world and all the creatures who have inhabited it. His literary device even provides unlimited opportunity for criticism of contemporary society. In substance, therefore, the *Divine Comedy* is a sort of encyclopædia, like those of the schoolmen;[12] yet in form it is a vernacular poem, combining and developing elements drawn from the epic, romantic, and lyric compositions of the preceding two centuries. The poet who could conceive such a work, perfect a language in which to express it, and then complete it with

[12] See below, pp. 361-62.

sustained artistry must always be recognized as a towering genius.

For most of the story itself the reader must be referred to the original or to one of the many translations. Dante, escorted by the pagan Vergil, first makes a tour of hell, which is a hollow cone reaching down into the spherical earth. Next, climbing by means of a passage to the opposite hemisphere, he ascends the mountain of purgatory. On its top he finds the earthly paradise, and there Beatrice assumes charge of his further progress. She, by mystic power, draws him up to the encircling spheres of the seven planets and finally, after passing through the heaven of the fixed stars, rewards him with a brief glimpse of God, enthroned in the Empyrean. Throughout this marvelous journey Dante meets the famous persons—good, bad, and indifferent—of all generations. In hell, well towards the bottom, he finds many clergymen, including a pope who predicts that Boniface VIII will soon arrive and then be joined by Clement V. In one or another of the heavens he encounters Justinian, who sketches for him the tragic history of the Roman Empire; a crusading ancestor, who castigates the present rulers of Florence and predicts the undying fame of Dante's book; St. Benedict, who discourses at length on the degeneracy of monastic orders; and lastly St. Peter, who approves Dante's theology and bids him speak boldly with regard to the corruption of the papacy. Quite apart from the quality of the verse, which has been applauded by numberless critics, the *Divine Comedy* is a magnificent work—sincerely religious, prodigiously learned, and yet amazingly human.

Exiled along with Dante was a Florentine notary who **Petrarch** established his residence on the papal territory near Avignon. **(1304-74)** His son, illustrious under the name of Petrarch,[13] first studied law at Montpellier and Bologna, but abandoned the legal profession to take holy orders. His motive, presumably, was to obtain means and leisure for a literary career; at any rate, he never allowed priesthood to interfere with either his love

[13] In Italian Petrarca—to which the poet changed his father's name, Petracco.

of women or his pursuit of worldly fame. Petrarch's activities as a humanist will be examined in the following section; here we are concerned with his early verse. Laura, he tells us, he first saw in 1327. She seems to have been married to a gentleman of Avignon and never to have paid the slightest attention to the poet who worshiped her from a romantic distance. Altogether, Petrarch inscribed over three hundred sonnets to Madonna Laura. Some of them are spoiled by the customary overindulgence in tricks of versification; many, on the other hand, are ranked among the lyric masterpieces of the world. Best of all are his less pretentious songs—as when he praises his lady's golden hair, blesses the grass that bears the imprint of her foot, or celebrates the glove that covers her hand.

Boccaccio (1313-75)   Of Petrarch's literary associates the most talented was Giovanni Boccaccio. The son of a Florentine merchant and a Parisian woman, Boccaccio was brought up in his father's trade and for a time lived in France. There he seems to have interested himself in French literature rather than in business; and as he grew to maturity, he devoted more and more of his time to writing. In honor of a certain Fiametta he composed a variety of lyrics, romances, and allegories, largely imitated from the French. It was only after coming to know the works of Petrarch that Boccaccio despaired of equaling his friend's sonnets and wisely confined his further efforts to prose. The result was the famous *Decameron*, a collection of stories presumed to be told by a company of ladies and gentlemen who have isolated themselves to escape the Black Death. Although Boccaccio's description of the pestilence is one of the classics on the subject, it serves in the Decameron merely to introduce the series of tales that, in large part, he borrowed from the French *fabliaux* or from such ancient authors as Apuleius. The originality of the book lies in its graceful, smooth-flowing style, which admirably reflects the changing moods of the narrative. The tales, as is well known, vary from the extremely delicate to quite the reverse. But as yet no one dreamed of expurgating this kind of literature; many generations were to pass before refined language became fashionable even in aristocratic circles. The *Decameron*, whatever may be thought of its subject-matter, is an artistic triumph which, as the first noteworthy composition in Italian prose, deserves mention along with the masterpieces of Dante and Petrarch.

While Italian was thus acquiring glory as a literary language, what we know as English was just beginning to take form. In the fourteenth century French was still spoken at the royal court of England and was learned as a matter of course by educated persons generally. In both town and country, however, the ancient vernacular had steadily gained among all classes of the people. There were many dialects. That of the north we know as Scottish; that of the south lingers on in rural communities and occasionally appears as a quaint or comic touch in modern novels. Our English is based rather on the speech of the Midlands, the ancient Anglo-Saxon of Mercia modified by and largely mixed with the spoken French of the Normans. It was this English which, after obscure development in various minor books, was brought to splendid maturity by a series of distinguished writers in the latter half of the fourteenth century. One of them was Wycliffe, whose religious teachings will be considered in the following section. To English literature his great contribution was the Bible that bears his name. Precisely what part he had in the translation remains doubtful, but in the later version of it we find emerging the majestic prose that was to reach such perfection in the Bible of King James two hundred years later. *(margin: Beginnings of modern English)*

One of Wycliffe's contemporaries, and one who shared many of the great preacher's convictions, was the author of the remarkable *Vision of Piers Plowman*.[14] Whether or not his name was Langland is a matter of no importance; we know him only through his poem, which is written in rather archaic English and employs the ancient alliterative verse of the Anglo-Saxons. In it we hear about a series of marvelous *(margin: The Vision of Piers Plowman)*

---

[14] See especially the modernized English version by Skeat, from which some of the following phrases have been taken.

visions. The first is an allegory of the earth and its inhabitants, most of whom are rascals. The dreamer, it is true, perceives a few honest men and good Christians. But they are all too rare among the hordes of others: "jugglers and jesters, all Judas's children"; beggars and beadsmen, intent on filling their bellies; pilgrims and palmers, who are no better than professional liars; pardoners, who cheat the people into buying indulgences;[15] all sorts of friars, who preach solely for profit; masters and doctors, who desert their parishes to hold easy jobs in London; serjeants of law, whose mouths will open only for pounds and pence; and unworthy laborers who loaf and sing all day. The other visions include a great lawsuit over the marriage of False to Lady Meed, the personification of unjust reward, and a pilgrimage to the shrine of St. Truth, led by Piers Plowman, the only person who knows the way. This poem, with its realistic sketches of contemporary society, is an eloquent commentary on the conditions that produced the Great Revolt of 1381.

Chaucer (d. 1400)

Geoffrey Chaucer, unlike the embittered author of *Piers Plowman*, seems never to have lacked the good things of life. He inherited considerable property from his father, a prosperous vintner of London, received a good education, traveled extensively, held various posts in the royal government, and enjoyed high favor at court. Although he composed many works, including numerous translations and adaptations from the French and the Italian, Chaucer remains chiefly famous for the *Canterbury Tales*—like the *Decameron* a collection of retold stories held together by means of a very obvious literary device. Writing in this way, an inferior poet would have produced little more than poor imitations. That Chaucer, despite his borrowing of subject-matter and literary forms, produced a great work of art is sufficient proof of his genius. To the old-fashioned language of *Piers Plowman* Chaucer preferred the colloquial English of the capital, with its rich intermixture of French; and the fact that we can read it with such ease shows how our speech is descended

---

[15] See below, p. 356 n.

from his rather than from Langland's. Since his own day Chaucer's popularity has never waned; for the *Canterbury Tales* have never been surpassed for graceful, witty, and entertaining narrative. Whatever the special merits of his individual stories, either in prose or in verse, the historian finds particular significance in Chaucer's prologue. This matchless series of portraits is too familiar to need even a summary here. It may, however, be pointed out that Chaucer could draw his characters with a good-humored objectivity that would have been impossible for a man in less easy circumstances. Chaucer launches no diatribe against the upper or middle classes; his gentle irony develops into biting satire only when he comes to certain members of the clergy—the worldly monk, the hypocritical friar, and the swindling pardoner. It should have been a fact of deep interest to the rulers of the church that in these respects Chaucer agreed with Langland, Wycliffe, Dante, Boccaccio, and a host of other critics, both heretical and orthodox.

The fifteenth century, for reasons already seen, brought a tragic relapse of culture on both sides of the Channel. England, to enjoy a great revival, had to wait for the Tudors, but under Louis XI the glory of French literature was restored by Philippe de Commines[16] and François Villon. It is no exaggeration to say that within the field of prose memoirs the standard set by Commines has never been surpassed, and that Villon may be called the greatest ballad-writer of all time. He certainly is one of the most famous characters in literary history. Born of a poor Parisian family in 1431, the boy was adopted by a certain Guillaume de Villon, a chaplain attached to the church of Saint-Benoît near the Sorbonne. Thanks to this worthy man, François acquired not only the name of Villon but also a superior education. In due course he became a master of arts at Paris and for a while continued in theological study. By this time, however, he had already developed the roistering habits that were to debar him from ecclesiastical preferment. Such as it was, his academic career

François Villon

[16] See above, p. 310.

ended with his killing of a priest in a fight over a girl, after which his associates became even more disreputable. Like so many others in that lawless age, Villon turned to thieving for a livelihood, and his downward path led him eventually to prison—just in time to be released by Louis XI as part of the usual ceremony attending a king's accession.

Villon had long been famous for his light verse. On hurriedly leaving Paris some years before, he had composed his *Petit Testament*, a series of humorous bequests in the form of a will. Now, in a very different mood, he wrote his *Grand Testament*, one of the greatest poems in any language. It is not merely clever and amusing; fundamentally, it is the poet's lament for a wasted life—as sincere and moving as if told in the confessional. His youth is gone, and with it are gone yesterday's boon companions and lights of love. He is left alone with his poverty. There is only one consolation:[17]

> Ofttimes my heart to me hath said, . . .
> "Better to live and rags to wear
> Than to have been a lord and, dead,
> Rot in a splendid sepulchre."

Death follows on his track; yet for a time he at least has life. So he inserts a number of his finest ballads on the two themes, the grim and the gay. And he continues the same alternation in the testament proper, bequeathing a lovely prayer to the Virgin for his mother, who cannot write, and ending with a mock epitaph for himself, in which he asks to be buried in a nunnery while the great bells of Notre-Dame celebrate his funeral. Villon lived to write one more great poem in 1462, when he expected to be hanged for his part in a stabbing affray. Actually, he was again pardoned. When or where he died we do not know. That we should not was perhaps his final jest.

The advance of secular art

Looking back over the long development of vernacular literature in mediæval Europe, we may readily see that its later stages were no more inspired by the ancient classics

---

[17] The quotation is from John Payne's translation.

than its earlier ones had been. However original the works of the later writers in Italian, English, and French, none of them were produced in revolt against the traditions of the twelfth and thirteenth centuries. The story is one of continuous growth, not of a renaissance—unless that name be applied to the revival of French literature under Louis XI. To a considerable degree the same generalization holds in the history of architecture and the decorative arts. In those fields, however, another factor must be taken into account—the progress of secularism. Vernacular literature, though largely produced by ecclesiastics, was from the beginning dominated by a secular spirit because it was intended for a secular audience. This was not true of architecture and the allied arts in the earlier period because the great artists, while themselves laymen, were exclusively employed to build and adorn churches. It was only with the decline of ecclesiastical influence and the rise of bourgeois wealth in the thirteenth and following centuries that secular architecture, sculpture, and painting had a chance to flourish.

At the opening of the fourteenth century Gothic still remained the dominant style of architecture in the north, but its great age was past. Simpler forms of construction were superseded by the style known in England as Decorated and in France as Flamboyant, from the flame-shaped traceries that characterized it (see Figure 3). Although striking effects were occasionally obtained by the use of such ornamentation, it tended, especially in France, to obscure rather than to enhance the structural beauty of the framework.[18] By that time, however, the communes of Flanders and Brabant had begun to raise the splendid civic structures that yet give them such charm and distinction—notably the cloth hall of Bruges (see Plate XIII), the belfry of Ghent, the *hôtels de ville* of Louvain and Oudenarde, and the clustering gild houses of Brussels. The statuary of the fourteenth and fifteenth centuries tells the same story. The radiant beauty of the earlier French

[18] See Plate XII (York Minster) and cf. the upper façade of Amiens Cathedral, Plate VI.

sculpture yielded to a naturalism that was better suited to portraits than to expressions of the ideal. So it was characteristic of the later age that some of the best artists were employed in designing memorial statues to the departed great. Even the characters of sacred history came to be represented as persons subject to violent emotion. The pathos of life and the tragedy of death, so prominent in the literature of the fifteenth century, became favorite themes for the sculptor, as well as for the illustrator of books and the painter.

Flemish painting   Throughout the earlier age painting had been used to decorate ecclesiastical buildings in three principal ways: on glass, on the wooden panels of altars, and on plaster. This last use—the process known as fresco—had scarcely been applicable in Gothic churches for the simple reason that they had no plaster walls. And little remains of such work in other structures north of the Alps. Stained glass, as we have seen, was a highly specialized art which inevitably declined along with Gothic architecture. On the other hand, the painting of altars continued to fascinate artists of the fourteenth century, and in this pursuit they naturally followed the traditions of the illuminators. From an early time it had been customary to adorn the finest manuscripts with marginal illustrations. These miniatures, though usually symbolic, might deal with anything. When, for example, a book of devotion was made for a wealthy prince, it might be decorated with realistic scenes from everyday life—as in the case of the Book of Hours illuminated for the duke of Berry, the brother of Charles V (see Plate XIV). Shortly afterwards a famous altar-piece at Ghent was painted by the brothers van Eyck, Flemings in the service of the Burgundian duke. Earlier paintings of this sort had normally been in tempera, i.e., color mixed with egg or gum. The van Eycks, on the contrary, used oils—a process which they seem to have perfected. The work of Jan van Eyck, in particular, was remarkable for its realism. He was a consummate portrait-painter, as may be realized from his "Man with the Pink" (see Plate XIV) or the figures of the donors in his larger compositions. He also excelled in the painting of domestic interiors, reproducing with amazing skill the textures of rich fabrics, the sheen of polished wood and metal, the brilliance of a sunny window, or the depth of reflection in a mirror. Effects like this had never before been achieved by smearing paint on a flat surface; and the art was essentially a native product, untouched by classic influence.

Italy, meanwhile, had witnessed remarkable developments, not only in painting, but also in sculpture and architecture; and to some degree they were inspired by antique models. The craze for Roman writings begun by the humanists[19] was accompanied by a craze for the remains of Roman art. Since to the collector of antiquities everything mediæval was barbarous or "Gothic," a reaction set in against the exuberant and often meaningless style that had been imported from the north. Italians generally sought to restore their buildings to classic purity. Knowing nothing of Greek architecture, they tended to imitate such Roman monuments as the triumphal arches and the Colosseum, which had never been examples of perfect taste. Too often they were satisfied with the addition, to a Romanesque or Gothic structure, of pilasters, entablatures, and other superficial features. The first great church to be hailed as an expression of the new movement was the cathedral of Florence, on which Brunelleschi placed a dome some three hundred feet high. Constructed like a cupola on an octagonal base, it was a fine and original work, though hardly Roman in design. More Italian than classic were likewise the civic buildings and private residences, the best of which (for example the Medici palace in Florence, Plate XIII) owe their beauty to graceful proportions rather than to pseudo-Roman decoration. What is called Renaissance architecture thus began as a very haphazard style, resting on no logical development of structural principles. It was not until later that Italian architects sought to work out a complete system, and then they adopted the mathematical formulas of the Roman Vitruvius. The results were

Italian architecture

[19] See below, pp. 365-66.

not altogether happy, but the continuation of the story must be left to others.

Italian sculpture

On the whole, Italian contributions in sculpture and painting were superior to those in architecture, and as late as the fifteenth century the former owed little to classic art. Perhaps it was fortunate that there were no antique pictures and, for a while, very few antique statues to be copied. The first of the great Italian sculptors was the Florentine Ghiberti, whose masterpiece was the set of bronze doors for the baptistery of the local cathedral (see Plate XVI). His magnificent reliefs, to be sure, reveal touches of Roman ornamentation; yet the total effect is anything but classical. The scenes from the Old and New Testaments are infused with religious feeling, while much of the decoration is naturalistic. In the work of the slightly younger Donatello this latter characteristic is even more pronounced. His statues of saints, instead of being attempts to represent ideal Christian virtues, are individual men and women, modeled from life with all their peculiarities and imperfections. His angels are smiling robust children. His David is a graceful Florentine boy who, it must be admitted, looks more like a dancer than the slayer of Goliath (see Plate XVI). Such an artist was primarily a master of portraiture. His equestrian statue of the mercenary captain Gattamelata set a new standard for the representation in bronze of a horse as well as a rider. This was the beginning of an art that, with the better appreciation of antique sculpture, was to attain fresh glory under the hands of Michelangelo.

Italian painting

The history of Italian painting is a much more complicated subject, and one that can be no more than touched here. The man who laid the foundations for the splendid advance of this art in the following centuries was Giotto, the compatriot and friend of Dante. Breaking with Byzantine tradition, he covered walls with frescoes that sought to tell a story by direct expression in pictures. Such, for example, are his famous decorations at Assisi, which deal with the life of St. Francis. Each scene is in itself a dramatic episode, portrayed with what was intended for realism. Giotto's skill in drawing was limited, but the pictorial value of his compositions made him the founder of a new school (see Plate XV). The rest of the century saw little more than imitations of Giotto; then Florence produced the astonishing Masaccio, who died at the age of only twenty-seven. The vivid realism of his pictures became the inspiration of all the great Florentine masters who followed (see Plate XV). By way of conclusion, it may only be mentioned that Verrochio, a disciple of Masaccio and a pupil of Donatello, helped to develop the surpassing genius of Leonardo da Vinci.

These facts should at least indicate that the rich vein of naturalism in Renaissance art was independent of all classic influence and had its source in the later Gothic art of the thirteenth and fourteenth centuries. It was not that the Italians borrowed from the Flemings or vice versa; both groups started with a common inspiration and up to a certain point progressed together. That the van Eycks were of the same generation as Masaccio, Ghiberti, and Donatello is more than coincidence. Whatever may be decided concerning the mutual influence of the two schools, it must be admitted that the Flemings led the way in realistic portraiture and landscape painting, and that they improved the technique of mixing colors with oil. On their side the Italians excelled in fresco, and from them all Europe learned the art of pictorial composition. Although ecclesiastical influence remained, the old religious feeling that had inspired Dante and Giotto all but died under their successors. The art of fifteenth-century Italy was secular in spirit. The madonnas and saints of the great Italian masters were hardly less fleshly, though more fully clothed, than their Roman gods and goddesses. The Italian theorists, who wished to derive everything fine in their civilization from the antique, were right in at least one particular: their art was essentially pagan. Eventually, as the artists became more expert, they were better able to appreciate the finer qualities of classic work and to draw from it lessons of value for their own age. There was, nevertheless,

no rebirth of ancient art, no sharp contrast between that said
to be of the Renaissance and that said to be of the Middle
Ages.

5. RELIGION AND LEARNING

The In-
quisition

By the middle of the thirteenth century, as noted in a preceding chapter, the church was confronted with two grave
problems. One, in the sphere of university education, was
how to reconcile the great body of the new learning, mainly
the work of pagans and Moslems, with the traditional principles of Christianity. The other, in the sphere of practical
religion, was how to prevent the loyalty of the masses from
being destroyed by more or less heretical agitation. Of these
problems the second was the more vital to the church, which
proceeded to meet it by developing a twofold policy: while
actual heresy was to be extirpated through whatever means
could be found, justified criticism of the clergy was to be
counteracted by the establishment of needful reforms. For a
while both phases of this policy had considerable success.

To combat the Albigensians, Pope Gregory IX finally
authorized certain Dominican friars to hear and determine
causes of heresy in southern France; and the system thus inaugurated was eventually extended to most of Latin Christendom. The new series of papal courts was known as the Inquisition because, unlike the ordinary courts of canon law,
they developed an inquisitorial process. The judges themselves sought out and prosecuted suspects. Trials were held
in secret. A defendant was not faced by his accusers and was
not permitted to have an advocate. In theory, torture could
only be applied once and any confession thereby secured
had to be confirmed by the accused while under no compulsion. It was only later that the inquisitors learned to nullify
these restrictions by "continuing" the first torture until the
desired confession was obtained. For incurring suspicion of
heresy, or in any way aiding heretics, various degrees of
penance were imposed. One who confessed and recanted
might be subjected at most to imprisonment for life. The

obdurate or relapsed heretic was "relinquished to the secular arm" for punishment under the civil law. And whatever the formula by which the relinquishment was carried out, every one knew that in most countries the law now prescribed burning at the stake. In extenuation of such practices it can at least be said that the primary object of the inquisitors was to win converts rather than to produce victims and that, until the later years of the mediæval period, judicial persecution was only occasional. Furthermore, the church ought not to be blamed for the faults of the entire age. All criminals then received what we should regard as inhuman treatment. Secular princes were no more tolerant than the clergy, while armies and mobs proved that they were even less merciful than the law.

The Franciscan order, as we have seen, had been primarily established for the sake of charitable work and had done much to improve the moral and physical condition of the people. Violent criticism of the organized church nevertheless continued in the later thirteenth century—for example, in the enormously popular *Romance of the Rose*. Jean de Meun, a learned bourgeois, took the unfinished allegory[20] and made it into a satire against the follies of mankind. By putting words into the mouths of his characters, Jean speaks his mind on every subject. He cares nothing for convention and flays the great and respected of all classes. His most damning indictment is leveled against the clergy, whom he accuses of avarice, pride, sloth, and general worthlessness. Judged as a work of art, the *Romance of the Rose* can hardly be ranked with the *Divine Comedy*; yet Dante, in his attack on the corruption of the church, was only one of many who followed the lead of the French satirist. Especially after the papacy had come to be resident at Avignon, its mercenary character was bitterly assailed by scores of writers, both in Latin and in the vernacular. Among the abuses commonly denounced were the pope's provision (i.e., nomination) of candidates for ecclesiastical office in all parts of Europe, his development of

Anti-clerical agitation and the Franciscans

[20] See above, p. 247.

various taxes to be paid by the clergy everywhere, and his
indiscriminate sale of indulgences.[21] Before long even the
Franciscans were drawn into the thick of the controversy.

By the close of the thirteenth century the Friars Minor had
widely departed from their original ideals. Without holding
actual title to property, they had generally come to live in
houses and not infrequently to engage in other than charitable pursuits. The change of discipline was frankly recognized as necessary by the governing majority in the order; but
a zealous minority, called the Spiritual Franciscans, fiercely
resented all lax interpretation of the rule and insisted upon a
life such as had been led by the saint's early disciples. Some
went so far as to preach and write against the wealth of the
clergy, thus allying with numerous radical groups that had
waged a similar campaign for generations. Although Clement
V commanded the Spiritual Franciscans to obey their superi-
ors, many refused to do so and instead formed a separate organization styled the Fraticelli. Clement's successor, John
XXII, only made the situation worse by issuing extreme pro-
nouncements that antagonized the entire order. Some of the
more prominent Franciscans, including the distinguished
William of Ockham,[22] took refuge with the emperor Louis
of Bavaria, who had likewise become embroiled with the
pope. And at his court they joined a number of other scholars
in composing weighty volumes to refute the papal claims.

**Four-
teenth-
century
mystics**

The ultimate significance of this affair in the religious history of Europe is much too complicated a subject for discussion here; only a few of its major connections can be
briefly indicated. The papacy, of course, turned the machinery
of the Inquisition against the dissenters, whether Franciscan
or not; but the chronic disorder of the age, culminating in
the Great Schism of 1378, prevented the enforcement of decisive measures. As a result, the opposition continued to gain
strength, and some of its leaders, in the face of ineffectual

---

[21] The indulgence was supposed to be a remission of penance, not a forgiveness of sin (see above, pp. 45, 197). But the papal agents engaged in raising
money were only too likely to misrepresent their wares.

[22] See below, p. 364.

threats, became out-and-out heretics. A great number of the dissatisfied, on the other hand, refused to break with the traditional system and sought consolation in various forms of mystic faith. There were, for instance, many such persons associated with the Spiritual Franciscans, either as actual friars or as lay brothers pledged to an especially austere life. In the early fourteenth century two German Dominicans, Eckehart and Tauler, had an important influence as preachers of contemplative piety, and so helped to found the religious association of laymen called the Friends of God. Somewhat similar were the Brothers of the Common Life, established in the Netherlands by Gerard Groote. The New Devotion to which they were committed is eloquently revealed by the well-known *Imitation of Christ*, traditionally ascribed to Thomas à Kempis. The list of other mystics who gained fame by preaching or writing could be extended indefinitely. But the greatest of them was unquestionably St. Catherine of Siena, a simple Italian girl whose ecstatic visions led her to play an active part in the contemporary agitation for reform.

Keeping in mind the social and religious discontent that characterized the fourteenth century, we may now turn to the renowned leaders of the anti-papal movement. Foremost among the authors who distinguished the otherwise insignificant court of the German king were two Parisian masters: the Frenchman, John of Jandun, and the Italian, Marsiglio of Padua. As a feature of the campaign against John XXII, they collaborated in a remarkable book entitled *Defensor Pacis* (Defender of Peace). It is divided into two main parts, one dealing with the state and the other with the church. The first part, probably contributed by John of Jandun, is largely drawn from Aristotle's *Politics* and develops the familiar thesis that monarchy rests on a delegation of power from the people. The second part, on the other hand, is strikingly original—an ample justification of Marsiglio's lasting fame as a political theorist. Here is set forth the idea that the church is really the body of believing Christians. Within that congregation clergymen have the power to determine

Marsiglio of Padua

purely ecclesiastical questions; but they have no power to assess temporal penalties, for God alone may punish violations of His law. Nor have clergymen any just title to worldly goods; their sole function is to save souls by preaching the Gospel and by administering the sacraments. The pope is merely the elected head of the clergy. His alleged plenitude of power is sheer usurpation. Sovereign authority within the church lies with the community of Christian citizens. A general council representing them not only can but must carry through a sweeping reform. Until that is done, there will be no lasting peace in the world.

Wycliffe and the Lollards

Marsiglio's book, to be sure, was only a theoretical discussion; yet it was one that could be turned to excellent account by agitators of all kinds. Especially in England, where the French sympathies of the Avignon popes were hotly resented, the anti-papal movement gained rapid headway towards the middle of the fourteenth century. With the cordial support of the royal government, parliament forbade papal appointment to ecclesiastical office in England by the Statute of Provisors, restricted the carrying of appeals to the papal court by the Statute of Præmunire, and finally denied all papal lordship over the realm on the ground that King John's homage to Innocent III had been illegal. It was no wonder that powerful men at the court of Edward III now welcomed the learned essays of one John Wycliffe. Almost nothing is known of his early life. By 1360 he was a well-known master at Oxford and, as an ordained priest, was helping to maintain himself at. the university by holding a parish in the country. Since he had previously been a student at Oxford, he must have come under the influence of such famous men as William of Ockham. At any rate, when Wycliffe himself came to publish books, they developed arguments that had long been familiar in the controversial writings of the Franciscans and others—as that the rightful authority of a ruler, lay or clerical, is in direct proportion to the reciprocal service that he performs for his subjects; and that, at least in some cases, a state may be justified in confiscating ecclesiastical property. Wycliffe's favor at court stood him in good stead when Pope Gregory XI condemned as erroneous eighteen of his opinions, affirming that they were reminiscent of Marsiglio "of damned memory." For a time Wycliffe even kept his position at the university. Then, as he more and more became a rebel against ecclesiastical authority, he lost the support of the conservative elements at Oxford and retired to his parish of Lutterworth, where he died in 1384.

Until his later years Wycliffe remained essentially a scholar; and since his Latin works are filled with the fine-drawn distinctions of the schoolmen, it is often hard to determine his exact position. Some points, however, are certain. He repudiated the papal headship as a corruption of the primitive church. Without excluding all miraculous quality from the celebration of the mass, he denied transubstantiation as it had been defined since the days of Innocent III. And after his writings had been formally declared heretical, he naturally tended to press his argument to increasingly radical conclusions. Like the Waldensians, he came to emphasize the saving power of Christ rather than priestly mediation, and to prefer the authority of Holy Scripture to that of the organized church. Through force of circumstance he at the same time shifted his appeal from men in power to the ordinary inhabitants of town and country, preaching in the vernacular, supervising an English translation of the Bible, and inspiring disciples to adopt a life of poverty among the people for the sake of reform agitation. Although Wycliffe himself never justified political insurrection, some of his popular preachers may have done so. There were, we know, rebellious priests who encouraged the Great Revolt of 1381. In any case, the Lollards, as Wycliffe's disciples came to be known, multiplied rapidly during the troubled years that closed the fourteenth century. Then the Lancastrian Henry IV, anxious to obtain ecclesiastical recognition of his title to the throne, gave warm support to the orthodox cause. The punishment of heretics by burning, hitherto unknown in

England, was now established by act of parliament; and after a rising of the Lollard gentry had been suppressed, the law was rigorously enforced against the remnants of the sect.

Meanwhile, remarkably enough, the Wycliffite doctrines had become widely prevalent in Bohemia. There, even more than in England, men had been prepared for the reception of heterodox views by the preaching of Waldensians and other reformers during the previous two hundred years. And in so far as the Roman Church in Bohemia was identified with German domination, the cause of reform was eagerly adopted by all patriotic Czechs.[23] Among them, at the opening of the fifteenth century, was John Hus, a young theologian in the university of Prague, who became acquainted with the later books of Wycliffe when they were brought to him by Bohemian students returning from Oxford. However respectable as a scholar, Hus was chiefly famous as a preacher attached to one of the local chapels. The doctrinal extremes of Wycliffe he refused to accept; rather he emphasized the Lollard denunciation of abuses in the church and the need of practical reform in religion. His sermons, delivered in the vernacular, won great success. His views, taken up by a host of volunteers, quickly spread throughout the countryside, and there the agitation grew more and more violent. Quite inevitably Hus became embroiled with the ecclesiastical authorities who, in this instance, were supported by the royal government. The result has already been seen. Tried before the Council of Constance, Hus was found guilty of heresy and, on refusing to abjure, was burned in 1415. Yet the Czechs insisted on regarding him as the martyr of a holy and patriotic cause. Sigismund,[24] for ignoring the imperial letters of safe conduct that he had given to Hus, was driven from Bohemia. For over a dozen years the country was controlled by the rebels, who turned back no less than five crusades directed against them by the pope. Among themselves, however, the Hussites were divided into two main parties: the moderates,

---

[23] See above, pp. 185, 212.
[24] See above, p. 273.

who demanded only a few changes in ecclesiastical discipline and ceremonial, and the radicals, who tended to reject all beliefs and practices not directly justified by Scripture. It was by making peace with the moderates that the council of Basel was able to break the Hussite power and, after the radicals had been crushed, to pacify Bohemia in 1436.

In the course of the foregoing discussion it has been necessary to mention a number of university teachers; yet, on the whole, academic discussion remained apart from religious controversy. Although Albigensians and other heretical agitators might be condemned by the Inquisition and relinquished to the secular arm for legal execution, no outstanding scholar was thus punished in the Middle Ages. During the great age of the mediæval universities the freedom permitted to the teaching profession was much greater than it was to enjoy in the subsequent period. Early in the thirteenth century the papacy, perceiving especial danger in Aristotle's philosophy and the Arabic commentaries upon it, at first tried to·exclude the obnoxious books from the curriculum. But as students everywhere insisted on reading the whole of Aristotle, the later popes adopted the wise policy of encouraging its reconciliation with Christian dogma. For this task the Dominican friars, because of their devotion both to learning and to authority, were peculiarly fitted. In all university centers they maintained houses with resident masters, to whom the best of the pupils trained in their local schools were sent for advanced instruction. The most promising of their theologians naturally came to Paris, and it was this group in particular that now undertook the formidable task of combining the results of human learning. That the three greatest encyclopædists of the later thirteenth century were Dominican masters at Paris was no mere coincidence.

Dominican scholarship: Thomas Aquinas

Vincent of Beauvais was essentially a compiler. His *Speculum Maius* (Greater Mirror) is a prodigious book of 9885 chapters. In its three parts—the mirrors of nature, of doctrine, and of history—it covers the whole realm of contemporary knowledge, but is more remarkable for its comprehensive plan than for the quality of its thought. As a philosopher and as a scientist, Vincent was far surpassed by the German Albertus Magnus (Albert the Great), a renowned teacher and writer at Paris. He was the most learned man of his generation, and his monumental books—thirty-eight quarto volumes in the last printed edition—cover the entire field of contemporary education, with noteworthy sections devoted to mathematics, physics, biology, and Aristotelian philosophy interpreted in the light of Christianity. Though Albert wrote a *Summa Theologiæ* (Compendium of Theology), the finer work of this type was produced by his pupil, the Italian Thomas Aquinas. Whatever may be thought of the author's particular conclusions, the *Summa* of Aquinas is an intellectual achievement of the first magnitude. Its main purpose— to reconcile the truths of revelation, as found in the dogmas of the church, with the truths of reason, as set forth by Aristotle—is most admirably carried out. Every believer in traditional Christianity who is unwilling to abandon all reliance on the rational faculties must, indeed, arrive at some such compromise as that of the great Dominican.

The Franciscan opposition: Roger Bacon

Since the triumph of Aquinas in the field of academic instruction was also a triumph for the papacy, it is not surprising that his book has now been officially recognized as the basis of theological instruction in all Roman Catholic schools. Yet there was no unanimity with regard to the Thomist doctrine in the Middle Ages. At Paris the increasing power of the Dominicans was bitterly opposed by the other masters, who in this respect were quite as willing to quarrel with a pope as with any one else. And the anti-Dominican cause could always obtain vigorous support from Oxford, where the Franciscans, despite their founder's deprecation of book learning, had acquired intellectual leadership. In so far as the Dominican doctors became ardent Aristotelians, the Franciscan doctors eloquently defended the Platonic traditions of St. Augustine. The more radical of the Oxonians might go so far as to accuse the Parisians of neglecting the truly important sciences for the sake of deductive argumentation. At one time this opinion was exclusively accredited to Roger Bacon; now it is beginning to be understood that he was essentially the pupil of Robert Grosseteste. An English boy of humble birth, Grosseteste rose through sheer ability to be chief lecturer of the Franciscans at Oxford, chancellor of the university, and finally (1235-53) bishop of Lincoln. Though necessarily proficient as a theologian, he revealed a dominant interest in natural science by writings on astronomy, chronology, physics, and optics. He had a thorough knowledge of Greek and at least a smattering of Hebrew. It was these accomplishments and predilections that he passed on to Roger Bacon, whose alleged martyrdom for the cause of science has brought him posthumous fame in the modern world.

The known facts about Roger Bacon are far less romantic. He was an Englishman who, after studying at Oxford, became a master at Paris and there for a time taught the ordinary subjects in the ordinary way. Later, becoming dissatisfied with what he was doing and with the books that he was using, he joined the Oxford Franciscans in order to gain leisure for more original investigation and for learning the necessary languages. Eventually, after considerable reading of Greek and Arabic authors, he sent to the pope the sketch of a *Summa* which he never actually completed. In it he outlin d an improved scheme of education; and although he tended to minimize the achievements of his contemporaries, he admirably stated a number of theoretical reforms—especially the study of ancient writings in the original languages and a greater emphasis upon mathematics and experimentation. Bacon himself was interested in mechanical engines of one sort or another, in combinations of reflecting mirrors, and in the processes of alchemy. By developing Arabic science, he may have been able to produce an explosive substance like gunpowder. There is, however, no evidence that he ever constructed a telescope, a compound microscope, or a gun. It is very significant that his conception of experimental science did not exclude the mystic interpretation of dreams or the current lore of the alchemists and astrologers. And his supposed imprisonment on account of his scientific activities is no more than a legend.

William of Ockham

In the fourteenth century the feud with the Dominican scholars was continued by Duns Scotus and William of Ockham, both of them Franciscans of Oxford. The former was more a mystic than a scientist and more a critic than a systematic theologian. For his skill in dialectic he was called *Doctor Subtilis*, and he achieved great fame by defending the thesis that such doctrines as the existence of God and the immortality of the soul cannot be proved by reason. Logically carried out, his argument would have denied much of the Thomist system. Scotus, however, died prematurely in 1308 and within a few years his work had been largely superseded by Ockham's. That illustrious scholar revived the discussion over universals and particulars by re-examining the whole subject of human knowledge. Accepting the dogmas of the church as matters of divine revelation, Ockham discarded the rationalized theology of the schools as resting on false premises. General ideas, he declared, have in themselves no absolute truth. One idea we accept because it follows from another already held. But what is the origin of the latter? Its validity must depend on the extent to which it faithfully represents the objects of experience. This was to challenge not only the teaching of Aquinas but all rationalism that preferred logic to observation. It was an approach to the very threshold of what we call the scientific method, and momentarily it encouraged some promising developments in the schools. Despite Ockham's later denunciation of the papacy, the foremost Parisian scholars of the following generation were his disciples. Turning their attention to mathematics and the physical constitution of the universe, they vaguely anticipated many of the truths that were to be demonstrated by Galileo and other scientists in the seventeenth century. But with the growing anarchy in church and state many of the old universities fell into decay; too often scholastic education degenerated into mere repetition of ancient formulas and prolonged argument about very little.

In Italy, meanwhile, Petrarch had led the way towards a revival of humanistic study. In his time, as earlier, the humanist was essentially one who remained loyal to the ideal of the ancient grammarians—one who devoted himself primarily to *litteræ humaniores*, i.e., the "more humane" or secular literature of pagan antiquity. We have seen that the Latin classics had been continuously used throughout the preceding centuries; for such classics, indeed, Petrarch and his followers were entirely dependent on mediæval copies of the ancient books. But the educational system of the west, being governed by the church, had subordinated literary study to the needs of practical religion. The great revival of learning in the eleventh and twelfth centuries, though briefly characterized by renewed enthusiasm for grammar, had culminated in the development of the universities, where instruction was concentrated on professional subjects. It was inevitable that the weakening of ecclesiastical influence should produce a sharp reaction towards secular ideals in education. And in Italy, with its urban civilization and its pleasure-loving aristocracy, the emphasis of the schools tended to be æsthetic—to be placed on the study of literature for its own sake.

Petrarch and the humanist revival

Petrarch, whose example was largely responsible for the new movement, was a man of strange contradictions. Having won merited fame by his Italian verse, which displays a lively appreciation of the contemporary world, he came to affect a great disdain for the vulgar tongue and to express the wish that he could have lived in some age other than his own. Although he was a priest, he showed no understanding of Dante's Christianity and found his chief inspiration in pagan letters. With a very imperfect knowledge of the Latin classics and no knowledge of Greek at all, he denounced the barbarism of the schoolmen and sought to write as Cicero and Seneca had written. The result, naturally enough, was mediocre. For the sake of sheer delight, who today would read any of Petrarch's works except his sonnets? And much the same criticism holds for Boccaccio, who ranks among the immortals on account of his stories in the vernacular, not on account of his later attempts at elegant Greek and Latin.

Humanism and literary appreciation

A cause, however, should not be judged by the foibles of its leaders. The humanist enthusiasm for classical study, despite the extremes to which it was sometimes carried, was in itself admirable—as all lovers of great art will surely admit. Within the field of Latin literature it led to the rediscovery of many forgotten books and the truer appreciation of many that had been neglected. Within the field of Greek literature —as far as the western schools were concerned—it produced a revolution. Such of the ancient authors as had generally been known through poor translations now came to be used in the original, and beside them were now placed the masterpieces of prose and verse that the Latins, following the Arabs, had hitherto ignored. Study of this sort was a thousand years old, or more, in the cities of the eastern Mediterranean; but to the Italians of the later fourteenth century it was an exciting novelty. Once launched, the humanist education quickly became an academic craze. To satisfy the demands of students, old professorships were reformed and new ones were established. Great libraries were erected to house the treasures that were eagerly collected on all sides. Improved editions of Greek and Latin authors were brought out in beautiful handwriting. Scholars produced more adequate grammars, dictionaries, and other manuals. And as men sought to read the classics with a fuller understanding, they gained a better knowledge of the ancient world generally and so broadened their intellectual horizon. All this, it will be agreed, places us under deep obligation to the humanists, who came to dominate the universities of Italy in the fifteenth century and those of other countries in the centuries following.

Humanism and science

To praise the humanism of the later Middle Ages as an æsthetic revival is by no means to admit the once-honored thesis of the Italian Renaissance. However important in the field of education, humanism was no magical element by which mediæval culture could be transformed into modern culture. Will any one today care to assert that a finer appreciation of ancient literature produced the glorious arts of the fifteenth century, the growth of capitalism, the opening of the New World, the Protestant Revolution, or the triumphs of experimental science? Repetition of what has already been said about some of these developments will hardly be necessary. As far as architecture, sculpture, and painting are concerned, the influence of humanism was at most secondary. Vernacular literature, it may easily be perceived, progressed not by virtue of humanism but in spite of it. Economic development had absolutely nothing to do with changing academic fashions, and it was the former rather than the latter that determined the course of ecclesiastical history. There remains the question of scientific progress, and in this connection it must be granted that the chief credit goes to the schoolmen. The early humanists, by rejecting both the vernacular and the contemporary Latin for literary composition, made it difficult for their disciples to be more than antiquarians. Along with scholastic theology, they condemned original advance in law, mathematics, and the study of natural phenomena. In their zeal to extol Plato at the expense of Aristotle, they rejected all that antiquity and the Middle Ages had contributed towards the definition of scientific method. It is now coming to be understood that, without the preliminary work of Hellenistic, Arabic, and mediæval scholars, the magnificent achievements of Vesalius, Fabricius, Brahe, Kepler, Galileo, and Harvey would not have been possible.

How far the great age of the humanists was removed from the scientific attitude of the modern world is clearly shown by the fact that the fifteenth and sixteenth centuries marked the height of the witchcraft mania—a hysterical relapse into superstition for which little if any support can be found in the scholastic writings. All the theologians, to be sure, wrote at length on the origin of evil, the fall of the angels, and the power of Satan. Accepting the authority of Scripture, they had to follow the church fathers in emphasizing diabolic inter-

The witch-craft delusion

vention in human affairs. But in general they agreed that neither Satan nor his agents could in any way contravene the divine order of nature, as by changing a man into a beast. The witch of popular delusion seems rather to have been derived from the ancient folklore of werewolves and night-hags; and any one who believed in such things, the older writers declared, was sinfully yielding to Satanic deception. It was not until the fourteenth century that charges of sorcery began to be prominent in trials before secular courts and that the Inquisition began to take cognizance of witch-craft as a form of heresy. By the fifteenth century the educated apparently joined the uneducated in attributing the evil times to a devilish conspiracy for the ruin of the world, and the great witch hunt was on. To what extent the experts of church and state had now accepted the popular belief in witchcraft may be seen from three famous sources: the records of Jeanne d'Arc's trial in 1431, the witch bull of Pope Innocent VIII in 1484, and the *Malleus Maleficarum* (Hammer of Witches) published by his inquisitors in 1486. If one looks for such documents from the happier age preceding, he will not find them.

The printing-press

A few words, finally, may be devoted to the subject of mechanical invention. Of the much that we should like to know about the technology of the Middle Ages little can be positively stated. There were at least three great mediæval inventions: the magnetic compass, the gun, and the printing-press. The first was presumably brought by the Arabs to western Europe, where it was unknown before the twelfth century. The second, as we have seen, was apparently perfected by Europeans in the fourteenth century, though men had already learned how to make the explosive that came to be called gunpowder. It is only the third that has ever been attributed to the influence of humanism. But paper-making, we may be sure, had been brought westward by the Arabs, and with it the method of printing by means of carved wooden blocks. Such printing could be used either for pictures or for letters. Not infrequently whole books were thus reproduced. Whether the invention of the printing-press should be credited to Gutenberg of Mainz or to Coster of Haarlem is still disputed. In any case, what was invented was the casting of metal type that could be set in a frame and so used over and over again. Perfected about the middle of the fifteenth century, the new art spread rapidly, so that presses were working in practically every country of Europe before 1500. Was it the demand for books created by the humanists that led directly to the invention? First to be printed were Bibles, psalters, and scholastic texts, rather than editions of the classics. The earliest type to be used was that called Gothic, a reproduction of the decorated hand popular in the later Middle Ages. The primary contribution of the humanists seems to have been a preference for the type that became known as Roman—actually copied from the Carolingian minuscule.[25]

That the appearance of the printing-press revolutionized the intellectual history of mankind is another familiar statement. If taken generally to apply to a slow process, it is true enough. It does not, however, hold for the fifteenth and sixteenth centuries alone. Although the invention was welcomed as a useful method of producing books cheaply, it hardly induced anybody to read what he would not otherwise have read and it left unchanged the ideas of the masses. Here, as always, the historian finds that his epoch-making event was not a sudden innovation, but a gradual transition.

[25] See above, p. 128.

CONCLUSION

THE SIGNIFICANCE OF MEDIÆVAL CIVILIZATION

One who writes a book on the Middle Ages necessarily stops with the close of the fifteenth century, when he reaches the time-honored boundary between the mediæval and modern periods. Although that boundary is in some respects bad, it is no worse than most of the arbitrary divisions that have come to be accepted, and it has the advantage of leaving to other volumes such excellent starting-points as the discovery of the New World and the outbreak of the Protestant Revolution. To say this, however, is merely to adopt a convenience in historical narration; it is not to attribute a peculiarly modern character to voyages of exploration or to attacks upon the organized church. Without serious distortion of the truth, the Protestant Revolution might be called a chapter in the history of mediæval religion, the opening of the New World a chapter in the history of mediæval commerce. When used with more than a chronological implication, the terms "mediæval" and "modern" become only a source of confusion.

We cannot, for example, hold that the essence of mediævalism was feudal society without concluding that a good part of western Europe ceased to be mediæval in the thirteenth century; or hold that it was devotion to the papacy without admitting that a large section of humanity is still mediæval. We are told about a mediæval mind, perpetually fascinated by abstractions, merely to discover that few men outside the cloister ever thought in that fashion at all. For the sake of preserving historical sanity, it is better to forget such generalizations and to realize that in the so-called Middle Ages, as in other ages, ideas and habits and institutions varied enormously. To call anything mediæval is not to describe it. No single word should be expected to give precise information about peoples and customs throughout a span of a thousand years. A book on the period after 1500 can cover only a little more than four centuries; yet who will attempt a brief definition of "modernity" or a summary characterization of the "modern mind"? The search for the first modern man is as vain as that for the last man of antiquity. The deluded enthusiast who undertakes such a quest will inevitably lose himself in the Middle Ages.

As historical students, we cannot hope to isolate the typically mediæval or the typically modern; we can only try to explain what happened in a given period. If, without presupposing an Italian Renaissance or other miraculous transformation, we turn from the mediæval centuries to the sixteenth and seventeenth, we find, simply, a continuation of what we have already studied. For instance, we may see that the Habsburg inheritance of the Spanish throne was the lucky consequence of a policy that had been followed by every feudal house in Europe; that, by fighting the French kings for two hundred years, the Habsburgs prolonged an ancient feud which they had acquired with the Burgundian dominions. As a matter of fact, European politics are still permeated by traditions of the Middle Ages. The newspapers of today may not refer to the Holy Roman Empire; but recent events have served to replace it on the map. Almost invariably the present rivalries of nations in the Balkans, along the German-Slavic frontier, on the Baltic, or to the westward carry us back to the days of Jeanne d'Arc or earlier. Even to account for modern imperialism in Asia and Africa, we have to revert to precedents set by the crusaders.

In other fields the importance of the mediæval period is yet clearer. The constitutions of both England and France, as they were to be retained for centuries, had in substance appeared long before the end of the Hundred Years' War. From the towns of the twelfth century we derive such important features of our modern culture as local self-government, the free tenure of land, everyday business organization, banking practice, and other varieties of capitalistic enterprise. In navigation, warfare, and book-making the importance of mediæval invention will be recognized without further comment. The especial glories of the Middle Ages, however, must always be seen in the development of a rich vernacular literature, the perfection of a splendid native art, and the revival of learning that gave birth to our first universities.

For beauty and originality the monuments of the Romanesque and Gothic styles, the feudal epics, the songs of the troubadours, and the cycles of romances rank among the world's masterpieces. Many of them—together with the memoirs of Joinville and Commines, the stories of Boccaccio, and the immortal verse of Dante, Petrarch, Chaucer, and Villon—have held an unfailing charm for countless generations. Scholasticism is now generally thought of as something devoid of practical sense; yet the educational system of the mediæval schools was not sheer foolishness. It had at least the merit of demanding analytical thought—an intellectual discipline that, we may hope, will never be outmoded. The logic and the mathematics of the thirteenth century are, as far as they go, still valid. The theology of Peter Lombard and Thomas Aquinas, though discarded by most universities, continues official in the Roman Church and differs from Protestant theology merely in that the latter rests on another set of postulates. The study of law, with its necessary reliance on deduction from authoritative precepts, has never ceased to be thoroughly scholastic. The natural science of the schoolmen, for all its shortcomings, was the best that the world could then offer and prepared the way for the triumphs of the seventeenth and eighteenth centuries.

The traditional distinction between the modern and the mediæval is not, therefore, a distinction between the vital and the defunct. Many an institution that flourished after 1500 is today as dead as chivalry, while much from the Middle Ages remains a living heritage of the present.

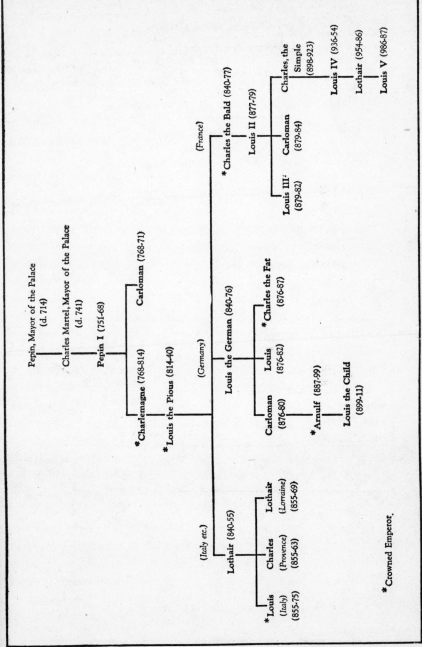

TABLE I. THE CAROLINGIANS.

Pepin, Mayor of the Palace (d. 714)

Charles Martel, Mayor of the Palace (d. 741)

Pepin I (751-68)

*Charlemagne (768-814)   Carloman (768-71)

*Louis the Pious (814-40)

(Germany)   (France)   (Italy etc.)

Louis the German (840-76)   *Charles the Bald (840-77)   Lothair (840-55)

Carloman (876-80)   Louis (876-82)   *Charles the Fat (876-87)   Louis II (877-79)   Louis (Italy) (855-75)   Charles (Provence) (855-63)   Lothair (Lorraine) (855-69)

*Arnulf (887-99)   Louis III¹ (879-82)   Carloman (879-84)

Louis the Child (899-11)   Charles, the Simple (898-923)

Louis IV (936-54)

Lothair (954-86)

Louis V (986-87)

* Crowned Emperor.

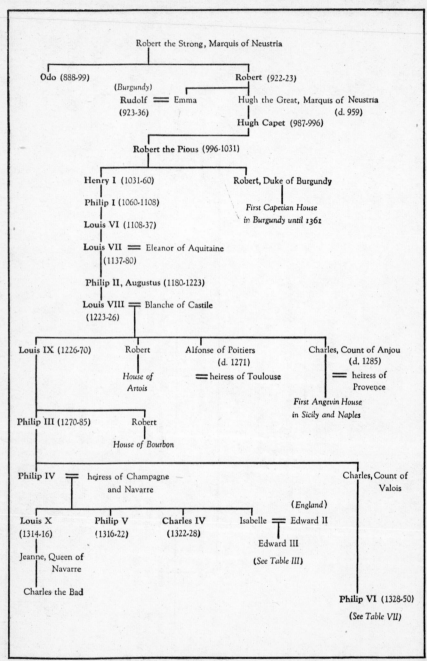

TABLE II. THE CAPETIAN HOUSE UNTIL 1328.

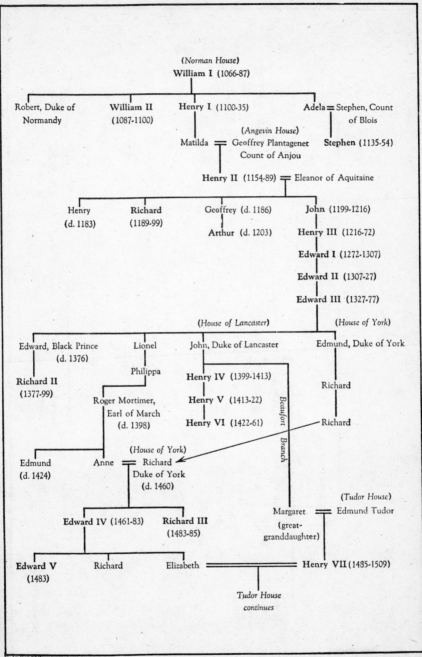

TABLE III. KINGS OF ENGLAND (1066-1485).

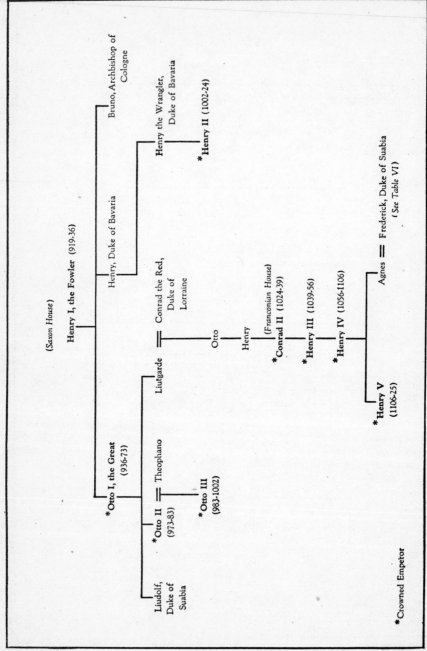

TABLE IV. SAXON AND FRANCONIAN KINGS OF GERMANY.

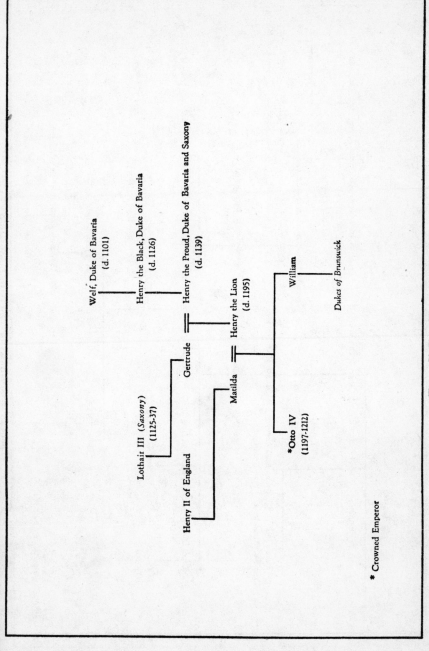

Welf, Duke of Bavaria
(d. 1101)

Henry the Black, Duke of Bavaria
(d. 1126)

Lothair III (*Saxony*)
(1125-37)

Gertrude

Henry the Proud, Duke of Bavaria and Saxony
(d. 1139)

Henry II of England

Matilda

Henry the Lion
(d. 1195)

*Otto IV
(1197-1212)

William

Dukes of Brunswick

* Crowned Emperor

TABLE V. THE HOUSE OF GUELF.

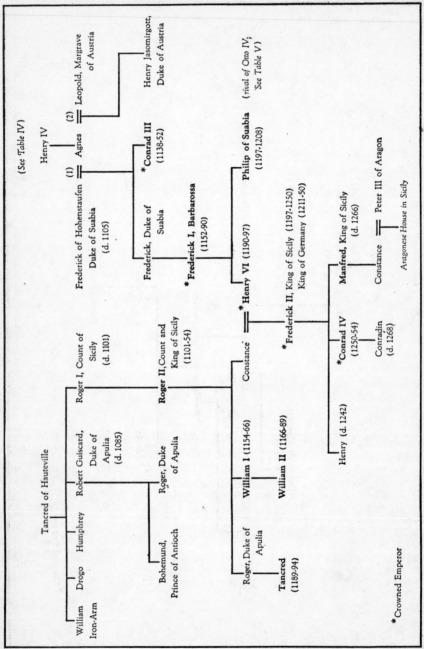

TABLE VI. THE HOUSES OF HAUTEVILLE AND HOHENSTAUFEN.

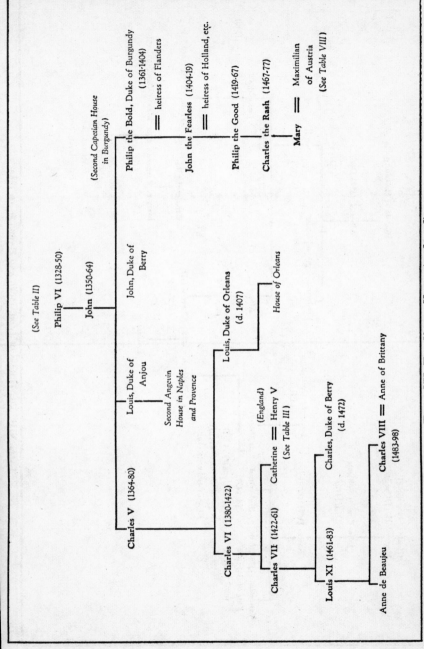

TABLE VII. THE VALOIS HOUSE (1328-1498).

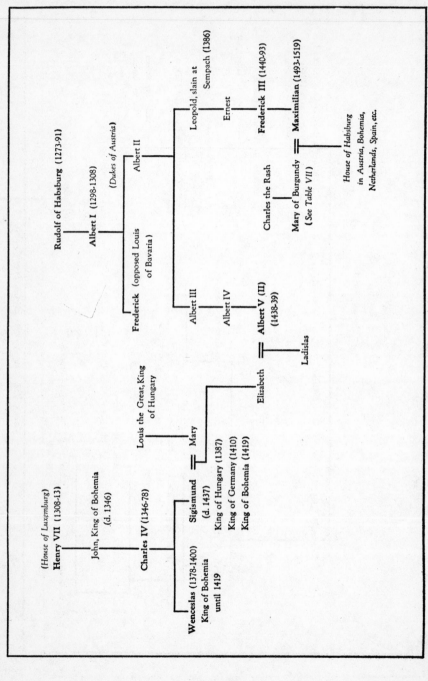

TABLE VIII. THE HOUSES OF LUXEMBURG AND HABSBURG TO 1498.

Abbreviations for
CHRONOLOGICAL CHARTS

K...King

D...Duke

C...Count

P...Pope

Æ...Archbishop

B...Bishop

d...died

m...married

† ..murdered

⚔ ..Battle of

FOURTH CENTURY

Date	ARTS AND LETTERS	THE CHURCH	ROMAN EMPIRE — WEST	ROMAN EMPIRE — EAST	THE BARBARIANS
300	Porphyry		Diocletian (284-305)		Franks and Alamans on the Rhine
10		Grant of toleration to Christians	Constantius (d. 306) / Constantine (306-37) / ✕ Milvian Bridge (312)	Galerius (d. 311)	Goths, Sueves, and other Germans on the Danube
20		Arian heresy		Licinius (d. 324)	
30		Council of Nicaea (325)	Constantine (d. 337)	Founding of Constantinople	
40		St. Anthony of Egypt		Sons of Constantine (337-61)	
350		St. Pachomius (d. 346)			Invasion of Europe by the Huns
60			Valentinian I (364-75)	Julian (361-63) / Valens (364-78)	
70	Vulgate of St. Jerome	P. Damasus I (366-84)	Gratian (375-81)		✕ Adrianople (378) / The Visigoths in the Empire
80	Gothic Bible of Ulfilas (d. 383) / Ammianus Marcellinus / Ausonius	St. Basil (d. 379) / P. Siricius (384-99)	Valentinian II (383-92) / Arbogast / Theodosius (d. 395)	Theodosius I (379-95)	Rise of Alaric
90	St. Augustine's Confessions	St. Ambrose (d. 397)	Honorius (395-423)	Theodosius I (d. 395) / Arcadius (395-408)	
400					

FIFTH CENTURY

	THE BARBARIANS IN THE WESTERN PROVINCES						ROMAN EMPIRE		THE CHURCH	ARTS AND LETTERS
Date	ANGLO-SAXONS	VANDALS	VISIGOTHS	FRANKS	ALAMANS	BURGUNDIANS	WEST	EAST		
400	Britain	Africa	South Gaul and Spain	North Gaul	Alsace and upper Danube	Rhone Valley	Honorius (d. 423)	Arcadius (d. 408)	P. Innocent I (402-17)	Claudian Symmachus Capella Macrobius
410							Stilicho (d. 408) Sack of Rome by Alaric (410)	Theodosius II (408-50)		
420										St. Jerome (d. 420)
430							Valentinian III (425-55)		Nestorian heresy	St. Augustine (d. 430) City of God — Theodosian Code
440	Permanent settlement begins		Theodoric	Salian and Ripuarian Kingdoms			Aëtius (d. 454)	Invasion by Huns under Attila (d. 453)	P. Leo the Great (440-61) Monophysite heresy	Orosius
450							✗ Catalaunian Fields (451)	Marcian (450-57)	Council of Chalcedon (451)	Byzantine architecture in the east and at Ravenna
460							Puppet Emperors (455-76)	Leo I (457-74)	St. Patrick (d. 461)	
470		Kingdom under Gaiseric (d. 477)	Euric (466-84)				Ricimer (d. 472)	Zeno (474-91)		
480				Clovis (481-511) ✗ Soissons (486) Conversion			Odoacer (476-93)	Rise of Theodoric the Ostrogoth	Schism between East and West	Apollinaris Sidonius (d. 488)
490							OSTROGOTHS Theodoric (493-526)	Anastasius I (491-518)		
500	Various small kingdoms continue	Conquered by Justinian in Sixth Century	Kingdom in Spain continues until 711		Conquered by Franks in Sixth Century	Conquered by Franks in Sixth Century				

Spanning notes across the Barbarians columns:

- Franks, Alamans, Burgundians, Vandals, and Sueves cross the Rhine into Gaul
- Angles and Saxons invade Britain
- Visigoths enter Gaul (412); Ataulf, Galla Placidia
- Visigoths under Wallia conquer Spain from the Vandals, who cross into Africa under Gaiseric (429)

	BRITISH ISLES	SPAIN AND AFRICA	FRANKISH KINGDOM	ITALY	BYZANTINE EMPIRE	ASIA	ARTS AND LETTERS
500	Continuation of Anglo-Saxon conquest	Vandals in Africa; Visigoths in Spain	Clovis (d. 511); Conquest of Aquitaine	Theodoric (d. 526)	Anastasius (d. 518)	Renewal of the Persian offensive	The Salic Law
10			Sons of Clovis (511-61); Conquest of Burgundy Provence Alamania Bavaria Thuringia		Justin I (518-27)		Boëthius (d. 524); Cassiodorus
20					Justinian (527-65); Theodora; Belisarius; Narses		St. Benedict's reform of monasticism
30		Justinian's reconquest of Africa and part of Spain		Justinian's reconquest (535-53)		Persistence of Nestorian and Monophysite (Jacobite) Churches	Justinian's Corpus Iuris Civilis
40							Splendor of Byzantine architecture
550				Exarchate of Ravenna	Council of Constantinople (553)	Invasion of Europe by the Avars, who conquer the Slavs, Bulgars, and other peoples. Together they overrun the Balkan peninsula	Church of St. Sophia
60	St. Columba (d. 597) at Iona		Grandsons of Clovis		Justin II (565-78)		Procopius
70			Decline of Merovingian power	Lombard invasion under Alboin	Tiberius II (578-82); Maurice (582-602) — Wars with Avars and Persians		Gregory of Tours (d. 594)
80	St. Columban (d. 615) to Gaul		Civil wars Austrasia vs. Neustria	Political chaos			Ecclesiastical History of the Franks
90	Mission of Augustine (597)	Visigoths recognize Roman Church		P. Gregory the Gt. (590-604); Extension of papal authority			Gregory the Great Pastoral Care Dialogues, etc.

SIXTH CENTURY

SEVENTH CENTURY

Year	BRITISH ISLES	SPAIN AND AFRICA	FRANKISH KINGDOM	ITALY	BYZANTINE EMPIRE	THE ARABS	ARTS AND LETTERS
600	Northumbria the dominant Anglo-Saxon kingdom		Great-Grandsons of Clovis	Gregory the Great (d 604) Papacy remains strong	Loss of Balkans to Avars and Slavs; Phocas (602-10)	Mohammed (d. 632) Preaching of Islam	Isidore of Seville (d. 636) *Etymologies*
10		Byzantine loss of Spanish coast	St. Columban (d. 615)		Heraclius (610-41)		
20				Lombards split into many small principalities	Successful offensive against Persia (622-29)	The Hegira (622)	
30				Byzantine control rapidly weakens	X The Yarmuk (636)	*Caliphate* Abu-Bakr (632-34)	The Koran
40		Arab conquest of Egypt	Dagobert (d. 639) *Rois Fainéants*		Successors of Heraclius	Omar (634-44) Conquest of Syria, Persia, Egypt. Othman (644-55)	
650			Mayors of the Palace		Collapse of the Byzantine Power. Losses: Syria, Egypt, North Africa, Spanish coast, Islands of the Mediterranean, Most of Italy, Interior of the Balkan peninsula	Civil war; Ali (655-61)	Learning of the Irish monks
60	Council of Whitby (664)					Muawiya (661-80) Ommiad Caliphs at Damascus until 750	Illuminated manuscripts
70	Theodore of Tarsus *AB* of Canterbury (669-90)	Arab campaigns in Tripoli and Tunis	Willibrord's mission in Frisia			Further conquests in Asia and North Africa	
80							
90		Arab conquest of North Africa			Defense of Asia Minor and Constantinople	Control of the Mediterranean	
700							

EIGHTH CENTURY

Date	BRITISH ISLES	SPAIN AND AFRICA	FRANKISH KINGDOM	ITALY	BYZANTINE EMPIRE	THE ARABS	ARTS AND LETTERS
700	Mercia the dominant Anglo-Saxon kingdom		Pepin II, Mayor of Palace in Neustria and Austrasia (d. 714)		Revival of Byzantine strength		Bede (d. 735) Ecc. Hist. of the English People
10		Moslem conquest of Visigothic kingdom	Charles Martel M. of P. (714-41)	Liutprand, K. of Lombards (712-44) Attacks Ravenna	Leo III (717-40) Iconoclastic Controversy	Siege of Constantinople fails (718)	Learning of Irish and Anglo-Saxon monks brought to continent by missionaries
20		Moslem raids in Gaul	Pacification of Aquitaine Burgundy Alamania Bavaria Thuringia Frisia	P. Gregory II (d. 731) Condemns Iconoclasts	Schism between East and West		
30		X Tours (Poitiers) (732)		P. Gregory III (d. 741) Appeals to Charles Martel			St. Boniface (d. 754) Organizer of the church in Germany
40			Pepin III, M. of P. (741-68)		Successors of Leo III		
750		Ommiad Emir at Cordova later styled Caliph	Pepin, K. by support of Pope (751)	Aistulf, K. of L. (750-56)	Palace revolutions	Fall of Ommiads (750)	Beginnings of Arabic Science
60	Viking raids along coasts of Britain and Ireland		Conquest of Septimania	P. Stephen II (752-57) Frankish intervention Takes Ravenna	Religious strife Bulgarian wars	Abbasid Caliphs at Bagdad until 1258 al-Mansur (754-75)	Translations from Greek
70			Charlemagne (768-81?) Conquest of Lombard Kingdom and Saxony	Donation of Pepin Papal States / P. Hadrian I (772-95) / Desiderius (757-74) last of the Lombards kings	Loss of all authority in Rome and North Italy		Libraries / Saracenic architecture and decorative arts
80		Morocco becomes independent	Reconquest of Bavaria Defeat of Avars Creation of Eastern Marches Spanish March			Harun-al-Rashid (786-809)	
90			Imperial coronation (Xmas, 800)	P. Leo III (795-816)			Carolingian Revival of Learning Alcuin (d. 804) Paul the Deacon
800							

NINTH CENTURY

Year	BRITISH ISLES	CAROLINGIAN EMPIRE	BYZANTINE EMPIRE	THE ARABS	ARTS AND LETTERS
800	Wessex the dominant Anglo-Saxon kingdom	Charlemagne (d. 814) Emperor — The Frankish Kingdom at its height	Paralysis under weak emperors	Harun-al-Rashid (d. 809)	Einhard (d. 840); Hrabanas Maurus; John the Scot
10	Increase of viking raids throughout British Isles	Louis the Pious (814-40) Emperor	Rise of Bulgaria	al-Mamun (813-33)	Carolingian minuscule
20		Weakening of the monarchy			Romance Languages; lingua romana
30		Civil war among sons			
40	Viking conquests: E. Ireland, W. Scotland, Most of Northumbria, Mercia, and E. Anglia	(Emperor) Lothair (840-55) Peace of Verdun (843); Louis the German (840-76) [GERMANY]; Charles the Bald (840-77) [FRANCE]	Michael III (842-67)	Disintegration of Arab Empire under rival caliphs and independent governors	Arabic culture: Literature, Music, Fine Arts, Commerce, Geography, Mathematics, Astronomy, Medicine, etc.
850		**GERMANY:** Viking raids. **CENTRAL KGDM.:** Division among three sons (855); P. Nicholas I (858-67); Extension of papal power. **FRANCE:** Viking raids; Settlement of Normandy	Viking raids down Dnieper to Black Sea; Russians		
60			Macedonian House	Sea power of African emirs	Hunain; al-Kindi; al-Farghani; al-Khwarizmi
70	Alfred, K. of Wessex (871-901)	**GERMANY:** Increasing power of dukes. **CENTRAL KGDM.:** Italy, Provence, Lorraine. **FRANCE:** Feudalization of kingdom; Great duchies; Emperor (875)	Basil I (867-86) Religious peace between East and West	Capture of Sicily, Crete, Sardinia, Corsica, and Balearic Is.	
80	Defense of Wessex, which comes to include all territory south of Thames; also W. Mercia	**GERMANY:** Charles the Fat (876-87). **CENTRAL KGDM.:** Charles the Fat Emperor (881); Deposed (887). **FRANCE:** Various Carolingians (877-85); Charles the Fat	Bulgarians under Boris I (852-84) accept Greek Christianity	Continuous raids along European coasts	Slavic alphabet invented by Cyril, missionary to Bohemia. Adopted by Bulgarians
90		**GERMANY:** Arnulf (887-99); Emperor (896). **FRANCE:** Odo of Paris (888-98)			
900		Political disintegration. Civil wars. Invasions of vikings, Hungarians, and Saracens.			

TENTH CENTURY

Year	ENGLAND	FRANCE (SPAIN)	GERMANY	ITALY	BYZANTINE EMPIRE	THE ARABS	ARTS AND LETTERS
900	Alfred (d 901) Edward the Elder (901-25)	Charles the Simple (898-923)	Louis the Child (899-911)	Degradation of the Papacy Control by local nobles Marozia	Macedonian Dynasty Hungarians in Pannonia	Caliphs at Bagdad become puppets controlled by military chieftains	Continuance of Arabic culture
10	Conquest of Danelaw begun	Recognizes duchy of Normandy (911) Acquires Lorraine	Conrad I (911-18) Virtually powerless Saxon House Henry I (919-36) Reorganizes kingdom Acquires Lorraine		Bulgarian Empire under Tsar Simeon (d. 927), then decline		al-Razi al-Farabi Ibn al-Haitham al-Battani
20	Aethelstan (925-37)	Kings of the Parisian House (922-36)					
30	Conquest of Danelaw completed	Kings of the Carolingian House (936-87)	X The Unstrut (933) Otto the Great (936-73) Lordship of Arles and Bohemia	Rise of Venice as an independent city state	Rise of Russia under Princes of Kiev		Anglo-Saxon literature Beowulf Song of Maldon Anglo-Saxon Chronicle
40	The Kingdom of England	Hugh the Great C. of Paris (d. 956)	Redistribution of duchies		Attack Constantinople and overrun Bulgaria		Translations
950				Assumes crown of Italy (951)			
		SPAIN Caliphate of Cordova at height		P. John XII (955-63)	Byzantine offensive in Cilicia	Byzantine conquest of Antioch and Cyprus	Revival of Learning under Otto I German schools and scholars
60	Edgar (959-75) Lordship of all Britain	Five Christian states in north: León, Castile, Navarre, Aragon, Catalonia (County of Barcelona)	Imperial coronation (962) The Holy Roman Empire	Imperial coronation (962)	Nicephorus Phocas (963-69) John Tzimisces (969-76) Defeats Russians		
70			Byzantine alliance Otto II (973-83) m. Theophano	Fails to conquer South Italy	Basil II (976-1025)		Scientific works of Gerbert (Silvester II) Study of the abacus
80	Aethelred (979-1016) Weak reign	Hugh Capet (987-96)	Otto III (983-1002)	Imperial dreams Neglect of Germany	Russians under Vladimir (d. 1015) accept Greek Christianity		
90	Renewal of Danish raids Danegeld	Robert (996-1031)	Hungary Christian under Stephen I (997-1038) Poland under Boleslav I (992-1025)	P. Silvester II (999-1003)			Beginnings of Russian culture
1000							

Eleventh Century timeline chart. Columns left-to-right: Arts and Letters, Arabs and Turks, Byzantine Empire, Italy, Germany, France (Spain), England. Dates in left and right margins: 1000, 10, 20, 30, 40, 1050, 60, 70, 80, 90, 1100.

Date	Arts and Letters	Arabs and Turks	Byzantine Empire	Italy	Germany	France (Spain)	England
1000	Continuance of Arabic culture	Emergence of Seljuk Turks	Basil II (d. 1025) conquers Bulgaria after long war	Silvester II (d. 1003) Papacy weakens Cluniac Reform	Otto III (d. 1002); Henry II (1002-24) Slavic offensive led by Poland German control of Bohemia	Robert (d. 1031)	Aethelred (d. 1016)
10	Avicenna (d. 1037) al-Biruni (d. 1048)					The Capetian kings accomplish little, but the French nobility is very active, especially the Normans in Italy and England	Danish Conquest Canute (1016-35) K. of Denmark and Norway
20				Pisa and Genoa lead offensive against Moslems on the sea	(Franconian House) Conrad II (1024-39)		Peace with Scots; cession of Lothian
30		Turkish advance into Persia	Decline under successors of Basil II; Macedonian house ends (1056)	Rise of the Lombard Communes	Acquires Kingdom of Arles (1032)	Henry I (1031-60) French recruits make possible Christian offensive in Spain Noteworthy expansion of León, Castile and Aragon	Sons of Canute (1035-42)
40				Four German popes P. Leo IX (1048-54) Reform councils Alliance with Normans	Henry III (1039-56) Reform of church Control of papacy Height of the H.R.E.		Edward Confessor (1042-66) (Son of Aethelred)
1050	Revival of Culture in Western Europe	Sultan Togrul Beg takes Bagdad (1055)	Final schism between East and West (1054)	Rise of Hildebrand	Henry IV (1056-1106) Regency to 1066		Advancing influence of Normans
60	Dialectic Nominalism vs. Realism	Alp Arslan (1063-72) Conquest of Persia and Armenia	Loss of South Italy; Romanus IV	P. Nicholas II (1058-61); P. Alexander II (1061-73)	Papal autonomy Cardinal College Robt. Guiscard D. of Apulia (1059-85)	Philip I (1060-1108); X Barbastro in Spain (1065)	Norman Conquest William I (1066-87)
70	Roscellinus Berengar of Tours	Malik Shah (1072-92) Conquest of Asia Minor and Syria	X Manzikert (1071) Loss of Asia Minor	P. Gregory VII (1073-85); Canossa (1077)	Saxon Wars Investiture Controversy		Introduction of feudal tenures French culture
80	Development of Romanesque Architecture		Alexius Comnenus (1081-1118) Norman War	Henry IV takes Rome (1084); P. Urban II (1088-99)	Constant civil war	Almoravids to Spain; X Zallaca (1086)	Domesday Book William II (1087-1100)
90	Bayeux Tapestry Song of Roland		FIRST CRUSADE — 1096 Arrival at Constantinople; 1098 Capture of Antioch; 1099 Capture of Jerusalem	C. Roger (d. 1101) conquers Sicily	Henry abandons Italy	Council of Clermont (1095); Crusade proclaimed	Anselm, AB of Canterbury
1100							

ELEVENTH CENTURY

TWELFTH CENTURY

Date	ENGLAND	FRANCE (SPAIN)	GERMANY	ITALY	EASTERN EUROPE	THE TURKS	ARTS AND LETTERS
1100	Henry I (1100-35) Coronation Charter Takes Normandy from brother	Philip I (d. 1108)	Henry IV (d. 1106)	Roger II (1101-54) Inherits Sicily	Alexius Comnenus (d. 1118) Recovers coast of Asia Minor War with crusaders over Antioch	Results of crusade: Latin Kingdom of Jerusalem County of Edessa Princ. of Antioch County of Tripoli Templars and Hospitallers	Omar Khayyam
10	Improved central government	Louis VI (1108-37) Consolidation of Capetian domain	Henry V (1106-25) Continued strife between Papacy and Empire				Idrisi
20	Exchequer Privileged boroughs Angevin alliance	Communes and privileged towns Suger (d. 1151)	Investiture Controversy ended by Concordat of Worms (1122)	Acquires Apulia and Calabria	Comneni continue until 1185		Averroës Rise of the Universities
30			Lothair III (1125-37)	K. of Sicily (1130) Anti-church agitation	Hungary remains strong; holds Croatia	Trade concessions to Pisa, Genoa, Venice	Scholastic theology Abelard Peter Lombard
40	Stephen (1135-54) The Anarchy Angevin War	Louis VII (1137-80) Rise ot Angevins Geoffrey Plantagenet Second Crusade	Guelf (G) vs. Hohenstaufen (H) (H) Conrad III (1138-52) (G) Henry the Lion Second Crusade (1147?)	Arnold of Brescia Peter Waldo Cathari (Albigensians)	Poland weakens Intermittent German lordship Bohemia loyal; part of H.R.E.	Zangi, Gov. of Mosul takes Edessa (1144) Second Crusade (1147-49) fails	Canon Law Gratian Revival of Roman Law Translations of Greek and Arabic science Adelard of Bath John of Salisbury
1150	Henry II (1154-89) m.? Constitutional reforms Common Law New taxes	Eleanor of Aquit. divorced (1152) SPAIN C. of Portugal recognized as K. by pope (1179) C. of Barcelona acquires crown of Aragon (1150)	(H) Frederick Barbarossa, (1152-90) Italian expeditions; conflict with papacy and communes	P. Hadrian IV (1154-59) P. Alexander III (1159-81) Fall of Milan (1162) Lombard League	Eastward expansion of Germans Slavic Marches Pomerania to Austria	Nur-ed-Din (1146-74) takes Damascus	St. Bernard Vernacular Lit.
60	† Becket (1170) Norman expansion in Wales						Chansons de Geste Lyrics of troubadours
70	Irish conquests Wars with sons		Old duchies broken up	X Legnano (1176)	Henry the Lion founds Lübeck	Saladin, Sultan of Egypt (1171-93) Acquires Mosul, Aleppo, Damascus	Romances; Marie de France Chretien de Troyes Drama and music
80	Angevin-Capetian War	Philip Augustus (1180-1223) acquires Picardy Third Crusade	Fall of Henry the Lion (1181) Sicilian alliance (H) Henry VI ('90-'97) Acquisition of Sicilian Kingdom	Peace of Constance (1183)	Russia disintegrates Isaac II (1185-95) Bulgaria again independent	Takes Jerusalem (1187)	Icelandic sagas Cid; Goliardi Transition to Gothic Arts Architecture
90	Richard I (1189-99) → Third Crusade John (1199-1216)	Contest with pope over divorce	(G) Otto IV vs. (H) Philip of Suabia	P.Celestine III ('91-'98) P. Innocent III (1198-1216)	Alexius III (1195-1203)	Third Crusade (1190-92) fails Teutonic Knights	Sculpture Stained glass
1200							

Year	ENGLAND	FRANCE	GERMANY	ITALY	EASTERN EUROPE	THE TURKS	ARTS AND LETTERS
1200	John (d. 1216) Loss of Normandy, etc. Quarrel with Pope (1207-13)	Philip Aug. (d. 1223) Conquest of Normandy, Anjou, Poitou, etc.	Frederick II, K. of Sicily (1197-1250) Philip of Suabia (d. 1208)	Innocent III (d. 1216) Height of the Papacy	Fourth Crusade Capture of Constantinople (1204) Latin Empire (1204-61)	Rise of Mongols under Jenghis Khan (1206-27)	Perfection of Gothic Arts; St. Francis
10		Albigensian Crusade (1208-29); X Bouvines (1214)	Otto IV put out by Frederick II (1215) Emperor (1220)	Franciscan order; Lateran Council (1215); Dominican order (1220); P. Honorius III (1216-27) Renewal of Lombard League	Maritime supremacy of Venice	Conquer all central Asia and Persia	Villehardouin; Fabliaux
20	Magna Carta (1215) Henry III (1216-72) Minority to 1227	Louis VIII (1223-26)					Romance of Reynard
	SPAIN						Aucassin and Nicolette
30	James the Conqueror of Aragon (1213-76) takes Valencia	Louis IX (1226-70) Blanche of Castile Regent to 1234	Crusade (1228-29) Sicilian Code Contest with Gregory IX	P. Gregory IX (1227-41) Canon Law Papal Inquisition	Teutonic Knights in Prussia (1230) Union with Livonian order (1237)	Frederick II recovers Jerusalem	German poetry; Nibelungenlied
40	Final union of León and Castile under Ferdinand III (1230)	Secures half of Languedoc; Constitutional advance	Italian Wars; Germany left to princes	X Cortenuova (1237); P. Innocent IV (1243-54)	Mongols invade Bohemia and Hungary	Mongols conquer Russia; Kiev destroyed; Fall of Jerusalem	Walther von der Vogelweide; Robert Grosseteste
1250	Takes Murcia, Cordova, Seville	Crusade (1248-54) disastrous	Conrad IV (1250-54)			Louis IX's Crusade in Egypt	Vincent of Beauvais
60	Provisions of Oxford (1258) Simon de Montfort Barons' War (1264-65)	Peace with England (1259)	Disputed Election (1257) Interregnum until 1273	Manfred, Regent, then K. of Sicily (1258-66); P. Urban IV (1261-64); P. Clement IV (1265-68)	Republic of Novgorod prosperous; Michael Palaeologus (1261-82)	Mongols end Caliphate of Bagdad (1258); checked in Syria by Mamelukes, who take Antioch (1268)	Albert the Great
70	Edward I (1272-1307)	Philip III (1270-85) Secures all Languedoc	Rudolf of Habsburg (1273-91)	Charles of Anjou K. of Sicily (1266-85); Ruin of Pisa; Rise of Florence	Restored Byzantine Empire; Bitter rivalry of Venice and Genoa for Black Sea	Kublai Khan (1259-94); Marco Polo's travels	Thomas Aquinas; Roger Bacon; University colleges
80	Conquest of Wales (1282-84) Statutes	Aragonese Crusade fails; Philip IV (1285-1314) m. heiress of Champagne	Takes Austria from Ottokar of Bohemia; Origin of Swiss Confederation (1291)	P. Martin IV (1281-85); Sicilian Vespers (1282) Island acquired by K. of Aragon			Growth of naturalism in art
90	Scottish Wars; Model Parl. (1295); X Falkirk (1298)	War with Edward I (1294-98)	Albert of Austria (1298-1308)	P. Boniface VIII (1294-1303); Clericis Laicos (1296)	Second Bulgarian Empire	Fall of Acre (1291); End of the original crusade	Joinville; Romance of the Rose
1300							

FOURTEENTH CENTURY

	ENGLAND	FRANCE	ITALY	GERMANY	EASTERN EUROPE	THE OTTOMAN TURKS AND THE BALKANS	ARTS AND LETTERS
1300	Edward I (d. 1307) Conquers Scotland	Philip IV (d. 1314); [Estates General; X Courtrai (1302)	Unam Sanctam Anagni (1303)	Wars of Habsburg (H), Luxemburg (L), Wittelsbach (W)	Teutonic Knights Headquarters to Prussia (1309)	Osman (1299-1326) and his Turks capture Brusa	Duns Scotus; Pierre Dubois; William of Ockham
10	Edward II (1307-27); Robert Bruce K. of Scotland; X Bannockburn	Trial of Templars (1307-14); Sons of Philip IV (1314-28)	P. Clement V (1305-14)	(L) Henry VII (1308-13) son; (W) Louis of Bavaria (1314-34); X Morgarten (1315)	John, K. of Bohemia (1310-46); Angevin House in Hungary (1309)		Marsiglio of Padua
20	Scottish independence	Law of Succession; Valois House	P. John XXII (1314-34); Contest with Franciscans and Louis of Bavaria	Growth of the Swiss Confederation		Orkhan (1326-59) Takes Nicaea and Nicomedia Organizes state	Italian Literature Dante (d. 1321) Divine Comedy
30	Edward III (1327-77)	Philip VI (1328-50)	Development of Canon Law	Rise of the Hansa		Serbian Empire under Stephen Dushan (1331-55)	Petrarch (d. 1374) Sonnets
40	Opening of the Hundred Years' War (1337); X Sluys (1340); X Crécy (1346)	Acquisition of Dauphiné	Papal Taxation	Independence of princes and Free Cities	Louis the Great (1342-82)	Decline of Bulgaria	Boccaccio (d. 1375) Decameron; Revival of Humanism Petrarch
1350	The Black Prince	John (1350-64)	The Black Death	(L) Charles IV (1346-78)	also K. of Bohemia Founds U. of Prague		Development of Painting
60	X Poitiers (1356); Anti-Papal Statutes	[Estates at Paris Etienne Marcel Jacquerie (1358); Victory of Charles V (1364-80)	Revival of mysticism Brothers of the Common Life	Abandons Italy; Golden Bull (1356) Seven Electors	Revival of Poland under Casimir the Great (1333-70)	Turks enter Europe (1356); Murad I (1359-89) Takes Adrianople Conquers Bulgars	Giotto (d. 1336); Miniatures
70	The English all but driven from France; Richard II (1377-99)	Foundation of absolute monarchy; Du Guesclin	St. Catherine of Siena; P. Gregory XI (1371-78) Returns to Rome; The Great Schism (1378-1417)	War of Hansa with Waldemar of Denmark; Peace of Stralsund (1370); Height of Hansa	Louis, K. of Poland (1370-82); also K. of Bohemia	X The Maritza (1371) Defeat of Serbs	Flamboyant style of Gothic; Secular architecture of Italy and Flanders
80	Great Revolt (1381); Growth of Lollardy	Charles VI (1380-1422); Philip of Burgundy acquires Flanders (1384)	Rome: Urban VI (d. '89), Boniface IX (d 1404); Avignon: Clement VII (d.'94), Benedict XIII (1394-1417)	(L) Wenceslas ('78-1400); Sigismund (brother) K. of Hungary (1387-1437); X Sempach (1386) Final Swiss victory	Jagiello of Lithuania acquires Polish crown (1386)	Vassalage of Byzantine Emperor (1381); X Kossovo (1389); Bayazid I (1389-1402)	English Literature Chaucer (d. 1400) Canterbury Tales; Wycliffe's Bible
90	Attempted royal absolutism; Revolution	Insanity of king; Orleans vs. Burgundy		Wenceslas deposed, keeps Bohemia	Union of Calmar (1397)	Hungarian Crusade; X Nicopolis (1396)	Langland Piers Plowman
1400							

Papacy at Avignon until 1376 (Italy column)

	ENGLAND	FRANCE	ITALY	GERMANY	EASTERN EUROPE	THE OTTOMAN TURKS AND THE BALKANS	ARTS AND LETTERS
1400	House of Lancaster Henry IV (1399-1413) Parliamentary government	Charles VI (d.1422) John of Burgundy (1404-19)	Innocent VII (d.1406) Gregory XII (1406-15)	(W) Rupert (1400-10) Preaching of Hus in Bohemia	Wenceslas, King of Bohemia (d.1419) Sigismund K. of Hungary (d.1437)	✗ Angora (1402) Victory of Timur (d.1405) Civil War	Pierre d'Ailly Jean Gerson Renaissance Arts
10	Henry V (1413-22) ✗ Agincourt (1415)	† Orleans (1407) Civil War Invades France † Burgundy (1419)	Council of Pisa (1409) (L) Sigismund Council of Constance (1414-18)	Hus burned (1415)	✗ Tannenberg (1410) Decline of Teutonic Knights	Mohammed I (1413-21) Turkish recovery	Painting Van Eyck
20	Henry VI (1422-61) Regency of Gloucester and Bedford	Peace of Troyes (1420) Charles VII (1422-61) Bedford	P. Martin V (1417-31) Restoration of papal monarchy		Sigismund, K. of Bohemia (d.1437) Hussite War (1420-36) John Zizka (d.1424)	Murad II (1421-51)	Masaccio (d.1428) Sculpture Ghiberti (d.1455) Donatello (d.1466)
30		Career of Jeanne d'Arc (429-31) Peace of Arras (1435)	P.Eugenius IV (1431-47) Contest with Council of Basle	Council of Basel (1431-49) Religious peace with Hussites (1434) Germany and Bohemia to Habsburg house			Architecture Brunelleschi (d.1466)
40	Defeat in France	Restoration of Charles V's government		Frederick III (1440-93) Failure of Conciliar Movement	Hungarian crusades; victories of Hunyadi Ladislas III, K. of Poland and Hungary slain at	✗ Varna (1444)	Dominance of Humanistic Study in Italy Poggio (d.1459)
1450	Insanity of King Yorkist rising House of York	Fall of Guienne End of Hundred Years' War (1453)	P.Nicholas V (1447-55) Papal triumph Relapse of Roman Church under Renaissance popes	BURGUNDY Philip the Good (d.1467) unites Netherlands	Revival of Russia under Princes of Moscow	Turks subdue all Balkans Mohammed II ('51-81) Fall of Constantinople (1453)	Perfection of Printing Coster and Gutenburg
60	Edward IV (1461-83) Warwick the King-Maker	Louis XI (1461-83) League of Public Weal (1465) Péronne (1468)	SPAIN Isabella of Castile m.Ferdinand of Aragon (1469)	War with Louis XI Charles the Rash (1467-77)	Peace of Thorn (1466) Polish dominance in Prussia	EXPLORATION Portuguese voyages under Prince Henry (d.1460)	French Literature Commines Villon
70	Extermination of Lancastrians	Royal absolutism acquires Burgundy, Provence, etc.	Latter inherits crown (1479)	Occupation of Alsace, Lorraine Defeat by Swiss Mary of Burgundy m.Maximilian son of Philip III (1477)	Discovery of Senegal, Niger, etc.		
80	Richard III (1483-85) House of Tudor Henry VII (1485-1509)	Charles VIII (1483-98) Anne de Beaujeu Regent	Establishment of royal absolutism	Foundation of Habsburg greatness	Diego Cam discovers Congo (1482) Diaz rounds Cape (1486)		Witch Bull of Innocent VIII (1484) Malleus Maleficarum (1386)
90	Establishment of royal absolutism	Charles m. to heiress of Brittany	Conquest of Granada (1492)		Columbus discovers America (1492) Vasco da Gama circumnavigates Africa (1498)		
1500							

FIFTEENTH CENTURY

SUGGESTED READINGS

In a little book like this any formidable bibliographies would be out of place. The following lists have therefore been restricted to a few suggestions, principally of source material in English and of rather general discussions by modern writers. The student or teacher who desires additional references may consult the author's *Mediæval History* (New York, 1935), pp. 746 f.; L. J. Paetow, *Guide to the Study of Mediæval History* (New York, 1931) ; J. W. Thompson, *Reference Studies in Mediæval History* (3 vols.; Chicago, 1925-30); or the bibliographies attached to the chapters of the *Cambridge Medieval History* (8 vols.; Cambridge, 1911-36). This collaborative work is the most comprehensive survey of the mediæval period in English. It can be relied on for a scholarly narrative of political events, and for occasional essays on particular phases of civilization. Such essays, however, provide no continuous account of cultural development. A much smaller history, but one larger than the ordinary textbook, is J. W. Thompson's *Middle Ages* (New York, 1932), which contains interesting chapters on arts, letters, and social conditions.

Useful collections of documents and other materials for study are the following: *Translations and Reprints from the Original Sources of European History* (U. of Pennsylvania Press, 1897 f.); E. F. Henderson, *Select Historical Documents of the Middle Ages* (London, 1896); O. J. Thatcher and E. M. McNeal, *A Source Book for Mediæval History* (New York, 1905); F. A. Ogg, *A Source Book of Mediæval History* (New York, 1907); J. H. Robinson, *Readings in European History* (Boston, 1904); J. F. Scott, A. Hyma, and A. H. Noyes, *Readings in Medieval History* (New York, 1933); R. C. Cave and H. H. Coulson, *A Source Book for Mediæval Economic History* (Milwaukee, 1936); F. Duncalf and A. C. Krey, *Parallel Source Problems in Mediæval History* (New York, 1912). More specific references to some of these collections will be given below; as also to the *Records of Civilization*, published by Columbia University, and to the *Berkshire Studies in European History*, a series of small but comprehensive books edited by R. A. Newhall, L. B. Packard, and S. R. Packard.

Chapter I.—The Roman World

A stimulating description of the later Roman Empire, with emphasis on institutions and culture, will be found in F. Lot, *The End of the Ancient World and the Beginnings of the Middle Ages* (New York, 1931) ; and much more detailed treatment of many fundamental problems in M. I. Rostovtzeff, *Social and Economic History of the Roman Empire* (Oxford, 1926). For adequate citation of reading on Græco-Roman civilization, the reader must be referred to histories of the ancient world; mention will be made here of only two useful summaries: *The Legacy of Greece*, edited by R. W. Livingstone (Oxford, 1921), and *The Legacy of Rome*, edited by C. Bailey (Oxford, 1923). The former includes good sketches of Hellenistic science. The ideas of the later Stoics can readily be learned from the works of Epictetus and of Marcus Aurelius, available in many translations; and any one who wants a taste of Neo-Platonism can obtain it from Plotinus, translated in the *Bohn Library*. The best source for early Christianity is, of course, the New Testament, which should be read—if for no other reason—as part of a historical education. Documents concerning the Christian persecutions have been published in the Pennsylvania *Translations and Reprints*, IV, nos. 1-2. See also H. B. Workman, *Persecution in the Early Church* (London, 1906); N. H. Baynes, *Constantine the Great and the Christian Church* (London, 1930); and (in the *Berkshire Studies*) E. R. Goodenough, *The Church in the Roman Empire* (New York, 1931). The religious background of Christianity is well set forth in T. R. Glover, *The Conflict of Religions in the Roman Empire* (London, 1909), and in F. Cumont, *Oriental Religions in Roman Paganism* (Chicago, 1911).

Chapter II.—The Barbarian Invasions and the Christian Church

The best description of the Ural-Altaic nomads in English is that of J. Peisker in the *Cambridge Medieval History*, I, ch. xii. For accounts of the barbarian invasions, see the other chapters in the same volume and those in Lot's *End of the Ancient World*. Every student of mediæval history ought to read the *Germania* of Tacitus—preferably in a recent translation, for the older ones are often inaccurate. Good examples of Germanic custom are provided by the Salic Law, partly translated in Henderson's *Select Documents*, and by the Anglo-Saxon dooms, as edited and translated in F. L. Attenborough's *Laws of the Earliest English Kings* (Cambridge, 1922). Selections are given in various source books, as in C. Stephenson and F. G. Marcham, *Sources of English Constitutional History* (New York, 1937). The famous *History of the Franks* by Gregory of Tours graphically depicts life in Merovingian Gaul: translated with an admirable introduction by O. M. Dalton (Oxford, 1927), and in part by E. Brehaut for the Columbia *Records of Civilization* (1916).

Innumerable books on the history of the Christian Church deal with the controversial subject of the episcopate. A clear sketch from the Protestant point of view is that contributed to the *Berkshire Studies* by S. Baldwin, *The Organization of Mediæval Christianity* (New York, 1929). For the Catholic tradition see P. Batiffol, *Primitive Catholicism* (London, 1912). Of the utmost value to the student of the mediæval church is the *Rule of St. Benedict*, of which an inexpensive translation has been published by the Society for the Promotion of Christian Knowledge (London, 1931). For interpretation see especially E. C. Butler, *Benedictine Monachism* (London, 1919), and J. Chapman, *St. Benedict and the Sixth Century* (New York, 1929). The life of a pre-Benedictine monk, St. Columban, appears in the Pennsylvania *Translations and Reprints*, II, no. 7. Also invaluable as historical materials are the works of the great church fathers. St. Augustine's *Confessions* and *Civitas Dei* are obtainable in numerous translations. Selected letters of St. Jerome have been translated by F. A. Wright for the *Loeb Classical Library* (London, 1933). The *Pastoral Care* and various other writings of Gregory the Great are included in the collection of *Nicene and Post-Nicene Fathers*, Second Series, vol. XII. Gregory's *Dialogues* in translation have been edited by E. G. Gardner (London, 1911). Biographies of these authors, as well as commentaries on their doctrines, are numerous. But this list will close with the mention of two excellent books that deal primarily with early mediæval education: E. K. Rand, *Founders of the Middle Ages* (Cambridge, Mass., 1928), and M. L. W. Laistner, *Thought and Letters in Western Europe, A.D. 500 to 900* (London, 1931).

Chapter III.—The Byzantine Empire and the Rise of Islam

Practically every phase of Byzantine history receives detailed treatment in the *Cambridge Medieval History*, vols. II and IV. Briefer sketches will be found in C. Diehl, *History of the Byzantine Empire* (Princeton, 1925); N. H. Baynes, *The Byzantine Empire* (London, 1925) ; and S. Runciman, *Byzantine Civilization* (London, 1933). The second volume of the *Cambridge Medieval History* also includes good chapters on the Slavs and the Avars by J. Peisker and on the Roman law by H. J. Roby. For a fuller account of Roman legal development, see F. P. Walton, *Historical Introduction to the Roman Law* (Edinburgh, 1912). Any one of a dozen histories of architecture will provide information about the Byzantine style, with adequate illustrations. But the student is referred in particular to T. G. Jackson's *Byzantine and Romanesque Architecture,* vol. I (Cambridge, 1913), which contains a wealth of drawings by the author, including reproductions of famous mosaics in color. See also E. W. Anthony, *A History of Mosaics* (Boston, 1936).

The career of Mohammed and the growth of the Arab Empire are clearly sketched by A. A. Bevan and C. H. Becker in the *Cambridge Medieval History*, vol. II. A fuller account is given in the recent and scholarly *History of the Arabs* by P. K. Hitti (New York, 1940). The indispensable source for a study of Mohammedanism is, of course, the Koran. The best translation is that of M. Pickthall, *The Meaning of the Glorious Koran* (New York, 1930), but there are numerous others. *The Legacy of Islam,* edited by T. W. Arnold and A. Guillaume (Oxford, 1931), serves as an excellent introduction to Arab civilization and indicates further readings.

Chapter IV.—The Carolingian Empire

The best review in English of the Carolingian Empire and its institutions is that of G. Seeliger in the *Cambridge Medieval History*, II, chs. xix, xxi. More illuminating than much of the modern writing about Charlemagne are the biography by Einhard, which has been translated a number of times, and the emperor's capitularies, some of which may be found in the Pennsylvania *Translations and Reprints*, III, no. 2, and VI, no. 5. On the imperial coronation of 800 see Duncalf and Krey, *Parallel*

Source Problems. The outstanding book on Latin education during the Carolingian age is Laistner's *Thought and Letters in Western Europe*, which includes a full bibliography. See also H. O. Taylor, *The Mediæval Mind* (2 vols.; London, 1930), chs. x-xi, and C. H. Haskins, *The Renaissance of the Twelfth Century* (Cambridge, Mass., 1927), introductory chapters. *An Encyclopedist of the Dark Ages*, by E. Brehaut (New York, 1912), summarizes Isidore's *Etymologies* and gives examples in translation. The more famous works of Bede are available in various English editions. E. A. Lowe's chapter in *The Legacy of the Middle Ages*, edited by C. G. Crump and E. F. Jacob (Oxford, 1926), sketches concisely the difficult subject of mediæval handwriting.

Among many recent books on the Vikings may be mentioned the following: T. D. Kendrick, *History of the Vikings* (New York, 1930); A. Mawer, *The Vikings* (Cambridge, 1913); A. Olrik, *Viking Civilization* (New York, 1930); Mary W. Williams, *Social Scandinavia in the Viking Age* (New York, 1920).

CHAPTER V.—FEUDAL SOCIETY AND THE REVIVAL OF TOWN LIFE

Nellie Neilson's *Medieval Agrarian Economy,* in the *Berkshire Studies* (New York, 1936), is the best account of the manorial system in English. There are numerous translations of manorial documents, but they are hard to understand without expert interpretation. See also Eileen Power's *Medieval People* (London, 1924); her chapter in the *Cambridge Medieval History*, vol. VII; and G. C. Homans, *English Villagers of the Thirteenth Century* (Cambridge, Mass., 1941). There is no good book on feudalism in English; but see the pertinent chapters in J. W. Thompson's *Middle Ages* and also S. Painter, *French Chivalry* (Baltimore, 1940). Feudal documents have been published in many source books, as in Stephenson and Marcham, *Sources of English Constitutional History*. A. Luchaire's *Social France in the Age of Philip Augustus* (New York, 1912) contains much interesting detail largely drawn from contemporary literature. The Bayeux Tapestry has been reproduced many times—excellently in H. Belloc's *Book of the Bayeux Tapestry* (London, 1914), though his comments are not always reliable. A volume on feudalism by C. Stephenson will appear in the *Berkshire Studies*.

Our finest survey of mediæval economic development is H. Pirenne's *Economic and Social History of Medieval Europe* (New York, 1937), which is to be supplemented by his *Mediæval Cities* (Princeton, 1925) and his chapter in the *Cambridge Medieval History*, vol. VI. Few illustrative documents have been translated except those pertaining to the English boroughs; see, for example, Stephenson and Marcham, *Sources of English Constitutional History*. See also the interesting little book in the *Berkshire Studies*, S. Baldwin, *Business in the Middle Ages* (New York, 1937).

CHAPTER VI.—POLITICAL AND ECCLESIASTICAL RECONSTRUCTION

Practically everything covered by this chapter is treated in considerable detail by the *Cambridge Medieval History*, vols. III and V. The sections on France and on early England are especially good. The *Berkshire Studies* include a number of useful volumes for supplementary reading: S. Baldwin, *The Organization of Medieval Christianity* (1929); S. R. Packard, *Europe and the Church Under Innocent III* (1927); F. Nowak, *Medieval Slavdom and the Rise of Russia* (1930); R. A. Newhall, *The Crusades* (1927). Further references may be found by consulting the bibliographies in these volumes. Interesting source material on the crusades is provided in the Pennsylvania *Translations and Reprints*, I, nos. 2, 4, and in A. C. Krey's *First Crusade* (Princeton, 1921). See also Duncalf and Krey, *Parallel Source Problems,* and the *Correspondence of Pope Gregory VII*, translated by E. Emerton for the Columbia *Records of Civilization* (1932). For the working of feudal institutions in England, see A. B. White, *The Making of the English Constitution* (New York, 1925); W. A. Morris, *The Constitutional History of England to 1216* (New York, 1930); G. B. Adams, *Constitutional History of England* (New York, 1921); Stephenson and Marcham, *Sources of English Constitutional History*. The feudalization of Germany and the expansion of the Germans to the east are emphasized in J. W. Thompson's *Feudal Germany* (Chicago, 1928). The famous exploits of the Normans are brilliantly set forth by C. H. Haskins, *The Normans in European History* (Boston, 1915). There are two fine books that deal with political theory in the Middle Ages: C. H. McIlwain, *The Growth of*

Political Thought (New York, 1932), and G. H. Sabine, *A History of Political Theory* (New York, 1937).

CHAPTER VII.—THE GROWTH OF MEDIÆVAL CULTURE

On particular subjects of study in the mediæval schools there are chapters, not always adequate, in the *Cambridge Medieval History*, vol. V; in Crump and Jacob, *The Legacy of the Middle Ages;* and in F. J. C. Hearnshaw, *Mediæval Contributions to Modern Civilization* (London, 1921). Mediæval dialectic, theology, jurisprudence, mathematics, and natural science can hardly be understood except by advanced students; for few scholarly works of the Middle Ages have been translated and even good summaries of them are almost impossible to find in English. Popular histories of science—such as those of W. T. Sedgwick and H. W. Tyler (New York, 1929) and W. C. Dampier-Whetham (Cambridge, 1930)—are exceedingly brief on the Middle Ages. Among more detailed studies are the following: D. Riesman, *The Story of Medicine in the Middle Ages* (New York, 1935); A. Castiglioni, *A History of Medicine* (New York, 1941); J. L. E. Dreyer, *History of the Planetary Systems from Thales to Kepler* (Cambridge, 1906); F. Cajori, *History of Mathematics* (New York, 1919); C. J. Singer, *From Magic to Science* (New York, 1928) ; G. H. T. Kimble, *Geography in the Middle Ages* (London, 1938).

A splendid introduction to the mediæval revival of learning in general is provided by C. H. Haskins, *The Renaissance of the Twelfth Century*. On the early universities see the same author's *Rise of the Universities* (New York, 1923) and H. Rashdall's *Universities of Europe in the Middle Ages* (new edition in 3 vols.; Oxford, 1936). Highly entertaining student letters have been translated by Haskins in his *Studies in Mediæval Culture* (Oxford, 1929). Many quotations from mediæval scholars will be found in H. O. Taylor's *Mediæval Mind* and in R. L. Poole's *Illustrations of the History of Mediæval Thought and Learning* (London, 1920). There are many books about Abelard and Héloïse, but their famous story can best be read in their own letters, as translated by C. K. Scott-Moncrieff. The student is warned against older books called *Letters of Abelard and Héloïse;* they are largely falsification.

Practically all the vernacular works referred to in the fore-going pages have been translated into English, and a good selection of them should be read by every one interested in mediæval civilization. For general comment see the *Cambridge History of English Literature*, vol. I (Cambridge, 1932); Bertha S. Phillpotts, *Edda and Saga* (London, 1931); G. Paris, *Mediæval French Literature* (London, 1903); A. Tilley, *Mediæval France* (Cambridge, 1922); K. Francke, *A History of German Literature* (New York, 1913); H. J. Chaytor, *The Troubadours* (Cambridge, 1912) ; Gustave Reese, *Music in the Middle Ages* (New York, 1940).

The only way to gain an understanding of art is to study either the original works or good reproductions. There are dozens of excellent books on mediæval architecture, sculpture, and painting, which include a wealth of illustrations. Even the beauty of stained glass can now be appreciated through color photography. No specific references will be included here, except by way of recommending two fine books of interpretation: E. Mâle, *Religious Art in France, Thirteenth Century* (London, 1913), and Henry Adams, *Mont-Saint-Michel and Chartres* (Washington, 1904).

On the problem of ecclesiastical reform, see the books cited in connection with the previous chapter. Villehardouin's famous account of the Fourth Crusade can be read in a volume of the *Everyman Library* called *Memoirs of the Crusades*; Robert of Clari has been translated by E. H. McNeal for the Columbia *Records of Civilization* (1936). The best sources for the life of St. Francis are his own writings, translated by P. Robinson (Philadelphia, 1906), and the biography by Thomas of Celano, translated by A. G. F. Howell (London, 1908). For additional references see A. G. Little's chapter in the *Cambridge Medieval History*, vol. VI.

CHAPTER VIII.—CHURCH AND STATE IN THE LATER MIDDLE AGES

The *Cambridge Medieval History*, vols. VI-VIII, provides good chapters with extensive bibliographies on virtually every phase of political and ecclesiastical history in the later Middle Ages. But to the usual biographies and narratives most students will prefer some of the famous sources. Joinville's *Life of St. Louis*, Marco Polo's *Travels*, and Froissart's *Chronicle* are all available in the *Everyman Library*, as well as in more scholarly editions. The first two are justly renowned as important historical works and as eminently good reading; the third, especially the part from 1386 to 1400, gives a vivid picture of decadent feudal society, if not of the Hundred Years' War. The *Memoirs* of Commines, translated in the *Bohn Library*, are a truly great classic. And the records of Jeanne d'Arc's trial, edited in translation by W. P. Barrett (New York, 1932), cannot be too highly recommended. These records, it should be noted, are a valuable source, not only for the life of the maid, but also for contemporary belief in witchcraft and for inquisitorial procedure in ecclesiastical courts.

CHAPTER IX.—SOCIETY AND CULTURE IN THE LATER MIDDLE AGES

Industrial and commercial developments in the later Middle Ages are brilliantly sketched by Pirenne in his *Economic and Social History of Medieval Europe*. On the Italian cities and the Hansa, see the pertinent chapters in the *Cambridge Medieval History*, vols. VII-VIII; on the Jews in mediæval Europe, *The Legacy of Israel*, edited by I. Abrahams and others (Oxford, 1927), and ch. xii (with its bibliography) in the *Cambridge Medieval History*, vol. VII; on the geographical background of the great explorations, G. H. T. Kimble, *Geography in the Middle Ages;* on the changes in warfare, C. W. C. Oman, *The Art of War in the Middle Ages* (London, 1924), and C. H. Ashdown, *Armour and Weapons in the Middle Ages* (London, 1925).

The older view of the Italian Renaissance is eloquently set forth by J. A. Symonds in his famous book on that subject. With it may be compared a number of more recent studies, including one by H. S. Lucas in this same historical series. Arthur Tilley's chapters in the *Cambridge Medieval History*, vols. VII and VIII, give the main facts about the Italian humanists, though he repeats too many catchphrases about the "mediæval" and the "modern." W. G. Constable's chapter in vol. VIII admirably summarizes the development of Gothic art and its relation to Renaissance art. For further suggestions the reader must be referred to special works on the fifteenth and following centuries.

There is, unfortunately, no good English translation of the *Romance of the Rose*. The best introduction to the study of Dante is K. Vossler's *Mediæval Culture* (2 vols.; London, 1929).

All of Dante's works may readily be found in English versions; see in particular C. E. Norton's prose translation of the *Divine Comedy*. R. Garnett's *CXXIV Sonnets* (London, 1896) include excellent renderings in English of various poems by Dante and Petrarch. See also Morris Bishop's *Love Rimes of Petrarch* (Ithaca, N. Y., 1932). The works of Boccaccio and Chaucer are too familiar to need citation of particular editions. The most usable version of *Piers Plowman* is that of Skeat, referred to in a footnote, above, p. 345. Payne's translation of Villon is better than many of the more recent attempts. Finest of all, however, are the few ballads put into English by Swinburne.

Although the *Summa Theologiæ* of Aquinas has been translated, most students will probably gain a clearer knowledge of his teaching from modern works about him: for example, E. H. Gilson, *The Philosophy of St. Thomas Aquinas* (Cambridge, 1924); M. Grabmann, *Thomas Aquinas* (New York, 1928); and M. C. D'Arcy, *Thomas Aquinas* (London, 1930). Roger Bacon's *Opus Maius* has been translated by R. V. Burke (Philadelphia, 1928). On Bacon's alleged cipher, see the book of W. R. N. Newbold on that subject (Philadelphia, 1928) and J. M. Manly , in *Speculum*, VI, 345 f.; cf. L. Thorndike, in the *American Historical Review*, XXI, 237 f., 468 f. The ideas of Ockham, Marsiglio, and other writers of the later Middle Ages are well discussed in McIlwain's *Growth of Political Thought* and in Sabine's *History of Political Theory*. See also D. S. Muzzey, *The Spiritual Franciscans* (New York, 1907), and J. N. Figgis, *Studies of Political Thought from Gerson to Grotius* (Cambridge, 1923). Marsiglio's *Defensor Pacis* has been partly translated by E. Emerton (Cambridge, Mass., 1920). The works of Wycliffe are practically all available in English, as are some of those of Hus. On the mediæval mystics, see Evelyn Underhill's chapter in the *Cambridge Medieval History*, vol. VII, and the numerous commentaries and translations there listed. A number of documents on witchcraft have been published in the Pennsylvania *Translations and Reprints*, III, no. 4. The *Malleus Maleficarum* has been translated and edited with an amazing introduction by Montague Summers (London, 1928). See also Thorndike's chapter in the *Cambridge Medieval History*, vol. VIII.

INDEX

(As a matter of convenience, Roman emperors in the east after Justinian are called Byzantine emperors; kings of the West Franks after 843 are called kings of France; kings of the East Franks after 843 are called kings of Germany.)

The
Last
Magazine

ALSO BY MICHAEL HASTINGS

Panic 2012

The Operators

I Lost My Love in Baghdad

The
Last
Magazine

A NOVEL

MICHAEL HASTINGS

BLUE RIDER PRESS   A MEMBER OF PENGUIN GROUP (USA)   NEW YORK

blue
rider
press

Published by the Penguin Group
Penguin Group (USA) LLC
375 Hudson Street
New York, New York 10014

USA · Canada · UK · Ireland · Australia
New Zealand · India · South Africa · China

A Penguin Random House Company

ISBN 978-1-62953-329-2

Printed in the United States of America

Book design by Meighan Cavanaugh

This is a work of fiction. Names, characters, places, and incidents either are the product
of the author's imagination or are used fictitiously, and any resemblance to actual persons,
living or dead, businesses, companies, events, or locales is entirely coincidental. The
sequence of real events has also been altered.

to Brent and Molly

The
Last
Magazine

INTRODUCTION: WHY I WRITE

My name is Michael M. Hastings, and I'm in my twenties. I'm sitting in a studio apartment on the Lower East Side in Manhattan. Second floor, overlooking Orchard and Rivington. There's snow dropping by the streetlights. It's three a.m., and I just got off work.

My magazine has a policy, a little item in the fifty-seven-page Human Resources manual called the "outside activities clause." It prevents employees from publishing journalism without the magazine's permission. That could apply to writing books like this one. So I want to say right now: This is fiction, it's all made up.

This book is a story about the media elite. Maybe you're interested in that world. I have the cc's and the bcc's and the reply-alls. Three years' worth, from 2002 to 2005, time- and place-specific, a very recognizable New York, at least for now.

I do have themes, too. Love, in a way, though it's not my love, and I can't say I understand it too well. Not murder, at least not in the whodunit sense. No ghosts or supernatural horrors or serial killers. Sex, yes, I have a bunch of sex scenes. There's war in the backdrop, looming and distant and not real for most of these characters, myself included.

Maybe I'm talking genres, and maybe the genre is *corporate betrayal*.

Including the big decision that the entire media world is so interested in: Who and what is left standing?

It'll take me about 300 pages, approximately 85,000 words, to get to that. By turning the page, you're 1 percent closer to the truth.

PART I

The Intern

1.

Morning, Tuesday, August 20, 2002

W hat's our take?"

That's Nishant Patel talking. He's the editor of the international edition of our magazine, available in eighty countries.

"It's a real genocide. We got A.E. Peoria there, got some great reporting. Guys on horseback burning a village, cleansing the place, poisoning wells. An interview with the IFLNP rebel leader."

"And?"

"Uh, we'll be talking about the genocide, that the UN called it that, great detail, how the catastrophic—"

"That's not new."

"The genocide?"

"Yes."

"It's new, it only started last week—"

"We've read it before."

Nishant Patel is hearing story pitches for next week's magazine. Tuesday mornings, ten a.m., in the sixteenth-floor conference room. He sits at the head of the table, thirteen swivel chairs in length. The section editors sit around him.

"It's an on-scener," continues Jerry, the World Affairs Editor. "Horseback riding, the rebel leader's got a motorcycle—"

"What are we saying? To have spent thousands of dollars so Peoria can land at an airport in Khartoum, tell us how hot and sunny it is, and bump his head in a Land Rover so we can read what we've already read in the *Times*?"

"Nishant, the *Times* only did one story on it—"

My job as an intern—or as a just sort of promoted intern—is to sit in the meetings and write down the story list, divided into the proper sections, with a note on how long the story might actually be. Length is measured in columns. There are approximately three columns to a page, about 750 words total, depending on photos. It's a rough list that changes throughout the week. On Tuesdays at ten a.m., I have to make a best guess at what stories are most likely to survive.

Jerry's story on the genocide is already on deathwatch.

The other editors are looking down, shuffling reading material, pretending to take notes. It's not proper etiquette to gawk at a drowning man. And if another section editor does speak up, it won't be to rescue Jerry. It will be to throw a life preserver with the intent of cracking the drowning man's skull so he sinks even quicker.

Like so:

"You know, Nishant," Sam, the Business Editor, says, "you're right. That story is stale. I saw a report this week that showed the fastest growth industry in East Africa is mobile phone sales. Up like eight hundred and thirty-three percent from two years ago. If that's going on across the continent, that's a story with regional implications."

Sam emphasizes the word "regional."

Nishant Patel nods.

"An outsourcing angle too," says Sam. "Americans outsourcing to the Indians, the Indians outsourcing to the Chinese, and the Chinese outsourcing to the Africans."

"Who are the Africans outsourcing to?" Nishant asks himself. "A great question. Yes, get Peoria to talk to someone who sells mobile phones there."

I write down the potential story: Mobile Phones/Outsourcing/ E. African Genocide (Peoria, 3 Columns).

Next up is Foster, the Europe Editor.

"The Islamic Wave Recedes. We have numbers showing that Islamic immigration is dropping. A huge drop, off a fucking cliff. Fears of Islamophobia? Unfounded. Townsend is writing from Paris."

"My sense is that the Islamic wave is cresting," says Nishant.

"Exactly. The Islamic Wave Is Growing. The numbers don't tell the whole story. Other factors that aren't being looked at show a real significant increase. Townsend can get that in by Wednesday."

"That sounds fine, yes," says Nishant.

"Cover: The Global Housing Boom," says Sam for Business. "The most expensive house in the world was just sold for two hundred fifty-three million dollars. It's happening everywhere."

"Good, good," says Nishant.

"Didn't we just do that story," says Jerry from World Affairs, but Nishant has moved on.

"We're reviewing three women novelists," says Anna from Arts & Entertainment and Luxury Life. "All are writing about ethnic marriages—I mean, they are, uh, beautifully written, and they take place in these settings that are just, really, they're about the experience of two cultures and how—"

"Fine, fine, but let's cut down on the novels."

"We have our story on Space Tourism," says Gary from Sci/Tech. "Our crack intern Hastings is working on it."

"Who's Hastings?" says Nishant.

Let me say that my heart—well, I like the attention. After working over the summer as an unpaid intern, I'd been hired as a temp just last week. I'd never had my name mentioned in a meeting before. Nishant Patel is about to see me for the first time. His gaze trails nine swivel chairs to his right. The eyes of Nishant Patel are deep brown, a set of chocolate emeralds that a profile writer for the *New York Herald* said were like an Indian Cary Grant, his lashes fluttering in sync with his melodious voice, British with a hint of the refined castes of New Delhi—the voice of an internationally flavored school tie.

"Thanks, everyone," Nishant says, and stands up.

Everyone thanked stands up too, and walks along the sides of the conference room, passing by the great big windows that look across 59th Street to a massive construction site of dual glass towers in Columbus Circle. Our competitor, the other weekly newsmagazine we call Brand X (and they call us Brand X), is getting ready to move into the towers when construction is complete. Brand X, as usual, is following our lead. We were here first. (You can also see an apartment building on Central Park West where everyone says Al Pacino lives.)

I step out into the hallway, and as I'm walking away, I overhear a brief exchange. I look back to see who's talking.

"Professor Patel," says a voice in the hallway with a southern drawl.

"Mr. Berman," Nishant Patel says.

It is the first time I see them side by side, Nishant Patel and Sanders Berman, sizing each other up.

2.

Tuesday, August 20, 2002

Magazine journalist A.E. Peoria is kneeling on top of a 1994 Toyota Land Cruiser in eastern Chad. It's night, and he's up on a small hill to get reception. The engine is running so that the electronics he has plugged into the jeep stay charged. A.E. Peoria is swearing. He believes that his Uniriya mobile satellite phone must be pointed 33 degrees southeast, and that should make it work.

The Toyota Land Cruiser is making a beeping sound because the keys are in the ignition and the door is slightly ajar. It's actually more like a dinging sound than a beep, and Peoria would close the door but he needs the interior ceiling light from the car to see what he is doing. His seven-inch black Maglite, which he usually would be gripping in his teeth, has run out of batteries. Or so he thinks.

Before climbing onto the roof of the Land Cruiser, he had tried to turn on the flashlight. When the light didn't come on, he checked the batteries to make sure the + and – were correctly in place. Unscrewing the top, he saw that the two double-A batteries inside weren't the Energizers he'd purchased at the Dubai Duty Free Travelers' Shop and Market at the Dubai International Airport. These were batteries with Chinese characters on them, the word MAJORPOWERY in pink English.

Someone had switched his Energizers for MAJORPOWERYs.

Why hadn't the person just taken the flashlight—that would have made more sense. Why did the thief bother replacing the Energizers with dead knockoffs? The thief either was trying to be clever and/or knew him, swapping dead batteries so he wouldn't notice the difference in the flashlight's weight. The prime suspect, he reasoned, was his translator, David D. Obutu from N'Djamena.

"It's dark, man, don't go up there. It's stupid shit," David D. Obutu had told him twenty minutes before Peoria had decided to drive the Land Cruiser to the top of the small hill.

"I have to get reception to check if there's anything from New York."

"Stupid shit, man. You have a light up there they can see for fucking kilometers, man. They'll start shooting again."

"They haven't shot in three days. I should be okay. I'll do it quick."

"It's some stupid shit, man."

"This *is* stupid shit. I'm here to do stupid shit. I'm not asking you, I'm just telling you."

"The villagers aren't going to be very happy with you."

"Fucking villagers have more to worry about than me checking my email for twenty minutes."

That was how he'd left things with David D. Obutu, translator turned battery thief.

Now kneeling atop the Land Cruiser, Peoria understands why David D. Obutu didn't want him to go up to the hill. Obutu knew he'd need his Maglite. When the Maglite didn't work, he might check the batteries. David D. Obutu's motives, A.E. Peoria thinks, were not pure. His motives were not to protect Peoria's well-being, or the well-being of the village (really a refugee camp), but to prevent the detection of the theft.

Still, magazine journalist A.E. Peoria knows that Obutu did have a point, even if it was secondary to hiding the double-A rip-off—kneeling atop a Land Cruiser at the crest of a hill next to the refugee camp that had been victimized, in the strongest sense of the word, by various tribal/warlord/bandit factions in the previous weeks, was stupid shit. Especially with the door to the Land Cruiser left slightly ajar.

He had thought he'd need the light for just a few moments—a minute at most—while he plugged the Ethernet cable connection into the Uniriya, then booted up his laptop, then aimed the Uniriya in the appropriate direction to pick up the satellite signal.

But the fucking thing isn't working, and he needs the light on as he keeps trying different angles and different settings.

It is doubly bad, MAJORPOWERY bad, because now the screen on his laptop adds to the illumination.

Ten minutes I have been fucking around with this thing, A.E. Peoria thinks.

He feels like he is being watched. What is that kind of feeling anyway? How does that work?

Sitting cross-legged, Native American style, on the roof of the Toyota Land Cruiser, he can see the tent village/refugee camp to the west and to the east he can't see anything clearly but knows there is a border. He sees that about one hundred of the refugees have crowded together near the bottom of the hill. It's so dark he knows people are there only because they are a mob of blackness, and he thinks this might be taken as a reference to skin color, but it's actually a reference to the fact that the gathered crowd has just taken on a shadowy shape. They are watching him; he is entertainment.

He uncrosses his legs and kicks the driver-side door shut. The interior car light stays on a few more moments, then turns off.

The dinging, too, ceases.

He decides to use his laptop screen for light, which is annoying because the dial that adjusts the angle of the Uniriya satellite modem is very small. The digital glow, even after he opens the laptop like a book, flattening it out so that he can get the screen close to the dial, isn't very helpful.

The laptop and the satellite modem are tethered together by a blue Ethernet cable, making the movement even more awkward. Other wires come down off the car through the rolled-down window on the driver's side to stay charged in a contraption hooked into the Land Cruiser's cigarette lighter. The cigarette lighter is rarely used for lighting cigarettes anymore, A.E. Peoria thinks.

What is that noise?

Oh, it's just a new dinging. It's his laptop making the new dinging noise, no longer the car door, which means the software for the Uniriya is trying to "acquire" the satellite, *ding, ding, ding.*

He presses the mute button on his laptop so it stops making the dinging noise. He's sweating and worried and very much discomfited. That fucking David D. Obutu. The country to the east, where the refugees came from and where the attackers came from, looks very flat and peaceful and serene and unthreatening—though admittedly he can't really see much of it in the dark. And A.E. Peoria knows that scenery in this region is not a good way to judge the chance of catastrophic violence occurring at any moment.

Satellite found. 123 bps.

Is that a whistling?

No.

He gets on his email. The web browser allows him to pull up his account, and there's the email he's been waiting for, the story list from some kid named Michael M. Hastings. Must be an intern.

He sees the list:

Cover: Global Housing Boom
Nishant Patel on TK
Rise of Islam In Europe?/townsend
Mobile Phones/Outsourcing/E. Africa Genocide/peoria
The Swedish Model
TK Columnist on Financial Scandal
Three Novels on Exile
Space Tourism

Mobile phones? Out fucking what? What moron wrote up this story list?

He refreshes his screen, and there's a new email from Jerry, the World Affairs Editor.

Hey A.E., the story is on for this week—just going to make it more of a business story pegged to a new report about the increase in mobile phone sales across Africa. Would be good if you interview a mobile phone vendor or talk to some Africans about their use of mobile phones. What colors, styles? What kind of brand? How many phones do most families have? How much do the phones cost in USD? What are the Chinese really up to? We'll have an intern here call the authors of the study, so no need to worry about that. We'll wrap your on-scene reporting lower down in the story. Can file thursday ayem? many thanks, j

A.E. Peoria is about to hit Reply, about to cc the entire top editorial staff. He gets only to the words "Jerry that sounds like" and doesn't get to "absolute bullshit" when he notices that the crowd that had gathered to watch him from the bottom of the small hill has dispersed. To move silently away, in a herdlike fashion, as if sensing an earthquake or a thunderstorm or some kind of major weather or geological event. He listens closely. There is actually a deep and frightening whistle. He understands that perhaps a mortar shell or a rocket is on the way. Right when he thinks that, he hears a very loud boom and grabs his laptop and satellite modem, and while flipping the screen down, he hits Send by accident and falls off the roof of the Toyota Land Cruiser. He protects his laptop, falling on his back, but the Uniriya satellite mobile modem, which looks like a gray plastic box, falls on the ground next to him. Peoria scrambles to his feet and opens the door to get back in the car and the overhead light goes on, and he thinks, Oh fuck, fuck me, this is stupid shit.

He slams the door and puts the Toyota Land Cruiser in reverse and starts driving down the hill, thinking he should try to get back to the refugee camp. The electronics he had been charging in the cigarette lighter are tangled on his lap, and the interior of the car is a fucking mess. He feels liquids, like spilled water bottles or something. *Ka thunk, ka thunk, ka thunk.* Without a seat belt, each twenty-foot stretch on the dirt path down to the village sends him up high in his seat. He keeps bumping his head. Finally he gets to the bottom of the small hill and stops outside the tent that he and David D. Obutu are sharing. David D. Obutu is standing outside the tent and smiling and shaking his head.

"You lucky the Ibo tribe can't shoot RPGs for nothing," David D. Obutu says.

"That was an RPG? I thought it was a mortar."

A.E. Peoria and David D. Obutu smoke a cigarette.

"We have to get back to N'Djamena tomorrow. We need to go to the market and talk to someone who sells mobile phones."

"No problem. Everyone in Chad has mobile phones now. Two years ago, nothing! Now we are all talking on the mobile phones. Makes a good story—I worked with Granger from *USA Today* last week, and we did a big report on how Africans love mobile phones. Big business. Fucking Chinese."

"That's what I hear. Did you take my fucking batteries?"

3.

Afternoon, Tuesday, August 20, 2002

My desk is on the sixteenth floor, at an intersection of cubicles and two hallways, a listening post for office gossip. Every day, the section editors gather on the other side of my cubicle wall before going out to lunch.

Today, Jerry is the first out of his office, then Gary, then Anna.

"Want to come to the Crater with us?" Gary asks me.

It's the first time I've been invited, suggesting I may not just be another temp, replaced each season.

The Crater is two blocks west from the office, on 57th Street. It's cramped and greasy, an atmosphere of frequent foodborne illnesses. We're at a table in the corner underneath framed pictures on the wall of unknown famous people who have dined there and have taken the precaution of bringing aspirational publicity shots, signed with Magic Marker, made just in case.

"Ask for the burger well done if you're going to get a burger," says Jerry. "Nishant is really getting to me."

"Did anyone read his book?" asks Anna.

Jerry and Gary don't say anything. I wait a second.

"I read it," I say.

"What did you think?"

What did I think of Nishant Patel's book? It doesn't matter what I think of his book. I bought the book to find out as much about the boss as possible, not for any particular love of the subject matter. Reading it gave me insight into his thinking, insight into who he was or at least what he pretended to think. It was preparation for the moment, assured by probability, when I would be stuck in the elevator with him and I could say, "Gee, Mr. Patel, I loved your book, especially Chapter Seven, where you talk about transparency and corruption."

"I thought it was good," I say. "Especially the parts about transparency and corruption."

"What's it about again?" says Jerry, who makes a point not to pay attention to anything Nishant Patel–related that does not directly affect his stories or mood or job security. "Outsourcing, right? That fucking bastard."

"Uh, sort of. It's really about benevolent dictatorships."

The editors are listening to me.

"Benevolent dictatorships. How, you know, democracies evolve, and how they really take time to evolve, and so, though human rights activists like to push for changes really quickly, stability is preferable to quick or immediate change, and expecting immediate change, you know, is really, really a folly. Illiberal democracies. You know, like Tiananmen Square was a good thing, because look at the economic growth of China, when a democracy there could have really fucked— sorry, excuse my language—really slowed everything down."

"What countries does he talk about?" says Anna.

"Oh, you know, the Middle East, China, Indonesia, Pakistan, the, uh, warm countries. But America too, and he makes this kind of interesting argument that the problem with our government is that it's too transparent, that it should, I guess, be a little more secretive—that the transparency sort of paralyzes us and prevents good decision making."

Jerry isn't really listening to what I'm saying.

"He's just getting on my nerves," Jerry says.

"He might not be with us much longer," says Gary.

"No way—he's staying," says Anna.

There are three competing Nishant Patel tea-leaf readings. (1) Nishant Patel might accept some kind of government position at the NSC or State. (2) Nishant Patel might accept some kind of position in academia, president of Princeton or something—considered the most unlikely, as he has already spent much of his time in academia (Harvard, Yale, Ph.D., youngest professor, youngest editor of *Foreign Relations*, etc.). (3) And this is the juiciest: Nishant Patel is a contender to take over the domestic edition of *The Magazine* after the editor in chief retires. The EIC is named Henry and he's been EIC for seven years, and seven years is the historic average for EICs.

"They're not going to give him EIC. That's what Berman is being groomed for," says Jerry.

Sanders Berman, official title Managing Editor of *The Magazine*, ranked number six on the *New York Herald*'s "Top 20 Media Players Under Age 38."

"Why do we keep coming here?" Jerry says, looking at his chicken potpie.

"It's cheap," says Gary.

"Do you guys like Berman?" I ask.

"Ummm," says Jerry.

"He's okay," says Gary.

"Don't really know him," says Anna.

"Have any of you read his book?" I ask.

The Greatest War on Earth. A book about World War II. It's currently competing with Nishant Patel's book on the national bestseller lists. I've been keeping track of whose book is up and whose book is down.

"I'm thinking of reading it," I say.

The editors give a smile, condescending.

"How old are you?" says Gary.

"Twenty-two."

"Twenty-two."

"So young," the three, in unison, say at the table.

"I remember when I was twenty-two, walking around, change jingling in my pocket," Gary says. "Got the assignments I wanted, the jobs I wanted. No responsibilities. Just wait for the disappointments."

The check comes, and Jerry says he'll pick it up and expense it—it's only $43.37, but he likes to stick it to the magazine when he can.

"Man, Nishant is getting on my nerves," says Jerry. "I've got to quit."

Out on 57th Street, cabs and delivery trucks don't slow at the Eighth Avenue crosswalk, and Anna tells me that Jerry has been saying he's going to quit for fourteen years.

4.

Wednesday,
August 21, 2002

Space Tourism.

I'm excited about this story, and I've been working on it for two weeks. The story is pegged—"pegged" is a news industry word—to an American centimillionaire who's scheduled to go up in a Soyuz rocket in Novorossiysk, Russia, on September 14. He'll be the seventh private citizen to make the trip to space, and the private company, working with the Russian government to send him up, is called Orbital Access Inc. Orbital Access Inc. has one industry rival, Great Explorations, and they aren't very friendly. The two CEOs are quoted in most stories on the subject explaining their two different business models on monetizing the "nascent space tourism industry."

I'm supposed to do an interview by phone, in fifteen minutes, with a businessman, an engineer who lives in Colorado and is designing a space hotel. I'm preparing for the interview. I had printed out a stack of clips about the gentleman two days earlier, and I'm trying to find those pages. They are somewhere in the vicinity of my cubicle, but I am very messy, and there are stacks of newspapers and magazines and Post-it notes and binders and folders left open and creased at the spine.

I start to dig for the papers, throwing open the metal cabinet drawers underneath the desktop, tossing and shifting piles of eight-by-eleven sheets.

My cubicle is in a process of fossilization. The process, as far as I can tell, began when the magazine started to rent space in this building in 1987. None of the interns who have sat in this cubicle has ever completely removed all of their belongings. Decaying bits of personality, deposits of forgotten headlines, inexplicable artifacts.

I've been getting the sense lately that someone, perhaps the Mexican cleaning service woman or the Polish cleaning service old man, is messing with my documents and cleaning my desk for me when I go home, so the papers could really be anywhere.

I pull open a drawer where I think the stack of papers could be.

Inside is a pile of comic books, with a graphic novel on the Palestinian territories on top of the stack, and I assume these are from four interns ago, because that was when A.E. Peoria started his career at the magazine. In this very cubicle. He'd become a star foreign correspondent, and it would make sense that a star foreign correspondent would be reading comics about war.

Tossing through another drawer, I find a green construction helmet and a gas mask with a broken rubber strap—I date this find to October 2001, after the terrorist attacks in New York convinced Human Resources to provide protection from chemical and biological threats targeted at media organizations. The construction helmet and gas mask are on top of a manila folder with notes from a story about the Supreme Court's 2000 decision to make George W. Bush president; those notes are piled on another folder, red, with photo caption information about the Balkans, notes on a graphic illustration breaking down population levels and ethnicities in the ratio of numbers killed in Bosnia-Herzegovina, Croatia, Serbia, etc.; there are lots of spelling mistakes and red pen on this document.

Underneath the folder is a pile of back issues, the newest one dating from 1996, working backward at uneven intervals to 1991. Whoever chose the issues to collect in this pile was making some kind of time capsule point or editorial critique. All the headlines on the covers either contain the word "new" ("The New Happiness," "The New War on Drugs," "The New Normal," "The New Hollywood," "The New Aging," "The New Parent Trap") or end in a question mark ("Did the President Lie?" "The Candidate to Beat?" "Is the Globe Warming?")—and sometimes have both ("The New Mystery of Mary Magdalene: Can Science Tell Us What History Can't?"). According to this compiler's count, marked by a yellow Post-it, either a question mark or the word "new" was used more than thirty-nine times in that five-year stretch.

What catches my eye is another Post-it note, hand-scrawled, on the last issue in the pile. There is no question mark or word "new" in it, so I wonder why it's there. The date says January 3, 1991. There is a picture of a desert and an American tank. "The Vietnam Syndrome," blares the headline.

This story is famous in the magazine's lore. It was written by none other than Sanders Berman while he was finishing up his final year at Tulane. Quickly flipping through the other issues, I see that a good 90 percent of them carry the Sanders Berman byline—it dawns on me that I might be sitting in the exact same cubicle that Sanders Berman once sat in, though I find that hard to believe. Legend has it that he was only in the cubes for three months before he got his own office, before he was made the youngest editor of the National Affairs section of *The Magazine*. Perhaps I am sitting in the cube of Sanders Berman's old assistant?

I place the "Vietnam Syndrome" issue on top of my desk—I'll get to this soon—and continue my search for the papers, when I'm distracted again.

Did I mention where *The Magazine*'s TVs are? It's a matter of some dispute, as there's a shortage of television sets. For some reason, most of the sets are on the fifteenth floor, where the production and photography staff are, not the news reporters. This helps the fifteenth floor follow important sporting events on Saturday, like the Kentucky Derby or March Madness. But in the southeast block, near me, there is only one television shared by sixteen cubicles—it's on a swivel attached to a column.

The column is outside Nishant Patel's office. The TV hangs over the three cubicles surrounding the column, and those three cubicles are manned by Nishant Patel's three assistants: Dorothy, Lucy, and Patricia. The highest person in the hierarchy of the three assistants is Dorothy, and Dorothy has been at the magazine for three decades. Dorothy does not like to have the volume of the television set on. Dorothy always puts it on mute.

So it is a fluke that in my search for the Space Tourism papers, I turn around 180 degrees to catch the BREAKING NEWS ALERT on MSNBC.

The vice president of the United States, Richard B. Cheney, is standing at a lectern, speaking to men and women in military uniform. You know what Dick Cheney looks like, so I won't waste time on that, and I can't hear what he's saying. Luckily, MSNBC has taken what it thinks are the most important themes in his speech and keeps scrolling them across the screen while he speaks.

VP CHENEY: IRAQ HAS CHEMICAL WEAPONS

VP CHENEY: IRAQ IS PURSUING NUCLEAR WEAPONS

**VP CHENEY: WE CANNOT ALLOW
IRAQ TO ACQUIRE WMD**

My phone rings and I pick it up.

"Michael M. Hastings."

"Mr. Hastings, this is Douglas Dorl, from Outerlimits Hotels."

"Mr. Dorl, great, thanks for calling me back. Is this a good time?"

"I called you, yeah."

"Great, great, great."

I spin back around, and though I'm not entirely prepared to do the interview, I do remember the list of questions that I more or less wanted answers or quotes about.

"Oh, so, uh, when will the space hotels be ready?"

"If our models are correct, we hope to get the first space hotel in orbit by 2015."

"And, uh, what, are, the, uh, challenges, to, uh, this?"

I have a tape recorder hooked up to the phone and press Play/ Record, so I'm not too worried about listening that closely.

"Customer confidence."

"What do you mean?"

"We have to avoid catastrophe. Look at the airlines. The first national airline began in the early 1930s. But it took years of proving to the consumer that it was safe to fly. Almost didn't—an accident in 1938, a crash over the Alleghenies that killed forty people, almost ruined the airline industry as we know it. There's a reason for that. There was a law in Congress trying to ban air travel! Can you believe that? So I'm talking bulk. We need to have regular tourist space flights, at cost, at a price point people can afford. One tourist flight blows up, and we're sunk as an industry. Funding dries up, the public won't have trust in us."

"So, your hotels, um, how expensive are they to build?"

"Cheaper than NASA."

"So is that like a couple hundred million?"

"We think we can do it for a couple hundred million. Hell, a new hotel that just opened in Las Vegas cost one hundred and twenty million, and that's on Earth."

"Right, right."

Phone tucked under my ear, typing what Douglas Dorl is saying, I peer over my shoulder at the television screen, and VP Cheney is still talking.

VP CHENEY: U.S. MUST TAKE ACTION, NOT APPEASE

"And how much a night, do you think?"

"Between three thousand and ten thousand a night."

"Does that include travel cost?"

"Goes back to what I was saying—making an economy of scale."

"Right, right. Tell me more about your company, how you founded it, why you're interested in space."

This is a throwaway question to get him talking—I'm distracted by the news on the television set, and I'm not as focused as I should be on what Mr. Dorl is saying: As a kid watched the moon landing. Worked for NASA. Designed a part of the shuttle. Enjoyed the film *The Right Stuff.*

Then I catch sight of the TV screen again.

Sanders Berman is on, as a guest, giving analysis.

"Okay, great. Yeah, thanks, um, if I have any follow-up questions, mind if I give you a call?"

"Be my guest."

I hang up the phone and walk quickly two cubicle rows over.

"Hi, Dorothy, mind if I turn the volume up? Sanders Berman is on."

"Ohhhhh, Sanders Berman," she says, her tone suggesting a familiarity with Sanders Berman, years of anecdotes about him that she's not about to share with me.

I kneel on the desk of one of Nishant Patel's three assistants and hit Volume Up once.

Sanders Berman is discussing what Vice President Cheney just said.

". . . certainly," Sanders Berman answers.

"Sanders, now, you're the expert, you're the historian, give us some historical idea of what you make of the vice president's speech."

"In 1940, President Franklin Roosevelt gave an underlooked address to a Lions Club in Decatur, Illinois. Now, no one pays attention to that address today, it's been overshadowed by the 'Day of Infamy' speech after Pearl Harbor. But what I hear in the vice president's language, in his somber delivery, his cadence, the timbre of his voice, is what FDR said in Decatur—he's quietly preparing the American people for what clearly is a dangerous and imminent threat. I suspect the discussion, going forward, is not going to be a question of *if* we should go to war in Iraq, but *when*. The vice president is warning of a great evil we face. It's not Japan or Germany; it's Iraq, Iran, North Korea. It's the 9/11 terrorists, a great evil. Of course the audience here is the American people, but there's also a second audience—our allies—and this is a call to the Winston Churchills out there, a warning to them that we need them, and I hope they will stand on our side."

The door to Nishant Patel's corner office opens, and he walks out.

"Dorothy, can you have Patricia bring my lunch?"

"Yes, Nishant," Dorothy says, and she stands and looks over the cubicle wall at Patricia, a thirty-seven-year-old Korean woman who lives with her family in Queens. Patricia is deaf in her right ear and blind in her left eye.

"Patricia," Dorothy says, "can you please go get Nishant his lunch."

"What, Dorothy?"

"Patricia, Nishant's lunch," she says.

Dorothy sits down, Patricia stands up, and Nishant Patel asks, "What are you all watching?"

"Mike turned the volume up, Dr. Patel," Patricia says.

Dorothy looks at me.

"Vice President Cheney, I think, just sort of said we're going to war in Iraq," I say.

"Oh, yes, of course, I had heard that the vice president was going to do that. I had dinner with the undersecretary in Washington on Monday."

Nishant Patel walks around the corner of the cubicles and looks up at the TV, just as the cable network is about to cut to a commercial.

"Mr. Berman, a pleasure as always," says the host. "*The Magazine*'s managing editor and also author of *The Greatest War on Earth: The New History of World War Two*," says the host, holding a copy of Sanders Berman's book.

I'm not looking at the TV; I'm looking at Nishant Patel. He winces when the MSNBC host bangs Sanders Berman's book on the table.

"We'll turn the volume down right away, Nishant," says Dorothy.

Nishant Patel goes back in his office. I go back to Space Tourism.

Three hours later, I get an email forwarded to me. It's a forward from Dorothy, forwarded from Sam, who forwarded it from Nishant Patel.

Subject: Fw: Int'l story list change
From: Dorothy
To: International Staff

See below from Sam/NP, dorothy

Subject: Int'l story list change
To: Dorothy

From: Sam
Subject: Int'l story change

All, we are going to go with a new cover this week. "The Case for War?"

Dropping sci/tech and Mobile phones.

Subject: [blank]
To: Sam
From: Nishant Patel

Change in cover. See me in my office. np

It's 5:30 p.m. and the editors are leaving the office. Gary stops by my cubicle.

"Hastings, you're off the hook for Space Tourism this week."

5.

Friday, August 23, 2002

Thirty-four-year-old magazine journalist A.E. Peoria sits in first class right now, right fucking now, just sits down, and there are two women standing over him. DBX to JFK. One has a tray of hot hand towels, and she gives him one and smiles; the other has a tray with a variety of liquids: booze, waters, juices—sparkling water, nonsparkling water, tomato, mango, grapefruit. Peoria takes three glasses—sparkling water, grapefruit juice, and wine—and he gulps them down and starts to pat himself down, rubbing the tiredness from his eyes, the days in the African bush getting soaked up in the warm hot towel. He removes the towel from his face and the three glasses have already been taken away, replaced with a four-page menu.

He didn't have to suffer the indignity of finding the menu in the seat-back pocket.

The flight attendant is asking him if he'd like something else to drink, and he says, "Yes, give me a gin and tonic," and as he is scanning the menu—whipped summer squash, couscous, goat cheese and beet salad, Asian wheat noodles with shrimp, a seven-ounce grilled flank steak, potatoes and chicken curry, and more, and flambéed ice cream and rice pudding and bread baskets with thirteen different kinds of bread and a cheese plate with grapes and orange slices and bananas and cheese and apples and olives—he gets the gin and tonic delivered to him, and it's in a glass glass.

Another indignity avoided: the woman—what a fucking angel—is unscrewing the cap of the small bottle of gin and pouring it into his glass and mixing it for him. Even as the cabin doors close, everyone in first class is still talking on their mobile phones, and even as the plane is taxiing, people are still talking on their mobile phones and the stewardesses are letting it happen, until the last possible moment, when they ask them, politely, to please finish their conversations, as we are about to take off.

Politeness, no glowers or glares, politely requesting that you turn off your mobile phone. They are treating him like some kind of human being up here, not an animal that needs to be prodded and kicked in the seat.

Eight hours or more and the magazine gives correspondents a first-class ticket. Until he became a star foreign correspondent, a roaming-the-globe international affairs reporter, he had flown first class only once. Sixteen, visiting a friend in the Bahamas for spring break, an upgrade. That wasn't real first class. That was Delta domestic first class. This is real first class, and real first class makes him wonder how he had ever traveled in economy/coach class without developing a severe class hatred. When did economy become coach and coach economy anyway? He thinks it was around 1997. Must have been an advertising or marketing study. *Coach* is a respectable word, he never thought anything was wrong with *coach*—stagecoach, almost classy-sounding, or even *coach* as in a bus, where everyone has an equally comfortable or uncomfortable seat. *Coach* is an equal opportunity word, a normalizing word. *Economy* is a word for "cheap."

Cheap.

It's another way, he thinks, the mix of liquids giving his thoughts the appearance of great profundity, for the airlines to subtly rub it in the passengers' faces that they are screwed in life and made bad decisions every step along the way and are forced to pay attention to money, forced to pinch pennies.

The airlines, he now realizes, had been trying to make him feel bad his entire life, or at least since 1997.

For years in coach, with the rest of the fellow failures, he had gotten off the plane last. This meant that he'd had to walk past the first-class seats and business-class seats. Before getting to the first- and business-class seats, he had to go through at least two or more cabins of economy.

Economy always looked like shit after a fourteen-hour flight. It looked like a bunch of preschoolers had been stuck in a fallout shelter. Empty plastic water and juice cups, tangled headsets, ripped plastic bags, crumbs from never-go-stale biscuits, bright blue thermonuclear fleece blankets, weird puke smells, torn packaging, yes, lots of shredded plastic and mutilated packaging, as if a scarce amount of resources had been consumed in a frenzy.

The flight attendants didn't bother with cleanup in coach—no, they wanted the evidence of the savagery on display. And by the time the disembarking economy passenger got through the coach wasteland, the single business-class cabin was a relief and went by in a blur. It wasn't so obvious that a major shift in socioeconomics had taken place. In fact, the business-class cabin seemed designed to ease the shock that those traveling in coach would have experienced if they'd just stepped directly from coach to first class, from one socioeconomic sphere to the other. Like letting a bum into the country club. Yes, that would have been too much of a shock, that might have backfired. Best to use business class as a buffer zone. The airlines wanted you to know what you were missing, but they didn't want to spark any social revolts, any impromptu pummelings, anyone to take a protest dump on an aisle seat.

So Peoria would walk through business class and see nine seats per row instead of twelve, and this wasn't too jarring, and then when he got to first class or, on some planes, just got a glimpse through the curtains ahead, there were only six seats—and what big and comfortable-looking seats they were. And where was the evidence of a fourteen-hour flight?

The evidence, Peoria now knew, had been quietly picked up and cleaned along the way by these angel flight attendants. Angels pushing dangerous and embittering illusions without rubber surgical gloves to protect their hands from economy-class parasites and filth. The evidence of the disgusting humanness of adults locked in a capsule of recycled air and sleep breath and hunger had been erased and sterilized even as the first-class passengers were getting off the plane. Even as the first-classers were exiting, the flight attendants, an entire team of them, would rush to perform an instant cleanup. It gave the passengers in economy, who had to pass through the cabin before deplaning, the unconscious impression that perhaps they were truly savages at heart, truly disgusting people who deserved to sit side by side in the cattle car, making a mess of their environment, using thin polyester pillows, hauling luggage with rolls and rolls of clear plastic tape and big handwritten notes with foreign names and impoverished zip codes, digesting single-serving chicken and beef on a single-page menu.

All of this, all the service, the high-touch service that had taken over his thoughts, had been so engrossing to him that he hasn't even bothered to look at who he is sitting next to or any of the other people sitting in his first-class cabin.

He is sitting next to a woman.

Two hours, four gin and tonics, and he is looking out the window of the plane.

Why so emotional on night flights?

Hour three and a half and he goes to the bathroom and snorts the cocaine he bought in Dubai on the twelve-hour layover.

Hour five, he is going to the bathroom, and he is talking to the woman.

"It's so rare to sit next to a pretty woman my age in first class," he says. "Usually they can't afford it or they're with some older rich guy."

The woman nods, and across the aisle, there's an older rich guy who smiles at A.E. Peoria.

"Oh shit, is that your boyfriend?"

Hour seven, there's a knocking on the bathroom door, a glowing sign that says PLEASE RETURN TO YOUR SEAT, with a little figure of a dickless man and an arrow.

"Sir, are you all right?"

Wobbling, A.E. Peoria opens up the bathroom door, which folds up like an accordion, and he laughs at this, and the pretty stewardess woman who gave him the menu and poured what he estimates to be five out of his seven drinks is standing there.

"You're the one who gave me that menu! Thank you, thank you. You're Miss Five-out-of-Seven, Miss Laila. 'Laila' is Arabic for what?"

"Look how much legroom I have," A.E. Peoria says, returning to his seat.

"I always wanted an electric chair as a kid, one of those electric La-Z-Boy chairs where I could move it around like this," A.E. Peoria is saying while he adjusts every control on the seat. There are sixteen different ergonomic portions of the seat to calibrate, five just for the upper torso and seven for different leg positions. How do you even describe all of these positions? Stretched, outstretched, slightly stretched, partially stretched, a quarter partial stretch, a half partial stretch, three-quarters partial stretch. He would need to resort to math to describe all the things his seat could do.

"You know what I like about first class," he says to the older man, who is now sitting next to him, having changed places with his girlfriend or wife. "I like that there's no evidence that I'm drunk. If I was back with the fucking beasts and vampires back there, sucking the fucking marrow from bones, you know, if I was fucking back there, there'd be all these little bottles in front of me because the service back there sucks and there's no way I could have even had that many drinks because the service is slow, so it's like a catch-22, you know?"

Hour nine.

"You don't fucking know what I saw out there, man. You don't fucking want to know what I saw. Heads on pikes."

Hours ten and eleven.

"Hey man, fuck, sorry dude. But here's the thing. Here's what you're missing. Don't worry about getting sleep and rest. I've been thinking about this, and the irony is, if you travel a lot, if you do a lot of travel, it's ironic, because nowadays . . ."

A.E. Peoria pauses.

"The irony of international travel is that you spend as much time or more time going nowhere as going somewhere. You spend time sitting in the same fucking place."

He pauses again.

"Even right now. You can't even tell that you're moving."

Hour twelve.

The stewardess hands A.E. Peoria an immigration card, and this reminds him to take one more trip to the bathroom, where he flushes the small and empty plastic bag of coke down the toilet after ripping it and licking the insides so he can numb his gums.

A car is waiting for him at the airport, and when the driver asks for directions, he tells him to bring him straight to the office, to West 57th Street. He wants to talk to someone, whoever the motherfucker was who killed his story.

6.

Saturday Night, August 24, 2002

Saturday night is closing night. By three on Sunday morning, the new issue is electronically transmitted to seven printers across the continental United States and twelve printers in different regions across the globe, where it is printed, tied in stacks, put in the back of delivery trucks, and distributed to newsstands and delis and bookstores, or shrink-wrapped and mailed to 2.2 million subscribers.

I treasure Saturday nights. The sixteenth floor clears out around three or four p.m., leaving a handful of editorial staffers, whose job it is to make sure all the stories, captions, pull quotes, photographs, and tables of contents make their way safely through the gauntlet of copy desk to make-up to production, to catch errors that might have slipped in along the way.

My role on Saturday night is to be available in case there are any last-second changes the correspondents want to put in the stories. They call me, I pull the story up in the computer system, and I make the changes. I'm the liaison between the correspondents in the field and the editors in New York, who by Saturday night are at home.

It's mostly downtime. The waiting begins mid-afternoon and ends between eleven p.m. and one a.m., when I get the word from the production staff that I can leave.

I've found comfort in waiting: the empty floor, the vacuuming, the dark offices, a warm feeling, a feeling that I am part of something *bigger than myself,* a dedicated servant to the magazine.

My friends tell me that it sucks that I have to work Saturday night. I don't mind at all—I have no problem working Saturday nights. I would not want to be anyplace else.

But what to do during those seven or so hours of waiting.

Get to know *The Magazine.* I want to learn as much detail as I can about the lives and careers and personalities of the people who work in our little universe. The histories, the disputes, the controversies, the raw copy sitting in the computer system—to know the real story of the stories. To know how the magazine got started, stretching back to 1934, its evolution and many incarnations, and to understand the different factions at work today.

Red Notes are a function in the computer system (called Agile). They allow editors and researchers and copy desk employees to ask questions by writing them in the actual file of the story. They are like the Track Changes function in Microsoft Word. Rather than simply delete something, the editor can write a Red Note so the changes can be seen by the person looking at the file but not by the reader when it finally gets published. The editor uses Red Notes to put questions in the text that the correspondent or writer has to answer, like so: <<this attribution okay?>>

The most important Red Notes are at the end of the story. These are the Red Notes that editors, on each level of the editorial chain, use to give praise. Or don't.

To know who is up and who is down, you have to look at the Red Notes.

I have access to all the stories in the domestic and international editions.

I can see all the Red Notes. I study what changes have been made and how they have been made and why.

I read the Red Notes at the end first. The praise in Red Notes is an indication of the star power of the writer or reporter, how valuable they are to *The Magazine*.

Nishant Patel's story "The Case for War?" is being published in both the domestic and international editions. In the international edition, it is the cover story. In the domestic edition, it isn't the cover story—the cover this particular week is about autism and twins.

I open the story, file name int0114, and scroll to the last page. Four editors have signed off on Nishant Patel's essay.

```
<<magnificent, thought provoking. Sure to
get us out front. excellent work Nishant//
jeff>>


<<superbly done. compelling, challenging,
deceptively entertaining. i second
jeff//nh>>


<<amen. you've blown us all away again with
your elegance, style, and fresh thinking.
this has national magazine award written
all over it. the greatest piece yet on the
argument for war. you've outdone yourself
mr. patel, many thanks.//sanders>>


<<couldn't agree more. a fluid, engaging,
comprehensive, persuasive, groundbreaking
```

```
essay. puts our competition to shame. glad
to have you here raj//henry>>
```

The effusiveness is not unusual. The effusiveness is what a figure like Nishant Patel would expect from Red Notes. What it means on this story is that Henry the EIC took the time not only to read the story but also to actually type a Red Note himself.

Alone, perhaps, this wouldn't mean much. Out of context, it might just seem the norm. But I contrast Red Notes on Nishant's story with Red Notes on the next story.

I open the essay Sanders Berman wrote this week, file na0214.

It is about FDR's speech in Decatur, Illinois.

I skip to the bottom of the page.

There are two Red Notes. Only two.

```
<<impressive, sanders//tom>>


<<excellent timing//nh>>
```

There is no comment from Henry the EIC. Again, alone, this wouldn't have much significance. Henry the EIC is a busy individual. He doesn't have time to read all the stories, so you could easily dismiss the non–Red Noting as an issue of scheduling and time management. But if you are a savvy user of Agile, you know that by clicking on one of the drop-down menus, a list of every user who has opened and made changes to the document is available. (For my Saturday-night readings, I use the "read only" function so my username, mhasti, doesn't appear on this list.) And sure enough, on the list is Henry the EIC's username, heic.

Which means Henry the EIC read Sanders Berman's column and didn't say anything.

He didn't leave a Red Note.

A shift in the power balance is occurring, not yet seismic but clearly felt.

I hear a loud banging on the glass doors down the hallway. Not unusual. Means someone has forgotten their company identification.

I get up from my cubicle and walk down the hall, past the men's and women's rooms, to the set of glass doors.

I jump back, slightly shocked.

A face is pressed up against the glass, mouth like a blowfish, the full weight of the figure propped up by the door.

The eyes on the face above the gaping mouth are closed.

The eyes open. Bloodshot, one thick eyebrow arching.

"You going to let me in," says the person. "It's me, A.E. Peoria. I fucking work here."

"You might want to step back," I say.

A.E. Peoria, in the flesh, stumbles back.

I pull open the glass doors.

"Where the fuck is he and who the fuck are you," A.E. Peoria says.

"I'm Michael M. Hastings, but I just got hired on—"

"Mmmmm, Mike Hastings . . ."

I am holding the door open; A.E. Peoria has yet to step through.

"You sent the story list."

"Yeah, I did this week . . ."

"Sh . . . Sh . . . Ssssssshhhhh."

There are two bags at A.E. Peoria's feet. His eyes are opening and closing as he rocks back and forth.

"It's not your fault, it's not your fault. You can get my bags, right, bro?"

A.E. Peoria walks past me, zigzagging and pushing off from one wall to the other.

"Watch the—"

On his third sequence of zigzagging, he pushes the door to the men's room. The door swings open easily, and he falls through, losing his balance. His legs are sticking out in the hallway. He groans.

I run up beside him.

"Here you go, let's get you to your office," I say, as his blowfish mouth is now half on the white-tile floor of the men's room.

Kneeling, I notice we are not alone in the bathroom—someone else is in there. I can see his shoes underneath the blue stalls. The shoes are pointed at the toilet bowl, not away from the toilet bowl, which means this person is either urinating standing up in the bathroom stall or doing something else. Whoever's toes, they have frozen still. Whoever it is, he's waiting to see if he will have privacy in the bathroom again.

"Thanks for the help, bro," says A.E. Peoria, getting up, then saying, "I don't need your fucking help, bro."

A.E. Peoria stumbles off down the hall, toward his office. I follow him to make sure he doesn't fall again. We get to his office and he throws himself into his chair.

"I gotta check my email," he says, sitting in the dark.

I flick on the light switch and go back to get his bags.

I pick up the bags. As I'm turning around, the door to the men's room swings open slowly and a head peeks out.

I freeze, carrying A.E. Peoria's baggage, a duffel bag and a North Face hiking backpack slung over my shoulders.

It's Sanders Berman.

This is the closest I've ever been to Sanders Berman, and I can now tell you what he looks like in person.

Sanders Berman looks like he got his wardrobe from raiding Mark Twain's closet.

"Mr. Berman," I say, "I'm Michael M. Hastings. I work in international, saw you on MSNBC, really fascinating what you were saying."

Sanders Berman shoots his eyes back and forth and he wipes his mouth. What is he wiping from his mouth?

"It's okay to call me Sanders," he says. "What are you doing here so late?"

"Oh, I'm here late every Friday and Saturday, making sure the magazine gets put to bed."

Sanders Berman looks at me.

"Going somewhere?"

"Oh, these are A.E. Peoria's bags. He just got back from eastern Chad, covering that, uh, mobile genocide there."

"That was Peoria on the floor?"

"Yes, he tripped."

Sanders Berman is wearing a bow tie and is hunched over slightly—he's a thirty-seven-year-old trapped in a sixty-seven-year-old's body, and from what I've read about him, he's been trapped in a sixty-seven-year-old's body since puberty.

"Did he hear anything?"

I don't quite know what he's talking about.

"I think he heard a lot, I mean, he was in Chad for, like, three weeks, so I'm sure he heard a lot."

Quizzically, Sanders Berman nods.

"It's been one of those days," he says.

"Really honored to be here, Mr. Berman," I say as he walks down the hall.

I wonder if I made a bad first impression. Fuck, I think. But I start to get a bit giddy, having finally introduced myself to Sanders Berman.

In one week, I'm now on the radar of the two really important men at the magazine. It is strange, though, Sanders Berman being here so late. I've never seen an editor that high up stick around to this hour on a Saturday.

Lugging the baggage, I go back to A.E. Peoria's office. He's not there. I put the bags down and walk back toward my desk, where I find a much more awake and lively A.E. Peoria sitting in my cubicle.

"I'm checking my email," he says. "This is my old cube. It's nostalgia. It's like instinct, me coming and sitting back down right here."

A.E. Peoria is wearing green work pants with extra pockets and black leather hiking boots. He doesn't look cool. I had this idea in my mind that because he was doing cool things, like traveling to eastern Chad and whatnot, and because he had kind of a cool byline, A.E. Peoria, no first name, that he would look more striking, more tall, dark, and handsome. Can't judge a man by his byline apparently. He's short and sort of dark, but he would not be mistaken for handsome, I don't think, unless we lived in a world where people who looked like pudgy gnomes were considered handsome. He does, though, have a bundled, intense energy around him, even while he is completely shit hammered.

My phone rings.

A.E. Peoria picks up.

He covers the mouthpiece.

"What's your name again?"

"Mike Hastings."

"Mike Hastings," Peoria says into the phone.

"Excellent, that's fucking excellent, bro."

He hangs up.

"That was production. We're free to go get a drink."

7.

Early Morning, Sunday, August 25, 2002

have a disorder," says A.E. Peoria.

It's two a.m. and we're sitting in O'Neil's Irish Pub and Tavern on 55th and 7th Ave. It's sort of shitty, but it's upper Midtown we're talking about, shabby since the 1950s. There aren't too many good places to go in upper Midtown at this hour. We're in a strange late-night dead zone. The nightlife in New York is to the north of us, to the south of us, but right here, it's lame places like O'Neil's Irish Pub and Tavern, a default location that seems to cater to tourists who don't have a good guidebook or the courage to go farther than five blocks from their hotel.

"CDD," he says. "Have you heard of that?"

"Is that like OCD?"

"Maybe it is. Want to take a shot?"

"No, remember, I don't drink."

"Really? That's fucked-up. Are you one of those Mormon interns?"

The Magazine had a special relationship with Brigham Young University, which meant Mormons had three guaranteed internship slots a year.

"I mean no offense if you are a Mormon."

"No, it's not for religious reasons. Moral reasons."

"What?"

"Moral reasons. When I drink, I lose my morals."

I'd been saving that line, thinking it was a clever way to parry questions about my nondrinking, but A.E. Peoria doesn't appear to find it funny. My clever lines rarely pay off in context of the conversation. The last time one worked was in AP History class in twelfth grade. A girl sitting in front of me was debating with another girl how to pronounce the word *schedule*—was it "sked-u-al" or "ssshed-u-al"? The girl asked me to weigh in. I did. "What ssshoool did you learn that at?" I asked. Meaning "school."

"That's good, man. Good for you for not drinking."

"Thanks."

"I'll take two shots then, one for you, one for me."

He orders two shots of tequila.

"Fuck I haven't slept in a while. What day is it?"

"Saturday."

"That's why not one of those fuckers was at the office. I got my date and time all wrong—it's all fucked-up. I'm something like six and a half hours ahead, which means I'd be just waking up, but I was in Thailand before Chad, and that's like thirteen hours ahead, and I went back four hours and never really adjusted to that, so I don't really know what time it is."

"I think it's two-thirty."

"Two-thirty for you, but for me I'm talking about."

A.E. Peoria, four-year veteran, with just over a six-figure salary as a staff correspondent. A.E. Peoria, living the dream. How did he do it? Like a sponge, I want to know.

"How was Chad?"

"Intense," he says.

The bartender puts two shots of tequila down in front of us. I thank the bartender and ask for a club soda. The bartender passes me a club soda and puts down a slice of lemon and a saltshaker next to it. A.E. Peoria licks his lips, licks the salt, throws the shot back, his blowfish mouth widening. He coughs and his eyes water.

"Cheers," I say, tilting my club soda in his direction.

"Ahhhhhahahhhahahhhahahhh," says A.E. Peoria. "That's better."

Here's what I know about A.E. Peoria. I got most of this information from the Meet the Staff link on *The Magazine*'s website and the rest from an online profile of him from a recent alumni newsletter posted on the Internet. I know he started at *The Magazine* in 1998. I know that he spent his early twenties working for a midsize newspaper in Virginia. He left the midsize paper and traveled across the country on a Greyhound bus. He talked to the passengers along the way, bag ladies, scratch-ticket junkies, blacks and whites and Hispanics, single mothers en route to visit deadbeat convict lovers housed in the federal and state prison system; dreamers, degenerates, dopers, hippies, whores, keno players, bingo fanatics. He wrote a book called *Desperation Points West*. I'd checked the book on Amazon, and its sales ranking was #1,934,987. It got one review by *Booklist*, a five-sentence critical summary that called it "disappointing" and said, "Hoping to hear from voices of America's economically deprived, we instead are treated to monologues from the painfully unaware narrator. . . . *Desperation Points West* points nowhere." Shattered by the absence of the book's reception, Peoria spent the next eighteen months in Cambodia. It was his magazine work there that got him back on the fast track. "There's nothing like seeing a field of skulls while listening to AC/DC's 'Thunderstruck' in a jeep full of ex–Khmer Rouge to give you a new perspective on life," he'd told his alumni newsletter. He got hired during flush times at *The Magazine*, and they outbid a competitor to bring him on staff as a roving-the-world writer for the international editions.

"Are you going to drink that?" he asks me, looking at the shot of tequila.

"No, I don't drink," I say.

"Oh that's right, a Mormon."

A.E. Peoria snaps up the other shot, quenchingly.

"I have a disorder," A.E. Peoria says again. "So I'm not going to be apologizing for this. CDD. Have you heard of it?"

"Is it like OCD?" I ask again.

"Yes, but reverse. Compulsive disclosure disorder. I have no filter, my shrink says. I don't know boundaries, I'm always revealing very personal and intimate details about my life, and there's nothing I can do about it unless I want to get on medication, and I just don't want to get on medication right now because I would have to give up drinking, and it's just not time for me to give up drinking."

I nod.

"See, right there. I don't even know you and I'm telling you I have a mental disorder and I don't want medication and I see a shrink. Blows my fucking mind. But I'm aware of it now, you know? I'm aware of it, and that's good progress, right?"

"Sounds like great progress."

A.E. Peoria orders another shot of tequila.

"How old are you, Hastings?"

"Me, I'm twenty-two."

This bit of information always has impact, and I don't really understand why. Age isn't a big deal to me (yet?). For most of my life, I've always been the youngest one at the table, and it's something I've come to expect, maybe take for granted. I can't imagine that when I'm older I'll ever ask that question.

"You're just a fucking baby, bro," says A.E. Peoria. "Let me tell you something about the magazine. The magazine is shit, but it's great for someone your age. You have to get out of the office. The office will steal your soul. The lights in the office—you've looked at them? Those fucking energy-efficient fluorescent things, the dimpled plastic, all of that, it's like it's radiating soul-suckingness. It's radiating deadly soul-destroying, like, radiation, and it will fucking kill you if you don't get out. You really want to end up like Jerry and Sam and Gary and all those guys? Fuck, I mean Gary and Jerry are cool, but shit, you really want to end up like them?"

I nod.

"Know what I should do? I should write up tips, a tip sheet for a successful career. You'd like that wouldn't you?"

"Yeah, that'd be great. I mean, I wanted to ask you, how did you end up—"

"How did I become A.E. Peoria," he says.

"Right."

"Never do the job you have—do the job you want to have. I kept asking for more when I was at the *Fairfax Gazette*. They wouldn't give it to me, so I left, and I wrote this book—maybe you heard of it, *Desperation Points West*—and then I went to Cambodia. Cambodia—let me say this: There's nothing like riding in a jeep with ex–Khmer Rouge in a field of skulls listening to AC/DC's 'Thunderstruck,' the wind blowing, high on hashish, to give you a real perspective on life."

I nod, and he starts nodding too.

"But I don't know if I'm hard-core enough. I really started to question that in Chad. Like Townsend."

A.E. Peoria reaches in his left pocket, then his right pocket, then notices that he placed his mobile phone down in front of him next to a bowl of popcorn, provided free of charge by O'Neil's Irish Pub and Tavern.

"Oh shit, I should go see my girlfriend. What do you think? I think I might love her. I gave her six orgasms. Big orgasms, huge orgasms. I'd never given anyone so many orgasms before. But I don't know if she's top tier, do you know what I mean? I want a top-tier girl, and I think she might be second tier."

Realizing the conversation is wrapping up, I try to think of any other questions I want to ask.

"I mean, how exactly did you become a foreign correspondent?"

"Look, I'm not going to lie. The job is fucking great. But it's also shit. I mean, my career is shit. Look, what have I done? Okay, so I wrote a book? So fucking what. Okay, so I've covered stories in thirteen different countries? Big fucking deal. Okay, so I'm only thirty-four and I've accomplished things that most people won't do in their entire lives. Okay, so I'm probably, give or take a few thousand, one of the highest-paid journalists my age in the country. None of it means shit."

"Well, I mean, you did write a book. How many people can say that? And like you said, you're only thirty-four."

"Yeah, I did write a fucking book. I guess that is pretty elite. Fuck, I really have to go. What do you say, time for one more shot?"

His phone vibrates.

"Oh shit, she just sent me a picture of herself. Here, take a look at her."

He slides his mobile phone to me on the bar as the bartender pushes another shot of tequila in front of him.

I snap open the mobile phone, and there's a surprisingly clear digital picture of A.E. Peoria's girlfriend. It's an impressive feat of self-portraiture. From knees to face. Shaved to drooping. Nimble fingers. Lips, a toy.

"She got cleaned up yesterday," says A.E. Peoria. "Timed for me. She's great like that, you know? She doesn't like to fuck on the day she gets waxed because her vagina gets irritated. But look at that—she has a really wet pussy. That ever happened to you? Very adventurous. She calls that one in her mouth the Contender. She's a little on the heavy side, you know, and she likes it doggy style the best. They have a name for that. I think it's like Dirty Sanchez or something. Six orgasms I gave her—incredible. She's a writer. She even does ghost-writing for *Penthouse* letters, but I don't think that's going to last much longer with all the porn on the Internet."

"You're a lucky guy," I say as he takes his phone back and stands up from the bar.

"What's your number? I'll send it to you," he says.

A.E. Peoria punches in my number and tries to send the photo.

"Thanks, man, I appreciate it."

"Bro, I'm fucking drunk. It's really amazing that you don't drink. I have a lot of respect for religions, though I think they're bullshit. Want to share a taxi? I'm going uptown."

"I'm heading downtown."

"I'm expensing all of these drinks tonight, fuck *The Magazine*. We deserve it."

I follow A.E. Peoria outside, and he ducks into a cab and shuts the door, and in the four seconds the courtesy light stays on after he closes the door, I can see his blowfish mouth has already opened to give directions and likely more to the taxi driver.

Seventh Avenue at 3:25 a.m. on a Sunday in August is hot and damp, wafting the smell of trash. Most of the cars are yellow taxis. The storefronts are shut, except for a few bars, chalkboard signs not yet dragged back inside, and the unnatural glow from twenty-four-hour corner delis shining through the temporary-looking but perma-nent plastic walls set up to protect the fruits, vegetables, and flowers. I wonder how those flowers sell. I decide to walk a few blocks before hailing a cab myself.

I wake up at 10:35 a.m. and leave my apartment to get iced coffee. I spend the day watching television.

On Monday morning, I take the F train to work. I stop at the newsstand underneath Second Ave. and Houston to look at *The Magazine*—"Autistic Twins" is the cover, but over the logo, on what's called the roofline, it says "Iraq: The Case for War?"

Exciting times, I think.

TOWARD A MORE
CYNICAL PROTAGONIST

We're about fifteen thousand words into the story, a good seventy thousand more to go. Adjust your schedule accordingly. If it took you thirty minutes to get this far, that means the running time for the remainder is, oh, four more hours.

Let me offer some preemptive criticism.

I see that I'm setting myself up as the coming-of-age protagonist, a naive and excited twentysomething hero named Michael M. Hastings, unleashed on the world, loose in the big city. Wet behind the earlobes, bright-eyed and puppy-tailed, the universe my own clambake.

But how *could I ever have been so naive?* How can anyone be naive these days? What's my excuse?

How could I have expected anything else besides what happened? The eventual disillusionment, the disappointment, the subtle corruption. Shouldn't I have seen it coming? If I'm a cliché, shouldn't I have been aware of why I'm a cliché—because my life story, my pattern, has been told and retold over and over again, the future for me was already written? Is it excusable to feel what I eventually feel—betrayed, disappointed, wronged, and upset by how *The Magazine* treated A.E. Peoria?

Aren't we in a new age? The end of naïveté?

I grew up reading media satires, reading about the corporate culture, massive layoffs, and polluted rivers, reading about censored stories and the national security state, our imperial sins, FBI investigations into masturbation in the executive office, reading Noam Chomsky and Howard Zinn and Tom Wolfe and Pat Buchanan and Hunter S. Thompson—what else could I have expected from *The Magazine* besides what I saw? I grew up reading Holocaust literature at the beach, Gulag literature on winter holidays, Vietnam memoirs on spring break. Histories of Gentiles and Jews and Germans playing poker and swapping wives at Los Alamos. The rap music I listened to was about dealing crack and dropping Ecstasy and cunnilingus. The television programs and films a constant stream of irony and mocking. How could all of that not have prepared me for the human condition, in the most extreme possible circumstances?

Isn't it somewhat preposterous, looking at the character that I'm presenting to you, for me to feel let down by the world? Isn't that narrative arc just a little tired?

Maybe that's the genius of it, then: because it is tired, it's easily recognizable. You can relate to me. And even with the knowledge of how the world works, we don't really know it until we see how the world works ourselves. Secondhand information doesn't do it.

Until your own hopes and dreams are shattered, or just slightly cracked, shouldn't you be allowed a bit of innocence?

I don't know. Maybe that's the growing-up part. Maybe I was just going through the motions, maybe I knew the fall was coming all along.

Anyway . . .

I'm going to give my past self a more cynical edge, whether or not I actually had it at the time.

I've taken a week off from the magazine to finish writing this. It's still snowing.

8.

Wednesday Evening,
October 23, 2002

The signs are up all over the lobby, in the elevator, in the cafeteria on the twenty-first floor, right outside the elevator doors on the sixteenth. The signs are big blown-up pictures of different scenes from World War II, and every picture—Stalin shaking FDR's hand, the flag show at Iwo Jima, seven slightly out-of-focus dead bodies floating up to the shore on Omaha Beach—has the big name under it: SANDERS BERMAN.

"You going to this thing?" Gary asks me, leaning up against my cubicle.

"The Berman thing?"

"Yeah."

"I was thinking about it."

"I'm going up now, you want to come?"

"Sure."

I prepared for Sanders Berman's book party accordingly. I read his book, *The Greatest War on Earth*. If I am in the mood to be cruel, I'd say his book does really well at nourishing our national myths. It's a real comfort, reading his book. It gives you a real warm feeling about that whole time between 1939 and 1945. A real black-and-white-photo wholesomeness to it, a breast-fed narrative of good versus evil. A time, thankfully, when there wasn't much ambiguity. Or at least that's what he's selling and that's what people like to read about, and Sanders does a good job at throwing around words like *tragedy* and *Holocaust* and *Stalingrad*, and does a real good job at making us all feel special about it.

You can say I'm something of a contrarian here, but I guess my reading list on the Second World War is a bit different—more *Thin Red Line*, memoirs from Auschwitz and Hiroshima, *The Battle for Moscow* and *Life and Fate*—stuff that when you read it, you don't come away feeling particularly enamored with the greatness of human beings and the exceptional nature of the American character. "Fuck my shit," is how war correspondent Ernie Pyle put it at the time. "That's what war adds up to."

So fuck my shit, *The Greatest War on Earth* reaches number one on the bestseller list, so Berman must be doing something right, and there's nothing wrong with admiring success. Can't argue with success, can't argue with this book party on the twenty-second floor to celebrate the success that he's having.

"I'm just going to use the restroom," I tell Gary, using the word *restroom* because I'm never really comfortable, at work or at home, saying things like "I have to take a piss"—or "a leak" or "drain the lizard" or "shake hands with the wife's best friend."

I push open the door to the restroom and hear what sounds like a retching, a *hughghghg*. The noise stops right when the door is in midswing. I can always tell when someone is standing still in his bathroom stall. It's as if by actively trying not to make a sound, he's making a silent dog-whistle-like noise that triggers a well-honed lavatory sixth sense—probably a survival instinct from when I was a little kid and public bathrooms were always a potential danger zone, booby-trapped with lurking perverts.

Walking up to the urinal, I glance down at an angle and see the same pair of shoes, pointed to the toilet, not away from it, that I saw a few months back on the night with A.E. Peoria.

I start urinating (or, if you like, I use the urinal, make water, piss, etc.), and it lasts about thirteen seconds. I probably have more left, but I'm a tad nervous with Sanders Berman standing behind the blue panel five feet to my left.

I flush. The man behind the stall flushes. I zip up; I don't hear a corresponding zip-up. I turn to take the three steps to the six sinks and six mirrors; the door to the stall opens, and there's Sanders Berman, taking his own two steps to the sink.

"Mr. Berman," I say, tapping the pink soap container screwed into the white tile just below the mirror. "On the way to your book party now."

"I'm running late," says Sanders Berman, and he's not so much washing his hands as looking in the mirror and wetting a brown paper towel and wiping his face, primarily around the mouth.

I think it might be best to wait it out, to let the water keep running, to take even more time so he finishes his cleanup first and leaves. Or should I finish washing my hands right now and leave first?

Leave first, I think, but in the seven awkward seconds it takes me to make that decision, Berman has turned off his sink, and we're both tossing crumpled brown paper towels into the steel wastebasket built into the wall next to the door.

Gary doesn't act surprised when he sees me coming out of the bathroom with Sanders Berman, and he cracks a joke.

"We're going up with the right company," Gary says, and all three of us walk through the glass doors on sixteen. I push the up button on the elevator, and we're in that waiting time when, really, it's proper etiquette for Sanders Berman to start asking Gary, a senior editor, questions about how life is going for him, etc.

But with the pressure of having a book party, I guess, Sanders Berman doesn't fulfill that etiquette duty, and as we step into the elevator, *bing*, I take up the slack.

"Really enjoyed your book," I tell him. "I'm a big fan of World War Two."

"Oh, thank you," says Berman.

"Hastings is the rising star in international," Gary says, getting in on the act. "He does great work—if you ever need another researcher, you should ask him."

Sanders Berman looks at me, nods, and says, "I'll keep that in mind."

Mercifully, we've arrived on the twenty-second floor, and both Gary and I say, in chorus, "After you," and Sanders Berman goes first, and Gary and I do what's proper and just hang back for an almost imperceptible split second so Berman can walk into the room on the twenty-second floor without us.

It's a good thing we do, because when Sanders Berman enters the dining hall, the crowd gathered inside starts to clap.

Gary and I look at each other—dodged a bullet there.

9.

Book Party, Five Minutes Later

The twenty-second floor is called Top of the Mag. A catered dinner is served to the staff there on Friday nights, the late nights at the magazine. It's classy, with nonindustrial-strength carpeting and rich, glossy brown-paneled walls. The best part is the view. For that brief moment on Friday, I feel like I'm part of the big time, one of those Captain of the Universe types, with a view of Central Park and Columbus Circle, breathtaking and unmolested greenery all the way to Harlem.

It's also where the magazine hosts events like this one.

Framed posters of Sanders Berman books are up on the wall, with pictures that I have seen before in history books but not pictures that I've seen in the context of the promotion of his book—the USS *Arizona* going down in Pearl Harbor, VJ-Day in Times Square, Churchill on some podium.

Gary and I head to the bar, something to do, and I get a club soda and he gets a Coke.

"You owe me one," says Gary.

"Thanks. No, that would be great, doing research for him."

"It'd be a real feather in your cap."

Gary often talks to me about feathers in my cap. Now, it isn't about the good of the magazine that Gary tells me to get as many feathers in my cap as possible—because I don't know anyone who hates the magazine as much as Gary does. He hates it, really detests it. Thinks it's a total piece of shit. "You don't think I don't think about quitting this fucking place every day of my life," he told me last week. "You don't have a mortgage, you don't have kids, you don't have responsibility, just walking around, the change jingling in your pocket"— he likes to tell me that, that I walk around with change jingling. But we do get along, and he wants to help me out in my career as much as he can, by assigning me that Space Tourism story, for example, or by putting a good word in for me with a guy like Sanders Berman.

Gary and I stand next to each other, sipping our nonalcoholic beverages, watching other people socialize.

There are some noticeable absences. Where's Henry the EIC? Nishant Patel? Every other bigwig is here, including Tabby Doling, the daughter of *The Magazine*'s owner, Sandra Doling, who, when she was alive, also owned a big newspaper in Washington and nineteen other media properties around the country, including local television and radio stations.

"That's Berman's source of power," Gary whispers to me, talking about Tabby Doling. "Her mom is the one who discovered him. Way back in the early nineties. I think he was still in school. She put that story of his, the famous one he did . . ."

"The 'Vietnam Syndrome'?"

"Yeah, that's the one. She put that story on the cover."

At that moment, a semicircle of people starts to form, the employees and famous and semi-famous guests (Kissinger, Stephanopoulos, Brokaw, etc.) step away, leaving Sanders Berman, Tabby Doling, and Delray M. Milius in the center. Milius holds up his glass and taps it, chinking and bringing silence to the room.

Delray M. Milius is doughy-faced and five-foot-seven, and I don't mention his height pejoratively, as I'm only five-foot-nine, and I've never put much stock in how tall somebody is in relation to their character. I know big pricks and little pricks, as I'm sure we all do. He's Sanders Berman's right-hand man, his hatchet man, if you will, or if you believe the story—and I believe it because it's true—he's "that glory hole ass gape cocksucker." I don't choose those words lightly, or to offend homosexuals, some of whom are my closest friends, but because those were the words that Matt Healy, a correspondent in the magazine's Washington, D.C., bureau, put in an email, accidentally cc'ing the entire editorial staff. This was back in '99, before my time, and when email mistakes like that were more common. It was also back when Healy was in New York. After that email, he was sent to DC in a kind of exile, while Delray M. Milius leveraged the potential sexual harassment suit to get a big promotion to assistant managing editor, where he's twisted Sanders Berman's bow tie ever since.

As you can probably guess, Milius isn't too popular at the magazine. There's a strong anti-Milius faction, and within this faction, there's always a running bet about how long Milius is going to last—this time. He's left and come back to the magazine five times in twelve years. "Don't let Milius bother you" is the conventional wisdom in how to deal with him. "It's just a matter of time before he wakes up one morning and just can't get out of bed and quits again. Paralyzed. By depression, fear, anxiety, who knows—it's happened before."

Delray M. Milius keeps tapping the glass.

"Thanks, everyone, for coming to Sanders Berman's celebration," Milius says. "I especially would like to thank our esteemed guests. Without going on, it is of course, and has always been, an honor to work with Sanders, and those of you who know him know that this success is the perfectly natural result we would have expected. But without going on, Tabby Doling would like to say a few words."

Tabby Doling is bone-thin, rail-like, brown hair held in a pretty coiffure. She's maybe sixty.

"When my mother first met Sanders, he was a senior at Tulane, and she was there on a speaking engagement. What, Sanders, you were still in seminary studies?" she says.

"God and war, my two favorite subjects," Sanders says.

Everyone in the room gives a nice and expected laugh.

"Sanders is a prize, and I'm very pleased so many of us are here to recognize this, especially my guests—"

Notice the word *my*. Tabby Doling's thing is that she's friends with a bunch of famous and important people, media types, heads of state, Academy Award winners from the '70s. Though she's partial owner of *The Magazine*'s parent company, on the masthead she's listed as "Special Diplomatic Correspondent," which is kind of a joke, because that would lead readers to assume there are people above her in the hierarchy, which there are not—she even has a floor to herself, the notorious twenty-third floor.

Tabby is one of those people who, if you bring up her name in conversation around New York, you'll most likely get three or four really great anecdotes about. Everyone who's met her has a moment to recount, told with the bemused acceptance that if you're that rich and that eccentric, it's par for the course. Gary's Tabby Doling story, for instance, is that he was standing in the hallway on the sixteenth floor when he heard a knocking on the glass; someone had forgotten their ID. When Gary went to answer it, he saw Tabby through the glass and decided to make one of his customary jokes. "How do I know you're not a terrorist?" he said, as if he wasn't going to let her in. And she responded, "I'm Tabby Doling," with a real flourish and emphasis on both her first and last names. Gary thinks that's why he got passed over for the domestic sci/tech gig and has been stuck in international. That's a pretty low-level story, too, not one of her best.

I don't know her at all and haven't spent time with her, which isn't surprising, as she has a $225,000-sticker-price Bentley and a driver I always see idling outside the entrance on Broadway for her—though she did say hello to me in the hallway once, so in my book that's a plus. She keeps talking about what a wonderful man Sanders Berman is, and everyone agrees and claps and laughs when appropriate.

I'm looking over the room, and I notice that most of the people look more or less like they're up here for a reason—because they're supposed to be—or are here because they're the kind of name that goes in a New York gossip column, which is great for Sanders Berman's book, because the gossip items, whatever they will say, will also mention *The Greatest War on Earth*. I'm not telling you anything groundbreaking or new, but it's good to explain a few things every once in a while.

There is one guest, a man, I'd say sixtyish, who would stand out less if he weren't planted back in the corner against the glossy brown paneling. I've never seen him before, which isn't that unusual, but he's wearing a baseball cap—the baseball cap says "POW/MIA," and so I think, If he's wearing a baseball cap, he probably works in the mailroom.

Sanders Berman starts to speak, a perfunctory address, and the book party—and the "party" part of book party is a bit of an overstatement, as there's not really much partying; a more accurate phrase would be something like "mandatory book gathering"—starts again.

The guy with POW/MIA is still planted there, and I end up next to him.

"How long have you been with *The Magazine*?" I ask.

"Not with the magazine, son," he says with a southern drawl. "That's my boy up there."

"You're Mr. Berman's father," I say, for lack of anything better.

"That's right."

Times like this are when it really pays off for having done so much research and reading about my colleagues. I did get around to reading the "Vietnam Syndrome" story, and in it there's a reference, in, like, the sixteenth paragraph, to Sanders Berman's father, a "Vietnam veteran." It stood out because Sanders Berman is never one to write about his personal life; I think that's the only reference to his personal life I've seen.

"That's great that you could make it up to New York," I say.

"He didn't ask me here. I don't think that boy wants me here. I'm here because I'm trying to save him," he says.

"Right, of course," I say.

"Did you know that Sanders, and that other one, Nishant Patel, are members of the Council on Foreign Relations?"

"That's right, I did know that."

"Did you know that Tabby Doling's mother, Sandra Doling, used to meet every year in Germany, a little something called the Bilderberg Group. Freemasonry, you know?"

"Yeah, I've heard of the Bilderberg Group."

"What does that tell you?"

What it tells me is that rich people like to hang out with rich people, and that guys who fancy themselves foreign policy experts like to hang out and talk about foreign policy, but I know he's looking for a more History Channel "Conspiracy Revealed" insight. The problem with talking conspiracies is like the problem with talking religion: you're either preaching to the choir or arguing with the inconvincible.

"You were in Vietnam," I say.

"I was. Phoenix Project. Air America. Blackest of black ops. Over the border, Cambodia, Laos. I drink because of it. I'm angry because of it. I killed people, and I don't say they were innocent—no one is innocent in this fallen paradise. I always told Sanders that killing and war are man's most horrible things, the most deadliest things. I will admit that it takes a lot of courage to kill like I have killed, and I made that clear to Sanders, but now here he is, hobnobbing with the Illuminatos."

"Illuminati?"

"Illuminatos, more than one. Hispanics influence nowadays. You know, Davos?"

"I see what you mean. So, you're from the South?"

"Rolling hills, bootlegging country, hollows. I haven't set my eyes on the boy in years, he doesn't visit much, but I tried to teach him as best I could. We're right near Chickamauga, and every weekend I would take Sanders out and let him loose, to teach him what it means to be afraid for your life, dress him in camo from the Army/Navy, face paint, and we'd play the special ops kind of hide-and-seek. He teethed on the KA-BAR. I think I failed, though. Look at him now."

I'm no Jungian, but the thought does occur to me that Sanders's loving embrace of Apple Pie and all that starts to make more sense after meeting his father and getting a glimpse of the kind of twisted upbringing in the American dream he was apparently subjected to. Rebelling in reverse—growing up under the PTSD fringe, when he was bombarded with all sorts of ideas about the bullshittingness of our national myths, it makes sense that he'd want to immerse himself in national myths, and in fact, start to believe in the exact opposite of what his father told him.

I'm sort of looking for a way out of this conversation when I see A.E. Peoria walk in, head straight to the bar, and say loudly, "No shots? Wine only?" And as Papa Berman keeps a running commentary on the insidious nature of his son's current endeavors—*The Greatest War on Earth* is published by Simon & Schuster, SS, the name of the elite Nazi unit, and Simon & Schuster is owned by CBS, and "CBS" backward is "SBC," and "SBC," in Greek letters, is the exact same sequence of letters engraved on the inside brass door knocker at the secret society, you guessed it, Skull and Bones, on the Yale campus in New Haven, the location of an underreported 1913 meeting where J.P. Morgan and some Jewish guy devised the illegal income tax—A.E. Peoria breaches etiquette by bumping up next to Tom Brokaw and Henry Kissinger, who is short, no comment, and they are talking to Sanders Berman and Tabby Doling, and even from thirteen feet away I can hear what he's saying—"Chad . . . *Penthouse* letters . . . where do you think I should go next?"

For five minutes Peoria stands there, before abruptly twirling around and leaving from where he came, and I hear Sanders Berman say, semi-uncomfortably, "That's a magazine foreign correspondent for you," and they all laugh at Peoria's expense.

By this time, I'm swept back toward Gary, and I ask him, "Did you see Peoria?"

"That was ugly," Gary says.

"Yeah, I think he was pretty drunk," I say.

"Hastings, you have ambitions to be a foreign correspondent, right? Just remember, really, do you want to end up like Peoria? I mean, he's a cool guy and all, don't get me wrong—but he doesn't have a home or a family or anything, and there'll come a time when you'll have to ask yourself, do you want to end up like that?"

10.

After the Party

Magazine journalist A.E. Peoria is in a career crisis. The crisis of what to do next. *Thirty-four, thirty-four, thirty-four.*

A.E. Peoria likes to say that he doesn't trust anyone who loves high school, and he especially doesn't trust anyone who loves college. He likes to say that the twenties are a time in life when things are uncertain and still painfully anxious, the twenties are rough, and he is suspicious of anyone who enjoys their twenties too much. He likes to repeat that it's the thirties, the fourth decade in life, when you really get that perspective and finally get that comfort of who you are. The thirties are when you begin to understand limitations in life, a time when the things that stressed you out so much in your twenties don't seem as important anymore. This is what he likes to say when he is invited to speak to young people at colleges and high schools: that by the time you reach thirty-two-ish, the childish dreams of childhood, the teenage illusions, and the stresses of the overreach of your twenties fall into their appropriate place in the memory bank.

Then why, he wonders, am I in a career crisis yet again?

He thinks it's the inverse proportional response to his CDD. It is the silent CDD. He is always compulsively disclosing and dissecting in his mind *to himself*. He has no control over it. He doesn't quite have the science to back it up, but it is this theory of his.

He cannot stop thinking about his career. What is *career*? There is no time to search for a meaning, because meaning cannot be found until the question of career is put to rest. Why is career always in crisis? It is a looping crisis. It is the crisis of reaching goals. The crisis of setting goals then reaching goals then setting more goals and reaching more goals. The crisis of five-year plans and ten-year plans and other evil baby boomer inventions. He cannot escape this vicious looping circle of career thinking. It is never far away from his mind. It's always there, career, he's always thinking about it, analyzing, plotting, planning, worrying, fretting.

He likes to think of himself as Icarus, probably because that's the only Greek myth he can remember accurately without the aid of a search engine. The only Greek myth that, after reading Sophocles and Euripides and all the other one-named Greek pederasts in school, he can remember and draw a detailed meaning from that he can relate to life today.

Icarus flies too close to the sun after his father gives him wax wings, and then the wings melt and Icarus falls into the ocean, maybe the Mediterranean, so it's not that bad, beats the North Atlantic, but he falls into the ocean and he drowns. A.E. Peoria likes to think of that myth and say to himself, or others if he's on drugs: Fuck you, father. Fuck you, Icarus. I am Kid Icarus, like in that Nintendo game from 1987, leaping from free-floating graphic structure to free-floating graphic structure. I fly too close to the sun and crash into the goddamn ocean! But I know how to swim, I know how to swim, I know how to swim to shore, and when I'm on the beach, I look at the sun again. The sun as it is drying the saltwater from my skin. I yell out to the sky, "Fuck you, Sun! I'll be back! With a new set of wings, just you wait, you shining, spotty-flaring, cancer-causing fuck."

Maybe it is New York.

A.E. Peoria likes to think maybe it isn't him, maybe it's this place, this city. New York, Peoria knows from reading Evelyn Waugh, is a city where "there is neurosis in the air which its inhabitants mistake for energy."

Couldn't say it better myself, A.E. Peoria thinks, could not say it better myself.

The city of New York is always causing this career crisis. An insidious conspiracy to remind him on every block about the state of his career.

What other reason for glass skyscrapers, glass windows everywhere, all this glass that was erected and positioned so that you cannot escape your own reflection—he is always getting himself bounced back at him in glass, as if whoever designed these glass buildings likes to keep putting him in his place. Look at what you're wearing.

The word *career*, A.E. Peoria knows, because he looks it up, comes from the Latin *carrus*, or "wagon," via the French *carrière*, or "road." A person's progress and general course of action through life or through a phase of life, as in some profession or undertaking. Success in a profession, occupation, etc. A course, especially a swift one. Speed, especially full speed. A verb meaning "to run" or "to move rapidly along." Careering, rush. "My hasting days fly on with full career"— John Milton. A third definition, *career*, a racecourse, the ground run over. Fourth, falconry, the flight of the hawk. "Careering gaily over the curling waves"—Washington Irving. Archaic: to charge ahead at full speed.

Rushing ahead at full speed on his life's vocation, in control, out of control, a little of both.

Up until when—recently?—he had viewed the path of career unimaginatively, like some kind of long hallway in a poorly designed international airport, where the architects seemed to have gotten

great pleasure making sure that every connecting flight was mathe-
matically at the farthest point away from any other point in the terminal. A long hallway, low music, beeping golf carts with oxygen
tanks. As if the architects had taken to heart Zeno's paradox of never
being able to cross a room and so designed an infinitely divisible
hallway between points A and B at each transit underpass.

In his imaginary career-fantasy metaphor, there are those who are
curiously choosing to walk the hallway, those who are standing to the
right on the people mover, and those who are walking on the left of
the conveyor belt, rushing along. That third lane was the lane he
thought—from the age of twenty-eight to thirty-four—he was finally
on. At some point he had jumped over the hand railing where he'd
been walking, paused for a brief moment, and then he'd stepped on
the fastest track, a track that he had just been watching other people
use, as if it had been protected by a thick plastic barrier. And he was
cruising along on this fast track, thinking, I did it, I am finally on the
fast track, I'm going to catch my flight—but until when—recently?—
that feeling changed.

A.E. Peoria had always thought of himself as lucky, and this luck,
he felt, made him somewhat superior to other people his age. It was
not the luck of good things happening to him, but the luck that he
could always say, "I know what I want to do with my life. I'm lucky."

A.E. Peoria never questioned that he wanted to be a magazine journalist. Had always known it. Even when it was rough during his twenties, when all of his wandering and drifting college classmates were
anguishing in this kind of existential variety of what to do. I just don't
know what I want to do, his friends would tell him, and that was
something he could sympathize with sort of, but not completely.
Because if the conversation continued, he would always say, "I'm lucky,
I've always known what I wanted to do," and they would respond,
"Yes, you are lucky. I wish I always knew what I wanted to do."

Peoria, though, was getting worried that maybe he wasn't lucky anymore. Maybe he'd made a grave mistake by becoming a magazine journalist. Maybe it wasn't what he'd always wanted to do.

So, in his office—though the career crisis wasn't limited to his time in the office; how he wished it was limited to his office and not his bedroom, his bed, his showers, his jogging, his dinners with his girlfriend, his phone conversations, his commute, how he wished it was just limited to his office!—he had started for the first time to think about other careers.

He looked on the CIA website. He looked at Harvard Law School. He looked at SUNY Upstate Medical University. He looked at NASA. He looked at MCATs and LSATs and GREs and the Foreign Service Exam. Film school. He looked at job openings with small news-papers in places like Malone, New York, and Yaak, Montana. He looked at business school—Stern, Wharton, Stanford. He looked at financial aid documents. He looked at everything, and he fretted about everything. He looked at doctoral programs and master's programs and technical institutes in TV/VCR repair and forensic criminology. Dental school. He looked at intensive language pro-grams for Urdu and Arabic and Russian and Spanish. He looked at teaching English in Katmandu and microfinance initiatives in Ghana. Those professions seemed so much simpler—doctor, lawyer, astro-naut, accountant, linguist—professions where the path to success was clear. Why had he stupidly chosen to be a magazine journalist—now, that was a career with pressure! That was a career with stress, with uncertainty. How much simpler life would be if he were a brain sur-geon or a physicist or designed helicopters for a defense contractor—a simple, stable career path with a well-defined destination, so much easier than this constant and vicious battle he was in with himself over this New York magazine media world he lived in. Those were careers with real skills, real sellable skills. What skills did he have?

Diagnose what? Consult on what? Fix what? No, he could gather information half decently and present that information half decently, but it was always other people's information, others' doings, always the observer—to make a career out of observing other careers, what did that say of him?

His girlfriend, to whom he had given six orgasms, had given him some of her Xanax, and that helped some.

Thirty-four, and never had a book party!

So, A.E. Peoria, door to his office closed, window shades clinched, drunk as fuck, pale light from the computer screen zebra-ing his face, is considering a change in careers, drastically, when he sees that another magazine has been delivered to his desk, the middle-highbrow magazine that Henry the EIC once clipped a cartoon from. He flips open to a story called "A Professor in Exile," and it's by a guy he's never heard of before but who seems very serious, and this guy's byline is Brennan Toddly, it's fifteen thousand words, very detail-oriented and persuasively reported from the halls of northeastern joint conferences and the cloistered monklike apartments off Ivy League campuses, leather-bound bookshelves, dust, reported with a forcefully humorless I-narrator, laying out in genius fashion the case for war against Saddam Hussein and Iraq, and predicting that the war will happen, needs to happen, within six months.

A.E. Peoria forgets about his career crisis and starts to make his own phone calls, all his anxiety relieved because he gets a urinary tract–like tingling that a big career-making story is on the way, something he can really sink his teeth into. He starts to think about the ways he can make sure that when this future war does start, he's in place to cover it. He sees the fast track again and its name is Brennan Toddly.

Before he gets too far, he passes out and falls asleep, curled underneath his desk, the book party six floors above him temporarily forgotten.

11.

Friday, October 25, 2002

D*ing.*
I get an email, and it shoots me up in my swivel.
Nishant Patel. No subject.

come by my office np

Do I reply? Or do I just go?
I hit Reply.
My fingers freeze over the keys.

Dear Nishant . . .

What else? How formal do I make it? Or should it be as informal as Nishant Patel's? Am I at a stage where I can write "ok" and put my own initials: "ok/mmh"? Or do I need to sign off with at least my first name?

Five minutes pass.

How deferential do I need to be? I freeze. Does Nishant Patel understand the impact of an email from a boss? To see his name in my inbox, to see it, and to think, How am I going to answer this?

Does he realize how much time it takes to compose a response? I want to choose the words perfectly. I am still at a stage where I think people are going to actually read my email somewhat closely, and there's all sorts of etiquette issues that will probably just disappear in the technological informality of communication that seems to be heading our way. No punctuation, no salutations, no goodbyes, just initials and shorthand and all caps or no caps.

I come up with:

Dear Nishant, I will come by now, if that's okay.

Sincerely,
Michael M. Hastings

I get up from my cubicle. I walk toward his office. The door is closed.

I stand next to Dorothy's cubicle for permission from her to go in.

Dorothy and Patricia are in dueling phone conversations. They aren't talking to each other. They seem to be in endless negotiations with other people's assistants. "Dr. Patel will call Mr. Rose back," says Patricia. "Yes, Dr. Patel called Mr. Rose and now Mr. Rose is calling Dr. Patel back."

The unknown figure on the end of Dorothy's line is acting pushy, and Dorothy is saying, "We very much understand how busy the Ambassador is, and I'm sure you can understand how busy Nishant is, and we appreciate Mr. Holbrooke's call and we're sure to find a time later this afternoon or tomorrow?"

Dorothy hangs up.

"Patricia, mark down that Nishant has a call to Holbrooke tomorrow," but Patricia doesn't hear Dorothy, over the cubicle divider and with that deaf ear. She just knows that Dorothy has commanded her to do something, so she says, "Yes, can you please hold, please hold, yes, is this Mr. Rose's office, this is Dr. Patel's office, please hold for a moment," and she covers up the mouthpiece with her hand and calls over to Dorothy, "What, Dorothy? What, Dorothy?" and Dorothy snaps, "Tomorrow, one-thirty, a call with Holbrooke's office," and Dorothy looks up at me.

"Yes, Mike?"

Dorothy, though aging, was once a real knockout, single but with former lovers who were diplomats and war correspondents, and weekend getaways with captains of industry and nights in the late sixties and early seventies in the West Village. She lives for the magazine now, and she is the gatekeeper, both physical and electronic, to Nishant Patel, the magazine's number-one or -two most valuable commodity, depending on who you ask. I'm lucky because Dorothy likes me, because if Dorothy doesn't like you, you have to wait in line.

"Hi, Dorothy, Nishant—I mean, Dr. or Mr. Patel asked me to come by."

Dorothy smiles, and nods.

"One second."

Dorothy stands up and says to Patricia, teaching her, "Patricia, we know the rule. If you have 'former' in your title, then we return the phone call in twenty-four hours. If you are current, then we return the phone call in six hours or less."

"What about Mr. Rose?" says Patricia.

"For TV, one hour or less," says Dorothy. "Go ahead and knock, Mike."

I knock on the closed door, and I hear the slightly accented British lilt of Dr. Nishant Patel, and he says, "Come in," and as I walk in, he's on the phone. He points to a seat in front of his desk.

I sit down.

Nishant Patel is in a corner office. There are hundreds of books, mostly his books, and they are all in different languages. German language, French language, Portuguese language. Spanish. Dutch. Italian. Indonesian. The books line the shelves and are neatly stacked on every free flat surface, tables, coffee tables. There are two couches and three chairs and a ledge on the window to sit, if he's having a meeting with everyone in his office.

Nishant Patel's legs are crossed, and he leans back in his Executive 3000 black swivel chair, perfectly tailored tan pants riding up to mid-ankle to reveal lightly patterned argyle socks, probably from Paul Smith, which are a perfect contrast to his brown Gucci loafers, going up to his thin waist and off–powder blue Ermenegildo Zegna dress shirt, knotted green silk cuff links from Bergdorf Goodman, silk Brooks Brothers–looking tie, though probably not Brooks Brothers, probably something a few steps above that, like Thomas Pink, hair cut and effortlessly styled every two weeks by the Grooming Lounge.

He's turned at about forty-five degrees to my right, his left, tilted a precise sixty-seven degrees backward, talking on the phone.

". . . Yes, it was an interesting meeting. . . . The undersecretary invited us there—Kaplan, Friedman, Haas, Brennan Toddly, a number of others from the Council on Foreign Relations. Oh, he wanted to get our opinions, our ideas. No, it was all very off-the-record. . . . We're not allowed to say anything or mention it in our columns. . . . No, Berman wasn't invited. . . . To convince us, and it was quite, quite convincing. I have to go. I'll be taping the show tonight, but I should be home after dinner."

Patel gently hangs up the phone and turns toward me.

"Hastings, thank you for coming. I need you to do research for my column this week. Have you seen this story?"

He tosses a copy of the middle-highbrow magazine on his desk, folded up to a story by a man named Brennan Toddly.

"Have you read this?"

I haven't read it, but nod yes, because I have learned that this magazine is the only one that the editors at *The Magazine* read on a regular basis—certainly, they never actually read our magazine, unless it is to see who got in the magazine that week and who didn't.

"He quotes an Iraqi man in there, and he cites Kenneth Pollack's book *The Threatening Storm*. Call Pollack and the Iraqi man, and have them say basically what they say in that story."

"Sure, Nishant, no problem."

"My column this week, to give you an idea, is going to go further than I had in my last cover story. I left my argument open—the case for war? Now I am going to answer the question. I will be making the argument primarily for national security reasons, but also, humanitarian reasons. We cannot forget about the Iraqi people, et cetera. You follow this stuff, don't you?"

"Of course, of course," I say.

"I'll be writing tomorrow afternoon, get it to me before then."

"Okay, Nishant, no problem."

And he doesn't say "Dismissed," but he does re-angle his chair, forty-five degrees back to the left, and hits the intercom button and tells Dorothy to get him the host of the TV show he's going to be a guest on tonight.

Taking the copy of Brennan Toddly's article with me, I go back to my desk, nervous and excited—getting to do research for Nishant Patel.

This is the big time.

12.

Two Hours Later

Before I look at the Brennan Toddly story, I want to find out who Brennan Toddly is. There is a Wikipedia entry for him, a single paragraph:

An author of three books, two nonfiction, one fiction.

1989: *A Peaceful Village*—an account of a Peace Corps building effort in Uganda. (Out of print.)

1996: *The Typewriter Artist*—a novel. The main character is a writer who lives in New York. He is a mild depressive and everyone ignores his work. (Out of print.)

1999: *Awash in Red*—a personal journey of self-discovery, as the author struggles with whether or not to remain a socialist.

I find out that Brennan Toddly, according to his bio, spent two years at *The Magazine* in the mid-nineties, has been the recipient of a number of government grants, and seems to have landed at his new magazine just this year. An impact hire, to be sure.

I power-read the story. It is impressively full of nuance. A representative paragraph:

> After the panel discussion, I made my way backstage, where I encountered Kanan Makiya. I introduced myself to Makiya. He invited me to his home for tea. We walked across the campus yard, where a new class of coeds had just arrived, playing Frisbee and hacky sack. Easy, carefree thoughts. The opposite of what Makiya was thinking. "This is what Iraq was like when I was a child, before I had to leave," he told me. "You Americans are finally paying attention. You must finally take action." Three hours later, I had left his office, a bladder full of sweet chai, convinced. But the arguments with myself would continue.

I call the university where Makiya is living out his exile and request an interview for a Nishant Patel column.

For Kenneth Pollack, I call his publisher and ask for a copy of his book *The Threatening Storm* to be sent over. It is getting so much attention, thanks to the Brennan Toddly story, that the publisher tells me they are doing a rush second printing of it. But he says they'll messenger me a copy and get Pollack to phone me later this afternoon.

Now I wait.

A blur of a human being passes by my cubicle, high-pitched voice trailing.

"Sanders, Sanders, Sanders."

I jump up in my seat to see the human comet. I recognize the man calling Sanders. It is Matt Healy, Chief Investigative Correspondent, based in DC.

Healy broke *The Magazine*'s (and the country's) biggest story in the nineties, the Pentagon Paper of Blow Jobs, that whole business with President Clinton and Monica Lewinsky. Without Healy, the nation might never have known the details of things like cigar vaginal penetration. Then where would we be? Well, the Internet would have solved that problem within a few years anyway.

Yes, there is no doubt in the mind of anyone at the magazine that Healy is the closest thing the magazine has to its own Woodward and Bernstein, rolled into one. A regular Neil Sheehan—revealing the past decade's version of Watergate, but easier for most to imagine, as it just involved a slightly chubby chick, infidelity, and a hard-on. The evolution of American journalism: three decades coming full circle, a source with the name Deep Throat leaking information about the chief executive's illegal behavior to investigating the actual mechanics of deep-throating a chief executive. There's no need to even point out that Healy himself isn't exactly a model citizen of marital behavior—the "ass gape cocksucker" email about Milius, for instance, a couple of divorces, smoking crack, rumored affairs, the whole deal—but of course, Healy never had the chance to lie about it under oath, in a grand jury, so ethically speaking, the magazine is in the clear from charges of hypocrisy.

Healy is pigeonholing Sanders Berman, right outside the men's room. A real bulldog type. Three spiral notebooks on his person. Two flopping out of his back pockets, one in his hand.

"We should make it a cover, a cover," he yells. "Three sources—CIA, DOD, the VP's shop—are all saying and confirming it. They are saying the links are there, they are saying there are links. Al Qaeda in Baghdad!"

Healy rushes off down the hall, his points made.

Sanders Berman comes wandering away from the men's room, as if in a daze, like he's just been hit by a dust storm.

I take the chance.

"Hi, Sanders, how's everything?"

He stops.

"Oh, hi—Walters, is it? Everything is good."

"Hastings, yeah, that's great, that's great. Yeah, I'm just research-ing Nishant's column for the week."

"What's he writing on?"

"The case for war, really coming down for it."

"He is? Darnit, that's what I was going to write this week."

I start nodding.

"I just had dinner with Ken Pollack last night. I was going to quote him, too."

Sanders Berman touches his bow tie. He puts his elbows up on my cubicle, a gesture of familiarity. He sees that I have the Brennan Tod-dly article on my desk.

"Don't tell me he's going to use that Iraqi gentleman's argu-ment . . ."

"Yep, I have a call in to his office."

He puts his knuckle under his chin, in thought.

Am I going to appear too precocious? Am I about to overstep my bounds? I mean, who am I to suggest any ideas? I'm a twenty-two-year-old former intern, a researcher and an occasional fact-checker.

"Oh, I'm sure you'll come up with something to say," I say. "Like, no one has made any American historical arguments for the war yet."

He looks at me, eyebrows up, as if he's considering humoring my suggestion.

"Hmm. And Hastings, if you had a column, that's what you'd say?"

"Uh, well, I mean, President James Polk has some good thoughts on these kinds of issues."

Sanders Berman smiles and starts to walk away. I think he's regret-ting even talking to me. He has his head down and I hope he's not regretting it, but that is the sinking suspicion I get. If I were a female intern, at least his ego could have received some flattery, but "There's never a reason to talk to a young male intern" is probably what he's thinking. I should have kept silent, mouth shut.

No time to worry or beat myself up over it.

The phone rings.

It's Kanan Makiya.

"Hi, uh, thanks for calling. Yeah, so, like you said in Brennan Toddly's piece—"

"Mr. Toddly took me out of context."

"No doubt, um, really, hunh."

"Have you read my book?"

"Um, no, it's on my list."

"Hmmm."

We go back and forth a few more times, until, twenty minutes later, he says more or less what he said in the Brennan Toddly story. I thank him and hang up.

My phone rings again.

Kenneth Pollack is on the line.

"Have you read my book?" he asks before we begin.

"Um, no, sorry. It's on my list, though."

"Hmmm."

"But I did see what Brennan Toddly wrote about it, and it sounds like a really great book."

"Yes, thanks, but that was taken out of context."

"Right, sure, no doubt."

"I mean, how do you summarize a five-hundred-and-three-page book in a single page?"

"Very carefully?"

"You lose the caveats."

Pollack starts in on his theory and doesn't let up for a good

twenty-three minutes. Nuclear programs. Weapons of mass destruction. Biological, chemical. UN reports, broken resolutions, aluminum
tubes, uranium enrichment, Israel's reactor strike in 1983. Secret
mobile weapons labs. I'm feeling good about it, because it's the stuff
that Nishant Patel wanted him to say, and all I have to do is keep
typing what he's saying.

I spend the next three hours correcting typos and condensing my
conversations with Kanan and Ken into a single page, taking the best
quotes and putting them up top.

I grab a quick dinner and come back to my desk after eating. Ago-
nizing over each sentence. This is the first time I've been asked to do
research, and I don't want to fuck it up.

While I'm proofreading and figuring out the best way to write it
up in an email to Nishant, another email appears.

From: Sanders Berman
Subject: James Polk

Mike, per our conversation, could you send me the Polk
citations you were talking about?

Regards,
SB

This really, really is the big time now.

I'M VERY SORRY

I think it's about time for me to apologize to all of my colleagues.

I'm sorry.

There, that's out of the way.

I don't want to hurt anyone's feelings. I'm a nice guy, at heart, and I have to say it weighs on me whether or not to write about everything that happened at *The Magazine*.

Thomas Jefferson said something once: "Don't mistake the facts for truth."

Actually, I said that, not Jefferson, but attributing my thoughts to him gave it more authority for a second.

It's true that without *The Magazine*, I'd never have gotten a platform. *The Magazine* gave me my start. Biting the hand that feeds and the like.

In my defense, I'd like to point out that we at *The Magazine* are always doing unseemly things, always taking other people's experiences and actions and desires and totally mangling them for our purposes. An intellectual journalist once wrote a book about it—I think she was working for the same magazine as Brennan Toddly. She said that what we do is morally indefensible. Yeah, probably, but who does anything that's really morally defensible these days? Politicians? Lawyers? Janitors maybe? Should we all be janitors? Construction workers? Cops? EMTs? Teachers?

Okay, maybe they are doing morally defensible things. Regardless, other people's experiences sell ads, make good copy, the usual. We're always sticking the long knife into someone's back, and with the right editing, we always manage to give that knife a little twist—we're professionals, after all.

Maybe I'm giving myself too much credit. Maybe my colleagues will read the excerpts (very little chance they'll buy the hardcover) and think, yes, that Hastings kid, he got it exactly right. Does anyone ever read something that's been written about them and think, "Yep, that motherfucker nailed me—all my faults and hopes and insecurities and dreams and all"?

Maybe they'll think, "What an asshole. Look at this, selling out his employer to make a quick buck." (Trust me: I make more working for *The Magazine* than writing a memoir about working for a newsmagazine. We're not Condé Nast, after all.)

Maybe some co-workers will read the book and think it's okay. And others will think it's shit. That's what I guess is called "a mixed critical reaction." My guess is that I won't have much future at the magazine once word gets out that I'm trying to publish this—which makes me a little sad. They have feelings, and I have feelings too.

So really, I'm sorry. Mr. Peoria, Mr. Berman, Mr. Patel, Jerry, Sam, Gary, Anna—it's not personal, or at least it's only as personal as anything else.

It's snowing still, December 2005. I've switched to drinking bottles of San Pellegrino mineral water because I like the feel of the weight of the bottle in my hand. Almost like I'm actually drinking.

I just got an email from Human Resources saying that the magazine is about to lay off one-third of its staff, thanks to the difficult

economic climate and "the rapidly changing nature of our industry."
So if the general thesis of the book is true, encapsulated in the title—
that this could actually be the last magazine of its kind—it's hard to
jeopardize a future if the place you're working for has none.

Which reminds me of a speech Henry the EIC gives to the new
interns. He says he keeps a cartoon in his office that's from that
middle-highbrow magazine, published in 1981. It's a dinosaur reading our magazine. We're a dinosaur, get it? Ready for extinction. The
point, he told us, twenty years later, is that critics and naysayers have
been heralding the decline of *The Magazine* forever and it's never
come to pass.

There's that other saying, too. I think Harry Truman said it: "If
you've worked in the kitchen, you won't eat at the restaurant." But if
it's a five-star restaurant, with a couple of celebrity chefs, wouldn't
you want to hear about the rats from a rat himself? The chefs might
think it's an unfair attack, because, if you *really* know restaurants,
you know rats are a big part of the business. All sorts of unsanitary
shit goes on that you wouldn't ever want the customers to know.

All that being said, I do and always will love *The Magazine*.

Approximately three hours and forty-eight minutes left.

PART II

Why We Fight

"There is no doubt that Saddam Hussein now has weapons of mass destruction."

—VICE PRESIDENT DICK CHENEY, AUGUST 2002

"Hard-liners are alarmed that American intelligence underestimated the pace and scale of Iraq's nuclear program before Baghdad's defeat in the gulf war. . . . The first sign of a 'smoking gun,' they argue, may be a mushroom cloud."

—*The New York Times,* SEPTEMBER 8, 2002

"The debate about whether we're going to deal with Saddam Hussein is over, and now the question is how do we deal with him."

—PRESIDENT GEORGE W. BUSH, NOVEMBER 2002

"These liberal hawks could give a voice to [Bush's] war aims. . . . They could make the case for war to suspicious Europeans and to wavering fellow Americans. They might even be able to explain the connection between Iraq and the war on terrorism."

—GEORGE PACKER IN *The New York Times Magazine,*
DECEMBER 8, 2002

"Barring a dramatic change of behavior by Saddam Hussein in the coming weeks . . . a military intervention to disarm Iraq would be justified."

—*Washington Post* EDITORIAL, FEBRUARY 5, 2003

"The president will take us to war with support . . . from quite a few members of the East Coast liberal media cabal. . . . We reluctant hawks . . . generally agree that the logic for standing pat does not hold. . . . Mr. Bush will be able to claim, with justification, that the coming war is a far cry from the rash, unilateral adventure some of his advisers would have settled for."

—*New York Times* COLUMNIST BILL KELLER, FEBRUARY 8, 2003

"The humanitarian case for war is strong enough on its own."

—BRENNAN TODDLY ON *Charlie Rose*, FEBRUARY 13, 2003

"We have to save the Iraqi people."

—NISHANT PATEL ON THE SAME BROADCAST

"What I'm suggesting is that if our goal is to bring democracy to the Middle East, there are better ways to do so then invading and occupying a country."

—JAMES FALLOWS ON THE SAME BROADCAST

"That's Munich talking."

—SANDERS BERMAN, *The Magazine*

"Every statement I make today is backed up by sources, solid sources. . . . What I want to bring to your attention today is the potentially much more sinister nexus between Iraq and the Al Qaida terrorist network. . . . As with the story of Zarqawi and his network, I can trace the story of a senior terrorist operative telling how Iraq provided training in these weapons to Al Qaida."

—SECRETARY OF STATE COLIN POWELL AT THE UNITED NATIONS, FEBRUARY 2003

"The detainee was not in a position to know if any training had taken place."

—JANUARY 2003 CIA REPORT ON POWELL'S SOURCE, AL QAEDA OPERATIVE IBN AL-SHAYKH AL-LIBI, WHO PROVIDED THE INTELLIGENCE AFTER HIS RENDITION TO EGYPT

"Yes, [Iraq] could be an incredibly dangerous war for journalists. But then, you know, we're in a situation that's fairly dangerous for those of us who live in places like New York and Washington."

—JOE KLEIN ON ABC's *This Week*, MARCH 9, 2003

"This is really bold. . . . Mr. Bush's audacious shake of the dice appeals to me."

> —*New York Times* COLUMNIST THOMAS FRIEDMAN, MARCH 2003

"The question is, is Saddam Hussein a threat to the world or not? I think he is. We should do it with or without the UN."

> —PETER BEINART, EDITOR OF *The New Republic*, MARCH 2003

"Iraq is a part of the war on terror. Saddam Hussein is a threat to our nation. September the 11th should say to the American people that we're now a battlefield, that weapons of mass destruction in the hands of a terrorist organization could be deployed here at home."

> —PRESIDENT GEORGE W. BUSH, MARCH 2003

"One Arab intelligence officer interviewed by *Newsweek* spoke of 'the green mushroom' over Baghdad—the modern-day caliph bidding a grotesque bio-chem farewell to the land of the living alongside thousands of his subjects as well as his enemies. Saddam wants to be remembered. . . . It is up to U.S. armed forces to stop him."

> —*Newsweek* COVER STORY, MARCH 17, 2003

"I believe that the Bush administration is right: this war will look better when it is over. . . . Weapons of mass destruction will be found. . . . Iraq is surely producing weapons of mass destruction."

> —FAREED ZAKARIA, *Newsweek* COVER STORY, MARCH 24, 2003

"Iraq is going to be a cakewalk."

"We'll be greeted as liberators."

"U.S. officials expect there to be less than 20,000 U.S. troops left in Iraq after the initial invasion phase of the war is over, anticipating a drawdown by December 2003."

"They'll be home by Christmas, I can tell you that much."

"We need to demonstrate the good intentions of Americans, but also our power. Shock and Awe, I dare say, did that beautifully."

"We forget, or pretend to forget, or convince ourselves that this time, this time it's going to be different, this time it really is evil versus good, good versus evil, this time, we swear it, the war is going to follow the script, even though in the first scene of the movie, you always have a savvy general ready to give a warning, ready to foreshadow what we all know, who says, wars never go as planned, wars never go how you want them to, wars unleash things— those dogs of war—that we have no control over, ripple effects and whatnot. But there is also the other general in the first scene, the fool to be sent up, ready to say, don't worry, it will all be over by Christmas."

—Very Important Thinkers from Very Important
and Well-Funded Think Tanks

PART III

The Invasion

13.

Wednesday, March 19, 2003

The desert, the steaming dry desert.

No, that image doesn't work. Deserts don't steam.

A fog, then?

Ten details.

If I force myself to write ten details, then I will always be able to paint word pictures for each scene.

A.E. Peoria leans back against the Humvee, thinking about the system of description he had devised, systematic, rigid, a format he could repeat. A disciplined way of reporting. He didn't want to rely on his memory as much as he had in the past—was it black or blue, three cars or six, a sparrow or swallow. He would write everything down.

He'd marked his notebook, spiral, with numbers 1 through 10. Page after page of 1 through 10.

A.E. Peoria stretches, shakes his head, wonders how bad his breath smells.

1. *I lean back against the Humvee.*
2. *Humvee is tan, sand-colored.*
3. *Five Humvees, parked in a row.*

4. *8 soldiers. 3 smoking.*

5. *Desert fog looks like steam.*

6. *Two soldiers in chemical biological nuclear suits. Astronauts. Scuba?*

7. *One soldier pulls off glove.*

8. *Shit, he says, my wedding ring flew off.*

9. *Other soldiers search for wedding ring.*

10. *Wedding ring glimmers in dirt.*

"There it is, sir," A.E. Peoria says, then immediately regrets saying it. Shouldn't have put myself in the story; now if I use that anecdote, I can't be in the objective third-person voice of *The Magazine*.

A.E. Peoria is holding his digital tape recorder under his notebook. Along with description, he wants to work on listening, or if not listening, recording.

The digital tape recorder is picking up this dialogue.

"That's fucking gay, dude," says Lenny.

"Ball flaps aren't fucking gay," says Tom Yelks, a twenty-three-year-old from Akron, Ohio. "I want to start a family when I get back, not just give fucking blow jobs like you. I'm keeping mine on."

Ball flap: a piece of Kevlar with Velcro that fastens onto the bottom of the flak vest.

Yelks holds it up, examining it under the early light.

"You gotta ask yourself, you know, will this actually stop a bullet? If a fucking bomb explodes, you think this will actually stop the shrapnel? Look at this piece of shit," says Lenny, waving it around. "It's thinner than a fucking pantyhose."

By this time, others in the squad have gathered around.

"It's better than nothing," says Staff Sergeant Gerome Phelps, twenty-six, from Midland Springs, Texas. "And all you guys are going to wear it. Captain's orders."

Lenny walks up next to A.E. Peoria and confides, "If you haven't noticed, the Army is a twenty-four-hour gay joke."

A.E. Peoria writes in his notes, "twenty four hour gay joke." That clicks with what he'd been observing. The gayness is everywhere: bursting, ironic, warmly comforting, a way to deal with the homo-eroticism of hanging out with a bunch of dudes.

Peoria divides men into two categories: those who like to shower with other dudes and those who don't. Peoria is very much in the those-who-don't category, but it has been his experience that athletes, frat types, golfers, and now soldiers fit in the showering-naked cate-gory, the ass-slapping, dick-hanging, towel-whipping category. This is not to say anything homophobic—god knows Peoria is against any kind of talk like that at all. He's had to deal with it his entire life.

When he was twelve years old, his father came out of the closet. When he was fourteen, his mother came out of the closet, a lesbian. Father was a professor at Harvard, mother taught at an elite all-girls college in New York. He didn't reveal this to the soldiers, though each brain cell, genetically wired by his compulsive disclosure disorder, wanted him to blurt it out. He resisted shouting: Stop with the gay jokes, my parents are gay. It's not cool. His therapy must be working. Was he betraying his roots and his parents by keeping silent? By letting words like "faggot" and "butthurt" slip by without comment? Should he explain how that kind of language might cause offense?

"Let's ask the reporter," says Yelks.

"Ask me what," Peoria says, realizing he hasn't been listening, only recording.

"Is wearing a ball flap fucking gay?"

This would be the moment to protest.

"Not if you care about your dick, I guess," Peoria says.

"Fucking Lenny loves dick!" says Yelks.

The argument continues, and Peoria starts to compose in his head something he can send back to New York. He is supposed to, according to his editors who are preparing a big package on the ground war, look for "examples of fear."

Soldiers afraid of gay men wouldn't cut it. But the fear of getting your balls blown off was something he could work with.

The soldier's number-one fear, Peoria writes in his mind, throughout the history of human warfare. An ancient anxiety, as large as death. Writings from Genghis Khan's time show that the Mongols were worried about a saber to the groin, putting a crimp on the raping. A legion of Romans in A.D. 23 refused an order for battle near the Sea of Galilee because the bronze cups they had requisitioned from Carthage—which all the other legionnaires from competing formations, even the African slaves, had been given—hadn't arrived yet. A near armed mutiny. On sea, conscripts in the British fleet under Nelson described a phenomena called splinter cock, the result of a cannonball crashing into the wooden deck, sending shards of handcrafted timber ripping through hammocks and pantaloons. Letters home from the Civil War—letters that aren't talked about too much—mentioned how Confederate soldiers had competitions to take aim "a smidgen lower south from the goddamned Yanks' belt buckles." In World War I, a French general famously gave a rousing speech, urging the young Frenchmen, already ravaged by two years of back-and-forth in slaughterhouses like Verdun and the Somme, to advance over the trenches *"avec courage,"* helmets *"sur la tête."* In the hush following the speech, one private, sick with louse bites and scarlet fever, quipped, "That's not the head I'm worried about." (*C'est ne pas cette tête qui me préoccupe!*)

Weapons manufacturers explicitly exploited this anxiety in the second half of the twentieth century, designing explosive charges that jumped from the ground to hip level before they exploded—the

Bouncing Betty, named after Betty Boop, the first hypersexualized female cartoon of the postwar era. The chant that Marines out at Parris Island introduced in 1966: "This is my rifle, this is my gun, this is for fighting, this is for fun." Lose either, and the fun ends.

The fears: soldiers spent a lot of time not really thinking to avoid them, and when they did think, it was about home and girlfriends and fiancées and sex, and after that, when they thought about the future, which seemed to loom in the country overheard to the north, it was about their balls. True fear and the language of courage. Testicles, *cojones*, testosterone to stand up under fire and not be a pussy.

Since arriving in Kuwait, Peoria had spent more than twenty days in the Humvees with the soldiers—mostly men, mostly nineteen to twenty-eight—prepared for the invasion. We need color, the editors had said, and maybe find a scandal too. War crimes are always good.

Peoria has assigned each of them a place in the group hierarchy. Characters, all of them. The staff sergeant is someone you could say is straight from central casting—is there a central casting anymore? The men are stereotypes with legs and animated mouths. They have affected their roles in the unit almost cinematically, so much so that Peoria feels like he has watched this scene before, certainly he has read about it in all the war novels, heard the banter, or a variation of it, in the dispatches from the front from every other war reporter he has ever studied. Chicken/egg, egg/chicken. What comes first: the drill sergeant or the drill sergeant in *Full Metal Jacket*?

Phelps is the badass, can-do NCO, a veteran of four deployments who has seen it all, no sweat, regularly abusive. Yelks is the typical private: talkative, youthful, running at the mouth in an ongoing and evolving profane banter with his buddy, Specialist Lenny. Yelks is always anxious to explain and make sweeping judgments on Army life and on his fellow soldiers, like "problem in the Army is that most of these guys didn't have friends in high school. I mean, they were picked on in high school. I mean, if they had friends, you know, they were fucking losers, to be honest, and now they've got guns?"

There's the large southern redneck, with a neck red from the sun, from Arkansas. A pair of black kids from Brooklyn and Jersey, who even today make jokes about the white man, though there is the double irony that they really don't feel very oppressed. The young lieutenant, an intellectual sort from one of the Ivy League schools who went against the grain and signed up to learn about war because, as he puts it, "it was such a part of human history, the human experience, and to understand myself and the world, I need to understand war," with whispers that he is thinking about a career in politics.

And then there is the quiet loner, non-aggressively awkward, effeminate, near pretty, always a half step behind, not on the ball, with a silent mystery hinting at some hidden depth, some sensitivity in a very insensitive environment—and in this unit, that soldier's name is Justin Salvador. From what Peoria has gathered, he's Puerto Rican, though he's often called Mexican or Honduran or Panamanian, and his nickname—as most in the unit have a nickname, just like soldiers in the movies—is Chipotle. He is the soldier the conversation seizes on in moments of silence. Rather than talk about the weather, a joke thrown Salvador's way acts as the icebreaker.

Salvador, slight and fair-skinned, is fumbling with the ball flap.

In the silence, the velcroing and unvelcroing can be heard.

Yelks turns to Salvador.

"Now Chipotle over there, he being a Mexican, it might not be a bad thing for him, you know, since his race breeds like field mice. We don't want your spawn taking over the country now, do we, Chipotle? New order—only the Mexicans don't need to wear the ball flap."

Everyone laughs, and Salvador mumbles a "Go fuck yourself" or something to Yelks.

The lieutenant walks up.

"Okay, guys, we got the word. We're gonna be going first. The convoy is gonna stay a couple klicks behind us. We're clearing the way. I remind you we are about to enter hostile territory, but we are liberators. As such, we will kill, but we will kill only those who are trying to kill us. Shoot if you are shot at, shoot if you are threatened. Make sure you get a positive ID. The S-2, the intel that we got, says there are unfriendlies. No shit, right? Sergeant Phelps will brief the ROEs and EOFs. All that being said, it is a free-fire zone, meaning, if you feel yourself threatened, do not hesitate."

Peoria is in the first vehicle, sitting on the hard metal seat behind the driver. Yelks is driving; Salvador stands on the .50 caliber machine gun; the lieutenant sits shotgun. The engine starts, the trucks roll off, kicking up dust.

The invasion is under way.

At the border, over the radio, the lieutenant announces, as hundreds of others did, "Welcome to Iraq." He smiles as he turns to Peoria, marking the time.

Two-thirty p.m., March 19, the year of our lord 2003.

The Humvees follow a main highway for a few hours.

There is dust, hundreds of vehicles, armored machines, loaded up, snaked out, rolling, churning a magnificent storm, choking, eye-irritating. Brown dust, and of course the dust is brown, brown dust hit by light particles, particles of sand and light, and the sun is rising up, the sun rising up in the east, and the dust becomes less brown and the dust becomes a big vocabulary word: *translucent*.

A road sign: BABYLON, 312 KM.

And over the radio, the redneck from Arkansas, who is also a Baptist, who also studies the Bible and knows it by heart, starts to recite:

"Thus saith the Lord, Behold I will rise up against Babylon, and against them that dwell in the midst of them that rise up against me, a destroying wind, And will send unto Babylon fanners that shall fan her and shall empty her land, for in the day of trouble they shall be against her round about and spare ye not her young men, destroy ye utterly all her host. . . . I will bring them down like lambs to the slaughter, like rams with he goats. Her cities are a desolation, a dry land, and a wilderness, a land wherein no man dwell, neither doth any son of man pass nearby. And thou shalt say, Thus shall Babylon sink, and shall not rise from the evil that I will bring upon her: and they shall be weary. Thus far are the words of Jeremiah."

A.E. Peoria is taking notes, thinking he needs to check that passage, or have someone in New York check it for accuracy. He doesn't want to interrupt the poetic moment by asking an intrusive journalist a question, but he does.

"That's, uh, Old Testament?" Peoria says over the net.

The redneck doesn't answer directly.

"And he cried mightily with a strong voice saying, Babylon the great is fallen, and is become the habitation of devils, and the hold of every foul spirit, and a cage of every unclean and hateful bird . . . And the light of the candle shall shine no more, and in her was found the blood of the prophets, and of saints, and of all that were slain upon the earth."

The Humvees are so enveloped in the dust that they can keep an eye only on the vehicle in front of them, staying a safe three hundred feet apart.

"He's fucking playing you, sir. Redneck can't even do a fucking briefing and he's saying he can say all that from the Bible by memory," says Yelks. "He's reading that fucking Bible of his, I bet."

The dust clears.

The lieutenant's five-Humvee reconnaissance convoy has put enough distance between itself and the main route of hundreds of vehicles that Peoria can now see clearly, and what he sees is shocking. He sees blue sky, an overwhelming blue above the desert.

He has a strange tingling sensation and a sentence goes through his head that takes him a second to place.

"Beware of blue skies and open horizons."

And A.E. Peoria remembers 9/11. 9/11 was a blue-sky day. In New York, he grabbed his notebook and jumped in a taxi and went down there to Chambers Street, and he stood next to a woman, a stranger, who had grabbed his arm as the two of them watched dark figures, one after the other, jump, fall, and the woman saying, Oh my god, oh my god. The woman gripped his arm tightly, but he didn't notice or didn't say anything, because he felt like he should be feeling pain. A terrifying rumble. Let's go, let's go, and that's when he started to run through the canyons of Lower Manhattan, and the dust was coming, the dust was coming. A man in a coffee shop kept the door open and yelled, "Get in here, get in here!" Everything was dark for forty-three seconds. Car alarms and coughing. Light came back in. He saw fingernail marks on his arm, deep cuts. He looked around for the woman, but the woman was gone.

Pearl Harbor, Hawaii, December 7. A passage from *From Here to Eternity*, something about the skies not showing any hint of clouds over the Pacific, clear blue.

He recalls an eyewitness at Nagasaki. A clear day. The city was the second choice—the first, Kokura, was covered in clouds. The bomber commander said he headed toward the blue skies. You could drop the atomic bomb only on a day that had excellent visibility.

Exterminate all the brutes, he thinks, remembering his Conrad. Exterminate all rational thought, he thinks, remembering his Burroughs. And between those two lines written sixty years apart, you have the entire canon of Western liter . . .

Dozing off.

Awake again.

Wake up, wake up, Peoria thinks, though nothing is happening. Here he is, in war, on the frontline of history, and there is just the dull engine noise that puts him to sleep, the helmet on his head, the body armor, the heat.

His senses are heightened and he looks around and the air seems much clearer, and he feels there should be ringing in his ears, an acute ringing in his ears, all the alarm bells in his mind, his senses overloading, like one of those hearing tests, an invisible high-pitched sound, as the truck bumps up and down. He has his helmet on; he has his body armor; the standard blue issue with the word PRESS across the front; he has his digital recorder, which he fumbles with as he forces himself to take notes and he feels so clumsy. There he is in war, fussing around in the backseat, with his seat belt, with his sunglasses, with his tape player, with a pen—why doesn't his pen work? The ink is not coming out of his pen, and he scribbles, and scribbles again, finally sticking the dead pen in his pocket and fishing out a new pen from his black shoulder bag—his larger backpack with his equipment is in the trunk of the Humvee. His shoulder bag, which has his satellite phone, computer, and extra pens, is at his feet. He finds another ballpoint, hits the record button, and writes down, "Welcome to Iraq, two-thirty pm, march 19, the year of our lord—" He realizes he has taken only a few notes since the invasion started, he didn't keep up with his system, he is far behind. He looks out the window and he sees dead cars and a dead tank from the previous war, and he sees shitty little mud huts with threadlike power lines, and he notes more road signs—BAGHDAD 400 KM, NAJAF 220—and tunes out the voices over the radio. He thinks to himself, Man, I am glad I'm not leading this convoy. I am glad all I have to do is watch. I am already disoriented. I have no idea where I am. I'm just along for the ride, and then he looks at his watch. Five hours have passed.

It is almost dark.

He feels something nudge his shoulder.

"Sir, excuse me, sir?"

It is Salvador, tapping him with his boot from his position in the machine-gunner slot.

"Sir, could you pass me a Mountain Dew? The cooler's behind you."

He looks up at Salvador, taking a few seconds to shake off the sleep. So he has been sleeping again. Dozed off in the back of the Humvee. It is hot, for sure, and with the weight of the helmet on his head, and the fact he's been awake for, like, twenty hours, it all keeps putting him to sleep, sleeping right through the story.

"Yeah, no problem."

He unstraps himself, turning in his seat to open the metal panel that divides the backseat from the trunk. He puts his notebook and tape recorder down on the floor. He uses both hands to pull it open. There is a red cooler in the back, the kind at every Fourth of July picnic. The ice hasn't melted yet, and he plunges his hand in, bobbing past water bottles and searching for a soda can.

"I think we're lost, sir."

It isn't Salvador speaking, but Yelks, to the lieutenant.

"This fucking GPS is shit."

Peoria doesn't know if he's heard correctly—he's not too concerned, after all, these guys are professionals. He feels the soda can. He succeeds in the small task of finding it, and is proud how quickly he did—prying open the sliding metal door to the trunk, having to find the right bolt to pull. The small satisfaction of accomplishing a simple physical action. He takes the soda can out of the cooler.

"Salvador, here you go."

Peoria doesn't get an answer.

The war is no longer silent.

"Engage, engage, engage," the lieutenant yells.

The machine-gun fire opens up three feet above his head. He sees the tracers flash, slanting down from the side window. There is a loud crash and a scream. He is thrown against the front seat, and because he is facing the wrong way, he feels the back of his helmet knock heads with Yelks, the driver. He is facing backward. The Humvee, he notices, is no longer moving. The other new sound is spinning tires in dirt.

Then the *ping*s start.

PING, PING, PING.

"That's fucking incoming. That's fucking incoming."

Scrunched up on the floor of the backseat, Peoria looks around for his tape recorder and notepad. They are somewhere on the floor. He finds the can of Mountain Dew. Where the fuck are they? *WHOOSH.* The Mountain Dew explodes; there is wet stickiness all over his hand.

Oh shit, hunh. So this is what combat is like.

He realizes the lieutenant has opened the front door, sticking his M-16 out. He is firing, and saying, "Yelks, you okay, man? Yelks, you okay?"

Peoria finds his notepad. Next to it is his tape recorder. He fumbles with it, pressing Play, then Stop, and then finally hitting Record in time to hear the lieutenant scream to Salvador, "Yelks is hit. Keep firing. I'm going to drive."

Peoria watches the lieutenant get out of the Humvee. He sees him run around the front, the truck's headlights lighting him up before he suddenly falls out of view and on the ground, the bullets passing through his body and shattering the windshield of the Humvee.

That is when he hears the first shriek. It is not human: it is the shrieking of explosives, in a shell, dropping down from the sky and dangerously close to the truck. Again, he is surprised about how accurate the movies really are in terms of sound effects. There is another shriek, and another. Peoria judges the situation, he assumes, rationally. He has heard that the Iraqis have poor aim, yet he senses that whoever is flinging those mortars his way knows what they are doing. It feels to him like he should get out of the Humvee. The engine has gone silent, but the headlights for some reason are on. They were supposed to tell him what to do if something like this happened, but no one is telling him what to do. He senses too, and then sees, that Yelks is dead, and he hasn't heard anything in a few seconds from the lieutenant either.

Then Salvador's machine gun stops, and the Puerto Rican is inside the truck, very close to his face, and telling him they have to get out, they have to get out of the Humvee now.

"Push in, then pull the handle, push in, then pull it toward you."

Peoria stuffs his tape recorder in his pocket with his notepad, and keeps trying the door, but it isn't budging, not giving as easily as the sliding metal one he had successfully opened to access the cooler.

"It's not working."

The Puerto Rican leans over him, the muzzle of his rifle hitting Peoria in the mouth, cutting his lip. He yanks on the door handle and pushes it open, almost falling out of the truck.

"Sir, we have to move, we have to move, come on."

There is another shriek. Peoria is outside, on his feet and running, or he is following, quickly following Salvador, down an embankment of pebbles and sand, moving through what feels like bushes, away from the road, and the next shriek he hears—he is losing track of how far he has run—seems far away, and the firing also seems distant. It is quiet again, until all he can hear is swearing in Spanish.

"Hey, hey, Salvador, where are we, man?"

"Shut up, shut up. We'll stop here."

There is no moon, or any stars. What happened to the blue sky at night? The two men are lying next to each other. Salvador is aiming his rifle in the direction they came from. Peoria looks at the Puerto Rican closely and sees that something is a little off. He isn't lying on his belly in the normal prone position, but off to one side.

"Where did the other guys go?" Peoria whispers.

"What?"

"The other Humvees. Where did they go?"

"They're gone, they're gone. You didn't see them? They kept driving."

"What?"

"Shit . . ."

Salvador has dropped his rifle, is clasping his hand across his belly.

More shooting starts. Peoria thinks the bullets are coming toward him. He finds it funny that his life actually does flash before his eyes. As if there is a chemical in the blood that is released only at certain moments in life, an endorphin with the flashback function. He sees things, collapsed, in seconds. Toddler. Graduation. Cambodia. Chambers Street. Dad and Mom.

He doesn't understand why they are shooting at him. He wants to stand up. He feels this urge to stand up and explain himself. He wants to tell them to stop shooting. You've got the wrong guy. There's no need to shoot at me. This is silly, you trying to shoot at me. This powerful urge to stand up and explain to the attackers that this must all have been some gigantic, enormous misunderstanding to have brought us to this point in time. It is counterintuitive—self-preservation would suggest hiding, but then why the desire to ask them to stop, to give up, to surrender?

But he sees Salvador lying there, and he knows that he can't stand up. If I stand up, he thinks, they will shoot me. So I must not stand up. I must stay here, down, hidden, and hope that they will go away.

Five minutes? Ten minutes?

No more shooting.

"The flashlight, get the flashlight. It's in my pocket, on my jacket."

Peoria inches closer to the Puerto Rican, placing his hand on his chest. He can feel his heart beating fast and is comforted by how warm the body feels. He touches a hard, round piece of metal through the cloth of the shirt. He unbuttons the pocket and pulls out the flashlight. Salvador makes a gurgling sound and wheezes.

"Sir, man, sir. I think I'm bleeding. I think I'm hit."

Peoria flicks the flashlight on, making sure to aim it down. A coffee-stained circle appears on the Puerto Rican's chest. As he moves the circle lower, the beam becomes darker. The beam lights up the top of a stain on the tan, desert camouflage uniform, right above the belly button. The beam follows the stain, which gets bigger, and he stops on the belt buckle. He doesn't want to look farther down. He knows it is blood. He knows there is a lot of blood.

"Sir, what's wrong, am I hit?"

Peoria nods.

The flashlight is now on Salvador's groin. The buttons on the pants are wet, and he catches the sight of flesh. It looks disfigured. He frowns. He starts to undo the buttons on the pants. Salvador groans.

"Oh god, not there."

"I need to administer, uuh, first aid."

Peoria's mind goes through the procedures he'd studied. He remembers the class he took in Virginia. An Australian special forces instructor, six-foot-four with a blond crew cut, saying: First, make sure there is no danger. Yell, "Clear." All clear, Peoria says to himself. Second, do a sweep of the body to make sure there are no other wounds and to find out where the bleeding is from. Peoria figures he's already done that. In his mind, he sees the instructor's PowerPoint presentation flip to the third slide—something about a tourniquet.

The fourth slide has a picture with it—a picture that was jarring at the time, as it was shown in such a clean and peaceful conference room, usually reserved for marketing presentations, and learning about war in that environment did feel a little odd. But that fourth PowerPoint slide and the Australian accent are coming back to him now, as big letters, big letters that say STOP THE BLEEDING. How do you do this, mate? You apply pressure. Does he have his first-aid kit? No, of course not—it's back in the truck. Salvador doesn't have one on him either.

The facts come to his head: Most deaths are from massive trauma and blood loss. With no bandages, he needs something else, anything. Perhaps his shirt. Okay, my shirt. He undoes his helmet, and unvelcros his body armor, slips off the North Face parka he's been wearing, and then the sixth slide pops into his head—don't let your patient lose consciousness.

"Hey, hey, Salvador, are you awake? Stay with me, man, stay with me."

"I'm with you, am I okay?"

"Yeah, I think so. You're bleeding and a little fucked-up, but you're okay, sure."

"What do you mean, I'm 'a little fucked-up'?"

Fuck. Peoria wishes there had been a seventh or an eighth slide that told him, When patients ask for their condition, lie. Tell them they are fine. Perhaps they figured that was common sense, and therefore unnecessary to teach, but if there was one thing Peoria had been told over and over again, it was that he lacked common sense.

"You're fine, you're fine. There's no bleeding. There is bleeding, but it's not bad. I think I've seen worse. I haven't, but I've seen worse on TV. Me, personally, I haven't seen worse. I'm taking my shirt off. It's clean, and I don't have any other bandages. It's not clean, actually,

I sweated like a bitch today. But once I get my shirt off and on you, I'm going to press it against your crotch and . . ."

"My crotch? My crotch? Is it gone?"

"I don't know. I haven't checked. I'm not a doctor, so I better leave it for them to check that. I'm just going to stop the bleeding. It's slide number four, you know. I learned all that from my first-aid class at the security training course in Virginia. That was a good time. There's a girl in the class who was really hot, you know. Fuck, I should really email her."

Peoria takes off his undershirt, and with both hands, presses it up against Salvador's crotch. He holds it there with both hands. He has to keep him awake. He has to talk to him. Peoria starts to talk.

"I'm thirty-four years old, and what do I really have to show for it, you know? I have a bunch of magazine articles to my name. I've been on TV a few times. I guess I've had some cool experiences, the kind no one else has had, or very few, but when you think about it, so what? So what that I've done things other people haven't. What does that really mean in the end? I haven't been able to write a best-seller, you know, and that's depressing, because I see so much that gets published that really is shit, and I'm like, Fuck, I could write shit like that. Really . . . I can't really believe this is fucking happening to me, you know? Here, you hold on to the T-shirt, just hold it tight against you."

Peoria searches his pockets. He freezes for a second—is his wallet there? Did I lose my fucking wallet? And then he goes anxiously through a checklist, out of instinct. Wallet, keys, gum, cigarettes. He checks his pockets to make sure of all his possessions. Wallet, keys, gum, cigarettes. Laptop, the laptop is gone. Recorder and notepad, okay. He takes out his wallet and finds a picture—six orgasms he had given this girl in one night—and he stares hard at the picture and asks himself, Is this it, is this her? It depresses him to think he could

die in the desert with some mediocre girl as his love, a third-tier girl.
He'd dated in New York for years, and he'd gone from relationship to
relationship, some lasting six months, a couple lasting a year or more,
and he didn't much see his family, and he didn't really have anything.
He had his career, and that was about it; he'd spent the last ten years
on his career, in the office, at work, all the time, and here he was going
to die at work, on the job, for his career. Not even a country. To die
for a 401(k) and health insurance and a vague idea of success. He
could feel the spleen, a fucking mediocre career too, not like his
bosses—not like fucking Nishant Patel and Sanders Berman—some
of his bosses were legitimate media superstars. He remembers once,
when he was on an assignment in Richmond, Virginia, doing a profile of a NASCAR driver, and he was sitting in the airport and watching CNN when Nishant Patel was being fawned over by a fake-blonde
anchor with nice tits, who was just pretty enough and had something
a little off-kilter about her mouth, which made her unique enough to
be on TV. He realized in Richmond that he had so far to go, and
wondered if he'd ever even get there. Richmond itself, a third-tier
city, and he was shocked when he saw people in Richmond go to
work—as a New Yorker, he had forgotten there were other cities put
there on Earth to live in, and he saw a guy with a suit and tie head to
a glass skyscraper and realized there were other lives he could lead. It
didn't have to be in the Big Apple, Gotham, formerly New Amster-
dam. Of course he didn't do anything about it; he did not make any
big career change or life choices. He went back to New York on the
727, back to the office, back to the dimpled plastic sheets hanging
over his head, shining that hard yellow light, convincing himself he
loved his job. Who could ask for a better job? His investment banker
and lawyer friends all hated their jobs. (Actually, does he really know
any investment banker friends, or is he just choosing that profession

as an East Coast resident chooses the town of Boise, Idaho, or his namesake, Peoria, Illinois, to score an easy point about the cultural backwardness of certain states?) I get paid to have new experiences, to do things no one else has done, and I get to do it for, like, two weeks, or a few hours, and I never have to get stuck with the grind of doing the same thing over and over again. It all became the same thing, it all was a grind, this whole life thing, the steady nasal drip of paychecks and bills and late nights and dinner dates that depressed him.

Peoria doesn't know if he has been saying these things out loud or just to himself, and he continues talking to Salvador.

"What the fuck . . . I think I'm depressed a lot of the time. I was going to show you a picture, but really, it's not even worth it."

It is getting cold. Another factoid from his security training class pops into his mind: People freeze to death in the desert. Despite the popular myths of deserts as sweltering death traps, they are just as likely to transform, once the sun sets, into freezing death traps, with temperatures dropping to near zero Celsius in the middle of the night. And now he doesn't have his shirt on, though he did put his parka back on. That brings another first-aid fact back to his mind: He needs to keep Salvador's body temperature up. He moves in closer to him, putting his hands over Salvador's hands to apply more pressure to the wound.

"Yes, yes," Salvador says.

He has never been in this position before, spooning with a dude whose balls were blown off, but he figures his best bet is to wait. He starts talking again.

"This is a little awkward, right, but it's best because we need to keep warm. We really do. I'm not gay. I don't have a problem with that or anything. I guess you would, because the Army does really have a problem with it, but I don't. My father's gay. So is my mother. Pretty fucked-up, right? I never really understood it. Freaked me out. I was twelve and I remember thinking, Does this mean my father wants to fuck me?"

Peoria goes on talking through the night. The bleeding appears to stop, though he is certain at times that Salvador is going to die.

14.

Wednesday, March 19, 2003

The countdown clock is running on the cable news stations, ticking away in the bottom right-hand corner of the screen, synced to President George W. Bush's final ultimatum to Saddam Hussein.

What's the ultimatum?

To hand over weapons of mass destruction. No one believes that Saddam is going to do that. Nobody wants him to do it either. It's too late in the narrative for anyone to back out now.

Back home after a long day, an exciting day at the office.

I can't sleep.

I don't want to sleep.

I have my television set on.

I have ordered *Double Penetration Sluts #4* on the Time Warner Adult Video on Demand. A twenty-four-hour rental. Channel 304.

From channel 304, I punch in the number for CNN, channel 35.

Then I hit the Last button on my remote control, so I can bounce back and forth between my two choices.

Stop, fast-forward the digital television, rewind, see it again.

I'm hammering away, touching myself, and it's onto the next scene. Waiting for the right moment. It used to be easier, but I've developed a strong resistance to pornography. As a young teen, the pages of a *Penthouse* were enough. Then old VHS cassettes, Internet, DVDs, Adult Video on Demand.

The bar for my porn watching keeps going higher. Rewind again. The man shooting his jizz in the faces of Ying and Yang doesn't do it tonight. The gaping holes don't do it. Fast-forward. Maybe the next scene with Gauge will. Gauge is dressed to look like a fourteen-year-old girl. She's earns her living the hard way—it's not fair to say just on her back, but with all different parts of her body flattened against floors, walls, designer chairs, soiled mattresses, leather couches, bent and acrobatic, ass pointed to the air, the weight of her body on her neck, knees somehow stretched backward behind her ears. I read on the Internet that she does five scenes a week in a good week.

I am waiting for what is making me come lately.

Ass to mouth—shorthand: ATM.

I watch the man, whose hair could have been styled in 1991 and never been changed, take his penis from her ass and then grab her by the waist to twist her face toward his cock. I wait for the moment when he puts his cock in her mouth, the moment of entry.

It doesn't happen. There's a jump cut.

I'm pissed. That is no good at all. I need to see the full-body motion, I need to see the uninterrupted movement from ass to mouth because I am savvy enough, my penis is savvy enough, to know that if there is a jump cut, then things could have been done, organs cleaned, wiped off, made more sanitary; my brain is trained to sense these kinds of illusions, to sense when it's not real enough—when it's too clean.

I am disappointed. I should never have trusted Time Warner Cable. They've given a nod to some kind of strange decency regulations. Is it a legal thing? Why did they edit it out? Who sets these standards? Who sat around the table, saying gaping assholes okay, assholes to mouth not okay? What does that look like in legal language? Was there a board meeting? "Non-explicit or internal visualizations of sex organs."

TWC isn't going to give me what I want to see, exactly, but I already have been charged $14.95, so I am forced to make do. I am forced to make do with the fact that I will have to settle for *representation* of ass to mouth. I will have to imagine what happened in the edit myself.

Fast-forward. Gauge is kneeling and spitting and the man's hand is on his penis, a point-of-view shot, and he ejaculates in her face. I shoot too.

Ahhhhhhhhhhhhhhhhhhhhhhhhhhhhhhhh.

Okay.

I hit the Last button and jump back to a CNN correspondent with the 1st Armored Division.

The correspondent has positioned himself on a road to somewhere, and the trucks are rolling by him.

I reflect. I know I am being somewhat self-conscious. I know I am somehow, in some inexplicable way, being ironic. But I am not being ironic. This is just what life is for me. What else am I going to do when sitting in front of a TV alone? Jerk off. And if my country is going to war, I'm going to watch my country go to war.

More channels. Anchors shouting about how wonderful the technology is, allowing them to stream live video while they are riding with the troops. Allowing us to see correspondents with satellite phones in Kurdistan, waiting with exiled groups. Allowing us to see inside the Bradleys. The live images of Baghdad getting bombed.

I'm tired now, so the only fighting I get that first night is a British journalist getting shot at with Americans behind a berm.

I jerk off three more times.

I watch the maps of Iraq and the columns of soldiers and I think I'm really missing out on this. I really should be over there. Maybe I'll go over there sometime. My eyes close, and I wonder how A.E. Peoria is doing.

15.

Thursday, March 20, 2003

Next morning, in the office.

My computer takes the required few minutes to load up. Iced coffee on the table, eating a croissant. Happy to be back in the office. Happy to be sitting there at the center of things in the newsroom of a major news organization while history shits itself around me.

Gary is there and he comes up to my desk.

"Have you heard the news?" Gary whispers.

"What?"

"Peoria is missing. The convoy he was with got attacked. They found his phone, and there was blood all around it. They hit Redial and got Dave at the news desk."

"No shit, oh my god. Fuck."

"Henry has called his parents. I mean, it doesn't look good."

"Fuck, wow, I can't believe that."

A wave of seriousness passes over me. It's not ironic at all. My friend and colleague A.E. Peoria is presumed dead.

But he isn't that good of a friend. I don't really know him that well.

I'm excited by the possibility that the war is real and that I have a connection to it. I have an anecdote that I can retell. I do.

"Did you hear the news? Peoria is missing. Yeah, apparently his convoy was attacked, found his phone in blood. I can't believe it either . . ."

16.

Friday, March 21, 2003

The sun comes up around five-thirty in the morning. There is an emptiness in the desert, a silence, a chill. It is at this time, though Peoria doesn't know it, that another convoy reaches the scene of the attack, finds Peoria's satellite phone and hits Redial.

Peoria is feeling a new level of all-time discomfort. An ache in the muscles, hugging himself, rubbing as fast as he can, desperate for friction and heat. Hugging himself with the strength he has never hugged another human being with. He feels damp, though he finds this hard to believe. How is he feeling damp when the temperature on the previous day had reached 90 degrees Fahrenheit? A dry heat, a very hot dry heat, but the chill has gotten so bad that it brings a feeling of cold moisture. Eyes half open, thoughts trailing, head on Salvador's knee, begging for the sun to return to its full power. Rolling over, out of the shadow of the berm he has been hiding behind and into a rectangle of sunlight, sunlight still weak, still not hot enough, the sunlight that's promise of warmth is still an hour or two or three away.

Peoria feels he should be more afraid. A dying man by his side, but he is pleasantly surprised that he has reached that point beyond fear.

That point that those on shipwrecked lifeboats feel hours before they start to poison themselves with saltwater.

A.E. Peoria doesn't care anymore if he lives or dies and he doesn't care anymore if Salvador lives or dies and there is a relief, a letting go. He feels he has found at the bottom of this berm that Zen place he has had such difficulty finding anywhere else, where fatigue and spent adrenaline and hunger and no cigarettes or caffeine have left him. The second, third, and fourth winds have blown in and blown away, and he isn't looking for the fifth wind to stand him upright. He's enjoying this bliss, and he keeps tapping his foot, tapping and tapping and looking up for the sun to start doing its daily life-killing damage on the landscape, tapping and tapping, and he thinks, Maybe this is the first sign of post-traumatic stress disorder, this constant tapping, and then he thinks, Oh boy, my lips are really dry, and he wishes he had his ChapStick, and despite his best efforts, that sixth or seventh wind is creeping up—that nagging for survival and living and action is creeping back into his bloodstream.

How he wishes he had his fucking ChapStick.

The Zen is going away. His brain is getting activated, as if by solar power, his brain and neuroses and anxieties are beginning all over again.

At around seven a.m., Peoria decides to assess the situation—these are the words in his head, "The situation needs assessing." He asks Salvador if he can walk. Salvador doesn't answer. Salvador is pale. His light brown skin is lighter. He is in a small dip in the ground in the desert. Peoria hasn't stood up since diving to the ground nine hours ago. He stands. He can see a long line of American vehicles. Then he understands that it is the noise of engines, that dull rumbling, that must have triggered him to stand, sensing vibrations in the air like a dog.

He looks down at the Puerto Rican and tells him to stay right there, and Peoria starts to run, waving his arms.

As he gets closer, he sees there are three men with rifles aimed at him. He puts his hands up.

"Don't shoot, I'm an American, I'm an American! I'm with the press!"

A soldier jogs out to him.

"What the fuck are you doing here?"

"We were attacked. There's a guy with me. He's bleeding bad. Chipotle."

The soldier yells back to another soldier, that soldier yells to someone else, the chain of command at work. Peoria points to where Chipotle is lying; he leads a squad to get him and helps as they put Salvador on a stretcher and carry him to what Peoria can now see is a tank. He jogs at Salvador's side, saying, "You'll make it, man, you'll make it."

The Puerto Rican's eyes flutter open. He sees Peoria and tries to say something. Nothing comes out, but later, when he thinks about it, Peoria is sure the words he mouthed were "Mountain Dew."

Peoria has a blanket around him and his laptop has appeared by his side. He is in the cocoon of a tank. He's been picked up and he gets handed things. Food, water, blanket, and his laptop bag reappears. How did it get to him, all these things happening? He is handed a phone, and he knows he needs to make the call back to *The Magazine* and tell them what happened. How information is getting conveyed to him and how he is conveying information back is a mystery, but he remembers that he should be doing his job.

He starts taking notes. He only gets two words down before a soldier leads him outside the tank. Another soldier, an officer, walks up to him, carrying his satellite phone.

"It's for you, sir."

Jerry is on the line.

"You okay? Fuck! Tell me what happened. We'll write it from here, just give me the details."

Peoria looks at his notebook and sees it isn't much help. Three pages, a few words a page, written as if he had been holding his pen with a fist. He starts talking, from the unit he was with to the ambush to the night in the desert and his girlfriend with six orgasms and how he wanted to stand up and say, Stop shooting at me, stop shooting at me. What the sound of a rifle fired sounded like and hitting the vehicle sounded like, *ping, ping, ping,* and Jerry keeps saying, My god, it's good you're alive, go on, my god it's good you're alive, go on. . . . Until he gets to the last act. The rescue, the chill of the morning, running with the stretcher, looking into Salvador's eyes, when the beep of a low battery starts on the satellite phone.

"What did Salvador say to you?" Jerry asks.

"He said—"

A crackle over the line.

"Mountain Dew."

"What? 'Saved you'?"

Peoria looks at the two words on his notepad.

Mountain Dew.

"Saved you?"

"Not him, me. He said, 'Mountain Dew.'"

Distance, six thousand miles, satellite interference.

"On the stretcher?"

The satellite phone dies.

The new convoy Peoria is with has to keep moving, so he can't make another call. He doesn't know that his story is going to be mentioned on the cover.

The headline is "You Saved Me."

PART IV

After the Invasion

17.

August 2003

To get the can of yellow spray paint, A.E. Peoria steps over the sleeping bodies of the bellhop and two other waiters passed out on the thin foam mats and wrapped in threaded blankets on the concrete floor in the Hamra Hotel's supply closet. Spray paint is a red-hot commodity in Baghdad, sales off the charts. The owner of the Hamra, Mr. Al Mansour, had been bragging that he'd bought ten cans just this morning and stashed them away for potential resale.

The collapse of Saddam's regime has brought a flood of new products to Iraq that people couldn't get before: satellite television dishes, air conditioners, extra-large flavored condoms, gumballs, new Toyotas, genetically modified nectarines from the European Union, premium whiskey, Turkish beer, and yes, spray paint—there had never been cans of spray paint in Iraq before, something to do with United Nations sanctions. All the paint in Saddam's regime had been in tin aluminum buckets that required a brush. But a shipment of spray paint had come in at the market, a few truckloads driven up from Dubai, and the stocks cleared out within hours, more truckloads ordered up.

Spray paint, A.E. Peoria has observed, was catching on like mobile phones in East Africa, the push-button aerosol technology a new blessing on the land.

The Iraqis were trying out these cans of wonder with gusto. An Aladdin's lamp of a free society: shake it, push, puff, and forty wishes of free expression granted before the hiss of an empty bottle.

In Iran, after the fall of the shah in 1979, there was an old man who made his living walking around the streets pulling down statues of the shah, with a simple noose and rope pulley device, reimbursed by the new fundamentalist government per statue. In Iraq there had been some highly publicized toppling of statues, some nice TV moments, but the real symbolism of the new era had been found in the cans of spray paint that had infiltrated Baghdad. Slogans spray-painted everywhere, showing the world that Iraq was still a literate cradle of civilization, the premier spot for poets and artists and love-sick songstresses in the Arab world, the first signs of a new age of legal vandalism and graffiti and contemporary writings. Messages, taunts, haikus, circles, squares, penises, threats, cubes spray-painted across the city in all colors—yellow, black, purple, green, blue, red—a rain-bow of spray paint on the sagging corners of wounded buildings, on the stone exteriors of government offices stripped bare of copper wiring and paper products and Apple IIe computers, on the strikingly white pillars of Saddam's now abandoned ninety-seven palaces, on road signs crossing out the name Saddam with the Arabic word for "free," *ahrar*, and on the newest feature of the city, the concrete blast walls, two tons of concrete each, eight feet by ten feet, a perfect canvas for the country's new identity.

The ten cans of spray paint, as bragged about by Mr. Mansour, are there, and Peoria grabs one, jumps back over the sleeping bodies, and heads back out to the pool.

Over the past five months, the pool at the Hamra Hotel has become the central meeting place for American and British journalists, and the home of *The Magazine*'s bureau. A.E. Peoria helped set up the bureau on the third floor, a deluxe suite, converted into a place of business, with a kitchen, desks, phone lines, running water, rent of three grand a week, and bad room service. Mr. Al Mansour was making up for lost profits after thirteen years of those same sanctions that kept the country spray paint–free.

It is A.E. Peoria's last night in Baghdad. A drive across the desert to Amman the next morning, then a flight to Bangkok, and he is letting loose. What a five months it has been. A real learning experience.

He barrels out onto the patio, poolside. He starts shaking the can. The party is in full swing.

There is a tray of kebabs, a feast of hummus and chopped cucumbers and eggplants and tomatoes, there is a platter of grilled fish, *masgouf*, the Iraqi delicacy. He sees his translator, Ahmed, grabbing a plate.

"Ahmed, my haji, come here, man, I'm leaving tomorrow, we need to talk before I go."

He grabs Ahmed by the shoulder and guides him over to a white suntanning chair under the glow of a tiki torch. Ahmed sits down, and so does Peoria.

"Have you tried the *masgouf*," Ahmed says.

"You know, I have to say, Ahmed, there's a fucking reason you don't see Iraqi restaurants anywhere, you know what I mean? Thai restaurants, Lebanese, even fucking Tibetan, Indian, Nepalese, every kind of cuisine in the world is in almost every big city, there's all these kinds of restaurants, you know? But there's not any Iraqi restaurants anywhere. I think that says something, man. You can't blame that shit on the sanctions. How many times can you have fucking boiled and grilled chicken and fucking cubes of cucumbers and tomatoes before it's like, shit, enough, let's get some flavor. . . ."

"The *masgouf* is our national dish," Ahmed says. "Saddam's favorite . . ."

"Would you think I would eat a fish caught in that fucking river? A fish from the Euphrates?"

"The Tigris."

"It is the Tigris, man. I have to thank you for correcting me, because without you I wouldn't know shit about this country. There's a new regulation that Americans aren't even allowed to swim in that river."

"It is not a problem."

"No, it is a problem. Don't give me that 'It's not a problem' shit. I'm leaving tomorrow, Ahmed, I'm leaving tomorrow and I need to know what you really think. We can drop the 'I'm your boss, thing,' you know we're friends. You've told me everything, bro, every fucking thing. Can you believe it, I didn't even know what a Sunni or Shia was—or I guess I did know it because, you know, I'd done the reading—but not what it really meant, you know? Like a fucking Catholic versus a Protestant a few hundred years ago, or maybe ten years ago if you're talking Northern Ireland."

"I don't even think your president knew the difference," says Ahmed.

"Isn't that the problem," says Peoria. "Look what's happening. You can't feel good about it, can you?"

"Feel good?"

Peoria knows that Ahmed doesn't feel good about it, because Peoria doesn't feel good about it, and Peoria is partially relying on Ahmed to get that feeling. Ahmed's unease is understandable: he was a translator in Saddam's Ministry of Information. He is a Sunni, from a prominent Sunni tribe, the Dulaimi. One of the other correspondents at *The Magazine* first met Ahmed while he was an official minder on the journalist's visit during Saddam's regime. He'd been assigned, up until the bombing, to keep watch on the journalists, and translate. After the bombs started, the journalist told Ahmed he could have a job working for *The Magazine*, now that his old job had been wiped out by the war.

Peoria doesn't feel good about the war because he feels fear all the time now. After he'd spent the night in the desert, darkness started to creep into his mind. A real darkness, because for the first time in his life, he'd actually experienced a trauma. A bona fide trauma. A life-or-death trauma, not the garden-variety American trauma of parents getting divorced, or deciding what graduate program to apply to, or as in his case, the more unique but still peculiarly American trauma of having two gay parents coming out.

Over the past five months, when self-assessing his own life and how that life shaped the person he was, those two events—what happened in the desert and his parents' homosexual revelations and divorce—were the two events that explained how he felt about the world, how he saw the world, what the world meant to him. Things weren't permanent, things could always fall apart, never get too comfortable, and even those you trust, those you trust as authority figures and role models, are liable to show themselves as illusions.

Yes, those two traumas were the first stories, right off the bat, he'd be sure to tell a shrink or a therapist or a psychologist when he got home. He had much experience with mental health professionals—a long list of them, his parents believed in therapy—and he'd always started with the divorce and the coming out to explain how, exactly, he had become the gnomish ambitious person sitting on the chair beside the expert and talking as the hour passed.

Now he had another trauma to add.

The desert, in his personal narrative, had radically altered his life. And though normally, as his compulsive disclosure disorder would dictate, he would spend the time talking about the trauma, ad nauseam, to whoever happened to be in his vicinity, he realized that this was a peculiar trauma in that he was very scared to talk about it. That was what was so unusual: the fear to bring it up. Unprecedented.

He had started to feel a great shame, an introspective sort of shame that he thought he'd dealt with. How long did it take him to get over the shame of, as he once heard a less than politically correct guidance counselor put it, "having two homos" as mom and dad? At least until he was twenty-three or twenty-two maybe twenty-four. But he still would talk about it! And what solid ground or semisolid emotional ground he felt he was on after talking about it. In his narrative, he was sure the gay divorce would always be the pantheon of trauma, the starting point of his life—if I survived that, I can survive anything, he would tell himself.

And then he actually—literally, with the reality of dirt—survived a night in the desert, an attack, an ambush. Seven Americans killed, he escaped. But how he processed this—how he processed this had made him pick away at the other scabs in his mind. So he felt shame (like the divorce), and he felt, on some profound level, that it was all his fault, like the divorce.

His CDD, usually, would handle this by just talking about what had happened—but he'd never felt so afraid of talking about anything else, so he didn't want to say a word about it anymore, but in every conversation, he found himself talking about it, again and again, getting more afraid each time he told his story, and he couldn't stop.

The desert—that's how he thought about what happened, as "the desert"—became the new prism upon which he reevaluated everything else that had happened in his life, and more specifically, everything that had happened since he had set foot in Baghdad. It had colored his views, it had made everything dark, and it had started to really frustrate him that not everyone could see just how dark things were, no matter how much he talked.

Peoria then did what he had always done: he threw himself into his work. He focused on the work.

Peoria had arrived in Baghdad with the convoy that rescued him and immediately disembedded from the unit and made his way to the Hamra. His story had made quite a splash—which brought attention to Peoria, an attention that he had once thought he craved but now wondered if it was such a good thing after all. He would be introduced, and the journalist would likely say, "Oh, you are the one who saved that soldier." Peoria would then have to explain that it was an editorial mistake. That no, he hadn't saved anyone, that he didn't have approval over the headline, that he was lucky to be alive and that he in fact was saved, not the other way around, that he had almost given up that night. But this didn't ease any of the suspicions. Journalists, Peoria knew, as a whole, were first and foremost suspicious of each other—especially if it was another's perceived successes, and especially if they had been writing about themselves; it was seen as cheating. Never write about your own problems, write only about the problems of others.

But Peoria started working, setting up the bureau, going out on the streets every day, looking for stories with Ahmed at his side.

Peoria had never experienced a city that had no rule of law. Rule of law had been a vague concept to him, something he didn't think too much about: parking tickets, speeding tickets, open-container laws. Even in Third World countries, where rule of law didn't necessarily live up to legal ideals, there at least were some laws at work, even if they weren't enshrined in a document that the brown-faced citizenry probably couldn't even read, or the white-faced citizenry didn't bother to read and just took for granted.

You could make sense out of corruption to the point where corruption started to make more sense than following the rules of the non-corrupt—why not take a bribe, after all? Playing by the rules means not playing by the rules. But you expected people to stop at traffic signs, or not to, or to drive on the correct side of the road, or not to, or to not just shoot you in the face because you're there, or to shoot you in the face because you're there. Other places had at least been predictably chaotic.

No consistency, though, was the problem in Baghdad, no way to guess the right patterns.

Over the past five months, he could actually feel the rule of law erode, the society's protective membrane disintegrating under the onslaught of a series of complex diseases. The attack on the immune system had sounds and smells to go with it. Symptoms.

In the first week, there was a light ringing in the ears, as if the whole city were on the verge of a stroke. As if the people of Baghdad woke up each day and tried to shake off a blood clot forming in the brain. All around the city, his inner ear would ring with too much blood and his nostrils would pick up an unidentifiable smell that might as well have been burnt toast, the telltale sign of a stroke. (Though not toast in Baghdad: What was the smell? Oil? Gunpowder? Trash? Flaming sewage?) And even walking in a straight line he would feel dizzy, as if he'd been turning around in circles, head spazzing to the right and left, trying to figure out exactly what was happening.

And like a stroke victim who tried to put his condition into words, he felt tongue-tied and slack-jawed and mildly retarded trying to explain what was happening, groans and grunts, indecipherable— "Fucked-up, this is fucked-up"—and this inability to string words together was reflected in his reporting among the general population, quotes from Iraqis that didn't get past three or four words, strung together, and jotted down with his handwriting that resembled a palsy case.

By week two, the medical condition shifted from signs of a stroke to a hypomanic episode. The ringing was still there, but now every-one had too much to say—the Iraqis couldn't tell him everything fast enough, especially those who spoke English, and notebooks filled up, three a day, filled with long passages and monologues. The smells floated in the air, but a man in the throes of mania finds joy even in the scent of wafting dog shit and bitter unchlorinated feces.

He inhaled the smells, absorbed them in his pores along with everyone else in the city, and it didn't seem to matter that the toast was still burning and the city was on fire; hysteria made all of it irrel-evant. And, as is true for a small percentage of manic cases, some Iraqis and American soldiers and Western mercenaries turned to vio-lence: rioting, looting, checkpoint killings, criminal acts, rape, and it didn't matter what you were stealing or killing—throwing a ripped mattress on the back of a truck was as good as smashing a priceless vase, ripping off a flat tire the equal of a brick of gold, a book to a crate of milk and cheese, a schoolteacher in a car to a terrorist with a rocket-propelled grenade, an ugly woman to a beautiful teenage starlet—no it didn't matter, as mental illness can give everything perceived the same exaggerated value, worth and worthless indistinguishable. It wasn't about value: it was about letting the mania take hold, allowing the mania to equalize all things considered, with the only solution for the hysteria to wind itself down, exhaustion the only cure.

Following the mania there was a depressive crash. With it came deep and profound questions that had no answers, or answers that could never satisfy. After two months of insomnia, months of only blackout sleep, and not wanting to get out of bed—just a rest, just a timeout from life is what everyone seemed to need. No timeout was coming. Such difficult questions in the morning, in the afternoon, at night. What is going on in life? What's the meaning of all this? Is there someone who can tell me?

And Peoria bopped around the city streets, windows of the car rolled down, no traffic laws still, asking these questions—asking these questions, he thought, on behalf of the Iraqi people and the American people. And the answers he was getting—what were the answers? Uncle Fadil says the answer is that freedom is here, thank you George Bush, goddamn Saddam. Another, when Peoria ran into a funeral procession, answers: What have you done to my family, my life—is this what freedom means, does freedom mean the death of my family? And the Americans, most of the Americans, they had answers, the least satisfying of them all—answers that hinted at such a lack of answers that the only possible response was to hope they were right. They could give you answers, yes, very good at providing answers—the answer is, everything is going great, democracy is going to be established, the rule of law and the new Iraqi government shall be here. Yes, the Americans were sure confident they had the right diagnosis, the right meds, the right brand of therapy and treatment—this is a traumatized country! Thirty years of brutal repression—how do you expect them to behave? Of course there is anger and violence, this is normal, this is expected, but within six months, they'll be on their feet, and we'll all be home by Christmas.

"Do you think," Ahmed says to Peoria, "your country will be home by your Christmas, as your general says?"

"I'm going to be home by Christmas," says Peoria. "Thanksgiving too."

"I've seen movies of your Christmas and Thanksgiving."

"Yeah, there are some good movies about them."

Yes, the American general in charge of American Forces in Iraq said this: we should have the bulk of Americans home by Christmas, and this was reported, and Peoria knew this wasn't an unusual comment for a general to make. Home by Christmas had been promised before. Pope Gregory VIII, setting off the Third Crusade in the twelfth century, issued a papal bull exhorting his allies to war. The bull promised that after a journey to retake Jerusalem, your men will be able to return in two years' time to celebrate the birth of Christ on our land, which will be made so much sweeter, so much sweeter knowing that we have retaken the holy city of Jerusalem and restored its rightful place. Longer travel times, in those days, of course, but getting everyone home for the holidays was a major concern—a concern that Napoleon ignored to his everlasting historical shame when he decided to invade Russia, and when one of his sultry little French advisers said, "Emperor, we might get stuck in the Russian winter, the mud, the cold—why don't we bring clothes for the winter?" And Napoleon didn't believe him. When winter comes, Napoleon wrote, our soldiers will be celebrating Noel in Paris—*Joyeux Noël pour toute la France!*—or the anterooms of Saint Petersburg. In World War I, the Brits promised the war would be done soon enough. Hitler expected a comfortable O Tannenbaum as well. In Korea, after MacArthur turned the tide, just to push the Chinese back over the Yalu River, word was that we'd be out of there by the New Year. In Vietnam, Lyndon Johnson, on tape, after making a massive bowel movement, grunted that he wanted to make sure Robert McNamara understood that no tour of duty should span two Christmases—we can't have them missing two holiday seasons, bad for morale.

The promise of Christmas was given, and it was a promise that the Americans believed, at least temporarily, that they could keep.

Peoria gets up, grabs a chair and drags it along the patio.

"Sit, Ahmed, sit," he says.

Ahmed sits.

"What do you think of this spray paint? Look at this, the stars, the tiki torch, the hummus—you and me? What is it? What do you think it is?"

"Peoria, I remember the day your country was attacked on the September the eleventh. I cheered."

Ahmed laughs, Peoria laughs.

"But I would not have cheered if I knew you would come here. You don't understand these people, these Shiites," Ahmed says. "They are no good, they are Muppets of Iran."

"Puppets?"

"Yes, Muppets of Iran. Saddam knew this. They are worse than the Kurds. We Sunnis, we are better well educated, you see," Ahmed says. "We respected the Shiites, we understood them, we knew they were not well educated. The engineers, the doctors, the lawyers, they are Sunni, not Shiite. But these Shiites, these Muqtada Al-Sadr and the Abdul Aziz and all of them, are not well educated. That is why we did not let them rule Iraq."

"Right, right," Peoria says.

"You see this now, in the government—sixty-five percent of the seats to the Shia? This is another Iranian lie—you Americans say Sunnis are thirty percent?"

"Twenty-four percent."

"Lies, this is not true. Sunnis are the majority and have always been here—how else do you think we have led Iraq?"

"Right, right."

"This is very dangerous, you see," Ahmed says. "Think of the niggers."

"You can't say that word, dude. You have to say 'blacks.'"

"Really? Why not? I have seen it in the *Police Academic* movie."

"Yeah, they can say it in *Police Academy*, but you and I can't say it, you know?"

"Okay. Think of the blacks slaves when your Lincoln let them out of their caves. He did not make them president! He did not make them secretary of defense! He did not put slaves to run your army! Because they still did not have the education. This is like the Shiite."

"I don't know, dude. That sounds like a bit of a stretch."

"You want another example? South Africa! Before the war, I worked with a white man from South Africa, a journalist, and he agreed with me. He said, 'When our government changed, we did not just give all the jobs to the blacks—they needed time, they were not educated, they were not ready.' And he says to me, 'If there is democracy here, if the Americans do come, I agree, you can't just give all of the country to the Shiite. They are not the engineers!'"

The Iraqis, Peoria knew, held engineers in very high esteem. Engineer, a sign of great respect and prestige. He'd never met a people who were so keen on engineering degrees. More engineers per capita than anywhere else, if the Iraqis were to be believed, and really, there wasn't much to show for it—shit still looked like it was falling apart, everywhere, and he didn't think the bombs changed all that much.

Click, click, click, Peoria is shaking the spray paint can with one hand, drinking a beer with the other.

"I need another drink," he says, and leaves Ahmed in his patio chair, and heads over to the bar, three wine buckets filled with ice, half-empty cans of Diet Coke, Arabic lettering and with the European openers—which don't just click and pop, like the American cans do, but peel back, leaving what Peoria thinks is a dangerous metal edge. You could easily cut your lip on the foreign Diet Coke. There are two shot glasses and a bottle of tequila.

"Is this Turkish tequila?"

"Fuck yeah," somebody shouts.

Peoria pours two shots for himself, takes the two shots, gulps them, down, done, finished, refreshing. He keeps shaking the spray paint can, turning it upside down and right side up, the noise like a sprinkler system, upper torso rotating, falling a bit back on his heels.

He sees Christine, a girl he would classify as top tier. Christine works for Sky News and has a British accent. She is blonde and large-breasted and she's right now stripping off her polo shirt to put on a T-shirt that another enterprising soul has made, a T-shirt that says BAGHDAD HOT.

Peoria walks up to Christine.

"Baghdad Hot."

"Peooorrrrriiiiaaaaa, my hero," she says, and tosses him her polo shirt. "Do you think this fits?"

Peoria takes a step back, his foot resting on the filter for the pool, and grabs the silver tube railing on the pool steps for balance.

Christine's breasts, as Peoria has already noticed, are large. The cotton T-shirt stretches around them.

"Headlights," Peoria says.

"Headlights?"

She looks down.

"You mean my nipples," she says.

"Who made that T-shirt?"

"Crazy Dave the German," she says. Crazy Dave, a German, had driven an RV from Germany to Iraq, crossing at the border point in northern Iraq, and set up his RV like a trailer at a parking lot across the street from the U.S. embassy. He had a line of T-shirts—"Stay Classy Iraq," "I've Been Fucked in Baghdad," "Stuck Between Iraq and a Hard Cock," "Major League Infidel," "I ♥ Sunnis," and other sexually suggestive and culturally charged lines—creating his own little logo of a female by the name of Baghdad Betty. The term "Baghdad Hot" became popular about month four, when the first significant group of female contractors, soldiers, and NGO workers started to show up. If the normal scale for attractiveness in the real world was, say, one to ten, the term "Baghdad hot" meant an additional two or three or four bonus points were added, thanks to the sheer dilemma of the male-to-female ratio. A girl who was, say, a four or a five or maybe a six in Kansas or New York or wherever would become a seven or an eight or a nine in Baghdad. "Do you think I'm Baghdad hot?" Christine says.

"Yeah, I think you're top tier wherever. Didn't you go to fucking Yale?"

Instead of answering, Christine dives into the pool. The shallow end.

She skims the top and pops up.

The splash draws the attention of the other partygoers, thirty or so of them now, all watching Christine break the surface and pull back her hair.

Peoria, with his years of being trained in the art of American safety—always wear a helmet, always wash your hands, always look both ways before crossing the street, always wear a mouthpiece, even in soccer—realizes it is very dangerous, the pool.

The shallow end is five feet deep, the deep end, ten feet deep, but the way the lights bounce off the pool, in the darkness of the tiki torches and the heavy shades of booze, presents an optical illusion of the same depth.

He cringes.

The signs around the pond in New Hampshire that he visited as a kid, the stick figure with a slash through the chest, the long list of rules at the country club. (1) No running. (2) No diving. The statistics he had memorized after reading the story of a local boy in the eerie dive-accident-prone summer of 1986, a total of 757 diving incidents in New York, Massachusetts, New Hampshire, and Connecticut, two or three fatal, the others causing lifelong spinal cord injuries.

These warnings, he knows, are part of his culture, and that culture grabs hold of him.

Holding the spray paint, he steps up to where the water laps against the filter, and he stares at the concrete, water from the pool gathering in small rivulets.

He thinks of two words

NO DIVING.

There is no "No Diving" sign, no warning!

Christine swimming, the crowd getting noisier, louder.

Peoria bends over, arm outstretched, the spray paint can good and shaken.

He starts spraying, in large, yellow, sloppy letters: NO DIVING.

The next few hours: black, image, black, black, image—a face.

The face of Brennan Toddly.

A conversation—no, an altercation.

"I think," says Brennan Toddly, sitting next to Christine, Peoria sitting next to her poolside, "that what you did was disrespectful."

"Christine jumping in?" Peoria says.

"No, you. Your spray-painting. That was a sign of disrespect."

Peoria, yelling, now five months or seven months of what—of anger, of disillusionment, and thinking about the dead Americans and Chipotle without a dick and how cold he was that night in the desert and thinking of those slaughtered goats and donkeys and Iraqis he'd seen on the side of the road on the way into Baghdad, the piles of man shit in the terminals at the newly liberated international airport—is screaming: "Aren't we a little late for that, Brennan, disrespect? You're the motherfucker who said this was going to be a great idea, you're the motherfucker who advocated bombing a city and occupying a country and killing all sorts of fucking people, and you think I'm the one who is being disrespectful? I read your shit, man!"

A salsa bowl spills, a table gets turned over, crashing drinks.

"And why are you talking to her, aren't you married?"

Black, black.

In the bed. Christine without her shirt. Peoria apologizing for some reason.

The next morning.

Peoria dragging a duffel bag into the tight elevator, inhaling a sick breath of Turkish tequila, green and gilled-up and unshaven—*ding*, the elevator door opens—and through the glass doors to the pool.

There are beer bottles and plastic cups filled with cigarettes and spray paint everywhere: no running by the pool, no smoking by the pool, no minors not accompanied by an adult. A whole list of rules now spray-painted around the Hamra pool: no invasions by the pool, no English by the pool, no naked tits by the pool, no pornography by the pool, no Christians by the pool, no Muslims by the pool, the Jews run the pool, no pools by the pool, no journalists by the pool without adult supervision.

How many rules had he written? Was it even him? Fuck! There were some rules in Arabic too, written by Ahmed—yes, he remembers handing Ahmed the spray paint at some point.

What a mistake.

Peoria's fear breaks through the tequila sweat, one fear undiluted, and coming through with clarity: I need to flee. I need to get out of here.

I need to get out of here right now.

Two SUVs are waiting for him in front of the hotel.

He throws the duffel bag in the back of one of the SUVs, a drive out in the early morning, echoes of minaret calls heard through the tinted windows, before the sun comes up and the depression sets in again.

The trip to the border will take about eight hours, and he knows he'll fall asleep by the time they reach Fallujah.

THE PLOT MUST ADVANCE AT A QUICKER PACE

That's fun. That's what it was like. I'll tell you how I know later.

I leave you with Peoria on his way to Bangkok.

The plot needs to advance back in New York.

Time capsule: George W. Bush lands on an aircraft carrier. "Mission Accomplished."

No one ever accuses America of being a nation of historians. Our impressions over the long run are formed by a few vivid pictures and a tagline.

Nixon and Watergate: "I'm Not a Crook." Bill Clinton: "I Did Not Have Sex with That Woman." Gerald Ford: Tripping. Jimmy Carter: Malaise, though he never actually said that word. Reagan: Tear Down That Wall. Morning in America. Kennedy in black-and-white: Ask not what. Kennedy in color: Back and to the left.

War happens and life goes back to normal for the headquarters staff.

Michael M. Hastings, me, now one year employed at *The Magazine*. My attention strays from the war after the first summer of the invasion.

Anyway, mission accomplished.

You might forget that at the time, people took that seriously.

18.

September to December 2003

W e've won the war, Hastings," Nishant tells me. "Now, how do
we win the peace?"

I take notes.

"Post-conflict situations. The Balkans, Japan, Germany—those three should do for now. How long did the occupation last? How much money was spent? How did we enable the local government? How did we get them up on their feet?"

I do my research and get the answers for Nishant. We had 465,000 Americans in Japan in 1945 for the occupation, which lasted till 1952. Germany, well, we had only half of that country to take care of—luckily, it turned out, the good half.

The Balkans are a different story—we didn't fight those wars; we just came in on the end to broker a peace agreement and use some tactical airstrikes. De-arming programs, weapons for bread.

I dig up all this information and write it up in about ten pages, single-spaced.

My point, and I try to stress this to Nishant, is that these historical examples don't really apply to Iraq. That Iraq, in a lot of ways, seems sort of unique, at least in American history. The closest example is

Vietnam, or the Philippines, and that isn't an example anyone wants to bring up.

Nishant uses lots of the numbers in the final piece and takes a quote or two from the experts I'd interviewed, but doesn't seem to appreciate my analysis.

At the time, though, it is popular to say that we did it for the Germans and the Japanese, we can do it for Iraq too.

The story runs in September, and I stop paying attention to the war.

The U.S. presidential election is under way, and I start to write stories for the magazine's website. It's the only place I can get my political stories published. To work for the printed domestic magazine, you have to be a political correspondent, and I'm not that—technically, my title is still part-time temporary researcher.

In October, I write a story about a candidate for president named Howard Dean. He has basically been ignored by the media, and so when his camp finds out that the magazine is going to do a story on him (even for the website), they jump. My angle is his celebrity connections: a bunch of left-wingers in Hollywood want to support him, and because they are more famous than the actual candidate, the website takes the story. I get to interview Rob Reiner, Alec Baldwin, Ed Norton, and Ben from Ben & Jerry's, the ice cream maker.

By the end of the month, it's clear Dean's candidacy is making an impact—he starts speaking out against the war in Iraq, and a lot of people, it turns out, are willing to listen. *The New Republic* puts him on the cover, and they quote my story from the magazine's website. Then, the political correspondents at the magazine realize they'd better get on this story, so they decide to put Howard Dean on the cover. Brand X, our main competitor, puts him on the cover the same week we do.

In December, months after Nishant runs his "How to Win the Peace" story, Sanders Berman calls me into his office, on the other side of the building.

"The Vietnam syndrome, Hastings," he says.

"Yes, Sanders?"

"Don't repeat what I'm going to tell you, but that story we ran—'How to Win the Peace'—that's classic Vietnam syndrome thinking. It's bet-hedging, Hastings—Patel is hedging his bets, already. That was the problem with Vietnam—everyone in the news business started hedging their bets at the first sign of trouble," he says.

"We have to give Rumsfeld the benefit of the doubt, we have to give the president the benefit of the doubt, we have to give our military the benefit of the doubt—a few months into this thing and already we're throwing them to the wolves."

"Yes, it seems like there is a souring," I say.

"So we haven't captured Saddam? Doesn't matter. These things take time. Capturing Saddam wouldn't make a real difference anyway, tactically, strategically, or psychologically speaking. Not a lick of difference. I spoke to Henry about this, and we agreed to do a story—'Don't Let Vietnam Happen to Us Again.'

"My story was supposed to be on the cover this week. But do you know who is going to be there instead? Howard Dean! Howard Dean, a governor from Vermont—Howard Dean, the so-called antiwar candidate. The second time we'll have put him on the cover. He's calling Iraq 'Vietnam,' and we're putting him on the cover and doing a profile of him! And how does the profile begin? It begins with him crying because he lost his brother in Vietnam. He doesn't have the distance to understand what Vietnam was about. To understand what war is about. He's just playing to people who don't get why we need to make the sacrifices. And my story, 'Don't Let Vietnam Happen to Us Again'? One page, I'm getting one page, while Dean is getting fifteen, with pictures. It's bad, it's bad news for me and our country, don't you think?

"Our problem with Vietnam was our high expectations. We can't expect our leaders, in a time of war, to meet these expectations. We need to respect them more than that. That's why Patel's story really is aggravating—just weeks after the invasion—"

"Months, I think," I say.

"And he's holding the bar so high? We beat Saddam, we beat a horrible, disgusting, despicable regime, and there are a few riots and we're supposed to start saying it might not have been the wisest move. No way," he says. "Let me tell you this: it's a quote from Winston Churchill. Churchill."

Sanders Berman stands up in his office, walks back and forth, and looks out the window over Central Park, a classic pose.

"He carried on his shoulders a horrible burden, a horrible burden—he's like Bush in that way, a war leader. I've always been fascinated by war leaders. What great decisions they have to make. The burden they carry, the price they pay. Don't go wobbly! Nineteen forty-one, mid-Atlantic, the two boats meet in the dark. Roosevelt's ship blew a horn thrice. The response from Churchill's vessel: a magnificent ray of light from a single lamp, held for fifteen seconds. Destroyers, medium-class, circled the two ships, keeping an eye out for German U-boats—perhaps the Nazis had cracked their code? Perhaps they knew that these two great leaders would be meeting at dusk, mist curling up from the ten-foot swells. Roosevelt, huddled over in his wheelchair, covered in a shawl knitted by Eleanor. Churchill, five drinks into the evening. Their aides stand off to the side, trying not to get seasick—neither Winston nor Franklin got seasick. Franklin, a sailor from his younger days, Winston, permanently drunk. Didn't really make a difference if the floor dipped to the right and left—a hard drinker is always prepared for the sea. . . ."

A knock on Sanders Berman's door.

I turn to see who it is, but even before I get halfway around, I can feel a presence, feline, predatory. Delray M. Milius's voice follows.

"Umm, Sanders, can I interrupt you for a moment?"

"Sure, Milius, what's the daisies?"

"Breaking news, Sanders," he says, smiling. "We captured Saddam."

Sanders leans back in his chair. A look of intensity, betraying his casual southernness, flashes to his eyes.

"Does Henry know?"

"Not yet, I don't think."

Sanders picks up the phone and dials Henry's extension.

"Henry, it's Sanders. We got Saddam."

Delray M. Milius moves up from the door, and with the contempt of a Prada clerk, seems to look down at me in my chair. I'm moving in on his turf.

"We have to bump Dean. This changes everything about the war. Tactically, strategically, philosophically. I can write it. We were about to fall into the Vietnam syndrome, you know? But now we've really won the war."

Howard Dean gets bumped. Sanders Berman gets to write his story—"How Saddam's Capture Changes Everything." Without a leader, the dead-enders will soon reach the dead end.

19.

A.E. Peoria Goes on Holiday

After the flight attendants tell you where the exits are and how the oxygen masks drop down, most airlines don't play videos about why it's bad to sleep with twelve- and thirteen-year-olds, thinks magazine journalist A.E. Peoria. But Thai Airways is a little different, due to its clientele, and sure enough, before takeoff from Dubai to Bangkok, there is a seven-minute public service video that reminds him of his destination.

A red curtain in a back alley opens, a naked leg on a bed, hookah smoke hovering, a seductive haze. The camera sneaks in, creeps into the bedroom, and there is this beautiful young girl lying on the bed, wide eyes, and instantly Peoria thinks, that girl is fucking hot. The director ruins the erotic moment by flashing *14 ans*, right there, a chyron at the bottom of the screen to trigger what Peoria guesses is supposed to be a response of shame or revulsion, or self-flagellation. The video does the same trick, again and again, showing these preteens made up to look like postteens in very seductive settings, high production values in the brothels creating a romantic sleaziness. *12 ans*, *15 ans*, *17 ans*, and in small writing at the bottom, there is a message, in French, about who paid for the video, the Thai and French tourism boards, with a grant from Interpol's anti-human-trafficking division.

It was stupid of them to let a Frenchman produce that kind of video—this is no moment for edginess. But if I was on my way to Thailand to sleep with fourteen-year-old girls, Peoria thinks, would this public service announcement stop me? Or was it just an FYI to the regular old sex tourists—for your information, be careful that you could accidentally sleep with a fourteen-year-old, even if you're aiming for eighteen? Or, if you wanted to pretend it was an accident, now you have no excuse, because you were warned that a lot of the girls on the street—over two hundred thousand of them in Thailand alone, according to a statistic at the end of the video—are selling themselves.

Seven hours later, after landing and checking into a hotel, Peoria remembers the video, rather uncomfortably. He is staring at what looks like a children's playroom, a romper room. He is looking through a Plexiglas window of the kind used at a supersize McDonald's or a Burger King to separate the toddlers' play area from the restaurant. There is a carpeted floor with no sharp edges. All it's missing are a trampoline and a container full of colored balls. The room has levels of large carpeted steps, with spaceship-like oval chairs and a half-dozen oversize fuzzy building blocks to sit on.

Sitting, sprawling, in positions from prim to proper to sultry, legs crossed or uncrossed, vectors of narrow panty lines, thirty-five young Thai women, peasant dark to Victorian pale, stare out at the darker room where Peoria sits, deciding.

Can they see me? Are they looking? Does it matter?

He had told himself, upon arrival, that he was going to resist. See the temples, walk the famous streets of Patpong, get a tuk-tuk ride and a cheap silk suit, maybe a massage. Research. At the most, he'd get a blow job. Then technically, he could say that, like great American leaders before him (never wanting to rule out future career options, such as one in the legislature), he had never had sex with a prostitute, per se, and technically, he wouldn't be lying. He didn't think the press corps would push him on this point—there wouldn't be specificity in the question, words like "blow job" or "hand job" or "happy ending" would not be used. "Sex act," perhaps. Have you ever had a sex act with a prostitute? A question to laugh off, not worth answering. In a scenario that was admittedly more realistic, he doubted that any girl he would date would ever dig that deeply on the subject. It was a perfectly natural question, he believes, for a girl to ask if he'd ever slept with a hooker. His denial then would be honest and pure and he wouldn't be lying—blow jobs didn't count.

If only it would have stopped at the blow job.

From a hash-and-booze daze, his eyes focus on a white pin with a red number that says 72 hanging off the chest of one of the Thai women.

He's made it this far in life, thirty-four years of putting up the boundaries, of never breaking his own rule. Now he finds himself (because he's never *gone* to these places, he's only found himself there) telling a man that he's chosen 72.

Over the intercom, piped into the playroom, the manager says 72.

"Handsome man, so handsome," 72 says.

She takes his hand and they get into an elevator, up two floors. They are greeted by a smaller Thai woman, a maid with darker skin and two towels.

"So handsome," the maid says, handing 72 a key.

The key is for door number 11, three down the hallway on the left. Peoria feels like he is in some kind of '80s health club, catching a smell similar to that of a newly opened container of blue racquetballs.

There is a Jacuzzi bathtub and a shower and a roll futon with clean sheets, raised two or three feet off the floor.

72 takes her clothes off and turns on the water in the bathtub.

Peoria takes his clothes off.

72 fiddles with the temperatures. She asks a few questions in English.

"You here for fun?" 72 asks.

"No, business," Peoria says.

"What job you do?"

"I'm a journalist, a reporter, a writer," he says, and he pretends to write in the air.

"A writer?"

"Yes, for a magazine," he says, pretending to open a magazine.

"Oh, magazine," she repeats.

"*Time* magazine," he says.

She points to the bath. He doesn't know what she's asking.

"Go in."

He steps in, and she unhooks the showerhead and starts to spray him down, scrubbing him with soap—she scrubs parts of his body that have never been scrubbed so clean since childhood; she starts scrubbing his testicles, she scrubs his ass. She puts her hand right up there with soap and his rectum tingles as she scrubs away at it. She starts to scrub herself, too, and whenever she touches her shaved vagina, she smiles and giggles and says, "Don't look, don't look."

She hands him a towel to dry off. He lies down on the futon. She straddles him and starts to rub his shoulders.

She reaches, with great dexterity, into a small plastic water-resistant cabinet, like the kind you get at the Container Store, or whatever the Bangkok equivalent would be. She pulls out a Durex Ultra Thin condom in a yellow wrapper. She starts to jerk his penis, and he becomes hard. She puts the condom in her mouth, and, with the same kind of dexterity, 72 slips her mouth onto his penis, unrolling the condom skillfully as she goes.

Peoria has thoughts of safe sex—if her saliva is on the condom, on the inside of the condom, would that contaminate it? Could he get HIV/AIDs from that?

He closes his eyes and remembers what his doctor friend told him the last time he got a blow job from a prostitute in Mexico. He called the doctor upon returning home and asked: Should I get tested?

"She use a condom to blow you?"

"No, she didn't."

"Did it look like she had any sores or anything on her mouth?"

"No, I don't think so."

"You're probably good on herpes. You didn't go down on her, did you?"

"No, of course not."

"The rate of HIV in Mexico," his friend said, looking up the information online at the CIA *World Factbook*, "is about one in three hundred fifty thousand. The at-risk populations are gay men and intravenous drug users. I'd consider prostitutes at risk too. No track marks?"

"No track marks."

"Okay. And you didn't have any cuts or anything on your dick, did you?"

"Fuck, I don't think so."

"Chafing?"

"A little chafing, but I think that came from later, after showering too much and watching porn in the hotel."

"Okay. Now, if you were having sex with her, and she was having a full-blown HIV outbreak—just vaginal sex—if you were having vaginal sex with her, the chance of you, a heterosexual male, getting HIV would only be at like five percent. That's if she was all-out HIVing it. And since you weren't the one giving the blow job, it's not like you're ingesting any semen or anything. Were you? You can be honest."

"No, dude. Fuck you."

"So you're probably good to go."

Now, as number 72 lowers herself down on his penis, he opens his eyes and grabs her waist to stop her. He runs the calculations in his head. Thailand, he'd read, had done a surprisingly good job protecting its citizens from HIV—you want to protect your natural resources—and the rate of infection of females was one in one hundred thousand.

"Wait, wait," he says.

72 stops, half submerged.

"Do you do drugs, needles," he says, tapping his inner arms along the veins.

"No way, man," she says. He can tell he's almost ruined the mood.

"And you're clean," he asks her.

"Very clean! We just took bath. You have very nice . . ."

She looks at his face, searching for a feature to compliment—whether the size of his dick or his nose or his smile.

"Hair on your eyes," she says, running her finger along his eyebrows.

"Eyebrows?"

"Very handsome eyebrows."

And she lowers herself the rest of the way and starts to bounce up and down, move around, and it feels pretty good, Peoria admits. He thinks of his girlfriend back home, and knowing that it has been three weeks since the last time he spoke to her and that he wondered if they were actually going out anymore, and that as the days go on, he keeps getting email messages that vary wildly in length, from two paragraphs to three thousand words, explaining all the reasons why he should break up with her: that she waited for him patiently even after he almost got killed, what a stress that was for her, and rather than go straight back to New York for his break, he decided to go to

Thailand for a month. To Thailand—and so he should now consider himself to be broken up with her, unless he has decided otherwise. And Peoria knows how to respond—he knows what he needs to write back to save the relationship with the girl he gave six orgasms to, but he doesn't want to say it, he doesn't want to say it.

And as he starts to fuck 72, or 72 starts to fuck him, he realizes it doesn't matter if he just blows his load now, or ten minutes from now, or forty-five minutes from now; there is no pressure to perform sexually, and if 72 judges him, she will judge silently, or at least in a language he doesn't understand, and at least pretend to be satisfied—her satisfaction comes from the baht, his from the orgasm. What liberty! So he doesn't wait to come. In fact, with health and safety reasons lingering in the back of his head, he wants to get it over with quickly.

"Ah ah aha . . ."

She pops up. His cum drips back down the condom, a gooey ring around his pubic hair.

She hands him a piece of tissue paper. He plucks the condom off his cock, handling it like a dirty diaper covered in seaweed, and jumps up, his penis withdrawn in its foreskin. He drops the dead condom in a wastebasket by the door.

72 grabs a pack of Marlboro Lights and hands him one.

They smoke in tandem.

"Where are you from?" she asks.

"New York, but I haven't been home in a while."

Should he tell her? Yes, he has to. As he starts to talk, he knows he can't blame it on the unmedicated CDD. Mentally ill or not, he would have talked. He sees why men open up to whores, why they feel the need to share the dark and deep secrets, to water the ego, to repeat, I am a man and paying for sex will not change that. The desire to open up, to talk, to puff himself up, as well as his accomplishments, is irresistible. Peoria's view on prostitutes until now has been only a matter of literature and the tabloids—he has always been surprised how call girls manage to get so much out of men, enough for $100,000 paydays. But he realizes now that they didn't even need to try to learn the secrets; the men would start divulging state secrets and professional gossip as naturally as they would orgasm and roll over—because the talk was part of the process, part of the sex act, as certain as a lake level rises after a storm.

"Baghdad, I've spent the last few months in Baghdad," he says.

She doesn't understand.

"Iraq, you know, the war."

She looks at him, smiling.

"No, no, the war, you know? Boom, boom, pop-pop, pop, shooting, fighting, you know, the war?"

72's face becomes very serious.

"Oh no, the war. It is bad?"

"Very bad, very bad. I was almost killed, you know—"

He's never said those words—he'd written them when the first erroneous magazine piece was published, but he had never said it like that, with such bluntness, which was so unlike him, to have gone months without saying something like that, something so obvious and self-absorbed and to the point. *I almost was killed, you know.* He has an audience, an audience that has no agenda, an audience that could just sit there and listen, and just get the emotion of it. He doesn't care if she misses the details. The details don't matter. It's the emotion of it, the fear of it, the goddamn danger of it, that's what she can understand and that's what he wants her to understand.

"The war in Iraq is very bad," he says.

"You fight?"

"No, I don't fight. I'm a writer, a writer," he says, writing in the air. "I was there during the morning of the invasion, and then . . ."

So number 72 is Peoria's number one. After one come two, three, four, five, six, seven, eight . . . Like pills, like shots, like hands of blackjack and lines of cocaine and potato chips and cheese fries.

And what number would be next? How many days has he been here, how much baht spent, how many girls? He tries all the girls, two girls at a time, upping it to three girls. The numbers keep piling up, and he thinks, Do I count whores when I count the number of women I've slept with? Do they count toward my number? Is it demeaning to them, antifeminist, not to count them as part of my total number of sexual partners? The girls: he touches and pokes and prods them because he can, because he's paid, and they giggle or scowl or blank out or look at him with suspicion. He mostly overcomes his health concerns after number three—he even makes his way back to find 72 and really fucks her, flips her around, donkey punches, doggy style, reverse cowgirl suplexes, titty slapping, truly aimed ejaculates. To really try to make her moan—making a whore moan, he'd once read, being the true test of a man, but he doesn't even really believe in things like true tests of manhood, and he has to admit, it doesn't matter.

There are occasional complications in the transactions. He learns that whores have feelings too. Who would have thought or known that these girls had feelings? That they are people in their own right, their soft skin a membrane holding blood and organs and brain and keeping the universe outside. He encounters these feelings with a thin nineteen-year-old girl who, after the ritual bathing, starts to blow him and swing her pussy around to his face, to the numeraled position, and though it looks clean and tempting to lick, he doesn't stick his tongue out. He doesn't plunge in. A few seconds pass, then fifteen seconds, and the thin nineteen-year-old takes her mouth off his cock and glances over her shoulder, a stern, confused look, and says, "You don't want me?" No, he did want her. But did she not know that he couldn't just lick her where she had snuggled hundreds, if not thousands, of cocks? He can stick his in there, sure, with the Durex for protection, but his mouth? He still has his boundaries. She is pissed. She feels rejected, he knows, and though he fucks her quickly, she isn't into it. He wants to get out of there—it's uncomfortable for him. He doesn't get the chance for conversation—they just walk out of the 250-baht-a-half-hour hotel room in Nana Plaza, and part in the night.

Jilted. He didn't get his part of the transaction, the talk. He didn't get the chance to explain how very important and special he was, how very dangerous his job was, what it means, what his emotional state means to him and them after spending all those months running around the streets with Ahmed, and after each dead condom, each encounter, he would say, "I am a writer, I am from Baghdad, it is a war there, it's now raining car bombs, don't you see it's raining car bombs? *Time* magazine!"

He has spoken only to whores and concierges and maids for two weeks now. Conversations, one-sided as was his way, but conversations with people there to serve him. Should he feel bad about that?

20.

The Frenchman and A.E. Peoria's Last Night in Bangkok

A.E. Peoria steps into the lobby of the Bangkok Mandarin Oriental. It is lit up and white and marble with hundreds of dollars' worth of white flowers arranged in vases and the soothing light tones of Orientalish music playing: *pong dong ping*. Through the glass windows at the back of the lobby are the hotel's two pools: one pool, still water, with cabins, shallow, private, more for lounging; and the other pool, for more active swimmers. Even at one a.m., there is a fleet of Thais to greet him as he comes in. Bowing and saying hello as he steps through the first doors, bowing and saying hello as he rounds the corner to wave at the check-in desk, bowing and saying hello as he gets to the entrance to the bar, and, finally, as he takes a seat at the bar, the waitress and bartender both bow and say hello.

At this bar, Peoria thinks, what history. The Oriental: the hotel of Graham Greene and Joseph Conrad and Somerset Maugham and James Michener. Did they, like me, partake in the city's number-one attraction, the girls? Or wasn't Maugham homosexual? The boys, then? Hard to know. Greene almost likely did, and had Peoria ever managed to get through volume 2 of his 3,400-page, three-volume autobiography, he'd probably have found the passage about Greene's slipping out in the middle of the night to congenially and guiltily cheat on his wife, who refused him a divorce. It is a city of blue-movie possibilities. Conrad, the failed suicide, multitongued linguist, waited—in this very bar, or a version of this bar—for his first commission to captain a vessel. Maugham rode out a nasty bout of malaria in a guest room, near dying. And apparently James Michener, whose books Peoria had never read but had seen on the shelves of his grandmother's home, in paperback, made a reputation there, too. Such a list of greats who'd stayed and slept and suffered from various tropical maladies and more typical Western guilt on the floors above him!

Would that ever be me, Peoria wonders. Or am I going to be left with that one book, that *Desperation Points West*, and that one story: the night I spent with a Mexican—nay, a Puerto Rican—who got his balls blown off.

What could he say about everything he'd done? Would the sum total of his life be conflict zones plus the peyote eaten in New Mexico plus the rim job from three nineteen-year-olds two days ago? All of it had been research. But to what end?

He had pursued the life of a great writer because he wanted to be a great writer. Isn't this what they did? Screw whores and get shot at and ingest large quantities of booze and drugs? Isn't the Oriental—this very bar—proof? These were not lightweights: the Greenes, the Maughams, and the Conrads. These were greats, men of true literary heft. They had passed through here and left with the valued and vaunted experience needed to write. But what is the point of all of it, Peoria thinks, if all his material never comes out, if all of it just stays endlessly circling in his head?

His thoughts are pressing up against his own career irrelevance—he can feel himself slipping off the escalator, getting sucked back toward the emergency stop button, no longer on the fast track.

All he has to do is look at the lives of these writers and he will know.

He'd gotten into a very bad habit, a reading block. He tried to read the classics, but the classics had failed him. Or he had failed the classics. Invariably, he failed at the preface and the introduction, at the author's biography and timeline. The writing was secondary to the life—the facts and details of what they did and why, where they slept and who they slept with captured his interest. The very fact that he could be reading a book written decades ago held more power than the book itself. The words, the sentences, the language—his mind wouldn't last past page 10. And so he has great knowledge of the life without knowledge of the art; he can guess at the art, talk intelligently about it, but he will admit that he really hasn't gotten past Queequeg's hug of Ishmael—pretty fucking weird, that!—but he does know that Melville worked on a dock in Battery Street in Lower Manhattan, that he'd been penniless, that after *Moby-Dick* he had said he'd never write a novel again (the critics hated it, the critics killed him, the critics said he was a loser, a dope, a maniac, a fool); Peoria found that anecdote comforting after *Desperation Points West* received its cold shoulder. But he was sure that almost every author, if they had the chance, would embrace the Melville example as their own—they'll be sorry in twenty years when they discover that they missed a masterpiece, that it was sitting right under their noses all these years and they were too stupid and small-minded to see it!

Melville. *Typee*. The South Pacific. Melville had visited Siam— that's Thailand—for a fortnight. Three nights his vessel had pulled into the kingdom of Siam, en route to Australia. Those savages. According to his description of Bangkok, the city was steaming, low-lying, waterlogged.

Melville, his son's suicide. Melville and Mount Greylock. Melville dedicated *Moby-Dick* to Hawthorne—and at the book's hostile reception, did Melville wonder if Hawthorne was ashamed to have his name associated with it? Did Melville worry that he had embarrassed Hawthorne by putting his name on a book massively considered at the time a piece of shit? Yes, he is sure Melville had those doubts. The personal humiliation of a failed novel, three years of his life, vanquished in a few afternoons of critical thought set in type.

Conrad—who hated Melville's *Moby-Dick* and who missed Melville in Bangkok by less than a decade—surely nursed a depressed beer right here. Conrad's life gives him hope—he bucked the mold. He didn't write anything of genius until he was almost forty, older than Peoria. Greene was something of a prodigy, so fuck him. Maugham, again, the details are blurry, but all of this happened in this hotel. He could feel it, live it, kick it around, be initiated by it, be daunted by it, and think that the task of equaling . . .

A man next to him at the bar taps him on the shoulder.

"There is no pride," the Frenchman says, "on being the best-looking man in a whorehouse. This is a shame."

Peoria looks at him.

"Here."

The Frenchman pushes over a small glass of blue liquid, his fingers brushing the top with a strip of something that looks like sandpaper.

"I've seen you at the hotel before. Where's your wife?"

"She is upstairs right now, in rest."

The Frenchman is the same height, Peoria guesses, five-foot-seven, with thin brown hair combed over on the front of his skull and dropping back below his ears, his head a few years away from accepting baldness by his early fifties. The kind of haircut that the man had probably had since he was twelve or thirteen.

"Marcel," he says, making a gesture with his hand that isn't a shake, just putting it on the bar.

"Peoria," A.E. says.

"You are here for work?"

"Because of work," Peoria says.

"We will have a drink and then we will discuss," Marcel says.

Peoria downs the blue liquid, feeling a lime taste on his lips around the glass where Marcel had rubbed the strip of sandpaper.

"I have spiked your drink," he says. "But it is a good spike, no?"

"Tastes like lime," Peoria says.

"We have twenty minutes here before we will go on a walk," Marcel says.

"That's great, it's just great to be able to talk to someone who knows English so well. I haven't had a full English conversation in three weeks, you know, and I have to say that it gets lonely. You don't think it would, but it does get lonely traveling alone."

"Yes, I will comfort you."

Peoria nods, not listening, already revving up.

"I've been to Paris a couple times. I think it really is a beautiful city, and I've never really got the sense that they hate Americans there."

"We do," Marcel says.

"And it's like, well, the taxi drivers don't like it that you can't speak French, so they can be dicks, but I didn't think that anyone else was really, you know what I mean? But it's really nothing compared to when you're in a place where they really hate Americans, you know? It's such a relative scale now because you go to places and you're a target. People really want to kill you."

"And what places are those?"

"I'm talking right now about Baghdad, that's where I've been, fuck, since March, since the invasion there. I know you guys weren't happy with the invasion, and you know, shit, you're right, probably right, you know, the whole thing was such a fucking stupid debacle, but that's the way history goes I guess sometimes."

"*Ah, la guerre d'Irak.*"

"Yeah, yeah, the Iraq War."

Peoria launches into his story. The Humvees, the convoy, the boredom, the fear, and the massacre. Seven soldiers killed at one time, the worst incident of that day, and the only survivors were Chipotle and him, in the desert, holding a rag to Chipotle's groin. The Frenchman listens, shaking his head, looking at his watch.

"Do you know the Jewish author Elie Wiesel?" Marcel asks.

"Yeah, the Nazi hunter," Peoria says.

"No. But he tells of a story, in a novel. I do not recall the name, but it is fiction. The plot is about a man, the narrator, who has stepped in front of a car to kill himself. An attempt at suicide, yes. He had survived the Holocaust, our narrator. And we are in his coma, seeing his flashbacks. He is on a boat, crossing the Atlantic, and he is looking out over the railing of this boat. He is thinking deep thoughts, profoundly deep thoughts of why. Of why he is going to jump and sink. He longs for the sinking, for the feeling of the boat leaving him in its cruel wake. Another passenger on the boat sees our narrator, and says to him, 'Do not jump. Do not jump, *monsieur.*' '*Mon ami,*' our narrator says, 'you do not know my story, and if you did know my story, you would not be so quick to stop me.' The other passenger says, 'There can be no story that would make me say that. I can see in your eyes, in your pain, that you are a victim, and the victim's story should not end at the bottom of the sea.' So our narrator, he tells his story to the curious passenger, this would be the Good Samaritan. Of the camps, of seeing his mother and sister for the last time. Of living for three years with shit and death on his plate. All the time, of walking, on the last push, from Buchenwald to—and this is the twist—to Auschwitz. This is where our narrator ends up when he thinks he has gotten free and it is on this walk, this march. His father, still alive, takes sick in the cold and his father dies. Our narrator catches a fever as well, and somehow he finds a girl, a twelve-year-old girl, who takes his hand, who keeps him walking as the snowflakes fall. A Nazi officer approaches the girl. The Nazi grabs her by the arm and starts to pull her away from him. But the girl will not let go of our narrator's arm. She is crying hysterically, so the Nazi officer says okay, you can come too, and he brings both of them to a private room, a private house in the northeast corner of Auschwitz, almost a barn—you can visit this private house on tour, I have visited it myself. And in this private room, that is when the shooting starts. Our narrator can hear the shooting through the walls, and he understands that this officer was saving the girl because of this liquidation. The Allies are on the way, of course, the Allies are always on the way, but always too late, no? The Allies are rolling in, but that is still days later. And as our narrator hears this racket, this utter racket, this Nazi jazz jam of bullets and cocked triggers and grenades, wiping the grounds of Gypsies and Jews and Communists and undesirables—while our narrator is hearing this soundtrack, do you know what is in front of his eyes? He is seeing this Nazi pet the girl on her head to keep her calm. This Nazi is a man of strong sexual desires—he can get hard in the middle of a bloodbath. That is sexual potency. To get an erection inspired by liquidation. He starts to kiss the girl and take the girl's shirt off. If this was Nabokov describing this scene, he would talk about pale raisins on a plain pudding. He would write of the dry well that is more pure than a flooding and somewhat older spring. But our narrator is no Nabokov. He just sees the Nazi's pants drop, the SS eagle clinking on the floor, and the cot springs going up and down. The girl closes her eyes, and when the girl closes her eyes, our exhausted narrator, he closes his eyes too. Exhausted, no food, eighty pounds underweight. When he opens his eyes, it is the next day and the officer is gone. He looks around to see the girl and he does see her. She is on the bed, dead now, suffocated, or so it seems. By what? Blunt force trauma to the throat, we assume, though this detail is too horrible to make explicit. And the Nazi officer has left! He has left! Why did he not kill me, our narrator wonders, why did he not kill me then? Must he have thought I was already dead? Our narrator staggers out of the barn and all the Nazis have fled—back to their old cushy jobs in Wiesbaden and Frankfurt, to be sure!—and all the prisoners are all dead. The bodies, even these emaciated bodies have so much blood. He can't smell anything anymore and can't feel anything and so he collapses in the pile of cordwood flesh and is only woken up by an American fellow. A black man is tugging on his feet with a bandana over his face from the stench—they gave the Negros this cleanup duty; do your histories tell you that of this liberation?—the sick stench and his eyes open and our narrator is saved. Our narrator is saved. He says these words out loud. The passenger on the boat has listened, without interruption. The passenger would look seasick but anger is a cure for seasickness. Contempt cures seasickness. The Good Samaritan walks away, leaving the narrator alone, or so our narrator says. Our narrator knows why, why even the Good Samaritan is disgusted by such a story. Our narrator concludes: he was affronted by the very fact that the story was told to him."

"Wow," A.E. Peoria says.

"It has been twenty minutes. Let us walk. There is a place I'd like to show you."

A.E. Peoria and Marcel leave the hotel, and the mild hallucinogen laced with amphetamines is taking effect, the Oriental music *ding-dong*ing, sounding like the French song "Frère Jacques" to Peoria. Peoria thinks that's pretty hilarious, and they are both talking, fast, talking back and forth and over and under each other, and the blocks pass by like nothing. On Patpong Road there is a Thai teenager with baggy pants and a skateboarding decal on his shirt, handing out flyers, and Marcel approaches the Thai teenager and says they would like to see a show. A.E. Peoria says, Wait a minute, Marcel, the guidebook says never trust the touts, never go with a tout anywhere, and then they are walking up to a second-floor club. Never go up to the second floor of any club on Patpong. Marcel says that is the very reason he has chosen a tout and that he has gone up to the second floor: because the guidebook says no. You must not ever pretend the guidebook has wisdom, Marcel says.

They are sitting in the back corner and they are the only two men in this club and a horn blows when they walk in, and a woman walks out onstage and starts a performance; she takes a cigarette and smokes it with her pussy, she puts a straw in her pussy then puts a dart in, and from across the stage she shoots a green balloon and the balloon pops; she takes a Ping-Pong ball and pops it up, and then she does one that Peoria has never heard of before. Peoria is called to the stage, and there is a green bong with water at the bottom and a bowl filled with weed. The Thai woman sits on the bong and says, Light me, and he lights the bowl of the bong and the water starts bubbling up when her vagina begins to suction the marijuana in. This goes on for fifteen seconds, until the translucent bong is now filled with smoke, and the Thai woman stands up and quickly covers the bong to keep the smoke in. Then she takes her hand away and puts the bong to Peoria's mouth and he inhales the hit, takes it down, and he can feel it work inside his head and he falls backward. He can't see where Marcel went, but the girl who is onstage is now walking over to him. She has a collection jar and Peoria puts a few hundred baht in, but as he reaches in his pockets, he is swarmed by other Thai girls, and none of them are pretty; they are just female, they are the women who have been broken by selling themselves and are now in their late twenties and thirties and too old to make a good living doing straight-up sex, so they must debase themselves like this, taking vaginal bong hits and smoking Marlboros from their twats. He is getting clawed at and is nervous and he can't find any money—he knows the money is there but his hand in his pocket keeps going down and down like his arm is rubber and plastic and it could keep going through his pockets until it reaches the floor. He starts to yell, Get the fuck off me, feeling all the tentacles of five Thai girls, zombie squids with slanted eyes. They want his money, that's all they want.

Marcel and the tout come charging back to his rescue. Marcel starts slapping the girls and pushing them and kicking them like mangy dogs, screaming at them in French, *"Allons-y, allons-y."* The girls are recovering the baht notes on the floor and the tout and Marcel usher Peoria out of the second-floor club.

The street brings the hallucinations back to a manageable level.

"This is not the place that I wanted to bring you," Marcel says. "It is a few blocks more."

They start walking, this pair, and there is another neon sign that says "Farang Vilvage," which Peoria thinks is supposed to mean "village."

The word *farang* is familiar, he thinks: it means "foreigner." It is like those few Thai phrases he's learned—*soi dee kap*, thank you, or hello, one of those two, whatever one it is.

The girls inside are taller than those in the other massage parlors he's been in.

Marcel is handing over money, and then the host and a tall girl are grabbing Peoria by the arms and pushing him into another room. Water is spilling down over him now, and Marcel is in the same room with another girl. Marcel is giving Peoria a sign, the A-okay sign, and Peoria is surprised that despite the drug, he's got an erection. The girl goes down on him and starts to suck away.

It is the most amazing blow job he has ever experienced. It is something about the mouth, about the throat, about the grip of solid hands.

Marcel is laughing hysterically, and even the laugh sounds like "Frère Jacques."

"You see, you see how good this is?"

The tall girl then says to Peoria, you want to blow me now? And Peoria starts to laugh and doesn't understand, until she lifts up her skirt and there is a penis.

He remembers what that other Thai word means—ladyboy, ladyboy, ladyboy—and Peoria gets up and says no thanks.

Marcel, what have you done?

But he's not angry, because the spike is good, and Marcel says, okay, we will have them blow each other. They both sit back and watch the two ladyboys give each other blow jobs, for a good fifteen minutes, then Peoria says, I'm tired, man, I'm tired.

They are trying to wave down a tuk-tuk, and they get one. The man who steps out of the tuk-tuk is an Arab gentleman in a nice suit.

The Arab gentleman in the nice suit is not getting out of the way. He is engaged in a conversation with the tuk-tuk driver, an argument, scary tonal highs and lows.

Peoria feels an onrush of the psychedelic fear—the corners of all objects and shapes in his sights pop out, the carriage top of the tuk-tuk taking the neon colors from the signs and the puddles of dead rainwater in the streets and reflecting them back in lines and patterns that jump out at his retinas like a magical net capturing imaginary sea creatures, dancing on a slimy coral reef.

Accented English of the Arab and broken English of the tuk-tuk driver.

"My tip, my tip," says the tuk-tuk driver.

"Too long, too long," says the Arab. "In circles you've driven me."

"No, no," wails the tuk-tuk driver.

Marcel, stringy brown mane, bouncing, hunched energy of a five-foot-seven man, raises his left hand above his shoulder and, in a swooping pass with his crusty melanin-spotted and freckled paw, strikes the Arab gentleman on the face.

A bright flash on the slap's impact. A.E. Peoria knows that his pupils are well past dilated, both shallow and gaping shiny black holes, and it's as if he's watching a panel in a comic strip. Out of the corner of his eye he sees the bubble words ZAM WOW speed off quickly.

"Marcel, dude!"

The Arab gentleman, shocked, looks at Marcel, and now it is Arabic and French screaming.

"Allez-vous en!" and Marcel is shooing the Arab gentleman away from the tuk-tuk, kicking at his heels, arms now windmilling, light touches on the nice suit. Peoria hears a rumbling, a gurgling coming from Marcel's throat, as if he'd adjusted the treble dial on his own voice, and Peoria can hear the scratchy expectorate forming like angina crackling in a blood vessel, and the sound-expanding properties of the hallucinogen allow him to hear each molecule of the phlegm convalescing into a blob darkened by the red inner walls of Marcel's esophagus, up past the tonsils, and the image flashes through Peoria's mind as if he is standing right in front of the jaw and staring down the gullet of Marcel. The blob of spit and mucus flies out with a *whoot*. The Arab gentleman, arms raised in surrender, is backing away from the tuk-tuk when the loogie takes flight and lands solidly on his lapel.

Peoria grabs Marcel and dives into the back of the tuk-tuk, holding on to him. The tuk-tuk driver is laughing, and Peoria yells, Go, go, and the tuk-tuk driver starts off and speeds down the street. The Arab gentleman is running behind them, yelling and spitting and screaming, swatting the back of the tuk-tuk, its weak diesel engine accelerating to the speed of a man sprinting, and finally, to a nice twenty-two miles an hour, which leaves the Arab gentleman standing on the street corner, screaming obscenities foreign to Peoria's ear.

"To the Oriental," Marcel says, sitting up.

"Thank you, sir, *soi dee kap*," says the tuk-tuk driver. "The Arabs here are bad, very bad. They come for the Russian girls and they are very cheap. No money they give us. The girls say they smell."

"Yes, of course, my friend," Marcel says.

Regaining composure and seriousness, Marcel turns to Peoria in the back of the tuk-tuk.

"You are listening, Mr. Peoria, to what he is saying? We from the West, we say everyone is equal, that there are no differences or that the differences are a matter of ignorance. This is fantasy, this is fantasy. We have the Arabs in Paris and you must treat them like that—with spit and kicks. They talk of human rights, these Arabs, and this is the most disgusting of subjects. We are all human, *oui*, we are. But that is where it ends. The Arabs, you see, think they are better than the West, that is what they think, and like Nazis, they would enslave us all under their sultans and dashikis. They would treat us all like they treat their women, you understand this? This is how they treat other beings that threaten them, these Arabs. They treat them like slaves if they can get away with it. They come here and treat Mr. Tuk-Tuk as if he is a Pakistani servant cleaning the shit off the bowls of the Royal Palace in Riyadh. We are supposed to respect them for it? No, we cannot, we cannot respect them for it. Because we know that they are different—these are traits of humanity, and the Arab is still stupid, he is still stuck with the bedouins, with the nomads. He does not even understand how to use bombs and bullets—they say the Arab understands power only, but he does not even understand what power is today—he understands how to use the clubs, to club his goats and his women, to herd them, and his only power is making more of himself, his only power is fucking his women with their veils off so they produce more like him, they keep coming. Look, they cannot defeat the Jews, ten countries surrounding a speck and they cannot defeat the Jews because the Jews have learned the West's ways of the bombs and the bullets—the Jews invented them! The Jews have said, No we will not be clubbed like curs, like dogs from beyond the Pale, no, never again. So the Arabs have more children and more children and hope to overwhelm the bombs and bullets with offspring, and this offspring they will call democracy and human rights. Then they will win. And they will go and exterminate the Jews, if they could, with their democracy, they would exterminate them. The Jews know this—they are clever—and the Thais know this. Monsieur Tuk-Tuk, he knows this. Yet your dinner- and drinking-party friends in the West do not know it at all; they want to drown in their fantasy of the liberalism, they want to drown there."

Marcel pauses for breath, and as he inhales, Peoria, as if a tele-prompter were scrolling across Marcel's face, sees the words roll by: democracy, human rights, the West, liberalism, ballot box, Israel, free speech, habeas corpus, the United Nations.

"When your war in Iraq started, we in France, our politicians and our people said: No, you should not. It is stupid for you Americans. *L'invasion est une connerie*—it is bullshit. We know this of course had nothing to do with morality, the morality of your cause. We French know that this is not what our objections were truly about. It was about the Arabs. We know from Algiers that it is such a foolish game to try to change these minds. We know it is senseless, pointless, and so we offered a warning, and your politicians said, 'Who is France, on their high horse, with their memories of Vichy, to tell us what is moral? Who are the French, who did nothing while Sarajevo died! You have no high ground!' And your politicians were correct. We had no high ground; we only had practical advice disguised as morality, disguised as the international community. And this advice was ignored and now you will learn what we have learned: that there is nothing worthwhile, that it is all savage and torture and Islam." He spat. "Islam."

"Oh, you can't say that about just Islam, dude, all religions are fucked."

"Can I not, Mr. Peoria?"

"I mean, look at the Crusades, look at the Inquisition, look at Northern Ire—"

"The Crusades! The problem with the Crusades, Mr. Peoria, is that they did not go far enough—they were not successful! That was our chance to rid the world of this Islam, and our forefathers failed at it. Now, with information technology, with such good record keeping, with silly ideas of human rights, the time has passed when you can get away with such a thing."

"I don't know, this all sounds like, I mean everybody is violent. I'm a journalist and—"

"You need a fatwa!" Marcel screams.

"What?"

"You need a fatwa against you, you need a jihad against your name. You need for the ayatollahs and mullahs to condemn you. Then perhaps you will understand, then perhaps your career, which you worry so much about, will be saved," Marcel says.

"I think you have to be Muslim to get a fatwa," A.E. Peoria says. "But that would be pretty cool, I guess."

"Cool," Marcel says. "You Americans and your cool."

The tuk-tuk pulls into the arching brick drive of the Mandarin Oriental.

"Have you looked in your dressers by the bedside?" Marcel says. "There are now two books there at these five-star hotels that cater to all the rich international clients: there is the Christian Bible and there is also a Koran. I will show it to you in my room."

The hallucinations are wearing off, and Peoria is left with a general brightening of his vision, a false sense of energy running through his system, keeping him awake as the alcohol exits his bloodstream. He can feel the high coming down and he realizes he needs a drink.

"I need a drink," he says.

"Yes, in my room as well."

Inside the lobby, Marcel hits button 16, the top floor, and the soothing music makes Peoria more anxious.

The two men walk down the hall to room 1614, the corner room, and Marcel takes out a plastic swipe card, thinks about putting it in, then stops.

He knocks instead.

A five-foot-nine Thai man, in his early twenties, opens the door. Marcel and the Thai man stare at each other. A soft voice comes from inside the room.

"C'est toi, Marcel?"

"Oui," says Marcel, and he walks into the room, the Thai man stepping out of the way. Peoria follows him in, impressed with what a few hundred more dollars a night can get you at the Mandarin Oriental. The suite is two rooms, a living room with a stylish sofa that leads to an even larger master bedroom with a view of the river and the Peninsula Hotel across it. On the couch is a woman, late thirties, lying in a hotel-supplied bathrobe, untied, left breast open to view under the light of one of the two high-definition television sets— both sets are on, and both sets are airing pornography, which in its

repetitive casualness is somewhat disturbing to Peoria's now fragile mental state.

"You are standing there like a eunuch, but I know you are not," Marcel says to the Thai man. "Exit, you can leave now."

The Thai man pulls on a pair of jeans, bows, and slips out the door.

Marcel starts to hunt around the room, moving from one waste-basket to the other, before going into the bathroom.

"Aha!" he yells.

He jumps back into the living room, holding two spent condoms in his hand.

"This is all, two hours I am gone and the man has only filled up two of these? This is not our money's worth," Marcel says, throwing the condoms back into the wastebasket.

The woman, whom Marcel introduces as Valerie, sits up from her languorous film noir pose and looks at Peoria.

"You have arrived just in time. I was about to fall asleep," she says.

Marcel has disappeared inside the bathroom, keeping the door open but turning the water on in the shower, behind a plate-glass see-through stall. The steam starts to fill up the stall, and as Marcel gets naked and steps in the shower, Peoria loses sight of him.

Peoria goes to the minibar and takes out three small bottles and drinks them. He has reached a point of what might be called a moment of clarity—in the span of two hours he has had oral sex with a transvestite, taken a mild hallucinogen with an obvious non-mild amphetamine base, and broken up a shouting match on the street with an Arab. He is taking stock of the evening. It has been a clear case of one thing leading to another. Now he is in Marcel's hotel room and he doesn't quite know what to make of it all and is staring at a woman who he assumes is Marcel's wife. Marcel's wife, Valerie, has already thrown her bathrobe off, just a little bit more, and is massaging her pussy with a half-smile, seemingly enjoying watching the American's uncomfortableness.

It's all very French, Peoria thinks.

His response is instinctual—it's either fuck or flight, either slip out the door, following the Thai male prostitute, who, as the evidence in the wastebasket makes clear, had already made love (is that an appropriate expression here?) to Valerie at least twice, not really knowing what other sexual acts they might have engaged in.

Peoria, as a modern American male, had been exposed to these kinds of fantasies via the Internet from a very early age. Even before the speed of the Internet allowed users to download highly graphic pixel images and video clips of every debased act there was a market for, he'd been reading erotic stories on what was the most extensive erotic database of stories in English that he'd ever seen. It was quite a collection of stories, this particular website, and it opened his eyes to all manner of perversions by category: teen, bondage and sadomasochism, big beautiful white, groping, bisexual, lesbianism, glory holes, homosexuality, bestiality, pedophilia, gang bangs, orgies, rapes, violence, snuff, kidnappings, granny porn, MILFs (moms I'd like to fuck), GILFAs (grandmothers I'd like to fuck anally), celebrity fantasies, mind control, incest, interracial, Asian, swingers, nonconsensual, military, extra hair, no hair, smoke. In fact, with all of these stories in such a public and easily accessible venue and seemingly legal—words can say whatever words want to say—he had in his later years wondered if there were any taboos left that he hadn't seen or read about. He came up with a resounding no: other things, like vomit porn, water sports, scatological porn, fuzzies, plushies (where people like to have sex with stuffed animals or people dressed in animal costumes), had all, at various points, made their way into popular culture, usually in gross-out comedies, and he wasn't even getting into the hours of Japanese anime he'd watched, with cartoon demons and monsters from other dimensions manhandling and raping unsuspecting Japanese teenagers and children. By the time the Internet caught up to the videos, what he could now watch online didn't surprise him at all. He had examined, on occasion, the moral implications of this new industry—whether he was some kind of degenerate for consuming the product, and what the effects were on his sex life. Did they give him a false sense of what sex was? And after masturbating to what, if admitted publicly, would seem particularly heinous, he often felt like he'd just eaten a Big Mac and pre–trans fat fries in secret—instant gratification wasn't very good to the soul. But who believed in souls anymore anyway? Certainly, this trip to Bangkok would suggest a negative correlation with his sexual habits.

There was another category that he was drawn to that he would probably never admit to any of the women he dated. It was a subcategory of general male-on-female porn called "Fuck my wife," academically known as cuckolding. Cuckolding had been getting readers turned on and intrigued since Jesus' time—Joseph was cuckolded by God himself—and in more obvious ways over the next two thousand years, in *The Canterbury Tales*, throughout Shakespeare plays and other Elizabethan literature, and the like, the cuckold held particular fascination to readers. In the past decade of easily produced and distributed pornography, the cuckolding genre had taken a more explicit turn. If cuckolding was a subcategory of straight male-female sex, a subcategory of the subcategory was something called a cream pie.

It took a lot of work to be innocent, and Peoria didn't seem biologically inclined toward innocence.

"And so?" Valerie says.

Peoria readjusts his gauge of Valerie's age. Early forties. Under the high-definition glow of the 1080 pixels of Korean-manufactured

Samsung color, the Mandarin Oriental's courtesy bathrobe open to the hotel's air conditioner, he got a good look at her breasts. They sagged a bit under the weight of two decades' worth of topless sunbathing. Nude beaches in the Riviera, cigarette butts stubbed out in a pile of sand next to her beach towel. Without a bikini top, she had a body that American men would look at as they walked past on the shore, partially intrigued by the woman's attractiveness, partially by her comfort in exposing a pair of naked breasts. If she was so casual about allowing gazes to come her way, in view of running toddlers, German beer guts, Swedish Speedos, local teens hawking bottles of Coke and *croque-monsieurs*, one could only imagine what she would do behind closed doors; there was an openness to her sensuality, an openness that with a few bottles of wine might be persuaded to try anything.

Valerie slides her panties down, feet coming out carefully, sure of her balance. She hangs the panties on the tip of her finger. She motions, with that same finger, for Peoria to approach her, the panties swaying as if they were resting on a clothesline.

Peoria steps next to her. She pushes her panties to his face, her finger in his mouth. He starts to suck on her finger, mild saltiness.

Valerie touches his groin with her other hand and starts to rub his penis. He leans forward and kisses her, keeping her finger in his mouth, off to the side, like a hooked fish, lips making contact around the crumpled edges of the silk.

She takes her finger from his mouth and the panties stay in between their lips. He unbuttons his pants and unzips them and steps back and her panties fall to the floor. He pulls down his boxers and he can feel the crust from his own sperm, the stains of sexual moisture that the tissues in the brothels didn't wipe up. She kneels down and takes his penis in her mouth. Peoria closes his eyes and wishes that he will get hard, because there are a few seconds when he wonders if he has enough blood left in him to fill up.

He opens his eyes and Marcel is out of the shower, standing at the bathroom door, smiling.

Peoria feels a mild shock. His penis, which was becoming harder, becomes temporarily less so. How do I feel that he is watching me? Can I let go in this setting, this hotel room? It's not the intimate professionalism of a whorehouse, where if a friend was watching him get a blow job, it would seem okay, part of the atmosphere and ambience . . .

Valerie is squatting, mouth on his cock, with two hands free, she shakes off the Mandarin Oriental's courtesy bathrobe and places one hand back under her for balance, then with her other hand begins to finger herself.

"Look at me, look at me," she says.

Peoria looks down and her eyes are rolled back up staring at him. He moves his eyes from Valerie, at his knees, to Marcel, still standing in the shower door.

"Do not let him come yet," Marcel says, and goes into the other room, the bedroom.

Valerie gets up from her knees and takes Peoria's hand and leads him into the bedroom.

The bed is well used, the one-thousand-thread sheets pushed to the bottom of the king-size mattress, the decorative pillows tossed off on the bedside tables. It's a bed that has not been available for a turn-down service and a mint on the pillow in days.

Marcel is lying on his back, towel still on. He hangs his head down over the side of the bed, looking at the world upside down.

Valerie walks over to Marcel. The bed is four feet off the ground. She climbs onto the mattress and then puts one leg on one side of Marcel's head and her other leg outside of his shoulder, knees straddling his face. With her teeth, she undoes Marcel's towel and uncovers the Frenchman's erection. She turns around to look at Peoria.

"Doggy style, yes?"

Peoria moves up behind her and feels another hand on his cock, from below. Marcel opens Valerie's pussy for him and directs his cock in.

Peoria is not tall enough to be having standing-up sex while Valerie is on the bed and his feet are planted to the ground. He gets up on his tiptoes and holds on to her waist for balance.

He starts to move in and out of her, Valerie ducking her head down every fourth insertion to lick Marcel's cock, and Peoria can feel a kind of tingling on his alcohol-constricted testicles, the sandpaper of another tongue, and he remembers a line he'd read in a prison memoir, a mouth is a mouth and a tongue is a tongue, one brand of sandpaper the same as any other, and he lets himself go with the groans and the groans coming from Valerie's mouth ahead of him. He sees the digital clock that says 2:15 a.m. and he spaces out. He has a flight to catch tomorrow. Distracted, he slips out of her, and before he can get back in, he feels another mouth on his penis.

"I'm cleaning you off," says Marcel.

He can see Marcel, buried underneath her ass and pussy, in glimpses when she rises up off his face, and he can see Marcel's tongue flutter into her asshole and out of her asshole. She climbs off her husband and tells Peoria to join her on the bed.

She rolls to one side and Peoria moves in behind her. He starts fucking her ass quite hard, and he feels that he is going to come.

"Put it in my pussy, you want to put it in my pussy?"

Marcel is jerking off, lying next to them on the bed.

"My head is full of blood from being upside down," he says. "I am dizzy."

He holds Valerie's hand. What tenderness.

Peoria takes his cock out of her ass and finds her pussy.

There is an anticlimax before the climax because he has to ready himself again, to get to the point where he can come. He starts thinking even dirtier thoughts than what he is doing—he starts piling on the dirt, splashing the dirt in his head in scenarios that he plays out in his mind's eye, outrageous thoughts, more outrageous than fucking the wife while her husband jerks off and watches and holds her hand on the same hotel bed. He starts thinking: strange to have to imagine a fantasy when you have such a real-life fantasy right here. Odd, but he must focus if he wants to come. He focuses. He starts thinking: all the cocks that have ever been where he is fucking her now, and he sees them all, lined up in a row, Valerie, on a beach, on that beach in the Riviera, under a lifeguard chair—there are no lifeguard tents in the Mediterranean—no, he sees her between a sand dune and he imagines the line of men coming to take their turn with her, one after the other, stretching back into the waterfront restaurants, the jism dripping from her ass and her pussy and her mouth and her sunburned breasts, and then he comes . . .

Peoria falls over onto the bed. Valerie rolls to her back. Marcel gets to his knees, and starting at his wife's breasts, licks and caresses her body, moving toward her belly button, moving toward her pussy. Valerie puts her hand on his head and pushes lightly, her fingers tangled in her husband's thinning hair. Valerie puts her left hand on the top of her pussy, and in a move that Peoria has seen only on a computer monitor and television screen, she squeezes and a dollop of his sperm pops up.

Clams, seashells, mollusks, mussels, oysters. White discharge. Membranes and inverse epidermal layers. Pink jowls, a string of soy milk drool. A raw baked good, doughy, whipped egg-white batter uncooked.

Pushing himself up on his elbows, Peoria sees for the first time—in the dimming lights of the HDTV and the digital clock and the faint city lights cutting through the open drapes—what a cream pie looks like.

The sight is too organic and messy for him to find beauty in it. . . .

Peoria wakes up twelve hours later. He has a flight to catch.

PART V

Homecoming

21.

Morning, Monday, January 12, 2004

Unbundling, I sit down in my cubicle.

It's either the coldest January in New York on record, or I'm getting old. I've lived most of my life in the Northeast, and Manhattan is the farthest south I'd ever called home. But this is my fourth year in the city, and my tolerance for zero degrees Fahrenheit has disappeared. A coldness without the warm feelings of FAO Schwarz and Radio City Music Hall and Macy's window-shopping. A dead month, January is, another New Year's without a terrorist attack on Times Square, and I, perhaps stupidly, blame the weather for how everyone acts.

Seasonal affective disorder. It's a real phenomenon. The medical explanation, not enough sunlight. Depression and listlessness are the two well-known side effects, but there's another one: paranoia. Self-preservation instincts, from the sidewalk to the corner office. If the sun isn't hitting me, it's got to be hitting someone else, much to my disadvantage. The bitterness of Fifth Avenue winds, from apartment door to subway, melted slush and running noses—the lack of eye contact noticeable. It's like just looking someone in the eye lets a few degrees of heat escape from my eye sockets.

It's the worst month for office intrigue.

My computer whines and sputters on. Other bundled figures limp by, fifteen minutes or so behind the usual schedule. Everyone is feeling the cold.

My Outlook program comes to life, closing a series of warnings and updates and pop-ups. The server searches something, whatever a server searches, and downloads the crate of electronic mail that has entered my address and domain overnight.

An email from Judy Givens, subject: On behalf of Henry the EIC.

Dear Staff:

After thirty-three years at the magazine, I'm announcing today that I will retire my position as editor in chief, effective January 2006 . . .

Before I get to the two remaining paragraphs of the thank-yous and the memories, Gary's head appears over my cubicle wall.

"Did you see the email," he says.

"Reading it right now."

"Announcing so far in advance that he's leaving. Don't you find that strange?"

"Maybe he wants to do a farewell tour."

"Maybe, but the big news is what's not in the email. He didn't name a replacement."

"Really?"

"Yeah, and he says that a search for the replacement will start ASAP, once various factors are considered and weighed and everything."

"The race is on, I guess."

My computer beeps, another staff-wide email.

It's a reminder. This afternoon, at four p.m., there's a homecoming

party at the Top of the Mag for the staff who have returned from
covering the war. It gives the list of attendees, including A.E. Peoria,
Townsend, Charles, and Lee.

> Please join us to welcome and celebrate the work of our brave
> and courageous correspondents who are back after giving
> the magazine incredible coverage of our nation's most
> important story.

"You going to this?" I ask.

"Yeah, why not. Should be interesting—Nishant and Sanders and
Henry will probably be there. Good time to do some body-language
reading."

I hear the glass doors open at the end of the hallway, and rushing
past in a blur is A.E. Peoria. It is his first day back in the office. I
don't get a look at his face, only the top of his head as he blows by my
cubicle.

I want to say hello, but I don't want to be too aggressive. I'll let
him unbundle, de-thaw, and fire up his Dell before I go greet him.

"Hastings?" I hear the singsong voice of Nishant Patel.

I jump.

"Hi, Nishant, how's it going?"

"Fine. I'm giving a speech at the American Enterprise Institute in
honor of the economist Milton Friedman. Could you write up about
nine pages or so of research on him for the acceptance speech?"

"Sure, Milton Friedman award, no problem at all. Who's getting it?"

"Hernando de Soto—you've heard of him?"

"The explorer or the economist?"

"The economist."

"Yep, sure, I'm on it."

I always try to slip a few notes of humanity into these conversations to build my bond with Nishant.

"Are you going to the homecoming party tonight?"

"Hm?"

"For the correspondents coming back from the war."

"I don't know if that's in my schedule. Patricia, Lucy, have you scheduled me to go to the homecoming event?"

A furious exchange of recriminations and accusations.

"Henry the EIC is going to be there, I think," I say.

"Henry is going to be there," he says, his thoughts taking over, and he heads back into his office, followed by Patricia and Lucy.

I walk down the hallway to Peoria's office. The lights are off and he's sprawled in his swivel chair, eyes closed.

"My girlfriend broke up with me, bro," he says as I walk in the door.

"Hey, man, great to see that you're back."

"She broke up with me."

"That sucks—the six-orgasms girl?"

"I should never have told her about the spot, the questions just kept coming after that."

"The spot?"

"You want a cigarette?"

"I don't smoke, but I'll go outside with you."

From the elevator ride to the street, he recounts the conversation with his girlfriend.

"I got back and we went out to dinner and she asked me if something was wrong and I was, like, no, nothing is wrong," he says. "But she kept asking and asking and asking, and so finally I told her about the spot."

The spot. He'd been back in New York four days when he'd noticed, above his pubic hair, a red dot. Then, after foraging and brushing aside in front of a full-length mirror for self-examination, he noticed two red spots. He freaked out. He first called his doctor friend, who'd given him the odds on getting HIV after the trip to Mexico. His doctor friend recommended going to a walk-in clinic to get it checked out. Peoria did that, finding himself in a doctor's office out of the Third World, a doctor's office that smelled of rotting tobacco.

"Rotting tobacco. It's fucking cold out here," Peoria says. "Let's go back inside."

We go back inside and he gets to the point. The doctor, asking a series of invasive and highly personal questions, after drawing his blood and getting him tested, brought out a medical textbook and flipped it to the page with a large M in the corner.

"Molluscum contagiosum," Peoria says. "That's what I have. Molluscum contagiosum. I'd never heard of it. Toddlers get it—it's like the chicken pox. Toddlers and sexually active adults, you know. But it's not really an STD—it's, like, not really one. It's benign, you know, it doesn't do anything. It's just a spot, and there's a pretty easy procedure where they pluck it out."

"That sucks, that sucks," I say.

"Have you ever had a bandage on your dick?" he asks me.

"Not that I can remember," I say.

"I have a bandage on my dick right now."

I had thought, on some level, I was immune to conversational surprises, especially when sex was concerned. That over my approximately twenty-five years I had been told such a massive amount of personal information and sexual detail that very little would catch me off guard. I'm from the first totally coed generation. By the third grade we had textbook, graphic descriptions of sex. By middle school, survivors of herpes and genital warts and even HIV spoke as guest lecturers. I know sex is a beautiful living act between two adults; sex is something to discuss with your partner, in detail, before, after, and perhaps during. But I've never been confronted with a friend who has a bandage on his dick.

"I had to lie down on the table, and the doctor, a schlubby doctor too, the kind of guy you'd meet in AA, pulled down my pants, and he swabbed the two dots. And he found even more dots, he found five more, on the underside of my dick, and took a needle. He popped the head. They're like zits, I guess, that they have a head, and you need to remove the head so they stop spreading. There was a little blood. He put a patch of white bandages around my dick and then he snipped away my pubic hair. If you shave, apparently it can spread, and I guess that's why on gay guys it can spread, because they shave their pubic regions. Then he picked them out with a needle."

"Sounds pretty shitty," I say.

"Very vulnerable," he says. "After the procedure, he asked me if I took drugs and if I was depressed. I told him that I had been taking a lot of pills and drinking a lot since I left Baghdad. He thought I had some kind of post-traumatic stress. Had I taken pills recently? I had four Percocet and two Xanax that I got from my girlfriend that morning, and he wondered if it was an unhealthy relationship for me to be in. With her giving me pills and everything. If I was self-medicating."

We're back in his office. He tells me to shut the door and then he sits down.

"So I went out to dinner that night with her and she asked if something was wrong, and I said, yes, I have this spot, because the doctor recommended me to tell my sexual partners about it. That was a fucking mistake. Herpes or syphilis or chlamydia or something, I should have told her. But you know this molluscum contagiosum is benign. Most girls are pretty good about getting checked out regularly, so she would have found it eventually if she had it. Then she asked if I'd been, you know, unfaithful."

"Had you?"

"Not emotionally, you know, but I had a couple of run-ins."

Though I never could say that Peoria looked like a particularly healthy person, he looks particularly ill this morning. I picture him naked, bandaged dick, his cheeks not quite red enough from the frostbite temperatures. He looks like his stomach hurts, like coffee and a half quart of stale wine are swirling in his gut. He keeps talking, not stopping. He takes sharp, wheezy inhales, a two-pack-a-day cigarette habit. His teeth have a dull yellow sheen of moss. He looks like he has bad breath. He looks like he might never get up from his swivel chair again. He looks like he hasn't showered (he has, he tells me, but not completely because he didn't want to get the bandages wet).

And he details to me what he had the previous evening detailed to his girlfriend (leaving out a few things both to me and to Six Orgasms, as I will learn later): a sexual encounter poolside near the patio (Brennan Toddly was hitting on her too, and that motherfucker is married), and he refers vaguely to a number of unpaid sexual encounters in Thailand (though it isn't until a year later that I learn about the ladyboy). No, Peoria does not look very fit for the homecoming party this afternoon.

"She called me a rat," he says. "Do you think I'm a rat?"

A buzzing. His cell phone frog-crawls across his desk.

"It's her. I better take this."

He answers. He hits the mute button.

"Hastings, the thing is, I think I'm self-destructive, you know. Because I don't really want to be dating her, you know, because I don't love her. Anyway. Talk to you later."

He hits the unmute button.

I get up, close the door to his office, and go back to my cubicle.

22.

Early Evening, Monday, January 12, 2004

Gary and I take the elevator up to the homecoming party. A line has already formed, people standing and chatting along the windows, bulging out in the middle of a scrum centered around Henry the EIC, who accepts congratulations and regrets, even from the three other correspondents that had been to the war and come back.

With club soda in hand, I watch the progression of magazine dignitaries approaching Henry, saying a few words of consolation, shaking the hands of the three other war correspondents. Sanders Berman arrives, Delray M. Milius on his heels. Fashionably late, Nishant Patel strolls in, his assistants Patricia and Lucy behind him, carrying two of his BlackBerrys and his personal mobile telephone.

And as Nishant and Sanders go up the line, each working different sides of the room, they are both headed to meet at the towering figure in the center, Henry the EIC.

As the two contenders to his throne are about to meet, I move closer to listen. I feel a sharp stab in my side, then a liquid discharge, and looking down I see I've been bumped out of the way by Matt Healy, the crack investigative reporter, blue ink on my shirt leaking from his busted pen.

"Argrg, excuse me," he mumbles, timing his break in the scrum for when all three editors meet.

Henry, enjoying the moment, silences Berman and Patel, opening the floor to Healy.

"Matt, great you could make it," Henry the EIC says.

"I'm on deadline, so I can't stay long, but I want to make the case for going big on this," he says. "I've uncovered allegations of abuse by Americans of Iraqi detainees. You wouldn't believe what I'm hearing is coming down the pike."

Healy goes into some detail—blaring loud music, standing in stress positions, dogs sniffing, laughing, and other indignities that will be very well known by next summer. But, it's not well known now—the photos from Abu Ghraib aren't going to be released for months.

"Matt, it sounds like a great story, but making these accusations without having seen anything more than some government report that might or might not come out, that's dangerous. We need something more solid," says Henry.

It's always a risk for a subordinate to jump into a conversation with four elders, with four people who can make or break your career, who may not be too keen on your insight. You never want to contradict them in public or to say something unwise, but I feel I have something that they may not know of.

It's a file that A.E. Peoria had written for one of the larger Iraq stories; he'd filed ten thousand words, twenty-five pages single-spaced, and there's a good chance that I was the only one in the building who had actually read every last page. I'd come across two paragraphs where A.E. Peoria had described the interrogation of Iraqi prisoners, as told to him by an American officer at a detention facility in Baghdad. It was the kind of confirmation that Healy didn't have.

A.E. Peoria isn't here yet, so I figure I'm doing him a favor—dropping his name among the power elite at the magazine.

"Um, you might want to read A.E. Peoria's file too," I say.

The four esteemed gentlemen stop talking. Nishant Patel gives me a look that means, You have overstepped your precociousness. Sanders Berman, a fan of hierarchy, also looks uncomfortable. Healy, though, doesn't give a shit, and says, "Peoria? What does it say?"

"It quotes an American captain about some of the things they do to detainees, and—"

I catch a whiff of cigarette and vomit covered over with cologne, and Peoria enters the conversation.

"Sorry I'm late. I've had a hell of a time, you wouldn't believe what happened today—"

Peoria is lucky that Healy has another skill of the reporter—the sharp question to redirect a talkative subject back to where he wants the conversation to go. If he hadn't, Peoria probably would have started talking about molluscum contagiosum and his breakup.

"This guy says you have a detainee file?"

"Oh, yeah, I never knew why Jerry cut that out, it was great stuff. They've taken detainees, the real Islamic-types, and started slapping them around with the Koran, literally, the captain slapping, pissing on it, bringing it in the shower with them, even. I think they said they were jerking off in it, saying that Allah likes sticky pages, tossing it in the toilet, all sorts of stuff like that. Yeah, I don't know why—"

I back away, my place in pushing the story done, a role that would be forgotten by everyone (except for Delray M. Milius, whose eyes are on me, gauging the threat).

Henry the EIC, Nishant, and Sanders all agree that it sounds like a great story. It gets the cover. Healy and Peoria get the byline.

HOW A MAGAZINE
STORY GETS WRITTEN

I'm around twenty-five now—I think I've said that. I feel like a relic, like an ancient. I feel like I'm a blacksmith in the days of Henry Ford's assembly line, an apprentice scroll writer in the months following Gutenberg's great invention, or a poet in 1991.

Meaning: I feel my skill set is obsolete.

This book is an insurance policy against my dying field: maybe I can write novels, and if that's not a sign of desperation, a jump from one sinking ship to another, I don't know what is.

But for the sake of history, I'll explain the soon-to-be-lost art. Take my descriptions with you into the next century for research when Disney or some other corporation decides to build a tourist trap of what late-twentieth-century America was like, like they do now with those old villages of Pilgrims and settlers in funny hats and clothes: demonstrations of manual butter churning, candle making, and typesetting in a printing press.

This is what, the tourist guide will say, is called a "newsroom"; it's where they produced information content on paper, like newspapers and magazines. (Kids will nod: Oh, that's where the word *paper* comes from in *newspaper*.)

A slice of life: the cubicles, animatronics or live action—dozens of people to put out one single page of print, how extraordinarily quaint.

This is how a magazine story gets written.

Before 1969, stories in *The Magazine* had no bylines. There's a single authorial voice, the voice of *The Magazine*, omniscient in its power of observation, a fullness of perspective that transcends individual insight to bring the hefty weight of an institution. It works to much effectiveness.

But then 1969 happens. *The Magazine* catches up to the culture. The individual man, the yippie, the hippie, the hip and the square. Voices that are too institutional and too authoritative are suspect. Institutions inherently are co-opted by the immoral status quo, all slightly to massively oppressive, all involved in the insane desire of the Establishment to keep Blacks feeling Black, to keep White Kids from smoking dope and feeling love, to make the Working-Class Man consume, to reduce all the peoples of the world to their sole human value of becoming efficient actors in our economic system, and to keep undermining the beliefs of the Vietnamese people, particularly in the northern part of that country.

The Magazine, to its credit, adopts positions throughout the '60s that start to border on the radical, at least compared with those of its main competitor, Brand X. It is, as the editors see it, a time when smart business strategy and positive social policy converge. *The Magazine* promotes Negro rights, peacenik rights, Mexican rights, worker rights, and occasionally the rights of napalm victims. *The Magazine* mourns equally for Altamont and Kent State and Watergate.

In practice, though, it is undermining the labor movement. *The Magazine* writers don't have a union. The writers live with the hypocrisy until 1971. The writers go on strike.

It is a brief moment in history: magazine writers will never have the chance to go on strike again.

The writers and reporters win an important concession: the byline. The institutional voice of the magazine is never the same again.

But the byline, too, is misleading to the laymen. A magazine story is not the work of one man or one woman.

The byline gives the impression that the name on top actually wrote and reported the story. Not true. The writer, in this ancient formulation, takes the reporting from others and weaves it into a narrative. There are also layers of editors and copy editors and fact-checkers and writers and reportorial changes.

Each paragraph and each sentence that finds its way into print, hand-delivered to subscriber homes, resting casually and arrogantly on the newsstands, takes at least eight or nine hours of close inspection: tweaking, polishing, rubbing, beautification, sullification, hyping. These hands are hidden; it is the writer with the byline who gets the glory.

Drawback: the writer also gets the blame.

Advantage: the name in bold print is treated as if the brilliant insights and omniscience are all his own.

The '80s and '90s: The byline takes on a life of its own. The byline separates itself from *The Magazine* brand. Bylines become brands. Layoffs mean that there are no more layers of fact-checkers and researchers and editors. The strategy of *The Magazine* is to enhance its many brands by making brands of bylines.

Healy is a brand. A.E. Peoria is a brand in the making.

23.

Mid-January 2004

'm anticipating the reaction, monitoring the media waves from my cubicle.

Peoria and Healy's story is met with silence. Nothing. Doesn't crack the ether. Doesn't make *The Magazine* part of the conversation. Doesn't move the debate or get any television hits or radio hits. No responses from the White House or the State Department. Even Amnesty International and Human Rights Watch shrug it off.

The Magazine's public relations department is disinclined to touch it. Nobody wants this story. Complaining about Iraq when Saddam Hussein has been captured?

Three days, nothing.

What happens during those three days? *The Magazine* goes global. It is translated into six different languages: Polish, Russian, Korean, Japanese, Turkish, and Arabic.

By Thursday, an Islamic cleric in Najaf, a man who you wouldn't think would be in the magazine's target demographic—though, to be honest, by the year 2004, anyone who picks up the magazine is welcomed into its demographic—has a copy in his hands. It gets delivered to his mosque. (Or maybe he found it in the seat-back pocket on a first-class flight from Tehran to Baghdad, thanks to a promotional deal *The Magazine* has with Royal Jordanian Airlines.)

The cleric does what all truly holy men do when they come across an outrage, an indignation, an affront to what is good and decent in the world: he calls a press conference.

Only the Arabic-language press attends—the video shows, with the production value of a New England public access channel, a card table, and a filter of cigarette smoke in an elementary school classroom, Arabic script and loud trumpeting music on, a scratchy audio.

It's another twelve hours before what he says gets translated back into English. That's when I pick up on it. That's after the damage is done. The Internet has the story.

By Friday, followers of the cleric have taken to the streets in Najaf, waving copies of *The Magazine*, burning copies of *The Magazine*, and even mentioning things like death threats (though not taking it as far as a fatwa).

The Magazine's role gives a new theme to the usual riots and fighting following Friday prayers.

The local authorities, called in to stop the riots, are persuaded, after having the damning allegations on page 21 paraphrased for them— probably an inaccurate paraphrase, at that—to join the riots as well.

Furious excitement—religious, political, illiterate, a change of pace from relaxing though resentful unemployment—sweeps the streets outside "one of Islam's holiest shrines." It means only one thing: a trampling.

Crowd deaths follow. More deaths come after unknown guns fire bullets lengthwise.

Thirteen is the total.

It's clear in the first headlines I read from the Associated Press and

Reuters how this story is going to play: *The Magazine* is the cause of the riots.

The political fallout in America begins.

The administration in Washington goes on the offensive—an example of the liberal media, the pantywaist liberals in New York trying to undermine the war effort. Because of reckless reporting, the White House spokesperson says, thirteen people are dead.

The spokesperson pauses at the lectern.

Thirteen, he repeats.

The right-wing websites seize the deaths to attack *The Magazine*'s credibility. "The Magazine Murders," writes one blogger. "Thirteen innocents dead at the hands of the MainStreamMedia. Despicable."

There is no room in the discourse to mention the hypocrisy that in other circumstances, these same people would be cheering the deaths of thirteen Islamic extremists. But today they have taken up their cause with mourning blog posts.

I'm waiting for *The Magazine* to respond, to issue a statement.

Nishant Patel ducks by the cubicle, Sanders Berman hustles past. No time for chitchat today. I hear an "Arrgh" from Healy, notepads flapping in his pockets. Peoria, three Xanax already ingested, wearing an off-the-rack suit and tie, is the only one who stops by to tell me what's going on.

"Healy's sources are backing off," he says.

"What about your captain?"

"He's not answering emails. Fuck, he might be dead for all I know. I haven't heard from him in months."

"So what are you going to do?"

"They want me to go on TV to defend it."

Peoria says this and leaves me at the cubicle.

Choosing Peoria to go on TV? Bad idea. The two people who can offer the best defense for *The Magazine*: Nishant, a man many Americans assume to be Muslim because of his darker skin and accent, and Sanders Berman, a southerner who counts conservatives among his most devoted readers. Or Healy, whose reputation—the Pentagon Paper of Blow Jobs—could survive the blistering assault.

But Peoria, God bless him, so deranged from painkillers, war flashbacks, and the trauma of a benign STD, has been chosen to take the fall.

I hear a whispered conversation outside my cubicle.

The voice of Delray M. Milius, echoing off his hand, which he has put to his mouth. Sanders Berman stands next to him, looking panicked.

". . . stay out of the way . . . lay low . . . don't be associated with this story . . ."

I have an urge to pop up, to say, What the fuck, guys? But I don't. I just take a few notes. The time of the conversation, the words that I heard, the participants.

A door in the corner office shuts.

"Patricia, Lucy, is my car waiting for me?"

"Yes, Nishant," says the chorus.

Delray M. Milius's hand drops from his mouth. Sanders Berman stands upright. Nishant, a Burberry peacoat hanging over his arm, comes around the corner.

"Professor," Berman says.

"Milius, Sanders," he says.

"Off to CNN?" Sanders asks, a note of hopefulness.

"Oh, no, no time for television today," Nishant says.

"Me either," Berman says.

Two men who, as their reputations confirm, find it very difficult to go forty-eight hours without finding a way to a television studio, who carry makeup removal swabs in their pockets, are now both unavailable.

"I have a speech to give on Milton Friedman," Nishant Patel says. "An award ceremony. Hastings, you have that speech for me?"

"Right here, Nishant," I say.

Delray M. Milius's doughboy face flinches; he hadn't seen me, hunched behind the velvet cubicle walls.

"Lucy, Patricia, is my car ready?"

"It's waiting, Nishant," they respond.

Patricia snatches the manila folder from his hand, and Nishant leaves two of his assistants trailing.

Sanders Berman gives me a pained smile and turns the corner back to his office. Delray M. Milius follows him.

Peoria comes charging out of his office next.

"I'm supposed to be on CNN in forty-five minutes," he tells me.

I follow Peoria outside while he smokes a cigarette. The CNN studios are only two blocks away on Columbus Circle.

"Peoria, man, I think they want you to take the blame for this," I say.

He looks at me, inhaling, his cheeks turning Granny Smith–apple green in the cold.

"We have nothing to apologize for," he says. "All sorts of fucked-up shit is going on at these detention facilities. I know that, Healy knows that. We just need to stand by it, you know, and since I'm the one who was over there, I really have the credibility—that's what they told me, and I liked that, having the credibility to speak for the magazine. It shows that they really have put their faith in me, to choose me to do this, you know?"

"I don't think so, man. I think they're ducking for the fucking hurricane shelters while you're standing out there with the microphone, dodging telephone polls."

"You're a fucking cynical person for your age. You know, I was never that cynical when I was coming up. Now . . ."

Maybe it's the drugs or another hangover or the prescription meds or just the numb stressed-out feeling he's described to me since coming back. He doesn't get it.

24.

Mid-January 2004, Continued

Forty-five minutes later, I turn up the volume on the television on the pillar next to Dorothy's and Patricia's cubicles.

"A CNN exclusive interview," the anchor says, "with the reporter who wrote the now infamous story that sparked the *Magazine* riots in Iraq."

Although Peoria has gone to the studio, they don't actually put him in the same room with the anchor. He is, as he tells me later, brought down to a dark room on the second floor, behind a wall of glass, where production assistants and assistant producers and other young-looking people in headsets mill around, slamming phones down, rushing, wound-up. The anchor is on the fifth floor. Peoria is put on a chair to look straight into the camera.

They at least have given him a spray of makeup, I think, as his face flashes on screen, the green tone of his cheeks removed.

Isolated below, he doesn't have the comfort of seeing a human face—he feels trapped, cornered, staring at a camera with the words of what the anchor is reading scrolling underneath.

"In Iraq's holiest city, riots broke out after allegations in a *Maga-*

zine story offended tens of thousands of Iraqis and others across the Muslim world. The story alleged that Iraqi detainees were victims of abuse at the hands of U.S. soldiers, a claim that both the White House and the Pentagon have strongly denied. The riots have now claimed the lives of thirteen Iraqis. With us is A.E. Peoria, the *Magazine* reporter who wrote the controversial story. First, let's look at the words that have caused the deadly violence."

On screen, the offending paragraph is put up, with a number of ellipses.

According to a U.S. military official, detainees were told to strip naked . . . subjected to "debilitating noise levels" of rock music like AC/DC . . . and told to flush the Koran down the toilet. In one incident, the Koran was used to capture the ejaculate of a soldier who was reading aloud a page of *Hustler*'s letter section to the captured insurgents. . . .

I hear Peoria clear his throat.

"Do you think you owe the Iraqi people an apology?" the anchor asks, as a way to ease into the conversation.

"An apology, I mean, I'm sorry that they got so offended, but—"

"The sources in the story—everyone has backed off this. Our own CNN reporting also couldn't confirm your story. You can't really confirm it, can you?"

"I mean, we quoted—we had quotes from an eyewitness."

"But you never saw this yourself?"

"No, we had quotes from an eyewitness, like I said, uh, I never saw this myself, but I think, you know, we reported on this investigation that is going on into it—"

"But the government says that this investigation doesn't contain anything like what you described, that it is just a routine checkup of the facilities, and the claims that you make in the story haven't been confirmed by the investigation."

"Right, well, the other reporter, who wrote this, his sources told him that they saw a draft of the report—"

"A draft, so this was just a draft of a government report? And you're blaming Matthew Healy, one of the most well-respected journalists in the profession? As I know, from personal experience covering the government, the final version often has many things that are taken out, and so don't you think it was reckless to go ahead with this?"

"I don't think, I mean, you have to understand that I'm sorry that this rioting happened, but you know that cleric, that guy, he's a real jerk—he's not like a good guy, you know?"

"We have to go to a commercial, and when we get back, we'll bring in a Middle East expert to discuss the fallout. To join in the discussion, log on to CNN.com."

It is the first time I have seen a friend melt down on live television. It is a brutal experience. I want to give him the benefit of the doubt. I know the adrenaline is flowing through his mind. I know what he should say, I know that he should just say, Stop this madness, your questions are asinine. It's worse, too, when I put myself in the place of an average viewer who happens to be tuning into CNN at an airport lounge or as background noise as he makes the second pot of coffee in the kitchen, or the first pot of coffee if he's watching on the West Coast.

I know they will take one look at Peoria and think: This guy is fucked-up, this guy doesn't know what he's saying, he's not making any sense at all. Because the words Peoria says jumble together. They don't fit in sound bites. I know he needs time to explain himself, to explain the story, to have the viewers see the context. He just wants context. If he can just give the context of the story, if he can just make a few simple points—that the story is accurate, that perhaps they could have been more careful in how they reported it, but that other reporters had been digging around, hinting at similar activities by American forces. If he could have cited an Associated Press story from November, if he could have cited a Reuters story from last week, if he can just explain himself. But Peoria can't explain himself, because once you start trying to explain yourself on television, it's hard to win—you can't explain; you just have to state yourself, without hesitation.

I want to give him the benefit of the doubt—to take out the "ums" and "ahs" and how his eyes keep darting to the left and right. (He will explain later that his eyes were looking at the other television monitors, and he will swear the producers were cutting back to him at exactly the wrong moments.)

"We're back with noted Middle East scholar Daniel Tubes. Daniel, what did you make of the—"

"Can I just respond to what Mr. Peoria said first? What he's doing is classic. He's blaming the victims for his own reckless reporting."

"How is he blaming the victims?"

"He's saying it's their fault for rioting, their fault for reacting to the erroneous information he put out. And I think that's just despicable."

"Uh, no, I'm just saying—"

"He obviously knows nothing of Middle Eastern culture," Tubes continues. "I hate to be blunt, but that's so clear to me."

"Why do you say that?" the anchor asks, lobbing another softball to Tubes.

"*Hustler*? The Arabs don't have a culture of masturbation," Tubes says. "The story has so many holes in it, it's an embarrassment. It's offensive, because in the Arab world, and I don't think I can put this more politely, there just isn't the culture of masturbation that we have in the West."

"Mr. Peoria," the anchor says. "Is this true? Were you unaware of the cultural sensitivities you were reporting on?"

"No, I guess I wasn't aware of the, uh, lack of cultural, um, in that sense. I mean, the Iraqis I knew, um, they really liked looking at pictures of naked women and things. Um, I mean, they didn't even need to be naked, just like, you know, advertisements of a girl in a robe or a bra, or a girl in a dress that doesn't fully cover, you know, that was pretty shocking to them—"

"And so you thought it was a good idea to write about *Hustler* magazine?"

"I mean, I'm there to report on what's happening. I don't really—"

"This is the smoke screen that the liberal media have been hiding behind: they want to do their best to undermine the Americans. They hate the troops, they don't care that what they report actually puts American lives at risk. And by the way, a source at the Pentagon told me that pornography isn't even allowed among Americans in Iraq! It's against General Order Number 1. So how did they get this so-called *Hustler* magazine, this so-called November edition? How, I ask, did they get that? And flushing the Koran down the toilet? I spoke to another high-level source who told me that there are no flushing handles at the detention facility Peoria so inaccurately depicts as hostile. They don't even have toilets; they have little holes to squat in—and they have porta-johns."

"I mean, it is just to get at the idea they were throwing the Koran in the toilet, you know?" Peoria says.

"Oh, so he's changing his story again, right here! Admitting to another mistake! They don't flush; they throw! Next think you know, it's going to be, Well, there was a Koran that fell off a table in the room next door!"

"All right, we're going to turn to the viewer email, see what our audience is saying. Sam from Georgia writes, 'Peoria is a disgrace to

America. I'd cancel my subscription to *The Magazine* but I don't even have one.'

"Caroline from New Mexico says, 'I'm so disappointed in how the media always gets things wrong and no one holds them accountable. Kudos to your show for calling that reporter out for his bad news.'

"We're heading to commercial. Mr. Peoria, thanks for your time. Daniel Tubes will stay with us, and we'll be right back. You're watching CNN."

Peoria disappears from the screen, scratching his nose.

I turn off the television and go back to my cubicle. Within minutes, a story appears on the wires: "Journalist apologizes for erroneous story."

I click on the story and scroll down. In the second paragraph, the story says *The Magazine* has released a statement. This is news to me. The statement says that A.E. Peoria is suspended from his duties at the magazine, and the magazine is instituting new regulations to prevent this kind of mistake from happening again. The story quotes Delray M. Milius. It's clear they had the statement ready before Peoria even went on air.

25.

Mid-January 2004, Continued

know I'm jeopardizing my job, for sure, but every once in a while, I'm supposed to stand up for what's right—at least that's what I'd absorbed from all sorts of morality tales I'd heard over the years.

What can I really do, as a cubicle slave, as a desk jockey, as a kid just one step removed from an internship?

I know what I can do, actually—I can leak the real story. I know I can go to Wretched.com.

I type in the URL, and wait for the screen to upload. I open another window to log into my personal email account, on Gmail. The Wretched.com site is coming up. It's the most popular media gossip site on the web.

The top story that day happens to be about an assistant producer at Fox News who'd gotten drunk at a party and had an accident in her pants that was picked up by a camera phone video. The editors at Wretched.com are loving that story, but I think after Peoria's appearance on CNN, they'll probably write something about him, too.

Sure enough, after I refresh the screen, there is a YouTube clip with Peoria, with the choice quotes printed below.

On the sidebar, there is a link for people to send anonymous tips to Wretched.com. I start writing up an email, putting down the real story, the cover-up.

Thirty minutes later, I see my email, name redacted, printed in full.

It would have worked, or perhaps helped save Peoria's reputation, but at almost the exact same time, the governor of Virginia got caught getting a blow job in the bathroom of the Amtrak Acela Express, DC to New York. The guy who broke the story? Healy. He must have been saving that one.

If Peoria had just waited a few hours, maybe he could have survived the damage, as the *Magazine* riots were forgotten with the new round of blow job news.

But then I hear screaming down the hall.

26.

February 2004

Reeling, reeled, rocked, slipped, sliding. What is the right word? A.E. Peoria stares at his computer screen, sitting in his boxers, the white bandage visible through the slit for his penis. He scratched another bandage on his thigh covering up a puncture wound.

The Word document is opened up to his journal, file name wd35. When he had started this Word file during his senior year of college, he didn't want to name it something like "diary" or "aejournal," because if he ever lost his computer or if someone was looking in it—"someone" meaning a girl he was dating—then they'd know where to look, they could go straight to the source. He had transferred and resaved the file thirty-five times since that first document, in one of the early versions of Microsoft Word, and making its way from outdated laptop to outdated laptop, the journal now stretched to 1,700 single-spaced pages.

It isn't the most coherent document. There are so many spelling mistakes and typos that the red-line function, which marks a misspelled word, stopped working in late 2001.

But on the evening after the CNN appearance, it is to the wd35 that A.E. Peoria turns.

He knew that it couldn't have gone well. In the five minutes after removing the earpiece, being shuttled into the elevator by another large-breasted assistant producer, and being dumped out onto the street in the cold, he kept waiting for his mobile phone to light up with text messages and voicemails from friends and family who'd seen him on the program. Usually, after a TV appearance, he would be flooded with words of encouragement and support: great job, you looked great, excellent. He'd get notes from people he hadn't seen or heard from in years, all of a sudden impressed with him because he had managed to get onto a television screen.

Nothing this time.

When he got back to the office, the silence was even louder. He passed the security guard, and in the lobby there was a TV screen turned to CNN, and the security guard, a large African American woman, asked him for his ID.

"I was just on TV," he told her.

She looked at him.

And she waved him by. The doors opened to a crowd heading out for lunch, the clique that always seemed to hang out together, a group of assistant editors and senior editors who, Peoria had always felt, were replaying their high school fantasies of being the cool kids—and how he wanted to be among the cool kids! And Peoria thought that he had been finally making inroads into this crowd: one of them had asked him, at the homecoming party, if he would join their table for dinner Friday night, and this little group had come out in a bunch and blown past him, pretending they didn't recognize him, or at least pretending that they didn't know him well enough to say hello in the hallway.

On his floor, he walked by that kid Hastings's desk, and even Hastings just said hi, nothing special, no "Great job, man," and he knew Hastings was the kid who would have said "Great job" no matter what he had done.

And then he sat down at his desk and the email from Delray M. Milius was there, asking him to come into his office.

Peoria walked down the hallways again, and stood in front of the secretary sitting outside Delray's office.

"It was that bad, hunh?" Peoria said, fishing for at least a little encouragement. The woman at the desk didn't even smile and waved him in without answering his question.

"Alex, sit down," Delray M. Milius said. "We need to talk."

Peoria sat down and inhaled.

"We're putting you on administrative leave. We think you should take some time off."

"I don't think I need to take time off," Peoria said. "I don't think the story is getting any bigger now, I mean, what more could we do?"

"No, we think it's best for you to take time off, at least for a few weeks."

The conversation went back and forth like that for fifteen minutes, and Peoria finally agreed that he would take time off.

"Okay, Milius, I'm a team player and everything and I don't mind doing that at all, you know, so I only ask that we keep this confidential, because you know if it gets out that I'm taking time off, it's like I'm admitting I'm guilty and admitting I fucked up, and I really don't think I did, you know. I mean it was Healy's story and I just added that quote, so I don't—"

"Right, right," Milius said.

"I guess, because I don't want this to hurt my career here at *The Magazine*, so if we could keep this confidential, that would be great, you know, between us."

"Yes, of course, it won't go farther than this room."

"Thank you, I appreciate that," Peoria said, mildly shocked. Was he really getting suspended? He couldn't really believe it, and he felt like he wanted to do something—cry maybe, and if he were a girl, he probably would have started to cry, but Peoria really didn't cry when he was sober.

He got up and actually started to thank Milius for *The Magazine*'s generosity, for keeping quiet about his leave, and started to convince himself, feeling the bandage on his dick and the extra two Xanax in his pocket, that maybe taking a few weeks off to let this story die down wouldn't be the worst thing in the world. And as he left, he looked back to thank Milius one more time, and saw Milius had picked up his phone.

Five minutes later, back at his office, he looked on the Drudge Report to see if the story was still getting top billing. It had been moved above the headline.

There was a new headline, which said "RIOT JOURNALIST SUSPENDED."

Healy got suspended? Strange that Milius hadn't mentioned it. He clicked on the story.

He read it. He saw a quote from Delray M. Milius, a statement that said they had grown concerned with A.E. Peoria's behavior and they were suspending him, pending further investigation.

Peoria sat back in his chair, numbed, and took out a Xanax. He reached into his desk drawer and found a bottle of whiskey and took two quick shots. There must be some mistake. He started to feel a number of uncomfortable sensations that reminded him of the humiliation he hadn't felt since *Desperation Points West* was reviled in a *Booklist* review.

It was as if he'd been kicked in the nuts—and for some reason he thought of Chipotle for a moment, Chipotle squealing and bleeding from the groin. He thought of Chipotle and knew, or had some idea of, what it must have been like to get shrapnel in the balls, to feel like the world had betrayed him with a quick and unexpected blast to the groin—even knowing that these things happened and it was a cutthroat world and reputations rose and fell. Peoria had been lied to by the best of them over the years as a journalist who had been shot at, had been rocked by explosions, but none of it had felt personal, none of it had felt like he had been betrayed—politicians lie, people lie when they talk to journalists, bad guys and insurgents try to kill you, nothing more or less should be expected of them, but there was no sense in taking it personally.

This, however, felt personal.

His first instinct was to write an email, a scathing email, but he stopped himself, remembering a line he'd read in a business memoir: Make war by phone, make love by email.

Okay, he thought, so maybe sending an email wouldn't be the right move. Then how could he get proof that Delray M. Milius had lied to him?

He would have to talk to him again, that's how. He was a reporter and he'd go over there right now and get him to go on the record, get him to admit that he had lied.

He grabbed his digital tape recorder and a notepad and a newly sharpened pencil, and holding them in his fists (the Xanax, or was it Percocet he'd been taking, made his hands feel heavy; he felt like he was in physical therapy, the way he was moving his hands around the pencil), and he took off down the hallway, choosing another route, past the cubicle area where the cool kids hung out, swinging past Sanders Berman's office, until he saw Delray M. Milius standing at his door and talking to his secretary.

And then Peoria tripped, stumbled over a man purse that had been left out in the hallway, and the strap, as if it were a bear trap, snagged his leg and he tumbled over, falling. He saw the corner of the secretary's desk and jerked his head out of the way quickly. He felt a squishy feeling on his thigh and wondered if his pen had busted, then he stood up, rocked backward, and looked at Milius.

"You said you were going to keep it confidential—"

That's when the secretary who hadn't even smiled started screaming.

Delray M. Milius had a disgusted look on his face.

"What? What are you screaming at? I want you on the record. I want you to tell me that you lied."

With his left hand he grabbed the notepad and with his right he searched for the pencil.

He put his hands in his pocket and it wasn't there.

Delray M. Milius was staring at Peoria's lower half.

Then Peoria looked down and saw that the pencil was sticking out of his leg.

Perhaps it was the Xanax that hit him, or the Percocet, or the shots of whiskey he had taken, but he all of a sudden felt both heavy and light-headed and he fell backward, this time not missing the sharp edge of the desk.

Peoria felt comfortable on the floor and closed his eyes. He heard shouts of "Nine-one-one," and he felt he could open his eyes, but thought it was better to just lie there. His eyes were closed and Delray M. Milius moved next to him.

He heard the southern drawl of Sanders Berman, and Milius saying, "We clearly made the right decision." Fifteen or twenty minutes passed, and in that time he lost consciousness and started to snore, and he woke up with a paramedic looking down on him.

"Are you Nicolas Cage?" Peoria asked.

The paramedic pulled the pencil out quickly. The secretary screamed again.

"We need to take your pants off to put the bandage on," the paramedic said.

"No, I need my pants," Peoria whispered.

"We need to take them off," the paramedic said.

"No, I already have a bandage on my dick," he said. "Let me keep my dignity, let me keep them on."

Peoria grabbed hold of his belt, as if he were protecting his chastity, and closed his eyes. He was much drunker than he'd originally thought.

"Okay, but that means I'm going to have to cut a patch out."

He felt the cold metal of scissors clipping away around his pants, and then he passed out again. He woke up on a stretcher in the back of an ambulance.

He was released from the emergency room six hours later. He put his pants back on, a large hole in the leg, and on the subway, normal businessmen and good-looking women gave him space as he sat in the car, with his legs crossed, hoping that no one could see through the large patch in his left leg and up to the bandage. He should have taken a cab, he thought.

He didn't feel well at all, and everything that had just happened seemed like some kind of nightmarish dream—that dream where you try to confront your boss and end up impaling yourself on a pencil.

So there he is, back in his one-bedroom apartment on the Upper West Side, staring at the screen at wd35.

Reeled, reeling, slipping, sliding. He starts to write about how he has ended up alone, in his apartment, and almost out of a job.

PART VI

Disgruntled Employees

QUOTES I WOULD LIKE TO HAVE STARTED THE BOOK WITH

"Never mistake the facts for truth."

—THOMAS JEFFERSON, 1803

"Make love by email, make war by phone."

—K. ERIC WALTERS, FROM HIS 1997 BESTSELLER
21st Century Business: 101 Survival Tips

"They say war is hell. I disagree. War is war. Hell is reserved for the folks who start wars."

—FROM THE UNPUBLISHED JOURNAL OF A REPORTER WHO
WAS KILLED IN 1944 BY A SNIPER IN THE SOUTH PACIFIC

"I had inflicted terrible violence on my body, on myself. I had only two things to show for my suffering, and both were double D's."

—FROM AN ANONYMOUS SUBJECT IN A RESEARCH STUDY
PUBLISHED BY THE *American Medical Journal*,
"BECOMING ME: PLASTIC SURGERY IN PURSUIT OF
GENDER-BASED WISH FULFILLMENT"

27.

February 2004, Continued

I more or less forgive *The Magazine* for how they've treated Peoria. I'm not a suspect for the leak to Wretched.com, either. *The Magazine* is just relieved that Peoria's later incident—when he fell on his pencil—didn't make it onto the blogs.

Maybe Delray M. Milius thinks it might have been me, but he can't prove it. I'm starting to have second thoughts about the leak as well—was it worth the risk of getting caught just to try to defend A.E. Peoria (and my guilt is probably why I stop feeling bad for Peoria). I don't know him very well, really, and though I admire the reporting he's done—and *Desperation Points West* actually is a decent book—I also know he's pretty fucked-up.

Why so quick to risk everything to come to his defense? Especially now that I'm making some real progress in my career.

I'm working eighty hours a week, in the office six out of seven days. I've started to write a few stories a month for *The Magazine*'s website.

What I did realize about Wretched.com is that if I don't start writing online on a regular basis, I won't be very well positioned down the line as a journalist. The online editors at *The Magazine* really like what I'm doing for them, and so when an associate Web editor position opens up, I apply, and they offer me the job. The associate editor gig will finally make me a full-time staff member—I've been working full-time, but my title is still temporary researcher—and give me a salary, a job title, and benefits.

Then Nishant Patel calls me into his office.

"You're better off staying here at the international edition," Nishant Patel says.

"I'd like to, I guess, but the Web is offering me a permanent position."

Nishant Patel leans back in his chair, glancing at his monitor to see if any critical emails have popped up, and shakes his head.

"The Web is a black hole," he says. "There's not a future on the Internet."

You might think that this is a funny thing to say now. Maybe you would have expected a guy like Nishant Patel to say that in 1999 or 2000, or even 2001.

"But the Web is offering me a permanent position," I say, not wanting to get into the whole future-of-journalism debate. Maybe Nishant Patel doesn't even really believe what he's telling me; maybe he's more interested in getting me to stay so he doesn't have to find another research assistant.

"No, no, I think, for your career, you're much better off staying with the international edition. You can still write for the Web, of course, but it's much better for you to stay here. I spoke to Sandra this morning, and she agreed."

That's when I realize that I'm not really being given a choice. Sandra is the Web editor, and I had spoken to her yesterday, and she had been very excited about having me. Nishant pulled rank. I'm not going anywhere.

"We'll find a permanent position for you here soon," he says. Then he goes back to checking email, and I know I've been dismissed.

I'm pretty pissed off. On the one hand, I feel like Nishant Patel is really fucking with my career. I'd worked hard to get the job offer, and once I was in position to take it, Patel blocked it—more for self-interested reasons than anything about my future, I think. On the other hand, it's kind of a backhanded compliment—they feel I'm so important that they don't want to lose me. So I guess that's a good sign.

Sanders Berman is waiting for me at my cubicle.

"Hastings," he says.

"Oh, I was just talking to Nishant," I say.

"How is the professor?"

"He's good. I think he's doing *The Daily Show* tonight."

"*The Daily Show*? Good for him. I probably won't be able to catch it, as I'm going to be filling in for Chris Matthews."

"Oh, that's great. I'll have to make sure to TiVo them both."

"I'm due in DC in about five hours," he says.

"Taking the Amtrak?"

"No, that's what I'm here to ask you about."

I'm wondering what research I'm going to have to do. Probably something for the news of the day because Sanders is filling in for Matthews.

"Could you go pick up a pillow for me?"

"Sorry?"

"A pillow. One from Duane Reade would be fine. Just drop it off with my assistant."

I'm wondering why his assistant doesn't go buy him a pillow, and as if he knows what I'm thinking, he says, "I asked Nancy to get it for me last time, and I don't like her doing too many things like that. I don't want to get a reputation as a prima donna."

"Okay, right. Um, why do you need a pillow?"

"For the trip to DC. My car is picking me up in forty-five minutes."

Right: Sanders Berman hates to fly, and he also hates trains. He doesn't feel comfortable waiting in Penn Station, his assistant told me. Too many people who could recognize him. So when he goes to DC, he hires a car service.

Car services are the big topic of conversation around the office, especially for those editors who don't get cars all the time. Jerry got all the numbers, and he likes to recite them. Nishant Patel's car service bill: $7,323 a month. Sanders Berman's: $9,356. Sometimes they take them five blocks. Five blocks! Do you know how many reporters we could hire for that bill, Jerry likes to say.

"Sure, I'll grab you a pillow."

"Thanks."

I take the elevator down, and I'm getting kind of annoyed again. If I were an associate editor, I wouldn't have to be doing this kind of gofering anymore. As long as my title remains researcher, I'm more or less the office bitch. I have to figure out a way to get on staff, and I guess buying pillows is a step in the right direction.

I pick up two pillows at Duane Reade—one is from this foam material, another is designed for people with bad backs. I want to cover my bases, do the job right.

Sanders's door is open, and he's on the phone. I leave the two pillows with Nancy.

"I'll put this with his travel bag," she says, tapping a pile of folded sweatpants and a blanket on the desk. "Sanders," Nancy whispers, "likes to put these on in his car so it's more comfortable."

"Oh, right."

I see Sanders hang up, and I think maybe I should ask him if he'd step in to talk to Nishant about letting me go to the Web.

"Sanders, I just have a quick question. I applied for the associate editor job at the Web, and Sandra seemed really keen on having me there, but I don't know if Nishant wanted me to go for it. But I think it would be really good."

"The Web," Sanders says, like it's something he's never heard of.

"Yeah, the magazine's website."

"You mean Sandra the Web editor?"

"Yeah, that's who I mean."

"Oh, you don't want to go to the Web. Nothing good is happening there," he says.

I go back to my cubicle and I don't do much for the rest of the afternoon. I don't feel like working. What's hard work gotten me?

I leave an hour earlier than usual and take the F train back down to my apartment on the Lower East Side. I go to the dry cleaners to pick up clothes I'd dropped off yesterday.

In line at the dry cleaners, I notice a girl standing ahead of me. She's cute, and I recognize her face because her picture is always up at Wretched.com. She's the editor, and I know she lives in the neighborhood as well.

"Hey," I say to her.

She looks at me like I'm a danger.

"My name is Mike Hastings. I'm a writer for *The Magazine*," I say.

"Oh, okay, I thought you might be some crazy asshole stalking me. I've been getting a lot of that kind of email lately."

"No, I'm just a fan of Wretched.com."

"I'm sorry for you."

"Yeah, right. Actually, you guys posted something I sent in—I probably shouldn't bring this up—but yeah, I sent you guys an email about the *Magazine* riots and how they were, uh, blaming . . ."

"Oh yeah, sure, I remember that. Uh, thanks."

I give the Chinese woman my dry cleaning ticket.

"We should hang out sometime," I say.

"Yeah, that would be cool. Send me an email."

"I will."

She leaves the dry cleaners. And that's how my relationship with Wretched.com begins.

TOWARD A MORE LIKABLE NARRATOR

The disgruntled employee—it's hard not to sound like a loser, a whiny bitch, ungrateful. Noticing it just now—rereading where we're at in the story.

What gave me the right, at twenty-four or twenty-five, to expect my goals and desires to be taken seriously at *The Magazine*? Why did I expect them to care or to give a shit? Let's get my head out of my ass here: this is a magazine, part of a company that routinely hires and fires and thwarts much bigger plans than mine. Why would I expect anything other than frustration and dues-paying?

Don't they say that nothing in life is easy, and if it's easy, it's not worth it?

Maybe they do say that.

I read this book on twenty-first-century business survival tips, written by a guy named K. Eric Walters.

Walters, see, he opens the book with an anecdote about Tom Cruise. Nothing beats the wisdom of celebrities, Walters gets that, and so he brings us to Tom Cruise talking on the Letterman show.

Tom says: "People look at me now and think that my life has been smooth sailing. That I got everything that I wanted, and that my career just happened to take off. No. It didn't. I had to fight to get my foot in the door, and every day, people tried to slam that door shut, right in my face. And finally I did get my foot in, and they tried even harder to kick my foot out of the door, to shut it tight. I didn't let them. I kept my foot there. And one day, it opened. That's my advice."

So yeah, maybe I was having a bad day back then, and I wasn't able to get the needed perspective.

What's a few years of hard work unrewarded? Sounds like life to me, says K. Eric Walters.

Anyway.

And so on.

Can you believe I've made it to page 232? Passed the halfway mark by far. It's still December where I'm at in 2005, and I'm still trying to get this over with before the new regime takes over in January. I think that's when it'll be the best time to bring the book to market—right when the new editor of *The Magazine* is taking over.

28.

Winter–Spring 2004

The darkness, the darkness, oh the darkness. His pillows off the bed, sheets crumpled on the floor, shades drawn, four stale glasses of water on the bedside table. The darkness in his bedroom had even taken on his scent. He could smell himself, he could smell his days without a shower and the trip to the laundromat that kept getting put off and delayed and delayed. He could hear the buzz of his laptop, the keyboards sticky from who knows what delivery food residue, the fan on the laptop clicking away. Cooling down, screen saver jumping in and out, breaking through the darkness in some sick technological light, a sick mechanical glow, an unhealthy light— but even an unhealthy light was better than the darkness.

A.E. Peoria had hated the lights at the office, the radiating lights, the plastic dimples parceling out the fluorescent rays, sucking the soul, draining life from the skin. But how he missed those lights now.

A leave of absence. Yes, he was given a leave of absence.

Hugging himself in his bed, he wished he could have embraced the leave of absence. And he had, for the first seventy-two hours of darkness. He thought, I deserve a rest, a break; it's not really a leave of absence or a suspension; it's a much-needed respite. It would not be held against him, it would not hurt his career, he could just ride it out, like Milius said, until that entire story blew over, until the news had moved on to the next big story and all that was left from the *Magazine* riots was a vague memory, a memory that he would remember certainly but that most people would forget and move on from, so that in the future, in conversation, perhaps the riots would trigger some association with him, but not the kind of detailed association of fresh scandal—"Oh, didn't you have something to do with . . ."— and there would be more stories for him to write, more stories attached to his name, and eventually the riots would get pushed back, another chapter, another life lesson, just one more step in his career.

And who needed the magazine, really, he'd told himself, on the third evening of his leave of absence, garbage overflowing, bathroom floor littered with cardboard toilet-paper rolls. I don't. I had a life before the magazine—I had a life and a career before the magazine, and I will have a life and career after the magazine, so fuck them.

But the darkness was creepy. The lack of phone calls, the lack of supportive email, the fact that the six-orgasms girl had broken up with him—and he didn't even love her, what did he care that she'd broken up with him—but now he had faced the darkness for three days and he didn't want to move.

When he dreamed, he would dream of his past horrors; he would see pencils sticking up along desert berms, flames, tanks exploding; he would dream of TV appearances gone bad, the camera frozen on him, scratching away at the earpiece until blood started to shoot out, as if the earpiece were like a small worm, a bug in a science fiction novel that had traveled into his brain and made his voice sound silly and his brain stop working. That made him stutter, drilling away, and behind the camera he could see his friends and family looking at him, he could see Nishant and Sanders and the intern Mike and yes, there, holding a pencil between his legs, he could see Chipotle, the Mexican—or was it a Puerto Rican he had saved?

He would dream of cell phones not working, of plane tickets that weren't good, of unavailable seats and long lines at security checkpoints. He would dream of getting drunk, shitfaced, and waking up trying to figure out what thing he had done that he should be ashamed of, then realizing he had done nothing, smelling his darkness, and that he had not moved from his bed for two weeks.

His laptop had been on the entire time, picking up a wireless signal, but he could not check his email—he knew messages and emails and voicemails and texts had been building up over those two weeks but he did not want to look at them. He could not stand the sight of them, because they would just be bringing more bad news, more blog postings and stories about how he had failed, fucked up, screwed the pooch, about how the *Magazine* riots had been his fault, that he had killed, by accident, by dint of bad reporting, seventeen Iraqis (the death toll had risen).

This wasn't true—he knew he had been the victim of a great crime, a great conspiracy, a great cover-up, and he wanted *The Magazine* to go to hell, he wanted *The Magazine* to burn.

But then, like a slave, he thought, he wanted *The Magazine* to forgive him, he wanted *The Magazine* back. He rationalized that the magazine was doing what it did best, that it was just protecting itself. That by protecting itself it was protecting him, too. That he was still part of *The Magazine*'s family, and that he just wanted their forgiveness. He just wanted to become A.E. Peoria, *Magazine* Journalist, again.

And after week three, he had said, I will get out of bed. I will get out of the darkness. I will forgive and let live. Let the bygones go their merry way—what the fuck is a bygone? I will check my email and voicemails, and I will be very Zen about it.

The three weeks of cleaning his system. Of no pills or booze, of cold turkey that had added to his general feeling of despair, of mild drug and alcohol withdrawal, shakes and tears and self-recriminations.

On week three, he cracked the blinds and saw the snow falling, and said to himself: It's not that bad, it's not that bad, it's not that bad. I'm okay, I'm okay, I'm okay.

He finally left his apartment to go down to the STD clinic that smelled like wet cigars.

"All looks okay under here," the doctor, a small man with a gray beard and yellow teeth, said. "Have you found any more spots?"

"No, I haven't," Peoria said.

The doctor tossed the bandage into a wastebasket.

"Okay, then," he said. "Your blood tests came back negative on other STDs."

"Great, that's great."

"Last time we talked," the doctor said, looking at his chart, "I suggested you go to AA."

"Oh, I haven't, but I've stopped everything. I've stopped everything, and it hasn't been easy, because I'm sort of in a tough spot vis-à-vis my employer right now. I'm sort of out of a job."

"You still have insurance?"

"Yes, I have insurance, but I'm on, like, administrative leave, I didn't even know journalists could get that. It's like something they give cops after they shoot a black kid intentionally by accident, you know. But yeah, I'm on administrative leave."

"And you haven't done any traveling, no more trips back to . . . Thailand?"

"No, I haven't really left my apartment."

"Because sex addiction, you wouldn't believe it, men, once a month, take these trips, rack up all kinds of debts, tens of thousands of dollars in debt. Disappear for a long weekend, a long weekend or five days, halfway around the world, that's what their sex addiction does to them. Like I said before, one sign of sexual addiction is if you have an STD—it's the equivalent of drunks having a blackout—and so it's prudent to look at those signs carefully."

"No, I'm not a sex addict, I don't think. I don't know if I'm really an addict at all," he said. "Not in the traditional sense."

The doctor looked at him skeptically.

"You should check out the meetings."

Peoria left the clinic, no more bandages, free at least temporarily from molluscum contagiosum, feeling, for the first time in weeks, prepared to confront his inbox, his voicemail, his backlog of unanswered communications.

He felt okay.

He went into his apartment, breathing deeply, forcing energy upon himself, forcing the darkness away—I can do this.

Then he got the last message.

He'd been fired again.

The Magazine, the message from Delray M. Milius said, thought that maybe Peoria should take another six months, perhaps a year or more, of leave of absence before he returned—before he discussed returning. He would be able to keep his benefits but he would not be getting a regular paycheck anymore.

Back to the darkness he went. Back to the darkness, for another three-week stretch, the bills and dirty laundry piling up, redux. Resorting to reusing the coffee filter in his coffee machine after running out of paper filters, ordering groceries and deliveries, ordering everything and keeping the door shut. Vowing to never again check his email, never to look at what other news it would bring—the wound on his leg had healed, the puncture wound had healed, the molluscum contagiosum had run its course, but a new wound had opened up.

The darkness didn't help him heal that wound. The darkness hid it from him, hid what he didn't want to recognize. He went over the scenarios in his head again and again. This wound was deep, cut to his core. He tried to ignore the wound, tried to pretend it wasn't there, but he knew he was burying his feelings, burying his emotions, burying the truth. I'm a journalist, he thought, and if I can't look at truth within myself, how can I see the truth out there in the world?

And the truth was he was terrified about his leave of absence—terrified and angry and dreading all social interaction. For the first time in his life, he didn't want to see, didn't want to spill.

What would he tell people he did? What could magazine journalist A.E. Peoria now say when asked what his job was?

The truth: The fuckers had stolen his identity. By firing him, they had taken away what he held dear—he didn't even know he'd held it dear, he didn't know how much his identity had been wrapped up in *The Magazine*'s brand: that for the past few years he had thought of himself primarily as *Magazine* Journalist first, a person and human being second. He felt like he was one of those kids who went to Yale or Princeton or Harvard and for the rest of their lives clung on to that as their calling card, as the most important part of their identity, even years after graduation day, years after it was all over for them—years after the rest of the world had moved on, they saw themselves as the Ivy League (he didn't get into Ivy League schools, true).

Was that now him? Would he now only be able to say, when introducing himself, that he used to write for *The Magazine*? A former *Magazine* journalist! Pathetic!

How did he allow his identity to become so entwined with some pieces of paper printed weekly? How did he fall for the prestige and structure—though he had chafed under the prestige and structure, he had fallen for it, more than he would have thought possible. He had fallen for it, and then they had taken it away, they had snatched

his identity from him during the worst time of his life: Six Orgasms
had broken up with him, a public humiliation on television, reputation raped on the blogs, a dent in his otherwise skyrocketing career.
Yes, he had been bumped off the fast track, the people mover at the
airport. He was back on the other side of the plastic barrier. Even
worse, he was on his knees, on his stomach, his face getting hit by an
imaginary janitor's mop, soaking the floors to make them nice and
shiny for those who did have real careers and who did not stumble,
who did not fall. For those on the fast track, the floors were clean,
while he was licking the dirty end of the mop, drinking from the
murky waters of the mop bucket, the janitor standing on the back of
his neck, saying, You thought you almost made it, you thought you
were almost there, but you weren't! You fool, how could you have
believed that you were going to be one of them? One of the brands,
one of the bylines that people recognized? How could you ever have
thought that was where you were headed?

How could you have thought you were going to be your own
brand?

No, you were a failure, a fuckup, a fucktard, a dipshit, a loser, a
skank, a donkey-ass weak bitch motherfucker. Yes, these words and
even worse passed through his mind—a cunt snorter! Yes, he was a
cunt snorter, an abysmal failure, a catastrophic embarrassment, that's
what he was. He could feel it on his teeth, even after brushing and
flossing, he could smell the failure through the darkness, he could
taste the failure on his pillows. The crust in his eyes: he would wipe
it out, place it on his tongue, and he knew. The dried sperm in his
pubic hair: he would reach down and touch and then taste the musk.
He could taste the failure all over his body, a disgusting taste, with no
career future to cleanse it away.

What else did he have besides a career? What did anyone in his
peer group have besides a career? No close family, no God, what else

was there to fall back on? To make sense of the world, to give his life meaning besides his career, his once promising career, his career that he had taken for granted. He had taken it for granted: the flying first class, the phone calls returned, the pickup lines—I write for *The Magazine*. What do you do?

Yes, the career had been his life. The career at *The Magazine* had been his id, his ego, and his soul. He didn't know it at the time. He didn't care enough about it. He just took pills and got drunk and passed out under his desk because he thought that he had it locked up. But one mistake—fuck, and it wasn't even a mistake! But maybe it was a mistake, the more he thought about it. Certainly running after Milius with a pencil was a mistake—maybe he did fuck up. Objectively, he had to admit, it appeared that he had fucked up. After all, he was in the darkness. He was living in the darkness while Healy went on to break more blow job stories and Delray M. Milius collected his six figures and Nishant and Sanders showed up again on television—yes, all of these things were as true as his unwashed sheets.

If only he could just allow himself to give up. To say, It's okay, it doesn't matter, life is too short. If only he could just knock off the ambition, if he could just take a deep breath and say, It's all going to be all right. Then he would be okay, then he could let go of the career, then he could fall back on something. But that wasn't in him. He knew it would be like telling a lion not to bite, an elephant not to deposit large amounts of excrement; no, there was no way the gears in his mind would stop turning over and over and over again. Why couldn't he just lie in bed? Why couldn't he just accept the darkness, postpone the heat death of the universe, still and silent? Or, perhaps, open the windows and open the doors and accept the light?

One night the buzzer to his apartment rang. He had ordered no food deliveries, so he didn't know who it could be. He hit the intercom button.

"Yes?"

"Alex, it's your mother."

He pushed the buzzer to let her in.

He poked his head out the door and saw his mother, with her partner, Amy.

"You two shouldn't come in here," he said. "It's a mess."

"We'll be okay."

Amy and his mother walked into the apartment, grimacing, almost coughing: dishes piled in the sink, cardboard containers on the kitchen counters, smears and stains on the glass living room tables, wadded tissues and toilet paper.

His mother opened the drapes and then the window. She and Amy moved aside a blanket and tossed a few empty boxes of television-series DVDs onto the floor.

"We're worried about you," his mother said.

"Well, I didn't want to tell you, but I got fired."

"We know," his mother said. "Amy read about it online."

"Ahahahfgahrh," he cried out.

"But that's why we're here. Amy, as you know, works with the dean of faculty, and they're looking for a part-time professor to teach journalism. We think you could do that, while you're waiting to go back to work."

"Teach?"

"Yes, teach journalism," Amy said.

"A professor," A.E. Peoria thought, and he had the first positive emotion he'd had in a while, the first stirring to his soul, because—as if it were the first tingling of exoskeleton, of another system of verte-brae spawning—being a professor was a career too, and that was something he could hold on to, that was something with backbone. It was as if the dendrites in some paralyzed part of his inner being that had dried up and contracted were firing again, new nerve endings flourishing, a network of new nerves that could take the place of A.E. Peoria, Magazine Journalist: A.E. Peoria, Professor of Journalism.

"Don't I need a master's?"

"No, you have a book published—that's a terminal degree, and you have years' worth of reporting behind you, so I think that should be enough."

And with his mother and Amy there, he felt the sparks of the old A.E. Peoria, the compulsive disclosure disorder persona. He started to describe to them the darkness, the darkness that he could breathe in, the loss of Six Orgasms, the humiliation on television, and three hours later, he had finished dumping, unloading, and his mother and Amy left, like angels of mercy—if he had believed in angels or mercy—but angels carrying something that could give him real meaning again, another career path. He wrote all of this down in his journal.

He turned on the TV, which he hadn't used to watch anything besides DVDs, and switched to a news channel.

On it were pictures from a prison called Abu Ghraib, naked Iraqis in a pyramid, a girl holding a man on a leash, even a picture of a soldier drop-kicking a Koran.

His story had been right after all.

29.

Sunday, May 16, 2004

I email Sarah to say hey. She emails back: Want to come to a book party? But I'm not calling it a first date.

Her job at Wretched.com is all-consuming. Up at six a.m., reading at least four newspapers and ten other blogs by seven a.m., twelve posts a day, a thirty-minute lunch, and then at night she goes to different events across the city to stay on top of things.

The book party is for a daughter of a famous writer who wrote a women's liberation classic back in the '70s. The daughter's memoir is one of those tell-alls about what it was like growing up around all these other famous writers. About all the fucked-up shit she saw at a young age, about the different men who passed through her mother's life, and how that led, inevitably, to promiscuity, drug addiction, expulsion from high-priced schools, and, finally, a career in writing, the shadow of her mother looming over her.

The shadow has its advantages, like the fact that her mom is a famous writer with a really nice corner apartment on 81st and Park, a perfect place to host a book party.

I meet Sarah in Midtown. I'm coming from work, and she takes the train up from the Lower East Side. We grab a coffee at Starbucks.

She's in sandals and a light blue dress that's pushing the boundaries of summer.

"Thanks for inviting me to this," I say.

"It sucks, I really don't want to go," she says. "This job is taking up way too much of my life. And I think my boss is going to be there."

Timothy Grove. A media mogul in training. Reputation is that he's something of a "new media" genius. He's the first person to make a business out of blogging. He found a way to monetize it. He's not considered really respectable though—maybe a step above a pornographer.

The theory behind his success at Wretched: We live in a society of assholes. The media is a reflection of these assholes. We'll show you what the inside of the asshole's asshole looks like.

It's been an effective tactic so far—nine million unique visitors a month.

Taking the elevator up, I walk into the room with Sarah. My first New York media party. I'm part of the scene. I recognize the people eating hors d'oeuvres and holding drinks, not because I know them but because I've read about them. My inspirations.

I stand halfway off to the side. Sarah works the room. The room pays its respects to Wretched.com.

Sarah introduces me to the daughter whose book is being released, Eleanor K.

"Eleanor, this is Mike Hastings," she says, and tells her the name of the magazine I work for.

"Oh," says Eleanor, "I think your magazine is running a review of my book next week."

"I work mostly for the international editions," I say.

"I don't know who's writing it, but it would be great to get a copy before it came out," she says. "To know what to expect."

Eleanor K. and Sarah look at me.

"So, do you think you could send me a copy? I mean, if it's not too big of a hassle, if it's not too big of a deal."

"Um, yeah, I guess I could look into that, sure," I say, knowing that I wasn't going to look into that at all. I do have access to the system of all the stories that are scheduled to run, but I'm not going to risk sending a copy of a story to someone I don't know.

"Mom, come over here, meet Mike Walters," she says.

"Mike Hastings," Sarah corrects.

Eleanor K.'s mother comes up, and I say hello to Mrs. K.

"Obviously, I know I'm a guy, but I was, uh, am, a big fan of your book, Mrs. K." I say. I've never read the book, but I've seen the paperback enough times to get the gist of what it's about.

"Thanks so much," she says, as insincere as my compliment.

Mrs. K. looks like she's from the '70s: ashram-chic clothes, long hair that used to flow and fit in a ponytail now dry and long and puffy. She has all sorts of bracelets and necklaces hanging off her wrists and necks.

"Mike's going to send me an early review," Eleanor K. says to her mom.

"How kind of you," Mrs. K. says. She seems spaced-out, as if she had traded in the pot and acid of the '60s for the lighter mood-stabilizing drugs of the late '90s, like Wellbutrin and Prozac. A pharmaceutical sellout.

"Eleanor, are you going to read soon?" her mother asks.

The room is filling up, getting to that point where the number of people will only go down throughout the rest of the evening.

Mrs. K. clinks her glass and Eleanor K. picks up a copy of the book that had been displayed on a small round table near the door.

Mrs. K. says something about how this is a very personal book to her daughter—and a personal book to her as a mother too.

I have a flash of envy for a second, watching the two. Wouldn't it all be easier if one of my parents were some famous writer? Who knew all the book editors and agents and could stock a room full of gossip columnists and book reviewers and magazine editors? I'd have that good material right off the bat—how Philip Roth taught me to masturbate on a grapefruit, how Bill Styron once called looking for his wallet, which he thought he'd left in the couch, how I read about one of my parents in a first-person account by Norman Mailer of an orgy where he'd sat on his/her face.

Eleanor K. introduces the passage she's going to read.

"Because you're all here, and many of you know, my mother has had this apartment since 1985," she says. "'Eighty-five was the year they turned her classic book into a movie, so she could afford a place like this"—everyone laughs, somewhat uncomfortably—"but it's also when everything came . . . I don't know. Crashing down."

She has a page marked, about fifteen pages in.

"'Early night. I don't want to go to bed. Park Avenue isn't a place for children after nine o'clock, my mother tells me. I want it to be a place for children. I am not a child anymore, but I want my home to be for me. I still take childish pride in answering her phones. Is your mother home? the voice asks. I'm proud that the voice asks for my mother. When I ask the voice his name, I can see his name in front of me on the bookshelf. Does your mother get calls from bookshelves? No? Mine does. It's like the boy in my second-grade class who bragged his father had climbed Mount Everest. That boy was lying, but I wasn't lying when I said that I had met the man who'd written a book about climbing Mount Everest. He was a friend of my mother's; everyone with a name was a friend of my mother's.

"'I climb up the stairs, running my hands along the cold metal from the spiral case to the second floor. The spiral staircase is my favorite part of the new home. It's neat.

"'I climb up the stairs and I look down. I am fourteen years old and already I know I'm a woman, my mother's daughter. I catch the eye of a Famous Writer. The Famous Writer with dark eyebrows. He catches my eye. He asks me if I want to hear a bedtime story. I'm too old for bedtime stories. He tells me this is a bedtime story that I'd never heard before.'"

Eleanor K. flips to another chapter.

"'How could you have done this to me, how could you? I scream at my mother, eighteen now, drunk on booze stolen from the cabinet. She didn't bother marking the levels of the bottles anymore. I didn't try to hide it. I knew the combination to the padlock. He had shown it to me while she was at a benefit, at a concert, at a panel discussion, a book tour, a play, a guest lecture, a talk show, a radio show, at a reading, at a book party.'"

Silence in the room, ironic laughter—this is a book party.

I start to sidestep toward the balcony to get out of the room. I haven't been out there yet.

I recognize the silhouette of the tallest man on the balcony. Timothy Grove. In all the profiles I'd read about him, the writers mention his unusually tiny head on a skinny six-one frame. Massively tiny, almost like a headshrinker, like the guy sitting next to Beetlejuice in the waiting room to purgatory. You had to think that a smart guy like Grove has a pretty big brain, and that his brain must be really pressing against his skull, trying to squirt out his ears. There are three other guys standing around him, leaning up against the balcony, listening to him.

I stand back from the circle, waiting for a break in Grove's monologue to introduce myself. I can hear his heavy British accent.

"See what they've done, the *New York Post*? Taking four items from Wretched—four items, ripped right off our pages. No credit, not a single credit given to Wretched. A travesty, innit?"

Grove looks at me.

I feel a bit strange at the party, wearing what I'm wearing. I don't really dress like the normal media type. My hair is a bit mussed—an ex-girlfriend, in one of her parting shots, told me I should keep my hair messy because otherwise I look like a dork—but I don't wear tight jeans or American Apparel T-shirts to work, or button-down shirts with open collars. A blue blazer and tie and gray flannels—I've always gotten a lot of shit from colleagues about it. They ask me whether I'm going to a job interview, or going on television, or if I'm thinking about becoming a banker. But Nishant and Sanders Berman wear blazers and ties, and most of the senior editors do too, so if I want to climb up, it makes sense for me to wear them as well.

But seeing Grove and his posse, gelled, hair product, hair fibers, hair molding, sculpturing crème, with Diesel jeans and pointy-toed cowboy boots or shoes, tight T-shirts, also designer, that probably cost fifty dollars a pop, I feel a bit underdressed, even though I'm wearing a tie. I probably look more like I belong in DC than in New York, but that's not a compliment in this city.

"Oh, this lad right here looks like he might work for the *Post*," he says, and his coven of straight males laughs.

"Hah. Nah, I'm just coming from work. Mike Hastings, nice to meet you, Mr. Grove."

I tell him I work for *The Magazine*.

"Ah? Another dead-tree'er come to say hullo," he says, and the young men laugh again.

"What's the readership of your dead tree?" Grove asks.

"I think they say it's like twenty million readership, three million circulation," I say.

"Twenty million, my arse. Three million copies for the doctor's office and dentist rooms, a whole forest chopped up for stale news, innit?"

"We definitely use a lot of paper," I say.

"See, boys, the blogs, the blogs are good at tearing things down. Ants and the like. Tearing it down. Throw it up, tear it down, break it apart, piece by piece. You get the scale, you get the ad dollars. Low overhead, scale, ad dollars, tear it down," he says. "What do you think of that, Hastings?"

"Wretched certainly seems to be where the industry is heading," I say.

"So, you here looking for a job?" he says, and his circle chuckles.

"Not really," I say.

"Well he should be, innit!"

Grove's small head shakes when he laughs, like a steamed pea rolling atop a telephone pole.

I laugh along too, wanting to seem like I'm cool with being from the old media.

"Lookie who's arrived," he says.

As a Wretched.com reader, I recognize the face of Rohan Mais, another up-and-coming media guru (also on the list of "Top 20 Media Players Under Age 38"). Grove's been directing his bloggers to post at least a half-dozen items on Rohan's own start-up print publication—he sees him as his "homo-competitor" for the crown of new media guru.

"You boys see what he's doing here," Grove says. "Might have some questions, privy like, for Mr. Hastings here."

Three of the twentysomethings fan out, leaving Grove and me alone on the balcony.

"A tad of a shake-up at your pub," he says.

"The pub?"

"Publication, the dead tree."

"Yeah, there's some readjusting going on."

"So whosit going to be?"

"Pardon?"

"Who's gonna take ol' Henry's place?"

"Either Sanders Berman or Nishant Patel," I say.

"Right, right, that's obvious, innit—I'm asking Patel or Berman," he says.

I'm tempted to tell him something—a little nugget of inside dope. I should have inside dope, shouldn't I? And part of me wants to tell him—to impress him. Am I after a job? I'm not averse to the possibility. There's something enticing about the world of Park Avenue book parties and instant New York media celebrity—a touch of power—and I can see that's why the twentysomethings hover around Grove, to get a sense of that power that comes with having a platform where what you say can shape reputations, kill reputations, make reputations. It's part of the fun, I suppose.

"Oh, I think, that at least right now, Nishant has the lead . . . I mean, he's a minority, there's never been an Asian editor, he's still riding that wave from 9/11, he's got a TV show, so his brand recognition is way up . . ."

"I hear Henry likes Berman better," he says.

"Maybe, but the last time I saw them"—and here I'm lying—"they were talking and, and you know, Henry ignored Sanders, at his own book party, and talked to Nishant, so I think that was a sign."

Spastically, his head nods up and down.

"So you think it's a lock for Patel, innit?"

"Not a lock, but if I had to say who was ahead in the sweepstakes . . ."

"Right, right, natch, right. You see the magazine stories before they hit, right? You could send us along a little peek every once in a while, do ya think?"

"I could give your name to the publicist," I say.

"Don't want no publicists, mate. I want to get the scoops before the scoops, you follow?"

I follow.

I leave the party an hour later with Sarah. We take a taxi back down to the Lower East Side. We don't make out. I probably should have made a move, but I'll leave it at that, because I hate those books or stories about guys who agonize for one hundred pages about not making a move. It's not usually my style—usually I make the move—but I don't want to complicate things, at least not yet, especially if I'm maybe going to try to get a job there. Instead we talk about her boss.

"I talked to Grove," I say.

"Oh? I'm sure he loved you."

"What do you mean?"

"He does that, he likes to surround himself with twentysomething straight guys. It's a thing he has."

"Oh."

The next morning, Sanders Berman walks by my cubicle. He's leaving the bathroom, wiping at his face.

"Hastings, can you believe the nonsense these bloggers write? I'd never even heard of a blog until this morning," Sanders says. "No standards."

"Yeah, blogging is a big thing, everyone is reading them."

A look of fear.

"Everyone?"

"Well, depends."

"Heard of Wretched.com?"

They say when you lie your eyes dart to the side. My eyes really want to dart to the side.

"Sure, yeah, it's popular."

"Popular? How popular?"

I've never heard a southern drawl reach such a high pitch.

"Pretty popular."

"They wrote some trash about me this morning, saying I wanted to take Henry's place, and then that Henry hadn't talked to me and that Nishant was going to take it over. Unbelievable."

"Oh, yeah, wow, that's horrible. Who knows where they get their stuff from."

"Milius is writing them right now to correct the record."

"That's a good idea, yeah."

Sanders continues down the hall.

I check Wretched.com. Under Sarah's byline, there's an item that, almost verbatim, though unnamed, repeats the conversation I had with Grove.

I've never been a deep-background source before. It gives me kind of a thrill, to be honest.

30.

Later, 2004

The winter and spring have vanished, and the clothing on women in the city has vanished with it. A.E. Peoria walks down the street, and he swears there must be an uptick in emergency room visits from men running into parking meters, newspaper stands, lampposts, doors, taxis, heads whiplashing at what the city has hidden in the winter months, bounciness, unfettered gravity, bare skin, and Peoria wonders if women have always dressed like this or is it just another sign of the times.

There is a determined shuffle in his steps, head up. A peppiness through his entire being that is the spiritual correlation to the perky breasts and large breasts and mountain breasts and canyon breasts and fake breasts and real breasts that rise and fall so confidently, so healthily, that like him, shout out life.

A.E. Peoria has broken out of the darkness. He is working on himself.

Self-acceptance.

Embracing the teaching gig. Embracing therapy. Embracing salads and 2,500 calories a day. Embracing friends who he felt betrayed him. Embracing emails that went unreturned. Embracing time, embracing taking a nap. Embracing sweatshop Bikram yoga. Embracing moments of solitude, meditation, clearheadedness. Embracing three hours a day of work. A tentative embrace of sobriety and a marijuana- and pill-free existence, of higher powers and powerlessness and fate. Embracing the idea that it is possible to heal. Embracing working out. A surprising embrace of the gym culture.

A.E. Peoria is on his way to see his personal trainer, part of the six-month membership he has with the Platinum New Members Package at the Ultimate Fitness gym on West 83rd Street.

"Five minutes' warm-up on the 'mill," Norm says.

Peoria, in blue and white Nike sneakers and breathable nylon-blended shorts and a gray T-shirt that hangs out over his gut—a gut that is already getting smaller—starts walking on the treadmill, four minutes, three minutes, two minutes, one minute, a sip of water at the fountain before the workout session begins.

Norm, big eyes, thick-muscled body, specializes in self-acceptance, three or four mornings a week, at the gym. Two days for legs, two days upper body, fifteen minutes of core, cardio up to Peoria. His core starts to feel better. His core is something that exists somewhere in between his legs and arms and chest, some strange network of muscles that ties his entire body together that can be reached with strange duckwalks and massive green-and-yellow ball exercises and squats.

"You better not puke again," Norm shouts, his way of encouragement.

In the sweat and the claustrophobia of the low-ceilinged workout room at Ultimate Fitness, the treadmills and all these different machines, these weight machines bending this way and that, twenty reps, twenty reps, twenty reps—"Feel the burn," Norm yells at him, feel the burn, and he feels the burn, and between sickening gasps, he explains to Norm that, wow, working out really makes a difference. It's all part of accepting himself even as he's changing himself—

he is getting into shape, and it doesn't take long before he is in some kind of shape, the fifteen pounds he put on since the age of twenty-seven dropping to only twelve pounds, but it's twelve pounds of near muscle.

"Feel the burn!" Norm says, as Peoria lies over on a reverse lateral pulley system, ass up high, knees jerking back with the weight of fifty-five pounds.

Triceps, biceps, lats, squats, thrusts, mountain climbers, steps, push-ups, sit-ups, crunches, and curls—he sees why the exercise industry booms. He's never really been a fan of gyms before, never really understood them. There are two kinds of dudes, Peoria has always said, dudes who like to shower with other dudes and dudes who don't like to shower with other dudes. Gym culture reeked of the former. He hadn't minded sports in high school, played soccer, kept fit, but then didn't go out of his way to embrace the unnatural experience of the gym—too artificial. He now sees why they've become so popular—working out feels good, right, it's supposed to feel good, with all the endorphins and such.

He can now be one of those people who say, "Yeah, just going to the gym." Or, "Man, what a great workout it was today." To talk of the natural high. It hasn't taken long for him to look at those around him, on the street, who clearly aren't working out, who clearly aren't taking care of their bodies, and feel some measure of superiority over them.

And Norm, he can talk to Norm between suction pops of oxygen. Norm doesn't care about the Internet or the front page of *The New York Times*. Norm doesn't care about scandal and disgrace.

Norm cares about the burn, about the core, about his progress, about his health.

Because, as he has told Norm, there are still wounds, still things that protein shakes and chocolate milk can't fix, torn muscles of his heart and brain that just won't go away. Things he can't face. Like newspapers and magazines and the Internet. Peoria has stopped reading them. He can't stomach Googling his name anymore. He can't stomach more than a glance at the front page of *The New York Times*. He can't stomach any magazines, because he doesn't want to know what's going on in that world, his old world. It hurts too much to think about it, and so, he believes, it's better to just accept the fact that he can't look at it.

"I get how celebrities feel," A.E. Peoria tells Norm, sweat-soaked T-shirt and face splashed with water from the fountain. "Why so many television and film stars don't watch TV and film. You know why George W. Bush doesn't read the newspapers? It hurts."

"I hear you, man," Norm says. "Let's stretch you out."

And on his back, leg bending, Norm's weight pushing into his chest, Peoria explains how a television star, career up and down, can't stand to watch a half-hour drama because he's thinking, I could have gotten that part! I auditioned! I had that part, I was once that person, and then the industry cast me aside. Or how a director whose film had bombed doesn't want to hear of other films. He doesn't want to see interviews of other directors. No, an actor who has tasted success and then has that success pulled away is not too interested in watching *Inside the Actors Studio*, of course not. It's too painful to see: the actor knows the fates of career paths, and career implosions and explosions are the only difference between why he's sitting on the couch and flipping past *Actors Studio* and why the actor is sitting in the studio basking in his actingness.

And so it is the same with him—no CNN, no MSNBC, no Fox News or *Time* magazine or *Atlantic*.

"I hear you, man," Norm says. "Like these dudes over at Crunch. I left after some bullshit, and it took me like a year before I'd set foot in a Crunch again. Any branch."

Peoria leaves in the early morning to work out; he slides on flip-flops and a Nike tracksuit, sneakers tossed in his gym bag, and he likes that. Like a doctor who wears his scrubs at any opportunity for comfort and as a status symbol, he likes his workout clothes, his workout bag slung over his arm, dried sweat at the corner deli, dried sweat at Gristedes, dried sweat while walking the aisles of Whole Foods, getting healthy drinks of organic cherry and bunches of organic bananas, and he can feel that he is part of this elite club, the club of those who have worked out, and that his dress, his comfortable tracksuit, is accepted as the sign of a man who has released all the bad energy in the gym, the sign of someone who has learned to accept himself.

Self-acceptance.

Three hours a day, that's how much A.E. Peoria works out now. Three hours a day—self-acceptance.

Or is it all work? Working on himself.

After working out, a coffee in the morning, a walk to get the coffee. An hour of writing in his journal. An hour of thinking about the syllabus. An hour or two of reading *Teaching for Dummies*, where he learns tips about how to relate to students, how to present himself, how to share his experiences and his learning in a way that is engaging, Socratic, compelling, fascinating, thought-provoking. Tips like "Treat the students like equals, but remember they aren't your friends." Tips like "To relate to students, make sure to use references to cultural phenomenon that they understand—for instance, *Laverne and Shirley* might mean something to you, but don't be surprised if your group of students reacts to dropping that reference with blank stares."

And he swears he's okay. It's true he's not going totally unmedicated. How can one go totally unmedicated and why would he go totally unmedicated? He doesn't want to go back to that darkness, he doesn't want to go there. So he is medicated, yes, a mild antidepressant, a few hundred milligrams a day, just to take that edge off a little bit, just to give his emotions some space from his brain.

The excitement, the buoyancy, of the teaching gig lifts his spirits. Barnard College, an all-girls Ivy League school. He will be teaching undergraduates at this school the art of journalism, a little subject called narrative nonfiction. He will mold and guide and show the way forward into promising careers, careers with the promise that his career once had, careers that he will not envy. No, he's now, at least on some days, accepted his fate, accepted the fact that sometimes in life you need to take a break, sometimes it's okay to take a nap.

His friends call—he realizes he does have friends, he supposes. He tells them all what he is telling himself. I'm not drinking. I'm not taking pills. I'm not even missing *The Magazine*. Life is more important than *The Magazine*. You know, it's time for me to do something else anyway, time for me to try something else. Really, they haven't totally fired me, I think, once things settle down, I probably can go back—if I want. If I want. My choice.

And he says this to Norm and to whoever will listen. He's come to embrace this summer as part of him. The summer after high school was the summer he lost his virginity, and the summer after that was the summer he tried LSD, and the summer after that was the summer he had an affair with an older woman, and the summer after that was the summer he traveled to Europe, then came the summer of an internship at the magazine, then the summer he wrote *Desperation Points West*, then the summer of Baghdad and Iraq—how far away that seems. (A quick flash of Chipotle in his mind that he shakes off.) And so, if every summer in his mind has a theme, the theme this summer is self-acceptance. I'm okay, I'm okay.

31.

Time Passes

I t's like *Laverne and Shirley*," Peoria tells his class of twenty-six students. "You want the beginning of the story to grab the readers' attention, whether you're writing a nonfiction book, like *Desperation Points West*, or an article. You want to really get them into it. So, like *Laverne and Shirley*, that opening sequence—'We're going to do it!' Laverne is putting a glove on the beer bottle in Milwaukee. Lenny and Squiggy. You get the sense that it's a comedy, it's about friendship, it's set in Milwaukee—you get all of that just from the opening sequence."

Very little reaction.

"But you know, that theme song—rules are meant to be broken. That also applies to narrative nonfiction. I'm going to give you rules, but you can break them. But like that show, if you're going to break them, it better be, you know, brilliant.

"That's called, in journalism, we call that the lede. The opening paragraph is the lede.

"There can be an anecdotal lede.

"An analytical lede.

"A news lede.

"An omniscient-narrator lede.

"A lede in the second person. You.

"Most popular is probably the anecdotal lede, at least as far as magazines go."

He's scanned the list of students in his class, and there they are sitting in front of him. He knows that it's only natural for him to find the most attractive students first—he knows that he will not be able to resist that. There are three, two blondes and a brunette, and there is a fourth, a Mexican woman who makes fierce eye contact with him. She isn't really as attractive as the other three, but there is something appealing about her body language. He doesn't know if he's imagining it—perhaps it's something in Mexican culture where eye contact doesn't mean as much as it does in the States. Like in France, where women stare down men all the time and that's just part of the deal.

No, he scans his class of twenty-six, and he says what he says about *Laverne and Shirley,* and the rest of his first class is a rambling blur of handouts, stapled pages going back over back, of explanations about what he hopes to accomplish, about the different books on the syllabus, about how many papers he expects, about how he isn't going to accept just anything, he really wants reporting, about where they can obtain copies of the books on the syllabus—including, for extra credit, *Desperation Points West,* which, although out of print, can be ordered through a variety of websites for a good price: only 7 cents plus $1.35 shipping.

After the first class ends, he takes a breath and shuffles papers on his desk, finding it funny that he is the teacher, the professor. How very strange that is, waiting for the class to file past, smiling at the students, organizing, flushed, waiting to see if there is going to be anyone with questions or comments or concerns, waiting to see who is going to brownnose, who the kids are who don't care, looking for signs of drunkenness and drug abuse. He remembers college well.

He's pleased that one of the blonde girls stays behind and tells him that she has already read *Desperation Points West*. She has a copy. Will he sign it?

He smiles—"Karen, right"—and makes it out to Karen and then talks to her for five minutes, explaining how it was an important book, probably an overlooked classic, and that he appreciates greatly this kind of reader feedback. And while he's talking, he notes that his instincts were right about the Mexican, because she's also staying behind, waiting patiently for Peoria to finish speaking with the blonde.

The Mexican woman approaches his desk.

"Hi there, what can I help you with?"

"Professor Peoria," she says.

He looks at her, perplexed, and has a jolt of fear. Did he at some point hook up with this woman somewhere? She does look somehow familiar. Strong, slanted cheeks, a thick build for a woman, definitely third tier, maybe second tier. Certainly not first tier. He knows he must have hooked up with her or hit on her. Maybe he hit on her at some bar at some point during one of his periods in New York when that's what he was doing. Or maybe this woman is a friend of his ex-girlfriend's? Could that be? She would be the type that his ex-girlfriend would hang around—not quite that attractive, not much competition.

"Justina, is it?"

"Yes, Justina."

She waits.

He waits.

Does she want him, in this first class, to put a move on? This does seem like something out of a porn fantasy, something that isn't supposed to happen to a professor until at least mid-semester. No, Peoria resists the impulse to try something, and instead says, "I've blacked out a lot," he says.

She doesn't respond.

"What'd you think of the class?"

"You don't recognize me?"

"Oh, shit—I mean, excuse my language. Sure, I recognize you."

"You do?"

"You're a friend of my ex-girlfriend's, right? I met you at a slam poetry event?"

"No."

"Okay, we didn't, and I mean, this is awkward, we didn't hook up before, did we? Because if we did, I don't know what the school policy is about that. Fuck, I'm sure it's against policy."

"No, we never hooked up."

"Shit, then I'm sorry—did I interview you for an immigration story?"

"You saved my life."

32.

August 2005

'm working on the cover story when I get the email from Peoria. I figure it's one of those mass emails to all the people on his contact list. Hi all, here's my new information, just in case you want to ever reach me.

"Hey, Mike, how is everything at the magazine? I'm in the neighborhood today. Let's grab coffee if you can."

I say okay, but I think it's strange. Why would he want to talk to me?

Peoria says he'll be around in two hours. Both Nishant and Sanders are waiting on files from me, so I hurry to get those done.

It's a Monday, and the television outside Nishant Patel's office has been showing footage of a hurricane that hit New Orleans, and things seemed to be deteriorating real quick there. There's no way the story I'm working on is going to run on the cover.

Sanders walks by, on the way to the bathroom, and I say to him, "This hurricane in New Orleans looks pretty bad. Are we going to send somebody down there or do something about it?"

"Maybe a news brief," Sanders Berman says.

Nishant comes in from a television appearance. I mention the hurricane to him.

"We don't do hurricanes, Hastings," Nishant tells me.

"Okay, right, well, I'll get back to work on the files."

I go ahead on the cover story. Now, more than two years after the invasion of Iraq, it's called "How They Got It Wrong (And What They Can Do to Make It Right)." Both Nishant and Sanders are writing big pieces chastising various elements of American society and government. Nishant wants to aim at the Bush administration for being so stupid and incompetent. Nishant tells me—and this is a bit out of the ordinary for him, to make such a declarative statement—that he wants to call the decision "the most catastrophic foreign policy decision to be made in the twenty-first century."

"Do a little historical research, Mike, find examples of our history in war where we've launched an ill-fated foreign adventure then managed to settle for a less-than-satisfactory result, a result that doesn't meet our ridiculous expectations going in. Korea, perhaps. Vietnam, naturally." He pauses. "Get a few of the most outrageous examples in the media too—Robert Kagan, Brennan Toddly, that Kanan Makiya fellow—how the media didn't look critically at this case for war. But, you understand we need to be realistic here—we can't just leave. It's no use to just throw up our hands."

Sanders is going to give more or a less a historical defense too—yes, they made a mistake; what were we thinking?—but all great leaders make mistakes, and it is too early to count out Bush as a great leader. He is, after all, leading the country in two wars, one that is proving eminently successful in Afghanistan and one that is faltering in Iraq. "Historic examples, Hastings—I'm thinking here what Lincoln had to tell the American people after Bull Run, what FDR had to say to Americans after North Africa. Teddy up San Juan Hill . . .

History isn't made by losing our nerve . . . No, I don't think history is made by that, do you?"

I do my due diligence, digging up the most pertinent anecdotes for both sides of the argument. I start searching for embarrassing media examples and find a website that tracks those kinds of things. I edit out Patel's and Berman's own entries on the list before I send it along to them.

For Nishant, I find Eisenhower's decision to get us out of Korea. I get a great speech from our pullout in '75, in Vietnam. "We settled for half the country," Nishant writes in a draft. "And years later we've seen the benefits—a democratic regime, Samsung, Hyundai. Second-largest oil exporter in Asia. Second-fastest growth, beaten only by China." He wants to make the argument that by losing, we actually won in Vietnam. Look at the country now, thirty years later. Couldn't ask for better capitalists in training. So perhaps the same thing is true in Iraq—there's been enough creative destruction there that things will naturally take their course.

I send Sanders a Korean anecdote as well—a comment General Douglas MacArthur had made before he called it quits from both the military and life. "If we had pursued Korea to the fullest, perhaps we wouldn't be dealing with the nightmarish Kim Jong Il regime today," Sanders writes.

I figure one of them is going to have to lose the Korean anecdote in the final copy—we don't want to confuse our readers with contradictory historical precedent.

I send the files and go out to meet Peoria at Starbucks.

I order a large iced coffee. The kid behind the counter looks like he's been shipped in from the Bronx to fill up the minimum-wage jobs on the Upper West Side. He didn't understand what I wanted. Venti? he says. Yes, a large, I say.

I like Starbucks, but I refuse to speak Italian for them. Nothing against Italians—I'm not going to allow a corporation to rename a serving size.

Peoria arrives a few minutes later. He's wearing a blue Nike tracksuit.

"Just went to the gym," he says, after I stand up to shake his hand.

He orders a Grande iced coffee and we sit back down.

"Good to see you, man, you're looking well," I say.

"Thanks, bro."

I wait for him to fill the silence in the conversation. But he doesn't. It's odd to see him so healthy-looking; I wonder what kind of medication he's on, and how long it's going to last. There's something in his eyes, a layer of air bubbles in an algae-covered pond. Distracted. His upper lip keeps making a quick motion, like a snarl, the meds going to work on his synapses as they battle his true nature and find expression in a twitch. He's trying hard to seem calm and relaxed and to not just spaz out, right there at the table.

"We miss you at the magazine," I try.

He exhales.

"Wow, that's good to hear, man, because that's why I'm here. I don't want to get too specific, and I can't really tell you, but you should know. Because I'm supposed to come back."

I know he wants to get very specific—he wants to spill.

"Oh right, when?"

From what I've been hearing, it doesn't look good at *The Magazine* for Peoria. Some of the editors want administrative leave to mean he was basically fired and just hasn't been told yet, and they weren't officially informing him because they didn't want to seem like they would just abandon an employee that quickly if he was perceived to have made a mistake. Gary, representing the smart money, says that "there's zero chance he'd work at the magazine again."

"March. I was supposed to come back in March. A year off. But that was too soon, they said. Though now I have something, I have something real big. I'm working on something real big, you know, that might get me back there sooner, if you know what I mean."

"Right, sure, of course."

"It's a big story. I wanted to get the sense from you, as you always seem to know all the gossip, if you think I'd have a chance of coming back earlier if I had a big story."

I don't know if I should tell him the truth or even the truth about what the rumors say.

"Is, like, the coast clear?"

"There's some discussion about you, yeah."

"They're talking about me, so that means they haven't forgotten me. That's a good sign, I think."

"No doubt, like Wilde said, they haven't forgotten about you."

"That's what I wanted to hear. I mean, I can tell you, and this is between you and me, I've really been working on self-acceptance this summer, and I've accepted, you know, that the magazine doesn't really mean much to me. Can you believe that? I mean, when I was your age, I would have dreamed for the job I had, and then when I got it, I didn't know how dependent I became on it for my own self-worth. I, like, started to identify with the brand. I started to say things like I love *The Magazine*. I started to see it as family and as a place where they really, you know, cared about me as an individual, and man, I loved telling people I worked for them—it made me feel like I had some worth. I guess I took it for granted and I didn't see that if I lost that, if I lost that, I didn't think it would be that big of a deal, but it was like my whole identity got shattered. My entire identity. So I worked on self-acceptance, and I think now, you know, it's not a big deal at all. *The Magazine* isn't life. But I also realize, you know, how much it means at the same time, you understand what I'm saying? When I had my class—I'm teaching up at Barnard—you know, something really strange happened and my reporting instincts just *BAM!*, just pounced, and I said, Wow, this is such a blockbuster I can't even begin to say. I didn't get much sleep thinking about it, which really, I think, hurt my workout. I almost puked again, but then I had a protein drink and a slushy and that settled my stomach."

"You're teaching? That's great."

"Yeah, our semester just started. But that's how I got this story, or at least what I think might be a story. But I really can't tell you about it right now, I really can't."

"Okay, dude, sure, if you don't want to tell me about it, that's cool. But you can, like, trust me, you know?"

"Well fine, I'll tell you."

For the next fifteen minutes, Peoria launches into a bizarre story that I really don't believe. I think he might be having some kind of psychotic episode, or breakdown—a cousin of mine had had that once, and, as is strangely the case with psychotics, when the brain breaks down, it seems to break down in the same way for everyone. This cousin believed that evil alien ghosts were trying to do something with his genitalia and that the signals to these extra-dimensional creatures were coming from a place on the far side of Lake Superior. Peoria's story had whiffs of that, and the other signs seemed to fit: wearing a Nike tracksuit in the afternoon, talking fast, a stream of consciousness that, really, I could barely follow. Something about Babylon, a Mexican food dish, Thailand, and the GI Bill.

I don't know what to say, he's acting so strangely. I just want to get out of there. Yes, it sounds like a story, I tell him, but no, you should not approach Delray M. Milius about it.

Maybe I should tell him to forget it, that there's no rush, that I think he should think about it more. I think that's the best chance for him surviving at *The Magazine.*

And that he didn't have a chance to survive at *The Magazine* anyway.

But I don't say that, I don't, and maybe I miss a chance to save him, but I don't know that until later.

I go back to the office. Both Nishant and Sanders have responded, asking me to get a few more details, and maybe talk to a couple of historians to back up their respective cases. I'm keeping an eye on the news—all this Katrina stuff looks pretty bad—but it's a Monday and only a handful of people are in the office and it definitely doesn't seem like anyone else thinks it's a big deal.

Tuesday, Sanders runs the story meeting. He says we are going ahead with the Iraq cover, and that the "website can handle the hurricane."

On Wednesday afternoon, Delray M. Milius runs by my desk, hissing on the phone, "I know I told you not to go when you called on Monday, but we didn't realize how big this was. We need you to get down there now!"

On Thursday, Sanders runs the story meeting again. Henry the EIC is on vacation.

"Clearly, we're doing Katrina on the cover for this week."

During the international story meeting on Friday, Nishant Patel relents.

"Okay, we'll hold off on our covers and do this hurricane."

I get a frantic email from Sanders on Friday night, asking me to do some research for the editor's note.

"I want more details on how LBJ handled that natural disaster in . . . whenever that was."

I have to fact-check his editor's note on Saturday. It reads:

I, for one, have given the President the benefit of the doubt. But it's clear by his failure to realize how catastrophic the events in New Orleans were, how long he delayed before responding, how—and I'm going to use a word that the kids these days use—how clueless our President has been, I am disgusted. How could they not have seen how big this was? Why did it take them 72 hours, until Wednesday, to get into action? I have written before, that the President, a commander of two wars, is, by his very nature, a hero-prophet. After observing his reaction to this hurricane, I would be forced to admit that perhaps my estimation has proven premature.

All of this means that I forget about Peoria. I won't hear from him again until he sends me his journal months later.

THE PRE-DENOUEMENT

Okay, so the book is getting a little out of hand. I'm aiming to wrap it up at 80,000 words, and we just hit 80,000 words now. The plot is just beginning to materialize in full force, and there are all sorts of other threads and developments that, if I'm going to get to them, would add an extra hundred fifty pages to the book.

I'll spare you.

We get the joke quickly. I don't want to be tedious about the whole thing.

Most of the top media folks are a bunch of clueless assholes, egotistical, vainglorious, pompous, insecure, corrupt—you get the picture, right? Not that they're bad people—they're not out there running death camps—but it's just who they are. If it weren't them, it'd be someone else, right? And if I'd worked at another magazine, they'd be someone else too.

Like my uncle used to say—he's a priest—about giving homilies at a Catholic mass: Make it three minutes long and mention basketball.

Keep it simple. Grab the reader by the throat. A fact in every sentence.

I'm breaking these rules, and as Peoria tells his students, many of whom I've interviewed, I'm trying my best to do it brilliantly.

We're coming up on the end here—I'd say less than an hour left in the show.

33.

October 2005

A.E. Peoria sits at a table of his favorite Italian restaurant on the Upper West Side, pondering what he should call the individual sitting across from him.

Justina. Justin. Chipotle. He saw a documentary once about Muhammad Ali, and the writer was having that same problem—should I call him Muhammad Ali or Cassius Clay? Lew Alcindor or Kareem Abdul-Jabbar? The Artist Formerly Known as Prince and Sean Combs also pose that problem.

Justina is talking, laying it on heavy, dropping the wisdom. Justina is explaining the conversion.

"A belief in war," Justina says, "is like a belief in God. Comforting until you look too closely at the facts."

Peoria doesn't quite know what to say, but he does know he should write this down.

"Science," Justina says, "science is a religion that can prove its miracles."

Peoria keeps taking notes.

Ten details.

Thick bowl of pasta, penne Bolognese.

Four slices of garlic bread.

Justina is wearing a white sweater, preppy, for the fall, jeans that don't quite fit comfortably on her hips.

Black heels.

Dusky light.

Couple next to them glances over.

Table leg is shorter than the other; waiter kneels to slide a piece of cardboard underneath the dwarf leg.

Thinks: Good Justina isn't wearing a dress.

Elaborate silver jewelry.

Elaborate earrings: big hoops, bumblebee yellow.

Dark olive complexion contrasts against pale creamy sweater.

Chardonnay, lipstick trace on glass.

A.E. Peoria is surprised by the amount of wisdom she has, and wonders if that's some kind of stereotype—the wise transvestite or shemale, hard-earned packets of knowledge, dropped out, like crumbs on a trail to self-acceptance.

"I'm a miracle of science, Alex," Justina says. "I'm a miracle of fate."

It is their second meeting, not quite the third, not yet the meeting when things go wrong.

A.E. Peoria has promised that he will write about Justina only when Justina gives him permission to do so. Justina explains that she is at Barnard College on the GI Bill. But, as she explains to Peoria, there is a debate in Barnard about whether to accept transgendered students who were once male. It is a raging debate—protests, petitions, clauses in the student handbook. So, Justina hasn't mentioned her unique circumstances to anyone else. She also is fearful that the funding for the GI Bill could be taken away if it became public that it was supplying funds for the education of a transgendered individual.

Peoria knows this, has nodded and sworn the vow of secrecy, but he is already mentally preparing to back out of that promise. He hasn't quite admitted to himself that he is going to back out of the promise—he hasn't quite accepted the fact that he's ready to give Justina the major burn. He is telling himself that he should just be prepared to write about Justina now, or next week, or three weeks, in case he or she changes his mind, or whenever he has enough to tell her story, whenever he can go to his editors at *The Magazine* and say, I've got something for you, an exclusive. It involves an Ivy League school, a transvestite, and a Purple Heart. Can't beat that for a story.

Justina trusts him, as he is the man who saved his life, and especially since he agreed to the preconditions of the interview. She explains that the school has the most powerful LGBT organization in the country, so that is why she went there, that leaders of the LGBT know of her case and helped grease the paperwork, helped her in, but they are keeping her hidden, a shemale Trojan horse. She worries it could be a case that would have to be tested in court—if your gender has changed since leaving the armed forces, does your status as veteran change? She knows the conservative elements in the nation might be outraged, might say they do not want their taxpayer dollars paying for a transsexual to go to school, even a veteran transsexual with a Combat Infantry Badge. Already, explains Justina, she has lost her family and she does not also want to lose her benefits.

"So like, uh, how did you pay for the operation?"

She smiles.

"There wasn't much to pay for . . . I came back, you know, and it was gone. It was gone completely, a scar, a hole with a catheter. I was in my bed at Walter Reed for months, for months, and they would come in and say prayers and I would get balloons and flowers and even the president and celebrities would come by. One celebrity, a Hollywood star who had just tried to kill himself on painkillers and

heroin, three weeks later he came by Walter Reed. Like he wanted to
see how good his life was compared with people who really can com-
plain. I couldn't even look at him. I was so angry those first months.
They started giving me pills, testosterone supplements, to make up
for everything that I had lost. But the pills, they made me so angry! I
just got angrier and angrier. And then they would cut my hair, they
would still pretend I was in the service, still pretend that I was still
part of this army, and I knew that wasn't true anymore. So when they
let me out, I wanted to die. I wanted to curl up and not wake up and
just let myself die. It couldn't be done in the hospital—they were
watching you, therapy groups, post-traumatic stress discussions, very
well regulated on the pills that one could take lethal dosages of.

"They kept a close eye on me, because they say the wound I have
is called, in psychiatry, is called a non-threatening terminal wound.
Non-threatening, in that, physically, the damage was minimal! Minimal! Terminal in that it could lead to my death by my own hand
later on. This is the wound, I have heard soldiers say, they would
rather die than have. Do you know what is the best piece of your
body to lose?"

"Uh, your hand?"

"No, they say, BK, below the knee, non-dominant leg—that is the
best leg to lose if you have to lose something, I have heard them say.
Maybe they didn't know about me when they said it, that at least they
still had their penises, at least they did—because if they didn't, they
would rather have died out there, on the field, in the sand. Bleed out.
And where am I? What am I supposed to say to that, me with no
penis, no testicles, a scar on skin? I wanted to die. I do not think I am
being unreasonable . . ."

Peoria hasn't touched his pasta, and Justina hasn't really made
headway on her grilled chicken salad. She's ordering like a girl, Peoria
thinks, ordering a salad for a main course at dinner.

"At Walter Reed, there were reading groups. Discussion groups. A reading group, one of the books we were given was *Born on the Fourth of July* by Ron Kovic. Have you ever read this book? It is a powerful, disturbing book—it gives lie to everything that we fought for in Vietnam, in Iraq, in most wars. My fellow soldiers, they couldn't see it like that. They believed the book was interesting because it showed how bad VA care used to be, compared with what it is now. They found the positive message in the book—only in the modern-day American volunteer Army could you have soldiers find a positive message in that book, even the disfigured soldiers, soldiers with nine reconstructive operations on the face, soldiers whose arms have been sheared off at the shoulder, who cannot move anything below the Adam's apple, only among these soldiers could you have someone say, '*Born on the Fourth of July* is a book about the improvement in health care.'"

"I guess my question is, you didn't think that the book was about improvements in health care? Sorry, I've like, only seen the movie, a long time ago."

"No, it is not about health care. I found the book to be about transformation. Kovic's trauma transforms him from the soldier, born on the Fourth of July, the patriot, to an influential antiwar activist. It is about how this spirit of resistance was in him the entire time but it was not until he was shot, twice, until he lost the movement in his legs, that he realized that the surface, the patriot, was not who he really was—or no, I should say that he was always a patriot, it is just that his expression of patriotism did not fully form until the trauma. What was hidden inside him was a true patriot, his true self, a self that was prepared to go out and take criticism for revealing the government's lies. We are beyond that, we are beyond that, don't you see? We have to know the government lies, there is no shocking us— every soldier, or most, with a brain, know on some level that the government lies. So the transformation in this war, well, it is very hard to be the same—the veteran who comes back and says 'I was lied to' is greeted with a shrug—well, yes, of course you were, didn't you see Oliver Stone's film with Tom Cruise in it?"

"Shit, Justin, Justina, you're losing me—a bit. I don't quite get it—I'll rent the movie again, I have Netflix, so I can put it in my queue and everything."

"The transformation, for me, it could not just be political. It had to be more fundamental than that. It had to be a transformation of nature, my human nature, and what is more fundamental to human nature than gender?"

"Right, good question."

Peoria has this strange sense, forcing himself to listen again, that Justina had rehearsed this quite well, and he wonders how an enlisted soldier had that much education. Most didn't, most would have trouble answering Jay Leno's on-the-street stumpers: What two countries share the border with the United States? Who is the senator from Puerto Rico? Mexico City is the capital of what country? Who was the third president of the United States? You didn't get the rare intellectual or philosophizer unless you were talking to an officer.

"I don't understand, though, why you enlisted. I mean, you're obviously pretty smart."

"My family is very rich, a rich Hispanic family in El Paso. I had a very good education. I could have been an officer, I would have been accepted quickly, but I felt that if I was to understand what my family and the other immigrants went through, then I would have to join up as an enlisted man. Like Charlie Sheen in *Platoon*."

"Right, like, you would have to be rich to think like that."

"*Exactamente.*"

Peoria has been listening for close to forty-five minutes straight, and this is about his maximum attention span—this is the point where he nods and hopes that his digital tape recorder keeps capturing the seconds ticking away on the display counter so he can go back and listen to it later.

He looks down to make sure the little red light is still going, sees that it is, pushes it a little closer to Justina, making sure that it is not being blocked by the edge of a bread plate, and exhales.

"Anecdotes, do you have any more, you know, like I talk about in class?"

"Anecdotes?"

Justina pauses, and Peoria recognizes the subtle shift in the eyes—the shift that indicates the brain is about to disassociate with the words she is about to speak, because whatever it is, whatever sentences are arranging themselves in her head already have warned the brain that protective barriers of enzymes and neurons are necessary, walls must be erected on the sides of her syntax, to keep the language away from the emotional side of her brain, the tear ducts and the heart.

"Cindy Sheehan. She is the mother who camped out at President Bush's ranch after her son was killed in Iraq. You remember her?"

"Yeah, Cindy Sheehan."

"She came to Walter Reed. She was not allowed in, and I don't know if she wanted to come in, but she stood outside the Mologne House, the brick buildings, for three weeks, with a group of antiwar protesters. She stood outside the gates with her signs, and in my ward, we would come and look. Protesting outside Walter Reed. We would peek outside and see her and we would be filled with rage. With absolute rage. What is she doing here, tormenting us? The man in the bed next to mine, Lucas, he had lost his left leg above the knee. A full hip disarticulation, or FHD. He could not stand seeing her out there. He would say, 'The lying bitch! Her son did not even like her'—and he would tell me how he had heard from someone who knew her son, someone in her son's unit, that they were estranged, that she was not on good terms, and there she was, an impostor, outside the walls of the pain box, the pain house, marching to make a political point of her tragedy, exploiting her son's death, the fucking bitch, the fucking slut bitch whore. This became an accepted fact among the men of our ward, of the Army, I think. That she and her son were not close and that she should not be there. She should shut the fuck up and honor her son's sacrifice, like the rest of us. Lucas wanted to make her shut up. He would wish he had his thirty-thirty hunting rifle that he would use to bag bear and deer and sometimes to help with the local wild boar problem in Georgia. He would say to the CO, a doctor, when he came by, 'Sir, you've got to give me a shot at her. You got to let me get my rifle in here. All it will take is one, one shot. I'm a good shot and no one will be none the wiser.' He yelled this to the doctor one day, and the response from around the ward was incredible, like some kind of prison movie with the inmates banging tin cups on the bars, this steady beat of clinking and clanging started across the third floor. It was dinnertime and we had forks—men with one arm and one leg hitting against the metal bars of the hospital beds. The rhythm began, swelling up, and we all felt very good, and the shouts started, 'Sheehan, Sheehan, Sheeeeeeehhannnnnnnnnnnn.'"

"That's some heavy shit," Peoria says, thinking it makes the perfect anecdote to begin his piece, one certain to spark controversy and discussion.

"That night, as it happened, she was going to hold a candlelight midnight vigil to mark the last night of her three weeks. I believe it was even on Veterans Day. Lucas believed it would be his last chance. He plopped into his wheelchair and rolled over to my bed. 'My prosthetic is working well enough, and I know you can walk, so tonight is our last chance,' he told me. 'We have to go outside and we have to take her out. It's our duty,' Lucas whispered to me, 'we must do it.'

"Did I want to take part in such an adventure? Yes! I did. I did not think twice about it, I did not have a moment of reflection. We would again be in a small unit—it was such a relief to have a mission for us to do, another high-value target for us to take aim at, as Lucas put it. At twenty-three thirty, silent, like we were trained, a whole group of us gathered: me, dickless; Lucas, minus a leg; Payton, a quiet type, no right arm; Jack, two below-the-knees—yes, a half-dozen of us. Like a crippled A-Team. We could be a black humor sitcom. We did not feel at all ridiculous. Fuck them, we had a mission tonight, and if you would have seen us limping along, down the fire exit, one floor, two floors, three floors, down to the ground level, where we would walk out the back and circle around the side of the building, leave at Gate 3, and come up the sidewalk, where we would change into civilian clothes rather than hospital garb, maybe you would have laughed or felt sympathy or started to cry or sneered about how pathetic we looked. But we did not feel ridiculous. We were motivated. Very highly motivated. We were the volunteer army of 2002, and this was not some kind of pussywhipped Vietnam veterans who were just going to sit back and take it. We were making a preemptive, Rambo *First Blood* strike. We were not going to take this kind of abuse from a lying whore like Cindy Sheehan. Lucas led the pack, around the sidewalk, and as we came closer, we could start to hear the sounds of a song, a song they were singing, and we could see lights for television cameras. They were singing for the cameras. They had been silent all night but now the lights and the sound boom were there, and so they started to sing. They started to sing that very stale song 'We Shall Overcome,' as if they were King or Chavez—they shall overcome? They shall overcome what? Who were they, when we were the wounded, missing our manhood and our dignity and keeping our head held high. They were going to tell us, what, that it wasn't worth it? What the fuck do they know about Iraq? What the fuck do they know about costs, about it not being worth it? They have no idea, and especially that Sheehan, who hated her son and whose son hated her, had no right, no right to be overcoming anything at our expense. Lucas walked with his hand out, already in a grip, imagining Sheehan's neck in his hands, ready to strangle her to death. He would strangle her—he could taste how satisfying it would be. Army hand-to-hand combat training, army grappling is based on numerical superiority. You get the enemy down, you grapple him, immobilize him, and the others come to your help to finish the beating or detention. We, the other six, would run interference, form a tight circle around him, and therefore there would be no witnesses. There would be no one to see who did it and we would all say nothing. We would all say she had attacked first, and it would be the word of seven veterans against the word of what—a hippie peace activist, a radical tormenting the wounded warriors. Radicals versus veterans. We knew that in any court of law, we would win, the troops would be supported. We turned the corner and there Sheehan was standing, at the head of the crowd . . ."

Peoria tunes out. The whole thing sounds ridiculous now, and he wants to direct Justina back on track to the more important story, the story about her. All this bullshit about Sheehan is getting tiresome.

"Okay, yeah, yeah, so it didn't happen, and when you looked into her eyes or something, you came to realize something about yourself?"

"Yes, that's right, I—"

He cuts her off. "Great. Okay, so you go back to El Paso and your family isn't like, what, supportive?"

"Oh, they were supportive. They wanted me to be a hero. They presented me to friends saying I was a hero. My mother would cut in front of lines at Applebee's or Outback and say, we should sit first, our son is a hero, a veteran, a wounded soldier. They didn't tell anyone what my true injury was. They didn't want that information to get out—they just said I was shot in the lower regions and that I was recovering."

"Right, right."

"I curled up in a little ball in my house. My bedroom that I had had as a teenager, there I was, supposed to be a man in his twenties and living in his parents' house, in his old bedroom, same posters, same desk for studying, same all of this. I acted like I couldn't walk, like I was too sore, and my parents, they accepted this. I could have walked, but I didn't want to. I wanted to stay in bed. I wanted to just wither away. I stopped cutting my hair. I stopped taking those testosterone pills. I stopped those things, and I drifted, for weeks.

"My anger, after I stopped taking the pills, my anger started to go away. Like a eunuch. At first, I missed my anger—my anger was all that I had—but I didn't want to take some pills to be a man. For three days, I shook—I shook with the emptiness of these fucking hormones to make up for what would have been in my testicles! I woke up—"

"When?"

"This was five months after my Alive Day, they call it. Alive Day. A sick fucking joke, someone at HBO must have devised it, I don't know, to make us feel good, rather than call it Blown-to-Shit Day. The shakes had stopped—I had stopped shaking from lack of anger—and no, it was no peace, but I walked by the Dallas Cowboys poster, I walked by the picture of Miguel Fernandez in his Tecate-sponsored open-wheel racing car—we had gone down to, my father and I, to watch him race and got a picture, all of us smiling, the sponsored beer, red and green in the backdrop. I went to the bathroom and I took a shower and I picked up a shampoo—my mother's shampoo, a coconut-scented flavor from Vidal Sassoon, and I cleaned my long hair, down to my shoulders, and I stepped out and tied a towel around my head like I had seen my sisters do, and I saw how much weight I had lost, how thin I looked, and I looked down at the scar and it looked like a vagina. I smiled, I smiled and I batted my eyelashes, and I inhaled, and I felt at peace, because what I had been resisting, what I had been resisting was that I was no longer a man, yes, and that I was really a woman now, I was a female. I was thin and effeminate-looking always, and perhaps it would always have been so, but if it wasn't for fate, if it wasn't for that shrapnel, I would not have seen it, or it would have taken me years to see it, to act on it."

A.E. Peoria hits the stop button on the tape recorder and thinks, Man, this chick or dude is fucking nuts. He slips the tape recorder in his pocket and realizes that he has an erection.

34.

Later

don't expect to see Peoria back in the office so soon.

"Mike, dude, good that you're here," he says, elbows on the cubicle wall. "I took your advice—I decided to come and talk to Delray M. Milius, to make amends, you know, and to pitch that story I told you about."

"Cool, bro, that's cool."

I don't know what he's talking about. I gave him the exact opposite advice. But I suppose that's what he wants to do, and no matter what I had said, he had interpreted it as confirmation of what he had already decided.

I'm surprised that Milius even agreed to speak to him after the pencil incident—I thought for sure it was just a matter of time before Peoria got canned permanently.

"He said I could bring you in as a research assistant, you know, to help me get some background to the story. You have time for that?"

"Ah yeah, just doing a couple things for Sanders and Nishant, no worries."

"Okay, great. I gave you the details last time we met, right? About what I was sitting on? Swore you to secrecy, obviously too, as this can't leak out, you know? It's all very sensitive."

"Sure—"

The Peoria that I knew is back—divulging, disclosing, vomiting up his exclusive story. It's kind of mind-boggling to hear. I hadn't heard anything like it before. Sure, there are gays in the military stories, and there are stories over the past few years about transgendered kids in high school and college, and about how some state universities, like the University of Vermont, were creating unisex, or multisex, or transgendered bathrooms because the risk of attack on transgendered people is extremely high if they go into a men's room, and they aren't quite accepted in the ladies' room either. But never had I heard of a shemale war hero.

"Not 'shemale,' dude, that's not a politically correct term. Plus, she's got no junk anyway anymore, so it doesn't make you a shemale unless you have, like, a dick and breasts—she's working on the breasts, though. But really, what I need from you is to get me the science behind it, and some of the social context for this—talk to a few experts in the transgendered community. Don't quite tell them what we're talking about, you know, but we want to get the legal issues and everything resolved first, you know. We're really going to be doing Chipotle a favor, I think."

"So she's cool with you running the story?"

"Oh, you know, man, she doesn't really want to do a story about it, at least not right now, but sometimes the news value has to outweigh personal considerations. You can't just sit on a scoop like this because the person you know could get hurt by it."

"You don't want her to get kicked out of school and lose her benefits, though, right?"

"Yeah, that's probably going to happen, you know, but there are enough support groups and shit out there that if she does lose that, I'm sure someone will step in, you know?"

"Okay, right, maybe."

"Yeah, maybe, there's no guarantee in this business on anything, you know. Like that lady said: Anyone who does journalism and doesn't realize that what we're doing is totally immoral is a fucking clown, you know?"

"That's cool, dude, yeah, of course."

"Okay, man, I've got to run, because I'm, like, meeting her later tonight for what I hope will be the final interview—I've already got like thirteen hours' worth of audio files—maybe you can start working on transcribing those too? You have the Sony program, right? My other notes, you know, just keep them to yourself and everything."

Another assignment. If Delray M. Milius is willing to put his grudge behind him, I realize that this is probably going to be a big story to be part of, and I'm glad he thought of me to work on it. That means, including the Iraq stories, I will have contributed to more than thirty-five feature stories over the past year, which will put me way out ahead of the rest of the newbies.

Sanders strolls by my desk.

"Have my notes for the Imus show ready?" he asks me.

"Oh, coming along, no worries."

"I don't like to look bad on that show—he can throw some tough ones at you," he says.

Sanders has become a regular guest on the Don Imus program, one of the highest-rated radio shows in the country. Along with Oprah, Imus can move books like nobody else—and Sanders's book had moved, thanks to his regular appearances and endorsement by Imus. It's been a regular task for me to do, to get notes together on the possible subjects Imus might bring up on the show, maybe write a few jokes for him, or possible subjects. Not that Imus or his producers ever stick to the topics Sanders tells me they are going to talk about—a continuing source of annoyance for Sanders. I get to work writing up the notes.

35.

Sunday, November 20, 2005

Watching transsexual pornography started as research but it has become a compulsion within days. Men who are now women is the category that A.E. Peoria Googles. Full-blown transsexuals. Hundreds of thousands of links appear, safety filter off, images and video clips and paid sites. The shemales, the he-shes, the cross-dressers, the post-op and pre-op transsexuals, strap-on kings and queens—how much of this community, percentage-wise, he wonders, is involved in pornography or cabarets or strip clubs? And isn't it odd to base one's whole life around sex? Or did we all base our lives around sex, and if you could get a job focused on sex, perhaps you were ahead of the game? Perhaps the transsexuals understood something that no one else did? But what's the point of becoming a ladyboy if you aren't going to hustle on the street?

But Justina isn't a ladyboy or a shemale—she's a transsexual, and she wants to pursue a career in academia, in writing, in the arts or in advocacy, eventually. Advocacy, there's another popular profession for transsexuals. You either got a job in the sex industry or got a job advocating for transsexuals' rights. Advocacy and pornography and show tunes—the three primary industries of the transgendered community.

Peoria's morning research starts with his iced coffee and a check of the email and the list of phone numbers of experts he wants to call.

Up at six a.m., hitting his stride again, feeling for the first time since before the Iraq War that drive, that fulfilling call of work, a sense of purpose—a story to write and to tell and to understand. On his laptop, on his wireless, he streams a local news radio show—usually, the program he starts listening to is *Imus in the Morning*—but the pull of the boundless Internet, with all of its perversions, drags him back to free porn sites, and he lowers the blinds in his apartment, pulls down his track pants, and watches the explicit sexual acts.

As a young man growing up, photos in magazines were enough to get him off. First, publications like *Playboy* were good enough, but then he upgraded to *Penthouse*; the open vaginal and anal shots of *Penthouse*, still done respectfully, were the next level. Then, he discovered *Hustler*, and his masturbatorial bar was set even higher—*Hustler*, now that was explicit, threesomes, full penetration, dripping cum shots, and a new and enticing category called Barely Legal, which forever altered the way he viewed young female teenagers running cash registers at ice cream stands and in grocery stores and Japanese school uniforms and cheerleading outfits.

When he got his own apartment out of college, in the '90s, he was able to own his first VHS player and visit his first sex shops in the city, on 33rd Street: a candy store, all the different racks of various interests for sale, and all he had to do was duck in and buy the videotapes to see those still images that had worked for him for so long come to life. The sheer freedom of being able to rewind and fast-forward and pause, with no worries of parents or siblings ruining his privacy. That's freedom. He never bought another magazine again.

The Internet proved to be a disruptive force for self-abuse. With the Internet, the sheer range of digital images did the job at first—he was able to stop watching videos on the VHS and start watching, on his computer, acts that he had read about but never seen—women sucking off farm animals, women urinating on the faces of other women, women urinating on the faces of other men, men urinating in clear streams into the open mouths of women, defecating even, strapped and bound with metal and leather contraptions, penetrated with massive objects like baseball bats and giant rubber dildos, a foot in diameter, or shaken soda cans stuffed in rectal canals, and on and on. These images—who was putting them out there? Where was it all coming from? And what an amazing thing it was, all of this that previously one would have had to order via the U.S. Postal Service from a European country, now all available thanks to the spread of dial-up connections and 32-bit modems.

The Internet, he knows, had been developed by DARPA at the Defense Department, for war, but sex quickly took over as the primary innovator, from the days of the first chat rooms. Now, with DSL and cable connections and streaming video feeds, digital images of the most grotesque and enticing kind no longer worked to get Peoria off. He had to see the movement, he needed the image to be flashing at 32 frames a second, in a little box on his screen, uninterrupted—watching porn on a slow connection didn't even do it, he needed a high-speed connection or he just wasn't into it.

He was not terribly concerned about the moral implications until June 2002, when he'd gotten the fastest speed available and clicked on a link that said "vomit porn," and at that moment he had a crisis of faith, or the closest thing one who does not believe in anything can have to a crisis of faith.

A white girl, wearing a blue skiers' tuque with an embroidered golden star, had been kneeling down in front of a crowd and giving head to a black male of significant perpendicular length. Using the now ancient deep-throating technique, she worked the man's cock avidly, eyes watering, his large hands clasped around her ears, occasionally pulling out to the left or right to make a popping sound against the suction on her cheek. At minute 2:33 into the clip, the standard degradation went off course; at first, the male performer responded as if it were still part of the performance, but then she ripped his hands away and started to crawl away, a desperate move, as if she were a child with motion sickness in the back of the car trying to unroll the window, or a coed searching for a bathroom stall after expecting to come into the restroom only to touch up her makeup. She started to puke, a yellow and a watery flow, all over the ground, and the camera first zoomed in on her face as she vomited, and then the camera pulled back to get the reaction of the cheering crowd and the still-hard penis of the black performer, and then the video ended, and A.E. Peoria himself felt sick, he felt ill, and wondered if maybe he shouldn't be watching this stuff, maybe it was destroying his soul, if there was such a thing.

That didn't last long.

He thinks of it now because he'd had the same first reaction to the transsexual performers: that something was somehow unholy or desperately sick in the acts that were being performed, that it was somehow disturbing to his subconscious that the women being fucked in the ass used to be men. But as he watched, he instinctively started to touch himself, and he started to hold the images in his head of Thailand, enhancing a sexual experience that he had avoided masturbating to at all costs—he was straight after all, it was his parents who were gay—but the transsexual porn brought these memories back, and he no longer felt revulsion, and in fact, started to get off on the idea that the man fucking the woman was actually fucking a man, a dirty little secret that wasn't a secret but added a level of fantasy to the moving video clips, a level of fantasy that his own memories augmented.

After one week of research, he started to worry: In the same way that he was never able to go back to magazine porn after the Internet had evolved, would he ever be able to have normal sex again, with a normal female? Or had his fantasy wires been so crossed that he would need to keep upping the sexual illusions and delusions and confusion in order to reach a fulfilling orgasm? And then, he asked, in a rare moment of self-awareness, did he want to go back?

And then there is the issue that he tries to avoid. That he tries to sublimate with Oedipal and Freudian and Jungian rationalizations and all that—he tries to ignore that he really wants to fuck Justina.

PART VII

The Last Week

36.

Later

I'm preparing the notes for another Sanders Berman spot on the Imus show. I haven't heard from Peoria. That's not too surprising. He'd dumped his notes my way, emails and journals and audio files that I haven't yet bothered to look at. I had learned at the magazine to work on deadline, and even opening the email was effort I didn't want to expend until I was sure the story was going to go forward.

I'm surprised when I get an email from Sarah, the Wretched.com editor. She asks if I'd be able to fill in and guest edit Wretched the next week. Timothy Grove runs what is more or less the media equivalent of a sweatshop—no benefits, ten days of vacation, no extra time for holidays—and Sarah needs to go home for an emergency next week. Timothy Grove had protested and said that if she couldn't find a replacement, she would lose her job. So she asks me.

I should ask for permission from Delray or Sanders, to be safe. But I know they'll most likely reject it. Nishant might be more willing to say yes, because he doesn't really pay too close attention to the day-to-day, so as long as I ask him, I'm covered. I send an email to Nishant, and I never hear back. I take the non-response as his tacit permission.

Sarah invites me to a party that night at a bar on the Lower East Side called the Dark Room.

The Dark Room is on Ludlow Street, above Rivington. This doesn't mean much to most people—but as Greenwich Village was to the '50s beatniks and the '60s hippies, the Lower East Side is to this strange and much less influential crowd of the early '00s, at least in their minds. They are important, or believe in their own importance, even if only expressed with the required self-mockery. They aren't artists, and not really a community of writers, either: they are bloggers, and their focus is each other. They are hyper-consumers; they don't write, they create content, stripping away any pretense of some larger ethos or goal except that it is somehow hip, rebellious—though they'd never use those words and they mock hipsters and rebellion too. A desire to be noticed and to criticize the criticizers of the world, to gain its acceptance by rejecting it, breeding a strange kind of apathy and nihilism and ambition, floating in a kind of morally barren world where they say, Look, here is the asshole's asshole of the world, the New York media, and we will show you, minute by minute, post by post, what the rectum walls feel and taste like, and you will know even better these sensations because we ourselves are part of this intestinal lining, and we are okay with that, we have embraced it as our contemporary calling, at least until we can get real jobs or a book deal.

On the Lower East Side, where they live, gentrification on these blocks was more or less complete—the last remaining Jews had been pushed out a decade before, the Hispanics were still found but mostly outside the primary five-block radius, hanging around in small groups and whistling outside of the subway entrance to the F train on Second Avenue. Orchard Street is filled with luggage stores and leather stores and glasses shops, run by Pakistanis, storefronts selling junk and trinkets and passport photos, a slow death before developers can come in and create a trendy boutique.

But none of this is totally clear to me at the time—it seems like a cool crowd to be part of, it seems like the new new media is a place to visit, and here they are, in the Dark Room.

Sarah meets me outside the front door, where a Cadillac Escalade–size bouncer checks our out-of-state driver's licenses under the purple glow of a flashlight.

The bar is split into two rooms, to the left and right of the entrance, eight-foot ceilings, everything black. To the right is a stage, where live bands or DJs play next to a bar; and on the left, there are couches and tables.

Sarah points to the far corner where a table has been staked out. A group of about seven males and three females, all white, age range twenty-three to thirty-five, stand sipping beers and gin and tonics.

She starts making introductions, yelling the names and the blogs that they are associated with.

There is Allan Tool, who holds some kind of deputy managing editor title for Wretched; Franklin Liu, who blogs on Mediabistro; the other Sarah, Sarah Klein, who does Gothamist; some guy named Arnie Cohen, most notorious for his ability to get mentioned on everyone else's blogs without actually doing anything of note, except hitting on Sarah Klein in the back of a taxicab and then blogging about his rejection; Jennifer Cunningham, who would later have a "crisis of conscience" and leave Wretched to focus more clearly on herself; and on and on, names with a "blogspot" and a "dot com" attached, names that I've heard of before by reading one referring to the other. The closest thing to someone from a traditional media outlet, besides myself, is a kid with short dark hair and beady eyes and a skinny tie who works for the *New York Herald* named Jonathan

Lodello—he is here, Sarah whispers, to do a story on the new new media scene, a story that will surely then be linked to on all the blogs of everyone sitting around the table, generating traffic and page views that can help with the advertisers and buzz.

Franklin runs up to Sarah.

"Let's do coke."

Sarah looks at me.

"You want to come?"

"I'm good, thanks."

"Laaaammmmmme," says Franklin.

"Yeah," I concur.

He takes Sarah by the arm and they find a spot in line at the bathroom. I sit down next to another kid.

"Kelly," he says.

"Mike," I say. "Kelly, as in Kelly Treemont?"

"That's me."

"I've read your blog. I thought you were a woman. The name."

"I get that. You don't do the powder either?"

"Nah, I used to do that shit a lot but stopped."

"Me too," he says. "I'm very boring now. I live with cats. I'm in recovery."

"Great. I work for a magazine."

"Dead tree, oh no."

"Yeah, the trees are pretty dead."

"You know, to be honest, I take a little Adderall still," he says. "It helps me in my writing. I'm working on a memoir. About my experiences with drugs and alcohol, and I don't know if you know, but I'm gay, so it's about my experiences with drugs and alcohol and being gay and everything."

"Sounds great," I say.

"You know, I think it's been out there, a little, but my experience, I think I have a really unique perspective."

"How long have you been working on the book?"

"Three years. This blogging, you know. But I found an agent. She's excited."

"Very cool. Having fun?"

"I'm waiting for Timothy. He's supposed to show."

"Timothy Grove?"

"Of course. He doesn't like these places—he prefers Balthazar, a place where he can pretend he's Anna Wintour or Graydon Carter—I think coming here reminds him too much that he's not really one of them, no matter how hard he tries. He'll always be more Larry Flynt. But you should watch out. He's a collector of straights."

"Is that right?"

"Aren't you the one they have guest blogging this week?"

"Yeah."

"There are things you could do, you know, if you want to make it permanent."

"Things?"

"Yes, things."

"Good to know. Is that how, uh, I mean, has anyone else ever done those things?"

"Me, of course, but it was brief, and I thought I loved him, though he is such a fucking scumbag."

"Yeah, sounds like it."

"Oh, watch this, this should be good."

The other Sarah, Sarah Klein, stands up from the table and grabs Jonathan Lodello's hand.

"She has such huge tits," Kelly says. "You know the backstory?"

"Uh, no."

"Franklin broke up with her three days ago. She's totally pissed about it, and she is totally convinced that Franklin is going to go and sleep with Sarah, and so she has to make him jealous by dancing with Lodello. If you want to get laid tonight, you should really talk to her, I'm mean, she is going to be ready to go away with someone cute like you."

"Oh, thanks, right."

"You have very nice eyes."

"Yeah, I appreciate that. They work okay."

I get up to get a club soda at the bar. Kelly doesn't want anything, and while I'm waiting at the bar, Timothy Grove comes in. He looks lanky and recently showered, and there are three men, all in their twenties in a semicircle, the same group I had seen at Eleanor K.'s house. He's dressed in all black—black jeans and a black T-shirt, probably a two-thousand-dollar shirt, though—with black cowboy boots and silver rings on his left and right hand and two studded diamond earrings on his left ear, new additions, it looks like. He moves—"slithers" would be tipping my hand—he moves over to the table, looking like a Persian prince from some ancient time.

The other Sarah, Sarah Klein, appears next to me.

"Do you dance?"

"Not this early. Can I get you a drink?"

"Red Bull and vodka," she says.

"Very youthful."

"I'm going to be thirty-four next week, so I do everything I can do to be very youthful."

"Right, right."

Timothy Grove has taken over the corner table with his entourage. I walk up with my club soda.

"Ah, the dead-tree'er, innit? Dead man walking. You talk to old Sanders Berman and Nishant Patel about how they are running to the ground your old brand there? Third round of layoffs coming, innit, and what are they doing? The little princes are scrambling for the top editor job, trying to be the captain of the good ship *Titanic*. Make brands of themselves over it, and there you are, still the little drooge of them, eh, while they build up their names to trampoline off the dead tree, floating on the dead tree until it goes down? That was your original sin, giving it away for free, giving all that content away for free, what a sin that was! Didn't get the Internet, they did not at all, and opened the door for the likes of me to come and give 'em a good interrupting kick. Good to see you finally get it, Hastings. Good to see that you're wanting to work for us now."

"I appreciate the opportunity."

"You even speak in the dead-tree language. We don't 'appreciate opportunity' here, there's no need for the brownnosing and suck-upping here, Hastings, no need at all."

"Okay, right, well it should be fun."

"Here's a numbers game for you, some research I just had done for my empire. Your magazine circulation ten years ago? Maybe three million, and claiming a readership of twenty-one million. Highly unlikely, but still had impact, it still mattered who you decided to put on the cover. Had that lyric in a Paul Simon song, innit? Thousand words a page, eighty-three pages on average an issue. Now you're down to 725 words a page, and fifty pages an issue. Full staff of your foreign correspondents was thirty-five a decade ago, now you've got ten, but you're still holding on to them, just to tell your little adver-tisers that you have an international brand? Isn't that right, Hastings? You know how much that international brand is worth to your adver-tisers? Seven million dollars, my sources at your magazine tell me, seven million. No domestic bureaus—no more Detroit or Miami or San Francisco or Dallas, just DC and New York and a woman in Los Angeles. The dead tree, they didn't get it—and they laughed at me at first with my nonpaper. They said, 'Oh, there's no future in that,' but they weren't looking too closely, were they? They were blinded, stuck, a bunch of arrogant fools on the good ship *Titanic Lollipop*. I think you've seen the light, Hastings, seen the darkness, more like it, and you've become one of us. If, that is, you do a bangers job this week."

"Right, right, yeah, I'm looking forward to it."

Franklin rushes to the table, Sarah behind him, laughing, eyes darting, nostrils cherry red. He whispers something into Sarah's ear, and a few minutes later, when I look around to see if she wants to leave, she's already gone.

I walk outside the Dark Room. I feel a brush of long leather jacket charging inside.

"Whoa," I say, moving to the wall.

"It's you," Sarah Klein says.

We're standing in the dark alcove in front of the exit. The bouncer holds open the door, and in the light from the streetlamp, I can see her face.

"In or out," the bouncer says.

"Out?" I ask.

Sarah follows me out onto the street.

"I was about to leave too," she says.

"Sorry to hear about you and Franklin, that sucks."

"Fuck him, he didn't mean a thing to me. I was only out here looking for him because I forgot to tell him something about this post I'm writing."

"You were out here looking for him?"

"No, like I said, I just wanted to tell him something. I can't believe it. He's such a fucking asshole. Where's the other Sarah?"

"I think she left too."

"With him?"

"So it would seem."

There is the inevitable awkward pause.

"You're upset."

"Yes."

"If you want to talk about it, my apartment is just around the corner."

We start walking down the street, and I notice that Jonathan Lodello of the *Herald* has left the Dark Room at about the same time and sees us before we turn the corner.

37.

Later Still

A.E. Peoria tries to get comfortable in his bed, but he is lying on a hard object, buried beneath the sheets. He moves around restless, still can't figure out what it is, until in frustration he grabs the sheet and throws it up in the air.

"What's wrong?" Justina asks him.

"Oh fuck, I didn't mean to wake you."

"Does being with me make you nervous?"

"Ah, here it is, fuck," A.E. Peoria says, holding up the object. "The jar of Vaseline."

Justina laughs and rolls over, putting her head on his chest. Peoria places the Vaseline onto the nightstand, next to a cruddy box of condoms that he had purchased three years before, when he had moved into his apartment, but hadn't really used very much; the box just kept getting buried under papers and other junk that found its way into the nightstand drawer. His girlfriends were usually on the pill, so he hadn't had a need for them.

Did being with Justina make him nervous? Yes it did. Did he want to tell her that? No, but would he be able to stop himself?

What he really wanted to do was to call his doctor friend, and ask what his percentage chance of catching an STD is from sleeping with a transsexual. Have there been any studies done on that? What are the percentages? How many partners had Justina had before him? Does anyone really get infected with HIV from just one sex act? He supposes it's possible, but how unlucky would he have to be for that to happen? And really, he hasn't heard much about HIV in recent years, and he'd never had sex with African prostitutes, or gay men, or heroin users, so he had felt quite well protected and secure until now. Even the fear he'd felt in Thailand had been put to rest by a Reuters story saying that the Thai sex industry had really nipped the HIV problem in the bud, thanks to a public information campaign, symbolized by a cartoon figure named Pac Con-Dom-Dom, a lively semitransparent condom with a red sash and googly eyes, who would, like a Japanese spirit, swoop into brothels and teenage bedrooms moments before penetration, to say, at least in translation, Please remember to be safe. The cartoon worked, and practically eliminated that disease from the Southeast Asian nation, protecting its sex industry for at least another generation or two, until some new fucked-up supervirus came out that could kill every fornicator around.

But Peoria starts worrying about this midway through the second time they are having sex, after remembering that you aren't supposed to put Vaseline on condoms or something because the Vaseline eats through the rubber. Shit, there's even a Pac Con-Dom-Dom public service announcement about it on YouTube! But maybe that's inaccurate, referring to some outdated Vaseline in the developing world. Maybe Vaseline has gotten rid of that glitch; maybe it's now closer to the K-Y line of products, but it was the only lubricant that Peoria had available in his apartment—he had picked it up after broaching anal sex with his now ex-girlfriend, but when they finally did have anal sex, it was at her apartment, and she had K-Y.

Then there is the fact that he signed a contract with the school that said he wouldn't sleep with his students, at least while he was teaching them. He didn't ask about it at the job interview—he didn't think it would be a wise question—but he had read the paperwork carefully enough to see that professors were given a loophole that meant that as long as the student wasn't getting credit that semester and complied with other state and local laws, there was some room to maneuver. Finally, he started to feel a strong attachment bond, as his mother's partner would say.

"Yes, I think I am nervous. I mean, you are a student and I've never slept with a man before."

"I'm not a man."

"And what if the Vaseline ate through the condom?"

"What?"

Peoria pauses. He gets out of bed. He goes into the bathroom, closes the bathroom door, and turns on the hot water and starts to scrub himself.

What was it with this strong attachment bond anyway? She understood, Justina understood. She understood what it was like to be out there in the desert, and he had never really dealt with that. The I-am-going-to-die-amid-loneliness feeling, the absolute trauma of helplessness—no one had understood that, no one had gotten that, and maybe he had pretended that it didn't really matter to him that he had shrugged it off like the wannabe war correspondent is supposed to do. But it did affect him, and it was an experience that— despite his ramblings, despite throwing hundreds of thousands of words at it in conversation—that defied all conversation and writing and one that just required you to be there: you had to be there, and the only person close to the trauma of that night was Justina, and this is what is so powerful.

The door to the bathroom swings open slowly.

Peoria peeks around the shower curtain.

Justina stands there, flat belly, just thicker than a rail, tiny flat breasts with artificially puffy nipples, hairless vagina, if that was the right word, that even with reconstructive surgery resembled crushed Silly Putty wedged into an inverted ant hill.

She pushes the curtain aside and steps in, kneeling down. She starts sucking his cock.

A mouth is a mouth, a hole is a hole, Peoria remembers . . . Peoria gets hard.

He closes his eyes and rests his hand on the soap dish, knocking over a bottle of Gillette 2-in-1 shampoo-conditioner.

He usually has a hard time coming in hot water—he never masturbates in the shower, for instance—but he lets his imagination go, and his imagination goes back to the memory, the first time he had touched Justina, while he was still Justin, his hand warmed by blood, bodies pressed together, the absolute fear and excitement of death enveloping him, a memory so powerful he had pretended it didn't exist, and with the warm water falling off his short, five-foot-seven frame, splashing to the top of the long black hair at his knees, he lets the memory wash over him, maybe even washing it away however briefly, and he comes.

Swallowing, Justina looks up.

"I know what you were thinking about," she says. "I was thinking it too."

They both start to cry.

38.

Monday

Whoosh. I'm pulled into the blogosphere.

I'm at my cubicle at *The Magazine* at 6:45 a.m., a copy of the *New York Post* and the *Daily News* on my desk, scanning the papers for items that I can't find online. I'm hooked into Wretched's email system, where all the tips from readers come in, naming names, hinting at layoffs, leaking details to fuck somebody over. Wretched's slogan is "Envy is a beautiful thing," and it's apparent from the kind of correspondence that envy is the grease of the Wretched Empire.

I don't want to use my real name as a guest editor, so I come up with a pseudonym. I settle on K. Eric Walters, the name of a little-known and short-lived Irish revolutionary who had accidentally punched out a Brit in a drunken brawl, sparking a rebellion that Michael Collins would later take credit for. There is also a K. Eric Walters who spends his time as an amateur bass fisherman—the perfect name, one that gets plenty of Google hits, seemingly legit, and would cause a bit of confusion for anyone trying to figure out my identity—food critic? Bass fisherman? Molecular scientist at UCLA? Film critic for some site called Rotten Tomatoes? Yes, there were plenty of K. Eric Walterses to choose from.

Grove emails me.

Specting 10 posts a day? Use IDs.

I forward it to Sarah, with a "?"

Oh, he's obsessed with IDers. I don't know why. The guy is a freak. Something from his FT days I think.

Ten posts a day. Where to find them?

I check the story-tips email box. There is a forward from a publicist at a publishing house, a press release announcing that Stephen King's son has just published his first collection of short stories. "Think he deserves this on merit?" the emailer asks.

Okay, that works. Nasty potential there. I copy a chunk of the press release then write a few lines about how Stephen King's son got a book deal because he was Stephen King's son. Scathing.

And then I'm off, and I get a full sense of the power of the blog, like I'm walking a tightrope, a live piece of performance art. Hundreds of thousands of readers out there are responding within seconds and minutes to what I am writing, and I sense this sensation and the only thing I can think of is that it's like crack. This is a powerful drug, having the ability to communicate so freely and widely and instantaneously, and to get a response—yes they are reading my snark, hurrah.

The next few items are simple. A reporter for *The New York Times* has written a book about the three weeks he spent in Iraq at the paper's Baghdad bureau and has made up names for some of the Arabs they spoke to—probably true, and that is the problem with it, and Wretched is able to tee off, getting three posts out of it, until finally, one of his allies from the *Times* stands up for him in an email and says, Hey, if you want to really start talking about inaccuracies for the *Times*, try writing about our television critic—she has more corrections per story than any other *New York Times* person currently on staff. And with a bit of LexisNexis fun, I do a post on the television critic and how many mistakes she makes per column; by this time, I'm done, it's noon, the rush hour is over—the highest traffic is usually in the morning—and I go grab a sandwich at the corner store.

The subject heading of the email says: "Imus Racist comment."

"Hey, did you listen to the show today? Imus called the Rutgers women's basketball team a 'bunch of nappy-headed hos.' That's racist!"

The emailer is Sarah Klein, the other Sarah, who left my apartment earlier this morning. I know that she could use a link from Wretched. It would really drive the traffic her way. She has posted a partial transcript on her website.

I don't think much of posting it. It's one of many. It takes off.

39.

Tuesday

Like wildfire—cliché. Like flesh-eating bacteria? Closer.

The new new media, the new media, and the old media, go into action.

Again, at my desk, at 7:30 a.m. I'm not alone.

Sanders Berman, looking ill, leaves the men's room and walks by.

"What are you doing here so early, Hastings?"

"Oh, just working on some extracurricular stuff," I say. "Yourself?"

"Some silly thing with the blogosphere. Apparently Don Imus said something racist on air yesterday. I was on his show, and now the *Times* is doing a story on it, so I'm going to talk to their reporter in a few minutes. Have you heard anything about it?"

"Um, yeah. I saw something on Wretched.com."

"Wretched? Who reads that trash?"

"A lot of people, I think."

Berman leaves me at the cubicle.

Throughout the night, the Imus comments, the "nappy-headed hos" controversy, has swept away all other news. Bloggers on the East Coast and West Coast and in the American Midwest have listened to the show, in full, and started to dissect the entire transcript; the cable news networks are playing the audio recording, and "Is Imus a Racist?" columns are already being prepared for tomorrow's papers.

Fifteen minutes later, Sanders Berman comes back down the hall, his face greenish. He goes into the bathroom again and then comes back out.

"They said I laughed, Hastings."

"Laughed at what?"

"The reporter, the *Times* reporter. They said that Imus called the Rutgers team a bunch of nappy-headed hos, and I was on the line, doing my weekly interview, and they said I laughed at the joke."

"Wow."

"I cleared my throat, I recall, and unfortunately it happened to time with his comments. Have you seen Milius? Where is he?"

Berman disappears down the hall again.

Within minutes, the *Times* has posted a story on its website, including the Sanders Berman comment: "'I don't think we want to rush to judgment,' magazine editor Sanders Berman said. 'We should wait to see how it plays out.' Mr. Berman, a regular guest on *Imus in the Morning*, can also be heard apparently laughing after Mr. Imus's remarks. Mr. Berman said he was 'clearing his throat.'"

By noon, human rights groups, media watchdog groups, civil rights organizations, and the majority of mainstream media outlets are calling for an apology from Imus. Former guests on Imus's show, many of whose books had become bestsellers after their appearance there, are also demanding an apology. Imus refuses at first and strikes back at his critics, saying they are acting like "rats on a sinking ship. Not that this ship is sinking."

Nishant Patel, back from a meeting with European advertisers, strolls in around one p.m.

"Mr. Hastings, hope you are well, sir."

"Yes, Nishant, doing great, thanks."

"What have I missed?"

"The Imus controversy. He called the Rutgers basketball team a bunch of nappy-headed hos. They're black, so everyone is saying it was racist."

"Ah, I would visit Princeton when Yale played them, in American football."

"Sanders was on the show when he said it."

Nishant nods, then goes to his corner office.

"Dorothy, call Henry, tell him we should talk very soon."

"Yes, Nishant. You know, of course, that Henry is away, and Sanders is acting . . ."

Nishant nods and turns away.

Dorothy stands up and scans the room.

"Patricia?"

Patricia pops up from her cubicle, startled.

"Yes, Dorothy?"

"Call Henry the EIC and tell him Dr. Patel wants to speak with him."

"What is the EIC?"

"Not what, who—Henry, the EIC."

"Henry from the copy desk?"

"No, not the copy desk, the editor in chief."

"You want him to call you?"

"You won't get him, you'll get his assistant, and tell her to tell him to call."

I turn back to my cubicle. I've already posted three items on what is being called a "growing controversy." I'm getting a little nervous. Glad I have a pseudonym. I'm thinking that it might be smart to resign my position at Wretched for the week. That's when Grove pings me.

"Great job so far, keep this up and there might be a position for you here. Leave the dead trees once and for all."

I hear the hiss of Delray M. Milius, walking two steps behind Berman. They stop on the other side of the cubicle wall.

"Send another statement to the *Times*," Berman says. "Tell them *The Magazine* is no longer going on the show. Tell them I found his comments reprehensible—I scoffed at them on air! And let's get one of those staff meetings together. And make sure to invite all the . . . we need to get their input . . ."

Delray M. Milius sends out a company-wide email, calling for an emergency staff meeting to discuss the new policy in relation to the Imus show.

An hour later, the conference room on the fifteenth floor is filled up with staff. I'm about to sit down when Delray tells me that these four seats are reserved. I say okay and stand in the back of the room, by the door.

Charlotte, the youngest African American woman on staff, comes into the conference room.

"Sit right there," Delray tells her, pointing to the empty seat that I was going to sit in.

The three seats next to her are filled by the remaining three African American members on the magazine's staff.

Sanders Berman comes in, second to last, beaten in being fashionably late only by Nishant.

"Ladies and gentlemen, I'm sure you've all heard of the growing controversy surrounding Don Imus's appalling comments," Berman begins. "First, I'd like you to know that I had no idea that Imus would say such things."

Berman looks around the room, his eyes stopping on Janet, the woman who runs the magazine's public relations department and who regularly books the magazine employees for media appearances.

"Janet, I'm really disappointed that you never told me Imus ran this kind of a show. I'm really disappointed that no one warned me that he would say such horrible things."

Janet starts to respond, "You've been on the show for three years and—"

Sanders cuts her off. "Let's make sure it doesn't happen again."

He sweeps the conference room.

"So, our new policy. We're not going on *Imus* anymore. And we're going to address the issue of his comments in the next issue. I'd like you four," he says, pointing at the four African Americans on the staff who are sitting at the table, "I'd like you four—Charlotte, Sammy, John, and Lucas—to take the lead on this reporting."

"I don't cover media," says Charlotte.

"It's okay, and I think we really need your perspective. And if you have any problems, or would like to discuss this further, Delray is going to talk to each one of you individually. Obviously, this is not how I wanted my time as acting EIC to go, but Henry supports, and the Dolings support, my position to boycott Imus completely, and I support all of you to do the best damn story we can about it."

I go back to my cubicle. I figure I'd wait an hour before posting anything about the meeting on Wretched. Things are getting way too close to home. I have to tell Grove that I can't be guest editor the rest of the week—he has to take over the site himself.

I send him an email.

He responds.

"That's fine, but you did sign a weekly contract with us, but I see how you are in a bind, so just give me updates on what's going on inside your magazine. You don't have a choice, otherwise I'll do a post now saying you were the one who started this whole controversy."

Fuck.

"Mike, Nishant wants to see you," Dorothy calls out to me.

Shit.

I walk into Nishant's office. He's sitting there, reading the new issue of the *New York Herald*, its distinct pink paper standing out against the other papers on his desk.

"Have you read the *Herald* this week, Hastings?"

"Not yet, didn't know it was out yet."

"You're in it. I didn't know you were friends with these bloggers."

That Jonathan Lodello. He'd put me in his story. I wonder if he's mentioned that I'm guest editing under a pseudonym. If so, my career at *The Magazine* is about to end, and fast.

"Oh yeah, what did he say?"

"Nothing, except that you are dating a girl named Sarah Klein. Wasn't she the blogger who started this whole controversy?"

"I'm really sorry, Nishant. I'm no longer having anything to do with that crowd. It was a mistake being there, and it was a mistake guest editing this week—"

Nishant isn't listening.

"So, your girlfriend, don't you think she might find our meeting this afternoon with Sanders interesting?"

I suppose she would, but I don't know what Nishant is getting at right away.

"She's not my girlfriend, but—"

"I mean, to have the four African Americans reporting this story, doesn't that also have the faint stench of racism? After Berman laughs—scoffs—it seems rather clumsy to then have four blacks at *The Magazine* do the black story. You don't think so? Perhaps I'm mistaken."

"Oh yeah, I guess that could look bad."

"Hastings, you sent me that email, I don't think I ever responded, about you guest editing Wretched. Is it this week you're doing that?"

"Nishant, yes, but I'm not doing it anymore."

"And I never gave you permission, and you didn't ask Berman or Delray about it either?"

"I thought you knew, you were cool with it, no news is good news, and everything—"

"I would suggest you not doing it from this point on. That being said, I would not object to any further communication that you might have with Ms. Klein."

He turns back to his computer. I'm dismissed.

Back at my cubicle, I compose an email to Sarah Klein. I cc Timothy Grove. This is all I can give you, I tell them. He writes back, "Perfect."

This is how the scandal is propelled to the next level, wishing for another victim, full saturation, because this is a scandal that has started to drag others down with it, amplifying speculation, its tentacles grappling more boldface names into the abyss, into that area that got other boldface names to start speculating and hiding and focusing on survival—somebody is going to have to pay for Imus's comments, and if it is more than just Imus, all the better, as long as it isn't you.

There doesn't need to be any official words or messages; the instinctual calculations have been made—to risk a career and a family and a paycheck and a well-crafted brand name and status to defend Don Imus? Not likely. The indignation that can be found in the talking heads in the media elite is not so much over Imus's comments—after all, who truly gives a shit—but the indignation of almost getting dragged down too by his careless remarks. This feeling of a near-miss sparked the true outrage, which is expressed in comments about racism and demands for apologies, but it is truly just a cover for the outrage over Imus's misstep, and while making that gross misstep, to have threatened their own careers.

Danger looming, the momentum building up, an epic fall approaches. The knives are unsheathed, incisors sharpened, and enemies and targets of his scorn in the past are making phone calls, remarks on television, coming out of the media landscape, electronic specters with Rolodexes and grudges and access to editors, nudging the story along. Silently building, it expands and expands and by nightfall, the name Sanders Berman is on every Movable Type page and every gossip columnist's screen—will he go down too?

40.

Wednesday

I pick up the slow mumble of Berman's drawl as he leans up against the wall down from my cubicle. Delray M. Milius stands with his arms crossed. I figure they would have learned not to talk important business in the magazine hallways by now, but the crisis has made them more unsure of themselves, and they fall back into old patterns.

"Who's the leak? Who's the leak? . . . I can't even talk in my office because it could be her, my assistant . . . Lawsuits . . . I don't hate African Americans . . . You're right, we can't say that in a statement . . . All the advertisers have boycotted his show . . ."

"We need to change the subject," Milius says. "We need to change the subject soon. We don't want this to go on another week."

"How are they taking it?"

"Not well. Charlotte has offered her resignation, citing racial prejudices."

"Christ. This, this is bullshit—this is reverse racism. Just because I'm from Alabama, I'm a racist? Just because I laughed at a joke? And now that I've seen the clip of that basketball team, I can't deny that they do look like nappy-headed hos, one of them even has a tattoo that says 'ho,' I mean, this is just so incredibly unjust—"

"Sanders, Sanders, please, this isn't the time. Stay on message, and we'll change the message soon. We'll change the conversation."

"How?"

". . . A.E. Peoria . . ."

I'm surprised to hear A.E. Peoria's name.

Should I warn him? But warn him of what?

Three hours later, A.E. Peoria rushes in.

"Mike, fuck, hey. I'm meeting with Milius. They don't want to run the story this week, do they?"

41.

Wednesday, Continued

A.E. Peoria sits for a full five minutes without saying a word. He's sworn to himself that he is going to do a better job at listening. Receive mode. He is in receive mode, sitting in a chair across from Delray M. Milius. It is an accomplishment that he is even back in this office after the mistakes. At first, he wants to start apologizing for the pencil incident, to tell Milius about his transformation, to tell him about Norm and his iced coffees and self-acceptance, to tell him again about how he has changed and learned to love himself, somewhat, how it's a struggle he's working on every day. But then he thinks, No, I won't apologize, no need for me to bring up old news, he's probably forgotten about it anyway. I will just sit and listen and absorb and show that I have changed, that I am reliable, that I am a good citizen of the magazine.

"So, can you give us a draft of the story by tomorrow night," Milius says.

"The story?"

"About the transvestite."

"Transsexual."

"Right."

"Of course I can, no problem at all."

A good citizen of the magazine, he does not want to express any reservations; just say yes, agree to anything. Yes, that is his new philosophy of success, and this is the first time since his suspension that he is able to test it out.

So he says yes, I will do the story.

"All I have to do is get permission from Justina, you know, and then we should be okay."

"Permission?"

"Yes, need to get her approval, you know, so I can write the story."

"You haven't told her you're going to write a story about her?"

"No, not yet, you know, I was waiting, you know, but it's helped because I've gotten really good stuff, you know."

"Get her permission. We need this story. I don't have to mention that this is really your last chance."

A.E. Peoria leaves the office and walks out onto 57th Street. He has thirty blocks to go to his apartment on the Upper West Side. It is a fall day in New York, a beautiful fall day, and passing by Columbus Circle he nods happily at the immigrants waving laminated maps of the park and offering guided tours and he feels the need to walk. A walk in the city, what a pleasure, what a time to think, how amazing he feels, a man in the big city with a sense of purpose, with a renewed life. Is there any other street to have been walking on than Broadway with a view of Central Park, life, hustle, neurosis, energy, and attractive people? And it is only twenty minutes later that it sinks in what Delray Milius had actually said; he had said it so softly, with a strange inflection, that the offense wasn't processed at the time.

This story is his last chance. A threat, really.

Of course, he tells himself, Justina will be happy to help me tell this story. She'll be totally psyched about it, you know, I think she is going to be totally psyched. He has a date planned with her that night—he'll tell her after they see the movie.

He goes back to his apartment and starts to write. Where to begin?

No, I won't make this about me, he says. I will start with her, with Justina. I will start the story where it all began, back in Iraq at the invasion.

From memory he writes, chronology his friend, starting with the anecdote of the ambush, then her descriptions of her stay in the hospital, then her recovery process—the surgery, the day that she sat in her bedroom and realized looking downward that she was no longer a man and didn't want to be a man—then he writes about the GI Bill, and how it doesn't cover sex changes, and how that is unjust, and that she got into Barnard even though the documents on the GI Bill said she was a male. But that kind of subterfuge is for civil rights, heroic, and previously never disclosed—this is breaking news you are reading here people, this is a test case, this is a story generated and produced and distributed underneath a great brand by the great A.E. Peoria, Magazine Journalist. This is the story that will spark debate and conversation and change policy—yes, this is a great story.

All he needs is his last step. To tell Justina.

He emails Mike Hastings. He sends him what he's written so far. I need your files, he says, by tomorrow morning, the story is due tomorrow, and I need your files and you need to be ready to fact-check this fucker by Friday.

He closes his laptop. Tomorrow he will wake up and crash the rest of the story. The hours had disappeared as he'd entered his writing space, they'd just flown by, and the film he is scheduled to see with Justina starts in fifty-five minutes. He hopes they can still get seats.

He waits for her outside the theater on 68th Street, a massive Loews Cineplex, and he stands in front of a movie poster that has the tagline "Sometimes, it's only once." Apparently a love story, and this makes his eyes wet on the edges, thinking of Justina, the gift that has been brought into his life. He saved her life, and now she is going to save his career. An equal trade in his world. He got tickets out of the electronic kiosk—two adults for the film, a romantic comedy, that year's installment about a holiday get-together gone horribly wrong, dinner sequences with turkeys and cranberry sauce and accidentally offensive remarks and humorous, lighthearted, hilarious violence.

It is New York, so other pretty girls pass on the street, but he doesn't watch them with desire, which is his usual fallback position. He doesn't compare them on tiers or rank them with numbers; he feels no need to do that anymore. He has accepted himself, and yes, when he sees her, he thinks, Wow, this is the first time that I have waited for a girl outside the theater and felt lucky when she actually appeared. How strange is that? What am I to make of the fact that this feels so right?

Justina appears in a navy peacoat over a dress, her thin legs in black stockings coming out underneath. She has, out of self-consciousness, kept her female style quite simple, wearing knee-length skirts, pearls, peacoats, one season's worth of outfits from J.Crew—and yes, for a former man, she looks quite good—you can't tell.

"Popcorn?"

"Put extra salt on it."

After the film, they go to the Italian restaurant, only five blocks away, where they had their first date not long ago.

"I have really big news, so big I can't believe I was able to keep it in this long," he says.

"I can't wait to hear it," she says, squeezing his hand, in between a dish of olive oil and a brass candleholder.

"The magazine wants me to do a story for them this week," he says.

"That's so amazing. I'm so proud of you."

He waits. This would be the moment.

"I'm going to tell our story, your story," he says. "Isn't that great?"

"What do you mean?"

"I think we can get the cover, you know, I'm writing it, it will be your picture. I mean, it's going to be huge. You're going to be famous, and maybe we can get a book deal and a movie out of it too. I mean, I think it's that big, you know?"

Her face does not change into the shape he expects. It does not glow. He recognizes a kind of pained anger, and for a moment he sees the same face that had rested beneath the Kevlar helmet years ago, in Iraq. A masculine face, a face of rage.

"You can't do this. You can't write about me. I'm not ready, I'm not ready for it."

"But I thought you'd be cool with it. It'd be doing me a huge favor."

"Not yet. Can't you wait?"

"No, it really can't wait—the magazine asked and I said I would deliver. I mean, I'd been talking about it with them for months, you know."

"You've been talking with the magazine for months about this? And you haven't told me?"

"Uh, yeah, I mean, didn't I mention it?"

"I'm a fucking story to you," she says. "I'm a fucking story." She stands up from the table.

"If you do this, if you do this story, you will lose me."

"No need to be so dramatic—I know you're Latin and all—"

"Latina! A story! Throw our love away for what, for printed pages!" She leaves the restaurant.

"But I saved your life," he yells.

"Fuck you!"

"Don't get in the cab."

"I'm getting in the cab, get away from me."

"Don't get in the fucking cab."

"I'm getting in the cab."

He withdraws his hand before the yellow door slams on it, and he looks to see her through the window, but she has turned her head away. The only face he sees in the cab is on the small and newly installed video monitor, the face of New York City mayor Michael Bloomberg, reciting a public service announcement.

Relapse. Seven months of sobriety gone, just like that.

A.E. Peoria, magazine journalist, turns and walks into a bar, puts his credit card down, and starts to drink. Sober, yes, only drinking wine, which doesn't count, and now he knows that the only response is to get totally fucked-up, totally wrecked, to embrace that abyss that had been missing from his life. Justina's rejection has brought it back to him in full—oh, how good it feels, the beer and shot then another beer.

At 123rd and Lexington, three hours later.

"Put your fucking shirt back on, motherfucker," the drug dealer says.

"I saw the shoes up the telephone line, and I know that that means you sell crack, right?" A.E. Peoria says, putting his shirt back on. "See, I don't have a fucking wire."

"Shut the fuck up, man! Give me the cash."

"Give me the stuff."

"Shit, hold on."

The dealer goes over to a payphone.

"You still have payphones? That's so strange—isn't that, like, bizarre? I guess it's a class thing. But it's strange, I mean, even in Africa and shit, everybody has cell phones—they call them mobile phones, you know, because 'cell phone' isn't really accurate. They took the cells out of the phone a long time ago. And it's strange that only in America they still call it a cell phone."

A teenager runs down the street. He hands a small packet to the dealer, who goes up to A.E. Peoria and slaps his hand. Peoria takes the packet and kneels down.

"What the fuck you doing?"

"Oh, I keep my money in my sock when I come up here, but I guess I shouldn't have told you that."

"Man, just leave that shit on the ground and get the fuck out of here before I beat your ass."

"Okay, okay."

Peoria starts walking blindly down the street, crack secured. All he needs now is a way to smoke it. He threw out his crack pipe months before, during his self-acceptance and healthy-living phase. Which put him in a dilemma.

"Hey, handsome," a woman in tight black latex pants says. "You holding? Want to make a trade?"

"You have a crack pipe?"

"Shhhh, you're a crazy man, aren't you. Come with me."

"What do I get out of it?"

"I suck your dick for a hit."

She grabs his hand, and she presses a buzzer on an apartment building, where rent is clearly paid late each month and with cash.

A.E. Peoria stumbles into a room with a white mattress in the corner, three people passed out on the floor. He unzips his pants.

"Let's get high first."

He hands over the crack, and she takes a few minutes to stick it in a glass pipe. She sparks a Bic lighter, and he stares at her callused fingertips.

She exhales and passes the pipe to him.

He inhales and falls back.

She starts sucking his cock.

"Let me just finish my way," he says, looking at her and masturbating. She starts to push her breasts together and moan.

He stares at her breasts, but he isn't getting closer to ejaculating. He closes his eyes, and opens them, and closes his eyes again, fixing his mind on Justina, then opening them to get the image of the fat whore, then closing his eyes to fix on Justina, then reaching out and touching the breasts of the fat whore, and finally, thinking of Justina, coming.

He takes another hit from the crack pipe.

Fifteen minutes later, he jumps up.

"What the fuck am I doing here? What the fuck am I doing here?" he screams.

He sees the street sign—89th and Columbus. He's near Justina's place. His mobile phone says it's 5:45 a.m. He looks across the street and feels an agitating emptiness, an emptiness that stretches back years and years in his life that he can never quite fill, not with crack or with booze or a yearly gym membership or even with his career. No, this emptiness does not just reach across to the piled-up garbage bags and the trickle of yellow cabs crawling by in the empty streets— the only time of day when they travel under the speed limit, when the drivers drive cautiously, which is strange because it would be the safest time to go fast. The newspaper delivery trucks, and the neon sign promising the world's greatest coffee, and the other neon signs promising the world's greatest slice of pizza, and the emptiness of a metal grate pulled down over a fast-food juice and hot dog joint, or the emptiness of the Yemeni clerk in the twenty-four-hour bodega, guarding the stocks of booze in the back from drunks, having to say over and over again that he can't sell again until noon. This emptiness that he sees stretches everywhere and far back into his own past.

His own life. That he knows that there is no hope and no god, and nothing at all, and he knows that the story won't save him either, and he feels the crack leaving his nervous system raw and dry, and he knows the crack has abandoned him to life, and he wants to cry, and he wants to yell out, "Look, here I am world, on the corner of 89th and Columbus, coming down off crack, drunk, a magazine journalist, a New Yorker, a failure, and all I want is to be held."

She answers the buzzer on the third obnoxious ring.

42.

Thursday-Friday-Saturday

I don't have a good feeling about the email from Milius, summoning me to his office.

"Hi, Delray, what's up?"

"It's three p.m. and we just lost the writer on our cover story," he says.

"What happened?"

"Peoria isn't doing it. He won't write it. He's fired."

I nod.

Milius opens a drawer and pulls out a copy of the *New York Herald*, placing it on his desk.

"You're aware you were mentioned in association with these bloggers this week?"

"Oh, yeah, that was funny."

"You're aware that the magazine has had a series of leaks this week that have done a lot of damage to our brand?"

"Yeah, I saw something about that online."

Delray stands up, clasping his hands behind his back, and stares out the window.

He sighs, as if he had practiced the entire sequence of movements in front of a mirror, a corporate executive ballet.

Delray turns back around and sits.

"You have all of Peoria's files. What else?"

"His journals, his interviews, yeah, I have that."

"You've also done reporting, yes? He sent you pictures of Justina too?"

"I've talked to all sorts of experts, yes."

"Okay, you're going to do the story."

I don't say anything.

"You don't seem very excited, Hastings. This is your first cover."

"Oh, I am very excited, but you know, it's Peoria's story, and I'm sure if he doesn't want to do it, it's probably for good reason, right? Like that he doesn't want to screw over Justina."

"Do you know a blogger named K. Eric Walters?"

"Hmm."

Milius homes his eyes on me, stretches his face back, a flake of facial moisturizing cream falling onto his desk.

"This isn't ideal for anyone. But I promised Sanders this story, and so we are going to give Sanders this story. You're going to do it, you understand?"

"I understand."

I'd like to say that I agonized over the decision, that I thought twice about it—because I know by taking Peoria's story, I'm putting the last nail in the coffin of his career, and I know that I'm also jeopardizing the privacy and future of Justina. Who knows how the military is going to react to this? Most likely they'll strip her of the GI Bill benefits. Who knows how the liberals at Barnard are going to react to having been deceived? Maybe they will support her, maybe not.

But I don't agonize over it. I don't want to lose my job, and if Sanders finds out that I'm the leak, then I'm done for too.

Plus, this is a great opportunity. My first cover story for the magazine.

I go back to my desk, call up the half rough draft that Peoria had sent me the day before, and start to write, just like I had learned how.

EPILOGUE

You should feel like the story is over, like you're walking out during the credits, waiting for a few deleted scenes or bloopers. Like you want two or three more screens of text to explain what happened to who and how. Maybe then you'll watch the sequel, if one is made.

The next week, Henry the EIC decides who his successor is going to be. The decision doesn't become public until a few weeks later. They don't want it to have the taint of the nappy-headed hos scandal.

Henry offers the EIC job to Nishant Patel.

Nishant turns it down—he's just gotten his own cable news show.

Henry then decides that Sanders Berman, after all, is the right man to lead the magazine into the twenty-first century.

A.E. Peoria gets fired from Barnard.

Justina doesn't get expelled. She becomes a cause célèbre on campus.

There is talk of court-martial—defrauding the government—but the charges never go anywhere. The ensuing controversy outrages the LGBT community. A young woman is temporarily blinded by pepper spray during a protest. A defense fund is raised.

After the spring semester, A.E. Peoria and Justina get married in a civil union ceremony.

He sends me an email from their honeymoon in Thailand. He wants my notes and reporting, he says, because he is working on a book proposal. He doesn't seem very angry at me.

It's now 2008. I'm finished writing—finished three weeks ago.

I'm about to go into work at *The Magazine*. I should be hearing back about this book soon. I want to get mine out there before Peoria finishes his draft.

It's a story I should be able to sell.

ABOUT THE AUTHOR

Michael Hastings was a contributing editor to *Rolling Stone* and a correspondent at large for BuzzFeed. Before that he worked for *Newsweek*, where he rose to prominence covering the wars in Iraq and Afghanistan. He received the 2010 George Polk Award for his *Rolling Stone* magazine story "The Runaway General." Hastings was the author of three other books, *I Lost My Love in Baghdad*, *The Operators*, and *Panic 2012*. He died in 2013, and was posthumously honored with the Norman Mailer Award for Emerging Journalist.